THE FORMATION OF THE CLASSICAL ISLAMIC WORLD

General Editor: Lawrence I. Conrad

Volume 43

Education and Learning in the Early Islamic World

THE FORMATION OF THE CLASSICAL ISLAMIC WORLD

General Editor: *Lawrence I. Conrad*

1	**Byzantium on the Eve of Islam**	*Averil Cameron*
2	**The Sasanian East on the Eve of Islam**	
3	**The Arabs and Arabia on the Eve of Islam**	*Frank E. Peters*
4	**The Life of Muḥammad**	*Uri Rubin*
5	**The Expansion of the Early Islamic State**	*Fred M. Donner*
6	**The Articulation of Islamic State Structures**	*Fred M. Donner*
7	**Problems of Political Cohesion in Early Islam**	*R. Stephen Humphrey*
8	**Arab–Byzantine Relations in Early Islamic Times**	*Michael Bonner*
9	**The Turks in the Early Islamic World**	*C. Edmund Bosworth*
10	**Patterns of Everyday Life**	*David Waines*
11	**Production and the Exploitation of Resources**	*Michael G. Morony*
12	**Manufacturing and Labour**	*Michael G. Morony*
13	**Trade and Exchange in Early Islam**	
14	**Property and Consumption in Early Islamic Society**	
15	**Cities in the Early Islamic World**	*Hugh Kennedy*
16	**Nomads and the Desert in the Early Islamic World**	*Hugh Kennedy*
17	**Society and Individual in Early Islam**	
18	**Muslims and Others in Early Islamic Society**	*Robert E. Hoyland*
19	**The Christian Communities in the Early Islamic World**	
20	**The Jewish Communities of the Early Islamic World**	*David Wasserstein*
21	**Archaeology and Early Islam**	*Donald Whitcomb*
22	**Early Islamic Numismatics and Monetary History**	
23	**Early Islamic Art and Architecture**	*Jonathan Bloom*
24	**The Qur'ān: Style and Contents**	*Andrew Rippin*
25	**The Qur'ān: Formative Interpretation**	*Andrew Rippin*
26	**The Development of Islamic Ritual**	*Gerald Hawting*
27	**The Formation of Islamic Law**	*Wael B. Hallaq*
28	***Ḥadīth*: Origins and Development**	*Harald Motzki*
29	**Early Islamic Historiographical Traditions**	
30	**Early Islamic Theology**	
31	**Eschatology and Apocalyptic in Early Islam**	
32	**Early Islamic Visions of Community**	
33	**Shī'ism: Origins and Early Development**	*Etan Kohlberg*
34	**Khārijite Movements in Early Islam**	
35	**The Emergence of Islamic Mysticism**	
36	**The Early Islamic Grammatical Tradition**	*Ramzi Baalbaki*
37	**Early Islamic Poetry and Poetics**	*Suzanne Stetkevych*
38	**Early Arabic Prose Literature**	
39	**The Rise of Islamic Philosophy**	
40	**The Rise of Arab-Islamic Medicine**	
41	**The Exact Sciences in Early Islam**	
42	**Magic and Divination in Early Islam**	*Emilie Savage-Smith*
43	**Education and Learning in the Early Islamic World**	*Claude Gilliot*
44	**The Early Islamic Manuscript Tradition**	
45	**Early Islamic North Africa**	
46	**The Formation of al-Andalus I**	*Manuela Marín*
47	**The Formation of al-Andalus II**	*M. Fierro/J. Samsó*
48	**The Modern Study of Early Islam**	

THE FORMATION OF THE CLASSICAL ISLAMIC WORLD

General Editor: Lawrence I. Conrad

Volume 43

Education and Learning in the Early Islamic World

edited by
Claude Gilliot

ASHGATE
VARIORUM

Published in the series **The Formation of the Classical Islamic World** by

Ashgate Publishing Limited
Wey Court East
Union Road
Farnham
Surrey GU9 7PT
England

Ashgate Publishing Company
Suite 420
101 Cherry Street
Burlington, VT 05401-4405
USA

ISBN 978-0-86078-717-4

British Library CIP Data
Education and learning in the early Islamic world. – (The formation of the classical Islamic world ; v. 43)
1. Islamic education–History.
I. Series II. Gilliot, Claude.
370.9'1767-dc23

US Library of Congress Control Number: 2010933555

This volume is printed on acid-free paper.

MIX
Paper from responsible sources
FSC
www.fsc.org
FSC® C018575

Printed and bound in Great Britain by the MPG Books Group, UK

THE FORMATION OF THE CLASSICAL ISLAMIC WORLD-43

CONTENTS

Part III   Orality and Literacy

Part IV   Authorship and Transmission

Part V   Libraries

ACKNOWLEDGEMENTS

The chapters in this volume are taken from the sources listed below. The editor and publishers wish to thank the authors, original publishers or other copyright holders for permission to use their material as follows:

CHAPTER 1: Christopher Melchert, "The Etiquette of Learning in the Early Islamic Study Circle", in Joseph E. Lowry *et al.* (eds), *Law and Education in Medieval Islam*, Studies in Memory of Professor George Makdisi. Published by the E.J.W. Gibb Memorial Trust (Cambridge, 2004), pp. 33–44.

CHAPTER 2: Ignaz Goldziher, "Muslim Education", in James Hastings (ed.), *Encyclopedia of Religion and Ethics*, Edinburgh: T&T Clark, 1908–26, V, pp. 198–207; reprinted in his *Gesammelte Schriften*, ed. Joseph de Somogyi (Hildesheim: Olms, 1967–73) V, pp. 223–32.

CHAPTER 3: Albert Dietrich, "Some Aspects of the Education of Princes at the ʿAbbāsid Court", "Quelques aspects de l'education princière à la court abbaside", in George Makdisi Dominique Sourdel and Janine Sourdel-Thomine (eds), *L'enseignement en Islam et en Occident au moyen âge* (Paris: Paul Geunther, 1976: *Revue des études islamiques*, 44), pp. 89–104. Translation by Philip Simpson. Copyright © 2012 Ashgate Publishing Ltd.

CHAPTER 4: Richard W. Bulliet, "The Age Structure of Medieval Islamic Education", *Studia Islamica*, 57 (1983), pp. 105–17.

CHAPTER 5: Sebastian Günther, "Advice for Teachers: The 9th Century Muslim Scholars Ibn Saḥnūn and al-Jāḥiẓ on Pedagogy and Didactics", in S. Günther (ed.), *Ideas, Images and Methods of Portrayal. Insights into Classical Arabic Literature and Islam* (Leiden: Brill, 2005), pp. 89–128.

CHAPTER 6: Johannes Pedersen, "The Islamic Preacher wāʿiẓ, mudhakkir, qāṣṣ", in Samuel Löwinger and Joseph Somogyi (eds), *Ignace Goldziher Memorial Volume*, I, (Budapest, 1948), pp. 226–51.

CHAPTER 7: Claude Gilliot, "The Scholarly Formation of al-Ṭabarī", "La formation intellectuelle de Tabari 224/5–310/839–923", *Journal asiatique*, 276 (1988), pp. 203–44. Translation by Philip Simpson. Copyright © 2012 Ashgate Publishing Ltd.

CHAPTER 8: Jan Just Witkam, "The Human Element between Text and Reader: The *ijāza* in Arabic Manuscripts", in the *Codicology of Islamic Manuscripts: Proceedings of the Second Conference of al-furqan Islamic Heritage Foundation*, 4–5 December 1993 (London: Al-Furqan Islamic Heritage Foundation, 1995), pp. 123–36.

CHAPTER 9: Georges Vajda, "The Oral Transmission of Knowledge in Traditional Islam", "De la transmission orale du savoir en Islam traditionnel", *L'arabisant*, 4 (1975), pp. 2–8; reprinted in his *La transmission du savoir en Islam VIIe–XVIIIe siècles* (London: Variorum, 1983). Translation by Philip Simpson. Copyright © 2012 Ashgate Publishing Ltd.

CHAPTER 10: Max Weisweiler, "The Office of the *Mustamlī* in Arabic Scholarship", "Das Amt des *Mustamlī* in der arabischen Wissenschaft", *Oriens*, 4 (1951), pp. 27–57. Translation by Gwendolin Goldbloom. Copyright © 2012 Ashgate Publishing Ltd.

CHAPTER 11: F. Krenkow, "The Use of Writing for the Preservation of Ancient Arabic Poetry", in T.W. Arnold and Reynold A. Nicholson (eds), *A Volume of Oriental Studies Presented to Edward G. Browne* (Cambridge: Cambridge University Press, 1922), pp. 261–8. Copyright © 2004 Cambridge University Press, reproduced with permission.

CHAPTER 12: Stefan Leder, "Authorship and Transmission in Unauthored Literature: The Akhbār Attributed to al-Haytham ibn ʿAdī", *Oriens*, 31 (1988), pp. 67–81.

CHAPTER 13: Richard Walzer, "On the Legacy of the Classics in the Islamic World", in *Festschrift Bruno Snell zum 60. Geburtsag am 18. Juni 1956 von Freunden und Schülern überreicht* (Munich: C.H. Beck, 1956), pp. 189–96; reprinted in *Greek into Arabic: Essays on Islamic Philosophy* (Oxford: Bruno Cassirer, 1962), pp. 29–37.

CHAPTER 14: Johann Fück, "On the Transmission of Bukhārī's Collection of Traditions", "Beiträge zur Überlieferungsgeschichte von Buharis Traditionssammlung", *Zeitschrift der deutschen morgenländischen Gesellschaft*, 92 (1938), pp. 60–87. Translation by Gwendolin Goldbloom. Copyright © 2012 Ashgate Publishing Ltd.

CHAPTER 15: Isabel Fierro, "The Introduction of *Ḥadith* in al-Andalus", *Der Islam*, 66 (1989), pp. 68–93.

Chapter 16: Manuela Marín, "The Transmission of Knowledge in al-Andalus (up to 300/912)", *Al-Qantra*, 8 (1987), pp. 87–97. Translation by David McLoghlin. Copyright © 2012 Ashgate Publishing Ltd.

Chapter 17: Adolph Grohmann, "Libraries and Bibliophiles in the Islamic East", "Bibliotheken und Bibliophilien im Islamischen Orient", in *Festschrift der Nationalbibliothek in Wien, herausgegeben zur Feier des 200. Jährigen Bestehens des Gebäudes* (Vienna: Österreichische Nationalbibliothek, 1926) pp. 431–42. Translation by Gwendolin Goldbloom. Copyright © 2012 Ashgate Publishing Ltd.

Chapter 18: Ruth Stellhorn Mackensen, "Arabic Books and Libraries in the Umaiyad Period", *American Journal of Semitic Languages and Literatures*, 52 (1935–36), pp. 245–53; 53 (1936–37), pp. 239–50; 54 (1937), pp. 41–61; Supplementary notes to "Arabic Books and Libraries in the Umaiyad Period", 56 (1939), pp. 149–57.

Chapter 19: David Wasserstein, "The Library of al-Ḥakam II al-Mustanṣir and the Culture of Islamic Spain", *Manuscripts of the Middle East*, 5 (1990–91), pp. 99–105.

Every effort has been made to trace all the copyright holders, but if any have been inadvertently overlooked the publishers will be pleased to make the necessary arrangement at the first opportunity.

PUBLISHER'S NOTE

The pagination of articles originally published in English has been maintained for this volume. In articles translated into English, the original pagination has been indicated in the text in bold-face type.

GENERAL EDITOR'S PREFACE

Since the days of Ignaz Goldziher (1850–1921), generally regarded as the founder of Islamic studies as a field of modern scholarship, the formative period in Islamic history has remained a prominent theme for research. In Goldziher's time it was possible for scholars to work with the whole of the field and practically all of its available sources, but more recently the increasing sophistication of scholarly methodologies, a broad diversification in research interests, and a phenomenal burgeoning of the catalogued and published source material available for study have combined to generate an increasing "compartmentalisation" of research into very specific areas, each with its own interests, priorities, agendas, methodologies, and controversies. While this has undoubtedly led to a deepening and broadening of our understanding in all of these areas, and hence is to be welcomed, it has also tended to isolate scholarship in one subject from research in other areas, and even more so from colleagues outside of Arab-Islamic studies, not to mention students and others seeking to familiarise themselves with a particular topic for the first time.

The Formation of the Classical Islamic World is a reference series that seeks to address this problem by making available a critical selection of the published research that has served to stimulate and define the way modern scholarship has come to understand the formative period of Islamic history, for these purposes taken to mean approximately AD 600–950. Each of the volumes in the series is edited by an expert on its subject, who has chosen a number of studies that taken together serve as a cogent introduction to the state of current knowledge on the topic, the issues and problems particular to it, and the range of scholarly opinion informing it. Articles originally published in languages other than English have been translated, and editors have provided critical introductions and select bibliographies for further reading.

A variety of criteria, varying by topic and in accordance with the judgements of the editors, have determined the contents of these volumes. In some cases an article has been included because it represents the best of current scholarship, the "cutting edge" work from which future research seems most likely to profit. Other articles—certainly no less valuable contributions—have been taken up for the skillful way in which they synthesise the state of scholarly knowledge. Yet others are older studies that—if in some ways now superseded—nevertheless merit attention for their illustration of thinking or conclusions that have long been important, or for the decisive stimulus they have provided to scholarly discussion. Some volumes cover themes that have emerged fairly recently, and here it has been necessary to include articles from outside the period covered by the series, as illustrations of paradigms and methodologies that may prove useful as research develops. Chapters from single author monographs have been considered only in very exceptional cases, and a certain emphasis has been encouraged on important studies that are less readily available than others.

In the present state of the field of early Arab-Islamic studies, in which it is routine for heated controversy to rage over what scholars a generation ago would have regarded as matters of simple fact, it is clearly essential for a series such as this to convey some sense of the richness and variety of the approaches and perspectives represented in the available literature. An effort has thus been made to gain broad international participation in editorial capacities, and to secure the collaboration of colleagues representing differing points of view. Throughout the series, however, the range of possible options for inclusion has been very large, and it is of course impossible to accommodate all of the outstanding research that has served to advance a particular subject. A representative selection of such work does, however, appear in the bibliography compiled by the editor of each volume at the end of the introduction.

The interests and priorities of the editors, and indeed, of the General Editor, will doubtless be evident throughout. Hopefully, however, the various volumes will be found to achieve well-rounded and representative syntheses useful not as the definitive word on their subjects—if, in fact, one can speak of such a thing in the present state of research—but as introductions comprising well-considered points of departure for more detailed inquiry.

A series pursued on this scale is only feasible with the good will and cooperation of colleagues in many areas of expertise. The General Editor would like to express his gratitude to the volume editors for the investment of their time and talents in an age when work of this kind is grossly undervalued, to the translators who have taken such care with the articles entrusted to them, and to Dr John Smedley and his staff at Ashgate for their support, assistance and guidance throughout.

Lawrence I. Conrad

INTRODUCTION

Education and Learning in the Early Islamic World

Claude Gilliot

His amplius fili mi ne requiras faciendi
plures libros nullus est finis frequensque
meditatio carnis adflictio est
Ecclesiastes 12:12*

Preliminary notes**

The study of education and learning in Islam from 600 to 950 AD encounters at least two difficulties. The first is that the sources, especially the later ones, easily lend themselves to backward projection—the projection of later institutions and practices on to an ancient past. Indeed, religious scholars have taken great pains to establish the idea of an authentic and uninterrupted transmission (*mutawātir*) of religious knowledge and ancillary learning in order to show at all costs that their foundations lie in the time of the Prophet, or at the very least that they hark back to the very first Muslim generations, and take place within a continuum.[1]

The second difficulty lies in the fact that most of the existing studies are general, considering education and learning over practically the entire span of "classical" Islam, although it seems that there are exceptions. The fact remains that bringing the continuities and discontinuities of the subject and period of our interest to the fore is rarely an easy matter.

The First Orientalist Approaches to Education and Learning in Islam

While making no claim to set out the history of Western research in this area, it nevertheless seems useful at this juncture to broadly set out some of the stages of

* "And further, by these, my son, be admonished: of making many books [there is] no end; and much study [is] a weariness of the flesh.": *The Holy Bible: American King James Version*, Eccl. 12:12.

** Any incomplete reference made in the text or in the footnotes can be found in full in the bibliography that follows.

[1] See Juynboll, G.H.A. (ed.), *Studies on the First Century of Islamic Society*, Carbondale, IL, 1982, 1–2.

Western interest in education and learning in Islam up until around the twentieth century.

The Reformed theologian from Utrecht, Adriaan Reland (1676–1718), to whom we owe the first scientific exposition of Muslim institutions, set himself the goal of presenting his subject "as is taught in the Muslim churches and schools" (*uti docetur in templis et scholis mohemmedicis*), incidently something for which he advocated the necessity of knowing the Arabic language.[2]

Admittedly, certain travellers and missionaries of the Middle Ages, such as the Dominican Riccoldo da Monte di Croce (d. 1320), have given some indications about educational institutions in Islam. During his sojourn in Baghdad (*ca.* 1290–96) Monte di Croce attended lessons given by Muslim masters and frequented the libraries that had survived the partial destruction of the town at the hands of the Mongols in 1258.[3]

Yet it was not until the work of a Lebanese Maronite Christian, Abraham Ecchellensis (Ibrāhīm al-Haqilānī, d. 1664 in Rome),[4] that any fairly detailed information on teaching methods and pedagogy became available. Ecchellensis translated and annotated in Latin the *Instruction of the Student: The method of learning*[5] by Burhān al-Dīn al-Zarnūjī (d. 620/1223).[6]

Some 60 years later, Reland published al-Zarnūjī's[7] Arabic text with a Latin translation on the facing pages (pp. 1–165) by the Danish Fredrik Rostgaard (d. 1745); this was accomplished in collaboration with the Maronite Josephus Banesis (Yūsuf b. Jirjis al-Bānī al-Ḥalabī, called al-Muʿallim Yūsuf, of the Maronite College in Rome, d. 1725 in Aleppo),[8] from a copy belonging to Jacobus Salomon Damascenus (Sulaymān al-Aswad), an orthodox priest of Damascus. He added to this translation (p. 167 *et seq.*) Ecchellensis's rather different version with a commentary entitled *Semita sapientiae*, reproduced from a manuscript copy. Reland was apparently unaware that a printed edition already existed![9]

---

[2] Hadriani Relandi, *De Religione mohammedica*, 2nd edn, Utrecht, 1717, §XI. First edition published in 1705.

[3] Mérigoux, J.-M., "L'ouvrage d'un frère prêcheur florentin à la fin du XIIIe siècle. Le 'Contra legen Sarracenorum' de Riccoldo da Monte di Croce", *Memorie Domenicane*, n.s. 17 (1986), 117–21, ch. XIII; Ricoldo, *Itinerarium*, chs. XXI–XXIX, 131–35 (*Itinerarius Fratris Ricoldi*, ed. J.C.M. Laurent, *Peregrinatores medii aevi quatuor*, Leipzig, 1873, 105–41).

[4] Fück, J., *Die arabischen Studien in Europa*, Leipzig, 1955, 75–76; Troupeau, G., "Le rôle des chrétiens du monde arabe dans l'orientalisme en France, du XVIIe au XIXe siècle", in Musall, F. and Al-Mudarris A. (eds), *Im Dialog bleiben. Festschrift für Raif Georges Khoury*, Wiesbaden Harrassowitz, 2011, 232–33 (231–35).

[5] *Semita Sapientiœ sive ad scientias comparandas methodvs*, Parisiis, apud Adrianum Taupinart, 1646, 104pp.

[6] See "Pedagogy" *infra*.

[7] *Enchiridion studiosi*, Utrecht, 1709.

[8] Kaḥḥāla, *ʿUmar Riḍā, Muʿjam al-muʾallifīn*, Beirut, (reprint of the Damascus edn, 1957–61). XIII, 285.

[9] Smitskamp, R., *Catalog* 621 (Leiden, 1999), no. 606.

Al-Zarnūjī's treatise was then published in a new and better edition[10] taken from the text published by Reland and from five manuscripts, with a new Latin translation by Carl Paul Caspari (d. 1892).[11] The latter added to it variants and scholia taken from Ibrāhīm b. Ismāʿīl's commentary (written in 996/1588).[12]

The publication of the two volumes of *Bibliotheca Arabico-Hispana Escurialensis* in Madrid (1760–70) by the Maronite Miguel Casiri (d. 1791)[13] proved to be an important landmark in the field of our study and not only for the region of al-Andalus. Indeed, the author's scholarly notes do not merely include descriptions of written works, but also information on the scholarly production of the Arabs, on scholarship, on the transmission of knowledge, on libraries, schools and so on. This *opus magnum* practically became a source in its own right for several generations of orientalists.

As for the father of modern orientalism, Antoine Isaac Silvestre de Sacy (d. 1838), he made good use of the store of Arab manuscripts in the Royal Library, as well as the works of his predecessors, in order to write a long *mémoire*, in which he set out the history of Arabic writing along with the production of the ancient Arab poets.[14] Some of his other works also contain material on education and learning, notably his *Chrestomathie arabe*[15] and, more specifically, some edited and translated extracts from al-Maqrīzī and Ibn Khaldūn, among others.

On the Protestant side, the Lutheran theologian Heinrich Middeldorpf (d. 1861) published a dissertation in which he painted a literary landscape of Spain under the Arabs,[16] a landscape in which every feature was drawn from Casiri. This work notably examined the "Arab academies and schools" and libraries. Its concluding epilogue is dedicated to the Arabic translations of the Greek authors.

The Austrian diplomat Joseph von Hammer-Purgstall (d. 1856) published two large volumes *Encyclopädische Übersicht der Wissenschaften des Orients* (1804),[17] which covered the history of writing, grammar, historiography, philosophy, theology, law, medicine, magic, amulets and talismans and the like. He based this work on seven manuscript works in Arabic, Persian and Turkish, but most particularly on the *Kashf al-ẓunūn* of Ḥājjī Khalīfa (d. 1067/1657).

[10] Borhân-ed-dîni es-Sernûdjî, *Enchiridion Studiosi*, Leipzig, 1838.

[11] Fück, *Studien*, *op. cit.*, 199-200.

[12] Brockelmann, Carl, *Geschichte der arabischen Literatur* [hereafter *GAL*], I, 462; Supplement [hereafter *S*] I, 837.

[13] Fück, *Studien*, *op. cit.*, 125–26.

[14] "Mémoire" (1785), 248–348, 349–412; "Nouveaux aperçus" (1827), 209–31.

[15] Silvestre de Sacey, *Chrestomathie arabe*, 3 vols, Paris, 1826–27. First edition 1806.

[16] *Commentatio de institutis literariis in Hispania ...*, Göttingen, 1810.

[17] *Encyclopädische Uebersicht der Wissenschaften des Orients, aus sieben arabischen, persischen und türkischen Werken übersetzt. Den Freunden... der orientalischen Literatur gewidmet von einem derselben Beflissenen in Konstantinopel*, 2 vols, Leipzig, Breitkopf und Härtel, 1804, XIV+701 pp.

In 1838 Étienne-Marc Quatremère (d. 1857) published his famous *Mémoire sur le goût des livres chez les Orientaux*[18] which holds much information particularly on literary life and education at the time of the Umayyads and of the Abbasids, on the study sessions (*majālis*), the libraries and so on. He drew his material from the *Fihrist* [*Index of Books and Disciplines*] by Ibn al-Nadīm (d. 380/990 or 385/995), from Ibn al-Ḥakam (d. 257/871), Maqrīzī (d. 845/1442), Ibn Khaldūn (d. 808/1406), Maqqarī (d. 1041/1632), Ibn al-Athīr (ʿIzz al-Dīn, d. 630/1233), Abū al-Faraj al-Iṣfahānī (d. 356/967), among others. We have come a long way since the publication, in 1747, of J.J. Reiske's (d. 1774) *mémoire*, which still appears to be little known.[19] It should, however, be noted that the latter's *Dissertatio inauguralis exhibens miscellaneas aliquot observationes medicas ex Arabum monumentis*,[20] which was published in the preceding year, dealt with Arab medicine and thus held little interest for literary circles.

The Saxon Gustav Flügel (d. 1870) focused his energies on, among other things, cataloguing the Arabic, Turkish and Persian manuscripts of the princely library of Vienna. In addition to his edition and concordance of the Qurʾan (1837, 1875), he published two important sources for the knowledge of scholarship in Islam: the *Lexicon bibliographicum et encyclopaedicum* (*Kashf al-ẓunūn*) (1835–58) of Ḥājjī Khalīfa, with a Latin translation and scholarly notes, and the *editio princeps* of Ibn al-Nadīm's *Kitāb al-Fihrist* (1872), which was edited and published posthumously. He also published two monographs aimed at providing readers with a better understanding of scholars and scholarship in Islam: *Die Classen der hanefitischen Rechtsgelehrten* (*The Classes of Ḥanafī Jurists*) (1861) according to Ibn Quṭlūbughā (d. 879/1474), and *Die grammatischen Schulen der Araber* (*Arabic Grammatical Schools*) (1862). Several of his other writings followed in the same spirit.[21]

Ferdinand Wüstenfeld's (d. 1899) edition of the biographical dictionary *Wafayāt al-aʿyān* (*The Obituary of Illustrious Persons*) (1835–50) by Ibn Khallikān (d. 681/1282) gave access to a treasure trove of information concerning Arabic literary and scientific life. His *Die Academien der Araber und ihre Lehrer* (*The Academies of the Arabs and their Teachers*) (1837)—a German adaptation of the *The Classes of the Shāfiʿīs* by Ibn Qāḍī Shuhba (d. 851/1448)—made an important contribution to our knowledge of sources on teaching and scholarship. He also wrote on the history of Arabic physicians and naturalists (*Geschichte der arabischen Ärzte und Naturforscher nach den Quellen bearbeitet*, 1840). He then

[18] Quatremère, Étienne, "Mémoire sur le goût des livres chez les Orientaux", *JA*, 3rd series (1838), 35–78; Hammer-Purgstall, J., "Additions au 'Mémoire' de M. Quatremère sur le goût des livres chez les Orientaux", *JA*, 4th series, XI (1848), 178–98.

[19] *Dissertatio de principibus Muhammedanis* ..., Leipzig, 1747.

[20] *Lugduni Batavorum* (Leiden), 1746, 29 pp.

[21] Among others, "Einige geographische und ethnographische Handschriften der Refaïja auf der Universitätsbibliothek zu Leipzig", *ZDMG*, 16 (1862), 651–709.

published *Die Geschichtschreiber der Araber und ihre Werke* (*The Historiographers of the Arabs and their works*) (1882) and also compiled a wealth of information in the *The Classes of the Shāfiʿīs* of al-Subkī, al-Asanawī and Ibn Quṭlūbughā, which was published under the title of *Der Imâm el-Schâfiʿí, seine Schüler und Anhänger bis zum J. 300 d. H.* (*The Imām al-Shāfiʿī, his Pupils and Disciples until 300*) (1890–91).

In his dissertation, the Dutch theologian Pieter Johannes Veth (d. 1895)[22] investigated Arab institutions for the education of youth and the promotion of literatures.[23] He based this on the works of Casiri, Wüstenfeld, Hammer-Purgstall, G. Weil, Georg Wilhelm Freytag (d. 1861), William McGuckin de Slane (d. 1878), José Antonio Conde (d. 1820),[24] among others, as well as on edited Arab sources such as that of al-Zarnūjī and on Leiden manuscripts (Maqrīzī *et al.*).

In 1849 the orientalist Aloys Sprenger (d. 1893), an Austrian doctor, edited an important source for an understanding of the *ratio studiorum* and the Muslim classification of the sciences: the *Irshād al-qāṣid ilā asnā al-maqāṣid* (*s.t. Survey of the Mohammadan Sciences*)[25] by Ibn al-Akfānī (d. 749/1348), until then better known as al-Anṣārī or Shams al-Dīn Ibn Ibrāhīm. A few years later, Sprenger published an article on the subjects taught in schools and Muslim scholasticism.[26] Theodor Haarbrücker (d. 1880), the translator of Shahrastānī, had, however, previously partially translated al-Akfānī's text, notably the passages relating to pedagogy and the taught sciences (1859).[27] Having access to al-Akfānī's treatise in Arabic, and also partly in German, represented significant progress, particularly since this work is one of the sources for the *Miftāḥ al-saʿāda* (*The Key of Happiness*), a biographical/bibliographical work by Ṭāshkubrīzādah (d. 986/1651), which in turn is the principal source for Ḥājjī Khalīfa. Sprenger also oversaw, with W. Nassau Lees, the publication of the *Dictionary of Technical Terms used in the Sciences of the Musalmans* (1854–62) by al-Tahānawī (originally written in 1158/1745). Finally, he wrote a long article on the writing down of historical facts among Muslims.[28]

---

[22] Velde, Paul van der, *Een Indische liefde: P.J. Veth (1814–1895) en de inburgering van Nederlands-Indië*, Amsterdam, Balans, 2000, 451 pp.; id., *A Lifelong Passion: P.J. Veth (1814–1895) and the Dutch East Indies*, trans. Beverly Jackson, Leiden, KITLV Press, 2006, XVI+355 pp.

[23] Veth, P.J., *Dissertatio De institutis Arabum erudiendae juventuti ...*, Amsterdam, 1843.

[24] Conde, J.A., *Geschichte der Herrschaft der Mauren in Spanien*, trans. Karl Rutschmann, Karlsruhe, 1824–25 [*Historia de la Dominación de los Árabes*, 1820–21].

[25] *Two Works on Arabic Bibliography*, Calcutta, 1849, 14–99; reprint F. Sezgin *et al.* (eds), *Historiography and Classification of Science in Islam*, IX, Frankfurt, IGAIW, 2005, 187–275; Witkam, J.J., "Ibn al-Akfānī (d. 749/1348) and his bibliography of the sciences" *MME*, 2 (1987), 37–41.

[26] Sprenger, A., "Die Schulfächer und die Scholastik der Muslime", *ZDMG*, 32 (1878), 1–20.

[27] "Muhammad Ibn Ibrahim al-Anssâri's arabische Encyclopädie der Wissenschaften, vornehmlich in pädagogischer Beziehung", *Jahresbericht über die Louisenstädtische Realschule* (Berlin, Lange), 1859, 1–38; reprint in F. Sezgin *et al.* (eds), *Historiography and Classification of Science in Islam*, IX, Frankfurt, IGAIW, 2005, 1–25.

[28] Sprenger, A., "On the origin and progress of writing down historical facts among the Musulmans". *JAS of Bengal*, 25 (1856–57), 303–29, 375–85.

This same period saw several works contribute to a better understanding of the transmission of the *ḥadīth* and its terminology: L. Krehl's (1825–1901)[29] publication of the 20-verse didactic poem on the terminology of the *ḥadīth* by the Andalusian Ibn Faraḥ (d. 699/1300) was followed by an edition of Izz al-Dīn's (d. 819/1416) commentary, *Zawāl al-taraḥ fī manẓūmat Ibn Faraḥ*, edited, translated and annotated by F. Risch (1859).[30] In 1862 E.E. Salisbury (d. 1901) penned a long contribution on "the science of the Muslim tradition" made up of Arabic texts drawn from several sources and accompanied by a translation.[31]

The polyglot Benedictine abbot Daniel Bonifacius Haneberg (d. 1876) wrote a treatise in Latin on *Teaching and Instruction among the Mahomedans of the Middle Age*[32] in which he considered the relationship between schools and the state, the teaching of pupils, the method of instruction, and the formation of the various disciplines.

At the same time, much of what we know about Muslim Sicily has been culled from later Arabic sources and collated by the historian Michele Amari (d. 1889),[33] an effort that led him to compile a substantial work that was edited and published posthumously.[34] Towards the end of the eighteenth century, a work by the ecclesiastic, diplomat and historiographer Rosario de Gregorio (d. 1809)[35] was published in Palermo, but was made obsolete by the works of Michele Amari.

Certain general histories of education or teaching, based on monographs written by specialists, have included pages or chapters on Muslim Spain, one example being that by Auguste Vallet de Viriville (d. 1868).[36]

Because of a greater availability of Arabic sources edited in the West, lithographed or printed in the East, or, to a lesser extent, in the Maghreb, the last quarter of the nineteenth century to the first quarter of the twentieth century saw an increase in the publication of better-informed monographs, articles or book chapters on education than ever before. Thus, the Austrian Alfred von Kremer (d. 1889) devoted some chapters and pages of his *Culturgeschichte des Orients unter den Chalifen* (1875–77) to teaching and the *kuttāb*, other institutions, like mosques, study circles, *madrasas* (colleges), and diciplines, like poetry, science and literature, and libraries in the first four centuries of Islam. For his part, Julián

---

[29] Maqqarī, *Analectes sur l'histoire et la littérature des Arabes d'Espagne* (*Nafḥ al-ṭīb*), 2 vols, ed. R. Dozy *et al.*, Leiden, 1855–61, I, 819–20.

[30] *Commentar des Izz-ed-Dîn Abu Abd-ullah*, Leiden, 1885, VII+15+42 pp.; cf. Gilliot, "Textes arabes anciens édités en Égypte", *MIDEO*, 28 (2010), 400–402, no. 184.

[31] "Contributions from original sources to our knowledge of the science of Muslim tradition", *JAOS*, VII (1862), 60–142.

[32] *Über das Schul- und Lehrwesen der Muhamedaner im Mittelalter*, Munich, 1850.

[33] *Bibliotheca arabo-sicula*, Leipzig, 1857; reprint Baghdad, 1965; Beirut, n.d.

[34] *Storia dei Musulmani di Sicilia*, 2nd edn, 3 vols in 5, Catania, 1933–39; Firenze, 1854–72. Arabic trans. I. Muḥibb Sa'd, *Ta'rīkh Muslimī Ṣiqilliya*, 3 vols, Italy, 2003.

[35] *Rerum Arabicarum quae ad Historiam Siculam*, Palermo, 1790.

[36] *Histoire de l'instruction publique en Europe et principalement en France*, Paris, 1849, 103–10, on the Arabs and Jews in Spain.

Ribera y Tarragó (d. 1934) published two of his conferences—one on *Teaching among the Muslims of Spain* (1893)[37] and the other on book-lovers and libraries in Islamic Spain.[38] Moritz Güdemann (d. 1918) made a study of teaching among the Spanish Jews during the Muslim occupation,[39] and the American Duncan Black Macdonald (d. 1943),[40] published A Selection from the Prolegomena of *Ibn Khaldūn* in 1905.

In 1912 Ignaz Goldziher (d. 1921) published the first truly scientific article on education among the Muslims ever published in an encyclopaedia, which is as useful to us now as it was then (see Chapter 2, this volume). It benefited from Goldziher's previous research, which already included substantial relevant material such as his "Contributions to the History of Linguistic Scholarship among the Arabs"[41] and his *Muhammedanische Studien* (1889–90), which has now been partly translated into other languages, including French and English.

However, the great event proved to be the posthumous publication, in 1922, of Adam Mez's (d. 1917) *Die Renaissance des Islams* which has since been translated into several languages. This was the first attempt since that made by Alfred von Kremer to present a cultural history of Islam, here focusing on the fourth/tenth century.

The History of Education and Learning in Islam: General Notes

We have at our disposal a bibliography of Islamic education drawn up by A. Belambri (1988) almost up-to-date until around 1987, and also the *Bibliography of Islamic Philosophy* by Hans Daiber, the index of which includes an entry on "Education".[42] Furthermore, two Tunisian researchers, I. al-Najjār and B. al-Zarībī (1985), have collected numerous texts relating to education, teaching and pedagogy in Islam, drawn from Muslim sources; this anthology is of some use. Finally, the electronic site moderated by J.J. Witkam gives us direct access

[37] Ribera y Tarragó, J., *La enseñanza entre los musulmanes españoles. Bibliofilos y Bibliotecas en la España Musulmana*, 3rd edn, Córdoba, 1925, 120 pp./Arabic trans. al-Ṭ.A. Makkī, *al-Tarbiyya al-islāmiyya fī al-Andalus*, Cairo, 1981.

[38] Ribera y Tarragó, J., "Bibliófilos y bibliotecas de la España musulmana", dissertation, Faculty of Medicine and Science, Zaragoza, 1896.

[39] *Das jüdische Unterrichtswesen während der spanisch–arabischen Periode*, Vienna, 1873; reprint, Amsterdam, 1968.

[40] *Aspects of Islam*, New York, 1911, 288–322; id., "The moral education of the young among Muslims", *International Journal of Ethics*, XV/3 (1915), 286–304.

[41] "Beiträge zur Geschichte der Sprachgelehrsamkeit bei den Arabern". I. "Mit Mitteilungen aus der Refâ'ijja"; II. "Zur Gauharī-Literatur"; III. "Abu-l-Husein ibn Fâris"; SKAW, LXVII (1871), 207–51; LXXII (1872, 587–631; LXXIII (1873), 511–52; reprint in *Gesammelte Schriften*, I, Hildesheim, 1964, 7–51.

[42] *Bibliography of Islamic Philosophy*, 2 vols, Leiden, 1999; *Supplement*, Leiden, 2007, II, 107, under Education, and Supplement.

to numerous articles, and even to some works, on books, manuscripts and even scholarship on Islam.[43]

Shlomo Dov Goitein's (d. 1985) *opus magnum*, *A Mediterranean Society*, dedicated to the Jewish communities of the world, as portrayed in documents of the Cairo Geniza, is a treasure trove of information for the subject of our study, especially its sixth chapter entitled "Education and the Professional Classes".[44] Furthermore, it boasts an index volume, and access to the *materia arabica* has been made even easier by a special dictionary.[45]

Given the chronological parameters (from 600 AD to 340/950) assigned to this collection of essays, the *terminus ad quem* to which we have adhered is the creation of the *madrasas* (colleges), even though *madrasas* existed prior to the establishment of the Niẓāmiyya of Baghdad (457/1065), and even though the question of the origin, birth and evolution of these institutions remains highly controversial.[46]

We have not yet found a satisfactory work on the general history of education and learning in Islam, or even a monograph on this subject, for the formative period of Islamic history. It is no coincidence that the article "Tarbiyya" ("Education and Pedagogy")—referred to several times in the second edition of *The Encyclopaedia of Islam*—has an entry of merely a few lines.[47] The best work, which also relates to the concept of knowledge in medieval Islam, is the study by Franz Rosenthal, particularly Chapter 8: "Knowledge is Society: Education".[48] Arthur Stanley Tritton's 1957 study, *Materials on Muslim Education in the Middle Ages*, remains a mine of ever useful information, but it covers the whole of the medieval period and is in need of updating. Nevertheless, the author, being a good historian, often orders the material within the various chapters chronologically—for example, "Elementary Education", "Advanced Education", "Teachers and the Taught" and so on. Bayard Dodge's 1962 study, *Muslim Education Medieval Times*, is a short general synthesis. As regards the Qur'an, two articles in the *Encyclopaedia of the Qur'ān* address knowledge, learning and teaching.[49]

---

[43] http://www.islamicmanuscripts.info/reference/index.html.

[44] *A Mediterranean Society*, 6 vols, Berkeley, 1967–93; reprint, 1999, II, 171–272.

[45] Diem, W. and Radenberg, H.-P., *A Dictionary of the Arabic Material of S.D. Goitein's* A Mediterranean Society, Wiesbaden, 1994.

[46] Makdisi, G., "Madrasa", *EI*, 2nd edn, V, 1123–34 (French edn, V, 1119–30), V, 1126–27/1122–23; id., *The Rise of Colleges*, Edinburgh, 1981, 27–34. For a summary of Makdisi's ideas on these topics and the critique to them, see Lowry, J., "Colleges of law and the institutions of medieval Sunni Islam", in Lowry *et al.* (eds), *Law and Education in Medieval Islam*, Warminster, 2004, 1–4.

[47] "Tarbīya", *EI*, 2nd edn, X, 223a; French edn "Tarbiyya", X, 241a, with reference to Kuttāb, Madrasa, Djāmi'a, Kulliyya and so on; Berkey, J.P., "Tadrīs", *EI*, 2nd edn, X (1998), deals with teaching in the period of the *madrasas*.

[48] Rosenthal, F., *Knowledge Triumphant*, Leiden, 1970, 240–333.

[49] Walker, P.E., "Knowledge and learning", *Encyclopaedia of the Qur'an* [hereafter *EQ*], III, 100–104; Günther, S., "Teaching", *EQ*, V, 200–205.

A. Shalaby's thesis, *The History of Muslim Education with Special Reference to Egypt*, published in English (1954/1979) and in Arabic translation (1954/1973), certainly contains interesting material, yet suffers from a methodological insufficiency and a lack of historical objectivity. The last chapter of this work is dedicated to the Ismailis of Egypt[50] and does not seem to follow on well from what comes before. M. Hamiuddin Khan's first volume, *History of Muslim Education* (1967), considers the period between 712 and 1750 and offers little interesting information it its own right. S.M. Ziauddin Alavi's short book, *Muslim Educational Thought in the Middle Ages*, attempts to trace the development of Muslim education from the rise of Islam up to the fourteenth century and focuses on the ideas of Avicenna, al-Fārābī, Ibn Miskawayh, al-Ghazālī and Ibn Khaldūn. We were unable to consult ʿAbdul-Rahman Salih ʿAbdullah's (1982) thesis, nor even M.A. ʿAbdullatīf's (1997) large work in Urdu.

More works have been produced, either based on specific sources or on towns and regions. Accordingly, Munir-ud-Din Ahmed studied Muslim education and the status of scholars until the fifth/eleventh century using the *History of Baghdad* by al-Khaṭīb al-Baghdādī (d. 463/1071) as his principal source.[51] Similarly, on the basis of the *History of Damascus* by Ibn ʿAsākir, Malake Abiad has put forward a culture and education chart for Shām (Syria) during the first three centuries of Islam.[52] K.D. Zarw (1971), however, confined his study of Shām to its intellectual life solely during the first–third/seventh–eighth centuries. Ali Driss, for his part, wrote his 1979 doctoral thesis on education and pedagogic ideas in Muslim Barbary. In a work published in 1997 A. ʿU. Ḥijāzī set himself the task of drawing out the main characteristics of education among the Malikis, Fatimids, Sufis and Ibadites in Qayrawan (Fr: Kairouan) over the course of the three first centuries of the Hijra. Other works have focused on cultural life, teaching and transmission of knowledge in Sicily.[53]

Ibrahim Salama's 1938 publication on Islamic teaching in Egypt includes some pages on the first centuries of Islam. In 1992 Vernet made a written contribution to a volume on education in ancient and medieval Islamic Spain, while M. ʿA. ʿĪsā devoted a large work to the history of education in this same region (1982).

Although Charles Pellat's study of Bassora[54] at the time of al-Jāḥiẓ does not confine itself to education and learning, it remains a model of the genre for the *Geistesgeschichte* of this Muslim metropolis.

---

50 *Ta'rīkh al-tarbiyya al-islāmiyya*, 389–421.

51 *Muslim Education and the Scholars' Social Status*, Zurich, 1968.

52 *Culture et éducation arabo-islamique au Šām*, Damascus, 1981.

53 ʿAbbās, Iḥsān, *al-ʿArab fī Ṣiqilliyya. Dirāsa fī al-ta'rīkh wa-al-adab*, Cairo, 1959, 2nd edn, Beirut, 1975; al-Zahrānī, ʿA. b. M. b. Saʿīd, *al-Ḥayāt al-ʿilmiyya fī Ṣiqilliyya al-islāmiyya (212–484/826–1091)*, Mecca, 1996; Granara, W., "Islamic education and the transmission of knowledge in Muslim Sicily", in Lowry *et al.* (eds), *Law and Education in Medieval Islam* (2004), 150-73.

54 *Le Milieu baṣrien et la formation de Ǧāḥiẓ*, Paris, 1953/Arabic trans., 1961.

Several monographs have focused on non-Sunni Muslim groups, such as the Imamites[55] and the Ibadites,[56] among others.

Literacy in Pre-IslamicTimes and in the Time of Muḥammad[57]

When it comes to knowledge about the writings of the ancient Arabs,[58] the researcher is caught between a rock and a hard place. On the one hand, Muslim sources seek to convince us that the Arabs were illiterate (*umiyyūn*), thus seeking to establish the basis for the Muslim dogma according to which Muḥammad knew neither how to read nor how to write, in order to better establish the notion of the uniquely divine origin of the Qurʾan. On the other hand, over time, these same sources extended the list of those Muslims who would have commited the revelations of the Prophet of Islam to writing in order to emphasize the idea of the faithful transmission of the Qurʾan. We now know that if the word *ummī* came to be understood to mean "illiterate" it was probably in consequence of "a sectarian dispute about the probative value of the miracle in the Muḥammadan biography".[59]

Indeed, a debate broke out over whether or not Muḥammad knew how to write (or read). It is here, once again, that Aloys Sprenger emerges as a pioneer, even though the question had been raised a long time previously. According to him, Muḥammad probably did know how to read and write.[60] Indeed, Sprenger held that:

> ... the intellectual training of the Meccans or of the Qurayshites, as they were called, should not be disregarded. Most knew how to read and write; for their commercial travels had allowed them to acquire learning that cannot

[55] Fayyāḍ, *Taʾrikh al-tarbiyya ʿinda al-imāmiyya wa aslāfihim min al-shīʿa bayna ʿahday al-Ṣādiq wa al-Ṭūsī*, 2nd edn, Beirut, 1983; Qazwīnī, ʿA.A.M.M., *al-Fikr al-tarbawī ʿinda al-Shīʿa al-imāmiyya*, Cairo, 1985.

[56] Ḥijāzī (2000).

[57] For this whole section, see Gilliot, C., "Die Schreib- und/oder Lesekundigkeit in Mekka und Yathrib/Medina zur Zeit Mohammeds", in Groß, Markus, and Ohlig, Karl-Heinz (eds), *Schlaglichter. Die beiden ersten islamischen Jahrhunderte*, Berlin, Hans Schiler, 2008, 293–319.

[58] For the pre-Islamic period it is always worth consulting the following work, sadly lacking in references: Ālūsī, *Bulūgh al-arab fī maʿrifat aḥwāl al-ʿArab*, Cairo, 1923, III, 367–84.

[59] Calder, N., "The Ummī in early Islamic juristic literature", *Der Islam*, 67 (1990), 111 (111–23); Wansbrough, J., *Quranic Studies*, Oxford, 1977, 53–54, 63; Goldfeld, I., "Al-Nabiyy al-Umiyyʾ: an inquiry into the development of a dogma in Islamic tradition", *Der Islam*, 57 (1980), 58–67; Athamina, K., "Al-nabiyy al-umiyyʾ : an inquiry into the meaning of a Qurʾanic verse", *Der Islam*, 69 (1992), 61–80.

[60] Sprenger, A., *Das Leben und die Lehre des Moḥammad*, 2nd edn, 3 vols, Berlin, 1869, II, 398–402. See also ʿAlī, Jawād, *al-Mufaṣṣal fī taʾrīkh al-ʿarab qabla al-islām*, 2nd edn, 10 vols, n.p., 1413/1993 (1st edn, 1968–76), VIII, 91–143, which shows a certain critical distance, particularly concerning Muḥammad's illiteracy.

be underestimated, so that they could even boast before the Prophet of their knowledge (Koran 40, 83).[61]

Though sensitive to Sprenger's arguments, and that of others, Theodor Nöldeke does not follow suit.[62] Henri Lammens, on the basis of a passage from the *Sīra*, deduces that of the ten sons of ʿAbd al-Muṭṭalib, ʿAbd Allāh, Muḥammad's father, knew how to write.[63]

Investigation of the milieu that witnessed the birth of Arabic inscriptions[64] and the derivation of the Arabic alphabet has become a vexed issue among scholars.[65] Although everyone agrees that the Arabic alphabet is ultimately derived from some form of the Aramaic alphabet, some hold that it stems from the Nabatean, while yet others believe that it comes from the Syriac. The latter view is the older, harking back to the eighteenth[66] and early nineteenth centuries.[67] The small principality of Lakhm, and more specifically its capital Ḥīra,[68] could well be the birthplace of Arabic writing. This state welcomed the Manicheans persecuted by the Sassanids and, above all, Christians expelled from the Byzantine Empire for reasons of heterodoxy. The languages spoken there were Syriac and Arabic (they were also written down, but we do not know in what form). From a historical perspective, a likely hypothesis might be that Arabic script was created in Ḥīra in the fifth century for the purposes of the chancellery. It would then have been brought to Syria by Christians fleeing the Sassanid Empire at the beginning of

---

61 Sprenger, *Mohammed und der Koran: eine psychologische Studie*, Hamburg, 1889, 4–5.

62 Nöldeke, *De origine et compositione surarum qoranicarum ipsiusque Qorani*, Göttingen, 1856, 10–14; id., *Geschichte des Qorâns*, Göttingen, 1860, 7–15; id., *GdQ*, I, 11–15.

63 Lammens, H., *La Mecque à la veille de l'hégire*, Beirut, 1924, 123, n. 5; cf. Ibn Isḥāq, *Sīra*, (*Das Leben Mohammeds*), ed. Wüstenfeld, Göttingen, 1858–60, 97/trans A. Guillaume, *The Life of Muḥammad*, Karachi, 1978, 66. For Lammens, writing was very widespread in the "république marchande de La Mecque" (*La Mecque*, 192); id., "La république marchande de La Mecque vers l'an 600 de notre ère", *Bulletin de l'Institut d'Egypte*, 5th series, 4 (1910), 27, 46 and fn. 7.

64 Robin, C, "L'écriture arabe et l'Arabie", *Pour la Science*, Dossier (October–January 2002), 62–69; Endress, G., "Die arabische Schrift", in Fischer, Wolfdietrich (ed.), *Grundriss der arabischen Philologie*, I, Sprachwissenschaft, Wiesbaden, 1982, 166–70 (165–183); Gilliot, C, "Une reconstruction critique du Coran ou comment en finir avec les merveilles de la lampe d'Aladin", in Kropp, M. (ed.), *Results of Contemporary Research on the Qurʾan: The question of a historico-critical text*, Beyrouth, Orient Institut/Würzburg, Ergon Verlag, 2007, 66–76 (33–137).

65 Bellamy, J.A., "The Arabic alphabet", in Senner, Wayne M. (ed.), *The Origins of Writing*, Lincoln and London, University of Nebraska Press, 1991, 99 (91–102).

66 Silvestre de Sacy, A-I., "Mémoire", 1785, 266, 299–300, 306–307; id., "Nouveaux aperçus", 1827, 27 pp. He developed and reinforced through further arguments this idea which had already been proposed by others, such as: Adler, J.G.C., *De arte scribendi apud Arabes*, Hamburg, 1780; and Reiske, *Tharafae Moallakah cum scholiis Nahas*, Leiden, 1742.

67 Ewald, H. (G.H.A. von), *Grammatica critica linguae Arabicae*, 2 vols in 1, Leipzig, 1831–33, I, 34–36, giving the Arabic and Syriac alphabets side-by-side in a table reproduced in Troupeau, G., "Réflexions sur l'origine syriaque de l'écriture arabe", in Kaye, Alan S. (ed.), *Semitic Studies in Honor of Wolf Leslau*, II, Wiesbaden, Harrassowitz, 1991, 1567 (1562–70).

68 Thus al-Farrāʾ (d. 207/822), in Thaʿlabī, Abū Isḥāq, *al-Kashf wa l-bayān ʿan tafsīr al-Qurʾān*, 10 vols, ed. Abū M. ʿA. ʿĀshūr and Abū M. b. ʿĀshūr, Beirut, 2002, II, 281, *ad* Coran 2, 275.

the sixth century. This would, to some extent, agree with the accounts of Muslim historiographers.

Another hypothesis suggests that Arabic script could have its origins in the Arab Church of Syria, but this Church comprised tribes who would have had a centre only from the time of the establishment of the principality of Ghassān, towards 520, and it does not seem to have undertaken an Arabic translation of the Bible.[69] That said, the problem of pre-Islamic Christian literature in the East during the fifth century in relation to an Arabic Bible and liturgy has been considered by I. Shahid, who notably presented a *status quaestionis* of this subject.[70]

If we take a palaeographic approach to determining the origin of Arabic script we find two opposing currents. The first defends the Nabatean origin of the Arabic alphabet, claiming that the shape of the letters is the result of an evolution of the classical Aramaic alphabet (inscriptions in Jordan, southern Syria and north-west Arabia).[71] This thesis is generally agreed upon and originated with the publication of Sinaitic and Nabatean inscriptions in the nineteenth century, and, ever since, most scholars have followed the lead of Theodor Nöldeke who proposed the Nabatean origin, in 1865.[72]

However, beginning in the 1960s, several French researchers[73] revisited the old theory –that the Arabic alaphabet has a Syriac origin—this time backing up their thesis with more arguments. As was quite rightly written, "On est frappé de constater que les opérations au moyen desquelles l'écriture estranghelo a pu être transformée pour devenir l'écriture coufique concordent avec les données fournies par la tradition arabe"[74]—in other words, among others, a tradition transmitted by al-Kalbī (M. b. al-Sā'ib, d. 146/763) in a familial *isnād* that starts

[69] Robin, "L'écriture arabe", *art. cit.*, 65.

[70] Shahid, *Byzantium and the Arabs in the Fifth Century*, Washington, DC, 2006, 438–49, 449–58. First published 1989.

[71] Robin, "L'écriture arabe", *art. cit.*

[72] Nöldeke, T., "Bemerkungen zu den von de Voguë herausgegebenen nabatäischen und hebräischen Inschriften", *ZDMG*, 19 (1865), 638 (637–41); Euting, J., *Nabatäische Inschriften aus Arabien*, Berlin, 1885; Lidzbarski, M., *Handbuch der nordsemitischen Epigraphik nebst ausgewahlten Inschriften*, Weimar, 1898; Abbott, N., *The Rise of the North Arabic Script and its Kur'ānic Development*, Chicago, 1939, 1–5; Moritz, B., "Arabia (Arabic Writing)", *EI*, 1st edn (1913), I, 381–92, and more particularly 384, 387–89; Grohmann, A., *Arabische Paläographie*, II, *Das Schriftwesen. Die Lapidarschrift*, Vienna, 1971, 12–20; Gruendler, B., *The Development of the Arabic Scripts*, Atlanta, Scholars Press (Harvard Semitic Studies, 63), 1993.

[73] Starcky, J., "Pétra et la Nabatène", *Supplement au Dictionnaire de la Bible*, Paris, 1967, 932–34 (886–1017); Sourdel-Thomine, J., "Les origines de l'écriture arabe", *REI*, 1966, 151–57; Troupeau, "Réflexions", *art cit.*; Briquel-Chatonnet, F., "De l'araméen à l'arabe ...", in Déroche, F. and Richard, F. (eds), *Scribes et manuscrits du Moyen-Orient*, Paris, 1997, 135–49.

[74] "We are struck by the observation that the processes by which the estrangelo script could be transformed into the Kufic script tallies with the material supplied by the Arabic tradition": Troupeau, "Réflexions", *art. cit.*, 1539–70.

with his grandson al-ʿAbbās b. Hishām and Sharqī al-Quṭāmī al-Kalbī al-Kūfī,[75] who was the private tutor of Caliph al-Mahdī (d. 169/785) and Ibn al-Nadīm (except for the elements that refer to mythical figures such as Adam, Ishmael and others, which these notes contain).[76]

As for Irfan Shahid, he has presented the historical context within which the Arabic script was born.[77]

Muslim sources supply us with lists of those in Mecca who would have known how to write. Thus we have that of Wāqidī (d. 207/823)—which could belong to a chain of guarantors going back to Abū Bakr b. ʿAbd Allāh b. a. Jahm Ṣukhayr al-Qurashī[78] al-ʿAdawī—for Mecca: (1) ʿUmar b. al-Khaṭṭāb; (2) ʿAlī b. a. Ṭālib; (3) ʿUthmān b. ʿAffān; (4) Abū ʿUbayda b. al-Jarrāḥ; (5) Ṭalḥa (b. ʿUbayd Allāh al-Taymī); (6)Yazīd b. a. Sufyān; (7) Abū Ḥudhayfa b. ʿUtba b. Rabīʿa; (8) Ḥāṭib b. ʿAmr al-ʿĀmirī; (9) Abū Salama b. ʿAbd al-Asad al-Makhzūmī; (10) Abān b. Saʿīd b. al-ʿĀṣ b. Umayya; (11) Khālid b. Saʿīd, his brother; (12) ʿAbd Allāh b. Saʿd b. a. Sarḥ al-ʿĀmirī; (13) Ḥuwayṭib b. ʿAbd al-ʿUzzā al-ʿĀmirī; (14) Abū Sufyān b. Ḥarb b. Umayya; (15) Muʿāwiya b. a. Sufyān; (16) Juhaym b. al-Ṣalt b. Makhrama b. al-Muṭṭalib b. ʿAbd Manāf; and (17) al-ʿAlāʾ b. al-Ḥaḍramī.

Some sources also supply the names of women who were able to write:[79] (1) al-Shifāʾ bint ʿAbd Allāh al-ʿAdawiyya;[80] (2) Ḥafsa, wife of Muḥammad; (3) Umm Kulthūm bint ʿUqba b. Muʿīṭ; (4) ʿĀʾisha bint Saʿd; (5) Karīma bint al-Miqdād; (6) ʿĀʾisha, who read the Qurʾan in the codex (*al-muṣḥaf*), but did not know how to

---

[75] In Balādhurī (*viv.* third/ninth century), *Liber Expugnationis regionum*, ed. M.J. De Goeje, Lugduni Batavorum, 1866, 471; also *Futūḥ al-buldān*, ed. al-Ṭabbāʾ, Beirut, Muʾassasat al-Maʿārif, 1407/1987, 659–660.German trans. in Sprenger, *Leben*, 129. English trans. in Horovitz, J., "Ibn Quteiba's ʿUyun al-akhbar", *IC*, IV (1930), 488, n. 1; trans. and commentary by Gilliot, "Une reconstruction critique", *art. cit.*, 68-72; Ibn Khallikān, *Wafayāt al-aʿyān*, 8 vols, ed. I. ʿAbbās, Beirut, Dār al-Thaqāfa, 1968–72, III, 344, no. 457. Murtaḍā al-Zabīdī, *Ḥikmat al-ishrāf ilā kuttāb al-āfāq*, ed. ʿAbd al-Salām Hārūn, in *Nawādir al-makhṭūṭāt*, 2nd edn, Cairo, 1393/1973, II, 65, takes up the former. More developed in id., *Tāj al-ʿarūs*, ed. of Kuwayt, X, 386–87 (s. rad. *jdr*); XIV, 112–13 (s. rad. *mrr*); cf. Ibn Qutayba, *Ibn Coteibas Handbuch der Geschichte*, ed. Wüstenfeld, Göttingen, 1850, 273 *et seq.*/*Kitāb al-Maʿārif*, 2nd edn, ed. ʿUkāsha, Cairo, Dār al-Maʿārif, 1388/1969, 552–53; cf. Ibn a. Dāwūd al-Sijistānī, *K. al-Maṣāḥif*, ed. A. Jeffery, in *Materials or the History of the Qurʾān*, Leiden, 1937, 4.

Kitāb al-Kitāba wa al-Kuttāb by the blind grammarian Abū Mūsā (such was his *shuhra*) al-Baghdādī al-Ḍarīr (Abū al-Qāsim ʿAbd Allāh b. ʿAbd al-ʿAzīz), who was tutor (*ca.* 255/869) to the children of the caliph al-Muhtadī, gives a list of 11 scribes in Sourdel, D., "Le 'Livre des secrétaires' by ʿAbdallāh al-Baghdādī", *REI*, XIV (1954), 128–29 (116–53). Other accounts are also given by Ibn ʿAbd Rabbih, *al-ʿIqd al-farīd*, 9 vols, ed. Mufīd Qumayḥa *et al.*, Beirut, 1404/1983, IV, 239–40; Qalqashandī, *Ṣubḥ al-aʿshā*, 14 vols, ed. M. Ḥusayn Shams al-Dīn, Beirut, Dār al-Kutub al-ʿilmiyya, 1407/1987, III, 12–15.

[76] Ibn al-Nadīm, *al-Fihrist*, ed. Gustav Flügel, Leipzig, 1872, 4–5/German trans. by Sprenger, *Leben*, 129–30/English trans. by Dodge, 2 vols, New York, Columbia University Press, 1970, I, 6–9.

[77] *Byzantium and the Arabs in the Fifth Century*, 409–22.

[78] Mizzī, *Tahdhīb al-kamāl*, 23 vols, ed. A.ʿA. ʿAbīd and Ḥ.A. Āghā, Beirut, 1414/1994, XXI, 37–38, no. 78314.

[79] Balādhurī, *Futūḥ*, *op. cit.*, 662.

[80] We deduce from a tradition transmitted by Muḥammad that she would have learnt how to write to Ḥafsa; Mizzī, *Tahdhīb*, XXII, 355-356, no. 8458.

write; and (7) Umm Salama (Hind bint Abī Umayya, of the Makhzūm, the wife of Muḥammad) who knew how to read but not how to write.

We were also able to find the names of more literate women. In his Persian abridgement of the *Annals* of Ṭabari, Balʿamī (d. 363/974) writes that Khadija "had read the ancient writings and knew the history of the prophets, and also the name of Gabriel".[81] Of course, this tradition belongs in a Muslim apologetic context, but it is likely that this merchant-woman, cousin to Waraqa b. Nawfal, had at least some notion of reading and writing.

The same Wāqidī[82] mentions for Yathrib: (1) Saʿd ʿUbāda[83] of the Najjār (Khazraj); (2) al-Mundhir b. ʿAmr of the Sāʿida; (3) Ubayy b. Kaʿb of the Najjār (Khazraj); (4) Zayd b. Thābit of the Najjār (Khazraj); (5) Rāfiʿ b. Mālik of the Zurayq (Khazraj); (6) Usayd b. Ḥuḍayr of the ʿAbd al-Ashhal (Aws); (7) Maʿn b. ʿAdī of the Balī, a client of the ʿAmr b. Awf (Awf); (8) Bashīr b. Saʿd of the Ḥārith (Khazraj); (9) Saʿd b. Rabīʿ of the Ḥārith (Khazraj); (10) Aws b. Khawlī of the Aws (Khazraj); (11) ʿAbd Allāh b. Ubayy al-Munāfiq; (12) Suwayd b. al-Ṣāmit; and (13) Ḥuḍayr al-Katāʾib. In the list that he gives after that of Wāqidī, Qalqashandī mentions, in addition,[84] Abū ʿAbs b. Jabr of the Ḥāritha (Aws).[85]

In comparing Wāqidī's list with the corresponding notes of Ibn Saʿd (d. 230/845), who was the former's scribe, Michael Lecker[86] ascertained differences, some of which are highly significant, the most important being that Ibn Saʿd hushes up the fact that, because he had attended the Jewish school in this locality, Zayd b. Thābit knew how to write before Muḥammad came to Yathrib.

Thus the Muʿtazilite Abū al-Qāsim al-Balkhī/al-Kaʿbī (d. 311/931) quotes, and then criticizes, a tradition transmitted by al-Shaʿbī (d. 103/721):

> The Qurayshis were literate but the Helpers (*anṣār*) were illiterate. Therefore the Messenger of God ordered those [Qurayshis who were taken prisoner in the battle of Badr] who could not [pay ransom] (*man kāna lā māla lahu*) to teach writing to ten Muslim [helpers],[87] among whom was Zayd b. Thabit.

---

[81] Ṭabarī (that is, Balʿamī), *Muḥammad, sceau des prophètes*, trans. H. Zotenberg, Paris, 1980, 67 (originally 4 vols, Paris, 1867–74); cf. Sprenger, *Leben*, I, 151–52. For the possible literacy of her cousin, Waraqa b. Nawfal, see Gilliot, "Une reconstruction critique du Coran", 60–62; Sprenger, *Leben*, *op. cit.*, I, 124–34.

[82] Balādhurī, *Liber Expugnationis regionum*, 473/*Futūḥ al-buldān*, 663–664.

[83] Qalqashandī, *Ṣubḥ*, *op. cit.*, III, 15, gives Saʿīd b. Zurāra!

[84] Or at least according to *Futūḥ al-buldān*, ed. al-Ṭabbāʿ, 663–64.

[85] After correction, for in reality he gives Abū ʿAbs b. Kathīr, which is a misprint.

[86] Lecker, Michael, "Zayd b. Thābit, 'a Jew with two sidelocks': Judaism and literacy in pre-Islamic Medina (Yathrib)", *JNES*, 56 (1997), 267–68 (259–73).

[87] Cf. Ibn Saʿd, *Ṭabaqāt*, ed. Sachau *et al.*, 9 vols, Leiden, 1905–40, II/1, 14/ed. Beirut, Dār Ṣādir, 1957–59, II, 22.

Al-Kaʿbī continues:

> I asked those who were trained in the field of the life (*sīra*) [of the Prophet] about this, among others Ibn Abi l-Zinad, Muḥammad b. Salih (d. 252/866) and ʿAbdallah b. Jaʾfar, and they objected to this strongly, saying: "How could someone teach writing to Zayd, who had learned it before the Messenger of God arrived [to Yathrib/Medina]? There were more literate men (*kuttāb*) in Medina than in Mecca. In fact, when Islam arrived in Mecca, there were already a dozen there who knew how to write. When it was the turn of Medina, there were already twenty,[88] among whom was Zayd b. Thābit, who wrote in Arabic and Hebrew [other versions have Syriac or Aramaic], along with Saʾd b. ʿUbada, al-Mundhir b. ʿAmr, Rafiʾ b. Malik, etc."

Our hypothesis is that here we have a reversal of the situation. In Islamic times, the idea that the scribe of the Revelation could have written in Hebrew, Syriac, Aramaic, Arabic or another script prior to Muhammed coming to Yathrib became unacceptable, and so the account was reversed.[89]

If we turn our attention to the names of those who would have been Muḥammad's scribes (*kuttāb*, pl. of *kātib*),[90] we find more or less lengthy lists depending on the source. According to Yaʿqūbī (d. post 292/905)[91] we have: (1) ʿAlī b. a. Ṭālib; (2) Uthmān b. ʿAffān; (3) ʿAmr b. al-ʿĀṣ b. Umayya; (4) Muʿāwiya b. a. Sufyān; (5) Shuraḥbīl b. Ḥasana; (6) ʿAbd Allāh b. Saʿd b. a. Sarḥ; (7) al-Mughīra b. Shuʿba; (8) Muʿādh b. Jabal; (9) Zayd b. Thābit; (10) Ḥanẓala b. al-Rabīʿ;

[88] In addition to the 13 mentioned above, Lecker, "Zayd b. Thābit", 269–71, gives ten further names, bringing the total to 23. Among the 12 tribal representatives (*nuqabāʾ*) of the ʿAqaba meeting, seven were literate men (*art. cit.*, 271).

[89] For more sources, especially the *History of Damascus* of Ibn ʿAsākir, and details, see Gilliot, "Reconsidering the authorship of the Qurʾān. Is the Qurʾān partly the fruit of a progressive and collective work?", in Reynolds, G.S. (ed.), *The Qurʾan in its Historical Context*, Abingdon, 2008, 92–94 (88–108); id., "Une reconstruction critique du Coran", 62–66; Lecker, "Zayd b. Thābit: 'a Jew with two sidelocks'", 266, and n. 52.

[90] See a few references in *GdQ*, I, 46, n. 5. According to certain sources there would have been 26 scribes; Ḥalabī, Nūr al-Dīn (d. 1044/1635), *al-Sīra al-Halabiyya*, 3 vols, Beirut, n.d., III, 422. Ṣāliḥī, M. b. Yūsuf al-Shāmī, *Subul al-hudā [al-Sīra al-shāmiyya]*, 12 vols, ed. ʿĀ.A. ʿAbd al-Mawjūd and ʿA.M. Muʾawwaḍ, Beirut, 1993, XI, 375–94 gives the names of 34 scribes. According to al-ʿIrāqī, in his *Sīra*, there would have been 42; see Ḥalabī, *al-Sīra, op. cit.*; cf. Weil, G., *Mohammed der Prophet, sein Leben und seine Lehre*, Stuttgart, 1843, 350, n. 552. Ibn Sayyid al-Nās (d. 734/1334), *Uyūn al-athar*, 2 vols, Cairo, 1937, II, 315–16, also has a long list. Casanova, P., *Mohammed et la fin du monde*, Paris, 1911–13, 96–98, drew up a list of 40.

[91] *Historiae Ibn-Wādhih*, ed. M.Th.Houtsma, Leiden, 1883, II, 87. Abū Mūsā al-Baghdādī, *Kitāb al-Kuttāb*, *op. cit.*, 138, gives 11 names. It will be noted that Khalīfa b. Khayyāṭ, *Taʾrīkh*, ed. A.Ḍ al-ʾUmarī, 1st edn, Baghdad, 1967, 2nd edn, Damascus/Beirut, 1977, 99, only gives four names: 9, 4, 10 and 6 above.

(11) Ubayy b. Kaʿb; (12) Juhaym (or al-Juhaym)[92] b. al-Ṣalt b. Makhrama b. al-Muṭṭalib al-Muṭṭalibī; and (13) al-Ḥuṣayn (b. Numayr) (al-Anṣārī) al-Numayrī.[93]

According to Ṭabarī (d. 310/923)[94] we have: (1) ʿAlī b. a. Ṭālib; (2) Khālid b. Saʿīd; (3) Abān b. Saʿīd; (4) al-ʿAlā b. al-Ḥaḍramī; (5) Ubayy b. Kaʿb (it is said he was the first to write for the Prophet); (6) Zayd b. Thābit (when Ubayy was unavailable); (7) ʿAbd Allāh b. Saʿd b. a. Sarḥ (who customarily wrote for him, but who renounced his faith and then returned to Islam);[95] (8) Muʿāwiya b. a. Sufyān; and (9) Ḥanẓala al-Usayyidī.[96]

Ibn ʿAsākir (m. 571/1176)[97] records 24 scribes, listed here in Arabic alphabetical order: (1) Abān b. Saʿīd b. alʿĀṣ al-Umawī; (2) Ubayy b. Kaʿb Abū al-Mundhir al-Anṣārī; (3) Arqam b. Abī al-Arqam al-Makhzūmī; (4) Thābit b. Qays b. Shammās al-Anṣārī; (5) Ḥanẓala b. al-Rabīʿ al-Tamīmī al-Usayyidī; (6) Khālid b. Saʿīd b. al-ʿĀṣ al-Umawī; (7) Khālid b. al-Walīd Abū Sulaymān al-Makhzūmī; (8) al-Zubayr b. al-ʿAwwām Abū ʿAbd Allāh al-Asadī al-Qurashī; (9) Zayd b. Thābit Abū Saʿīd al-Anṣārī al-Khazrajī; (10) Sijill al-Kātib;[98] (11) (ʿAbd Allāh) Saʿd b. a. Sarḥ; (12) ʿAbd Allāh b. ʿUthmān Abū Bakr al-Ṣiddīq al-Qurashī al-Tamīmī; (13) ʿAbd Allāh b. Abī al-Arqam al-Makhzūmī; (14) ʿAbd Allāh b. Saʿd b. a. Sarḥ al-Qurashī al-ʿĀmirī; (15) ʿAbd Allāh b. Zayd b. ʿAbd Rabbih al-Anṣārī al-Khazrajī; (16) ʿĀmir b. Fuhayra *mawlā* of Abū Bakr al-Ṣiddīq; (17) ʿUmar b. al-Khaṭṭāb Abū Ḥafṣ al-Qurashī al-ʿAdawī; (18) ʿUthmān b. ʿAffān b. a. al-ʿĀṣ Abū ʿAmr al-Umawī; (19) ʿAlī b. a. Ṭālib Abū al-Ḥasan al-Hāshimī; (20) al-ʿAlā b. al-Ḥaḍramī (ʿAbd

[92] Zabīdī, *Tāj al-ʿarūs*, XXXI, 432b, gives two possibilities. He submitted to Islam (*aslama*) in the year of Ḥunayn, or during the conquest of Mecca; see Ibn al-Athīr, ʿIzz al-Dīn, *Usd al-ghāba fī maʿrifat al-ṣaḥāba*, 2nd edn, 7 vols, ed. Maḥmūd Fāyid *et al.*, Cairo, 1970, I, 369, no. 828.

[93] Ibn Qutayba, *Maʿārif*, ed. ʿUkāsha, 343—he was one of the hypocrites (*munāfiqūn*); Maqrīzī, *Imtāʿ al-asmāʾ bi-mā li-rasūl Allāh min al-abnāʾ wa al-amwāl wa al-ḥafada wa al-matāʿ*, 15 vols, ed. M. ʿAbd al-Ḥamīd al-Namīsī, Beirut, Dār al-Kutub al-ʿilmiyya, 1420/1999, II, 76; Ibn Ḥajar, *al-Iṣāba fī tamyīz as-ṣaḥāba*, 4 vols, ed. Ibr. b. Ḥ. al-Fayyūmī, Cairo, 1910, with, in the margin, Ibn ʿAbd al-Barr, *al-Istīʿāb*, Beirut, n.d, I, 339, no.1746.

[94] Tabari, *Annales*, ed. de Goeje *et al.*, I, 1782/*History*, trans. I.K. Poonawala, Albany, 1990, IX, 147–48.

[95] Sprenger, *Leben*, *op. cit.*, II, 407, n. 1.

[96] Maqrīzī, *Imtāʿ*, *op. cit.*, IX, 334: ten names; Ibn ʿAbd Rabbih,*ʿIqd*, *op. cit.*, IV, 250–51: ten names.

[97] Ibn ʿAsākir *Taʾrikh madīnat Dimashq, al-Sīra al-nabawiyya*, ed. S. al-Shihābī, Damascus, II, 1991, 328–52. This list and these notes (although abbreviated) are taken up, but with minor differences, by Ibn Kathīr (ʿImād al-Dīn, d. 774/1313), *al-Bidāya wa l-nihāya*, 2nd edn, 14 vols, Beirut/Riyad, 1978, V, 339-350 (1st edn 1966). The same was done by Ibn Ḥadīda (d. 783/1381), *al-Miṣbāḥ al-muḍīʾ fī kuttāb al-nabī*, Beirut, 1985, I, 27–28.

[98] According to Ibn ʿAbbās (*ad* Qurʾan 21 104) this was the name of one of Muḥammad's scribes! Tabari, *Tafsīr*, *op. cit.*, XVII, 100. Ibn Taymiyya and Mizzī considered this tradition to be a forgery. Al-Khaṭīb al-Baghdādī, *Taʾrīkh Baghdād* [hereafter *TB*], 14 vols, ed. M. Saʿīd al-ʿIrāqī, Cairo, 1931–49; reprint Beirut, Dār al-Kitāb al-ʿarabī, 1970–80, VIII (under Ḥamdān b. Saʿīd al-Baghdādī), 175 no. 4289: "The Messenger of God had a scribe whose name was Sijjil, and God revealed Q 21"; Dhahabī, *Mīzān al-ʿitidāl fī naqd al-rijāl*, 4 vols, ed. ʿA.M. al-Bijāwī, Cairo, 1963, I, 602, no. 2286. Thaʿlabī, *Kashf*, VI, 311 (*ad* Qurʾan 21, 104), according to Ibn al-Jawzā/ʿIkrima/Ibn ʿAbbās. But Thaʿlabī declares that this tradition is not sound, because the Prophet's scribes are all known, and he mentioned them in the *Rabīʿ al-mudhakkirīn*.

Allāh b. ʿAbbād or ʿIbād);[99] (21) al-ʿAlāʾ b. ʿUqba; (22) Muḥammad b. Maslama al-Anṣārī;[100] (23) Muʿāwiya b. a. Sufyān al-Qurashī al-Umawī; and (24) al-Mughīra b. Shuʿba Abū ʿĪsā al-Thaqafī.[101]

Ibn Ḥabīb al-Baghdādī (d. 245/860) in turn provides us with a list of 26 chancellery scribes in the service of the first caliphs or governors of towns and provinces in the decades following Muḥammad's death.[102]

Teaching and Learning: Places and Institutions

Places and Institutions of Learning

"Elementary schools" (kuttāb, pl. katātīb; or maktab) The origin of this institution remains problematic. While Gérard Lecomte and Marius Canard have drawn parallels between primary education in Byzantium and in Islam,[103] others believe that the term *kuttāb* was already in use in pre-Islamic times, bearing the Hebrew meaning of *beth ha-sepher* or *beth ha-midrash*.[104] According to Wāqidī, the Jews taught Arabic script in Yathrib and even at Medina's very beginnings.[105] As we have already seen, Zayd b. Thābit attended a Jewish school in Yathrib prior to Muḥammad emigrating there. ʿAlī b. a. Ṭālib would have learnt to read at the age of 14, although this would have taken place in Mecca.[106] As for Yathrib, among other towns, being the origin of Arabic writing, the town of al-Ḥīra equally comes to mind, for Arabic script most probably first saw the light of day there.[107] Indeed, Muslim sources tell us that a Christian from al-Ḥīra,[108] Jufayna, a slave and a foster son of Saʿd b. a. Waqqāṣ, had been brought to Medina to teach people how to write.[109] It should be emphasized that Arabia, and particularly Mecca and Yathrib, entertained relations with the Lakhmid kingdom and its capital.[110] Ibn

[99] Ibn al-Athīr, *Usd*, IV, 77, no. 3745.

[100] Ibn ʿAbd al-Barr, *Istīʿāb*, III, 1377, no. 2344.

[101] Nawawī (d. 676/1277), *Tahdhīb al-asmāʾ wa l-lughāt*, 4 vols in 3, Cairo, 1929; reprint Beirut, n.d., I, 29, takes up, with a few exceptions, Ibn ʿAsākir's list.

[102] Ibn Ḥabīb, *al-Muḥabbar*, ed. I. Lichtenstaedter, Hyderabad, 1942, 378–79.

[103] Lecomte, G., "Sur la vie scolaire à Byzance et en Islam, I. L'enseignement à Byzance et le kuttāb, II. (by Marius Canard), Falaqa = ΦΑΛΑΓΓΑΣ", *Arabica*, I (1954), 324–31, 331–36.

[104] ʿAlī, *al-Mufaṣṣal*, *op. cit.*, VIII (1993), 291.

[105] Balādhurī, *Futūḥ al-buldān*, ed. al-Ṭabbāʿ, 663.

[106] Alī, *Mufaṣṣal*, VIII, 292, according to al-Shaykh al-Mufīd, *al-Fuṣūl al-mukhtāra*.

[107] Shahīd, I., al-Ḥīraʾ, *EI*, 2nd edn, III, 463a (462–63)/III, 479a (478–79).

[108] On Ḥīra, see Rothstein, G., *Die Dynastie der Laḥmiden in al-Ḥīra*, Berlin, 1899. On Christianity in this town see Charles, H., *Le Christianisme des Arabes nomades ...*, Paris, 1936, 55–61; Fiey, J., *Jalons pour une histoire de l'Église en Iraq*, Louvain, 1970, index, 153a; ʿAbd al-Ghanī, ʿĀrif, *Taʾrīkh al-Ḥīra fī al-jāhiliyya wa l-islām*, Damascus, 1414/1993, 45–74, 471–95.

[109] Ṭabari, *Annales*, I, 2795, 2797 (*sub ann.* 23)/*History*, XIV, 161, 163, ʿAlī, *Mufaṣṣal*, VIII, 292.

[110] Kister, M.J., "al-Ḥīra: some notes on its relations with Arabia", *Arabica*, XV (1968), 143–69/ reprint in *Studies in Jāhiliyya and Early Islam*, London, 1980, no. III; Sachau, E., *Zur Ausbreitung des*

Ḥabīb (d. 245/860),[111] probably following Ibn al-Kalbī (d. 204/819), gives a list of eight Qurayshites who had been initiated to the *zandaqa* (here Manicheism?)[112] in al-Ḥīra. Several of them were massacred by Muḥammad, and the only one to finally submit to the yoke of Islam was Abū Sufyān b. Ḥarb,[113] the father of Muʿāwiya.

It is difficult to draw even an approximate picture of "primary teaching" in the Ḥijāz prior to Islam and in its very beginnings. We do have a study by Muhammad Hamidullah[114] at our disposal, but it is characterized by an apologetic mindset and lacks rigour in terms of its references and quotations.[115]

We have no comprehensive monograph on the *kuttāb* in the first centuries of Islam. The article in the second edition of *the Encyclopaedia of Islam* is very laconic on the matter.[116] One must therefore refer to general studies on teaching that contain a few pages relating to this period,[117] or to works on education among the Imamites, the Ibadites, to books on education and teaching in a region (see

Christentums in Asien, Berlin 1919; Andrae, Tor J.E., *Der Ursprung des Islams und das Christentum*, Uppsala, 1926, 137–38/*Les origines de l'islam et le christianisme*, trans. J. Roche, Paris, 1955, 32–37; Dussaud, R., *La pénétration des Arabes en Syrie avant l'islam*, Paris, 1955, 62–70; Trimingham, J.S., *Christianity among the Arabs in Pre-Islamic Times*, London and Beirut, 1979, 188–201, *passim*; Qanawātī (Anawati), Jūrj Shiḥāta, *al-Masīḥiyya wa al-ḥaḍāra al-ʿarabiyya*, 2nd edn, Cairo, 1992, 77–79; al-ʿĀyib, Salwā Balḥājj Ṣāliḥ, *al-Masīḥiyya al-ʿarabiyya wa taṭawwuruhā*, 2nd edn, Beirut, 1998, 53–59 (1st edn 1997).

[111] Ibn Ḥabīb, *al-Muḥabbar*, *op. cit.*, 161; Ibn Qutayba, *Maʿārif*, ed. ʿUkāsha, 621, does not give the names but writes instead: "The *zandaqa* existed among the Qurayshis; it came to them from Ḥīra."

[112] Van Ess, Josef, *Theologie und Gesellschaft im 2. und 3. Jahrhundert Hidschrah. Eine Geschichte des religiösen Denkens im frühen Islam* [hereafter *TG*], 6 vols, Berlin and New York, 1991–97, I, 421, with references to other sources and studies.

[113] ʿAlī, *Mufaṣṣal*, VIII, 494.

[114] Hamidullah, M., "Educational system in the time of the Prophet", *IC*, 13 (1939), 48–59, taken up, modified and argued for in French in id., *Le Prophète de l'Islam*, 4th edn, I–II, Paris, 1979, 1008 pp., II, 684-702, § 1219–70 (1st edn 1959).

[115] Among other examples in "Educational system", *art. cit.*, 53, it is said that Muḥammad "appointed Saʿīd ibn al-ʿĀṣ [read: ʿAbdallāh b. Saʿīd b. al-ʿĀṣ] to teach reading and writing", referring to ʿAbd ul Barr, *Istīʿāb*ʾ, [read: Ibn ʿAbd al-Barr]. In *Le Prophète*, II, 693: "ʿAbd Allāh b. Saʿīd b. al-ʿĀṣ, a calligraph [*sic*!] was appointed by the Prophet teacher of the wisdom", with no further explanation! At p. 692: "La Ṣuffah a été la première 'université' islamique [*sic*!]."

[116] Landau, J.M., "Kuttāb", *EI*, 2nd edn, V, 567 (567–70)/French edn, V, 572 (572–75); Brunot, L., "Maktab", *EI*, 1st edn, III, 177–80. On the other hand, Pedersen, "Masdjid", *EI*, 1st edn, III, 360–61 (Fred., III, 411–412), was far better with respect to the period of our interest. There is much to be gained from consulting Gilʿadi, A., "Individualism and conformity in medieval Islamic educational thought: some notes with special reference to elementary education", *Al-Qantara* (Madrid), 26/1 (2005), 99–121.

[117] Mez, *Die Renaissance*, *op. cit.*, 176–79/183–87; Tritton, A.S., *Materials on Muslim Education*, 1–26; Salama, *L'enseignement islamique*, *op. cit.*, 97–110; Pedersen, "Masdjid", *art. cit.*; Talas, *L'enseignement chez les Arabes: la Madrasa Nizamiyya et son histoire*, Paris, 1939, 7–12; Pellat, *Milieu*, *op. cit.*, 58–62; Shalabī, *Taʾrīkh al-tarbiyya al-islāmiyya*/id. (Shalaby), *History of Muslim Education*; Makdisi, "Madrasa", *art. cit.*; id., *The Rise of Colleges*, *op. cit.*, 19; Ahmed, *Muslim Education*, 40–46; Abiad, *Culture et éducation*, *op. cit.*, 213–19; Baer, E. "Muslim teaching institutions and their visual reflections: the *kuttāb*", *Der Islam*, 78 (2001), 73–102, deals with the way in which the *kuttāb* were seen and presented by the artists in later periods.

"Literacy in Pre-IslamicTimes and in the Time of Muḥammad" *supra*), or even to works examining childhood in Islam.[118] On starting at Qu'ranic school, and in addition to memorizing the Qu'ran, grammar, arithmetic and so on, boys had to learn the *ḥadīths* and elements of Islamic jurisprudence (*fiqh*) off by heart.

There are two so-called "institutions" that are problematic for the beginnings of Islam in Medina. The first is that which Muhammad Hamidullah calls a little hastily "the school of Suffah" and even "the first Islamic university".[119] Even if it is possible that the Medinian ʿUbāda b. Ṣāmit (ʿAwf Khazraj) could have taught literacy to the *ahl al-ṣuffa*,[120] it has been demonstrated that the reality on which the legend of the *ahl al-ṣuffa* is based is difficult to uncover,[121] and that, in any case, one cannot speak of an "institute".

The second is the *dār al-qurrāʾ* (at least this is how it is generally read) of Medina mentioned by Ibn Saʿd.[122] When Ibn Umm Maktūm ʿAmr/ʿAbd Allāh b. Qays b. Zāʾida al-Qurashī al-Maʿīṣī al-Aṣamm, nephew of Khadīja,[123] emigrated from Mecca to Medina, he resided in the *dār al-qurrāʾ*,[124] which was the dwelling (*dār*) of Makhrama b. Nawfal al-Zuhrī (d. 54/674), one of the three genealogists of the Quraysh who were ordered by ʿUmar to establish the state registers.[125] This was understood to be a "house of reciters of the Qurʾan", or even a "house of the Qurʾan".[126] But one may ask, given the context, if it is not here a matter of a *dār al-qarāʾ* (*hospitium*).[127]

The mosques The mosque (*masjid*) was the first institution of learning in Islam, and the term *majlis* gives philological evidence of this purpose.[128] It seems that Muḥammad and his Companions were quick to consider the mosque as both

[118] Gilʿadi, A., *Children of Islam: Concepts of childhood in medieval Muslim society*, Basingstoke, 1992, 61–66 (corporal punishment).

[119] Hamidullah, "Educational system", *art. cit.*; id., *Le Prophète*, II, 692–95.

[120] Ibn Ḥanbal, *Musnad*, 6 vols, ed. M. al-Zuhrī al-Ghamrāwī, Cairo, al-Maymaniyya, 1313/1895, V, 315/20 vols, ed. A.M. Shākir *et al.*, Cairo, Dār al-Ḥadīth, 1416/1995, XVI, 391, no. 22088; Abū Dāwūd, *Sunan*, 22, *Buyūʿ*, 36, *Bāb fī kasb al-muʿallim*, ed. M.M. ʿAbd al-Ḥamīd, III, 264, no. 3416; Ibn Māja, *Sunan*, 12, *Tijārāt*, 8, ed. M.F. ʿAbd al-Bāqī, II, 729–30; Bayhaqī, *al-Sunan al-kubrā*, 10 vols, Hyderabad, 1344–55/1925–36, VI, 125; Lecker, "Zayd b. Thābit", *art. cit.*, 270, n. 96.

[121] Watt, W.M., "Ahl al-ṣuffa", in *EI*, 2nd edn, I, *s.v.*

[122] Ibn Saʿd, *Ṭabaqāt*, ed. Sachau *et al.*, IV/1, 150/edn Beirut, IV, 205; Suyūṭī, *Ḥusn al-muḥāḍara*, 2 vols, ed. M. Abū l-Faḍl Ibrāhīm, Cairo, 1387/1967, I, 256, according to al-Wāqidī; Hamidullah, *Le Prophète*, II, 695.

[123] Ibn Athīr, *Usd*, IV, 263–64, no. 4005.

[124] The term *qurrāʾ* applied to a group that rebelled against ʿUthmān, and then against ʿAlī also creates a problem: see the works of M. Hinds and G.H.A. Juynboll on this subject, mentioned by T. Nagel, "Ḳurrāʾ", in *EI*, 2nd edn, V.

[125] Ṭabarī, *Annales*, I, 2750/*History*, trans. G.R. Smith, Albany, 1994, XIV, 115–16; Ibn Athīr, *Usd*, IV, V, 125–26, no. 4791; Ibn Ḥajar, *Iṣāba*, III, 370; ʿAlī, *Mufaṣṣal*, VIII, 331; IX, 377.

[126] Talas, *L'enseignement*, *op. cit.*, 8.

[127] Ibn Manẓūr, *Lisān al-ʿArab*, *s.v.* qarā: *qarā al-ḍayfa qiran wa qaraʾan*: *aḍāfahu*.

[128] Makdisi, *The Rise of Colleges*, *op. cit.*, 10.

a house of worship and their place of assembly. The following statements are attributed to Muḥammad. The first is: "He who enters a mosque either to teach or to be taught is like a warrior (*mujāhid*) who fights for God."[129] As it is permitted for a tradition to be transmitted according to its meaning, and not exclusively to the letter, it may be that this is an adaptation of a slightly different tradition: "He who enters a mosque either to teach good acts or be taught is like a warrior (*mujāhid*) who fights for God."[130]

The best writing on mosques and teaching is by the Dane, Johannes Pedersen (d. 1977), in his article on the mosque,[131] appearing in the first edition of the *Encylopedia of Islam* (*ca*. 1935). Here, he addresses, among other things, the genesis and evolution of teaching in the mosques, the subjects taught there, the teachers, their salaries and the students. This article was taken up, with an updated bibliography, in the second edition.[132] The section on teaching, however, was not kept but was instead rewritten by George Makdisi (d. 2002) in his article, "Madrasa".[133] Pedersen

> ... had been fascinated with al-Azhar, and during the last months of his stay [in Cairo] in 1921, he managed to study with an Azhari Shaykh .... But what really interested Pedersen was the teaching method, the meticulous transmission of knowledge from shaykh to student. For ever since his dissertation on the oath,[134] Pedersen had been particularly interested in Islam, not as ideas, but as a culture of learning. So he wrote on the mosque, the madrasa, the preacher (Chapter 6), the college, and the book. And in the book about the book, he wrote about how it was produced, traded, used, stored, even forgotten. Similarly, the book on al-Azhar[135] gives a rich portrait of a higher educational institution, its teachers and students, its incomes and salaries, its exams and careers, its disciplinary and health problems, its teaching methods, its buildings and its patrons and politics.[136]

129 Zarkashī, *Iʿlām al-sājid bi-aḥkām al-masājid*, ed. Abū al-Wafā Muṣṭ. al-Marāghī, Cairo, 1384/1964, 328 (2nd edn 1402/1982); Sibai, *Mosque Libraries*, 1987, 25.

130 Ibn Ḥanbal, *Musnad*, II, 350/VIII, 362, no. 8587; II, 527/IX, 574, no. 10758; Muttaqī al-Hindī, *Kanz al-ʿummāl*, 18 vols, Beirut, 1409/1989, X, 125, no. 28856–7.

131 Pedersen, "Masdjīd", *EI*, 1st edn, 1913–1933, III, 350–52, then "Special educational institutions", 352–53 (the whole article, 315–76); id., *The Arabic Book*, 20-26, *passim*.

132 Pedersen, "Masdjīd", *EI*, 1st edn, III, 315–76; French edn/reprint in *EI*, 2nd edn, VI, 644–77; French edn, VI, 629–64; id., *The Arabic Book*, 20–26, *passim*.

133 G. Makdisi, "Madrasa", *EI*, 2nd edn, V (French edn, V, 1120–21). Thus one should read the sections by both Pedersen and Makdisi on teaching in the mosques, for they complement each other.

134 Pedersen, J., *Der Eid bei den Semiten ...*, Strasburg, 1914, VIII+242 pp.

135 Pedersen, J., *Al-Azhar*, Et muhammedansk Universitet, Copenhagen, 1922.

136 Skovgaard-Petersen, J., "Johannes Pedersen in Cairo" at: http://www.dedi.org.eg/english/articles/johannes-pedersen-in-cairo/.

Other works had preceded Pedersen's article,[137] but those that came after tended, with little exception (Chapters 1 and 4),[138] to do little more than contribute additional information[139] on specific regions such as Muslim Spain,[140] or on more recent periods.[141]

Christopher Melchert's account (Chapter 1, this volume) of the etiquette of learning in early Islam is based on materials from the third/ninth century. It demonstrates that ninth-century forms continued to characterize Islamic learning for centuries to come "as becomes plain from comparison with an account by Samʿānī of teaching in the the twelfth century" (p. 1).

In a case study on Nishapur, Richard W. Bulliet (Chapter 4, this volume) gives the reasons why the age structure of the educational system is so difficult to ascertain with precision prior to the gradual introduction of the *madrasa* system—matriculation, graduation, set curricula, age limits, degrees, admission qualifications: "the whole panoply of modern educational administration was absent" (p. 51).

Following on, the organization of "advanced studies" was characterized by study circles (*ḥalqa*)[142] and "sessions" (*majlis*, pl. *majālis*)[143] that were not solely confined to the mosques. These sessions could be dictated and then edited, sometimes with the date and place given for where each (*jalsa*, *majlis*) had been held.[144]

---

[137] Mez, *Die Renaissance*, *op. cit.*, 320–24 and *passim*/*The Renaissance*, 332–36 and *passim*; Totah, K.A., *The Contribution of the Arabs to Education*, 39, 58–63; Khuda Bukhsh, S., "The educational system of the Muslims in the Middle Ages", 456–58; Mackensen, R.S., "Background of the history of Moslem libraries", *AJSLL*, 51 (1934–35), 122–23.

[138] Ahmed, *Muslim Education*, *op. cit.*, 115–64; Imamuddin, S.M., "Mosque", *art. cit.*, 159–70; Melchert, C, "The etiquette of learning", Chapter 1, this volume, 1–4; van Ess, *TG*, IV, index 1076b.

[139] Pellat, *Milieu*, *op. cit.*, 116–21, 243–45; Shalabī, *Taʾrīkh al-tarbiyya*, chapter I/8, 102–12/Shalaby, *History of Muslim Education*, the corresponding pages; Tritton, *Materials*, *op. cit.*, 61–22, 64, 89, 111, 117–20, but for all periods; Abrashī, *al-Tarbiyya al-islāmiyya …* (1969), 70–85; Fayyāḍ, *Taʾrikh al-tarbiyya ʿinda al-imāmiyya*, *op. cit.*, 72–82; Abiad, *Culture et éducation*, *op. cit.*, 246–59; Sibai, *Mosque Libraries*, *op. cit.*, 25–34; Khūlī, *Dawr al-masājid …*, Cairo, 1961; Ahmed, *Muslim Education*, *op. cit.*, 52, 115–17, addresses the subject until the fifth/eleventh century.

[140] Marín, M. "Learning at mosques in al-Andalus", in Masud, M. Khalid *et al.* (eds), *Islamic Legal Interpretation: Muftis and their Fatwas*, Cambridge, MA and London, 1996, 47–54.

[141] Berkey, J.P., *The Transmission of Knowledge: A Social History of Islamic Education*, Princeton, 1992, 50–56.

[142] Lewicki, "Ḥalḳa" (for the Ibadites), *EI*, 2nd edn, III, 95–98 (French edn, III, 97–101); Ahmed, *Muslim Education*, *op. cit.*, 52–54; Ephrat, D., *A Learned Society in a Period of Transition: the Sunni "ulama" of eleventh century Baghdad*, Albany, 2000, 76–85; see also the previously mentioned articles by Pedersen and Makdisi; Fayyāḍ, *Taʾrikh al-tarbiyya*, *op. cit.*, 87–90, for the *majālis* outside mosques; Sibai, *Mosque Libraries*, *op. cit.*, 27–33.

[143] Ahmed, *Muslim Education*, *op.cit.*, 55-85; Calder, *Studies*, *op. cit.*, 166–71.

[144] Thus that of Ibn Bābawayh, al-Ṣadūq (d. 381/991), *Amālī al-Ṣadūq*, 5th edn, Beyrouth, 1410/1985, 544 pp.; Fayyāḍ, *Taʾrīkh al-tarbiyya*, *op. cit.*, 89. On the connection between the following three titles—*Amālī* et *K. al-ʿArḍ ʿalā al-majālis* ou *ʿArḍ al-majālis* d'al-Ṣadūq—see Kohlberg, Etan, *A Medieval Muslim at Work*, Leiden, 1992, 119–21.

Other places of teaching Scholars' houses played an important role among the other places of teaching.[145] Instruction was sometimes also given from the doorsteps of their houses, in their shops (*ḥānūt*),[146] in a garden, in a marketplace and so on.[147] In order to collect the poetry of the ancient Arabs, and to enrich their language, certain scholars spent time among the Arab tribes in the desert.[148] Some caliphs[149] and great state officials invited scholars, theologians, jurists, poets and grammarians into various types of study circles, cenacles, "sessions" and "salons" (*majlis*).[150] They organized (or participated in) debates (*munāẓara*) between not only scholars, theologians[151] and jurists,[152] but also, notably, non-Muslims.[153] These debates also brought together other specialists, such as men of letters[154] or philologists. Thus, the grammarian of the school known as al-Baṣra, al-Mubarrad (210–285/826–898) and that of the school known as al-Kūfa, Thaʿlab (d. 291/904) held discussions in the palace of the Tahirid Muḥammad b. ʿAbd Allāh.[155] Al-Fatḥ b. Khāqān b. ʿUrtūj (d. 247/861),[156] the *kātib* and friend of al-Mutawakkil, was the mentor of the court literary circle.[157]

---

145 Shalabī, *Ta'rīkh al-tarbiyya, op. cit.*, 66–77; Fayyāḍ, *Ta'rīkh al-tarbiyya, op. cit.*, 83–86; Ahmed, *Muslim Education, op. cit.*, 135-140; Melchert, "The etiquette of learning", this volume, 2–3.

146 Ahmed, *Muslim Education, op. cit.*, 141.

147 Ibid., 112–14.

148 Blachère, R., *Analecta*, Damascus, 1950, 37–48; Fück, J., *ʿArabīya*, Berlin, 1950/*ʿArabīya*, Paris, 1955, *passim*; Jacobi, R., 'Rāwī', *EI*, 2nd edn, 466–67; Shalabī, *Ta'rīkh al-tarbiyya, op. cit.*, 96–101.

149 Bencheikh, J.E., "Le cénacle poétique du calife al-Mutawakkil (m. 247): Contribution à l'analyse des instances de légitimation socio-littéraires", *BEO*, XXIX (1976–77), I, 33–52; Hāshim, ʿAlī M., *al-Andiya al-adabiyya fī l-ʿaṣr al-ʿabbāsī fī al-ʿIrāq* ..., Beirut, 1982; Ḥulaybī, M. b. S., *al-Ḥaraka al-adabiyya fī majālis Hārūn al-Rashīd, 170-193 H*, 3 vols, Beirut, 2008.

150 Editorial [C. Pellat], "Madjlis", *EI*, 2nd edn, V, 1031–33 (French edn, V, 1027–29); Mez, *Die Renaissance, op. cit.*, 141–42/*The Renaissance, op. cit.*, 143–44, *passim*; Chejne, A.G., "The Boon-companion in early ʿAbbāsid times", *JAOS*, 85 (1965), 327–35; Blachère, R., *Histoire de la littérature arabe: des origines à fin du XVe siècle de J.C.* [hereafter *HLA*], 3 vols, Paris, 1952–66, III, 544–551 (poets and patrons of the arts); van Ess, *TG*, IV, 720.

151 Van Ess, J., "Disputations praxis in der islamischen Theologie. Eine vorläufige Skizze", *REI*, 44 (1976), 23–60; id., *TG*, IV, 725–730; cf. I, 48-55.

152 Makdisi, *The Rise of Colleges, op. cit.*, 109–11, but for a subsequent period than that which interests us.

153 Putman, H., *L'Église et l'islam sous Timothée. I. Étude sur l'Église nestorienne au temps des premiers ʿAbbāsides, avec nouvelle éd. du dialogue entre Timothée et al-Mahdī*, Beirut, 1975; Swanson, M.N., "The Christian al-Ma'mūn Tradition", in Thomas, F. (ed.), *Christians at the Heart of Islamic Rule. Church Life and Scholarship in ʿAbbasid Iraq: The History of Christian–Muslim Relations*, Leiden, 2003, 63–92; Moosa, Matti, "A New Source on Aḥmad ibn al-Ṭayyib al-Sarakhsī: Florentine MS Arabic 299", *JAOS*, 92 (1972), 21b (19–24).

154 Holmberg, Bo, "The public debate as a literary genre in Arabic literature", *Orientalia Suecana*, 38–39 (1989–90), 45–53.

155 Bernards, M., *Changing Traditions: Al-Mubarrad's refutation of Sībawayh and the subsequent reception of the Kitab*, Leiden, 1996, 28–30.

156 Sourdel, D., *Le vizirat ʿAbbāside de 749 a 936 (132* à *324 de l'hégire)*, 2 vols, Damascus, 1960, I, 282–86.

157 Ibid., 31.

Sometimes, this teaching took on a more "private" character, being reserved for a tribe or being under its direction, such as in Baṣra, where there was a "school" of the Banū Sakūn (Kindah) for the training of orators/preachers (*khaṭībs*).[158] The Ibadites of Baṣra had their own *majālis*, open to the members of the community, in which theological or juridic questions were addressed; these were also used for the training of missionaries, the "bearers of learning/knowledge" (*ḥamalat al-ʿilm*).[159] Such "sessions" could be held in private homes.

Teachers and Scholars

The education of princes at the Abbasid Court, as studied by Albert Dietrich (Chapter 3), is characteristic of the cultural patrimony of the time. The caliphs entrusted their sons to scholars of all types, particularly to philologists and traditionists, but also to poets and musicians.

With regard to "elementary school" schoolmasters, the private tutors of the sons of caliphs or high-ranking state officials or their families, or even "professors of higher education", the sources provide us with lists of their names until around 250/864.[160] We will begin with that of Ibn Qutayba (d. 276/889): (1) Abū ʿAbd al-Raḥmān al-Sulamī (ʿAbd Allāh b. Ḥabīb b. Rubayʿa al-Muqriʾ al-Kūfī, d. *ca.* 74), who was blind, taught the Qurʾan in Kūfa and was the master (*muʿallim*) of the sons of ʿAlī, Ḥasan and Ḥusayn;[161] (2) the Qadarite Maʿbad al-Juhanī (d. 80/700), who was a teacher in Baṣra and a private tutor to Saʿīd, son of the caliph ʿAbd al-Malik;[162] (3) the exegete, traditionist and storyteller al-Ḍaḥḥāk b. Muzāḥim al-Balkhī (d. 105/723), who had a school (*maktab*) that is said to have been attended by 3,000 children, and in which he used to ride up and down among his pupils on an ass;[163] (4) ʿAbd Allāh b. al-Ḥārith al-Anṣārī al-Baṣrī[164] (the two latter taught free of charge); (5) Qays b. Saʿd (b. ʿUbāda al-Khazrajī, d. at the end of the caliphate of Muʿāwiya); (6) ʿAṭā b. a. Rabāḥ (Aslam al-Qurashī al-Makkī,

---

158 Jāḥiẓ, *al-Bayān wa al-tabyīn*, 4 vols, ed. ʿAbd al-Salām M. Hārūn, Cairo, 4th rev. edn with index, Cairo, al-Khānjī, 1975 (1st edn 1948–1950, 2nd edn 1961), I, 135; Blachère, *HLA*, III, 731, n. 4; van Ess, *TG*, III, 112; IV, 720, n. 20.

159 Van Ess, *TG*, IV, 720–21; II, 203; Savage, E., "Survival through alliance: the establishment of the Ibāḍiya", *Bull. BriSMES*, 17 (1990), 5–15; id., *A Gateway to Hell, a Gateway to Paradise*, Princeton, 1997, 4, 24, 37–38, 45, 49.

160 Ibn Ḥabīb, *Muḥabbar*, 475–78; Ibn Qutayba, *Maʿārif*, 547–549; Talas, *L'enseignement*, *op. cit.*, 9.

161 Mizzī, *Tahdhīb*, X, 161–162, no. 3205. The date given for his death by some (105), notably Mizzī, according to Ibn Qāniʿ, must be corrected, according to Dhahabī, *Siyar aʿlām al-nubalāʾ*, 25 vols, ed. Shuʿayb al-Arnaʾūṭ et al., Beirut, Muʾassasat al-Risāla, 1981–88, IV, 272 (267–72). Correction should be made to the publication by Ibn Ḥabīb, *Muḥabbar*, who portrays Abū ʿAbd al-Raḥmān al-Sulamī and ʿAbd Allāh b. Ḥabīb as two different people.

162 Van Ess, "Maʿbad al-Ǧuhanī", in R. Gramlich (ed.), *Islamwissenschaftliche Abhandlungen Fritz Meier zum sechszigsten Geburtstag*, Wiesbaden, 1974, 49–77; Abiad, *Culture et éducation*, *op. cit.*, 263.

163 Yāqūt, *Dictionary of Learned Men*, IV, 272-3/*Udabāʾ*, ed. I. ʿAbbās, IV, 1452–53, no. 606.

164 Mizzī, *Tahdhīb*, X, 76–77, no. 3200.

d. 114/732);[165] (7) Qabīṣa b. Du'ayb (al-Khuzā'ī, al-Madanī al-Dimashqī, d. 86);[166] (8) Abū Umayya 'Abd al-Karīm b. a. al-Mukhāriq, d. ca. 140/757);[167] (9) Ḥusayn al-Mu'allim (or al-Mu'addib): Ḥusayn b. Dhakwān al-'Awdhī al-Baṣrī (al-Muktib, d. 145);[168] (10) al-Qāsim b. Mukhaymira (al-Kūfī al-Hamadhānī, d. 100), who was a schoolmaster in Kūfa before settling in Damascus, and who taught free of charge;[169] (11) al-Kumayt b. Zayd al-Asadī (d. 126/743), the Shī'ite poet who taught the young people in the mosque of Kūfa;[170] (12) Ḥabīb al-Mu'allim (Abū Muḥammad al-Baṣrī, Ḥabīb b. a. Baqiyya/Qurayba Dīnār/Zayd/Zā'ida) *mawlā* of the Companion Ma'qil b. Yasār al-Muzanī al-Baṣrī, who died during the caliphate of Mu'āwiya;[171] (13) 'Abd al-Ḥamīd al-Kātib (m. 132/750);[172] (14–15) al-Ḥajjāj b. Yūsuf (41–95/661–714) and his father, who both taught in Ṭā'if; (16) 'Alqama b. a. 'Alqama (Bilāl al-Madanī, d. *ca.* 158/775), *mawlā* of 'Ā'isha,[173] who had a school in which he taught Arabic, grammar and metrics; (17) Abū Mu'āwiya al-Naḥwī Shaybān b. 'Abd al-Raḥmān (al-Miṣrī al-Mu'addib, d. 164),[174] *mawlā* of theTamīm, a traditionist who was private tutor to the sons of Dāwūd b. 'Alī (b. 'Abd Allāh b. 'Abbās, al-Saffāḥ's paternal uncle);[175] (18–19) Abū Sa'īd al-Mu'addib Muḥammad b. Muslim b. a. al-Waḍḍāḥ al-Quḍā'ī (d. during the caliphate of al-Hādī),[176] who was named private tutor to Mūsā (al-Ḥādī) by this latter's grandfather al-Manṣūr, who then conferred this position to Sufyān b. Ḥusayn al-Wāsiṭī (d. *ca.* 150/767);[177] (20) Abū Ismā'īl al-Mu'addib Ibrāhīm b. Sulaymān (b. Razīn al-Baghdādī, d. 183),[178] a traditionist, who was private tutor to the sons of Abū 'Ubayd Allāh Mu'āwiya b. 'Ubayd Allāh al-Ash'arī al-Shāmī (d. 170), al-Mahdī's vizier;[179] (21) Abū 'Ubayd al-Qāsim b. Sallām (m. 224/838), was the *mawlā* of the Azd. In 191/806 this son of a slave captured in Byzantine territory became private tutor to the high-ranking

---

165 Dhahabī, *Siyar*, V, 78–88: *mu'allim kuttāb* (81).

166 Dhahabī, *Siyar*, IV, 282–83: *mu'allim kuttāb* (283), in his youth.

167 Van Ess, *TG*, II, 659–60, a Murjite from Baṣra, who established himself in Mecca, where he became a schoolmaster. His death being dated at 127 is probably the result of confusion with another, as shown by van Ess.

168 Dhahabī, *Siyar*, VI, 345–46; Jāḥiẓ, *Bayān*, I, 251; van Ess, *TG*, II, 316.

169 Dhahabī, *Siyar*, V, 201–203; Ibn Ḥajar, *Tahdhīb al-tahdhīb*, 12 vols, Hyderabad, Dā'irat al-ma'ārif al-niẓāmiyya, 1325–27/1907–09, VIII, 337–38.

170 According to Khalaf al-Aḥmar, in Abū al-Faraj al-Iṣfahānī, *Aghānī*, XVII, 2.

171 Mizzī, *Tahdhīb*, IV, 141–42, no. 1091; Dhahabī, *Siyar*, VI, 254.

172 Ibn Khallikān, *Wafayāt*, III, 228 (228–32, no. 405).

173 He transmitted some traditions by 'Ā'isha; Mālik b. Anas and Ibn Isḥāq transmitted from him: see, for example, Maqrīzī, *Imtā'*, IX, 31; Ibn Ḥajar, *Tahdhīb*, VII, 275–76.

174 Ibn Sa'd, *Ṭabaqāt*, VI, 377; Dhahabī, *Siyar*, VII, 406–408.

175 Van Ess, *TG*, I, 90, 99, etc.; Dhahabī, *Siyar*, V, 444–45; it was said that he was a Qadarite.

176 Ibn Ḥajar, *Tahdhīb*, IX, 453–54.

177 Dhahabī, *Siyar*, VII, 302–303.

178 Ṣafadī, *al-Wāfī bi-al-wafayāt*, 30 vols, ed. H. Ritter *et al.*, Istanbul, 1931, Beirut, 2004, V, 359.

179 Sourdel, *Vizirat*, *op. cit.*, I, 94–103. One of Abū 'Ubayd Allāh's sons was executed following an accusation by *zandaqa*.

Abbasid state official Harthama b. Aʿyān, then governor of Khorasān on behalf of al-Rashīd (d. 193/809).[180]

Ibn Ḥabīb al-Baghdādī (d. 245/860) list shares most of the names listed by Ibn Qutayba, but his list also includes: (22) the Christian Bishr b. ʿAbd al-Malik (al-Kindī) al-Sakūnī, brother of Ukaydir,[181] Christian king (*ṣāḥib*) of pre-Islam (*jāhilī*) Dumat al-Jandal. If Bishr is designated as *muktib* it is because, as we saw, he would have taught Arabic script in al-Ḥīra, and then in Mecca to Sufyān b. Umayya b. ʿAbd Shams, Abū Qays b. ʿAbd Manāf b. Zuhra b. Kilāb and others. He was married to the sister of Abū Sufyān, al-Ṣahbāʾ bint Ḥarb b. Umayya and is designated here symbolically as "the first master in literacy" for Mecca.[182] (23) Abū Qays b. ʿAbd Manāf, designated here as the "first teacher in literacy" for Mecca; (24) the poet (*mukhaḍram*) Ghaylān b. Salama b. Muʿattib al-Thaqafī, chief of the Aḥlāf clan (d. *ca.* 23/644);[183] (25) ʿUbayd b. Mihrān al-Muktib al-Kūfī, *mawlā* of the Ḍabba, who disseminated the traditions of Mujāhid b. Jabr (d. 104/722);[184](26) ʿAmr b. Zurāra[185] b. ʿUdus[186] b. Zayd (*jāhilī*) (al-Ḥanẓalī) al-Tamīmī, who was called al-Kātib; (27) ʿĀmir (b. Sharāḥīl) al-Shaʿbī al-Hamdānī al-Kūfī (d. between 103/721 and 110/728),[187] to whom ʿAbd al-Malik entrusted the education of his sons;[188] (28) Abū Ṣāliḥ (Bādhām), *mawlā* of Umm Hānīʾ bint Abī Ṭālib and master (*ṣāḥib*) of al-Kalbī, who was a teacher (*muʿallim*) according to Muḥammad b. Bakkār (al-Rayyān d. 238)[189]—he was also an exegete, but apparently couldn't read the Qurʾan very well (!);[190] (29) Ismāʿīl b. ʿUbayd Allāh[191] b. a. al-Muhājir, Aqram al-Qurashī al-Makhzūmī, *mawlā* of al-Dimashqī (d. 132), who was ʿAbd

[180] Lecomte, G., "Le problème d'Abū ʿUbayd: Réflexions sur les erreurs que lui attribue Ibn Qutayba", *Arabica*, XII (1965), 147.

[181] Lecker, M. in *EI*, 2nd edn, VI, under "Ukaydir".

[182] Ghanīma, Y.R., *al-Ḥīra, al-madīna wa al-mamlaka al-ʿarabiyya*, Baghdad, 1936, 56, according to al-Kalbī, via Balādhurī, etc.; ʿAbd al-Ghanī, ʿĀrif, *Taʾrīkh al-Ḥīra*, *op. cit.*, 353, 354.

[183] *GAS*, II, 302; *Aghānī*, XIII, 200–208.

[184] Ibn Saʿd, *Ṭabaqāt*, VI, 340; Mizzī, *Tahdhīb*, XII, 317–18, no. 4320.

[185] Zurāra was the chief of the Dārim in the second half of the sixth century. See Caskel, W., *Das genealogische Werk des Hišām ibn Muḥammad al-Kalbī*, 2 vols, Leiden, 1966, II, 613; I, table 60; *Aghānī*, XXII, 187–94; Abū al-Baqāʾ Hibat Allāh al-Ḥillī (lived second half of the fifth or first half of the sixth century of the Hijra), *K. al-Manāqib al-mazyadiyya*, ed. Ṣāliḥ Mūsā Darāka and ʿAq. Khuraysāt, Amman, 1404/1984, 354–55, gives the list of his ten sons, of which one was ʿAmr; cf. on Zurāra, Ibn Ḥabīb, *Munammaq*, 240–42.

[186] Zabīdī, *Tāj*, XVI, 235: ʿUdas can also be said, but, according to him ʿUdus is the correct form.

[187] Sezgin, Fuat, *Geschichte des arabischen Schrifttums*, I, [hereafter *GAS* I], Leiden, Brill, 1967. 277; Juynboll, in *EI*, 2nd edn, IX, s.v.

[188] Jāḥiẓ, *Bayān*, II, 251.

[189] Indeed, Ibn Ḥabīb, *Muḥabbar*, 475, provides a chain of guarantors.

[190] Ibn Qutayba, *Maʿārif*, 479.

[191] After correction of the text by Ibn Ḥabīb, *Muḥabbar*, 476, which has ʿAbd Allāh.

al-Malik b. Marwān's private tutor;[192] (30) ʿAbd al-Wāḥid b. Qays (al-Sulamī)[193], private tutor to the sons of Yazīd b. ʿAbd al-Malik; (31) the grammarian Yūnus b. Ḥabīb (al-Baṣrī, d. 182/798);[194] (32) Hārūn b. Mūsā al-Aʿwar al-Qāriʾ (al-Baṣrī al-Azdī al-ʿAtakī, d. before 200), who was a converted Jew;[195] (33) ʿUmar b. al-Faḍl (al-Sulamī) al-Baṣrī;[196] (34) Muḥammad (b. Muslim) Ibn Shihāb al-Zuhrī (d. 124/742). His first teacher (*muʾaddib*) was probably a *mawlā*, Ṣāliḥ b. Kaysān al-Madanī.[197] If Ibn Ḥabīb considers him a *muʿallim*, it is probably because he conducted dictation sessions (of traditions) for state officials during the Umayyad caliphates of ʿAbd al-Malik and Hishām;[198] (35) Ismāʿīl b. Jaʿfar b. a. Kathīr al-Madanī (d. 180), who was private tutor to ʿAlī, the son of al-Mahdī;[199] (36) Ḥajjāj b. Muḥammad al-Aʿwar, who was a *mawlā* (al-Miṣṣīṣi, d. 206, in Baghdad); (37) Yūnus b. Muḥammad al-Muʾaddib al-Baghdādī (d. 207 or 209); (38) Shaybān b. ʿAbd al-Raḥmān Abū Muʿāwiya al-Naḥwī (that is, of the Naḥw clan) al-Tamīmī al-Baṣrī, d. 164); (39) Ṣāliḥ b. Kaysān al-Madanī (d. after 140(?) at the age of about 80 years(?)),[200] who was *mawlā* of the ʿĀmir, Ghifār and others, and was named private tutor to ʿUmar b. ʿAbd al-ʿAzīz by ʿAbd al-ʿAzīz b. Marwān, then governor of Medina. When al-Walīd b. ʿAbd al-Malik acceded to the caliphate, he asked ʿAbd al-ʿAzīz, his governor in Medina, to send him over so that he could be private tutor to his son ʿAbd al-ʿAzīz and Umm al-Banīn, the daughter of ʿAbd al-ʿAzīz b. Marwān; (40) Abū ʿUbayda b. Muḥammad b. ʿAmmār b. Yasār al-ʿAnsī,[201] who succeeded Ṣāliḥ b. Kaysān as private tutor to ʿAbd al-ʿAzīz b. al-Walīd b. ʿAbd al-Malik; (41) the Murjiʾite ʿAwn b. ʿAbd Allāh b. ʿUtba b. Masʿūd al-Hudhalī al-Kūfī (d. between 110/728 and 120/738),[202] who was private tutor to Yazīd, son of Muḥmmad b. Marwān, the brother of the caliph ʿAbd al-Malik, but also to Ayyūb, the son of the caliph Sulaymān b. ʿAbd al-Malik; (42) Mundhir al-Afṭas al-Ṣanʿānī; (43) Abū Ayyūb Maymūn b. Mihrān al-Jazarī al-Raqqī (d. 118),[203] who was private tutor to the son of ʿUmar b. ʿAbd al-ʿAzīz; (44) al-Hasan

[192] Mizzī, *Tahdhīb*, II, 197–201, no. 459.

[193] Ibn ʿAsākir, *Taʾrīh madinat Dimashq*, 80 vols, ed. Muḥibb al-Dīn Abū Saʿīd ʿUmar b. Gharāma al-ʿAmrawī and ʿAlī Shīrī, Beirut, Dār al-Fikr, 1995–2001, XXXVII, 260–66, no. 4335. He was a scholar of grammar and private tutor to Yazīd's sons (264).

[194] *GAS*, IX, 57–58; Ibn Khallikān, *Wafayāt*, VI, 2850–52, no. 1262. If he is placed among the "teachers", it is probably because people flocked to his circle (*ḥalqa*).

[195] Mizzī, *Tahdhīb*, XIX, 207–209, no. 7124.

[196] ʿAbd Allāh b. al-Mubārak (d. 181/797) transmitted traditions from him; see Ibn Ḥajar, *Tahdhīb*, VII, 488–89.

[197] Dhahabī, *Siyar*, V, 456; Lecker, in *EI*, 2nd edn, XI, under "al-Zuhrī".

[198] Lecker, Michael, "Biographical notes on Ibn Shihāb al-Zuhrī", *JSS*, XLI/1 (1996), 21–63.

[199] Dhahabī, *Siyar*, VIII, 228–30.

[200] Dhahabī, *Siyar*, V, 454–56.

[201] Mizzī, *Tahdhīb*, XXI, 368–69, no. 8092.

[202] Van Ess, *TG*, I, 163–66.

[203] Ibn ʿAsākir, *Taʾrikh madinat Dimashq*, Beirut, LXI, 336–668; Dhahabī, *Siyar*, V, 71–78.

b. ʿArafa al-ʿAbdī al-Baghdādī al-Muʾaddib (born 150, d. 257(!));[204] (45) ʿUbayda b. Ḥumayd al-Ḥadhdhāʾ al-Naḥwī al-Kūfī (d. 190), who was private tutor to Muḥammad b. Hārūn (i.e. al-Amīn);[205] (46) ʿAbd al-Raḥmān b. Hurmuz b. Sarjis al-Madanī al-Aʿraj (d. 117);[206] (47) Shayba b. Niṣāḥ b. Sarjis al-Madanī (d. 130);[207] (48) the genealogist Daghfal b. Ḥanẓala al-Dhuhlī al-Shaybānī (d. 65/695) who was private tutor to Yazīd, son of Muʿāwiya; (49) Abū ʿAbd Allāh al-Muʿallim (?); (50) Maymūn b. a. Shurāʿa (?) –Yazīd b. Zurayʿ al-Baṣrī (d. 182), who is known to have transmitted from him; (51) Isḥāq b. a. Isrāʾīl Ibrāhīm b. Kāmjr al-Marwazī (b. 150/767, d. 246/860),[208] who taught a group (of children or youths) in Baṣra, at the door of Ḥammād b. Zayd al-Baṣrī (d. 199) and, according to ʿUbayd Allāh b. ʿUmar al-Qawārīrī al-Jushamī al-Baṣrī (d. 235),[209] like Ibn Abī Isrāʾīl, attended the lessons of Ḥammād b. Zayd. Muḥammad b. Ḥātim b. Sululaymān al-Zammī al-Muʾaddib al-Khurasānī al-Baghdādī (d. 246),[210] who is not mentioned by Ibn Ḥabīb and also belongs to this same generation of traditionists.

We could, of course, make the lists of Ibn Qutayba and Ibn Ḥabīb longer, but will confine ourselves to mentioning only a few more names. It is said that Muḥammad ordered al-Ḥakam/ʿAbd Allāh b. Saʿīd (Abū Uḥayḥa Dhū al-Tāj)[211] b. al-ʿĀṣ b. Umayya b. ʿAbd Shams (d. 8/629)[212] to teach literacy (*al-kitāb*) in Medina, or, alternatively, that he taught *al-ḥikma* before he was sent to al-Shām. In this context *al-ḥikma* seems to also mean literacy.[213]

The Shīʿīte ʿUmayr b. ʿĀmir al-Hamdānī (?) taught in a *kuttāb* in Kūfa;[214] when ʿUbayd Allāh b. Ziyād b. Abīhi (d. 67/686) had him released from prison, our teacher declared that he would never again teach young people, and that he would never again set foot in a school (*maktab*).[215] The poet Ṭirimmāḥ b. al-Ḥakīm (d. *ca.* 126/743) was once a schoolmaster in Rayy.[216] The Kūfian jurist and traditionist al-Ḥajjāj b. Arṭāt (d. 206/821) was part of Abū Jaʿfar al-Manṣūr's entourage. Al-Manṣūr charged him (*ḍammahu ilā al-Mahdī*) with the education

[204] Dhahabī, *Siyar*, XI, 547–51.

[205] *TB*, XI, 120–23. He was not a cobbler but he frequented the cobblers' quarter and thus came by this nickname.

[206] Dhahabī, *Siyar*, V, 69–70.

[207] Ibn Ḥajar, *Tahdhīb*, IV, 377–78.

[208] Dhahabī, *Siyar*, XI, 476–87; van Ess, *TG*, IV, 219.

[209] Dhahabī, *Siyar*, XI, 442–46.

[210] Dhahabī, *Siyar*, XI, 452–53.

[211] Zabīdī, *Tāj*, VI, 293b; V, 440b.

[212] Ibn ʿAsākir, *Taʾrikh madīnat Dimashq*, XXXI, ed. M. al-Ṭarābīshī, Damascus, 1986, 48–53.

[213] Lecker, "Zayd b. Thābit", *art. cit.*, 266, n. 52. Some might object that both *kitāb* and *ḥikma* mean "the Qurʾan" (Ṭabarī, *Tafsīr*, ed. Shākir, V, 576–79, *ad* Koran 2, 269), but, in agreement with Lecker's interpretation, we do not hold this.

[214] Fayyāḍ, *Taʾrikh al-tarbiyya*, *op. cit.*, 72, according to al-Imām M. ʿAbd Allāh, *Qurrat al-ʿayn fī akhdh thaʾr al-Ḥusayn*, Baghdad, 1957, 40.

[215] Fayyāḍ, *Taʾrikh al-tarbiyya*, *op. cit.*, 67.

[216] Jāḥiẓ, *Bayān*, II, 257; Talas, *L'enseignement*, *op. cit*, 9.

of his son, al-Mahdī, in whose company he remained until the latter's death.[217] The grammarian al-Kisā'ī (d. 189/805) bestowed his learning upon al-Rashīd, who entrusted him with the education of his sons, al-Amīn and al-Ma'mūn.[218] Ibn al-Sikkīt (d. 244/858) was private tutor to al-Mu'tazz (Abū 'Abd Allāh) and al-Mu'ayyad (Ibrāhīm), the sons of al-Mutawakkil;[219] with his father, he taught the children of the masses in Baghdad (Darb al-Qanṭara).[220] The blind grammarian 'Abdallāh b. 'Abd al-'Azīz al-Baghdādī was private tutor (*ca.* 255/869) to the children of the caliph al-Muhtadī.[221] Tha'lab (200–291/815–904), who was well known for his love of riches, was private tutor to the Tahirids, notably to Ṭāhir b. M. b. 'Abd Allāh b. Ṭāhir (d. 296/908),[222] but also to Muḥammad b. Dāwūd al-Ẓāhirī.[223] Finally, there is mention of Abū 'Alī Shaqrān (*sic*) al-Hamdānī;[224] one might speculate whether he might not be the Qayrawanian Abū 'Alī Shuqrān b. 'Alī al-Faraḍī (d. 186/802),[225] who was the Dhū al-Nūn al-Miṣrī's master.[226]

Given the informal nature of teaching in Islam,[227] no-one was under any compulsion to teach or to follow a teaching, and all who had been granted a licence (*ijāza*) to transmit part of a *ḥadīth* (or other text), a book or one of the 30 parts of the Qur'an (*juz'*), or even the unwritten *ḥadīth*, were authorized to do so. Occasionally, a master might attend the lessons given by one of his pupils.[228]

With regard to the relationship between scholars (*'ulamā'*), scholarship and teaching, and the relevant bibliography, one should refer to my article "'Ulamā".[229] Several researchers have addressed the question of leadership (*riyāsa*) among

---

[217] *TB*, VIII, 230, no. 4341.

[218] *GAS*, IX, 127; *TB*, XI, 403.

[219] Yāqūt, *Udabā'*, VI, 2841; "Ibn al-Sikkīt", an article by the editor [C. Pellat], in *EI*, 2nd edn, III, *s.v.*

[220] *TB*, XIV, 273.

[221] Sourdel, D., "Le 'Livre des secrétaires'", *op. cit.*, 116.

[222] Dhahabī, *Siyar*, XIV, 7. This provides an incomplete list that nevertheless suggests the scholars who taught the Abbasid princes. See Ahmed, *Muslim Education*, *op. cit.*, 96–100.

[223] Vadet, J.-C., *L'esprit courtois en Orient dans les cinq premiers siècles de l'hégire*, Paris, 1968, 281. For other schoolmasters or private tutors, see Talas, *L'enseignement*, *op. cit.*, 9.

[224] Talas, *l'enseignement op. cit.*, 9, according to the introduction by 'Abd al-Wahhāb to his edition of Ibn Saḥnūn.

[225] Muranyi, M., *Beiträge zur Geschichte der Ḥadīṯ- und Rechtsgelehrsamkeit der Mālikiyya in Nordafrika bis zum 5. Jh. d. H.*, Wiesbaden, 1997, 11–12.

[226] Ahmed, *Muslim Education*, *op. cit.*, 49–51, gives a list of 30 tutors with pupils.

[227] Van Ess, *TG*, IV, 720: "Der Betrieb war erfreulich 'ungeregelt'."

[228] See the comments by van Ess, *TG*, IV, 718–19, on the ambiguity of the term *ṣāḥib* (companion), which can be applied to a pupil or a master; also Arioli, Angelo, "*Ṣāḥib/aṣḥāb, waǧh/wuǧūh, 'ayn/'uyūn* nei testi di *'ilm al-riǧāl*", in Scarcia Amoretti, B. (ed.), *Onomastica e trasmissione del sapere nell'Islam medievale*, 6–17 (1–21).

[229] Gilliot, "'Ulamā' 1. In the Arab world", *EI*, 2nd edn, X, 801–804 (French edn, X, 865–68); also Modarressi, H., *Crisis and Consolidation in the Formative Period of Shi'ite Islam*, Princeton, 1993, 12–15.

the*ʿulamā*,[230] the mechanisms of inclusion and exclusion of scholars[231] and their relationship with the general public,[232] with one another[233] and with the government,[234] as well as the question of their financial condition.[235] Others have focused their attention on dynasties of scholars.[236]

Among the ancient Arabs, the art of the spoken word played a crucial role through poets (*shaʾirs*), orators/preachers (*khatibs*), and storytellers (*qussas*, sing. *qass*).[237] The poet, in particular, could pass for a rival of the Prophet, in so far as the revelations made (delivered) by the latter were reminiscent of poetry, or at least of rhymed prose (*sajʿ*).[238] As Johannes Pedersen states in Chapter 6 of this volume, "In Islam the poet maintained his influence in public life, and as the one who stimulated the Prince; and likewise poetry entered the service of religion" (p. 93). The preacher, however, gained standing "as the one who in continuance of the Prophet's function as a leader addressed the congregation from the *minbar* during Friday's service" (ibid.). As for the *qass* (often translated as "popular storyteller", "preacher", or "deliverer of sermons") in Islam, the origin, genesis and evolution of his role throughout the centuries have varied considerably: "[his] activity considerably varied over the centuries, from preaching in the mosques with a form of koranic exegesis to downright charlatanism".[239] The release of Ibn al-Jawzi's *Kitāb al-quṣṣāṣ wa-al-mudhakkirīn*[240] has brought new material to our understanding of this phenomenon; yet even prior to this publication, Léon

230 Mottahedeh, R.P., *Loyalty*, 1980, 135–57, 162–63; van Ess, *TG*, IV, 718–20. Asfaruddin, A., *Excellence and Precedence*, Leiden, 2002, deals with the discourse on legitimate leadership according to Jāḥiẓ and the Shīʿī Ibn Tāwūs (d. 673/1274). This does not relate to our subject, as it addresses the question of Muḥammad's succession. For "the scholars as heirs of the prophets", see Takim, Liyakat N., *The Heirs of the Prophet*, Albany, 2006, 1–36; Amir-Moezzi, M.-A. and Ch. Jambet, *Qu'est-ce que le shī'isme?*, Paris, 2004, 241–83; Amir-Moezzi, "Remarques sur les critères d'authenticité du hadîth et l'autorité du juriste dans le shi'isme imamite', *Stud. Isl.*, 85 (1997), 5–39.

231 Ephrat, *A Learned Society*, *op. cit.*, 95–124.

232 Ahmed, *Muslim Education*, *op. cit.*, 196–200.

233 Ibid., 201–23.

234 Ibid., 224–52.

235 Ibid., 252–54

236 See the references in Gilliot, "ʿUlamāʾ", *art. cit.*, 803b /867a; Bulliet, R.W., *The Patricians of Nishapur*, Cambridge, MA, 85–245; Ephrat, *A Learned Society*, *op. cit.*, 155–69.

237 ʿAlī, *Mufaṣṣal*, VIII, 371–79.

238 Gilliot, "Poète ou prophète? Les traditions concernant la poésie et les poètes attribuées au prophète de l'islam et aux premières générations musulmanes", in Sanagustin (ed.), *Paroles, Signes, Mythes*, Damascus, 2001, 331–96.

239 Pellat, C., "Ḳāṣṣ", *EI*, 2nd edn, IV, 733 (733–35); Goldziher, *Muhammedanische Studien*, II, 161–70/ *Muslim Studies*, II, 150–59;Mez, *Die Renaissance*, *op. cit.*, 313–20/*The Renaissance*, 325–32, and 344–52 (here trans. from Goldziher, *Muhammedanische Studien*, II, 161–70); Najm, W.Ṭ., *al-Qaṣaṣ wa-al-quṣṣāṣ fī al-adab al-islāmī*, Kuwait, 1972; Bosworth, C.E., *The Mediaeval Islamic Underworld*, I, Leiden 1976, 23–29; Leder, S., *Ibn al-Ǧauzī und seine Kompilation wider die Leidenschaft*, Beirut/Wiesbaden, 1984, 21–23; Athamina, K., "Al-Qasas", *art. cit.*; Toorawa, Sh.M., "Defining *adab* by (re)defining the *adīb*. Ibn Abī Ṭāhir Ṭayfūr and Storytelling", in Kennedy, P.F., (ed.), *On Fiction and Adab in Medieval Arabic Literature*, Wiesbaden, 2005, 294–302.

240 Ed. and trans. M.L. Swartz, Beirut, 1971.

Bercher had consulted one of its manuscripts and included some of its material in his translation of part of Goldziher's Muhammedanische Studien.

For Khalil Athamina, the main event to have influenced the nature of the *qaṣaṣ* was the civil war (*fitna*).[241] The battlefield preachers—for example, al-Ḍaḥḥāk b. Muzāḥim (d. 105/723) from Khorasan[242] and Muqātil b. Sulaymān (d. 150/767), among others[243]—played a role in this, even though they were probably not considered as "popular storytellers" in their usual working life. The progressive establishment of an orthodoxy was in large part responsible for some of their declarations being declared unacceptable.

Pedagogy

The history of childhood in Islam is becoming better known, even though there remains room for progress. Kūrkīs ʿAwwād (1908–1992) has compiled a bibliography of relevant sources,[244] and several works on children and childhood have been written.[245] Although he belongs to a later period than that which concerns us, we must mention Ibn al-ʿAdīm (d. 660/1262) from Aleppo, whose work, *al-Darārī fī dhikr al-dharārī* (*Stellae fulgentes de laudanda progenie*), has been the subject of two studies by Anne-Marie Eddé.[246]

We have seen from the first section of this Introduction how Western interest in education, teaching and pedagogy in Islam dates back a long time. With regard to pedagogy, some progress has been made since around 1950,[247] and more recently still, thanks to the work of Sebastian Günther (see Chapter 5, this volume; also the Bibliography).

---

241 Athamina, "Al-Qasas", *art. cit.*, 65.

242 Van Ess, *TG*, II, 508–509.

243 Van Ess, *TG*, II, 516–32; Gilliot, "Muqātil, grand exégète, traditionniste et théologien maudit", *JA*, 1–2 (1991), 39–92.

244 ʿAwwād, K., *al-Ṭufūla wa al-aṭfāl fi al-maṣādir al-ʿarabiyya al-qadīma wa al-ḥadītha*, Baghdad, 1979.

245 Rosenthal, F., "Child psychology in Islam" (1952); Adamek, G., "Das Kleinkind in Glaube und Sitte der Araber im Mittelalter", dissertation, University of Bonn, 1967; Motzki, H., "Das Kind und seine Sozialisation in der islamischen Familie des Mittelalters", in Martin, J. and Nitschke, A. (eds), *Zur Sozialgeschichte der Kindheit*, Freiburg and München, 1986, 391–441; Gilʿadi, *Children of Islam*, *op. cit.*: we will add to his list of sources (11–12) Nūr al-Dīn al-Sālimī al-Ibāḍī (d. 1914; *GAL S* II, 823), *Talqīn al-ṣibyān*, trans. A. Hamoud Al-Maamiry, Oman, 1989, 48 pp.; *Talqīn al-ṣibyān mā yalzamuhu al-insān*, Masqaṭ, 2004, 23rd edn (followed by other texts which are not by this author), also printed in Damascus, 1966. Abū al-ʿAbbās al-Baladī, A. b. M. (d. *ca.* 380/990) wrote *Kitāb Tadbīr al-ḥubālā wa-al-aṭfāl wa-al-ṣibyān wa-ḥifẓ siḥḥatihim*, ed. M.H. Qāsim, Baghdad, 1980, 335 pp.

246 Eddé, A-M., "Un traité sur les enfants d'un auteur arabe du XIIIe siècle", in Dubois, H. and Zink M. (eds), *Les Âges de la vie au Moyen Âge*, Paris, 1992, 139–49; id., "La représentation de l'enfant dans le traité d'Ibn al-ʿAdīm", in Jong, F. de (ed.), *Miscellanea Arabica et Islamica*, Leuven, 1993, 175–85.

247 Khan, M. Abdul Muʾid, "The Muslim theories of education during the Middle Ages", *IC*, XVIII (1944), 418–33.

As far as the sources are concerned, one of the first to have reached us in part is the treatise of Jāḥiẓ (d. 255/869), *The Book of Teachers*, the best edition being that of I. Geries.[248] Previously, some passages had been presented and translated,[249] or simply translated,[250] but not all of them came from the same origin.[251] Jāḥiẓ also tackled the issue of masters and teaching in several passages of his other books, notably in the *Book of Animals*.[252] His concept of pedagogy and the criticisms he directed against teachers have provided subject-matter for several studies in Arabic, particularly those of: al-Qazzāz (1995) and Shams al-Dīn (1985), works in Arabic, which also address the pedagogic ideas of Ibn al-Muqaffaʿ and ʿAbd al-Hāmid al-Kātib. The best developed studies on al-Jāḥīẓ remain those of Sebastian Günther (see Chapter 5, this volume).[253]

The publication by Ibn Saḥnūn (d. 256/870) from Kairouan, entitled *Rules of Conduct for Teachers* has been edited numerous times.[254] The author relied especially on material obtained from his father, in part orally, but also in writing from the Qāḍī of Tunis Shajara al-Maʿāfirī (d. 262/875).[255] This work has been translated,[256] and has also been the subject of several studies by Driss, Ahwānī, Ḥijāzī and Shams al-Dīn, among others.[257] More recently, Günther has devoted

[248] See the Bibliography, section V, under al-Jāḥiẓ.

[249] Hirschfeld, H., "A volume of essays by al-Jāḥiẓ", in Arnold, T.W. and R.A. Nicholson (eds), *A Volume of Oriental Studies Presented to Edward G. Browne*, Cambridge, 1922, 202–209.

[250] Partly adapted in German: Rescher, O., *Excerpte und Übersetzungen aus den Schriften des Philologen und Dogmatikers Gahiz aus Bacra*, Stuttgart, 1931; Pellat, C., *Arabische Geisteswelt: Ausgewählte und übersetzte Texte von al-Gahiz*, 181–84 (Rasāʾil, III, 38–42; ms. Rieu, Br. Mus., 1129, 10b–19b, for the whole of the treatise); id., *The Life and Works of Jahiz*, trans. D.M. Hawke, London and Berkeley, 1969.

[251] A passage from Ibshīhī, *al-Mustaṭraf*, ch. 76, s. 5, Cairo, 2 vols in 1, ed. M. ʿA. Ṣubayḥ, n.d., II, 318–19/trans. G. Rat, *al-Mostaṭraf*, 2 vols, Toulon, 1899–1902, II, 657–60; Basset, R., *Mille et un contes: récits et légendes arabes*, 3 vols, Paris, 1924–26, II, 159–61, corresponds to Rat, 658–60, but in a different translation. Pellat, *Milieu*, *op. cit.*, took up Basset's translation.

[252] Jâhiz, *Le Cadi et la mouche*, *op. cit.*, 138, 167–69.

[253] See also Günther, S. "Be masters in that you teach and continue to learn: medieval Muslim thinkers on educational theory", *Comparative Education Review* (Chicago) 50/3 (2006), 371–73 (367–88). In addition to his work still to be published, there are two other published contributions: Günther, "Praise to the book: Al-Jahiz and ibn Qutayba on the excellence of the written word", *JSAI*, 31 (2008); id., "al-Jahiz on the poetic of teaching", in Khalidi, Tarif (ed.), *al-Jahiz: A Humanist for our Time*, Beirut, 2008.

[254] Ibn Saḥnūn, *Ādāb al-muʿallimīn*. For the editions, see the Bibliography.

[255] Muranyi, *Beiträge*, *op. cit.*, 56–47, 66–67.

[256] Lecomte, G., "Le livre des règles de conduite des maîtres d'école par Ibn Saḥnūn", *REI*, 21 (1954), 77–105; *Eğitim ve öğretimin esasları. Ādābu'l-muallimīn*, trans. M. Faruk Bayraktar, İstanbul, 1996, 88 pp.

[257] Shams al-Dīn, ʿAbd al-Amīr, *al-Fikr al-tarbawī ʿinda Ibn Saḥnūn wa-al-Qābisī*, Beirut, 1985, 236 pp.; reprint Beirut, 1990; Ismail, S.M., "Muḥammad ibn Sahnūn [*sic*]: an educationalist and faqīh", *Muslim Education Quarterly*, 12 (1995–94), 37–54.

some well-informed pages to the latter, in preparation for a work he is putting together (see Chapter 5, this volume).[258]

Yet another writer from Kairouan, Abū al-Ḥasan al-Qābisī (d. 403/1012),[259] composed *al-Risāla al-mufaṣṣala li-aḥwāl al-muta'allimin wa aḥkām al-mu'allimīn wa al-muta'allimīn* (*Detailed Epistle on the Circumstances of Pupils, their Rules of Conduct and Those of the Masters*). Al-Qābisī is highly dependent on Ibn Saḥnūn's text and also frequently cites Ibn Ḥabīb ('Abd al-Malik, d. 238/853).

As for *Instruction of the Student: The Method of Learning* by Burhān al-Dīn ou Burhān al-Islām al-Zarnūjī (d. after 620/1223),[260] it became, after several translations into Latin, the subject of several other translations and presentations.

With respect to the teaching of philosophy, medicine and the true sciences, one should refer to the corresponding volumes of the series "The Formation of the Classical Islamic World",[261] as well as to the scholarly exposition of G. Endress with its copious bibliography.[262] Nor will we forget to mention here al-Fārābī (d. 339/950), who was among the first thinkers in Islam to formalize a theory of instruction[263] and to suggest an integrated curriculum for the higher learning of both the "foreign" and "religious" sciences, in which he affirmed the distinction between "human and divine knowledge": "It did not become an integral component of formal higher learning in Islam; yet it did have an impact on the philosophers who—in their private studies and in study circles—followed it to some extent."[264] Finally, A.'A. al-Qāḍī has studied the educational thought of the Mu'tazilites, the Asha'rites and of the philosophers.[265]

Several works have also been dedicated to instruction and pedagogy among the Brethren of Purity (writing *ca.* 350/961, 370/980),[266] Abū al-Ḥasan al-'Āmirī

[258] See also Günther, "Be masters", *art. cit*, 369–70; id., *Medieval Muslim Thinkers on Education*, *op. cit.*, to be published.

[259] Idris, H.R., "Deux juristes kairouanais de l'époque zīride: Ibn Abī Zaid al-Qairawānī et al-Qābisī", *AIEO*, 12 (1954), 181–83 (122–98); Muranyi, *Beiträge*, *op. cit.*, 271–96 and *passim*.

[260] *GAL S*, I, 837; Plessner, M. [Berkey, J.P.], *EI*, 2nd edn, XI, 462 (French edn, XI, 501). He was the student of Burhān al-Dīn al-Marghīnanī (d. 593/1197). Ibn Abī al-Wafā' held Zarnūjī's book in high esteem: see Ibn Abī al-Wafā' al-Qurashī, *al-Jawāhir al-muḍiyya fī ṭabaqāt al-ḥanafiyya*, 2nd edn, 5 vols, ed. 'Abd al-Fattāḥ M. al-Ḥulū, Cairo, 1993, IV, 365, no. 2065, 219: our Zarnūjī was in the same class as Nu'mān b. Ibr. al-Zarnūjī (d. 640/1242); *op. cit.*, III, 557, no. 1758.

[261] Vols 39–41 of this series.

[262] Endress, G., "Die wissenschaftliche Literatur", in *GAP* II, 431–60 (400–506); *GAP* III, 3–152.

[263] Haddad, F.S., "An Early Arab Theory of Instruction", *IJMES*, 5 (1974/3), 240 (240–59), only on Alfarabius.

[264] Günther, "Be masters", *art. cit.*, 374 (Fārābī, 373–76); Bayrakli, B., "The philosophy of education of al-Fārābī", *Hamdard Islamicus*, X (1987), 29–34; Reisman, D.C., "Al-Farabi and the Philosophical Curriculum", in Adamson, P. and Taylor, R.C. (eds), *The Cambridge Companion to Arabic Philosophy*, Cambridge, 2005, 52–71; cf. Asfaruddin, A., "Muslim views on education: parameters, purviews and possibilities", *Journal of Catholic Legal Studies*, 44 (2005), 143–78.

[265] al-Fikr al-tarbawī 'inda al-mutakallimīn al-muslimīn, Cairo, 1996.

[266] Gardet, L., "Notion et principes de l'éducation dans la pensée arabo-musulmane", *REI*, 44 (1976), 1–16; Shams al-Dīn, *al-Falsafa al-tarbawiya 'inda Ikhwān al-Ṣafā' min khilāl rasā'ilihim*, Beirut, 1988.

(d. 381/992),[267] Ibn Sīnā (d. 428/1037),[268] Miskawayh (d. 421/1030),[269] Ibn Ṭufayl (d. 581/1185)[270] and so on. With regard to the teaching of the *dāʿī* of the Fāṭimids and of the "Conference of Wisdom" (*majlis al-ḥikma*), we have at our disposal the pages that al-Maqrīzī (d. 845/1442)[271] devoted to the subject, based on ancient sources, mostly al-Muṣabbiḥī (d. 420/1030).

Many other similar works could be mentioned, [272] but among those that fit into our period of study we can cite *Riyāḍat al-mutaʿallim* (*Instruction of the Pupil/Student*) by the Shāfiʿite Abū ʿAbd Allāh Zubayr b. Sulaymān al-Baṣrī al-Zubayrī al-Ḍarīr (d. 317/929 or 323)[273] and the *Kitāb al-ʿilm wa l-taʿlīm* (*The Book of Knowledge and Teaching*) by the Muʿtazilite Abū Zayd al-Balkhī (d. 322/934) who was a schoolmaster.[274]

Although al-Ghazālī (d. 505/1111) does not belong to our period of interest, we will mention him here not only because of his ideas concerning pedagogy and education, but also because he bears witness to the previous eras. We know that the first book (*Kitāb al-ʿIlm*)[275] of his *Iḥyāʾ ʿulūm al-dīn* considers the subject, as well as books XXII and XXIII.[276] Ghazālī's ideas on education have also inspired numerous works.[277]

---

[267] Arkoun, M., "La conquête du bonheur selon Abū-l-Ḥasan al-ʿĀmirī", *Stud. Isl.*, XXII (1965), 55–90; Lacroix, M.-C., "Éducation et instruction selon Abū l-Ḥasan al-ʿĀmirī. Présentation et traduction d'un extrait du 'Kitāb al-saʿāda wa l-isʿād, [ed. Minovi, 348–88]", *Rev. Ph. de Louvain*, 87 (1989), 165–214.

[268] Stanton, C.M. *Higher Learning in Islam: The Classical Period, A.D. 700-1300*, Savage, MD., 1990; Shams al-Dīn, *al-Falsafa al-tarbawiya*, *op. cit.*; Günther, "Be masters", *art. cit.*, 376–80.

[269] Siddiqi, B.Ḥ., "Ibn Miskawayh's theory of education", *Iqbal* (Lahore), 11 (1961), 39-46; id., "The view of Miskawayh on the education of children", *Journal of the Regional Cultural Institute* (Tehran), 4 (1971), 49–56; Arkoun, M., *Contribution*, *op. cit.*, 294-302 *et passim*; Bhat, B., "Miskawayh on social justice, education and friendship", *Islamic Studies*, 25 (1986), 197–210.

[270] Shams al-Dīn *ʿAbd al-Karīm b. Muḥammad al-Samʿānī fī kitābihi Adab al-imlāʾ wa-al-istimlāʾ*, Beirut, 1984.

[271] Maqrīzī, *al-Mawāʿiẓ wa l-iʿtibār fī dhikr al-hiṭaṭ wa l-āthār*, Būlāq, 2 vols, 1270/1853, I, 390–97/ *Description topographique et historique de l'Égypte*, IV, trans. P. Casanova, Cairo, 1920 (reprint F. Sezgin, Frankfurt, 1992), 118–44.

[272] Totah, *Contribution*, *op. cit.*, 67–76, established a list of 42 works addressing the masters and the students as well as teaching methods.

[273] *GAS*, I, 495. This work is mentioned by Dhahabī, *Siyar*, XV, 58, etc.; Totah, *Contribution*, *op. cit.*, 68, n. 2, with this same title attributed to several other authors.

[274] Yāqūt, I, 141/I, 274 (274–78, no. 92). This title is not mentioned by Ibn al-Nadīm, *Fihrist*, ed. Flügel, 138, but is mentioned, nevertheless, by Ḥājjī, Khalīfa, *Lexicon biographicum*, V, 119, no. 10328; Ahlwardt, I, 53. On al-Balkhī see Rosenthal, F., "Abū Zayd al-Balkhī on politics", in Bosworth, C.E., *et al.* (eds), *The Islamic World from Classical to Modern Times: Essays in Honor of Bernard Lewis*, Princeton, 1989, 287–301.

[275] Ghazālī, *Iḥyāʾ ʿulūm al-dīn*, 4 vols, Būlāq, 1289/1872; reprint Cairo, al-Maṭbaʿa al-ʿUthmāniyya, 1933, Book 1, *Kitāb al-ʿIlm*, I, 5–79; *The Book of Knowledge*, 2nd edn, trans. Nabih Amin Faris, Lahore, 1966, 6+246 pp.

[276] Ghazālī, *Iḥyāʾ* Book XXII, Bayān 10, III, 62–64 (on child education); *On Disciplining the Soul and Breaking the Two Desires*, Books XXII and XXIII, trans. T.J. Winter, 1995; Abû Hâmid al-Ghazâlî, *Maladies de l'âme et maîtrise du cœur*, Livre XXII, intro., trans., notes by M-T Hirsch, Paris, 2007.

[277] El-Bagir, El-K.M., "Al Ghazali's philosophy of education, with special reference to Al Ihya, Book 1", PhD dissertation, University of Edinburgh, 1954; Dar, M.I., "Al-Ghazzālī on the problem of

Ibn Khaldūn (d. 808/1406) dedicated the sixth chapter of his *Prolegomena* to the "sciences" and to scholarship;[278] it includes a section entitled: "The Proper Method of Instruction".[279] In his autobiography Ibn Khaldūn gives an account of his own education, listing the principal books he read and describing the life and works of his main teachers.[280] Because the body of literature on Khaldūn is so enormous, we will confine ourselves here to mentioning just a few studies.[281] Ibn Khaldūn's educational ideas along with those of the Andalusian Ibn al-Azraq al-Aṣbaḥī (Muḥammad b. ʿAlī, d. 896/1491) have been discussed in a single book, with selected passages from both scholars.[282] Another author has presented the principles of education held by Zarnūjī, Miskawayh, Sharastānī, Ibn ʿArabī, al-Ghazālī, and Fārābī.[283]

Scholarship

The Transmission of Knowledge

Just as the transmission of the Qurʾan must be assured—that is, the believer must be certain that the Qurʾan he recites contains the *ipsissima verba Dei* proclaimed by Muḥammad and that it is transmitted in an "uninterrupted" (*mutawātir*) fashion by trustworthy readers—so the transmission of the *ḥadīth* must be established with the same degree of certainty, even though Muslim scholars admit that, to a certain extent, this transmission may be undertaken according to the meaning and not imperatively word-for-word so long as the meaning is not distorted. Indeed, many consider knowledge of the *ḥadīth* to be the "science" (*ʿilm*) *par*

education", in Abdullah, S.M. (ed.), *Armaġān-ʿilmī. Professor Muḥammad Shafiʿ Presentation Volume*, Lahore, 1955, 31–40; Sulaymān, F.H., *Madhāhib fī al-tarbiyya. Baḥth fī al-madhhab al-tarbawī ʿinda al-Ghazālī*, Cairo, 1964; Gardet, "Notion et principes", *art. cit.*, 4–8; Shams al-Dīn, *ʿAbd al-Karīm, op. cit.*; Günther, "Be masters", *art. cit.*, 380–85.

278 Ibn Khaldûn, *The Muqaddimah*, 3 vols, trans. F. Rosenthal, New York and Princeton, 1967 (1st edn 1958), III, ch. VI, 3–480.

279 Ibid., 292–98 *et passim*.

280 Ibn Khaldûn, *Le voyage d'Occident et d'Orient*, trans. A. Cheddadi, Arles, 1995 (Ist edn Paris, 1980), 45–71.

281 Sulaymān F.Ḥ., *Madhāhib fī al-tarbiyya*. Baḥth fī al-madhhab al-tarbawī ʿinda Ibn Khaldūn, Cairo, 1955; Qurayshi, M.A., "The educational ideas of Ibn Khaldun", *Journal of the Maharaja Sayajirao University of Baroda*, XIV, (1965), 83–92; Semaan, K.I.H., "Education in Islam, from the Jahiliyya to Ibn Khaldun", *MW*, 56 (1966), 188–98; Ahmad, A. "The educational thought of Ibn Khaldun", *J. of the Pakistan Historical Soc.*, XVI (1968), 175–81; Gardet, "Notions et principles", *art. cit.*, 8–9; al-Nuʿmī, ʿAl. al-Amīn, *Manāhij wa ṭuruq al-taʿlīm ʿinda al-Qābisī wa Ibn Khaldūn*, Tripoli (Libya), 1980; Bānabīla (1984); Cheddadi, A., 'Ibn Khaldun', *Prospects: The Quarterly Review of Comparative Education*, XXIV/1–2 (1994), 7–19.

282 Shams al-Dīn, *ʿAbd al-Karīm, op. cit.*: for Ibn Khaldūn, 5–98; Ibn al-Azraq, 99–114. For the *Muqaddimah*, 119–96; for Ibn al-Azraq's *Badāʾiʿ al-silk fī ṭabāʾiʿ al-milk*, 197–280.

283 ʿAbd al-Laṭīf, M., *Dirāsāt fī al-fikr al-islāmī*, Cairo, 1977, 190 pp., with the texts of several sources.

excellence, knowledge founded on certainty,[284] in contrast to dialectic theology (*kalām*) and lay knowledge such as literature, philosophy and so on; this is why it must be disseminated throughout all Muslim regions (see Chapters 15 and 16 in this volume). Moreover, among the traditionalist circles that claim to represent the Hanbalite theological perspective, in opposition to dialectic theology, those who have done nothing but devote themselves to the memorization, study and transmission of the *hadīth*, who basically have been nothing but traditionists (*muḥaddiths*), are presented as nothing short of saints.

The *ḥadīth* must be transmitted from master to disciple—at least this was how it was, in principle, until the beginning of the twentieth century, even though from the fifteenth century onwards this was no longer always the rule. In Islam, the Companions transmitted the Prophet's *ḥadīth* to their Successors, who transmitted what had been transmitted to them by the Companions, and so on and so forth, from generation to generation, or rather from scholarly "class" (*ṭabaqa*)[285] to scholarly class (a scholarly class might represent ten to 40 years, depending on the timespan between masters and pupils). From a certain period onwards, the transmitted *ḥadīth*s were preceded by a chain of guarantors (*isnād*): "So-and-so told me, he said: 'So-and-so told me'" and so on and so forth, until a Companion had related one of the Prophet's sayings, or a tale in which he figured. According to the Successor Ibn Sīrīn (d. 110/729):

> They were not used to inquiring after the *isnād*, but when the *fitna* [the civil war between Muʿāwiya and ʿAlī, 35/655] occurred they said: "Name us your informants." Thus, if these were *ahl as-sunna*, their traditions were accepted, but if they were *ahl al-bidaʿ* [innovators], their traditions were not accepted.[286]

It is difficult to give credence to this tradition, which contains an anachronism ("people of the sunna"), yet it remains likely that towards the end of the first/seventh century there was recourse to chains of guarantors, even if these were far from being commonly used. Thus there are few in Muqātil b. Sulaymān's (d. 150/767) Qurʾanic commentary, and most of those that are present have been inserted by one of the transmitters of this work. From the end of the second/eighth century, those who transmitted traditions without necessarily attributing them to Muḥammad were ridiculed as "storytellers" (*quṣṣāṣ*) and more often than

[284] Gilliot, "La transmission des sciences religieuses", in J.-C. Garcin *et al.*, *États, sociétés et cultures du monde musulman médiéval Xe–XVe siècle*, 3 vols, II, Paris, PUF (Nouvelle Clio), 2000, 327–29, 336–38 (327–51); "La transmission du message muhammadien. Juristes et théologiens", in Bianquis, T., *et. al.* (eds), *Les Débuts du monde musulman*, chap. XXV, 385–89; Nagel, Tilman, "Ḥadīth – oder: die Vernichtung der Geschichte", in Wunsch, Cornelia (ed.), *XXV. Deutscher Orientalistentag*, 1991, Stuttgart, 1994, 118–28.

[285] Marçais, William (trans. and annotation by), *Le Taqrîb de en-Nawawī*, Paris, Imprimerie Nationale, 1902, ch. 63; Gilliot, "Ṭabaḳāt", *EI*, 2nd edn, X, 7–10.

[286] Juynboll, *Muslim Tradition*, *op. cit.*, 17–18, according to Muslim, *Ṣaḥīḥ*, ed. ʿAbd al-Bāqī, I, 15.

not rejected. At the same time, a new discipline began to emerge within what was called "the sciences of the *ḥadīth*"—"disparaging and declaring trustworthiness" (*al-jarḥ wa l-taʿdīl*),[287] namely the criticism of traditions or, better, the critical examination of the qualities of a transmitter[288]—and this developed to a significant extent during the following centuries. Works were even penned that kept record of the transmitters who were "truthful authorities" (*thiqāt*), those who were "weak" (*ḍaʿīf*-s), "disparaged transmitters" (*majrūḥūn*) and so on. However, these distinctions were most often made according to doctrinal and moral criteria and hardly correspond to those of a dispassionate researcher.[289] From the sixth/twelfth century onwards, works were even composed on the "fabricated" (*mawḍūʿāt*) *ḥadīth*s, one of the most famous being that of the Hanbalite Ibn al-Jawzī (d. 597/1201).

Indeed, *ḥadīth* specialists were aware of the phenomenon of forgery from very early on, because the various groups (*firaq*) of politico-religious opposition had no qualms in attributing to Muḥammad traditions that would serve their position or their political or doctrinal ideas. Some of these *ḥadīth*s can even be found in collections of traditions that are said to be authentic. This is how Muḥammad came to say "The Qadarites are the Zoroastrians of this community". Yet the Qadarite movement that proclaimed, in one form or another, the principle of free will, which ran against the predestinationist "orthodoxy", only came into being around 70/689. Of course, one could always say that God had evidently granted his prophet a certain prescience for him to make this declaration!

Travel in Search of (Religious) Knowledge (al-riḥla fī ṭalab al-ʿilm)

Muslim scholars, especially *ḥadīth* scholars, travelled extensively in search of religious knowledge;[290] they were reputedly inspired by words attributed to Muḥammad, "'Seek knowledge even in China',[291] since the search for knowledge is an obligation for all Muslims".[292] This is the picture presented by the sources

[287] Marçais, *Le Taqrîb*, *op. cit.*, 80–101, ch. 23., Among the Imāmis one of the equivalents of Nawawī' Taqrīb, or of other books, is: Shahīd al-Thānī, Zayn al-Dīn ibn ʿAlī, *Munyat al-murīd fī ādāb al-mufīd al-mustafīd*, ed. al-Sayyid A. al-Ḥusaynī, Beirut, 1984, 214 pp.; cf. Scarcia Amoretti, Bianciamaria, "Sulla riwāya in ambito imamita", in Amoretti, Scarcia (ed.), *Onomastica*, 110–48.

[288] On the study of the ḥadīth in the Islamic East, see Mottahedeh, R., "The transmission of learning: the role of the Islamic East", 67–72.

[289] Gilliot, "Prosopography in Islam: an essay of classification", 5–36.

[290] On the ambiguity of the word *ʿilm*, see Nieuwenhuijze, C.A.O., *The Lifestyles of Islam*, Leiden, 1985, 115–22.

[291] The first part of this tradition is as famous as it is spurious; see Rosenthal, *Knowledge Triumphant*, *op. cit.*, 89, n. 4.

[292] Baghdādī, al-Khaṭīb, *al-Riḥla fī ṭalab al-ḥadīth*, 72–76; cf. Zarnūjī, *Instruction of the Student*, trans. von Grunebaum, 21, 28–29. The tradition "The search for knowledge is an obligation for all Muslims" has been transmitted in several "ways" (*ṭuruq*); see Suyūṭī, *Juzʾ fīhi ṭuruq ḥadīth: Ṭalab

and secondary literature on the subject.[293] Indeed, many scholars travelled extensively to hear the lessons given by masters in traditions. Once they had completed the training that was available in their village, neighbouring village or their region, the most talented students were sent "travelling" by their fathers, in order to collect as many prophetic, exegetic or even historiographic or other traditions as possible. This could be done for its own sake or as part of the pilgrimage to Mecca, in which case, whether on the way there or back, it was perfectly acceptable to make great detours in order to listen to the lessons of one or several renowned transmitters, in one location or another. This is how it was possible to retrace the "wanderings in pursuit of knowledge" undertaken by several Muslim scholars, such as those of Ṭabarī (d. 310/923)[294] (see Chapter 7, this volume). Such travels were also undertaken from the West (Muslim Spain[295] and the Maghreb) to the East. However, it has recently been shown that this custom was less widespread than was previously thought, not only among the philologists and grammarians, but even among the traditionists.[296] The practice was deep-rooted in a shared social and religious *imaginaire* (mindset):

> "The more teachers a scholar could boast of, and the more he knew to tell about the circumstances of their lives and studies, the more trustworthy he regarded himself .... An Egyptian scholar of the thirteenth century, who had made a dictionary of his 1,270 teachers, was asked by a friend how many were outstanding (*imāms*) and answered: 'Had I listed only *imāms*, I would not have reached the number five!'".[297]

Orality and Literacy

It was, in some ways, in the continuity of its oral transmission that the *ḥadīth*'s authenticity was meant to reside. Yet, even when delivering orally traditions they knew off by heart, many traditionists used "books of notes" dating as far back as to the first/seventh century, even though some were praised for "never" having done so. In the early days of Islam many opposed the writing down of

---

al-ʿilm farīḍah ʿalā kull Muslim, ed. in id., *Taḥdhīr al-khawāṣṣ min akādhīb al-quṣṣāṣ*, ed. M.Ḥ.M.Ḥ Ismāʿīl, Beirut, 2002.

[293] Kremer, *Culturgeschichte*, II, 436–39; Goldziher, *Muhammedanische Studien*, II, 175–93/*Muslim Studies*, II, 164–80/217–38/Études, 215–56; Shalabī, *Taʾrīkh al-tarbiyya*, 317–26; Juynboll, *Muslim Tradition, op. cit.*, 66–70; Gellens, S.I., "The search for knowledge in medieval Muslim societies" (1990); Ephrat, *A Learned Society, op. cit.*, 33–58.

[294] Gilliot, *Exégèse, langue et théologie en islam*, 19–37.

[295] Makki, M.ʿA., *Ensayo sobre las aportaciones orientales* ..., 1–58; Jarrar, M., *Die Prophetenbiographie im islamischen Spanien*, Frankfurt, 1989, 65–67.

[296] Bernards, M.M., "Ṭalab al-ʿilm amongst the linguists of Arabic during the ʿAbbasid period", in Montgomery, James E. (ed.), *ʿAbbasid Studies*, Leuven, 2004, 33–46.

[297] Goitein, reviewing Petry, *The Civilian Elite*, in *Speculum*, 59 (1984), 195.

the *ḥadīth* (*kitābat/kitāb al-ʿilm*), particularly in Bassora during the second/eighth century, but elsewhere too. On the one hand, it is said of the great Medinian traditionist Ibn Shibāb al-Zuhrī (d. 124/742) that he never wrote down a tradition or that he left no book, but, on the other hand, he is presented as an assiduous writer and even as the first to have written down the *ḥadīth*, which he would have done at the behest of the Umayyads. Those opposed to the writing down of the *ḥadīth* emphasized the tradition attributed to Muḥammad, of which one variant is: "Do not write what I say, except for the Koran. If someone writes down something other than the Koran, may God destroy him!"[298] One of the arguments put forward by Muslim scholars to justify such opposition was the fear that the Qurʾan and the *ḥadīth* might be confused! The question of the history and origins of the opposition to the writing down of traditions has been thoroughly addressed by Michael Cook.[299] He shows that, at an earlier stage, this opposition had existed in all major centres of learning, and that at one time it had been the prevailing attitude. He presents an argument for the Jewish origin of this Muslim hostility to the writing down of the traditions. He then sketches out a general explanation for the demise of the authentically oral tradition in Islam.[300]

Nevertheless, although over time the written took over from the oral, the latter continued to be regarded as an ideal; moreover, oral and written "reception of knowledge" (that is, of the traditions) (*taḥammul al-ʿilm*)[301] retained an ambivalence. Drawing on the practices of reception or transmission of knowledge, authors such as al-Khaṭīb al-Baghdādī (d. 463/1071) or al-Nawawī (d. 676/1277), among others, set out criteria for the quality of the transmission not only of the traditions, but also of books, without making the error of projecting into the most ancient past practices that only progressively came into being from the second half of the second/eighth century. These theoreticians enumerate some eight modes of transmission in descending order of value along with the terms designating the mode of reception (see also Vajda, Chapter 9, this volume). The first three modalities are as follows.

According to the authors, the best of these types of reception is "direct listening" (*al-samāʿ*): the disciple or the auditor listens to the traditions that are recited from memory or read from the master's "book" or "booklet" (*juzʾ*). In this case, the terms used in the transmission will be: "I heard" or "So-and-so

---

298 Cook, M., "The opponents of the writing of tradition", 459–66; Schoeler, *Écrire et transmettre dans les débuts de l'islam*, Paris, 2002,, 52–56/*The Oral and the Written in Early Islam*, trans. Uwe Vagelpohl, ed. J.E. Montgomery, London, 2006, 116–21, 124 *et seq.*

299 Cook, "Opponents", *art. cit.*

300 For the previous studies on this issue by Sprenger, Goldziher, Wansbrough, Sezgin, Schoeler, see Cook, ibid., 440, n. 23–27.

301 Sublet, J., "Le modèle arabe. Éléments de vocabulaire", in Grandin (ed.), *Madrasa*, 13–27.

transmitted to me/us".[302] Next comes "reading" (out loud—indeed, this used to be the only known way of reading) or "recitation" (*qirāʾa*) in front of the master.[303] The disciple or another person reads from the book, or booklet, or else recites from memory one or several *ḥadīths*, or even the entire book, in front of the master. The master listens and compares what is recited to his own copy or memory of it. In this case, the appropriate terms are "So-and-so taught me/us" or else "I read in the presence of" (*qaraʾtu ʿalā*). However, scholars of Islam do not agree over the question of whether recitation has the same value as direct listening from the very lips of the master. In both cases—direct listening or recitation—the disciple (or disciples) is authorized to transmit what they have received from the master. The third type of reception is the "licence to transmit" (*ijāza*)[304] (see Witkam, Chapter 8, this volume). Let us consider a couple of cases. First, the master specifies both the one whom he is licensing and the work which he gives licence to transmit, saying, for example, "I give you [So-and-so] licence to transmit *The Summa of the Authentic Traditions* of al-Bukhārī" or "all the works featuring on my syllabus", or even "my own work entitled ...". Alternatively, the master specifies the individual whom he licenses, but not the traditions to which he gives licence to transmit. There are also other types of licence, the validity or value of which are not unanimously agreed upon by all scholars.

In recent years scholars have turned their attention to the social aspects of the transmission of knowledge:

> Among these elements are different types of documents, whose significance varies over time and space; they include certificates of audition (*samāʿāt*)[305] noted on the margins, at the beginning or end of manuscripts and autobiographical reports about a scholar's studies that circulated as *fahrasa*, *mashyakha*, *barnāmaj*, *thabat* or *muʿjam*[306] .[307]

The ambivalence between the oral and the written is well illustrated in the certificate of listening (*samāʿ*) reproduced at the beginning of the publication of Ibn Hanbal's enormous *Musnad*[308] from the colophon of one of the manuscripts:

---

[302] Marçais, *Le Taqrîb*, *op. cit.*, 101–105, ch. 24.

[303] Ibid., 105–15.

[304] Ibid, 115–26.

[305] Leder, S., "Hörerzertifikate als Dokumente für die islamische Lehrkultur des Mittelalters", in Khoury, R.G. (ed.), *Urkunden und Urkundenformulare im Klassischen Altertum und in den orientalischen Kulturen*, Heidelberg, 1999, 147–66.

[306] Gilliot, "Prosopography in Islam", 47–78.

[307] Schmidtke, S., "Forms and Functions of 'Licences To Transmit', (Ijāzas) in 18th-Century-Iran:ʿAbd Allāh al-Mūsawī al-Jazāʾirī al-Tustarī's (1112-73/1701-59) *Ijāza kabīra*", in Krämer, G. and Schmidtke, S. (eds), *Speaking for Islam*, Leiden, 2006, 95 (95–127).

[308] Juynboll, G.H.A., "Aḥmad Muḥammad Shākir", *Der Islam*, 49 (1972), 221–47; Gilliot, "Textes arabes anciens", *MIDEO*, 23 (1997), 329–30, no. 62.

"certificate of reading" in the presence of the master Ibn al-Ḥuṣayn al-Shaybānī (d. 525/1121), in the "reading" mode; the chronologically preceding guarantor who "listened" to this recitation/lecture was Abū ʿAlī Ibn al-Madhhab (d. 444/1052), who held the licence to transmit this work through the reading mode from Abū Bakr al-Qaṭīʿī (d. 368/979), who in turn held it from the son of Ibn Ḥanbal, Abū ʿAbd al-Raḥmān ʿAbd Allāh (d. 290/902), the true editor of his father's book.

This mode of transmission sometimes leads to ambiguity concerning the author's identity. Thus, the *Kitāb al-Waraʿ*, the product of Ibn Ḥanbal's lessons, is sometimes attributed to the latter and sometimes to his pupil Abū Bakr al-Marwazī (d. 275/888), who was its ultimate editor;[309] this is not to mention the dozen collections containing Ibn Ḥanbal's "answers" to questions (*masāʾil*) addressed to him, put in order and amplified by his students.[310]

With regard to the relationship between the oral and the written during the pre-Islamic period[311] and the first centuries of Islam, Gregor Schoeler[312] has shed much light on the debate, distinguishing between—to use terms borrowed from the ancient Greek—the *hypomnēmata* (writings or notebooks for assisting memory) and the *syngrammata* (well-composed writings destined for publication).[313] In Chapter 11 of this volume F. Krenkow shows that occasionally some ancient Arab poets or their transmitters made use of writing.[314]

Books and Authorship

Books have been the object of praise by numerous scholars, including al-Jāḥiẓ.[315] The best reference work in terms of books, their composition, transmission,

---

309 Bousquet, G.-H and Charles-Dominique, P., "Le *Kitāb al-Waraʿ* ou Livre du Scrupule religieux selon l'Imām Ibn Ḥanbal, extraits traduits et annoté par Bousquet, G.-H et P. Charles-Dominique", *Hespéris*, 39 (1952), 97 (97–119); Levi Della Vida, G., "Une Addition aux dictionnaires arabes: la sottise est bien nommée", *AIEO* (Algiers), 12 (1954), 5 (5–30).

310 *GAS*, I, 507–508. Numerous other examples can be found for other "author" in Gilliot, "Textes arabes anciens", *MIDEO*, 19 (1989), 28 (2010) ; Gilliot, "La transmission du message muhammadien. Juristes et théologiens", art. cit., 396–97.

311 Pedersen, *The Arabic Book*, *op. cit.*, 3–11 (ch. I).

312 Schoeler, Écrire et transmettre, *op. cit.*, 15–29; id., *The Oral and the Written*, *op. cit.*, 28–44. Schoeler revised a collection of articles, published mostly in German between 1981 and 2000, and edited them in the form of a book in French, and then in English.

313 This distinction, without the Greek terms, had been suggested by Sprenger, *Leben*, III, p. XCIII–XCIV.

314 See also Jones, A., "Orality and writing", *EQ*, III, 587–89 (587–93); Blair, S.S., "Writing and writing materials" , *EQ*, V, 558–59; Maraqten, M., "Writing materials in pre-Islamic Arabia"; Rosenthal, F., *Technique and Approach*, 6–7: (Notebooks versus memory)/*Manāhij*, 22–26; Weil, G., "Arabische Verse über das Ausleihen von Büchern", *Islamica*, II (1927), 556–61; Weisweiler, M., "Arabische Schreiberverse", in Paret, R. (ed,), *Orientalische Studien Enno Littmann zu seinem 60. Geburtstag*, Leiden, 1935, 101–20.

315 Rufai, A., *Über die Bibliophilie im älteren Islam: nebst Edition und Übersetzung von Gâḥiẓ' Abhandlung Fî madḥ al-kutub*, Istanbul, 1935.

the scribes and booksellers, writing materials, Arabic script and calligraphers and so on remains that of Johannes Pedersen.[316] Since then, G. Endress has contributed an excellent bibliography on codicology:[317] the book in Muslim culture, writing materials, outside appearance, palaeography and the transmission of manuscripts.[318] We also have at our disposal an excellent monograph on the technique and approach of scholarship written by Franz Rosenthal from sources such Badr al-Dīn Ibn Jamāʿa (d. 733/1333)[319] and al-ʿAlmawī (d. 981/1573),[320] whose work is an abridgement of that of Badr al-Dīn al-Ghazzi (d. 984/1577).[321]

Max Weisweiler (Chapter 10, this volume) has written a scholarly article on the dictation of texts and works in preparation for his edition of Samʿānī's (d. 562/1167) *Adab al-imlāʾ wa l-istimlāʾ (The Methods of the Dictation Colleges)*.[322] For his part, Stefan Leder studied the manner and ways in which literary, historiographic or other traditions were transmitted and integrated into written works[323]—for instance, in *adab* collections—which in some cases compels us to redefine the notion of authorship (see Chapter 12, this volume).

The problem of the transmission of texts or textual units has also been considered with regard to the *belles lettres* (*adab*), as in *The Book of Songs* of Abū al-Faraj al-Iṣfahānī (d. 356/967) by M. Fleischhammer[324] and H. Kilpatrick,[325] or

[316] Pedersen, *The Arabic Book*, *op. cit.*, successively, 20–36, 37–53, 54–71, 72–88.

[317] Endress, G., "Handschriftenkunde", in *GAP* I, 271–91 (271–296); Atiyeh (ed.), *The Book*, with contributions by Mahdi, M., "From the manuscript age to the printed books", 1–5, and Rosenthal, F., "Of making many books there is no end: the Muslim view", 33–54.

[318] Akhtar, Q.A., "The art of *waraqat* during the ʿAbbasid period", *IC*, 9 (1935), 131–48; id., (1937); Ḥammūda, M.ʿA., *Taʾrīkh al-kitāb al-islāmī al-makhṭūṭ*, Cairo, 1994 (1st edn 1979; 2nd edn 1991); Jamil, M.F., "Islamic *Wirāqa* stationery during the early Middle Ages", PhD thesis, Michigan State University, 1985; Gacek, A., *The Arabic Manuscript Tradition: A glossary of technical terms and bibliography*, Leiden, 2001; Déroche, F., *Manuel de codicologie des manuscrits en écriture arabe*, Paris, 2001/*al-Madkhal ilā ʿilm al-kitāb al-makhṭūṭ bi-al-ḥarf al-ʿarabī*, trans A.F al-Sayyid, London, 2005; id., *Le livre manuscrit arabe. Prélude à une histoire*, Paris, 2004; Bloom J.M., *Paper before Print: the history and impact of paper in the Islamic world*, New Haven and London, 2001.

[319] Ibn Jamāʿa *Tadhkirat al-sāmiʿ...* (1934, 2005); on this book: Shams al-Dīn, *ʿAbd al-Karīm*, *op. cit.*

[320] al-ʿAlmawī, Abd al-Bāsiṭ b. Mūsa (*GAL S* II, 488), *al-Muʿīd fī adab al-mufīd wa al-mustafīd*, ed. A. ʿUbayd, Damascus, 1349/1930; Zayʿūr (1986, 1993).

[321] al-Ghazzī, Badr al-Dīn M. b. M. (*GAL S* II, 488), *al-Durr al-naḍīd fī adab al-mufīd wa-al-mustafīd*, ed. ʿAl. M. al-Kundarī, Beirut, Dār al-Bashāʾir al-islāmiyya, 2006, 304 pp.; Sharkas, A.H., Badr Al-din Al-Ghazzi, "Al-Durr Al-Nadid", PhD dissertation, Harvard University, 1976.

[322] Samʿānī, Abū Saʾd, *Adab al-imlāʾ wa l-istimlāʾ* [*The Methods of the Dictation Colleges*], 1952.

[323] Leder, S., "Prosa-Dichtung in der aḫbār Überlieferung", 1987: id., *Das Korpus al-Haiṭam ibn ʿAdī*, 1991; id., "The literary use of the *khabar*", 1992; id., "Materialien zum *Taʾrīḫ*", 1994; id., "Grenzen der Rekonstruktion alten Schrifttums", 1996; id., "Conventions of fictional narration", 1998; id., "Heraklios erkennt den Propheten", 2001; id., *Spoken Word and Written Text*, 2002.

[324] Fleischhammer, M., *Die Quellen des Kitāb al-Aǧānī*, Wiesbaden, 2004 (thesis University of Halle, 1969). Following the same orientation, the sources of another book by Abū al-Faraj have been updated: Günther, S., *Quellenuntersuchungen zu den Maqatil at-Talibiyyin des Abu l-Farag al-Isfahani (gest. 356/967)*, Hildesheim, 1991.

[325] Kilpatrick, H., "A genre in classical Arabic literature: the *adab* encyclopedia", in Hillenbrand, R. (ed.), *Proceedings of the 10th Congress of the Union Européenne des Arabisants et Islamisants*,

for the great collections of *ḥadīth* by Johann Fück (Chapter 14, this volume),[326] J. Robson[327] and others. The process by which the latter were canonized[328] and the transmission of texts in the formation of the Sunni schools of law has equally been examined.[329]

The prospect of recovering lost Arabic texts from later sources that quote from them has long tantalized modern scholars.[330] Yet, in many cases, it would be futile to seek a complete and final version of the works of the ancient historiographers. Thus the traditionist and historiographer Ibn Isḥāq (d. 150/767) never "published" a "complete" version of his *Universal Pre-Islamic History* (*Kitāb al-mubtada*ʾ) or of his *Biography of the Prophet* (*Sīra* and *Maghāzī*), but he delivered lectures on these subjects to various audiences. An "original" of his *Life of the Messenger of God* never existed. Nor was there ever a unified text for Ibn Ishâq's traditions; he delivered many of his traditions orally, at different times and on various occasions.[331] Thereafter, some of his listeners became transmitters of their master's lessons, which resulted in numerous versions, often concordant but also divergent or complementary.[332] Equal recourse was made to both oral and written transmission sometimes as early as the first/seventh century.[333]

As from about 1960, researchers began to set themselves the task of reconstituting sources, in which case "metamorphoses" in the transmitted texts

---

Edinburgh, 1982, 34–42; id., *Making the Great Book of Songs*, London, 2002, 288 pp.; id., "The transmission of songs in medieval Arabic culture", in Vermeulen, U. and De Smet, D. (ed.), *Philosophy and Arts in the Islamic World: Proceedings of the 18th Congress of the Union Européenne des Arabisants et Islamisants*, 1998, 73–82.

326 See now also Quiring-Zoche, R., "How al-Buḫārī's *Ṣaḥīḥ* was edited in the Middle Ages: ʿAlī al-Yūnīnī and his *Rumūẓ*", *BEO*, L (1998), 191–222. For a transmission of the "six books" and others among the Zaydis, see Traini, Renato, "Scienza senza confini: un caso singolare di 'clerici vagantes' nell'islam medievale", in Amoretti, Scarcia,(ed.), *Onomastica*, *op. cit.*, 149–93.

327 Robson, J., "The transmission of Muslim's Ṣaḥīḥ", 1949; id., "The transmission of Muslim's Ṣaḥīḥ", 1952; id,. 'The transmission of Tirmidhi's Jāmi", 1954; id., "The transmission of Nasāʾī's 'Sunan'", 1956; id., "The transmission of Ibn Mājah's 'Sunan'", 1958.

328 Brown, J.A.C., *The Canonization of al-Bukhārī and Muslim*, Leiden, 2007.

329 Melchert, C., *The Formation of the Sunnī Schools of Law, 9th–10th Centuries*; id., "The meaning of *qāla 'l-Shāfiʿī* in ninth century sources", in Montgomery, J. (ed.), *ʿAbbasid Studies*, Leuven, 2004, 276–301.

330 Conrad, L.I., "Recovering lost texts: some methodological issues", *JAOS*, 113 (1993), 258 (258–63); Landau-Tasseron, E., "On the reconstruction of lost sources", *Al-Qanṭara*, 25 (2004), 45–91; id., "Sayf ibn ʿUmarʾ in medieval and modern scholarship', *Der Islam*, 67 (1990), 1–27.

331 Schoeler, *Écrire et transmettre*, *op. cit.*, 8.

332 Al-Samuk, S.M., "Die historischen Überlieferungen nach Ibn Isḥāq: Eine synoptische Rekonstruktion", inaugural dissertation, University of Frankfurt, 1978.

333 For the transmission of the works on Muḥammad's biography, the various versions of the Sīra by Ibn Isḥāq, see Jarrar, *Die Prophetenbiographie*, *op. cit.*, 110–25, notably on the role of Ibn Malik (d. 238/852). The introduction of the prophetic traditions into Muslim Spain is attributed to Ṣaʿṣaʿ b. Sallām and Muʿāwiya b. Ṣāliḥ: see Fierro, Maria Isabel (Maribel), "Muʿāwiya b. Ṣāliḥ al-Ḥaḍramī al-Ḥimṣī. Historia y leyenda", in *Estudios onomástico-biográficos de al-Andalus* [*EOAB*], I, ed. M. Marín. Madrid, 1988, 282 (281–411). For the transmission of knowledge in Spain, one should refer to vols 46 and 47 of "The Formation of the Classical Islamic World".

can sometimes be noted.[334] This has been accomplished either through the analysis of the chains of guarantors or by the utilization of manuscripts or fragments of ancient manuscripts with their colophons, the certificates of listening, all combined with analysis of chains of guarantors leading to a more ancient dating of Arabic written production than that by J. Schacht,[335] J. Wansbrough,[336] N. Calder[337] and others.

F. Sezgin[338] distinguished himself in the first method—the analysis and dating of the chains of guarantors. The method proposed by Sezgin gave rise to a lively debate among the interested researchers. Doubt was cast over whether the formulas used in the chains ("So-and-so told us", "So-and-so related to/informed us" and so on) corresponded to the modes of transmission as defined in the works specialized in the "sciences of transmission", for the most part subsequent to the second/eighth century.[339] That said, and despite the justified criticisms levied against his method, Sezgin's work must be credited for having drawn attention to the fact that suspicion with respect to the chains of guarantors could not be a hard-and-fast rule. Thus, in his study on the beginnings of Muslim jurisprudence, H. Motzki[340] carried out fundamental work on the collections of traditions (*Muṣannaf*) of ʿAbd al-Razzâq al-Sanʿānī (d. 211/826), which came well before that of al-Bukhârî, seeking to discover, through this enterprise, former "sources"—in this case, material harking back to four of the masters whose lessons on traditions al-Sanʿānī followed: Maʿmar b. Rāshid (d. 153/770), Ibn Jurayj (d. 150/767), Sufyān al-Thawrī (d. 161/778) and Ibn ʿUyayna (d. 196/811). Motzki even went further back into the "sources" with regard to the materials transmitted by al-Zuhrī (d. 124/742).[341] He also responded to what he considers to be G.H.A. Juynboll's hypercritical tendency[342] which even calls into question the very existence of the ancient transmitters of *ḥadīth*.[343] Having said this, in comparing Sayf b. ʿUmar's traditions with reports from other sources, M. Murtaza argues

[334] Landau-Tasseron, "On the reconstruction of lost sources", *art. cit.*, 54 *et seq.*

[335] Schacht, J., *The Origins of Muḥammadan Jurisprudence*, Oxford, 1950, XII+348, in constant reprint.

[336] Wansbrough, *Quranic Studies*, *op. cit.*; reprint, Amherst, NY, Prometheus Books, 2004.

[337] Calder, *Studies in Early Muslim Jurisprudence*, *op.cit.*

[338] Sezgin, F., *Buhârî'nin kaynakları hakkında araştırmalar*, Ankara; reprint 2000, 399 pp.; id., *Geschichte des arabischen Schriftttums*, I, Leiden, 1967, and the volumes that followed; Sezgin, U., *Abū Miḫnaf. Ein Beitrag zur Historiographie der umaiyadischen Zeit*, Leiden, 1971.

[339] Motzki, H., "Dating Muslim traditions: a survey", *Arabica*, LII/2 (2005), 204–53; id., "Dating the so-called *Tafsīr Ibn ʿAbbās*: some additional remarks", *JSAI*, 31 (2006), 147–62.

[340] Motzki, H., *Die Anfänge der islamischen Jurisprudenz/The Origins of Islamic jurisprudence*, *op.cit.*

[341] Motzki, H., "Der Fiqh des Zuhrī. Die Quellenproblematik", English trans. at: http://webdoc.ubn.kun.nl/mono/m/motzki_h/juriofibs.pdf.

[342] Juynboll, "Nāfiʿ, the *mawlā* of Ibn ʿUmar and his position in Muslim Ḥadīth literature", *Der Islam*, 70 (1993), 207, n. 1 and other references.

[343] Motzki, "Quo vadis Ḥadīṯ-Forschung? Eine kritische Untersuchung von G.H.A. Juynboll: 'Nāfiʿ the mawla of Ibn ʿUmar, and his position in Muslim Ḥadīṯ Literature'", *Der Islam*, 73 (1996), 40–80.

that Sayf created companions, transmitters of traditions, battles, events and even geographical locations that had in fact never really existed.[344] In two studies from 2008, Tilman Nagel questioned the method of H. Motzki, G. Schoeler and others in their analysis of the chains of authority they use to illustrate the authenticity of historical or pseudo-historical narratives on the beginnings of Islam. In his large volume *Muhammad, life and legend*, written in German, Nagel shows that these texts cannot be interpreted without taking into account the fact that they are presented within the framework of an Islamic history of Salvation; they should be considered in the context of hermeneutic theology.

But we shall dwell no longer on this question of the transmission of the *ḥadīth* and of the law, for it is a subject that has been addressed in Volumes 27 and 28 of this collection.[345]

For the sources on the origins of Islam and the Arab conquests, one should refer to Volume 5 of this collection. Fred Donner has summarized the four types of approach to these sources taken by researchers: (1) the descriptive approach, (2) the source-critical approach, (3) the tradition-critical approach, and (4) the sceptical approach.[346]

Benjamin Jokisch has recently brought back to our attention the fact that "[t]he high density of cultural, religious and political connection between Islam and Byzantium/Orthodox Christianity contrasts with the traditional conviction that Islam is essentially an Islamic phenomenon". [347] Nevertheless, the efforts of several researchers, as well as joint initiatives between Byzantinologists and Islamologists, are beginning to change this state of affairs little by little, with, for example, the integration of the formative period of Islam into "Studies on late antiquity and early Islam" (see Walzer, Chapter 13, this volume).[348]

Previously we mentioned another method for recovering, identifying and/or reconstituting ancient sources, which can lead to a more ancient dating of the writing down of the *ḥadīth* and, juridic, historiographic or other texts; this is a method which can, at least in part, call into question what has been termed as the "visions of the skeptics".[349] Thus M. Muranyi, who has been working on the

[344] 'Askarī, Murtaḍā, *Khamsūn wa mi'at ṣaḥābı mukhtaluqa* [*A hundred and Fifty Falsified Companions*], Baghdad, 1387/1968; id., *Abdullah Ibn Saba and Other Myths*, 3rd edn, trans. M.J. Muqaddas, Tehran, 1995, 228 pp.

[345] Vol. 27, *The Formation of Islamic law*; vol. 28, *The Development of Ḥadīth.*

[346] Donner, F., *Narratives of Islamic Origins: The beginnings of Islamic historical writing*, Princeton, 1998, 5–25.

[347] Jokisch, B., *Islamic Imperial Law: Harun-Al-Rashid's Codification Project*, Berlin, 2007, 320.

[348] Cf. Leder, "Heraklios erkennt den Propheten", *art. cit.*; Conrad, *The Byzantine*, *op.cit.*. Cf. *supra* Shahid's work, to which we will add: id., *Rome and the Arabs*, Washington, 1984; id., *Byzantium and the Arabs in the Sixth Century*, Washington, 1995; Id., *Byzantium and the Semitic Orient before the Rise of Islam*, London, 1988.

[349] Muranyi, M., "Visionen des Skeptikers", *Der Islam*, 81 (2004), 206-17; id., "Die frühe Rechtsliteratur zwischen Quellenanalyse und Fiktion", *Islamic Law and Society*, 4/2 (1997), 224–41, which is a very critical review article of Calder's *Studies in Early Muslim Jurisprudence*.

rich contents of the ancient manuscripts in the ancient library of the mosque of Qayrawan and in Moroccan libraries since 1980, has revitalized our knowledge of ancient Malikism in the Maghreb and of its routes of transmission from the East or towards the East. [350] Such works lead us to revise certain opinions held on the beginnings of the written production in Islam, not only with respect to the *ḥadīth* and law, but also with reference to exegesis[351] and historiography.

The transmission of philosophical texts is addressed in this volume by Richard Walzer (Chapter 13), so we will not discuss this or the transmission of texts on medicine and the true sciences here. Likewise, we have chosen not to take up the question of the collection and transmission of the Qurʾan, for reasons of limited space. [352]

Libraries

Islamic libraries have been the focus of a number of general studies (see, for example, Grohmann, Chapter 17, this volume).[353] These particular studies have emphasized that "[e]very mosque of importance is likely to have had a library for, hitherto, it was the practice to bequeath books to them". [354]

We have at our disposal articles, monographs and chapters of works on the libraries of the Umayyad period. Ruth Mackensen's four articles need to

[350] Muranyi, M., *Materialien zur mālikitischen Rechtsliteratur*, Wiesbaden 1984; id., *Ein altes Fragment medinensischer Jurisprudenz aus Qairawān*, Stuttgart, 1985; id., ʿAbd Allāh b. Wahb, *al-Ǧāmiʿ*, Wiesbaden, 1992; id., *Tafsīr al-Qurʾān*, ed. M. Muranyi, Wiesbaden, 1993; id., *al-Ǧāmiʿ. Tafsīr al-Qurʾān. Koranexegese 2*, I, ed.Muranyi, Wiesbaden, 1995 with our reviews in *Stud. Isl.*, 81 (1995), 212–13; 86 (1997), 180–81; 90 (2000), 195–98; 93 (2001), 176–79.

[351] A change in orientation will be noted between Gilliot, C., "The beginnings of qurʾānic exegesis" and id., "L'exégèse coranique: bilan partiel d'une décennie", *Stud. Isl.*, 85 (1997), 155–62; id., "Exegesis of the Qurʾān: classical and medieval"; id., "Traditional disciplines of Qurʾanic studies", *EQ*, V, 318–39.

[352] Among others, one should consult Welch, A.T., "al-Ḳurʾān", in *EI*, 2nd edn, V; Motzki, H., "The collection of the Qurʾān ..."; Neuwirth, A., "Qurʾān and history – a disputed relationship ..."; Donner, *Narratives of Islamic Origins*, *op. cit.*, 35–36; Gilliot, "Reconstruction"; id., "Creation of a fixed text"; id., "Reconsidering the authorship of the Qurʾan".

[353] Krenkow, F., "Kitabkhāna" , *EI*, 1st edn, II, 1045–47; Heffening, W. [Pearson, G.], "Maktaba" , *EI*, 2nd edn, VI, 197–200/French edn, VI, 181–84, with bibliography; Sourdel, D., "Dār al-ʿilm", *EI*, 2nd edn, II, 130; Quatremère; Hammer-Purgstall; Mez, 172–78/164–61;Inayatullah, S. "Bibliophilism in medieval Islam", *IC*, 12 (1938), 154–69; Pedersen, *The Arabic Book*, *op. cit.*, 113–30;Qasimi, A.S., 'Libraries in the early Islamic world', *Journal of the University of Peshawar*, 6 (1958), 1–15;Eche, Y., *Les Bibliothèques arabes publiques et semi-publiques en Mésopotamie, en Syrie et en Égypte au moyen âge*, Damascus, 1967;Diwan, M., 'Muslim contribution to libraries during the medieval times', *Islam and the Modern Age*, 9 (1978), 19–34; Imamuddin, S.M., *Arabic Writing and Arab Libraries*, London, 1983; Endress, "Wissenschaftlische Literatur" , in *GAP* II, 448–60; Ibn Dohaish, A.A., "Growth and development of Islamic libraries", *Der Islam*, 66 (1989), 289–302; Elayyan R.M., 'The history of the Arabic-Islamic libraries: 7th to 14th centuries', *International Library Review*, 22 (1990), 119–35; al-Jawāhirī, K.M.M., *Min Taʾkhīr al-maktabāt fī al-buldān al-ʿarabiyya*, Damascus, 1992; Gilliot, "La transmission des sciences religieuses", 334–36; Touati, H., *L'armoire à sagesse*, Paris, 2003, *passim*.

[354] Mez, 172/164; Sibai, *Mosque Libraries*, 49–125.

be corrected and completed in several areas, but have been included here (see Chapter 18) because they constitute the first fundamental study of the subject, and also because we noticed that they are included in many biographies without actually having been read by their authors! The libraries of the Abbasid period are addressed in general works as well as in several articles (such as Pinto, 1928; English trans., 1929).[355] Others have focused on towns (for example, Mackensen, 1932, for Baghdad), or on regions (for example, Qazānjī, 1972, 2001; and in collaboration with K. ʿAwwād, 1975 on Iraq; Wasserstein, Chapter 19, this volume on Muslim Spain).[356] Still others have considered the debt which Islamic libraries owed to their forerunners and contemporaries of various nationalities, religions and civilizations;[357] some have also dealt with the relation between libraries and sectarian propaganda.[358]

Conclusion

We have come a long way since the early interest shown by Westerners towards education and learning in Islam. Important stages were reached in the nineteenth century and at the beginning of the twentieth century thanks to the works of Alfred von Kremer, Aloys Sprenger, Ignaz Goldziher, Adam Mez and Johannes Pedersen, among many others. Because of the work of Franz Rosenthal, we have a better understanding of the technique and approach of scholarship in Islam and the relationship between scholarship and knowledge. More recently, and due to the works of Christopher Melchert, we are better informed about the etiquette of learning in the first three centuries of Islam.

We now have at our disposal general histories of education in Islam, in Arabic as well as in other languages, although these remain too imprecise, often failing to make the required distinctions between periods. On the other hand, some works, bearing on a narrower period and drawing on more precise sources, cast an interesting light on the subject. Such is the case with, for example, Munir-ud-Din Ahmad's 1968 study up until the fifth/eleventh century, from *The History of Baghdad* by al-Khaṭīb al-Baghdādī (d. 463/1071).

---

355 Imamuddin, *Arabic Writing and Arabic Libraries*, *op. cit.*, 33–38.

356 Ribera, "Bibliófilos y bibliotecas de la España musulmana"; Imamuddin, S M., *Hispano-Arab Libraries*, Karachi, 1961; Marín, M., "Arabic–Islamic libraries and bibliography in Spain", *British Society for Middle Eastern Studies Bulletin*, 11 (1984), 180–84; Diyāb Ḥ.al-Sh., *al-Kutub wa-al-maktabāt fī al-Andalus*, Cairo, (1998); Prince, C., "The historical context of Arabic translation, learning, and the libraries of medieval Andalusia", *Library History*, 18, (2002), 73–87, at: http://everything2.com/index.pl?node_id=1042932.

357 Mackensen, "Background", *art. cit.*

358 Mackensen, R.S., "Moslem libraries and sectarian propaganda", *American Journal of Semitic Languages and Literatures*, 51 (1934-35), 83–113.

Numerous monographs, of varying quality, have been written in Arabic about the pedagogic conceptions held by several authors. Recently, Sebastian Günther has contributed writings on Ibn Saḥnūn and al-Jāḥiẓ, among others, which should lead to a book on Muslim thinking on education.

The works of Gregor Schoeler have developed the way in which we conceive of the relation between the oral and the written. In about the same timeframe, progress has also been made with respect to questions of authorship and the reconstruction or recovering of lost texts (Conrad, Kilpatrick, Landau-Tasseron, Leder, Motzki, Muranyi). This has caused several late datings of ancient texts by authors including J. Schacht and then J. Wansbrough and N. Calder to be called into question (by Motzki and Muranyi, among others).

Editor's Remarks

Some studies included in this volume, originally written in English, are old and contain errors which could not be corrected. This is the case in the four articles by R. Mackensen Stellhorn (e.g. p. 326: Asad ibn Mūsā, d. 133/749, leg. 212/827), which additionally suffer from occasional lack of historico-critical distance. There are some errors, of a lesser degree in the article by I. Goldziher (e.g. p. 228: Laith b. Mujāhid, leg. Laith *ʿan* Mujāhid), and in other articles.

As for the studies which were not originally in English, obvious mistakes have been corrected, but others may remain.

As the studies in this volume are reprinted in their original form, it is not possible to standardize the transliteration of words and proper names across the volume.

The volume contains a long index in which corrections have been made to proper names and words where errors appeared in the text, and some unidentified proper names have been identified. Dates have been checked, and corrected as necessary, and for this reason dates given in the index do not always agree with those given in the text. Where discrepancy occurs regarding proper names and dates, the reader is advised to refer to the index.

I should like to extend particular thanks to my colleague and friend Lawrence I. Conrad who advised on the choice of studies for this volume, the team at Ashgate Publishing, especially Mrs Rosalind Ebdon, the translators and all those without whom this book would not have been published.

SELECT BIBLIOGRAPHY

I Education and Learning (General), Related topics and Bibliographies

Sources

ʿAlmawī, ʿA.M, *al-Muʿīd fī adab al-mufīd wa al-mustafīd*, ed. A. ʿUbayd, Damascus, 1349/1930.

Ghazzī, B., *al-Durr al-naḍīd fī adab al-mufīd wa-al-mustafīd*, ed. ʿAl. M. al-Kundarī, Beirut, 2006.

Ibn Khaldūn, *The Muqaddimah: An introduction to history*, 3 vols, trans. Franz Rosenthal, New York, 1967 (1st edn 1958).

Nashshāba, Hishām, *al-Turāth al-tarbawī al-islāmī fī khams makhṭūṭāt*, Beirut, Dār al-ʿIlm li-al-Malāyīn, 1988, 267 pp.; 1. Ibn Sīnā [attributed to], *K. al-Siyāsa* (25–45) 2. Ghazālī, *K. Minhāj al-mutaʿallīm* (55–92); Ibn Jamāʿa, Badr al-Dīn Abū ʿAbd Allāh M., *Tadhkirat al-sāmiʿ wa al-mutakallim wa adab al-ʾālim wa al-mutaʿallim* (97–186); 4. Zakariyyāʾ al-Anṣārī, Abū ʿAbd Allāh, *al-Luʾluʾ al-naẓīm fī rawm al-taʿallum wa al-taʾlīm* (203–13); 5. Ibn Ḥajar al-Haythamī, *Taḥrīr al-maqāl fī ādāb wa aḥkām yaḥtāj ilayhā muʾaddib al-aṭfāl* (221–64).

Secondary Literature

ʿAbdullatīf, M.A., *Islām kā tarbiyatī, taʿlīmī aur tadrīsī niẓām*, Shivhar, Bihar, 1997.

ʿAbd al-Wahhāb, Ḥ.Ḥ., *Waraqāt ʿan al-ḥaḍāra al-ʿarabiyya bi-Ifrīqiyya* [*Studies on Certain Aspects of Arab civilization in Ifrikia*], 3 vols, Tunis, Maktabat al-manār, 1966–72.

Abrashī, M.ʿA., *al-Tarbiyya al-islāmiyya wa falsafatuhā*, Cairo, 1969.

Adamek, G., *Das Kleinkind in Glaube und Sitte der Araber im Mittelalter*, dissertation, University of Bonn, 1967.

Ahmed, Munir-ud-Din, *Muslim Education and the Scholars' Social Status up to the 5th Century Muslim Era (11th Century Christian Era) in the Light of Taʾrīkh Baghdād*, Zurich, 1968/Arabic trans., *Taʾrīkh al-taʿlīm ʿinda al-muslimīn wa al-makāna al-ijtimāʿiyya li-ʿulamāʾihim ḥatta al-qarn al-khāmis al-hijrī*, Dār Mazīkh, 1981.

ʿAwwād, K., *al-Ṭufūla wa al-aṭfāl fī al-maṣādir al-ʿarabiyya al-qadīma wa al-ḥadītha*, Baghdad, 1979.

Belambri, A., *Bibliographie systématique sur l'éducation islamique*, Paris, 1988.

Berkey, J.P., *The Transmission of Knowledge: A social history of Islamic education*, Princeton, 1992.

Dar, M.I., "Al-Ghazzālī on the problem of education", in S.M. Abdullah (ed.), *Armaġān-ʿilmī. Professor Muḥammad Shafīʿ Presentation Volume*, Lahore, 1955, 31–40; reprint in F. Sezgin, *Abū Ḥāmid al-Ghazzālī: Texts and studies*, V, Frankfurt, 1999, 183–92.

Dodge, B., *Muslim Education in Medieval Times*, Washington, DC, 1962.

Driss, A., "L'Histoire de l'éducation et des idées pédagogiques en Ifriqiya (depuis Ibn Saḥnūn jusqu'à Ibn Khaldūn)", thesis, University of Paris III, 1979.

Ecchellensis, Abraham, *Semita Sapientiæ sive ad scientias comparandas methodvs*, Parisiis, apud Adrianum Taupinart, 1646.

El-Bagir, El-K.M., "Al Ghazali's philosophy of education, with special reference to Al Ihya, Book 1", PhD dissertation, University of Edinburgh, 1954.

Fayyāḍ, ʿAl. Dakhīl, *Taʾrikh al-tarbiyya ʿinda al-imāmiyya wa aslāfihim min al-shīʿa bayna ʿahday al-Ṣādiq wa al-Ṭūsī* [*The Emamite and their Forefathers' Education: From the time of al-Sadiq to that of al-Tusi*], Baghdad, 1970, 1972 (2nd edn Beirut, 1983).

Gilʿadi, A., *Children of Islam: Concepts of childhood in medieval Muslim society*, Basingstoke, 1992. Review by A. Cheikh Moussa, in *JESHO*, 37 (1994), 344–48.

Gilʿadi, A., "Individualism and conformity in medieval Islamic educational thought: some notes with special reference to elementary education", *Al-Qantara* (Madrid), 26/1 (2005), 99–121.

Goldziher, I., "Education (Muslim)", *Hastings Encyclopedia of Religion and Ethics*, 1912, V, 198–207; reprint 1960, V, 198–207; reprint in Goldziher, *Gesammelte Schriften*, Hildesheim, 1964, V, 223–32.

Granara, W., "Islamic education and the transmission of knowledge in Muslim Sicily", in Lowry, J.E. *et al.* (eds.), *Law and Education in Medieval Islam*, 2004, 150–73.

Güdemann, Moritz, *Das jüdische Unterrichtswesen während der spanisch-arabischen Periode, nebst handschriftlichen arabischen und hebräischen Beilagen mit Berichtungen und Nachträgen*, Vienna, Carl Gerold's son, 1873; reprint Amsterdam, Philo Press, 1968.

Halm [Heinz], *The Fatimids and their Traditions of Learning*, London and New York, 1997.

Hamidullah, M., "Educational system in the time of the Prophet", *IC*, 13 (1939), 48–59.

Hamiuddin Khan, M., *History of Muslim Education*, 2 vols, Karachi, 1967–73.

Haneberg, D.B., *Über das Schul- und Lehrwesen der Muhamedaner im Mittelalter*, Munich, Abhandlungen der Königlichen Bayerischen Ak. der W., 1850.

Imamuddin, S.M., "Mosque as a Centre of Education in the Early Middle Ages", *Islamic Studies*, 23 (1984–83), 159–70.

Khan, M.A., "The Muslim theories of education during the Middle Ages", *IC*, XVIII (1944), 418–33.

Khuda Bukhsh, S., "The educational system of the Muslims in the Middle Ages", *IC*, I (1927), 442–72.

Khūlī, ʿA.M., *Dawr al-masājid al-taʾrīkhī fī al-tathqīf al-ʿilmī*, Cairo, 1961.

Landau, J.M., "Kuttāb", *EI*, 2nd edn, V, 567–70 (French edn V, 572–75).

Lecomte, G., "Sur la vie scolaire à Byzance et en islam". I. "L'enseignement à Byzance et le kuttāb". II (by M. Canard) Falaqa = ΦΑΛΑΓΓΑΣ, *Arabica*, I (1954), 324–31, 331–36.

Lowry, J.E. *et al.* (eds), *Law and Education in Medieval Islam: Studies in memory of Professor G. Makdisi*, Warminster, 2004.

Mahdi, M., "From the manuscript age to the printed books", in George N. Atiyeh (ed.), *The Book in the Islamic World: The written word and communication in the Middle East*, Albany, NY, 1995, 1–15.

Makdisi, G., "Madrasa", *EI*, 2nd edn, V, 1123–34 (French edn V, 1119–30).

Makdisi, G., *Religion, Law and Learning in Classical Islam*, London, Variorum (CS, 347), 1991.

Makdisi, G., *The Rise of Colleges: Institutions of learning in Islam and the West*, Edinburgh, 1981.

Makdisi, G., *The Rise of Humanism in Classical Islam and the Christian West with Special Reference to Scholasticism*, Edinburgh, 1990.

Makidisi, G., Sourdel, D. and J. (eds), *L'enseignement en Islam eten Occident au moyen âge/Medieval education in Islam and the West*, Paris, 1976 (1977).

Maʿlūm, Sālik Aḥmad, *al-Fikr al-tarbawī ʿinda al-Khaṭīb al-Baġdādī*, Riyad, Maktabat al-Rushd, 1413/1999.

Marín, M., "Learning at mosques in al-Andalus", in M.K. Masud *et al.* (eds), *Islamic Legal Interpretation. Muftis and their fatwas*, Cambridge, MA and London, 1996, 47–54.

Middeldorpf, H., *Commentatio de institutis literariis in Hispania, quae Arabes auctores habuerunt*, Göttingen, 1810.

Mottahedeh, R.P., *Loyalty and Leadership in Early Islamic Society*, Princeton, 1980 and London, 1999.

Mottahedeh, R.P., "The transmission of learning: the role of the Islamic East", in N. Grandin and M. Gaborieau (eds), *Madrasa: la transmission du savoir dans le monde musulman*, Paris, 1997, 63–72.

Motzki, H., "Das Kind und seine Sozialisation in der islamischen Familie des Mittelalters", in J. Martin and A. Nitschke (eds), *Zur Sozialgeschichte der Kindheit*, Freiburg and Munich, 1986, 391–441.

Nashshāba, Hishām, *Muslim Educational Institutions: A general survey followed by a monographic study of Al-Madrasah Al-Mustanṣirīya in Baghdād*, Beirut, Librairie du Liban, 1989.

Nashabi, H., "Educational institutions", in R.B. Serjeant (ed.), *The Islamic City*, Paris, 1980, 66–89.

Pickthall, M., "Muslim education", *IC*, I (1927), 100–108.

Pines, S., "Jāhiliyya and ʿilm", *JSAI*, 13 (1990), 175–94.

Reiske, Johann Jakob, *Dissertatio de principibus Muhammedanis qui aut ab eruditione aut ab amore literarum et literatorum claruerunt*, Johann Gottlob Immanuel Breitkopf, Leipzig, 1747, 20 pp.

Reiske, Johann Jakob (Ioann Jacobus), *Dissertatio inauguralis exhibens miscellaneas aliquot observationes medicas ex Arabum monumentis*, Lugduni Batavorum, Leiden, 1746, 29 pp.

Reland, A., *Enchiridion studiosi, Arabice conscriptium Borhaneddino Alzernouchi cum duplici versione Latina, altera a Friderico Rostgaard (1671–1754), sub auspiciis Josephi Banese, Maronitae Syri, Romae elaborata; altera Abrahami Ecchellensis, ex Museo Rostgardiano edidit Hadrianus Relandus*, Trajecti ad Rhenum (Utrecht), G. Broedelet, 1709.

Relandi [Reland], Hadriani, *De Religione mohammedica*, 2nd edn, Utrecht, 1717 (1st edn 1705).

Ribera y Tarragó, J., *Bibliófilos y bibliotecas en la España musulmana*, Zaragoza, 1896; reprint in *Disertacines y opúsculos*, Madrid, 1928, 181–218; Jamāl Muḥammad (trans,), "al-Maktaba wa huwāt al-kutub fī Isbanya al-islāmiyya", *Majallat Maʿhad al-makhṭūṭāt al-ʿarabiyya*, 4 (1958), 77–96; 5 (1959), 69–101.

Ribera y Tarragó, J., *La enseñanza entre los musulmanes españoles*, Zaragoza, 1893.

Ribera y Tarragó, J., *La enseñanza entre los musulmanes españoles. Bibliofilos y Bibliotecas en la España Musulmana*, 3rd edn, Córdoba, 1925; reprint in *Disertaciones y opusculos*, I, 1928, 229–359/Arabic trans. Makkī, al-Ṭāhir A., *al-Tarbiyya al-islāmiyya fī al-Andalus*, Cairo, 1981.

Rosenthal, F., *Knowledge Triumphant: The concept of knowledge in medieval Islam*, Leiden, 1970.

Rosenthal, F., "'Of making many books there is no end': the Muslim view", in George N. Atiyeh, (ed.), *The Book in the Islamic World*, Oxford, 1995, 33–54.

Rosenthal, F., *The Technique and Approach of Muslim Scholarship*, Pontificum Institute Biblicum, Rome, 1947/*Manāhij al-ʿulamāʾ al-muslimīn fī al-baḥth al-ʿilmī*, 3rd edn, trans. Anīs Furayḥa, Beirut, 1400/1980 (1st edn 1961).

Salama, I., *L'enseignement islamique en Égypte, son évolution, son influence sur les programmes modernes*, Cairo, 1939.

Shalaby, A., *History of Muslim Education*, Beirut, 1954 (2nd edn Karachi, 1979; PhD Cambridge, 1951)/Shalabī, A., *Taʾrīkh al-tarbiyya al-islāmiyya*, trans. A. Shalabi, Cairo, 1954 (4th edn 1973).

Sharkas, A.H., "Badr Al-din Al-Ghazzi (904/1499–984/1577), and his manual on Islamic scholarship and education 'Al-Durr Al-Nadid'", PhD dissertation, Harvard University, 1976.

Semaan, K.I.H., "Education in Islam, from the Jahiliyya to Ibn Khaldun", *MW*, 56 (1966), 188–98.

Silvestre de Sacy, Antoine-Isaac, *Chrestomathie arabe, ou extrait de divers écrivains arabes, tant en prose qu'en vers, avec une traduction française et des notes*, seconde édition, corrigée et augmentée, 3 vols, Paris, Imprimerie Royale, 1826–27 (1st edition 1806).

Sprenger, A., "Die Schulfächer und die Scholastik der Muslime", *ZDMG*, 32 (1878), 1–20.

Stanton, C.M., *Higher Learning in Islam: The classical period, A.D. 700–1300*, Savage, MD, 1990.

Taher, M. (ed.), *Encyclopaedic Survey of Islamic Culture*, 20 vols, Vol. VIII, *Educational Developments in the Muslim World*, New Delhi, 1997.

Talas, A., *L'enseignement chez les Arabes: la Madrasa Nizamiyya et son histoire*, Paris, 1939/*al-Tarbiyya wa-al-taʿlīm fī al-islām*, Beirut, 1957.

Tawfiq, M.A., "A sketch of the idea of education in Islam", *IC*, 17 (1943), 317–27.

Tibawi, A., *Islamic Education*, London, 1972.

Tibawi, A., "Muslim education in the golden age of the caliphate", *IC*, XXVIII (1954), 418–38.

Tritton, A.S., "Arab theories of education", *Journal of Indian History* (1925), 35–41.

Tritton, A.S., *Materials on Muslim Education in the Middle Ages*, London, 1957.

Tritton, A.S., "Muslim education in the Middle Ages (circa 600–800 A.H.)", *MW*, 43 (1953), 82–94.

Totah, K.A., *The Contribution of the Arabs to Education*, New York, 1926; reprint, Pistcataway, NJ, 2002.

Vernet, J., "La educación en la Hispania musulmana", in Buenaventura Delgado (ed.), *Historia de la educación en España y América*, I. *La educación en la Hispania antigua y medieval*, Madrid, Fundación Santa María, Morata, 1992, 179–204.

Veth, Pieter Jan, *Dissertatio De institutis Arabum erudiendae juventuti et literis promovendis inservientibus*, Amstelodami (Amsterdam), Müller, 1843, VIII+51 pp.

Wüstenfeld, Ferdinand, *Die Academien der Araber und ihre Lehrer*, Göttingen, 1837; reprint, Osnabrück, 1970; trans. S. Khuda Bukhsh in *Muslim Review*, I (1926).

Zahrānī, ʿA. b. M. b. Saʿīd, *al-Ḥayāt al-ʿilmiyya fī Ṣiqilliyya al-islāmiyya (212–484/826–1091)*, Mecca, 1996.

Zarw, K.D., *al-Ḥayāt al-ʿilmiyya fī al-Shām fī al-qarnayn al-awwal wa al-thānī*, Beirut, 1971.

Ziauddin Alavi, S.M., *Muslim Educational Thought in the Middle Ages*, New Delhi, 1988.

II Pedagogical Tradition

Sources

Ahwānī, A.F., *al-Tarbiyya fī al-islām*, Cairo, 1968 (1st edn 1955); review by Sartain in *JAOS*, 76/1 (1956), 46–48.

Ghazālī, *Iḥyā' 'ulūm al-dīn*, 4 vols, Būlāq, 1289/1872; reprint Cairo, 1933.

Ghazālī, *Al-Ghazali on Disciplining the Soul and on Breaking the Two Desires*, Books XXII and XXIII, trans. T.J. Winter, Cambridge, The Islamic Texts Society, 1995.

Ghazālī, *The Book of Knowledge, being a Translation with Notes of the* Kitāb al-'Ilm *of* Al-Ghazzali's Ihya' 'Ulum al Dīn, *by Nabih Amin Faris*, 2nd edn, Lahore, 1966.

Ghazālī: Renon, Albert (trans.), "L'éducation des enfants dès le premier âge, par l'Imam al-Ghazalî", *IBLA*, 1945, 57–74 (partial translation of *Iḥyā'*, Book XXII, *Bayān* 10, III, 62–64).

Ghazālī, Abû Hâmid al-Ghazâlî, *Maladies de l'âme et maîtrise du coeur* (Book XXII), intro., trans. and notes M-T. Hirsch, Paris, 2007.

Ibn al-'Adīm, Kamāl al-Dīn, *al-Darārī fī dhikr al-dharārī*, ed. M. 'Alā' 'Abd al-Wahhāb, Cairo, 1404/1984.

Ibn 'Arḍūn, Aḥmad al-Zajjālī, Paquignoni, P., "Le Traité du mariage et de l'éducation d'Ibn Abdoun", *Revue du Monde Musulman*, XV (1911), 1–59.

Ibn Ḥajar al-Haythamī, *Taḥrīr al-maqāl fī ādāb wa aḥkām yaḥtāj ilayhā mu'addib al-aṭfāl*, in Hishām Nashshāba, *al-Turāth al-tarbawī al-islāmī fī khams makhṭūṭāt*, Beirut, Dār al-'Ilm li-al-Malāyīn, 1988, 221–64.

Ibn Jamā'a, Badr al-Dīn, *Tadhkirat al-sāmi' wa-al-mutakallim fī ādāb al-'ālim wa-al-muta'allim*, Hyderabad, 1353/1934 in Hishām Nashshāba, *al-Turāth al-tarbawī al-islāmī*, Beirut, 1988, 97–186, ed. 'Abd al-Salām 'Umar, Cairo, 1425/2005.

Ibn Saḥnūn, M., *Ādāb al-mu'allimīn*, ed. Ḥusnī 'Abd al-Wahhāb, Tunis, 1348/1930.

Lecomte, G., 'Le livre des règles de conduite des maîtres d'école par Ibn Saḥnūn', *REI*, 21 (1954), 77–105.

Jāḥiẓ, *[Min] Kitāb al-Mu'allimīn*, in *Rasā'il al-Jāḥiẓ*, 4 vols, III, ed. 'Abd al-Salām M. Hārūn, Cairo, 196579, III, 27–51/ in *al-Mawrid*, 7 (1978/4), 149–58. Also in

Kitābān li-l-Jāḥiẓ [two essays by al-Jāḥiẓ: "On Schoolmasters" and "Refutation of Anthropomorphists"], ed. Ibrahim Geries, Tel Aviv, 1980, 57–87.

Qābisī, Abū al-Ḥasan al-Qayrawānī, *al-Risāla al-mufaṣṣala li-aḥwāl al-muta'allimin wa aḥkām al-mu'allimīn wa al-muta'allimīn* [*Detailed Epistle on the Circumstances of Pupils, their Rules of Conduct and Those of the Masters*], ed. and trans. A. Khālid, Tunis, 1986 (see Ahwānī *supra*).

Zarnūjī Burhān al-Islām or Burhān al-Dīn, *Enchiridion studiosi. Arabice conscriptium Borhaneddino Alzernouchi cum duplici versione Latina, altera a Friderico Rostgaard* [1671–1754, Danish], *sub auspiciis Josephi Banese, Maronitae Syri, Romae elaborata ; altera Abrahami Ecchellensis, ex Museo Rostgardiano edidit Hadrianus Relandus*, Trajecti ad Rhenum (Utrecht), G. Broedelet, Utrecht, 1709, 14+250 pp.

Zarnūjī Burhān al-Islām or Borhân-ed-dîni es-Sernûdjî, *Enchiridion Studiosi. Ad fidem editionis Relandianae nec non trium Codd. Lipss. et duorum Berlonn. denuo arabice edidit, latine vertit, praecipuas lectt. varr. et scholia Ibn-Ismaëlis selecta ex Cod. Lips. et Berolin. adjecit, textum et scholia vocalibus instruxit et lexico explanavit Carolus Caspari. Praefatus est Henricus Orthobius Fleischer*, Lipsiae Baumgartneri, 1838, XIV+82+48 pp.

Zarnūjī Burhān al-Islām or Burhān al-Dīn, *Semita Sapientiæ sive ad scientias comparandas methodvs (auctore Bourhan Al Din, Al Zarnoudji). Nunc primum latini juris facta, ab Abrahamo Ecchellensi Syriacarum & Arabicarum literarum christianissimi regis interprete, ac earumdem in Academia Parisiensi professore. Cum eiusdem notis, quæ ad calcem operis reperientur, Ex MS Arabico anonymo Bibliothecæ Mazarini*, Parisiis, apud Adrianum Taupinart, 1646, 10+104 pp.

Zarnūjī Burhān al-Islām or Burhān al-Dīn, *Ta'līm al-muta'allim ṭariq al-ta'allum*, ed. M. 'Abd al-Qādir Aḥmad, Cairo, 1406/1986/ed. Marwān Qabbānī, Beirut, 1981.

Zarnūjī Burhān al-Islām or Burhān al-Dīn, *Ta'līm al-muta'allim ṭariq al-ta'allum* [*Instruction of the Student: The method of learning*], trans. and intro. G.E. von Grunebaum and T.M. Abel, New York, 1947; reprint, Chicago, 2001; trans. O. Kattan, *Instrucción del estudiante, el método de aprender*, Madrid, 1991.

Secondary Literature

'Abdullah, 'Ar. S., *Educational Theory: A Qur'anic outlook*, Mecca, 1982 (originally a PhD thesis, University of Edinburgh, 1981).

Abdullatīf, M.A., *Islām kā tarbiyatī, ta'līmī aur tadrīsī niẓām*, Shivhar, Bihar, 1997.

Afsaruddin, A., *Excellence and Precedence*, Leiden, 2002.

Afsaruddin, A., "Muslim views on education: paremeters, purview and possibilities", *Journal of Catholic Legal Studies*, 44/1 (2005), 143–78.

Ahmad, A., "The educational thought of Ibn Khaldun", *Journal of the Pakistan Historical Society*, XVI, 1968, 175–81.

Ahwānī, A. Fu'ād, *al-Ta'līm fī ra'y al-Qābisī, min 'ulamā' al-qarn al-rābi'*, Cairo, al-Khānjī, 1945.

Baer, E., "Muslim teaching institutions and their visual reflections: the *kuttāb*", *Der Islam*, 78/1 (2001), 73–102.

Bānabīla, Ḥus., 'Al., *Ibn Khaldūn wa turāthuhu al-tarbawī*, Beirut, 1984.

Bayrakli, B., "The philosophy of education of al-Fārābī", *Hamdard Islamicus*, X/3 (1987), 29–34.

Bhat, B., "Miskawayh on social justice, education and friendship", *Islamic Studies*, 25 (1986), 197–210.

Cheddadi, A., "Ibn Khaldun", *Prospects: The Quarterly Review of Comparative Education*, XXIV/1–2 (1994), 7–19.

Eddé, A-M., "La représentation de l'enfant dans le traité d'Ibn al-'Adīm", in F. de Jong (ed.), *Miscellanea Arabica et Islamica*, Leuven, 1993, 175–85.

Eddé, A-M., "Un traité sur les enfants d'un auteur arabe du XIIIe siècle", in H. Dubois and M. Zink (eds), *Les Âges de la vie au Moyen Âge*, Paris, 1992, 139–49.

Gannūnī, 'A.A., *al-Madrasa al-qur'ānyya fī al-Maghrib min al-fatḥ al-islāmī ilā Ibn 'Aṭiyya*, Casablanca, 1981 (Vol. I: *Min al-fatḥ al-Islāmī ilā Ibn 'Aṭīyya*, thesis, Rabat, 1974).

Gardet, L., "Notion et principes de l'éducation dans la pensée arabo-musulmane", *REI*, 44 (1976), 1–16.

Günther, S., "al-Jahiz on the poetic of teaching", in Tarif Khalidi (ed.), *al-Jahiz: A Muslim humanist for our time*, Leiden, 2008.

Günther, S., "Be masters in that you teach and continue to learn: medieval Muslim thinkers on educational theory", *Comparative Education Review* (Chicago) 50/3 (2006), 367–88.

Günther, S., "Education: Islamic education", in *New Dictionary of the History of Ideas*, ed. Maryanne Cline Horowitz, Detroit, Charles Scribner's Sons, 2005, II, 640–45.

Günther, S., *Medieval Muslim Thinkers on Education: Insights into Islam's classical pedagogical theories*, forthcoming.

Hijāzī, ʿAr. ʿUth., *al-Madhhab al-tarbawī ʿinda Ibn Saḥnūn, rāʾid al-taʾlīf al-tarbawī al-islāmī*, Beirut, 1986 (with ed. of M. al-ʿArūsī al-Maṭwī of *Ibn Saḥnūn, Ādāb al-muʿallimīn*, 111–28).

Hijāzī, ʿAr. ʿUth., *al-Tarbiyya al-islāmiyya fī al-Qayrawān fī al-qurūn al-hijriyya al-thalātha al-ūlā. Al-madrasa al-mālikiyya, al-madrasa al-fāṭimiyya, al-madrasa al-ṣūfiyya, al-madrasa al-ibāḍiyya*, Sidon, 1997.

Hijāzī, ʿAr. ʿUth., *Taṭawwur al-fikr al-tarbawī al-ibāḍī fī al-shamāl al-ifrīqī min al-qarn al-awwal ḥattā al-qarn al-ʿāshir al-hijrī (713–1520)*, Sidon, 2000, 349 pp.

ʿĪsā, M. ʿA., *Taʾrīkh al-taʿlīm fī al-Andalus*, Cairo, 1982.

Jomier, J., *La pédagogie arabe*, Alexandria, 1949, 28 pp.

Lacroix, M.-C., "Éducation et instruction selon Abū l-Ḥasan al-ʿĀmirī. Présentation et traduction d'un extrait du 'Kitāb al-saʿāda wa l-isʿād' [ed. Minovi, 348–88]", *Revue Philosophique de Louvain*, 87/2 (1989), 165–214.

Marín, M., "Learning at mosques in al-Andalus", in M. Khalid Masud *et al.*, *Islamic Legal Interpretation: Muftis and their fatwas*, Cambridge, MA and London, 1996, 47–55.

Najjār, Ibr. and al-Bashīr al-Zarībī, *al-Fikr al-tarbawī ʿinda al-ʿArab*, Tunis, 1985.

Nuʿmī, ʿAl. al-Amīn, *Manāhij wa ṭuruq al-taʿlīm ʿinda al-Qābisī wa Ibn Khaldūn*, Tripoli (Libya), 1980.

Qāḍī, A., ʿA., *al-Fikr al-tarbawī ʿinda al-mutakallimīn al-muslimīn*, Cairo, 1996 (originally a thesis: "Falsafat al-tarbiyya ʿinda al-muʿtazila wa al-ashʿariyya", Cairo University, 1993).

Qazwīnī, ʿA.A.M.M., *al-Fikr al-tarbawī ʿinda al-Shīʿa al-imāmiyya*, Cairo, 1985.

Qazzāz, M.S., *al-Fikr al-tarbawī fī kitābāt al-Jāḥiẓ*, Cairo, 1995 (originally a Master's thesis, University of Ṭanṭā, 1981).

Qurayshi, M.A., "The educationnal ideas of Ibn Khaldun", *Journal of the Maharaja Sayajirao University of Baroda*, XIV, 1965, 83–92.

Reisman, D.C., "Al-Farabi and the Philosophical Curriculum", in P. Adamson, and R.C. Taylor (eds), *The Cambridge Companion to Arabic Philosophy*. Cambridge, 2005, 52–71.

Rosenthal, F., "Child psychology in Islam", *IC*, 26 (1952), 1–22; reprint in *Muslim Intellectual and Social History*, Aldershot, Variorum (CS, 309), 1990, No. XIII.

Rosenthal, F., "Abū Zayd al-Balkhī on politics", in C.E. Bosworth, *et al.* (eds), *The Islamic World from Classical to Modern Times: Essays in honor of Bernard Lewis*, Princeton, 1989, 287–301.

Saʿd al-Dīn, M.M., *al-Madrasa al-islāmiyya fī al-ʿuṣūr al-wusṭā*, Sidon, 1995.

Shahla, G.D., *The Arab Conception of the Ideal Teacher as Revealed in Arabic Pedagogical Literature*, MA thesis, London, 1939.

Shams al-Dīn, ʿAbd al-Amīr, *ʿAbd al-Karīm b. Muḥammad al-Samʿānī fī kitābihi Adab al-imlāʾ wa-al-istimlāʾ*, Beirut, 1984 (2nd edn 1986).

Shams al-Dīn, ʿAbd al-Amīr, *al-Falsafa al-tarbawiya ʿinda Ikhwān al-Ṣafāʾ min khilāl rasāʾilihim*, Beirut, 1988.

Shams al-Dīn, ʿAbd al-Amīr, *al-Fikr al-tarbawī ʿinda al-Imām al-Ghazālī*, Beirut, 1985.

Shams al-Dīn, ʿAbd al-Amīr, *al-Fikr al-tarbawī ʿinda Ibn Jamāʿah*, Beirut, 1990.

Shams al-Dīn, ʿAbd al-Amīr, *al-Fikr al-tarbawī ʿinda Ibn al-Khaldūn and Ibn al-Azraq*, Beirut, 1984.

Shams al-Dīn, ʿAbd al-Amīr., *al-Fikr al-tarbawī ʿinda Ibn al-Muqaffaʿ al-Jāḥiẓ ʿAbd al-Hāmid al-Kātib*, Beirut, 1985.

Shams al-Dīn, ʿAbd al-Amīr, *al-Fikr al-tarbawī ʿinda Ibn Saḥnūn wa al-Qābisī*, Beirut, 1985, 236 pp.; reprint, 1990.

Shams al-Dīn, ʿAbd al-Amīr, *al-Fikr al-tarbawī ʿinda Ibn Ṭufayl*, Beirut, 1984 (without references to the texts).

Shams al-Dīn, ʿAbd al-Amīr, *al-Madhhab al-tarbawī ʿinda Ibn Jamāʿa: Tadhkirat al-sāmiʿ wa al-mutakallim fī adab al-ʿālim wa-al-mutaʿallim*, 1988.

Shams al-Dīn, ʿAbd al-Amīr, *al-Madhhab al-tarbawī ʿinda Ibn Sīnā min khilāl falsafatihi al-ʿamaliyya*, Beirut, 1988, with 22 treatises which are listed in Daiber, *Bibliography of Islamic Philosophy*, I, 831–82, no. 8085.

Siddiqi, B.Ḥ., "Ibn Miskawayh's theory of education", *Iqbal* (Lahore), 11 (1961), 39–46.

Siddiqi, B.Ḥ., "The view of Miskawayh on the education of children", *Journal of the Regional Cultural Institute* (Tehran), 4 (1971), 49–56 (does not give references to the texts).

Sulaymān, F.Ḥ., *Madhāhib fī al-tarbiyya. Baḥth fī al-madhhab al-tarbawī ʿinda al-Ghazālī*, Cairo, 1964.

Sulaymān, F.Ḥ., *Madhāhib fī al-tarbiyya. Baḥth fī al-madhhab al-tarbawī ʿinda Ibn Khaldūn*, Cairo, 1955.

Walker, Paul E., "Knowledge and learning", *EQ*, III, 100–104.

Zayʿūr, S.M., *al-Fikr al-tarbawī ʿinda al-ʿAlmawī*, Beirut, 1986.

Zayʿūr, S.M., *ʿUlūm al-tarbiyya wa al-nafs wa al-ifāda fī tadbīr al-mutaʿallim wa siyāsat al-taʿallum. Al-Ghazzī wa al-ʿAlmawī, Kitāb al-Muʿīd fī adab al-mufīd wa al-mustafīd*, Beirut, 1993.

III Arabic Script: Beginning and Evolution

Sources

Abū Mūsā al-Baghdādī: see. Sourdel, "Le 'Livre des secrétaires' de ʿAbdallāh al-Baghdādī".

Ibn Qutayba, *ʿUyūn al-akhbār* [*Book of Useful Knowledge*]", 4 vols in 2, ed. A. Zakī al-ʿAdwī, Cairo, 1925–30, reprint Cairo, 1963, I, 42-51 ("On scribes and writing")/trans. Horovitz, Joseph, "Ibn Quteiba's ʿUyun al-akhbar", *IC*, IV (1930), 171–98, 331–62, 487–530; V (1931), 1–27, 194–224 ("On scribes and writing", *IC*, IV, 1930, 487–97).

Secondary Literature

Abbott, N., *The Rise of the North Arabic Script and its Kur'ānic Development*, Chicago, 1939.

Adler, J.G.C., *De arte scribendi apud Arabes*, Hamburg, 1780.

Bellamy, J.A., "The Arabic alphabet", in Wayne M. Senner (ed.), *The Origins of Writing*, Lincoln and London, 1991, 91–102.

Briquel-Chatonnet, F., "De l'araméen à l'arabe: quelques réflexions sur la genèse de l'écriture arabe", in François Déroche, and Francis Richard (eds), *Scribes et manuscrits du Moyen-Orient*, Paris, 1997, 135–49.

Endress, G., "Die arabische Schrift", in *GAP*, I, 165–83 (bibliography 190–97).

Grohmann, A., *Arabische Paläographie, II Das Schriftwesen: Die Lapidarschrift*, Vienna, 1971, 12–20.

Gruendler, B., *The Development of the Arabic Scripts: From the Nabatean area to the first Islamic century according to dated texts*, Atlanta, 1993; review by F. Scagliari, *Orientalia* (Rome), 63 (1994), 294–97.

Nöldeke, T., "Bemerkungen zu den von de Voguë herausgegebenen nabatäischen und hebräischen Inschriften", *ZDMG*, 19 (1865), 637–41.

Robin, C., "L'écriture arabe et l'Arabie", *Pour la Science*, Dossier (October–January 2002), 62–69.

Shahid, Irfan, *Byzantium and the Arabs in the Fifth Century*, Washington, DC, 2006 (1ST edn 1989).

Silvestre de Sacy, A-I., "Mémoire sur l'origine et les anciens monuments de la littérature parmi les Arabes", *Mémoires Académie Royale des inscriptions ...*, L (1785), 247–441.

Silvestre de Sacy, A-I., "Nouveaux aperçus sur l'histoire de l'écriture chez les Arabes du Hedjaz", *JA*, Series I, X (1827), 209–31 (or as part of a volume, 1827, 27 pp.).

Sourdel, D., "Le 'Livre des secrétaires' de 'Abdallāh al-Baghdādī", *REI*, XIV (1954), 116–53.

Sourdel-Thomine, J., "Les origines de l'écriture arabe", *REI* (1966), 151–57.

Starcky, J., "Pétra et la Nabatène", *Supplément au Dictionnaire de la Bible*, Paris, 1967, 932–34 (886–1017).

Troupeau, G., "Réflexions sur l'origine syriaque de l'écriture arabe", in Alan S. Kaye (ed.), *Semitic Studies in Honor of Wolf Leslau*, II, Wiesbaden, 1991, 1562–70.

IV Orality and Literacy

Cook, M., "The opponents of the writing of tradition in early Islam", *Arabica*, XLIV/4, (1997), 437–530.

Krenkow, F., "The use of writing for the preservation of ancient Arabic poetry", in T.W. Arnold and Reynold A. Nicholson (eds), *A Volume of Oriental Studies*

Presented to Edward G. Browne, Cambridge: Cambridge University Press, 1922, 261–68 (Chapter 11).

Lecker, Michael, "Zayd b. Thābit, 'a Jew with two sidelocks': Judaism and literacy in pre-Islamic Medina (Yathrib)", *JNES*, 56 (1997), 259–73; reprint in *Jews and Arabs in Pre- and Early Islamic Arabia*, Aldershot, 1999, no. III.

Maraqten, M., "Writing materials in pre-Islamic Arabia", *JSS*, XLIII (1998), 287–310.

Nasr, Seyyid Hossein, "Oral transmission and the book in Islamic education: the spoken and the written", *Islamic Studies*, 3/1 (1992), 1–14.

Schoeler, G., "Die Frage der schriftlichen oder mündlichen Überlieferung der Wissenschaften im Islam", *Der Islam*, 62 (1985), 201–30.

Schoeler, G., *Écrire et transmettre dans les débuts de l'islam*, Paris, 2002.

Schoeler, G., "Mündliche Thora und Ḥadīṯ: Überlieferung, Schreibverbot, Redaktion", *Der Islam*, 66 (1989), 213–51.

Schoeler, G., "Schreiben und Veröffentlichen: zur Verwendung und Funktion der Schrift in den ersten islamischen Jahrhunderten", *Der Islam*, 69 (1992), 1–43.

Schoeler, G., *The Oral and the Written in Early Islam*, trans. Uwe Vagelpohl, ed. J.E. Montgomery, London, 2006.

Schoeler, G., "Weiteres zur Frage der schriftlichen oder mündlichen Überlieferung der Wissenschaften im Islam", *Der Islam*, 66 (1989), 38–67.

Schoeler, G., "Writing and publishing: on the use and function of writing in the first centuries of Islam", with introductory remarks by Claude Gilliot, *Arabica*, XLIV (1997), 423–33.

Sprenger, A., "On the origin and progress of writing down historical facts among the Musulmans", *Journal of the Asiatic Society of Bengal*, 25 (1856–57), 303-29, 375–85.

V Scholarship and Attestation

Sources

Abū Ḥayyān al-Tawḥīdī, "L'épître sur les sciences d'Abū Ḥayyān al-Tawḥīdī", ed. and trans. Marc Bergé, *BEO*, XVIII (1963–64), 241–300; XXI (1968), 313–46.

Abū Hilāl al-ʿAskarī, *al-Ḥathth ʿalā ṭalab al-ʿilm wa-al-ijtihād fī jamʿihi*, ed. M. Qabbānī, Beirut, 1986.

Baghdādī, al-Khaṭīb, *al-Riḥla fī ṭalab al-ḥadīth*, ed. Nūr al-Dīn ʿIṭr, Beirut, 1975.

Ghazālī, Abū Ḥāmid [attributed to], *Kitāb Fātiḥat al-ʿulūm. Wa yalīhi Khulāṣat al-mafhūm fī takhrīj aḥādīth Fātiḥat al-ʿulūm, jamʿ M. Amīn al-Khānjī*, Cairo, 1904.

Ibn al-Afkānī, Shams al-Dīn al-Anṣārī al-Sakhāwī, *Irshād al-qāṣid ilā asnā al-maqāṣid fi anwāʿ al-ʿulūm*, ed. A. Sprenger, in *Two Works on Arabic Bibliography*, Calcutta, 1849, 14–99; reprint by F. Sezgin, Frankfurt 2005; reprint, Kessinger Publishing, 2010. Partial German trans. in T. Haarbrücker, "Muhammad Ibn Ibrahim al-Anssâris arabische Enzyklopädie der wissenschaften, vornehmlich in pädagogischer Beziehung", *Jahresbericht über die Louisenstädtische Realschule*, Berlin, 1859, 3–26; reprint in Sezgin, Frankfurt, 2005, 1–24.

Ibn al-Afkānī, *Irshād al-qāṣid ilā asnā al-maqāṣid fi anwāʿ al-ʿulūm*, ed. ʿAbd al-Munʿim M. ʿUmar, Cairo, Dār al-Fikr al-arabī, 1990, 232 pp.

Ibn al-Afkānī and Witkam, J.J., *De egyptische arts Ibn al-Akfānī (gest.749/1348) en zijn indeling van de wetenschappen. editie van het* Kitāb Iršād al-qāṣid ilā asnā al-maqāṣid, *met een inleiding over het leven en werk van de auteur*, Leiden, Ter Lugt Pers, 1989.

Ibn al-Ṣalāḥ al-Shahrazūri, *An Introduction to the Science of the Ḥadīth, Kitāb Maʿrifat anwāʿ ʿilm al-ḥadīth*, trans. Eerik Dickinson, Reading, Garnet, 2005, XXVI+359 pp.

Ibn Faraḥ al-Ishbīlī, Shihāb al-Dīn, *Qaṣidat Ibn Faraḥ: Gharāmī ṣaḥīḥ*, in Makkari (Maqqarī), *Analectes sur l'histoire et la littérature des Arabes d'Espagne* (*Nafḥ al-ṭīb*), 2 vols, ed. R. Dozy, G. Dugat, L. Krehl and W. Wright, Leiden, 1885–61; reprint, Amsterdam, Oriental Press, 1967, I, 819–20. For other editions see Gilliot, "Textes arabes anciens édités en Égypte", *MIDEO*, 28, 399–400, no. 183.

Ibn Jamāʿa, ʿIzz al-Dīn, *Zawāl al-taraḥ fī manẓūmat Ibn Faraḥ* in *Commentar des Izz-ed-Dîn Abu Abd-ullah über die Kunstausdrücke der Traditionswissenschaft, nebst Erläuterungen von Friedich Risch*, Leiden, 1885, VII+15+42 pp. (includes annotations from Ibn ʿAbd al-Hādī al-Maqdisī's commentary – see Gilliot, in *MIDEO*, 28, 399–402, nos 183–84).

Nawawī, *al-Taqrīb wa al-taysīr li-maʿrifat sunan al-bashīr al-nadhīr*, ed. M. ʿUṯmān al-Ḫušt, Beyrouth, Dār al-Kitāb al-ʿarabī, 1405/1985, 127 pp.

Nawawī, *Le Taqrīb de en-Nawawī*, trans. W. Marçais, Paris, 1902.

Samʿānī, Abū Saʿd, *Adab al-imlāʾ wa l-istimlāʾ* [*The Methods of the Dictation Colleges*], ed. M. Weisweiler, Leiden, 1952.

Secondary Literature

Bencheikh, J.E., "Le cénacle poétique du calife al-Mutawakkil (m. 247): contribution à l'analyse des instances de légitimation socio-littéraires", *BEO*, XXIX (1976–77), I, 33–52.

Bernards, M., "Ṭalab al-ʿilm amongst the linguists of Arabic during the ʿAbbasid period", in James E. Montgomery (ed.), *ʿAbbasid Studies*, Leuven, 2004, 33–46.

Bulliet, R.W., *The Patricians of Nishapur*, Cambridge, MA, 1972.

Chejne, A.G., "The boon-companion in early ʿAbbāsid times", *JAOS*, 85 (1965), 327–35.

Ephrat, D., *A Learned Society in a Period of Transition: The Sunni ʿulamaʾ of eleventh century Baghdad*, Albany NY, 2000.

Fayyāḍ, ʿAl., *al-Ijāzāt al-ilmiyya ʿinda al-muslimīn*, Baghdad, 1967.

Flügel, G., *Die Classen der hanefitischen Rechtsgelehrten*, in *Abhandl. d. Königl. Sächs. Ges. d. Wiss.*, Leipzig, 1861, 269–358.

Flügel, G., *Die grammatischen Schulen der Araber*, Leipzig, 1862; reprint, Nendeln, 1966.

Gelder, G.J.H. van, "The conceit of pen and sword: on an Arabic literary debate", *JSS*, 32 (1987), 329–60.

Gellens, S.I., "The search for knowledge in medieval Muslim societies: a comparative approach", in D.F. Eickelman and J.P. Piscatori (eds.), *Muslim Travellers: Pilgrimage, migration and the religious imagination*, London, 1990, 50–84.

Hammer-Purgstall, J. von, *Encyclopädische Uebersicht der Wissenschaften des Orients*, 2 vols, Leipzig, 1804.

Hāshim, ʿAlī M., *al-Andiya al-adabiyya fī l-ʿaṣr al-ʿabbāsī fī al-ʿIrāq ...*, Beirut, 1982.

Ḥulaybī, M. b. S., *al-Ḥaraka al-adabiyya fī majālis Hārūn al-Rashīd, 170-193 H*, 3 vols, Beirut, 2008.

Librande, L., "The supposed homogeneity of technical terms in hadith study", *MW*, 72 (1983), 34–50.

Nashabi, H., "The *ijāza*: academic certificate in Muslim education", *Hamdard Islamicus*, VIII (1985), 7–20.

Wüstenfeld, F., *Die Geschichtschreiber der Araber und ihre Werke*, Göttingen, 1882; reprint New York, n.d. (1964?).

Wüstenfeld, F., *Der Imâm el-Schâfi'í, seine Schüler und Anhänger bis zum J. 300 d. H.*, Göttingen, 1890–91.

Wüstenfeld, F., *Geschichte der arabischen Ärzte und Naturforscher nach den Quellen bearbeitet*, Göttingen, 1840; reprint Hildesheim, 1963, 1978.

VI Authorship and Transmission

Al-Samuk, S.M., *Die historischen Überlieferungen nach Ibn Isḥāq: eine synoptische Rekonstruktion*, Inauguraldissertation, University of Frankfurt, 1978.

Athamina, K., "Al-Qasas: its emergence, religious origin and its socio-political impact on early Muslim society", *Stud. Isl.*, 76 (1992), 53–74.

Blachère, R., "Les savant iraqiens et leur informateurs bédouins aux IIe–IVe siècles de l'hégire", in *Mélanges William Marçais*, Paris, 1950, 37–48; reprint in Blachère, *Analecta*, Damascus, 1975, 31–42.

Conrad, L.I., "Heraclius in early Islamic Kerygma", in Gerrit J. Reinink and Bernard H. Stolte (eds), *The Reign of Heraclius (610–641): Crisis and confrontation*, Leuven, 2002, 113–56.

Conrad, L.I., "Recovering lost texts: some methodological issues", *JAOS*, 113 (1993), 258–63.

Conrad, L.I., "The conquest of Arwād: a source-critical study in the historiography of the early medieval Near East", in A. Cameron and L.I. Conrad, *The Byzantine and Early Islamic Near East*, Princeton, 1992, 317–401.

Donner, F., *Narratives of Islamic Origins: The beginnings of Islamic historical writing*, Princeton, 1998.

Fleischhammer, M., *Die Quellen des Kitāb al-Aġānī*, Wiesbaden, 2004 (thesis, University of Halle, 1969).

Görke, A., and Schoeler, G., *Die ältesten Berichte über das Leben Muḥammads.* Das Korpus ʿUrwa Ibn az-Zubair, Princeton, NJ, 2008.

Kilpatrick, H., "A genre in classical Arabic literature: the *adab* encyclopedia", in R. Hillenbrand (ed.), *Proceedings of the 10th Congress of the Union Européenne des Arabisants et Islamisants*, Edinburgh, 1982, 34–42.

Kilpatrick, H., *Making the Great Book of Songs*, London, 2002, 288 pp.

Kilpatrick, H., "The transmission of songs in medieval Arabic culture", in U. Vermeulen and D. De Smet (eds), *Philosophy and Arts in the Islamic World: Proceedings of the 18th Congress of the* Union Européenne des Arabisants et Islamisants, Leuven, 1998, 73–82.

Landau-Tasseron, E., "On the reconstruction of lost sources", *Al-Qanṭara*, 25 (2004), 45–91.

Landau-Tasseron, E., "Sayf ibn ʿUmar in medieval and modern scholarship', *Der Islam*, 67 (1990), 1–27.

Leder, S., "Conventions of fictional narration in learned literature", in S. Leder (ed.), *Storytelling in the Framework of Non-fictional Arabic Literature*, Wiesbaden, 1998, 34–60.

Leder, S., *Das Korpus al-Haiṯam ibn ʿAdī (st.207/822)*. Herkunft, Überlieferung, Gestalt früher aḫbār-Texte, Frankfurt 1991.

Leder, S., "Grenzen der Rekonstruktion alten Schrifttums nach den Angaben im Fihrist", in *Ibn an-Nadīm und die mittelalterliche arabische Literatur*, Wiesbaden 1996, 21–31.

Leder, S., "Heraklios erkennt den Propheten: ein Beispiel für Form und Entstehungsweise narrativer Geschichtskonstruktionen", *ZDMG*, 151 (2001), 1–42.

Leder, S., "Hörerzertifikate als Dokumente für die islamische Lehrkultur des Mittelalters", in R.G. Khoury (ed.), *Urkunden und Urkundenformulare im Klassischen Altertum und in den orientalischen Kulturen*, Heidelberg, 1999, 147–66.

Leder, S., "Materialien zum *Taʾrīḫ* des Haiṯam ibn ʿAdī [d. 207/821] bei Abū Sulaimān Ibn Zabr ar-Rabaʿī [d. 379/989]", *ZDMG*, 144 (1994), 14–27.

Leder, S., "Prosa-Dichtung in der *aḫbār* Überlieferung: Narrative Analyse einer Satire", *Der Islam*, 64 (1987), 6–41.

Leder, S., *Spoken Word and Written Text: Meaning and social significance of the institution of* riwāya, Islamic Area Studies Working Paper Series, No. 31, Tokyo 2002, 16 pp.

Leder, S., "The literary use of the *khabar*: a basic form of historical writing", in A. Cameron and Lawrence I. Conrad (eds), *The Byzantine and Early Islamic Near East*, 1992, 277–315.

Melchert, C., *The Formation of the Sunnī Schools of Law 9th–10th Centuries*, Leiden, 1997.

Melchert, C., "The meaning of *qāla ʾl-Shāfiʿī* in ninth century sources", in J. Montgomery (ed.), *ʿAbbasid Studies*, Leuven, 2004, 276–301.

Motzki, H., "Dating Muslim traditions: a survey", *Arabica*, LII/2 (2005), 204–53.

Motzki, H., "Dating the so-called *Tafsīr Ibn ʿAbbās*: some additional remarks", *JSAI*, 31 (2006), 147–62.

Motzki, H., "Der Fiqh des Zuhrī: die Quellenproblematik", *Der Islam*, 68 (1991), 1–44; English translation at: http://webdoc.ubn.kun.nl/mono/m/motzki_h/juriofibs.pdf.

Motzki, H., "Quo vadis, Ḥadīṯ-Forschung? Eine kritische Untersuchung von G.H.A. Juynboll: 'Nāfiʿ the mawla of Ibn 'Umar, and his position in Muslim Ḥadīṯ Literature", *Der Islam*, 73 (1996), 40–80.

Motzki, H., "The author and his work in the Islamic literature of the first centuries: the case of ʿAbd al-Razzāq's Muṣannaf", *JSAI*, 28 (2003), 171–201.

Muranyi, M., "Die frühe Rechtsliteratur zwischen Quellenanalyse und Fiktion", *Islamic Law and Society*, 4/2 (1997), 224–41.

Muranyi, M., "Visionen des Skeptikers", *Der Islam*, 81 (2004), 206–17. See also A. Rippin's critique, "Studying Early Tafsir Texts", *Der Islam*, 7 (1995), 310–23.

Nagel, T., "'Authentizität' in der Leben-Mohammed-Forschung", to be published in *Arabica*, June 2012.

Najm, Wadīʿah Ṭāhā, *al-Qaṣaṣ wa-al-quṣṣāṣ fi al-adab al-islāmī*, Kuwait, 1972.

Pedersen, J., "The criticism of the Islamic preacher", *Die Welt des Islam*, NS, II (1953), 215–31.

Quiring-Zoche, R., "How al-Buḫārī's *Ṣaḥīḥ* was edited in the Middle Ages: 'Alī al-Yūnīnī and his *Rumūẓ*", *BEO*, L (1998), 191–222.

Robson, J., "The transmission of Abū Dāwūd's Sunan", *BSOAS*, 14 (1952), 579–88.

Robson, J., "The transmission of Ibn Mājah's 'Sunan'", *JSS*, 3 (1958), 129–41.

Robson, J., "The transmission of Muslim's Ṣaḥīḥ", *JRAS*, 1949, 49–60.

Robson, J., "The transmission of Nasāʾī's 'Sunan'", *JSS*, 1 (1956), 38–59.

Robson, J., "The transmission of Tirmidhi's Jāmi'", *BSOAS*, 16 (1954), 258–70.

Scarcia Amoretti, B. (ed.), *Onomastica e trasmissione del sapere nell'Islam medievale*, Rome, 1992.

Schmidtke, S., "Forms and functions of 'licences to transmit' (*ijāzas*) in 18th-century Iran: ʿAbd Allāh al-Mūsawī al-Jazāʾirī al-Tustarī's (1112–73/1701–59) *Ijāza kabīra*", in G. Krämer and S. Schmidtke (eds), *Speaking for Islam*, ed. Religious Authorities in Muslim Societies, Leiden, 2006, 95–127.

Schoeler, G., *Charakter und Authentie der muslimischen Überlieferungen über das Leben Mohammeds*, Berlin, 1996.

Zafar, Abdul Rauf, "Transmission of *ḥadīth* and biography", *Islamic Quaterly*, XXXV (1991), 117–39.

VII Libraries and Books

Akhtar, Q.A., "The art of *waraqat* during the ʿAbbasid period", *IC*, 9 (1935), 131–48.

Akhtar, Q.A., "More about the art of *waraqat*", *All-India Oriental Conference*, 9 (1937), 294–310.

Atiyeh, G.N. (ed.), *The Book in the Islamic World*, Albany, NY, 1995.

ʿAwwād, Kūrkīs, *Khazāʾin al-kutub al-qadīmah fī al-ʿIrāq, mundhu aqdam al-ʿuṣūr ḥattā sanat 1000 li-l-hijra*, Baghdad, 1948; reprint Beirut, 1406/1986.

Ben Aicha, H., "Mosques as libraries in Islamic civilization, 700–1400 A.D.", *Journal of Library History*, 21 (1986), 253–60.

Bloom, J.M., *Paper before Print: The history and impact of paper in the Islamic world*, New Haven and London, 2001.

Déroche, F., *Le livre manuscrit arabe: prélude à une histoire*, Paris, 2004.

Déroche, F., *Manuel de codicologie des manuscrits en écriture arabe*, Paris, 2001/ trans. A.F al-Sayyid, *al-Madkhal ilā ʿilm al-kitāb al-makhṭūṭ bi-al-ḥarf al-ʿarabī*, London, 2005.

Diwan, M.R.A., "Muslim contributions to libraries during the medieval times", *Islam and the Modern Age*, 9 (1978), 19–34.

Diyāb, Ḥ. al-S., *al-Kutub wa-al-maktabāt fī al-Andalus*, Cairo, 1998.

Eche, Y., *Les bibliothèques arabes publiques et semi-publiques en Mésopotamie, en Syrie et en Égypte au moyen âge*, Damascus, 1967.

Elayyan, R. Must., "The history of the Arabic–Islamic libraries: 7th to 14th centuries", *International Library Review*, 22 (1990), 119–35.

Gacek, A., *The Arabic Manuscript Tradition: A glossary of technical terms and bibliography*, Leiden, 2001.

Ḥamāda, M.M., *al-Maktabāt fī al-islām*, Beirut, 1978.

Hammer-Purgstall, J., "Additions au 'Mémoire' de M. Quatremère sur le goût des livres chez les Orientaux", *JA*, 4th series, XI (1848), 178–98.

Ḥammūda, M.ʿA., *Taʾrīkh al-kitāb al-islāmī al-makhṭūṭ*, Cairo, 1994 (1st edn 1979, 2nd edn 1991).

Ibn Dohaish, A.A. "Growth and development of Islamic libraries", *Der Islam*, 66 (1989), 289–302.

Imamuddin, S.M., *Arabic Writing and Arab Libraries*, London, 1983.

Imamuddin, S.M., *Hispano-Arab Libraries*, Karachi, 1961.

Inayatullah, S., "Bibliophilism in medieval Islam", *IC*, 12 (1938), 154–69.

Jamil, M.F., "Islamic *Wirāqa* stationery during the early Middle Ages", PhD thesis, Michigan State University, 1985.

Jawāhirī, K.M.M., *Min Taʾkhīr al-maktabāt fī al-buldān al-ʿarabiyya*, Damascus, 1992.

Mackensen, Ruth Stellhorn, "Background of the history of Moslem libraries", *American Journal of Semitic Languages and Literatures* 51 (1934–35) 114–25; 52 (1935–36), 22–33, 104–10.

Mackensen, Ruth Stellhorn, "Four great libraries of medieval Baghdad", *Library Quarterly*, 2 (1932), 279–99.

Mackensen, Ruth Stellhorn, "Moslem libraries and sectarian propaganda", *American Journal of Semitic Languages and Literatures*, 51 (1934–35), 83–113.

Marín, M., "Arabic–Islamic libraries and bibliography in Spain", *British Society for Middle Eastern Studies Bulletin*, 11 (1984), 180–84.

Pedersen, J., *The Arabic Book*, Princeton, 1984 (original Danish version, Copenhagen, 1946).

Pinto, O., *Le Biblioteche degli Arabi nell'età degli Abbassidi*, Firenze, 1928.

Pinto, O., "Libraries of the Arabs during the time of the Abbasides", trans. F. Krenkow. *Islamic Culture*, III (1929), 210–48.

Prince, C., "The historical context of Arabic translation, learning, and the libraries of medieval Andalusia", *Library History*, 18, (2002), 73–87, at: http://everything2.com/index.pl?node_id=1042932.

Qasimi, A.S., "Libraries in the early Islamic world", *Journal of the University of Peshawar*, 6 (1958), 1–15.

Quatremère, É., "Mémoire sur le goût des livres chez les Orientaux", *JA*, 3rd series (1838), 35–78

Qazānjī [Qaranchi], F., *al-Maktabat wa-al-ṣināʿa al-maktabiyya fī al-ʿIrāq*, Baghdad, 1972.

Qazānjī [Qaranchi], F., *al-Maktabāt fī al-ʿIrāq, mundhu aqdam al-ʿuṣūr ḥattā al-waqt al-ḥāḍir*, Baghdad, 2001.

Qazānjī [Qaranchi], F., *Libraries and Librarianship in Iraq*, Baghdad, 1972.

Qazanji, F. and ʿAwwād, K., *Marājiʿ al-kutub wa-al-maktabāt fī al-ʿIrāq. Thabt bi-mā nasharahu al-ʿIrāqiyyūn ʿan al-kutub wa-al-maktabāt wa-al-fahāris wa-al-makhṭūṭāt wa-al-bibliyūghrāfiyāt wa-al-khaṭṭ wa-al-ṭibāʿa*, Baghdad, 1975.

Ribera y Tarragó, J., "Bibliófilos y bibliotecas de la España musulmana", dissertation, Faculty of Medicine and Sciences, Zaragoza, 1896.

Ribera y Tarragó, J., *La enseñanza entre los musulmanes españoles. Bibliofilos y Bibliotecas en la España Musulmana, Córdoba*, 3rd edn, 1925, 120 pp./Arabic trans. Makkī, al-Ṭ.A., *al-Tarbiyya al-islāmiyya fī al-Andalus*, Cairo, 1981.

Rufai, A., *Über die Bibliophilie im älteren Islam: nebst Edition und Übersetzung von Gâḥiẓ' Abhandlung Fî madḥ al-kutub*, Istanbul, 1935 (thesis, University of Berlin, 1935).

Sibai, M.M., *Mosque Libraries*, London and New York, 1987.

Taher, M., "The book in Islamic civilization", 2000, at: http://taher.freeservers.com/ilm.htm.

VI Other References Cited in the Introduction

Sources

ʿAbd Allāh b. Wahb: see Muranyi *infra*.

Abū al-Faraj, al-Iṣfahānī, K., *al-Aghānī*, 24 vols, Cairo, 1927–74.

Balādhurī, Aḥmad b. Yaḥyā (lived III/IXth century), *Liber Expugnationis regionum*, ed. M.J. De Goeje, Leiden, 1866/*Futūḥ al-buldān*, ed. al-Ṭabbā', Beirut, 1407/1987.

Dhahabī, *Mīzān al-'itidāl fī naqd al-riğāl*, 4 vols, ed. 'A.M. al-Bijāwī, Cairo, 1963.

Dhahabī, *Siyar a'lām al-nubalā'*, 25 vols, ed. Shu'ayb al-Arna'ūṭ *et al.*, Beirut, 1981–88 [*Siyar* or SAN].

Dhahabī, *Ta'rīkh al-islām wa ṭabaqāt al-mashāhīr wa al-a'lām*, 17 vols, ed. B.'A. Ma'rūf, Beirut, 2003.

HKh [Ḥajjī Khalīfa], *Lexicon bibliographicum et encyclopaedicum*, 7 vols, ed. G. Flügel, Leipzig, 1835–58; reprint Beirut, Dār Ṣādir, n.d. (*ca.* 2000).

Ibn Abī al-Wafā' al-Qurashī, *al-Jawāhir al-muḍiyya fī ṭabaqāt al-ḥanafiyya*, 2nd edn, 6 vols, ed. 'Abd al-Fattāḥ M. al-Ḥulū, Cairo, 1993 (1st edn 1978–1982).

Ibn 'Asākir, *Ta'rīkh madīnat Dimashq*, 80 vols, ed. Muḥibb al-Dīn Abū Sa'īd 'Umar b. Gharāma al-'Amrawī and 'Alī Shīrī, Beirut, Dār al-Fikr, 1995–2001 [TD].

Ibn 'Asākir, *Ta'rīkh madīnat Dimashq, al-Sīra al-nabawiyya*, ed. S. al-Shihābī, Damascus, II, 1991.

Ibn 'Asākir, *Ta'rīkh madīnat Dimashq*, XXXI, ed. M. al-Ṭarābīshī, Damascus, 1986.

Ibn Ḥajar al-'Asqalānī, *Lisān al-Mīzān*, 7 vols, Hyderabad, 1911–13.

Ibn Ḥajar al-'Asqalānī, *Tadhdhīb al-tahdhīb*, Hyderabad, 1907–09 [TT].

Ibn al-Jazarī, *Ghāyat al-nihāya fī ṭabaqāt al-qurrā'* [*Das Biographische Lexikon der Koranleser*], 3 vols in 2, ed. G. Bergsträßer and O. Pretzl, Leipzig, 1933–35.

Ibn al-Jawzī, *Kitāb al-quṣṣāṣ wa-al-mudhakkirīn*, ed. and trans. M.L. Swartz, Beirut, 1971.

Ibn Khallikān, *Ibn Challikani Vitae illustrium virorum*, 13 parts in 2 vols, ed. F. Wüstenfeld, Göttingen, 1835–1850/*Wafayāt al-a'yān wa anbā' abnā' al-zamān*, 8 vols, ed. Iḥsān 'Abbās, Beirut, 1968–77.

Ibn al-Nadīm, *Kitāb al-Fihrist*, 2 vols, ed. G. Flügel, Leipzig, 1872; reprint, Beirut, 1964 and Frankfurt, 2005.

Ibn Qutayba, *Ibn Coteiba's Handbuch der Geschichte*, ed. F. Wüstenfeld, Göttingen, 1850/ *Kitāb al-Ma'ārif*, 2nd edn, ed. T. 'Ukāsha, Cairo, 1388/1969.

Ibn Sa'd, *Ṭabaqāt*, 9 vols, ed. Sachau *et al.*, Leiden, 1905–40/edn Beirut, Dār Ṣādir, 1957–59.

Ibn Wahb: see Muranyi *infra*.

Jâhiz, *Le Cadi et la mouche. Anthologie du Livre des animaux*, trans. L. Souami, Paris, 1988.

Mizzī, *Tahdhīb al-kamāl fī asmāʾ al-rijāl*, 23 vols, ed. A.ʿA. ʿAbīd and Ḥ.A. Āghā, Beirut, 1414/1994.

Qalqashandī, *Ṣubḥ al-aʿshā fī ṣināʿat al-inshāʾ*, 14 vols, ed. M.Ḥ. Shams al-Dīn, Beirut, 1407/1987.

Tahānawī, *Kashshāf iṣṭlāḥāt al-funūn wa al-ʿulūm*, 2 vols, ed. M. Wajīh ʿAbd al-Ḥaqq and Ghulām Qādir with Najm al-Dīn al-Kātibī al-Qazwīnī (d. 675/1276), *al-Risāla al-Shamsiyya fī al-qawāʿid al-mantiqiyya* [*The Logic of the Arabians*], trans. A. Sprenger, Calcutta, 1854–62; reprint, Istanbul, 1984.

Ṭāshkubrīzādah, ʿIṣām al-Dīn Abū al-Khayr, *Miftāḥ al-saʿāda wa miṣbāḥ al-siyāda fī mawḍūʿāt al-ʿulūm*, 4 vols, ed. Kāmil Kāmil al-Bakrī and ʿAbd al-Wahhāb Abū al-Nūr, Cairo, Dār al-Kutub al-ḥadīthiyya, 1969.

Thaʿlabī, Abū Isḥāq, *al-Kashf wa l-bayān ʿan tafsīr al-Qurʾān*, 10 vols, ed. Abū M. ʿA. ʿĀshūr and Abū M. b. ʿĀṣhūr, Beirut, 2002.

Baghdādī, *Taʾrīkh Baghdād*, 14 vols, ed. M.S. al-ʿIrāqī, Cairo, 1931–49.

Yāqūt al-Rūmī, *Irshād al-arīb ilā maʿrifat al-adīb* (*Muʿjam al-udabāʾ*), 7 vols, ed. D.S. Margoliouth, Leiden and London, 1907–27 (2nd edn 1923–31)/7 vols, ed. Iḥsān ʿAbbās, Beirut, 1993.

Secondary Literature

Abiad, M., *Culture et éducation arabo-islamique au Šām pendant les trois premiers siècles de l'Islam: d'après "Tarīḫ madinat Dimašq" d'Ibn ʿAsākir (499/1105–571/1176)*, Damascus, 1981.

ʿAlī, Jawād, *al-Mufaṣṣal fī taʾrīkh al-ʿarab qabla al-islām*, 2nd edn, 10 vols, n.p., 1413/1993 (1st edn Baghdad and Beirut, 1968–76).

Ālūsī, Jamāl al-Dīn, *Bulūgh al-arab fī maʿrifat aḥwāl al-ʿArab, I–III*, 3 vols, ed. M. Bahja al-Atharī, Cairo, 1342/1923.

Amari, Michele, *Storia dei Musulmani di Sicilia*, 2nd. edn, 3 vols in 5, Catania, 1933–39; Firenze, 1854–72. Arabic trans. I. Muḥibb Saʿd, Taʾrīkh Muslimī Ṣiqilliya, 3 vols, Italy, 2003.

Amir-Moezzi, M-A., and Jambet, C., *Qu'est-ce que le shīʿisme?*, Paris, 2004.

Anawati [Qanawātī] Chéhata, Georges [Jūrj Shiḥāta], "Textes arabes anciens édités en Égypte", *MIDEO*, 1 (1954);18 (1988).

Arkoun, M., *Contribution à l'étude de l'humanisme arabe au IVe/Xe siècle*, Paris, 1970.

Arkoun, M., "La conquête du bonheur selon Abū-l-Ḥasan al-ʿĀmirī', *Stud. Isl.*, XXII (1965), 55–90; reprint in id., *Essais sur la pensée islamique*, Paris, 1984, 149–84.

Bianquis, T., Guichard, P., Tillier, M. (eds), *Les Débuts du monde musulman*. De Muhammad aux dynasties autonomes, Paris, 2012.

Brockelmann, Carl, *Geschichte der arabischen Literatur* [*GAL*], I–II; Supplement [*S*] I–III, Leiden, E.J. Brill, 1937–49.

Brown, J.A.C., *The Canonization of al-Bukhārī and Muslim: The formation and function of the Sunnī ḥadīth Canon*, Leiden, 2007,

Calder, N., *Studies in Early Muslim Jurisprudence*, Oxford, 1993.

Casiri, M., *Bibliotheca Arabico-Hispana Escurialensis*, Madrid, 1760–70; reprint Osnabrück, 1969.

Cheddadi, A., *Ibn Khaldûn: l'homme et le théoricien de la civilisation*, Paris, 2006.

Conde, José Antonio, *Geschichte der Herrschaft der Mauren in Spanien*, trans. Karl Rutschmann, Karlsruhe, Gottlieb Braun, 1824–25 [*Historia de la Dominación de los Arabes en España, sacada de varios manuscritos y memorias arábigas*, Madrid, 1820–21].

Daiber, Hans, *Bibliography of Islamic Philosophy*, 2 vols and supplement, Leiden, 1999, 2007.

Diem, W. and H-P. Radenberg, A *Dictionary of the Arabic Material of S.D. Goitein's A Mediterranean Society*, Wiesbaden, 1994.

Encyclopaedia of the Qur'ān [*EQ*], 6 vols, ed. Jane Dammn McAuliffe, Leiden, Brill, 2001–2006.

EI: *The Encyclopaedia of Islam*, 4 vols and Supplement, Leiden, Brill, 1913–36

EI: *Encyclopédie de l'Islam*, 4 vols et Supplément, Leiden, Brill, 1913–38

EI: *The Encyclopaedia of Islam,* 13 vols, 2nd edn, Leiden, Brill, 1960-2002

EI: *Encyclopédie de l'Islam*, 13 vols, 2nd edn, Leiden, Brill, 1960–2009

Ess, J. van, *Theologie und Gesellschaft im 2. und 3. Jahrhundert Hidschrah. Eine Geschichte des religiösen Denkens im frühen Islam*, 6 vols, Berlin and New York, 1991–97.

Fischer, Wolfdietrich (ed.), *Grundriss der arabischen Philologie.* I: *Sprachwissenschaft* [*GAP* I], Wiesbaden, 1982.

Fischer, Wolfdietrich (ed.), *Grundriss der arabischen Philologie.* III: *Supplement* [*GAP* III], Wiesbaden, 1992.

Fück, J., *Die arabischen Studien in Europa*, Leipzig, 1955.

GAL: see Brockelmann, *supra*.

GAP I: see Fischer, 1982 *supra*; *GAP* II: see Gätje *infra*; *GAP* III: see Fischer, 1992 *supra*.

GAS I–IX: see Sezgin, *infra*.

Gätje, Helmut (ed.), *Grundriss der arabischen Philologie.* II: *Literaturwissenschaft* [*GAP* II], Wiesbaden, 1987.

Gilliot, C., *Aspects de l'imaginaire islamique commun dans le Commentaire de Tabari*, 2 vols, Thèse pour le doctorat d'Etat, Université Paris-III, Sorbonne Nouvelle, September 1987.

Gilliot, C., "The beginnings of Qurʾānic exegesis", in A. Rippin (ed.), *The Qur'an: Formative interpretation*, Aldershot, 1999, 1–39 [trans. of "Les débuts de l'exégèse coranique", *REMMM*, 58/4 (1990), 82–100].

Gilliot, C., "Collecte ou mémorisation du Coran: essai d'analyse d'un vocabulaire ambigu", in Rüdiger Lohlker (ed.), *Ḥadīṯstudien – die Überleferungen des Propheten im Gespräch. Festschrift für Tilman Nagel*, Hamburg, Verlag Dr Kovac, 2009, 77–132.

Gilliot, C., "Creation of a fixed text", in Jane Dammen McAuliffe (ed.), *The Cambridge Companion to the Qur'an*, Cambridge, 41–57.

Gilliot, C., "La transmission du message muhammadien. Juristes et théologiens", in Bianquis, T., *et al.* (eds), *Les Débuts du monde musulman*, chap. XXV, 373–406.

Gilliot, C., 'Die Schreib- und/oder Lesekundigkeit in Mekka und Yathrib/ Medina zur Zeit Mohammeds', in Markus Groß and Karl-Heinz Ohlig (eds), *Schlaglichter: die beiden ersten islamischen Jahrhunderte*, Schriften zur frühen Islamgeschichte und zum Koran, 3, Berlin, Verlag Hans Schiler, 2008, 293–319.

Gilliot, C., *Exégèse, langue et théologie en islam: l'exégèse coranique de Tabari*, Paris, 1990.

Gilliot, C., "Exegesis of the Qurʾān: classical and medieval", *EQ*, II, 2002, 99–124.

Gilliot, C., "La transmission des sciences religieuses", in J-C. Garcin *et al.*, *États, sociétés et cultures du monde musulman médiéval Xe–XVe siècle*, II, Paris, 2000, 327–51.

Gilliot, C., "Muqātil, grand exégète, traditionniste et théologien maudit', *JA*, 1–2, 1991, 39–92.

Gilliot, C., "Poète ou prophète? Les traditions concernant la poésie et les poètes attribuées au prophète de l'islam et aux premières générations musulmanes", in Floreal Sanagustin (ed.), *Paroles, signes, mythes*, Damascus, 2001, 331–96.

Gilliot, C., "Prosopography in Islam: an essay of classification", *Medieval Prosopography*, 23 (2002), 19–54.

Gilliot, C., "Reconsidering the authorship of the Qur'ān. Is the Qur'ān partly the fruit of a progressive and collective work?", in G.S. Reynolds (ed.), *The Qur'an in its Historical Context*, Abingdon, 2008, 88–108.

Gilliot, C., "Ṭabaḳāt", *EI*, 2nd edn, X, 7–10.

Gilliot, C., "Textes arabes anciens édités en Égypte", *MIDEO*, 19 (1989); 28 (2010).

Gilliot, C., "ʿUlamāʾ", *EI*, 2nd edn, X, 801–804; French edn, X, 865–68.

Gilliot, C., "Une reconstruction critique du Coran ou comment en finir avec les merveilles de la lampe d'Aladin", in M. Kropp (ed.), *Results of Contemporary Research on the Qur'an*, Beirut and Würzburg, 2007, 33–137.

Goitein, Shlomo Dov, *A Mediterranean Society: The Jewish communities of the Arab world as portrayed in the documents of the Cairo Geniza*, 6 vols, Berkeley, 1967–93; reprint 1999.

Goldziher, Ignaz, *Muhammedanische Studien*, 2 vols, Halle, 1889–90; reprint Hildesheim, 2004/*Muslim Studies*, 2 vols, ed. S.M. Stern, trans. C.R. Barber and S.M. Stern, Chicago, 1967/*Études sur la tradition islamique*, trans. L. Bercher, Paris, 1952.

Goldziher, Ignaz, "Beiträge zur Geschichte der Sprachgelehrsamkeit bei den Arabern. I. Mit Mitteilungen aus der Refâʻijja". II "Zur Gauharī-Literatur". III "Abu-l-Husein ibn Fâris", *SKAW*, LXVII (1871), 207–51; LXXII (1872), 587–631; LXXIII (1873), 511–52; reprint in *Gesammelte Schriften*, I, Hildesheim, 1964, 7–51.

Gregorio, Rosario, *Rerum Arabicarum quœ ad historiam Siculam spectant ampla collectio, opera et studio Rosarii Gregorio*, Panormi (Palermo), Ex Regio Typographeo, 1790.

Hamidullah, M., *Le Prophète de l'Islam: sa vie, son oeuvre*, 4th edn, I–II, Paris, 1979 (1st edn 1959).

Hirschfeld, H., "A volume of essays by Al Jahiz", in T.W. Arnold and RA Nicholson (eds), *A Volume of Oriental Studies Presented to Edward G. Browne*, Cambridge, 1922, 202–209.

Jokisch, B., *Islamic Imperial Law: Harun-Al-Rashid's Codification Project*, Berlin, 2007.

Juynboll, G.H.A., *Muslim Tradition: Studies on chronology, provenance and authorship of early ḥadīth*, Cambridge, 1983.

Juynboll, G.H.A., "Nāfiʿ, the mawlā of Ibn ʿUmar, and his position in Muslim ḥadīth literature", *Der Islam*, 70 (1993), 207–44.

Kaḥḥāla, *ʿUmar Riḍā, Muʿjam al-muʾallifīn*, 15 vols in 8, Beirut, al-Muṯannā/Dār Iḥyāʾ al-turāth al-ʿarabī, s.d. (reprint of the Damascus edn, 1957–61).

Kremer, Alfred von, *Culturgeschichte des Orients unter den Chalifen*, 2 vols, Vienna, 1875–77; reprint Aalen, 1966.

Lammens, H., *La Mecque à la veille de l'hégire*, Beirut, 1924.

Lammens, H., "La république marchande de La Mecque vers l'an 600 de notre ère", *Bull. Institut d'Egypte*, 5th series, 4 (1910), 23–54.

Leder, S., *Ibn al-Ǧauzī und seine Kompilation wider die Leidenschaft*, Beirut and Wiesbaden, 1984.

Macdonald, D.B., *Aspects of Islam*, New York, 1911; reprint Freeport, NY, 1971.

Makki, M.ʿA., *Ensayo sobre las aportaciones orientales en la España musulmana y su influencia en la formación de la cultura hispano-árabe*, Madrid, 1968.

Mez, A., *Die Renaissance des Islams*, Heidelberg, 1922/*The Renaissance of Islam*, trans. S. Khuda Bukhsh and D.S. Margoliouth, London, 1937; reprint New York, 1975/*El Renacimiento del Islam*, trans. from the German by Salvador Vila, Madrid, Escuelas de Estudios Árabes de Madrid y Granada (Publicaciones de las Escuelas de Estudios Arabes de Madrid y Granada Serie A., no. 4), 1936/*al-Ḥaḍāra al-islāmiyya fī al-qarn al-rābiʿ*, trans. M. ʿAbd al-Hādī Abū Rīda, Cairo, 1940/*Renesans Islamu*, trans. Janusz Danecki, Warsaw, State Publishing Institute, 1980.

Motzki, H., *Die Anfänge der islamischen Jurisprudenz: ihre Entwicklung in Mekka bis zur Mitte des 2./8. Jahrhunderts*, Wiesbaden, 1991/*The Origins of Islamic Jurisprudence: Meccan* fiqh *before the classical schools*, trans. M.H. Katz, Leiden, 2002.

Motzki, H., "The collection of the Qur'ān ...", *Der Islam*, 78 (2001), 1–34.

Muranyi, M., *Beiträge zur Geschichte der Ḥadīṯ- und Rechtsgelehrsamkeit der Mālikiyya in Nordafrika bis zum 5. Jh. d. H.*, Wiesbaden, 1997.

Muranyi, M., *ʿAbd Allāh b. Wahb, al-Ǧāmiʿ: die Koranwissenchaften*, ed. with commentary by M. Muranyi, Wiesbaden, 1992.

Muranyi, M., *al-Ǧāmiʿ: Tafsīr al-Qurʾān*, ed. with commentary by M. Muranyi, Wiesbaden, 1993.

Muranyi, M., *al-Ǧāmiʿ: Tafsīr al-Qurʾān. Koranexegese* 2, I, ed. with commentary by M. Muranyi, Wiesbaden, 1995.

Muranyi, M., *Die Rechtsbücher des Qairawāners Saḥnūn b. Saʿīd*, Stuttgart, 1999.

Muranyi, M., *Ein altes Fragment medinensischer Jurisprudenz aus Qairawān. Aus dem Kitāb al-Ḥaǧǧ des ʿAbd al-ʿAzīz b. ʿAbd Allāh b. a. Salama al-Māǧišūn (st. 164/780-81)*, Stuttgart, 1985.

Muranyi, M., *Materialien zur mālikitischen Rechtsliteratur*, Wiesbaden, 1984.

Nagel, T., *Allahs Liebling*. Ursprung und Erscheinungsformen des Mohammedglaubens, München, 2008.

Nagel, T., *Mohammed. Leben und Legende*, München, 2008.

Nagel, T., "'Authentizität' in der Leben-Mohammed-Forschung", to be published in *Arabica*, June 2012.

Neuwirth, A., "Qurʾān and history – a disputed relationship ...", *Journal of Qurʾānic Studies*, V/1 (2003), 1–18.

Pellat, C., *Arabische Geisteswelt: Ausgewählte und übersetzte Texte von al-Gahiz, 777–869*, trans. Walter W. Müller, Zurich, 1967.

Pellat, C., *Le Milieu baṣrien et la formation de Ǧāḥiẓ*, Paris, 1953/Bilāt, Shārl, *al-Jāḥiẓ fī al-Baṣra wa Baghdād wa Samarrāʾ*, trans. Ibr. al-Kaylanī, Damascus, 1961.

Pellat, C., *The Life and Works of Jahiz: Translations of selected texts [by] Charles Pellat*; trans. D.M. Hawke, London and Berkeley, 1969.

Petry, C.F., *The Civilian Elite of Cairo in the Later Middle Ages*, Princeton, 1982.

Reynolds, G.S. (ed.), *The Qurʾān in its Historical Context*, Abingdon, 2007.

Sezgin, Fuat, *Geschichte des arabischen Schrifttums*, 9 vols, Leiden, Brill, 1967–84 [GAS I–IX].

TB: see Baghdādī, *Ta'rīkh Baghdād*, *supra*.

TT: see Ibn Ḥajar, *Tahdhīb*, *supra*.

Touati, H., *L'armoire à sagesse: bibliohèques et collections en Islam*, Paris, 2003.

Vadet, J-C., *L'esprit courtois en Orient dans les cinq premiers siècles de l'hégire*, Paris, 1968.

1
THE ETIQUETTE OF LEARNING IN THE EARLY ISLAMIC STUDY CIRCLE

Christopher Melchert

Compendia of hadith from the ninth century, including most of the Six Books, for example, normally devote a section to *adab*, the etiquette of a religiously serious life. Compendia with and without separate chapters on *adab* consider many questions of etiquette elsewhere, such as in chapters dealing with mosques. Naturally, for books from legists, they pay disproportionate attention to how one should conduct oneself at meetings for the transmission of religious knowledge (*ᶜilm*). In details as small as the proper way to sit, one may observe central features of Islamic religious culture. In arguments over disputed questions, one observes the very emergence of a religious culture.

A. S. Tritton and George Makdisi have already given us valuable accounts of the forms Islamic education took.[1] The account that follows is based more strictly on materials from the ninth century C.E. These often describe the seventh and eighth centuries, but one usually presumes that norms of the ninth century have been projected backward. Sunni Islam crystallized in the ninth century. In consequence, ninth-century forms continued to characterize Islamic learning for centuries to come, as becomes plain from comparison with an account by Samᶜānī of teaching in the twelfth century. At the same time, evidence survives in ninth-century accounts of both earlier versions of the classical forms and of rejected alternatives to those forms.

Sitting in the Mosque

From as far back as the sources will take us, the site of most religious learning, whether in law or hadith, hardly distinguishable before the late ninth century, was the mosque.[2] The normal procedure was to sit (*jalasa* or, less often, *qaᶜaḍa*) on the ground in a circle (*ḥalqah*). The place where one sat was his *majlis*, a term referring to a particular place in the circle, but most often to the place in a mosque where a

---

[1] A. S. Tritton, *Materials on Muslim Education in the Middle Ages* (London: Luzac & Co., 1957), and George Makdisi, *Rise of Colleges: Institutions of Learning in Islam and the West* (Edinburgh: Edinburgh University Press, 1981).

[2] See Makdisi, *Rise of Colleges*, 1–12, "The Term Majlis and the Primacy of the Mosque."

particular teacher held forth.[3] Thus, "He sat with so-and-so" was equivalent to saying "He learnt from him."[4]

The foregoing characteristics of teaching are apparent, for example, in Ibn Sa^c^d's biography (before 230/845) of the Medinese Follower (*tābi^c^*) Sa^c^īd b. al-Musayyab (d. 94/712–13). On one occasion, when the governor of Medina (later caliph) ^c^Umar b. ^c^Abd al-^c^Azīz sent someone to question him, he supposedly returned with the messenger to appear before the governor himself. The governor apologized, explaining that he had meant for the messenger to ask his advice there at his *majlis*; that is, his place at the mosque where he normally made himself available to answer questions. An actual caliph, less worthy than ^c^Umar b. ^c^Abd al-^c^Azīz, came to the mosque of Medina and saw Sa^c^īd at his *ḥalqah*, but Sa^c^īd refused to get up and come to him. Ibn ^c^Umar referred petitioners whose questions were difficult to Sa^c^īd, "for he has sat with the pious"; that is, learnt from them. Presumably considering the bare ground good enough, Sa^c^īd dismissed prayer rugs as an innovation. Naturally for the early period, Sa^c^īd^ʾ^s teaching was not specialized, comprising hadith reports from Companions (he was called *rāwiyat ^c^Umar* for relating more than anyone else from that caliph, although by one report he denied ever meeting him), his own opinions on juridical questions (Ibn Sa^c^d distinguishes between his *^c^ilm* and *ra^ʾ^y*, authoritative opinions he quoted and his own), and even the interpretation of dreams. Additionally, his personal example was supposed to establish norms of dress, adornment, and so forth.[5]

After the mosque, the site of teaching most frequently mentioned is the teacher's own home.[6] Ibn Hurmuz (d. 145/762–63?) would meet at his house in Medina with various jurisprudents for *fiqh* and hadith.[7] The house of Shaybānī (d. 189/805) was said to fill up when he related hadith of Mālik but not when he related that of

[3] For one's place in a circle, see the many hadith reports, "Let not a man make a man get up from his place (*majlis*), then sit in it," as in ^c^Abd al-Razzāq, *Muṣannaf*, 11 vols., ed. Ḥabīb al-Raḥmān al-A^c^ẓamī (Johannesburg: Majlis Ilmi, 1970–72), 11:23, no. 19793; Dārimī, *Musnad*, *isti^ʾ^dhān*, 24, Aḥmad b. Ḥanbal, *Musnad*, 6 vols. (Cairo: al-Maṭba^c^ah al-Maymanīyah, 1313), 2:16–17, 45, 84–85, 121, 124, 126, 149, 338, 5:48; al-Dārimī, *Sunan*, *isti^ʾ^dhān*, *bāb lā yuqīmanna aḥadukum akhāh min majlisih*; al-Bukhārī, *Ṣaḥīḥ*, *isti^ʾ^dhān*, 31, *bāb lā yuqīmu al-rajul al-rajul min majlisih*; idem, *al-Adab al-mufrad*, *bāb idhā qāma lah rajul min majlisih lam yaq^c^ud fīh*, no. 1153, idem, *Ṣaḥīḥ*, *isti^ʾ^dhān*, 31, *bāb lā yuqīmu al-rajul al-rajul*; Abū Dāwūd, *Sunan*, *adab*, 18, nos. 4827–28, etc. Tritton reports a first-century *majlis* as an entire hall, built of tree trunks, but the site in question may have been an administrative center: see Tritton, *Materials*, 98, citing Ibn Sa^c^d, *al-Ṭabaqāt al-kubrā*, 9 vols., ed. Eduard Sachau, et al. (Leiden: E. J. Brill, 1904–40), 7:88 = (Beirut: Dār Ṣādir, 1957–68), 7:122.

[4] One avoided sitting in filth, but the dry earth was presumptively clean, so that one did not need to sweep it before praying on a spot, let alone before sitting there. The earth is a pure place of prostration according to Aḥmad b. Ḥanbal, *Musnad* 5:145, 148, 161, 383; also Abū Dāwūd, *Sunan*, *ṣalāh*, 24. No need to sweep the earth according to Ṭabarānī, *al-Ṣaghīr*, as reported by Ibn Ḥajar al-Haytamī, *Majma^c^ al-zawā^ʾ^id wa-manba^c^ al-fawā^ʾ^id*, 10 vols. (Cairo: Maktabat al-Qudsī, 1352–53), 8:61. Of course, mosques normally were swept out; e.g., Abū Dāwūd provides a hadith report that refers to specks put out of mosques under the title *kans al-masjid*, *Sunan*, *ṣalāh*, 16.

[5] Ibn Sa^c^d, *al-Ṭabaqāt al-kubrā*, vol. 5 (Leiden ed.):88–106 = vol. 5 (Beirut ed.):119–43.

[6] Mostly later examples in Tritton, *Materials*, 34–35, 98, 100.

[7] Ibn Sa^c^d, *al-Ṭabaqāt al-kubrā; al-qism al-mutammim*, ed. Ziyād Muḥammad Manṣūr (Medina: al-Jāmi^c^ah al-Islāmīyah and al-Majlis al-^c^Ilmī, 1983), 327. Mālik b. Anas is also quoted as saying, "I used to go to Ibn Hurmuz early in the morning and not leave his house till night," ibid., 436.

Kufans.[8] One Yaḥyā b. ᶜUthmān (d. 255/868–69) had sessions at his house in Homs.[9] Rather than going to the palace himself, Bukhārī (d. 256/870) bade the *amīr* of Bukhara come to hear him relate hadith in his mosque or in his house.[10] In 270/883–84, the Baghdadi Shāfiᶜi Maḥāmilī (d. 330/941–42) convened a session for jurisprudence at his house.[11] The house presented advantages over the mosque to the teacher who wanted to offer hospitality to his auditors, such as the Kufan Ḥafṣ b. Ghiyāth (d. 194/810?), who declared, "Whoever has not eaten of our food, we will not relate hadith to him."[12] It likewise presented advantages to the less reputable teacher who demanded payment for his hadith, such as the Baghdadi Ibn Abī Usāmah al-Tamīmī (d. 282/896). A traditionist related finding a crowd of booksellers (*warrāqūn*) in his vestibule, whose names Ibn Abī Usāmah was writing down. Each was to pay him two *dirhams*.[13] Finally, it was easier to withdraw from a session at one's house, as did the Nishapuran traditionist Muḥammad b. Rāfiᶜ (d. 245/860) when a bird soiled someone's hand and pen and another auditor laughed out loud, spoiling the solemnity of the occasion.[14] In addition to the mosque and house are also mentioned *ribāṭ*, *khāniqāh*, and, already in the third Islamic century, the *madrasah*.[15]

The teacher in the mosque normally sat against a pillar (*usṭuwānah* or *sāriyah*). No prophetic example is cited for sitting by a pillar, presumably because traditionists did not conceive of the Prophet's mosque in Medina as originally having had pillars. But numerous later teachers are described as sitting against pillars; for example, Abū Bakr b. Abī Shaybah (d. 235/849) quotes the Medinese jurisprudent Maᶜn b. ᶜĪsā (d. 198/814) as listing one Companion and three Followers who were seen sitting against pillars.[16] To sit against a pillar was so strongly identified with teaching that the Kufan traditionist Sufyān b. ᶜUyaynah (d. 196/811) metonymically referred to the first person to ask him to relate hadith, Misᶜar b. Kidām (d. 155/771–72), as "the first to make me lean against the pillar."[17]

Maᶜn b. ᶜĪsā also named two Followers who were not seen sitting against pillars.[18] It was presumably modesty that impelled at least one of the two, the famous Kufan

---

[8] Dhahabī, *Siyar aᶜlām al-nubalāᵓ*, 25 vols. (Beirut: Muᵓassasat al-Risālah, 1981–88), 8 (ed. Nadhīr Ḥamdān):67f.

[9] al-Khaṭīb al-Baghdādī, *Tārīkh Baghdād*, 14 vols. (Cairo: Maktabat al-Khānjī, 1349/1931; repr. Cairo: Maktabat al-Khānjī and Beirut: Dār al-Fikr, n.d.), 11:137.

[10] al-Khaṭīb al-Baghdādī, *Tārīkh Baghdād*, 2:33; Dhahabī, *Siyar*, 12 (ed. Shuᶜayb al-Arnaᵓūṭ and Ṣāliḥ al-Samar):464.

[11] al-Khaṭīb al-Baghdādī, *Tārīkh Baghdād*, 8:22; Dhahabī, *Tārīkh al-islām*, ed. ᶜUmar ᶜAbd al-Salām Tadmurī, 65 vols. to date (Beirut: Dār al-Kitāb al-ᶜArabī, 1987–), 24:282.

[12] al-Khaṭīb al-Baghdādī, *Tārīkh Baghdād*, 8:194.

[13] Ibn Ḥajar, *Lisān al-mīzān*, 7 vols. (Hyderabad: Majlis Dāᵓirat al-Maᶜārif, 1911–13; repr. Beirut: Muᵓassasat al-Aᶜlamī, 1986), 2:157–58.

[14] Samᶜānī, *Adab al-imlāᵓ wa-al-istimlāᵓ*, ed. Max Weisweiler (Leiden: E. J. Brill, 1952; repr. Beirut: Dār al-Kutub al-ᶜIlmīyah, n.d.), 141, with other examples; cf. Dhahabī, *Tārīkh al-islām*, 18:431, with the same story of Muḥammad b. Rāfiᶜ but a different name for the narrator.

[15] Tritton, *Materials*, 102, 108.

[16] Ibn Abī Shaybah, *al-Muṣannaf*, 9 vols., ed. Saᶜīd al-Laḥḥām (Beirut: Dār al-Fikr, 1989), 6:255, *adab*, 206.

[17] *Awwalu man asnadanī ilā 'l-usṭuwānah*: al-Khaṭīb al-Baghdādī, *Tārīkh Baghdād*, 9:176.

[18] Ibn Abī Shaybah, *Muṣannaf*, ed. Laḥḥām, 6:255, adab, 207. Ibrāhīm's refusal is also mentioned by Aḥmad b. Ḥanbal, *Kitāb al-ᶜIlal wa-maᶜrifat al-rijāl*, 4 vols., ed. Waṣī Allāh b. Muḥammad ᶜAbbās

Ibrāhīm al-Nakhaᶜī (d. 96/714–15), not to sit against a pillar. Fasawī (d. 277/890) asserts that Ibrāhīm would leave the circle if it expanded in such a way as to make him sit by a pillar.[19] He normally sat with just five or six auditors.[20] The Basran Follower Abū al-ᶜĀliyah (d. 90/709) would leave if more than three or four came to hear him.[21]

It was good form to face the *qiblah*; that is, the direction of the Kaᶜbah in Mecca. Ibn Abī Shaybah cites a number of favorable reports.[22] Presumably, the leader of the circle normally leant against the side of the pillar facing the *qiblah* while his auditors sat fanned out before him.

Although the teacher normally sat on the ground with his auditors, he might sometimes be distinguished by sitting on a pillow. By order of the governor, the jurisprudent Ibn Abī Najīḥ (d. 131/748–49?) was provided with a doubled-up pillow in the mosque at Mecca to sit on when giving opinions.[23] Ibn Abī Shaybah quotes four hadith reports, two Prophetic, in favor of offering someone a pillow as a particular honor.[24] There are also occasional references to teachers on benches. People put the Basran traditionist Ismāᶜīl b. ᶜUlayyah (d. 193/809) on a *masṭabah*, a bench or raised platform.[25] The Baghdadi Abū al-Qāsim al-Baghawī (d. 317/929) signalled that he would dictate by getting onto a *dikkah* or bench and sitting down.[26] Presumably, benches made it easier for a teacher to be seen and heard by the extraordinarily large audiences sometimes attracted to the dictation of hadith.[27]

How Auditors Sat

Hadith collections present various rules for joining a circle. "The best sessions are the widest" (*khayru 'l-majālisi awsaᶜuhā*) is a widely-attested formula.[28] One story relates how three men came up to the Prophet's circle. One of them saw a gap and sat down there, one sat behind the rest, and one turned away. The Prophet thereupon

---

(Beirut: al-Maktab al-Islāmī, 1988), 1:178 = *Kitāb al-Jāmiᶜ fī al-ᶜilal wa-maᶜrifat al-rijāl*, 2 vols., ed. Muḥammad Ḥusām Bayḍūn (Beirut: Muᵓassasat al-Kutub al-Thaqāfīyah, 1990), 1:86.

19 Fasawī, *Kitāb al-Maᶜrifah wa'l-tārīkh*, 4 vols., ed. Akram Ḍiyāᵓ al-ᶜUmarī (Medina: Maktabat al-Dār, 1989), 2:607; Abū Nuᶜaym, *Ḥilyat al-awliyāᵓ*, 10 vols. (Cairo: Maṭbaᶜat al-Saᶜādah and Maktabat al-Khānjī, 1932–38; repr. with index, Beirut: Dār al-Kutub al-ᶜIlmīyah, n.d.), 4:219.

20 Khalīlī, *al-Irshād fī maᶜrifat ᶜulamāᵓ al-ḥadīth*, abr. Silafī, ed. ᶜĀmir Aḥmad Ḥaydar (Mecca: al-Shāmīyah, 1993), 171.

21 Abū Khaythamah, *Kitāb al-ᶜIlm*, ed. Muḥammad Nāṣir al-Dīn al-Albānī (Beirut: al-Maktab al-Islāmī, 1983), 13; Abū Nuᶜaym, *Ḥilyah*, 2:217–18.

22 Ibn Abī Shaybah, *Muṣannaf*, 9 vols., ed. Muḥammad ᶜAbd al-Salām Shāhīn (Beirut: Dār al-Kutub al-ᶜIlmīyah, 1995), 5:267, adab, 298, nos. 25928–32.

23 Fasawī, *Maᶜrifah*, 1:702.

24 Ibn Abī Shaybah, *Muṣannaf*, ed. Shāhīn, 5:235–36, *adab*, 34, nos. 25575–78.

25 Aḥmad b. Ḥanbal, *Jāmiᶜ*, ed. Bayḍūn, 1:35.

26 al-Khaṭīb al-Baghdādī, *Tārīkh Baghdād*, 10:114.

27 On large meetings, see Tritton, *Materials*, 35f; on the special popularity of hadith, ibid., 130, 148.

28 Bukhārī, al-Adab *al-mufrad, bāb khayru ᵓl-majālisi awsaᶜuhā*, no. 1136; Abū Dāwūd, *Sunan*, *adab*, 14, no. 4820; al-Bazzār, apud Ibn Ḥajar al-Haytamī, *Kashf al-astār ᶜan zawāᵓid al-Bazzār*, 2 vols., ed. Ḥabīb al-Raḥmān al-Aᶜẓamī (Beirut: Muᵓassasat al-Risālah, 1979), 2:421, *adab*, 23; Ṭabarānī, *al-Awsaṭ*, apud Ibn Ḥajar al-Haytamī, *Majmaᶜ*, 8:59.

explained that God would reward the first two but turn away from the last.[29] It was definitely forbidden to make someone get up, and then sit in his place.[30] This prohibition is sometimes combined with the injunction to spread out and make room for a newcomer.[31] Rising to salute someone was in any case discouraged. The Prophet is quoted as telling a man not to rise for another "as the *aᶜājim* do," "as Fārs and the Rūm do," or "as the people of Fārs did to their mighty."[32] Aḥmad b. Ḥanbal stated directly that it was discouraged (*makrūh*) to stand for someone.[33] Some ambivalence may be indicated by contrary hadith reports, according to which the Prophet enjoined the Jews of Banū Qurayẓah to stand for their master (*sayyid*), the arbiter who was about to condemn them to death and slavery, and also by reports of Fāṭimah's always standing for her father.[34] There are, of course, reports that various traditionists rose to honor someone or other. Aḥmad b. Ḥanbal allowed a returning pilgrim to rise for elders coming to salute him based on the example of the Prophet's rising for Jaᶜfar.[35] Abū Zurᶜah al-Rāzī (d. 264/878) would not rise for anyone or seat anyone in his place save Ibn Wārah (d. 270/884).[36]

Ambivalence is also indicated by contradictory reports of where in a circle to enter. On the one hand, as one might expect, we have multiple reports enjoining indifference to where one sits. Abū Khaythamah (d. 234/849) assures us there was never any jostling for position among the Companions.[37] Bukhārī devotes a section to *man qaᶜada ḥaythu yantahī bihi ᵓl-majlis*, "those who sat wherever the session ended."[38] On the other hand, again as one might expect, there is much evidence that later men did pay keen attention to where in the circle they sat, much preferring the honor of sitting near the master.[39] There is some encouragement for such attention in various Prophetic hadith reports. Perhaps we see an attempt at harmonization (and acceptance of inevitable human frailty) in injunctions that allow one to claim a place other than "wherever the session ends," but one must not claim his place arrogantly; for example, "Whoever divides two in a session so as to put himself above them

---

[29] Mālik, *Muwaṭṭaᵓ*, rec. Yaḥyā, 2 vols., ed. Muḥammad Fuᵓād ᶜAbd al-Bāqī (Cairo: Dār Iḥyāᵓ al-Kutub al-ᶜArabīyah, 1951; repr., n.d.), 2:752, *salām*, 3; Aḥmad b. Ḥanbal, *Musnad* 5:219; Muslim, *Ṣaḥīḥ, kitāb al-salām*, 21, *bāb man atā majlisan fa-wajada furjatan fa-jalasa fīhā wa-illā warāᵓahum*; Tirmidhī, *al-Jāmiᶜ al-ṣaḥīḥ, kitāb al-istiᵓdhān*, 2723, *bāb fī 'th-thalāthati 'lladhīna aqbalū fī majlisi 'n-nabī*.

[30] See note 3 above.

[31] Aḥmad b. Ḥanbal, *Musnad* 2:16–17, 102, 338, 483 (the last from Abū Hurayrah rather than the Prophet); Dārimī, *Sunan, istiᵓdhān*, 24; Bukhārī, *Ṣaḥīḥ, istiᵓdhān*, 32, *bāb idhā qīla lakum tafassaḥū*; idem, *al-Adab al-mufrad, bāb al-tawassuᶜu fī 'l-majlis*, no. 1140.

[32] Abū Dāwūd, *Sunan, adab*, 165 (*aᶜājim*); Muslim, *Ṣaḥīḥ, ṣalāh* 413, *bāb iᵓtimām al-maᵓmūm bi'l-imām* (Fārs and Rūm); Ibn Mājah, *Sunan, duᶜāᵓ*, 2, *bāb duᶜāᵓ rasūl Allāh* (the people of Fārs).

[33] Ibn Hāniᵓ al-Naysābūrī, *Masāᵓil al-imām Aḥmad*, 2 vols., ed. Zuhayr al-Shāwīsh (Beirut: al-Maktab al-Islāmī, 1980), 2:180.

[34] Bukhārī, *Ṣaḥīḥ, istiᵓdhān, bāb qūmū ilā sayyidikum*; Muslim, *Ṣaḥīḥ, jihād, bāb jawāzu qitāli man naqaḍa 'l-ᶜahd*; Abū Dāwūd, *Sunan, adab*, 155.

[35] Ibn Hāniᵓ, *Masāᵓil*, 2:183.

[36] Dhahabī, *Tārīkh al-islām*, 20:177.

[37] Abū Khaythamah, *ᶜIlm*, 25.

[38] Bukhārī, *Ṣaḥīḥ, ᶜIlm*, 66.

[39] See Makdisi, *Rise of Colleges*, 91-92, for place in the circle as an indication of rank in the eleventh century.

(*takabburan ʿalayhimā*), his place is in Hell."[40] If someone left a circle, then returned, he had the right to reclaim his place.[41]

The Prophet expressly cursed whoever sat in the middle of a circle.[42] His precise objection is not made clear. Khaṭṭābī, the tenth-century commentator of Abū Dāwūd, proposed that this was either to prevent someone from stepping over people's heads or because whoever sits in the middle of a circle blocks the view of some.[43] It was acceptable to sit in front of a *shaykh* with one's knees touching his to ask a question, even though this evidently must have put one at least inside the circle. The angel Gabriel did so in the famous story of his eliciting from the Prophet the basic elements of Islamic belief, and Zuhrī (d. 125/743?) is quoted as saying metonymically, "My knees touched those of Ibn al-Musayyab for eight years"; that is, he continually asked him juridical questions for that long.[44]

Two postures of sitting are recommended. First is to sit with knees drawn up and held either by a cord or one's turban (*iḥtibāʾ*) or simply by the hands (*qurfuṣāʾ*). Second is to sit with legs folded (*tarabbuʿ*).[45] The latter posture must have taken longer to become generally accepted, for Ibn Abī Shaybah records a Follower's pronouncement against it, calling it *jilsat mamlakah*, "the posture of kingliness."[46] Perhaps sitting with legs folded seemed aggressive because one took up more space that way. One posture was forbidden: wrapping one's body in a garment so that one cannot raise the ends or take out one's hands (*ishtimālu 'ṣ-ṣammāʾ*).[47] Additionally, the Prophet forbade one to draw up the knees if one was wearing only one garment and therefore liable to expose his private parts.[48] The warning against *iḥtibāʾ* in just one garment helps explain why an Abū Ṣāliḥ (unidentified Follower, probably Kufan)

[40] ʿAbd al-Razzāq, *Muṣannaf*, 11:23, no. 19794.

[41] ʿAbd al-Razzāq, *Muṣannaf*, 11:23, no. 19792; Aḥmad b. Ḥanbal, *Musnad*, 2:263, 283, 342, 389, 447, 483, 527, 3:32; Dārimī, *Sunan*, *istiʾdhān*, 25, *bāb idhā qāma min majlisihi thumma rajaʿa ilayhi fa-huwa aḥaqqu bih*; Bukhārī, *al-Adab al-mufrad*, *bāb idhā qāma thumma rajaʿa ilā majlisih*, no. 1138; Muslim, *Ṣaḥīḥ*, *salām*, 23, *bāb idhā qāma min majlisihi thumma ʿād*; Abū Dāwūd, *Sunan*, *adab*, 38; Ibn Mājah, *Sunan*, *adab*, 22; Bazzār, *Kashf*, 2:424, *adab*, 26.

[42] Abū Dāwūd, *Sunan*, *adab*, 17; Tirmidhī, *Jāmiʿ*, *adab*, *bāb karāhīyatu 'l-quʿūdi wasṭa 'l-ḥalqah*, no. 2754.

[43] Khaṭṭābī, *Maʿālim al-sunan*, apud Abū Dāwūd, *al-Sunan*, 5 vols., ed. ʿIzzat ʿUbayd al-Daʿʿās and ʿĀdil al-Sayyid (Beirut: Dār Ibn Ḥazm, 1997), 5:106.

[44] For Gabriel, see Nawawī, *al-Arbaʿūn al-nawawīyah*, no. 2; for Zuhrī, see Aḥmad b. Ḥanbal, *ʿIlal*, ed. ʿAbbās, 1:183 = *Jāmiʿ*, ed. Baydūn, 1:87.

[45] Bukhārī, *Ṣaḥīḥ*, *istiʾdhān*, 34, *bāb al-iḥtibāʾ bi-'l-yad wa-huwa al-qurfuṣāʾ*; idem, *al-Adab al-mufrad*, *bāb al-iḥtibāʾ*, no. 1182; Bazzār, apud Ibn Ḥajar al-Haytamī, *Kashf*, 2:426; Ṭabarānī, apud Ibn Ḥajar al-Haytamī, *Majmaʿ*, 8:60; for the Prophet seen sitting cross-legged, Bukhārī, *al-Adab al-mufrad*, *bāb al-tarabbuʿ*, no. 1179; Abū Dāwūd, *Sunan*, *adab*, 27. Note that the chapter title in Bukhārī's *Ṣaḥīḥ* expressly equates *iḥtibāʾ* and *qurfuṣāʾ*, whereas some authorities rather equate *iḥtibāʾ* with *tarabbuʿ*; e.g., Samʿānī, whose chapter title reads *yustaḥabbu lahu an yajlisa mutarabbiʿan mutakhashshiʿan* but whose illustrative hadith report speaks of the Prophet as *qāʿidu 'l-qurfuṣāʾ* (*Adab*, 36).

[46] Interpreting *mamlakah* as a *maṣdar mīmī*: Ṭāwūs (d. 106/724–25?), apud Ibn Abī Shaybah, *Muṣannaf*, ed. Laḥḥām, 6:113, *adab*, 24.

[47] Bukhārī, *Ṣaḥīḥ*, *istiʾdhān*, 42, *bāb al-julūs kayfamā tayassara*.

[48] Bukhārī, *Ṣaḥīḥ*, *libās*, 21; idem, *al-Adab al-mufrad*, *bāb al-iḥtibāʾ fī al-thawb*, no. 1175; cf. Mālik, *Muwaṭṭaʾ*, 2:718, *libās*, 8.

is quoted as saying, "All I used to want in the world was two white garments in which to sit with Abū Hurayrah."[49]

Opinion was divided about sitting or lying in the mosque with one leg over the other. Ibn Abī Shaybah first quotes fourteen hadith reports in favor of putting one leg over the other, mostly in sitting, some in lying down. One concerns the Prophet's example.[50] ᶜAbd al-Razzāq, Bukhārī, and others offer further reports of the Prophet's lying in the mosque with one leg over the other.[51] But then Ibn Abī Shaybah quotes seven hadith reports against crossing legs.[52] In other sources, the Prophet himself forbids putting one leg on top of the other.[53] ᶜAbd al-Razzāq quotes Zuhrī as saying regretfully that the people raised a great controversy over the matter.[54]

Ibn Abī Shaybah relates this controversy to the customs of non-Muslims. In favor of sitting or lying with legs crossed, he quotes the Medinese Follower ᶜIkrimah (d. 107/725–26?) as saying dismissively, "Only *ahl al-kitāb* forbid that."[55] His Basran contemporary Abū Mijlaz (d. 106/724–25?) said, "It is just something the Jews disliked. They said He created the heavens and earth in six days, then settled (*istawā*) on the Sabbath and sat (*jalasa*) in that posture."[56] Al-Ḥasan al-Baṣrī (d. 110/728–28) is quoted as saying, "The Jews used to dislike it, so the Muslims contradicted them."[57]

There was also disagreement over sitting with legs stretched out. At one end of the spectrum, the Prophet himself is said to have modelled this posture, for he once received a delegation with his legs extended, leaning on a corner of his outer wrap (*ridā*ᵓ) with his hand.[58] A middle position is indicated by the story that the Damascene Kathīr b. Murrah (d. 70–80/690–700?) entered the mosque and found the Companion ᶜAwf b. Mālik al-Ashjaᶜī sitting in a circle. He had extended his legs in front of him. When he saw Kathīr, he pulled up his legs (*qabaḍa rijlayh*), then said, "Do you know why I stretched out my legs? That a good man should come and sit."[59] Apparently, ᶜAwf's previous companions had not been up to the standard that required pulling up the legs. At the other end of the spectrum, the Prophet is said to have passed a Companion leaning back on his left hand and asked him, "Will you sit as do those who have incurred God's wrath?" (an allusion to Qurᵓān 1:7, conventionally indicating the Jews).[60] It is easy to imagine that stretched-out legs

---

[49] Abū Khaythamah, *ᶜIlm*, 22, no. 84.

[50] Ibn Abī Shaybah, *Muṣannaf*, ed. Shāhīn, 5:228–29, *adab*, 23, nos. 25492–510.

[51] ᶜAbd al-Razzāq, *Muṣannaf* 11:167, no. 20221; Bukhārī, *Ṣaḥīḥ*, *istiᵓdhān*, 44, *bāb al-istilqā*ᵓ; idem, *al-Adab al-mufrad, bāb al-istilqā*ᵓ, no. 1185; Abū Dāwūd, *Sunan*, *adab*, 36; Nasāᵓī, *masājid*, 28.

[52] Ibn Abī Shaybah, *Muṣannaf*, ed. Shāhīn, 5:229–30, adab, 24, nos. 25511–17.

[53] Aḥmad, *Musnad* 3:42; Abū Dāwūd, *Sunan*, *adab*, 36; Bazzār, apud Ibn Ḥajar al-Haytamī, *Kashf*, 2:445, *adab*, 49, *bāb idhā 'stalqā aḥadukum fa-lā yaḍa*ᶜ *iḥdā rijlayhi* ᶜ*alā al-ukhrā*; Ṭabarānī, apud Ibn Ḥajar al-Haytamī, *Majma*ᶜ, 8:100.

[54] ᶜAbd al-Razzāq, *Muṣannaf*, 11:167, no. 20221.

[55] Ibn Abī Shaybah, *Muṣannaf*, ed. Laḥḥām, 6:111, *adab*, 23.

[56] Ibn Abī Shaybah, *Muṣannaf*, ed. Shāhīn, 5:229, no. 25502 = ed. Laḥḥām, 6:112, *adab*, 23.

[57] Ibn Abī Shaybah, *Muṣannaf*, ed. Shāhīn, 5:230, no. 25514 = ed. Laḥḥām, 6:113, *adab*, 24.

[58] Bukhārī, *al-Adab al-mufrad, bāb hal yuqaddimu al-rajulu rijlahu bayna aydī aṣḥābih*, no. 1198.

[59] Bukhārī, *al-Adab al-mufrad, bāb hal yuqaddimu al-rajul rijlahu bayna yaday jalīsih*, no. 1147.

[60] Abū Dāwūd, *Sunan*, *adab*, 26. For *al-maghḍūbi* ᶜ*alayhim*, see commentaries *ad loc.* Q.1.7. I have found no evidence in the Talmud of Jews being encouraged to sit leaning back on the left hand, nor have several Talmudic scholars I have asked recalled any. References in hadith to Jewish practices are most

seemed too casual for respectfulness; however, the prohibition on leaning suggests either that more than casualness was at stake or that the opponents of casualness in the mosque took it seriously indeed.[61]

Finally, some wished to forbid one to sit with the fingers intertwined. According to a hadith report related by Aḥmad b. Ḥanbal in slightly different versions from Kufan authorities, the Prophet once pointed out a man in the mosque who was sitting with his knees raised and his fingers intertwined (*muḥtabiyan mushtabika aṣābiᶜihi baᶜḍihā fī baᶜḍ*). He commented to those with him, "When one of you is in the mosque, let him not intertwine (his fingers), for intertwining (*tashbīk*) is of Satan. So long as you are in the mosque, you remain at prayer." Alternatively, he said (with stronger emphasis on prayer), "When one of you prays, let him not intertwine his fingers, for intertwining is of Satan. One of you remains in prayer so long as he is in the mosque."[62] The crossed fingers presumably had some magical significance. But Bukhārī reports that the Prophet himself once intertwined his fingers (*shabbaka aṣābiᶜah*) as he said that the believers were like the bricks of a wall, reinforcing one another.[63] And Nasāʾī reports that Ibn Masᶜūd intertwined his fingers (*shabbaka bayna aṣābiᶜih*) and put them between his knees at the inclination in prayer (*rakᶜah*), expressly saying he had seen the Prophet do so.[64] The campaign to forbid intertwining the fingers, whether in prayer or simply in sitting, appears to have failed.

Once the newcomer had taken his place in the circle or in the next rank outside it, he was supposed to remove his sandals and put them to his left side.[65] As one put on the right sandal first, then the left, so also one put off the left one first, then the right.[66] Furthermore, one was not to put them on or take them off while standing.[67]

Proper Dress and Other Rules

As indicated by Abū Ṣāliḥ's desire for two white garments, traditionists were recommended to wear white.[68] For example, Ibn Mājah successively quotes the Prophet as telling his Companions, "The best of your clothing is white, so wear it and

often intended to suggest that Muslims should do otherwise. Usually, neither archaeology nor the non-Islamic literary record confirms that the Jews actually had the practice in question. See G. Vajda, "Juifs et musulmans selon le hadīth," *Journal asiatique* 229 (1937):57–127, esp. 62–63, 83.

[61] In Egypt in the 1980s, some Christians urged me to uncross my legs while holding the Bible, and a son would normally refrain from crossing his legs in the presence of his father.

[62] Aḥmad b. Ḥanbal, *Musnad* 3:42–43, 54.

[63] Bukhārī, *Ṣaḥīḥ*, *ṣalāh*, 88.

[64] Nasāʾī, *Sunan*, *masājid*, 27.

[65] Bukhārī, *al-Adab al-mufrad*, *bāb ayna yaḍaᶜu naᶜlayhi idhā jalas*, no. 1190.

[66] Mālik, *Muwaṭṭaʾ*, rec. Yaḥyā, 2:717, *libās*, 7; ᶜAbd al-Razzāq, *Muṣannaf*, 11:166, no. 20215; Bukhārī, *Ṣaḥīḥ*, *libās*, *bāb yanzaᶜu naᶜl al-yusrā* and *bāb lā yamshī fī naᶜl wāḥid*; Muslim, *libās*, *bāb istiḥbāb lubs al-naᶜl*; Abū Dāwūd, *Sunan*, *libās*, 44; Tirmidhī, *Jāmiᶜ*, *libās*, *bāb bi-ayyi rijl yabdaʾu idhā 'ntaᶜal*; Ibn Mājah, *libās*, *bāb lubsu 'n-niᶜāli wa-khalᶜuhā*; Ibn Ḥibbān, *al-Iḥsān fī taqrīb Ṣaḥīḥ Ibn Ḥibbān*, 18vols., ed. Shuᶜayb al-Arnāʾūṭ and Ḥusayn Asad (Beirut: Muʾassasat al-Risālah, 1984–91), 12:270–71, no. 5455, 275, no. 5461.

[67] Abū Dāwūd, *Sunan*, *libās*, 44; no. 4135; Tirmidhī, *Jāmiᶜ*, *libās*, 31.

[68] See Tritton, *Materials*, 59, for disagreement.

wrap your dead in it," "Wear clothes of white, for it shows more clearly and is purer (*aṭyab*)," and "The best [clothing] in which to visit God in your cemeteries and mosques is white."[69] The famous Baghdadi renunciant Bishr al-Ḥāfī (d. 227/841) was said to have been kept out of the mosque by the doorkeepers, who had mistaken him for a beggar.[70] Presumably this was for wearing clothes not up to the standard of traditionists. Naturally, white conflicted with Abbasid black, worn at court and by qadis. Sufyān al-Thawrī (d. 161/778) is quoted as saying, "Whoever sees a black cloak (*khirqah*), let him trample it and not touch it at all."[71] The most traumatic single incident, that finally reduced Aḥmad b. Ḥanbal to tears, occurred when he was brought before the caliph and his son at Samarra and his own garment was taken off and replaced with a black cloak.[72] One suspects that Abbasid custom provoked traditionists to harden their call for white.

As for headgear, turbans are recommended but there are many variations of form and color, and strong local custom must have prevented traditionists from ascribing to the Prophet any strong endorsement of one. In the early second/eighth century, for example, the jurisprudents of Basra all wore a *miẓallah*, a type of headgear which served to shield one from the sun. When Shuᶜbah (d. 160/776) showed up not wearing one, perhaps shortly after transferring there from Wāsiṭ, Yūnus b. ᶜUbayd (d. 139/756–57?) warned him not to leave it at home.[73] I have not come across any prophetic precedent for the *miẓallah*.

A widely reported rule is that one should salute both on joining a circle and, unless it is breaking up altogether, on leaving it again.[74] Aḥmad b. Ḥanbal adds a report by which someone leaving the circle refrained from saluting because the Prophet was still speaking. His refraining was not taken as politeness, for the Prophet complained when he was gone, "How quickly comes forgetting."[75]

It was forbidden to sit at the edge of the shade. Ibn Abī Shaybah quotes seven hadith reports, two prophetic, against sitting at the edge of the shade or between sun and shade, that being the place where Satan sits.[76] Aḥmad b. Ḥanbal quotes one such hadith report.[77] Abū Dāwūd reports that the Prophet enjoined his Companions to get up if the sun shifted such that one was partly in shade, partly in sun, and once commanded a man to move who took up such a place while the Prophet was

---

[69] Ibn Mājah, *Sunan*, *adab*, 5. Many further references in A. J. Wensinck, *A Handbook of Early Muhammadan Tradition* (Leiden: E. J. Brill, 1927), s.v. "Clothes, white – preferable."

[70] al-Khaṭīb al-Baghdādī, *Tārīkh*, 13:227–28.

[71] Aḥmad b. Ḥanbal (attrib.), *Kitāb al-Waraᶜ*, ed. Muḥammad al-Sayyid Basyūnī Zaghlūl (Beirut: Dār al-Kitāb al-ᶜArabī, 1988), 79, no. 355.

[72] Ṣāliḥ b. Aḥmad, *Sīrat al-imām Aḥmad b. Ḥanbal*, ed. Fuʾād ᶜAbd al-Munᶜim Aḥmad (Alexandria: Muʾassasat Shabāb al-Jāmiᶜah, 1984), 102.

[73] Aḥmad b. Ḥanbal, *ᶜIlal*, ed. ᶜAbbās, 3:142–43 = *Jāmiᶜ*, ed. Bayḍūn, 2:136.

[74] The hadith report usually concludes, "the first has no better claim than the second": Aḥmad, *Musnad* 2:230, 287, 439; Bukhārī, *al-Adab al-mufrad*, *bāb al-taslīmu idhā qāma mina 'l-majlis*, no. 463; Abū Dāwūd, *Sunan*, *adab*, 150, no. 5208, Tirmidhī, *Jāmiᶜ*, *al-istiʾdhānu wa-'l-adab*, 15.

[75] Aḥmad b. Ḥanbal, *Musnad*, 3:438.

[76] Ibn Abī Shaybah, *Muṣannaf*, ed. Shāhīn, 5:268–69, *adab*, 101, nos. 25948–54.

[77] Aḥmad b. Ḥanbal, *Musnad*. 3:413–14.

preaching.[78] Without reference to Satan's place of sitting, Aḥmad b. Ḥanbal disliked that a teacher should sit in the shade while his auditors copied in the sun, once reproaching someone for doing this. "Do not do it again," he said, "but sit with the people."[79]

Three Centuries Later

The rules for proper teaching laid out in ninth-century hadith remained in effect for centuries, as is evident in the book on the etiquette of giving and taking dictation by ᶜAbd al-Karīm al-Samᶜānī (d. Marv, 562/1166). Most of the same rules reappear; to wear white, to sit with knees drawn up, to face the *qiblah*, to lay one's sandals to the left, and not to make another give up his place among others.[80] This is as one would expect: once the sound hadith had been sorted out and the law justified on their basis, the main point of studying hadith was to reproduce the experience of virtuous Muslims in the past, or at least to establish oneself at the end of a chain of virtuous Muslims reaching back to the Prophet. It was religiously satisfying to hear prophetic hadith in just the manner of the Companions' hearing it.[81]

As one also expects, there are nonetheless some differences between Samᶜānī's presentation and practice in the ninth century. Sometimes, Samᶜānī lays down as a rule what was only becoming general in the ninth century; for example, to relate hadith directly from one's notebook, not from memory.[82] Aḥmad b. Ḥanbal almost never dictated hadith without his notebook at hand, but no one asserted that this had been the normal practice a century before.[83] Other rules laid down by Samᶜānī plainly reflect the greater formality and differentiation one would expect three centuries later; for example, rules for checking the auditors' notes and for the *mustamlī* who repeats what the *shaykh* has said so that a large number may hear.[84] Missing from Samᶜānī's account are attempts to distinguish Islamic practice from that of Jews, Christians, and *aᶜājim*.

---

[78] Abū Dāwūd, *Sunan*, *adab*, 15. Although Abū Dāwūd puts it in his *bāb fī al-julūs bayna al-ẓill wa'l-shams*, the second report does not expressly mention shade; therefore, it might have originally had to do with a discouraged austerity, deliberately staying in the hot sun, on which see further Ignaz Goldziher, "De l'ascétisme aux premiers temps de l'Islam," *Revue de l'histoire des religions* 37 (1898):159–69, at 165; Mālik, *Muwaṭṭaʾ*, 2:387, *al-nudhūr wa-'l-aymān*, 4; Bukhārī, *Ṣaḥīḥ*, *aymān*, *bāb al-nadhr fīmā lā yamliku wa-fī maᶜṣiyah*.

[79] Tritton, *Materials*, 157, citing al-Khaṭīb al-Baghdādī, *Tārīkh Baghdād*, 14:22.

[80] Samᶜānī, *Adab*, 29–30 (white), 36 (*qurfuṣāʾ*), 44 (*qiblah*), 123 (sandals), 126–27 (make another give up).

[81] For the religious significance of hadith, see Aziz al-Azmeh, "Muslim Genealogies of Knowledge," *History of Religions* 31 (1992):403–11, stressing reproduction, and William A. Graham, "Traditionalism in Islam," *Journal of Interdisciplinary History* 23 (1992–93):495–522, stressing the chain through time.

[82] Samᶜānī, *Adab*, 46–48.

[83] Abū Nuᶜaym, *Ḥilyah*, 9:165.

[84] Samᶜānī, *Adab*, 77–79 (notes), 84–100 (*mustamlī*).

Conclusions

When one comes across an exposition of Islamic law in dialogue form, as in Shāfiᶜī's *Kitāb al-Umm*, or Shaybānī's *Kitāb al-Aṣl*, one infers a literary convention rather than actual composition by the recording of conversation.[85] Still, it is pleasing to be able to picture the scene in the mosque that originally gave rise to the literary convention. Descriptions of how the Prophet sat with his Companions are naturally about ideals, not observed reality; however, because these particular ideals make such modest demands, we may reasonably infer that they roughly describe ninth-century practice as well. Responsiveness to objections, as when the prohibition of intertwining the fingers was abandoned, also suggests a fairly close correspondence between ideal and reality. Disagreements show how Muslims interpreted their culture, as in the insistence that one not sit as Jews do.

It is notoriously difficult to date hadith reports unless one simply assumes that *isnāds* (chains of transmitters attached to hadith reports) are reliable.[86] Examination of the *isnāds* for the hadith reports cited here confirms my impression that they become progressively less meaningful the further back in time one goes. Traditionists often transmitted hadith by paraphrase (*al-riwāyah bi'l-maᶜnā*) rather than verbatim (*ar-riwāyah bi'l-lafẓ*); and feedback from contemporaries (by which a hadith report with one *isnād* picked up wording from another report with its own distinct *isnād*) was not rare. Scholars commonly work on the assumption that a report contradicting later orthodoxy is likely to be early, while a report confirming it more likely to be a retrojection. This principle would suggest that discussions among eighth-century wise men and observations of how they conducted themselves were an older source of norms than the documented practice of the Prophet himself. In other words, one sees in ᶜAbd al-Razzāq and Ibn Abī Shaybah, with their continual appeal to the doctrine and practice of eighth-century jurisprudents, an earlier stage of the development of Islamic law than one sees in the Six Books, which appeal almost exclusively to the doctrine and practice of the Prophet. Inferring the law from the behavior of its wisest teachers is consistent with Rabbinic Jewish practice. This, together with disappearing polemics about distinguishing the Muslims from the Jews, suggests that the matrix for the material in Ibn Abī Shaybah and ᶜAbd al-Razzāq was more likely sectarian polemics in Iraq, as Wansbrough has suggested for other material, than the Medina of Islamic tradition.[87]

---

[85] See Norman Calder, *Studies in Early Muslim Jurisprudence* (Oxford: Clarendon Press, 1993), 8–12, 49–53, chap. 7, et passim.

[86] The skeptical case (expressly contra van Ess but also against Juynboll, Motzki, and others) is put by Michael Cook, *Early Muslim Dogma* (Cambridge: Cambridge University Press, 1981), Chap. 11, "The Dating of Traditions." For a survey of the authenticity debate, see now Herbert Berg, *The Development of Exegesis in Early Islam* (Richmond, Surrey: Curzon Press, 2000), esp. chap. 1.

[87] For Jewish law inferred from the behavior of rabbis, see, for example, Jacob Neusner, "Judaism," in *Sacred Texts and Authority*, ed. Jacob Neusner (Cleveland: Pilgrim Press, 1998), 1–30. For sectarian polemics in Iraq as the matrix of Islamic religious culture, see John Wansbrough, *The Sectarian Milieu* (Oxford: Oxford University Press, 1978); more transparently, Andrew Rippin, "Literary Analysis of Qur'ān, Sira and Tafsir: the Methodologies of John Wansbrough," in *Approaches to Islam in Religious Studies*, ed. Richard C. Martin (Tucson: University of Arizona Press, 1985), 151–63, 227–32, also *idem*,

Finally, prescriptions of how to sit in the mosque are useful in characterizing Islamic law. Rules about sitting in the mosque are presented in the same style, with the same safeguards against imposture, as rules about, for example, sales, inheritance, and retaliation for homicide. Breaches of etiquette are notoriously detected and punished more swiftly and surely than breaches of the moral law. Thus, prescriptions of proper etiquette make it difficult to distinguish "legal" from "non-legal" concerns in books of Islamic law even by the criterion of consequences in the world: the Muslim gauche enough to sit down in the middle of a circle must normally have seen consequences a great deal sooner than if he had deliberately neglected to wash before that morning's dawn prayer, or even if he had committed a grievous sin such as adultery half an hour before.[88] The law treats all of life.

"Quranic Studies, part IV: Some Methodological Notes," *Method and Theory in the Study of Religion* 9 (1997):39–46.

[88] The most sophisticated attempt to distinguish between legal and non-legal concerns in Islamic law has been Baber Johansen, *Contingency in a Sacred Law* (Leiden: Brill, 1998).

2
MUSLIM EDUCATION

Ignaz Goldziher

1. Education in the early history of Islām.—The value set upon education in Islām is indicated by certain *hadīth* sayings which, though they may have no claim to rank as authentic, yet undoubtedly reflect the educational ideals of Islām in its early days, and may be taken as representing the prevailing views of the first generations. Thus it is handed down as a saying of the Prophet himself, that 'A father can confer upon his child no more valuable gift than a good education'; and, again, 'It is better that a man should secure an education for his child than that he bestow a *ṣā'* in charity.'* The boon thus commended extends also to slaves. It is regarded as a work of specially meritorious character 'to educate a slave-girl well, then set her free, and give her to a husband.'[1]

It may be safely said that Islām raised the Arabs to a higher level of civilization, and at the same time introduced amongst them the elements of education, in which they had hitherto been rather deficient.[2] That Muhammad himself—partly, it may be, on utilitarian grounds—attached considerable importance to the acquisition of the most indispensable elements of knowledge, may be inferred from the conditions on which he released prisoners of war after his victory at Badr. He employed several Quraish captives to teach the boys of Medīna to write, and this service counted as their ransom. Twelve boys were assigned to each of the Meccan prisoners who were capable of giving the required instruction, and, as soon as the pupils had attained the stipulated degree of progress, their teachers were set at liberty.[3] The Quraish, as a people largely engaged in commerce, had naturally more occasion to practise writing than the date-planters and husbandmen of Medīna,[4] and it was, therefore, easier to find penmen among them than in Yathrib—a consideration which may perhaps also dispose us to accept the view held by certain Muslim theologians,[5] though condemned as heresy by the orthodox school, viz. that Muhammad was not the 'illiterate' that Muslim orthodoxy, with its mistaken interpretation of the epithet *ummī*, tries to make out.[6] Mention is even made of a list of contemporary Meccan women who were familiar with the art of writing; but this group did not include the youthful 'Ā'isha, who, though she had the advantage over her companions in being able to read, yet had never learned writing.[7] We may, therefore, infer that among the men of Mecca the ability to write was nothing out of the common.[8] Mu'āwiya distinguished himself as the Prophet's secretary. Penmanship was not quite so common among the Arabs of Medīna. To the Khazrajite Ubaiy b. Ka'b, who made a name for himself by recording the revelations of the Prophet, is ascribed the exceptional distinction of having been skilled in penmanship before the rise of Muhammad.[9] In Medīna, those who, in addition to certain other accomplishments, possessed also the art of writing—acquired perhaps from the Jews resident there[10]—were deemed worthy of the title of *kāmil* ('perfect').[11]

It would also appear that, once the young Muslim community had been constituted, a primitive system of education, embracing at least the bare elements of knowledge, was set on foot. In no long time we begin to meet with references to the *kuttāb* ('elementary school'). We would cer-

* Tirmidhī, *Ṣaḥīḥ*, Cairo, A.H. 1292, i. 354.

1 Bukhārī, *Kitāb al-'atq*, no. 16; Jāḥiẓ, *Kitāb al-ḥayawān*, Cairo, A.H. 1323, i. 28, mentions a slave-girl who was conversant with Euclid.

2 Cf. the present writer's *Muh. Studien*, i. (Halle, 1889) 112.

3 Sprenger, *Mohammad*, Berlin, 1861–9, iii. 131; D. S. Margoliouth, *Mohammed and the Rise of Islam*, London, 1905, p. 270, at foot.

4 Cf. Caetani, *Annali dell' Islam*, Milan, 1907, ii. 702 ff.

5 *e.g.* the Andalusian Abu-l-Walīd al-Bājī († A.H. 474 = A.D. 1081), who incurred great hostility in consequence; cf. the present writer's *Ẓāhiriten*, Leipzig, 1884, p. 171, note 1; Dhahabī, *Mīzān al-i'tidāl*, Lucknow, A.H. 1301, ii. 41, *s.v.* ''Abdallāh b. Sahl of Murcia' († A.H. 480 = A.D. 1087); 'Between him and Abu-l-Walīd al-Bājī there were great disputes over the writing question.'

6 On this question, see Nöldeke-Schwally, *Gesch. d. Qorans*², i. (Leipzig, 1909) 12.

7 Balādhorī, ed. de Goeje, Leyden, 1870, p. 472.

8 Cf. Lammens, 'La République marchande de la Mècque,' p. 24 (*Bull. de l'inst. égyp.*, 1910, p. 46, note 7).

9 Ibn Sa'd, III. ii. 59; Caetani, *op. cit.* iv. 201.

10 Balādhorī, 473.

11 Cf. the passages quoted by Lammens, *Études sur le règne du Calife Mo'āwiya*, Beirūt, 1906, p. 630; also *Aghānī*, ii. 169, at foot; Ṭabarī, *Annales* (ed. Leyden, 1879 ff.), i. 1207, where the reference is not to Arabs in general, but to natives of Medīna. For the full connotation of *kāmil*, see Ibn Sa'd, v. 309, line 7 ff.

tainly not lay much stress upon the mention of a 'companion' called Mirdās,[1] and surnamed *al-mu'allim* ('the teacher'),[2] as there is but little evidence to show that such a person ever existed.[3] Even in the early period, however, we find better attested notices of the *kuttābs* and the *mu'allims* who taught in them. Umm Salīm, mother of Anas b. Mālik, the Prophet's attendant (or, according to other accounts, Umm Salama, one of the Prophet's wives), asks a *mu'allim kuttāb* to send her some schoolboys—preferably of the slave class—to assist her in wool-carding.[4] 'Amr b. Maimūn al-'Audī († c. A.H. 74–77 = A.D. 693–6) gives the text of an apotropæic formula which the 'companion' Sa'd b. abī Waqqāṣ taught his children, 'as the teacher instructs his scholars in writing.'[5] Another reference tells how Abū Huraira, Ibn 'Omar, and Abū Usaid (who fought at Badr) on one occasion passed by a *kuttāb*, and attracted the attention of the boys.[6] There is also evidence to show that the *lauḥ* (tablet for practice in reading and writing) was in use at a very early period; the female 'companion' Umm al-Dardā writes on such a tablet some wise sentences as reading lessons for a boy ('Abd Rabbihi b. Sulaimān b. 'Omar).[7]

Elementary education seems to have been thoroughly established in Islām by the early Umayyad period.[8] It is true that we cannot decide whether sound evidence on this point can be drawn from an anecdote telling how the facetious grammarian Sa'd b. Shaddād jocularly sold the pupils of his elementary school as slaves to 'Ubaidallāh b. Ziyād, governor of 'Irāq.[9] We are on surer ground when we read that the poet Kumait and the formidable vicegerent and commander Ḥajjāj b. Jūsuf were schoolmasters—the last-named, of course, in the years before his remarkable political career. Just before the time of Ḥajjāj, again, Jubair b. Ḥayya taught in a school at Ṭā'if, and likewise rose afterwards—in 'Irāq—to high rank, being promoted by Ziyād from the position of a clerk to that of administrator of Iṣfahān.[10] Ḍaḥḥāq b. Muzāḥim († A.H. 105 = A.D. 723) kept a *kuttāb* in Kūfa, making no charge for instruction.[11] In the 2nd cent. A.H.—the date cannot be fixed more precisely—we even hear of a Bedawi of the tribe of Riyāḥ who settled as a *mu'allim* in Baṣra, and conducted a school for payment (*bil-ujra*).[12] There is, of course, nothing surprising in the fact that in the lands conquered by Islām, such as 'Irāq, a Muslim system of education should take root and develop in the centres of an older civilization; but the foregoing references to schools in Arabia proper are more pertinent to the subject in hand.

Even in the early Umayyad period the education of the young princes at court had reached a high standard of excellence, but it is not necessary here to describe it in detail. A spirited account of it, dealing with all its phases, and furnished with copious references to sources, has been given by H. Lammens, and we need only call the reader's attention to his work.[1] The *mu'addib* ('instructor') was a standing figure at the Umayyad court, and was admirably supported in his work by the fathers of the princes.

'Omar II. took his children severely to task when they violated the rules of grammar.[2] He had, in his own youth, a most lugubrious *mu'addib*, and the ascetic character of the future khalif might perhaps have been anticipated from the fact that this tutor is described as a person negligent of externals; he wore a coat that reached to his heels, and his moustache hung down over his lips[3]—a trait at variance with Arabic ideas of elegance, which, in accordance with a primitive *sunna*, enjoined the trimming of the moustache (*qaṣṣ al-shārib*).[4]

The development of scientific knowledge under the Abbāsids in the 2nd cent. A.H. naturally carried with it a corresponding advance in preparatory education. There is also evidence of the fact that the younger generation were encouraged, by the prospect of public recognition, to give themselves heart and soul to the task of acquiring the elements of learning. It is recorded that in the early years of this period deserving pupils of the elementary schools in Baghdad were rewarded by being carried through the streets on camels and having almonds thrown to them. It was on an occasion of this kind that the poet 'Akawwak lost his sight, his eyes having been seriously injured by the almonds meant for the clever scholars. In this period, moreover, we find mention of institutions for higher education (*majālis al-adab*).[5] About the same time the Fāṭimid administration, now established in Egypt, took steps towards founding academies (*dār al-ḥikma* or *al-'ilm*) in Cairo, where the theological tenets of the Shī'ite school, as also—in eclectic fashion—the rich stores of learning inherited from the Greeks and the Persians, were studied. When the Fāṭimid dynasty was overthrown, the Ayyūbids superseded their academies by high schools conducted on Sunnite principles, and the wide spaces of the mosques were utilized for teaching purposes. This use of the mosque as a *madrasa* had a notable influence upon the architecture of the mosque itself.[6] The sultanates under the sway of the Abbāsids continued to vie with one another in the promotion of higher education—largely confined, it is true, to theology and its subsidiary sciences[7]—as also in the erection of suitable *madrasas*,[8] which find mention from the 4th cent. onwards. An epoch-making advance in the development of the higher school was made by the enlightened Seljūk vizier Niẓām al-mulk (middle of 5th cent. A.H. = 11th cent. A.D.), whose institutions—the *Niẓāmiyya*-academies—in various parts of the empire were devoted chiefly to the higher theological studies.[9] In the same period, however, we note a growing tendency to free the studies of the *madrasas* from their theological onesidedness. Separate institutions were founded, and became famous, for the study of the exact sciences. The observatories which sprang up everywhere became centres for the teaching of astronomy, while the numerous

1 Ibn Ḥajar, *Iṣāba*, no. 2008, iii. 818 (Calcutta ed.).

2 This title might also, as in Ibn Sa'd, III. ii. 103, lines 7–9, signify one who instructed the people in the citation of the Qur'ān.

3 The doubtful traditions referring to him are given by Suyūṭī, *Al-La'ālī al-maṣnū'a fi-l-aḥādīth al-mauḍū'a*, Cairo, A.H. 1317, i. 107.

4 Bukhārī, *Diyāt*, no. 27.

5 *Ib.* no. 24.

6 Ibn Sa'd, IV. i. 133, line 4; cf. the present writer's *Vorlesungen uber d. Islam*, Heidelberg, 1910, p. 148, at top.

7 Nawāwī, *Tahdhīb*, ed. Wüstenfeld. Göttingen, 1842–47, p. 860, line 6 from foot.

8 Kremer, *Culturgesch. d. Orients unter d. Chalifen*, Vienna, 1875–7, ii. 132.

9 In Suyūṭī, *Bughjat al-wu'āt*, Cairo, A.H. 1326, p. 253.

10 Ibn Ḥajar, *Iṣāba*, i. 460.

11 Ibn Sa'd, vi. 210, line 12.

12 Yāqūt, *Dict. of Learned Men*, ed. Margoliouth, 1909 ff. (*Gibb Memorial Series*, vi.), ii. 239.

1 *Études sur le règne du Calife Mo'āwiya*, p. 331 ff.

2 Yāqūt, ed. Margoliouth, i. 25, at the foot.

3 Ibn Qutaiba, *'Uyūn al-akhbār*, ed. Brockelmann, Berlin, 1900 ff. (in the series *Semitische Studien*, ed. C. Bezold), p. 351, line 15.

4 Bukhārī, *Libās*, no. 63.

5 *Aghānī*, xviii. 101.

6 See Max v. Berchem, art. 'Architecture,' in *Spécimen d'une encyclopédie musulmane*, Leyden, 1890, col. 16; also artt. ARCHITECTURE (Muhammadan in Syria and Egypt), above, vol. i. p. 757 f., and ART (Muhammadan), p. 878 f.

7 For Muslim higher education in the periods referred to, cf. Haneberg, *Über d. Schul- u. Lehrwesen d. Muhammedaner im Mittelalter*, Munich, 1856; Kremer, ii. 479 ff.; Winand Fell, *Über d. Ursprung u. d. Entwickelung d. höhern Unterrichtswesens bei d. Muhammedanern* (*Program d. Marzellen-Gymnasiums in Köln*, for the year 1882–83).

8 Important data regarding the older types of *madrasa* which preceded the *Niẓāmiyya*-schools are found in Subkī, *Ṭabaqāt al-Shāfi'iyya*, Cairo, A.H. 1324, iii. 137.

9 Julian Ribera, 'Origen del Colegio Nidami de Bagdad,' in *Homenaje a Francisco Codera*, Saragossa, 1904.

hospitals now being instituted—served as they were by the most renowned physicians of the day—attracted students of medical science, as is shown by numerous references in Ibn abī Uṣaibi'a's *Biographies of the Physicians*. In the present article, however, we propose to confine our discussion largely to elementary education.

2. The subjects of primary education; forbidden books.—In a series of sayings showing no trace of theological influence, advice is given regarding the subjects which should have a place in the education of children. Khalīf 'Omar I., for instance, is said to have counselled parents in these words: 'Teach your children to swim and to throw darts; charge them that they must be able to mount a horse securely, and make them recite appropriate verses.'[1] 'Omar was himself a renowned horseman, and is said, in picturesque phrase, to have sat in the saddle 'as if he had been created on the horse's back.'[2] Amongst these attainments the art of swimming was specially prized. Khalīf 'Abdalmalik gave his sons' tutor the following injunction: 'Teach them to swim, and accustom them to sleep little.'[3] Ḥajjāj (who, according to another report, laid most emphasis upon the religious training of his children, and therefore refused to engage a Christian teacher)[4] gave a similar charge to the preceptor whom he had selected for his sons: 'Instruct them in swimming before you teach them writing, for they can at any time easily find one who will write for them, but not one who will swim for them.' Jāḥiẓ, to whom we owe this item of information about Ḥajjāj, supplies further details indicative of the importance attached to the art of swimming in the educational practice of the higher ranks. A saying of Ibn al-Tau'am commends writing, arithmetic, and swimming as the accomplishments which, above all others, a prudent father should seek to procure for his children. As between writing and arithmetic, the latter should have precedence, since it is not only of more value in business, but is actually more easily learned, while its eventual advantages are also greater.[5] The traditional view, with a slight variation, finds expression in a modern Arabic proverb current in 'Irāq: 'Learn to write, to make the calamus, and to swim in the river.'[6]

It would, of course, be absurd to suppose that the educational maxims which assign so prominent a place to swimming had their origin in Arabia, as that country could provide but few opportunities for practising the art.[7] The present writer is of opinion that—as is suggested by the grouping together of riding, dart-throwing, and swimming—such educational ideals were largely influenced by foreign, and especially Persian and Greek, views; and, indeed, the pedagogic maxims in question are but the echoes of such views.[8] In especial, the importance ascribed to swimming is doubtless to be traced to Greek ideas: to be able 'neither to swim nor to read' (μήτε νεῖν μήτε γράμματα [Plato, *Leg.* iii. 689 D]) was a Greek equivalent for the absolute lack of culture. It was likewise under the same influence that swimming found a place in the educational maxims of the Talmud.[9]

The subjects recommended in the sayings just quoted form no part of the distinctively Muslim theory of education, which was governed by principles of an entirely different character. The general course of training for young males is set forth in the *ḥadīth* as follows:

'On the seventh day after the child's birth, the *'aqīqa* ("hair-cutting," together with the sacrifice of an animal) is performed, and he receives his name and is made secure against all harm; when he is six years old, his education begins; at the age of nine, he is given a separate sleeping-place; at thirteen years of age, he receives corporal punishment when he omits his prayers; at sixteen, his father gives him in marriage, then grasps him by the hand and says: "My son, I have trained you and had you taught, and I have given you in marriage: now I beseech God for help against your temptations in this world, and against your being punished in the Last Judgment."'[1]

As regards the elementary curriculum in particular, the relevant sources furnish us with the following details. When the child begins to speak, he should be taught to repeat the Muslim article of belief, *Lā ilāha ill' Allāh*; he must then learn the words of Qur'ān, xxiii. 117*b*: 'Exalted is Allah, the king in truth; there is no god but Him, the Lord of the stately throne of Heaven'; then the 'throne-verse' (*āyat al-kursī*, ii. 256), and the last two verses of sūra lix. (*sūrat al-ḥashr*): 'He is Allah; there is no deity but Him, the Holy King,' etc. Those who teach their children so will not be brought to judgment by God.[2] At the age of seven, when the child becomes responsible for the *ṣalāt*, he is to be sent to school, and the teacher must begin to instruct him systematically in the Qur'ān itself. Children should not be sent to school before the age of seven, as is the practice of some parents, who wish merely to spare themselves the trouble of looking after their offspring.[3] The teaching of the Qur'ān should be combined with instruction in the more important religious precepts and usages: the proper response to the *adhān*, the different kinds of washings, the prayers in the mosque to which children should be taken whenever possible; they must without fail be familiarized with the practice of joint-prayer (*ṣalāt al-jamā'a*), even in the school, where one of the older boys acts for the time as leader in prayer (*imām*). Instruction in reading and writing, of course, must also be proceeded with. The children practised writing on tablets (*lauḥ*, pl. *alwāḥ*); the words employed were usually taken from passages in the Qur'ān.

Ibn Jubair († A.H. 614 = A.D. 1217), in his sketch of the state of education in Damascus, says that in the elementary schools of that city—where writing (*taktīb*) and recitation (*talqīn*) of the Qur'ān were taught by different masters—the passages for exercise in reading and writing were taken, not from the Qur'ān, but from poetical texts of secular character, as the act of wiping inspired words from the tablets seemed to cast dishonour upon the sacred book.[4] The cleansing (*maḥw*) of the tablets marked the close of the first period of morning school: the allotted hour for this was eight o'clock a.m., and the teacher must then grant a short pause (*tasrīḥ*, 'leave').[5] For the act of wiping the *alwāḥ*, when they contained verses of the Qur'ān, various precautions are recommended by the more strait-laced theologians. It must be performed in a clean and well-guarded place, not open to be trodden upon, so that the water used in wiping out the sacred words shall not subsequently suffer any desecration. The best way to dispose of the water is to pour it into a river or a pit, or to collect it in a vessel for those who wish to use it medicinally,[6] as it is believed to possess magical virtues. A pious resident of Cairo, Muhammad Tāj al-dīn († A.H. 707 = A.D. 1307), who founded a school in the Qarāfa, inserted in the deed of foundation a clause to the effect that the water used in that institution for cleansing the *alwāḥ* was to be poured upon his grave.[7] Even the pieces of rag with which the tablets were wiped must be wrung out with the greatest care, lest the water that dripped from them should be profaned.[8]

Concurrently with exercises in reading and writing from the Qur'ān, the pupils were taught the rudiments of arithmetic. To these were added

[1] Mubarrad, *Kāmil*, ed. Wright, Leipzig, 1874, p. 150.
[2] Jāḥiẓ, *Bayān*, ii. 54, line 8 from foot.
[3] Mubarrad, p. 77, line 6.
[4] *Aghānī*, xviii. 37, line 20 ff.
[5] Jāḥiẓ, *Bayān*, i. 218.
[6] Weissbach, ''Irāḳ-arab. Sprichwörter,' no. 121, in *Leipziger Semitistische Studien*, iv. (Leipzig, 1908).
[7] Lammens, *Études*, p. 330.
[8] The like holds good of the *kāmil* ideal current in Medina (see above, p. 108[b]).
[9] Bab. *Qiddūsh*. fol. 29*a*.

[1] In Ghazālī, *Iḥyā 'ulūm al-dīn*, Būlāq, A.H. 1289, ii. 198.
[2] MS in the Ducal library of Gotha (Arab.), no. 1001, fol. 34*a*.
[3] 'Abdarī, *Madkhal al-shar' al-sharīf*, Alexandria, A.H. 1293, ii. 164, line 7.
[4] Ibn Jubair, *Travels*, ed. Wright and de Goeje, *Gibb Memorial Series*, v. [1907] 272, line 17.
[5] *Revue africaine*, xli. [1897] 283, at the foot.
[6] *Madkhal*, ii. 165.
[7] Ibn Ḥajar al-'Asqalānī, *al-Durar al-kāmina* (MS in Vienna Hofbibliothek, Mixt. 245), iii. fol. 350*b*.
[8] *Madkhal*, *loc. cit.*

also legends of the prophets (*aḥādīth al-anbiyā*) and anecdotes from the lives of godly men (*ḥikāyāt al-ṣalīḥīn*).[1] In early times the parts of the *ḥadīth* most in favour for educational purposes were the legends about the *Dajjāl* (Antichrist),[2] by which are probably meant the traditions regarding the Mahdī period and the Last Things. Finally, the children had to learn selections from the poets; and with these the elementary curriculum seems to have reached its term. In an ordinance regarding the education of the young, 'Omar I. enjoined that popular proverbs (*al-amthāl al-sā'ira*) and beautiful poems should form subjects of instruction.[3] As regards the kind of poetry to be selected for children, the writers who discuss the course of elementary education are all most emphatic in demanding that moral pieces alone should be allowed, and that verse of an erotic character should be strictly excluded. It is interesting to read what the philosophers—to leave the theologians out of account—have to say on this subject.

Ibn Sīnā (Avicenna) recommends the following course of instruction: 'When the boy's limbs have become firm and he has attained to some readiness of speech, when he is able to assimilate the coherent materials of language and his ear has become perceptive, he should begin to receive instruction in the Qur'ān, the letters of the alphabet should be drawn for him to copy, and he should be taught the precepts of religion. As regards poetry, it is desirable that the boy should acquire the *rajaz* poems to begin with, and only afterwards the *qaṣīdas*, for the recitation of the *rajaz* is easier and its retention in the memory more certain, as its verses are shorter and its metre simpler. The teaching of poetry should commence with pieces which find themes in the advantage of good morals, the praise of science, the reproof of ignorance, and the rebuke of stupidity, and which enforce the honouring of one's parents, the practice of good deeds, and other noble qualities.[4]

Ibn Miskawaih reproaches parents for teaching their children to recite licentious poetry, to repeat the lies found in such poems, and to take pleasure in what they tell of vicious things and the pursuit of lewdness, as, *e.g.*, the poems of Imru-ul-Qais, al-Nābigha, and others like them; 'one so taught will go to live with princes, who summon him to their presence in order that he may recite such poems, and even compose in a similar strain.'[5] And in the directions drawn up for the *muḥtasib* ('chief of police'), as recorded by Ibn Bassām (13th cent. A.D.), that official is charged to see that schoolboys do not learn the poems of Ibn Ḥajjāj or the *Dīwān* of Ṣarī' al-dilā, while boys who read such poems by stealth must be deterred by corporal punishment.[6]

The strictness with which the young were guarded from the influence of erotic poetry will not surprise us when we remember the attitude of the Sunnite theologians towards narrative literature of a secular stamp. In the extant *fatwā* of a fanatically orthodox theologian of the 11th cent. A.D., people are warned against the possession not only of metaphysico-theological and philosophical works, but also of poetic and entertaining writings, and especially of certain frivolous books of the day. Contracts relating to such literary products are null and void. Writings of this character should rather be destroyed by fire and water.[7] Muhammad al-'Abdarī goes so far as to maintain that a paper merchant should not sell his wares to one who, to the best of his belief, will use the paper for reproducing the stories of 'Antar or Sīdī Baṭṭāl, and similar tales, as the diffusion of such writings falls under the category of *makrūhāt* ('reprehensible things').[8]

There were, however, other grounds upon which certain kinds of poetry were withheld from the young. Thus 'Abdallāh b. Ja'far b. Abī Ṭālib forbade his children's tutor to read with them the *qaṣīdas* of 'Urwa b. al-Ward, as they might thereby be incited to leave their native soil and seek their fortunes elsewhere.[1] There is also a *ḥadīth* saying which assigns the 'books of the Christians' likewise to the class of writings that must not be taught to the young.[2]

3. Status of the elementary teacher.—The importance attached to the work of the elementary teacher—the person from whom the young received their earliest knowledge of Allāh—is by no means reflected in his social status. The prevailing attitude of Muslim society towards the teacher of children (usually called *fiqī*; in the Maghrib also *dārrār*, 'little child,' from *dhurriyya*, pl. *dharārī*) is represented in Arabic literature as one of extreme disrespect. His position is on a level with that of weavers, blood-letters, and other despised trades.[3] Teachers were universally spoken of as a stupid and brainless class. 'Seek no advice from teachers, shepherds, or those who sit much among women'[4]—an adage which, as applied to teachers and weavers, and with the addition of the explanatory clause, 'for God has deprived them of reason and withheld His blessing from their trade,' is quoted as a saying of the Prophet.[5] The phrase *'aḥmaq min mu'allim kuttāb* ('stupider than a schoolmaster')—with variations in the wording—has passed into a proverb.[6]

There is also a group of anecdotes, forming a permanent element in the Adab literature, which turn on the same point—the teacher as dunce.[7] 'How should we look for sagacity in one who is beside his wife in the evening, and in the early morning goes back to the society of little children?'[8] This contemptuous attitude found expression in the epigram:

Kafā-l-mar'a naqṣan an juqāla bi'annahu
Mu'allimu ṣibyānin wa'in kāna fāḍilā,[9]

i.e. 'It is a sufficient indication of a man's inferiority—be he never so eminent—to say that he is a teacher of children.' The teacher's occupation, in fact, works almost like a specific for generating stupidity. Ibn al-Jauzī († A.H. 597 = A.D. 1200), who wrote two books, treating respectively of 'the shrewd' and 'the stupid,' sets forth in the second of these the relative stupidity of various classes of people according to the following table:—'The rationality of women [who are universally regarded as *nāqiṣāt al-'aql wal-dīn*,[10] i.e. 'deficient in rationality and religion'] equals that of seventy weavers; that of a weaver equals that of seventy schoolmasters.'[11] When 'Abdallāh b. al-Muqaffa' was asked to give a weekly lesson to the son of Ismā'īl b. 'Alī, a dignitary of State, he refused the engagement, with the remark, 'Do you really wish me to have a place on the register (*dīwān*) of numskulls?'[12] It is not surprising, therefore, that the satirical poems directed against Ḥajjāj b. Jūsuf take full advantage of the fact that he, as well as his brother, was once a schoolmaster at Ṭā'if, and remind him of the time when he was still 'a humble slave, who early and late kept company with the village boys';[13] a person whose loaves were always of different shapes—'one without any visible rounding, another round as the full moon'—because he received them as payment from the parents of the children whom he primed with the *sūrat al-kauthar*.[14]

This literary mockery of the elementary teacher, however, was not so damaging as the scorn which found its way into the *ḥadīth* in the form of sayings ascribed to the Prophet; for here the criticism was no longer confined to humorous sallies against the

[1] Ibn al-'Arabī, in 'Abdarī, iii. 311, line 15.
[2] Nawāwī, *Tahdhīb*, ed. Wüstenfeld. p. 239, line 6 from foot.
[3] Jāḥiẓ, *Bayān*, i. 213, 3 from foot.
[4] *Risālat al-siyāsa*, MS in Leyden University Library, no. 1020, fol. 67a = *Mashriq*, ix. 1074.
[5] *Tahdhīb al-akhlāq*, p. 44, foot.
[6] *Nihāyat al-rutba fī ṭalab al-ḥisba*, in *Mashriq*, x. 1085.
[7] Cf. *ZDMG* lviii. (1904) 584.
[8] *Madkhal*, iii. 127, 131, line 1.

[1] *Aghānī*, ii. 191, 9. The reference is probably to such verses as are found in the *Dīwān*, ed. Nöldeke, Göttingen, 1863, iii. verse 5 ff., v. 1 ff., vi. 7 ff., xxxii. 4.
[2] *Lisān al-'arab*, s.v. 'Bkr,' v. 145, line 3: *lā tu 'allimū abkāra aulādikum kutuba-l-naṣārā.*
[3] Cf. the present writer's art. 'Die Handwerke bei d. Arabern, in *Globus*, lxvii. (1894), no. 13.
[4] Jāḥiẓ, *Bayān*, i. 180, line 1.
[5] Dhahabī, *Mīzān al-i'tidāl*, i. 66.
[6] Burton, *Unexplored Syria*, London, 1872, i. 285, no. 132.
[7] Ibn Qutaiba, *'Uyūn al-akhbār*, p. 442; Ibn al-'Adīm, in *Thalāth rasā'il*, ed. Stambul, p. 88; the same anecdote, as told of *mollāhs* in Turkestan, appears in F. Duckmeyer, 'Unbefangene Beobachtungen aus Russisch-Turkestan,' in the *Beilage zur Münchener Allgem. Zeitung*, 1901, no. 250.
[8] Jāḥiẓ, *loc. cit.*
[9] *Muḥāḍarāt al-udabā*, Cairo, 1287, i. 29.
[10] *Musnad Aḥmed*, ii. 67, at top; *Ṣaḥīḥ Muslim*, i. 159; cf. Goldziher, *Muh. Studien*, ii. 296; the idea is elaborated in a poem ascribed to 'Alī, and found in Bahā al-dīn al-'Āmilī, *Mikhlāt*, Cairo, A.H. 1317, p. 72.
[11] *Thamarāt al-aurāq* (ed. in margin of *Muḥāḍarāt al-udabā*), i. 194 (with many anecdotes about teachers).
[12] *Muḥād. udabā*, i. 29.
[13] Mālik b. al-Raib, in Ibn Qutaiba, *Poesis*, ed. de Goeje, Leyden, 1904, p. 206, line 14; cf. Lammens, p. 360, note 2.
[14] Jurjānī, *al-Muntakhab min kināyāt al-udabā*, Cairo, 1908, p. 118.

[202] 227

intellectual poverty of teachers, but fastened with special keenness on their moral shortcomings.

'The teachers of our children are the vilest among you; the most deficient in pity for the orphan, the most churlish towards the poor.' 'What thinkest thou of teachers?' asked Abū Huraira of the Prophet, whose answer was: 'Their *dirham* is forbidden property, their livelihood is unjust gain, their speech hypocrisy.'[1]

The odium thus expressed made itself felt also in the treatment meted out to teachers. Yaḥyā b. Aktham († A.H. 243 = A.D. 857), judge under Khalīf Ma'mūn, even refused to accept teachers as satisfactory witnesses in a court of law.[2] This disqualification has been explained on the ground that the profession taught the Qur'ān for hire. But the teacher could, of course, make the retort that the judge himself takes a reward for dispensing Divine justice.[3] The hapless pedagogue gave further offence by drawing attention to the better treatment accorded to his calling among other peoples. Such comparisons evoked severe strictures from the religious standpoint, and were actually declared by the Meccan theologian, Ibn Ḥajar al-Haitamī († A.H. 973 = A.D. 1565)—on the authority of earlier writers—to be one of the recognized criteria of unbelief:[4]

'When a teacher of children says, "The Jews are a great deal better than we Muslims, for they fulfil the obligations due to the teachers of their children,"—any one who so speaks is to be regarded as a *kāfir*.'[5]

It is possible, of course, that this depreciation of the indispensable profession of teacher may be due simply to the haughtiness inherent in the Arabic race.[6] In passing judgment upon it, however, we must not forget that analogous features appear in the educational annals of Greece and Rome.[7] Moreover, it may be said in favour of Muslim society as a whole that this far from creditable attitude towards the elementary teacher was by no means universal. We know of Muhammadans of unbiased mind who made a stand against the hackneyed judgments of the populace, and attained to a more appreciative estimate of an undeservedly maligned vocation. As the representative of this point of view, we may single out Jāḥiẓ († A.H. 255 = A.D. 869), who in this, as in other matters, criticized the prejudices of the masses in an independent spirit.

Jāḥiẓ maintains that the traditional estimate of the schoolmaster held good only of those in the lowest ranks of the profession—the ignorant *fellāḥ* teachers; and he points to the men of high intellectual distinction who had taught in schools, and had in some cases exercised great influence as the instructors of princes.[8] He also cites an imposing list of illustrious scholars, poets, and theologians (Kisā'ī, Quṭrub, Kumait, etc.) who had adorned the profession, and he sets beside them a number of contemporary teachers. 'Here in Baṣra we have never had men of greater learning in various branches of science, or of more lucidity in the expression of thought, than the two teachers, Abu-l-Wazīr and Abu-l-'Adnān.' Hence it was sheer folly and crying injustice to reproach the profession as a whole with stupidity.[9]

In order to gain the prestige of authority for this more favourable view of the teacher's calling, attempts were made to trace it likewise to utterances of the Prophet himself. Al-Qurṭubī († A.H. 671 = A.D. 1272), the great commentator on the Qur'ān, gives his imprimatur to one such deliverance, viz.

'The best of men, and the best of all who walk the earth, are the teachers. When religion falls into decay, it is the teachers who restore it. Give unto them, therefore, their just recompense; yet use them not as hirelings, lest you wound their spirit. For, as often as the teacher bids the boy say, "In the name of Allāh, the merciful, the compassionate," and the boy repeats the words after him, God writes for the teacher, and for the boy and his parents, a record which shall surely save them from the Fire.'[1]

It is true that the scholar who thus lent his sanction to a *ḥadīth*[2] usually branded as apocryphal was an Andalusian. In Andalusian Islām, no doubt, a higher value was placed upon the function of the teacher than was the case in the East—a result due in great measure to the flourishing system of elementary education that had grown up in the Western khalifate.[3] Here, therefore, the alleged utterances of the Prophet in honour of teachers would tend to be more favourably received. The same thing holds good of Islām in Sicily.

Speaking of Palermo, the Arab traveller Ibn Ḥauqal († A.H. 367 = A.D. 977) puts on record that he found over three hundred elementary schools in that city, and that the inhabitants regarded their teachers 'as their most excellent and distinguished citizens,' speaking of them as 'the people of Allāh, their witnesses [before God], and their trusty friends.' It is true that Ibn Ḥauqal, in explanation of the scornful attitude towards the intellectual capacities of teachers prevalent elsewhere, adds that 'they choose this profession in order to evade enrolment in the army.'[4]

4. Payment of teachers.—As has been indicated in the foregoing, the gravamen of the strictures urged against the teaching profession from the religious side was the fact that teachers asked and took payment for giving instruction in the Qur'ān. The moral propriety of taking wages for religious teaching was a question frequently debated among Muslim jurists. It is to be presumed that in Islām, as in other religions,[5] the devout were in favour of gratuitous religious instruction. In spreading the knowledge of Divine things the teacher should have no other design (*niyya*) than that of doing a work well-pleasing to God, and thereby attaining nearness to Him. No financial consideration should attach to such 'near-bringing works' (*qurāb*), any more than—on similar grounds—to the *ādhān*,[6] the *ṣalāt*, the diffusion of the *ḥadīth*, etc. All such acts must be done only *iḥtisāban* ('for God's sake'), not *iktisāban* ('for gain'). In support of this view, and in evidence of its being the only legitimate one, there were numerous traditions to hand;[7] nor were typical examples lacking to commend its acceptance.

One such example was found in 'Abd al-Raḥmān al-Sullamī, a man of devout spirit, who had actually heard *ḥadīths* from the lips of 'Othmān and 'Alī, and who, at the time of his death (during the khalifate of 'Abdalmalik), was *imām* of a mosque in

---

1 In Zurqānī, on *Muwaṭṭa*, Cairo, A.H. 1279-80, iii. 7.

2 *Thamarāt al-aurāq*, loc. cit.

3 *'Uyun al-akhbār*, p. 91, line 9; cf. Bukhārī, *Aḥkām*, no. 17 (Qasṭallānī, x. 268).

4 *Al-I'lām bi-qawāṭi' al-islām* (ed. in margin of this writer's *Zawājir*, Cairo, A.H. 1312, ii. 74).

5 As illustrating the reverse side of the matter, we may quote what Wilhelm Burchard, a native of Saxony, who was held captive by the Turks in the 17th cent., says with regard to the position of teachers in Turkey: 'Man hält die Schulmeister in Türckey sehr wehrt und thun kein Überlast, lassen auch nicht geschehen, dass ihnen ein eintzig Leid wiederfahre, worinnen sie uns Teutschen hefftig beschämen, als da viele gar Fuszschemel aus ihren Schuldinern machen und alles Hertzeleid den armen Leuten zufügen' (W. B., *Eines in die 19 Jahr von Türcken gefangen gewesenen Sachsen auff's neu eröffnete Türckey*, Magdeburg, 1688, ²1691, cap. ix.).

6 Cf. Goldziher, *Muh. Studien*, i. 110.

7 Ussing, *Darstellung d. Erziehungs- u. Unterrichtswesens bei d. Griechen u. Römern*, Altona, 1870, p. 102.

8 The tutor sometimes took his *nisba* from a family of repute in which he had served: thus the philologist, Abū 'Amr al-Shaibānī, who taught the son of Yazīd b. Manṣūr, adopted the surname Yazīdī (Suyūṭī, *Bughjat al-wu'āt*, p. 192).

9 Jāḥiẓ, *Bayān*, i. 100 ff. = *Khams rasā'il*, Stambul, A.H. 1301, p. 187.

1 Quoted by 'Abdarī, *Madkhal*, ii. 158.

2 Ibn al-Jauzī pronounces the following verdict on this *ḥadīth*: 'It is not permissible to use this saying as an argument [in the question as to payment of teachers], for it is a concoction of Aḥmed b. 'Abdallāh al-Harawī al-Jūyibārī, who was a liar, and fabricated *ḥadīths*—a matter in which all critics of tradition agree' (MS in Leyden Univ. Library, no. 1772, fol. 132*a*). In Suyūṭī's work on spurious traditional sayings likewise, this and other similar utterances regarding *mu'allim* are marked with a warning rubric (*Al-La'ālī al-maṣnū'a fi-l-aḥadīth al-mauḍū'a*, p. 103 ff.).

3 Cf. Schack, *Poesie u. Kunst der Araber in Spanien u. Sicilien*, Berlin, 1865, i. 52; Dozy, *Gesch. d. Mauren in Spanien*, Leipzig, 1874, ii. 68.

4 *Bibl. Geogr. Arab.*, ed. de Goeje, Leyden, 1870 ff., ii. 87, top.

5 Cf. Manu, xi. 63, where the act of teaching the Veda for hire, or learning it under a paid teacher, is declared to be a sin of the second degree.

6 Goldziher, *Muh. Studien*, ii. 390.

7 These traditional testimonies were collected by the Hanbalite Ibn al-Jauzī (MS in Leyden Univ. Library, no. 1772, fol. 131*b*).

Kûfa, and in that capacity had devoted himself to teaching the Qur'ān. It is recorded that once, on coming home, he found a number of cattle which a grateful father had sent him as a honorarium for instructing his son in the sacred volume. He at once returned the gift, with the message: 'We take no payment for the Book of God.'[1] Other teachers of the Qur'ān gave similar practical expression to this point of view;[2] and, in support of the theory that religious instruction should be given *majjānan* ('gratuitously'), appeal was made also to an admonition 'from the ancient books' which, in point of fact, may be identified as a Talmudic maxim.[3]

But, while the demand for free religious teaching might be good enough as an ideal, and while some even tried to carry it into effect, it was naturally left behind in the march of practical life. It was, after all, necessary that the wretched beings who, without much moral support from their fellows, engaged in the work of teaching should at least make a bare subsistence out of it. In this, as in many other things, the religious injunction, with its ascetic ideal, could not be put in practice so ruthlessly as to maintain a universal interdict against the merest pittance of payment.[4] As a matter of fact, besides the more austere *ḥadīths*, there are others of a more humane character, and more favourable to the practice of taking wages for religious instruction; and the teacher who was not in a position to prosecute his calling for a purely spiritual reward could always derive comfort from these.[5]

Even Bukhārī himself finds a place in his *Corpus Traditionum* for a saying ascribed to Ibn 'Abbās: 'Nothing has a better right to be rewarded than [instruction in] the Book of God.' It is true that he appends to this the condition laid down by Sha'bī, viz. that the teacher may on no account negotiate for his wages, but may accept what is voluntarily given him. Bukhārī finally cites the testimony of Ḥakam b. 'Uyaina: 'I have never heard it said of any of the *fugahā* that he disapproved of the teacher's remuneration. Even Ḥasan Baṣrī paid a teacher ten dirhams.'[6] From Mālik b. Anas comes the still more decisive statement that in the holy city of Medīna none has ever taken umbrage at the teacher's receiving a reward even in this world—and that not merely as a voluntary honorarium from the parents, but as a fixed monthly fee (*mushāhara*).[7]

Accordingly the payment of teachers became the rule actually recognized in practice by Muslim law,[8] and was vindicated, with the support of the sources quoted above, by authorities of the highest repute.[9]

The adherents of the more rigid view, in giving their consent to the practice of paying teachers—this payment, however, they preferred to call *'iwaḍ* ('recompense')—sought to solace their feelings by qualifying the teacher's right by certain *pia desideria*, which, it is true, made very little difference. They appealed to the moral sense of the teacher. He must look upon his wages, not as professional emoluments, but as a gift (*fatḥ*)[10] Divinely bestowed upon him in order that he may pursue a calling well-pleasing to God.[11] The all-important thing is the inward purpose (*niyya*); he must devote himself to the work from purely spiritual motives, and without any worldly considerations whatever. To this 'Abdarī adds the naive admonition that the teacher should make no public profession of his motives, as it is quite like 'the people of our time' to take him at his word, and deprive him of his material recompense.[1] Further, he must not let his continuance at work depend rigidly upon his being paid regularly. Should his allowance cease in any particular case, he must attend all the more zealously to the children of parents who, owing to their poverty, have fallen behind in their payments.[2] From the children themselves he must not receive presents without the knowledge of their parents or guardians.[3] In general, he must be satisfied that the money tendered him is above suspicion as to its source, and that it has not been gained dishonestly, or by methods obnoxious to religious precept; he should, for instance, have nothing to do with the money of a tax-gatherer. With respect to this counsel—it was, of course, simply a wish—it is interesting to note the qualifying clause annexed to it, viz. that in such cases the teacher need not refuse money from the hands of the mother or grandmother of his pupil, so long as he can assure himself that the immediate source has the warrant of religious law.[4] But he must avoid all intercourse with fathers whose occupation is at variance with the strict demands of religion; and, as long as they make their living in that way, he must not greet them, or hold himself accountable to them.[5]

Stories of the exorbitant charges made by eminent teachers come down from every period, though it must be admitted that this applies only to those branches of learning which were not in the strict sense religious.

The grammarian Muhammad b. 'Alī al-Mabramān († A.H. 345 = A.D. 956), pupil of Mubarrad, had a name for excessive avarice. He would not give instruction in the *kitāb* of Sībūyah under a fee of one hundred dīnārs.[6] Muhammad Shams al-dīn al-Suyūṭī († A.H. 808 = A.D. 1405) charged a dirham for every line of the grammatical poem *Alfiyya*,[7] which comprises about a thousand lines.

5. School administration.—Muslim literature treats in great detail of the teacher's demeanour towards his scholars,[8] and the conditions applying to the conducting of schools. As regards the relation of teacher to pupil, the fundamental principle is the just and equal treatment of all scholars. Laith b. Mujāhid affirms that at the Day of Judgment God will subject the schoolmaster to a special interrogation as to whether he maintained strict impartiality between pupil and pupil, and that, if he is found guilty in this respect, he will be set beside the workers of iniquity.[9] A whole series of apparently trivial points relating to the child's presence in school are brought by 'Abdarī under the principle that no distinction shall be made between children of the rich and children of the poor.[10] Nor must the scholars be employed in the private service of the teacher's household, without the express sanction of their parents;[11] and from this it was argued that the teacher must not make use of orphan children for such work *under any circumstances*.[12]

It is the law in Islām that all teachers should be married;[13] a similar requirement is found in the Talmud.[14] A typical indication of the ethical standpoint of Eastern peoples is seen in the regulations designed to obviate the very suspicion of evil communications. The rule that the work of elementary teaching must be done, not at the teacher's own

1 Ibn Sa'd, vi. 120, line 3 ff.
2 *Ib.* p. 210, line 12; 213, line 14.
3 Goldziher, *Muh. Studien*, ii. 181 f.; also quoted as from 'ancient writings,' in Māwardī, *Adab al-dunyā wal-dīn*, Stambul, A.H. 1304, p. 71.
4 Cf. Lammens, *Études*, 360.
5 The *ḥadīths pro* and *con* are brought together in the Ahlwardt MSS, Berlin Royal Library, no. 145.
6 Bukhārī, *Ijāra*, no. 16. That giving instruction in the Qur'ān might have a pecuniary equivalent is shown by a story which relates how a man who was too poor to give his bride money or money's worth as a wedding-present (*mahr*) was allowed by the Prophet to teach her several sūras of the Qur'ān in lieu thereof (Bukhārī, *Nikāḥ*, no. 40; cf. Zurqānī on *Muwaṭṭa*, iii. 7).
7 The present writer has not succeeded in tracing this regulation, as cited by Mālik, in the *Muwaṭṭa*.
8 *Revue africaine*, xli. 281.
9 Kamāl Pashāhzādah wrote a special *risāla fī jawāz al-istījār 'alā ta'līm al-Qur'ān* (Ahlwardt, Berlin MSS, no. 439).
10 For this term, see *WZKM* xiii. (1899) 49.
11 'Abdarī, *Madkhal*, ii. 158, line 13.

1 *Madkhal*, ii. 159.
2 *Ib.* i. 345, line 14 ff.
3 *Ib.* ii. 161, line 17.
4 *min wajhin mastūrin bil-'ilmi* (*Madkhal*, ii. 159, at the foot).
5 *Ib.* 160, line 2.
6 Suyūṭī, *Bughyat al-wu'āt*, p. 74.
7 *Ib.* 37.
8 Ghazālī has a short paragraph on the *ādāb mu'allim al-ṣibyān* ('manners of the teacher of children') in his *Al-ādāb fi-l-dīn* (*Majmū'at*, ed. Ṣabrī al-Kurdī, Cairo, A.H. 1328, p. 67).
9 Ibn Qutaiba, *'Uyūn al-akhbār*, p. 98, line 6.
10 *Madkhal*, ii. 158, 162, 167.
11 Ibn Bassām, in *Mashriq*, x. 1084; *Rev. africaine*, xli. 283.
12 *Madkhal*, ii. 166, line 19.
13 *Ib.* 167.
14 Mishn. *Qiddûsh.* iv. 13.

residence, but in a specially appointed public place (*ḥānūt*, pl. *ḥawānīt*) within sight of the people was intended to prevent every suggestion of scandal.[1] Nor could the halls of the mosques be used for this purpose, as little children might unwittingly defile the walls and flooring of the sacred edifice. This prohibition was supported by a saying of the Prophet: 'Keep your boys and your lunatics away from your mosques'; but the precept was not strictly observed in practice. It has been a favourite custom from olden times to conjoin the elementary school and the public fountain (*sabīl*); the institution of the latter is often combined with that of a school in the upper storey (*maktab sabīl*). It is interesting to note 'Abdarī's criticism of certain practices common among teachers in his day. He holds it unworthy of the profession that a teacher, at the inauguration of his school—or afterwards, if he finds his undertaking insufficiently supported—should try to draw the attention and invite the patronage of the public by setting up placards before the school-gate. It is likewise unbecoming that a teacher, in requesting the parents to attend the school-festivals (*afrāḥ*), should in his letters of invitation (*aurāq isti'dhānāt*) flatter them with high-flown epithets and titles, or compose the invitations in verse.[2]

The pupils must also have their off-days. The school must be closed for two days of every week, viz. Thursday and Friday, and also for a period of from one to three days before and after the *'īd* festival.[3] The Thursday holiday gave occasion to the proverbial phrase, 'to be as happy as a teacher on Thursdays' (*kamā fariḥa al-mu'addib bil-khamīs*).[4] The scholars are also granted a whole or partial holiday whenever any one of them has finally mastered a section of the Qur'ān.[5] The parents of a boy who has succeeded in doing this celebrate the event by a festivity (*iṣrāfa*),[6] and bestow upon the teacher a special gift, the acceptance of which is not frowned upon even by the precisians. When a youth completes his study of the Qur'ān, the occasion is celebrated in a feast called (in Mecca) *iqlāba*, or (in the Maghrib) *takhrīja*.[7] 'Abdarī's minute account of the more extravagant—and to him obnoxious—forms sometimes assumed by these functions reveals an interesting phase of contemporary life.

The question of corporal punishment was also discussed among those with whose educational methods we are now dealing. The 'rod' is regarded as a valuable auxiliary of the teacher's art. The 'strap'—quite characteristically—becomes an object of comparison: 'In the Prophet's hand was a whip, like that used in school' (*ka-dirrat al-kuttāb*)—a simile often employed.[8] The teacher is sometimes held up to derision by being described as 'one who brandishes the whip' (*ḥāmil dirra*) and takes reward for the book of God.[9] Even the philosopher Ibn Sīnā, in his treatise on the education of children, speaks of the 'assistance of the hand' (*al-isti'āna bil-yad*) as a useful adjunct of instruction.[10] The tutors of the young sons of khalīfs did not spare the rod,[11] nor did the fathers disapprove.

Al-Mubarrad describes a scene in which the Khalīf 'Abdalmalik leads by the hand Prince Marwān, 'crying because of the whipping his teacher had given him.'[12] Abū Maryam, preceptor of the Abbāsid princes Amīn and Ma'mūn, was apparently given to a too drastic use of the ferule. On one occasion he chastised Prince Amīn so severely as to make his arm black and blue. The prince complained to his father, and showed him the maimed arm. The Khalīf invited the stern pedagogue to dinner; and when the latter, in no little apprehension, specified the offence for which the prince had been so sharply dealt with, the father reassured him with the words: 'You are at liberty even to kill him: it were better that he die than remain a fool.'[1]

A further form of punishment was 'keeping in'; but, in the one instance of this known to us, it is the father, not the teacher, who administers the correction.[2]

It was to be expected that, in order to protect the children against the undue severity of irascible masters, Muslim jurisprudence would endeavour to regulate the penalties applied, both as to their form and as to their degree. It sanctioned corporal punishment, especially for religious offences,[3] but only in the case of children over ten years of age; while, as to the amount of punishment, the extreme limit was variously laid down as between three[4] and ten 'light strokes.' Nor must the teacher resort to any instrument used by the judge in administering legal penalties (*ḥadd*). The *Madkhal* speaks severely of contemporary teachers who chastise with 'dry almond rods, bushy palm-branches, Nubian switches, and even the instrument called the *falaqa*'[5] ('stocks'), and used for the bastinado. The supervision of the teacher in this, as in other matters, was assigned to the chief of police. In the directions drawn up for this officer he is instructed to be observant of the way in which children are treated at school, and to protect them from maltreatment by hot-tempered teachers.[6]

6. **Education of girls.**—It must be borne in mind that the maxims relating to the training and instruction of the young apply only to boys (*ṣabī*). The education of girls did not fall under these rules except in one single particular, viz. that, as set forth in the police directions recorded by Ibn Bassām, the female teachers of girls (*mu'allimāt al-banāt*) are to be more strictly looked after in regard to the poetical pieces which they set before their pupils.[7] While it was deemed necessary to instruct girls in moral and religious things, there was no desire to lead them through the portals of intellectual development. Woman's proper sphere centres in the spindle,[8] and this requires no training in letters. Even the philosophic thinker and poet Abū-l-'Alā al-Ma'arrī († A.H. 449 = A.D. 1057) endorses this maxim,[9] which became a veritable household word in the ancient Muslim world. The following utterance of the Prophet regarding females—said to rest on the authority of 'Ā'isha—is frequently quoted: 'Do not let them frequent the roofs; do not teach them the art of writing; teach them spinning and the *sūrat al-nūr*.'[10] But it were surely preposterous to regard this sūra

1 Ibn Bassām, in *Mashriq*, x. 1084; *Madkhal*, ii. 163; *Rev. africaine*, xli. 281.
2 *Madkhal*, ii. 169 f.
3 *Ib.* 168.
4 Balawī, *Kitāb Alif-bā*, Cairo, A.H. 1287, i. 208.
5 *Rev. africaine*, xli. 284, at top.
6 We find also the term *ḥudhāqa* (*Madkhal*, ii. 179, line 16).
7 Snouck Hurgronje, *Mekka*, Hague, 1889, ii. 146; Marçais, *Le Dialecte arabe parlé à Tlemcen*, Paris, 1902, p. 246.
8 *Usd al-ghāba*, iii. 50, line 6; iv. 284, line 9; v. 553, line 1.
9 Yāqūt, ed. Margoliouth, i. 60, line 7 from foot.
10 *Mashriq*, ix. 1074.
11 Yāqūt, i. 223.
12 *Kāmil*, p. 578, line 11.

1 *Muḥāḍarāt al-udabā*, i. 30.
2 *Aghānī*, IX. 111, line 6 from foot.
3 In the instructions regarding the training of children it is usually stated that 'they shall receive corporal punishment for neglecting prayer from the age of thirteen' (*e.g.* Ghazālī, as above); in other versions (e.g. *Mīzān al-i'tidāl*, ii. 364) the *terminus a quo* is given as ten years.
4 The maximum of three was deduced from the *ḥadīth* by certain Mālikite theologians; see Qasṭallānī, x. 40, line 12 (on Bukhārī, *Muḥārabūn*, no. 29).
5 *Madkhal*, ii. 105. Regarding the instruments of punishment employed in Oriental schools, cf. the interesting notes, with illustrations (including the *falaqa*), in the *Rev. du monde musulman*, xiii. [1910] 420–428, and xiv. [1911] 67, from which we learn that in one Muslim country or another the various penalties mentioned by 'Abdarī were all in actual use.
6 Ibn Khaldūn, in *Mashriq*, x. 963; cf. *ib.* 966; Ibn Bassām, *ib.* 1084.
7 *Mashriq*, x. 1085.
8 Mubarrad, *Kāmil*, 150. An almost verbally identical saying of the Rabbis occurs in the Bab. Talmud, *Yōmā*, fol. 66*b*, on which cf. S. Krauss, *Talmud. Archäol.* i. (Leipzig, 1910) 558, note 260.
9 Kremer, *Culturgeschichte*, ii. 133.
10 *Mīzān al-i'tidāl*, ii. 335. This *ḥadīth* is reproduced in the *Mustadrak* of Ḥākim as an authentic saying of the Prophet.

(xxiv.) as suitable for the training of young girls, containing as it does the revelations which refer to women of known or suspected immoral life. The most emphatic warnings of all are uttered against teaching women to write. Ibn Miskawaih († A.H. 421 = A.D. 1030), in spite of all his schooling in philosophy, finds nothing strange in this prohibition. In his *Jāwidān Khirad* he adopts a pronouncement of 'Omar I. which, in counselling the stringent control of women, lays an interdict upon their being taught to write.[1]

It is told of Luqmān the sage that, when on one occasion he passed a school, and noticed that a girl was being taught, he asked, 'For whom is this sword being polished?' implying, of course, that the girl would be her future husband's ruin.[2] It is not surprising to find this view reflected in the police instructions handed down by Ibn Bassām: 'He [the teacher] must not instruct any woman or female slave in the art of writing, for thereby would accrue to them only an increase of depravity.' It is a current saying that 'a woman who is taught to write is like a serpent which is given poison to drink.'[3]

Girls must be kept from the study of poetical literature; here there is no concession whatever, such as is made in the literary education of boys.[4]

These views, however, belong rather to the sphere of ethnology than to that of religion, and it would be absurd to regard them as expressing principles inseparable from the fundamental teachings of Islām. The history of Muslim civilization, even in periods which show no deviation from the line of strict orthodoxy, would supply many a refutation of such a theory. When we bear in mind how many women had a share in the transmission of *ḥadith* works,[5] we see the untenability of the view that in religious circles the art of writing was withheld from women on principle. The daughter of Mālik b. Anas was able to correct the errors of those who recited and transmitted her father's *Muwaṭṭa*.[6] That the rule against teaching women to write was of universal validity is disproved by the very name of a learned lady of Damascus, viz. *Sitt al-kataba* ('mistress of the writers') *bint abi-l-Ṭarḥ*, who supplied Jūsūf b. 'Abdal-mu'min of Nābulūs with traditions.[7] The learned woman is found even among remote tribes in the heart of the Southern Sahara, where women are apparently not prohibited from cultivating Muslim learning.[8]

'The nomads of this region of the Sahara possess books, precisely as do the settlers; nor do they abandon them even in their wanderings; their migratory habits do not prevent their devoting themselves to intellectual activities, or allowing their children, *even girls*, to share in such studies.'[9]

Above all, however, it is the position of women in the learned life of Andalusian Islām, as portrayed by such writers as al-Marrākushī,[10] and verified by the facts of literary history, that shows to what a small extent the prohibitory maxims were applied in actual religious practice.

[1] MS in Leyden Univ. Library, no. 640, p. 202.

[2] Ibn Mas'ūd, in Ibn Ḥajar al-Haitamī, *Fatāwī ḥadīthiyya*, Cairo, 1307, p. 63, among other warnings against educating girls.

[3] *Mashriq*, x. 1085. Cf. Muhammad ben Cheneb, *Proverbes arabes de l'Algérie et du Maghreb*, ii. (Paris, 1906) 246 f., no. 1685.

[4] Jāḥiẓ, *Bayān*, i. 214, line 1; Ibn Bassām, *loc. cit.*

[5] The instances given in the present writer's *Muh. Studien*, ii. 405-407, might be largely added to. We take occasion to refer only to the many women mentioned by Tāj al-dīn al-Subkī († A.H. 771 = A.D. 1370) among the sources of his knowledge of tradition; see, *e.g.*, *Ṭabaqāt al-Shāfi'iyya*, i. 49, lines 16, 17; 51. 16; 69. 7; 72. 16; 74. 12; 76. 6; 80. 3 from foot; 82. 3; 107. 7 from foot, etc. The number of women referred to as sources of tradition by al-Suyūṭī († A.H. 911 = A.D. 1505) in the list of his *Isnāds* (in appendix to his *Bughyat al-wu'āt*, pp. 440-461) is surprisingly large.

[6] *Madkhal*, i. 179.

[7] Ibn Rajab, *Ṭabaqāt al-Ḥanābila* (MS in Leipzig Univ. Library, Vollers, no. 708), fol. 149*a*.

[8] For a notable example from the 17th cent. see *Rev. du monde musulman*, xiv. [1911] 7.

[9] Ismā'īl Hamet, 'La Civilisation arabe en Afrique Centrale' (*ib.* 11). The author contrasts the ignorance prevalent among women in the Northern Sahara with the culture which is widely diffused among those of the Southern tribes (*ib.* 22).

[10] *Hist. of the Almohades*², ed. Dozy, Leyden, 1881, p. 270.

Besides the women who attained eminence in various branches of science and literature, and especially in poetry, we find several who were active in civic service, as, *e.g.*, 'Muzna (secretary to the Emir al-Nāṣir li-dīn-Allāh [† A.H. 358 = A.D. 969]), the learned, gifted with a beautiful handwriting.'[1] Such examples show at least that the prohibitive sayings referred to were a dead letter in practical life; and they also prove that the education of women actually attained a very high standard, and went far beyond the prescribed limit of the *sūrat al-nūr*. Hence the endeavours made within recent times in various parts of the Muslim world to raise female education to the level of Western civilization may be justified by an appeal to the past history of orthodox Islām.

7. Education in ethical and political writings.— The problem of elementary education has not been ignored in the literature of ethics and politics. The somewhat mechanical precepts of the older theological writings have been furnished with a deeper foundation in ethics and philosophy, and enriched with the ideas of a more worthy conception of life. As in ethics and philosophy generally, so also in education, we must recognize the powerful effects of that Hellenistic influence which we have already noted in some matters of detail. Reference was made above to an educational excursus which Avicenna († A.H. 428 = A.D. 1037) incorporated in his tractate on government (*risālat al-siyāsa*).[2] But Avicenna dealt with little more than the formal elements of the question, and it was really al-Ghazālī († A.H. 505 = A.D. 1111) who first brought the problem of education into organic relation with a profound ethical system. Starting from the Hellenistic idea of the infant mind as a *tabula rasa* susceptive of objective impressions,[3] he urges upon parents and teachers their solemn responsibility for the principles which they may stamp permanently upon the young soul. The child is given them as a trust, and it is their part to guard it well and faithfully. They must not only fill the young mind with knowledge, but—and Ghazālī lays special emphasis upon this—must seek to stimulate the child's moral consciousness, and train him to the proprieties of social life.[4]

It is somewhat remarkable that in the discussion of problems in the theory and practice of education the literature of Western Islām (the Maghrib) takes the lead. In the East, it is true, Ghazālī's vigorous dissertation makes up for the more abundant products of the West, and has, moreover, had a great influence upon the latter. As early as the 4th cent. A.H., however, we find a reference to a work called *Kitāb al-tafḍīla fī ta'dīb al-muta'allimīn* ('On the Education of Pupils'), by 'Alī b. Muhammad b. Khalaf al-Qābisī († A.H. 403 = A.D. 1012), of Gabes in Southern Tunis,[5] who enjoyed a high repute as one of the Mālikite traditional school.[6] The present writer has, however, sought in vain for any further mention of this presumably pedagogical work of al-Qābisī. In regard to the legal provisions bearing upon education, again, the great authority

[1] *Al-Dabbī*, ed. Codera, no. 1590 (*Bibl. Arab. Hisp.* vol. iii.).

[2] Published in the Arab magazine *Mashriq*, ix.

[3] Cf. the Arabic proverb *Al-ta'allum fi-l-ṣighar kal-naqsh fi-l-ḥajar* ('Learning in youth is like engraving upon stone'), Jāḥiẓ, *Bayān*, i. 102, line 10 from foot.

[4] This most important treatise by Ghazālī has been translated into English and appreciatively criticized by D. B. Macdonald, 'The Moral Education of the Young among the Muslims,' in *IJE* xv. [1905] 286–304; cf. also al-Ghazālī, *Lettre sur l'éducation des enfants*, tr. by Muhammad ben Cheneb, in *Rev. africaine*, xlv. [1901] 241 f.

[5] Balawī (likewise a native of the Maghrib), *Kitāb Alif-bā*, i. 76, line 6.

[6] Ibn Khallikān, ed. Wüstenfeld, Göttingen, 1835–40, no. 457 (tr. de Slane, London, 1843-71, ii. 263); Abū Bakr ibn Khair (*Bibl. Arab. Hisp.* ix. x.), p. 296.

is Abu-l-Walīd ibn Rushd the elder († A.H. 520 = A.D. 1126), qāḍī of Cordova, and grandfather of the famous philosopher of the same name (*i.e.* Averroës). Abū Bakr ibn al-'Arabī († A.H. 543 = A.D. 1148), qāḍī of Seville, who expounded his educational ideas in a work entitled *Marāqī al-zulfā* ('Stages of approach,' *i.e.* to God), is also frequently indebted—even in his language—to Ghazālī's treatise. The *Marāqī* is apparently lost, but numerous excerpts are quoted in a work by another Maghrib writer, the *Madkhal al-shar' al-sharīf* ('Introduction to the Sublime Law' of Muhammad ibn al-Ḥājj al-'Abdarī († A.H. 737 = A.D. 1336–7). This work, which has in view the reform of Muslim life on the basis of the ancient Sunna, devotes a number of sections to the subject of education and training, and has on this account been used as one of the sources of the present article. It is worthy of remark that in the scheme of education set forth in 'Abdarī's quotations from the *Marāqī* of Ibn al-'Arabī, the latter lays great stress upon hardening the body: the young should sleep in hard beds, and be trained in physical exercise; they should be urged to bodily activity, and inured to pain by corporal punishment. He also pleads strongly for games and hours of recreation.

'If a child is kept from play, and forced to work at his tasks without intermission, his spirit will be depressed; his power of thought and his freshness of mind will be destroyed; he will become sick of study, and his life will be overclouded, so that he will try all possible shifts to evade his lessons.'[1]

Ghazālī likewise had spoken emphatically on the evils of overpressure. Next in order after 'Abdarī comes another Maghrib authority, Ibn Khaldūn († A.H. 808 = A.D. 1405), renowned as a writer on the philosophy of history, who devoted great attention to educational problems, and especially to the spirit of primary education, its gradation, the methods of teaching the Qur'ān and philological subjects, and even the question of school-books (*mutūn*);[2] a lucid account of his educational ideas will be found in D. B. Macdonald's *Aspects of Islam.*[3] A work treating of married life (*muqni' al-muḥtāj fī ādāb al-ziwāj*) by the Maghrib writer Abu-l-'Abbās b. Ardūn al-Zajlī († A.H. 992 = A.D. 1584) contains a long chapter on the education of children; this was published recently by Paul Paquignon.[4] Reference may also be made to a compendium of the maxims relating to education, the work of a Maghrib author whose name is not given; it is based largely on the treatise of 'Abdarī, and has been published in the original, together with a French translation, by the Algerian professor, Muhammad ben Cheneb.[5]

A word may be added, for fullness' sake, regarding the educational 'guide' of Burhān al-din al-Zarnūji (*c.* A.H. 600 = A.D. 1203), introduced into Europe under the title of *Enchiridion Studiosi.*[6] This work, the author of which was a native of the East, deals, not with primary education, but with the study of theology, and gives pious counsels for the successful prosecution thereof. From the educational standpoint the sixth chapter is worthy of attention, as it contains suggestions regarding the first steps in study, the amounts to be mastered in the early stages, the repetition of what has been learned, etc. The author, conformably to time-honoured maxims, advises students to begin a study so far as possible on a Wednesday, as it was on that day that God created light.[7]

8. Modern movements towards reform.—So long as the social life of Islām remained impervious to Western influence, and even to-day in circles that are still unaffected by it, the instruction of the young proceeded mainly on the lines laid down in the older theological writings (see above, § 2). The best descriptions of this traditional stage are found in the works of E. Lane[1] and Snouck Hurgronje[2] (for Arabic countries), and H. Vámbéry[3] (for Turkey proper).[4] But, while this primitive and patriarchal form of instruction still holds its place—even amid the influences of foreign culture with which it will have nothing to do—there has meanwhile arisen in various Muslim countries a system of education which comes more and more into harmony with modern requirements. The new movement was initiated by the Egyptian pasha Muhammad 'Alī, the founder of modern Egypt, whose educational reforms, begun in 1811, were at first, it is true, of a somewhat circumscribed character. A further advance was made in 1824 by the erection of training schools in various departments, and the movement was partially organized and consolidated in 1836.[5] On this basis all branches of education have made rapid progress in Egypt. In Turkey, the reform of primary education was inaugurated in 1845, under Sultan 'Abdulmajīd, by the institution of the so-called *Rushdiyya* schools, while in 1868 his successor, 'Abdul 'Azīz, established a lyceum in Galata-Serai.[6] But, in spite of ceaseless efforts to raise the standard and widen the scope of education throughout Turkey, the results still fall far short of a general diffusion of knowledge, and in many parts of the Ottoman Empire there has been no advance whatever upon the crude institutions of primitive times. It should be added, however, that in Turkey and elsewhere the more liberal-minded Muhammadans, in default of adequate institutions of their own, send their children of either sex to non-Muslim schools established by European and American agencies.

It will be readily understood that, in countries under European rule having a Muslim population, the various Governments have greatly promoted the cause of education by the establishment of distinctively Muslim schools, as, *e.g.*, in India,[7] and, since the English occupation, also in Egypt. In the Muslim colonies of France and Holland likewise,[8] the respective administrations have devoted great efforts to the task of bringing the native educational methods nearer to the standards of modern culture. It is a remarkable fact that the Muhammadan subjects of the Russian empire (Tatars) are spontaneously and independently making strenuous and successful efforts to develop a modern system of education,[9] and, under the leadership of enlightened co-religionists, are able, in all social and intellectual concerns, to combine an unswerving loyalty to their faith with an earnest striving after progress on modern lines. The advance thus being made in various branches of education embraces also the instruction of girls, which is coming to be recognized more and more

1 In *Madkhal*, iii. 312 ff.

2 *Prolégomènes*, ed. Quatremère, Paris, 1858, iii. 248; tr. de Slane, Paris, 1862–68, iii. 271 f.

3 New York, 1911, pp. 309–316.

4 *Revue du monde musulman*, xv. [1911] 118–123.

5 'Notions de pédagogie musulmane,' *Rev. africaine*, xli. [1897] 269–285.

6 ed. Caspari, Leipzig, 1838.

7 *Ta'līm al-muta'allim ṭarīq al-ta'allum*, with a commentary by Shaikh ibn Ismā'īl 'Alī (dedicated to Sultan Murād III. [1574–1595]), Malmaniyya Printing Office, Cairo, A.H. 1311, p. 31.

1 *Manners and Customs of the Modern Egyptians*[5], i. (London, 1871) ch. ii. ('Early Education'), p. 73 ff.

2 *Mekka*, ii. 143 ff. For East India, cf. the same writer's *De Atjèhers*, Leyden, 1894, ii. 1 ff.

3 *Sittenbilder aus dem Morgenlande*, Berlin, 1876, p. 120 ff.

4 Cf. also *Voyages du Chevalier Chardin en Perse*, ed. Langlès, Paris, 1811, iv. 224 ff.

5 Cf. Dor, *L'Instruction publique en Égypte*, Paris, 1872; Yakoub Artin Pasha, *L'Instruction publique en Égypte*, Paris, 1890. The latest statistical information regarding Muslim and Coptic education in Egypt is given in a little work entitled *Al-ta'līm fī Miṣr*, Cairo, A.H. 1329, by Shaikh 'Alī Jūsuf.

6 The main particulars are given by Carra de Vaux, *La Doctrine de l'Islam*, Paris, 1909, p. 210 ff.

7 On the present state of Muslim education in India, see *Revue du monde musulman*, xv. [1911] 118–123.

8 J. G. Hockman, 'L'Enseignement aux Indes Orientales Néerlandaises,' in *Bibliothèque Coloniale Internationale* (Institut Colon. Intern., Brussels), 9th ser., vol. i.

9 See Molla Aminoff, 'Les Progrès de l'instruction publique chez les Musulmans russes,' in *Rev. du monde musulman*, ix. 247–263, 295; Sophie Bobrovnikoff, 'Moslems in Russia,' in *The Moslem World*, ed. Zwemer, i. (1911) 15 ff.

as a matter of vital moment for the Muhammadan world. The more important phases and incidents of the whole movement are chronicled in the *Revue du monde musulman* (Paris, since 1906), which deals with all Muslim countries, and has now completed its sixteenth volume.

Among specifically Muhammadan tendencies making for educational reform, we may mention the Bābī movement, which arose in Persia in 1844 (see art. BĀB, BĀBĪS, vol. ii. p. 299 ff.), and which, as Bahā'ism, has since then been constantly extending its influence. From the outset the principles of this sect have embraced an endeavour to raise primary education to a higher level and to relieve it of its long legacy of prejudice—aims which have been most strenuously pursued by the Bahā'i. Their more exalted conception of woman and of her function in family life, and their abolition of the restraints placed upon the female sex by ancient convention, are naturally coupled with efforts to improve the education of girls.

With the progress of primary education the development of the higher grades of instruction goes hand in hand. In many parts of the Muslim world, indeed, the latter has outstripped the former. A considerable number of colleges for the study of special subjects—military, medical, legal, and technical—and designed primarily to meet economic and political requirements, have been established, and in some centres these are combined to form a kind of university (*dār al-funūn*).[1] A large institution, designed to perform the function of a university, was quite recently erected in Cairo[2] (President-Rector, Prince Aḥmed Fu'ād Pasha, great grandson of Muhammad 'Alī). In Aligarh, India, the endeavour to form the academy founded there in 1875 into a university is within sight of success—a movement which, with Agha Khān at its head, finds generous support among adherents of Islām throughout India.[3] Ṭeherān likewise has a college which does its work under the style of a *dār al-funūn*. By way of providing stepping-stones towards such higher institutions, effective progress is being made in Turkey and Egypt with the system of preparatory or *i'dādī* schools.

These institutions are all conducted according to detailed instructions of the respective Governments, and the instructions are printed and made public. Various reforms, especially in regard to the system of examination and granting diplomas, have been recently effected by the Government in the great *madrasa* of the Azhar mosque in Cairo, in which the study of the various branches of theology is pursued on traditional lines; as also in the schools associated with that *madrasa* at Ṭanṭa (the Aḥmediyya mosque), Damietta, and Alexandria.[4] The need for reform in higher theological education has asserted itself also in more sequestered localities.[5] Among other agencies aiming at the diffusion of culture among Muhammadans, mention may be made of the Khaldūniyya institution at Tunis,[6] which takes its name from the Ibn Khaldūn referred to above. All these manifold activities are but so many endeavours to arouse, strengthen, and apply in practice, among the Muhammadan peoples, the conviction that their religion does not prohibit them from rising to the demands of a progressive civilization, or pursuing the intellectual life.

LITERATURE.—This has been given fully in the footnotes.

1 As regards Turkey, cf. M. Hartmann, *Unpolitische Briefe aus der Türkei*, Leipzig, 1910, p. 127 ff.

2 *Rev. du monde musulman*, xiii. [1911] 1–29. The courses given in Cairo University by native and European scholars (Guidi, Littmann, Nallino, etc.) in Arabic have now been published.

3 *Ib.* xiii. 570–573; as to the objects of the university, cf. *ib.* xiv. [1911] 100 ff.

4 P. Arminjon, *L'Enseignement, la doctrine, et la vie dans les universités musulmanes d'Égypte*, Paris, 1907.

5 As, *e.g.*, in Bukhāra; cf. *Rev. du monde musulman*, xiv. [1911] 143.

6 The official organ of this establishment is *Al-madrasa*, edited by 'Abdalrazzāq al-Niṭāsī; it contains reports of the courses in the various subjects taught in the Institution.

3
SOME ASPECTS OF THE EDUCATION OF PRINCES AT THE ʿABBĀSID COURT

Albert Dietrich

[**89**] The various observations which I propose to make here take as their point of departure a simple enough assertion, this being that for the Muslim historian the caliph only exists in practical terms from the moment that he is seen as the guide of the State, as the *imām* reorienting history. It is true that then – however insignificant his reign may be – he becomes the fulcrum around which all events gravitate. But for the purposes of knowing more about the infancy and education of the heir to the throne – an essential tool for the appreciation of the true worth of his future style of government – the written materials at our disposal are sporadic and not particularly fruitful, and furthermore are supplied to us only in cases of direct overlapping with the reign of the predecessor (since it is only under this heading that the chronicler judges them worthy of transmission to posterity). It may be recalled briefly that education is a phenomenon with diverse aspects – anthropological, ethical, genetic, sociological, etc. – not confined, in different languages, to a single exclusive notion. In German the concepts of *Erziehung* and *Bildung* are treated separately; in Russian there is an even more rigorous distinction between *vospitaniye* and *obrazovaniye*; similarly, in French, there is a distinction between *éducation* and *culture*, *formation*, while the English language encompasses both notions with the term "education". [**90**] In the survey which follows, "education" is taken to mean everything which models the character of the child-pupil, everything that conveys to him, by way of apprenticeship, theoretical discernment and practical knowledge.

At first sight, the task seems easy. Arabic and Persian literatures are quite rich in writings which, so it seems, inform us directly about princely education: writings dealing with the princely style of life, either imitating the model of a particular sovereign or seeking to define the essence of the sovereign's role in general terms, and works of the "Manual of princely education" genre, known in German as *Fürstenspiegel*. Other literatures supply famous examples, from the *Cyropaedia* of Xenophon, via Machiavelli's *Prince* and Fénelon's *Télémaque* to the *Anti-Machiavelli* of Frederic the Great. Islam supplies them to us fairly frequently in the form of memoranda personally addressed to one or another prince, such as that for example dedicated by al-Jāḥiẓ to the caliph al-Muʿtaṣim and intitled: "An appeal to teach children matters of knowledge and the categories of education".[1] We also have at our disposal a number of "logia" and testaments of an ethical and didactic character, whereby sovereigns, on their death-beds, sought to exercise a pedagogic influence over their sons.[2] But the fact is: the only elements which can be extracted without too much difficulty from all these literary genres are educational maxims, norms intended to idealise, to create types, and not necessarily the pedagogic measures effectively put into practice. We have here the discrepancy between the Renaissance prince as conceived by Castiglione in his *Cortegiano*, and the figure presented to us by Jacob Burckhardt in his concrete historical reality.

The questions thus arise: 1) What was, in the classical Islamic era, the cultural patrimony of the upper classes, specifically of the sons of caliphs? 2) Who were the educators of princes? 3) How was this cultural property conveyed to the princes? What were the particular features of ʿAbbāsid princely education?

[91] The cultural patrimony is divided into *ʿilm* and *adab*[3] – or more precisely in the plural, *ʿulūm* and *ādāb* – a duality which recurs throughout Islamic spiritual history and which corresponds approximately to the distinction which we make between "knowledge" and "culture, conditioning". Similar dualities occur almost everywhere: *dānish* and *farhang* in Persian, *eruditio* and *humanitas* (or *urbanitas*), *episteme* [G] and *paideia* [G], etc. The ideal, in Islam as elsewhere, was to be versed in both domains: "*ʿIlm* without *adab*, is like fire without wood, and *adab* without *ʿilm* is like spirit without body, al-ʿAnbarī tells us,[4] or indeed: "*ʿIlm* and *adab* are two treasures which are never exhausted, two flames which are never extinguished, two garments which are never discarded; who possesses them possesses reason; he knows his true position when facing the beyond and his life transcends the existence of

[1] Al-Ḥuṣrī, *Jamʿ al-jawāhir*, ed. al-Bijāwi, Cairo 1372/1953, p. 142 and f.

[2] This institution dates back to the earliest times in Oriental antiquity: see for example the instructions of Jacob (Genesis 48 and 49); cf. also 2 Samuel 17, 23; 2 Kings 20, 1 (=Isaiah 38, 1) where the Hebrew *ṣiwwā* corresponds to the Arabic *waṣṣā* – Concerning the subject in general, cf. the overall view, succinct but comprising the essential, of H. Busse, *Fürstenspiegel und Fürstenethik im Islam*, in *Bustan*, 9, Vienna 1968, pp. 12–19.

[3] It is very difficult to determine the content and the evolution of these two terms, as Arabic literature uses them in a highly inconsistent fashion. Even a systematic study, citing as many examples as possible, would be a futile exercise. The two articles *adab* (F. Gabrieli) and *ʿilm* (ed.) in *EI*[1] constitute useful introductions. Cf. also G.E. von Grunebaum, *Der Islam im Mittelalter*, Zurich 1963, pp. 300–304, pp. 319–328, and footnotes to p. 547 and p. 558.

[4] Samʿānī, *Adab al-imlāʾ wa-l-istimlāʾ*, ed. M. Weisweiler, Leiden 1955, p. 2.

slaves," according to al-Ḥuṣrī,[5] etc.; it is said of the grammarian Abū ʿUbayd that he "possesses the broadest *ʿilm* and the most profound knowledge of *adab*"[6] – to quote only a few appropriate examples to show the extent to which these two notions were inseparable in the classical period. There is sometimes a third which is postulated – or affirmed – as an attribute of members of the reigning dynasty: nobility (*sharaf, ḥasab*): this should not however be taken to mean hereditary nobility, which comes automatically, but nobility of character, acquired through education of the self. This is illustrated by the funereal eulogy dedicated to Ibn al-Muʿtazz, that most cultivated of princes who died a violent death: "How sublime he was in *ʿilm, adab* and *ḥasab*", i.e. in knowledge, education and nobility of spirit."[7]

ʿIlm, the first of these two concepts, could be defined approximately as follows: it comprises, at the start of the ʿAbbāsid era, the study and exegesis of the Qurʾān, canonical law, Tradition, i.e. the religious sciences which the Arabs had always claimed as their own domain. [**92**] There is a whole series of traditions according to which the Muslim is urged – or even obliged – to acquire this *ʿilm*[8] and to put it into practice: "Knowing and acting should not be separated"[9] and "Knowledge without action is a tree without fruits".[10] Thus we have for *ʿilm* the four above-mentioned, specifically Arab disciplines. This is normally regarded as sufficient, and although an erudite writer of the fourth/tenth century, al-Khwārizmī, lists a total of fifteen categories of *ʿilm*, the fact remains nevertheless that as early as this period, the majority of them were attributed to the *ādāb*. Six autochthonous, meaning Arab, sciences are listed (canonical law, theology, grammar, administrative science, poetic art, history and nine foreign sciences: philosophy, logic, medicine, arithmetic, geometry, astronomy, music, mechanics and alchemy.[11]

This brings us therefore to the *ādāb*, which are not easily encompassed, and which have undergone many changes in the course of time. The vizier al-Ḥasan b. Sahl is credited with this revealing definition, which may well have been valid for all of the early ʿAbbāsid era: "The *adab* are ten in number:

[5] *Zahr al-ādāb*, ed. Zakī Mubārak, Cairo 1952, ii, p. 189.

[6] Abū ʿUbayd al-Qāsim b. Sallām, apud Ibn al-Anbārī, *Nuzhat al-alibbāʾ*, ed. al-Sāmarrāʾī, Baghdad 1959, p. 96.

[7] Al-Khaṭīb, *Taʾrīkh Baghdād*, x, p. 101; al-Ḥuṣrī, *Zahr al-aḍāb*, ii, p. 201: Ibn Khallikān, *Wafayāt*, ed. M.M. ʿAbd al-Ḥamīd, ii. p. 264; Ibn al-ʿImād, *Shadarāt al-dhahab*, ii, p.223.

[8] A large number of significant traditions may be found *apud* Wensinck, *A Handbook of Early Muhammadan Tradition*, Leiden 1960, under "Knowledge". Al-Ḥuṣrī, *Zahr*, ii, p. 260, nominates "aspiration to knowledge" as one of the nine cardinal virtues of the believer.

[9] Ḥujwīrī, *Kashf al-maḥjūb*, tr. R.A. Nicholson, Leiden and London 1911, p. 11.

[10] Al-Ḥuṣrī, *Zahr*, ii, p. 77.

[11] Al-Khwārizmī, *Mafātīḥ al-ʿulūm*, ed. van Vloten, Leiden 1895, p. 5 f.

three of them are *shahrajāniyya*, three *anoshirvāniyya* (we shall return to these expressions), three of them are Arab and there is one which dominates them all. The *shahrajāniyya* are: playing the lute, chess and polo; the *anoshirvāniyya* are: medicine, geometry and horsemanship; the Arab ones are: poetry, genealogy and the history of tribal conflicts. But the one which outranks all the others consists of the short stories and the conversations in which people display their aptitude on the occasion of social gatherings."[12] The two foreign designations refer to Shahrajān and to Anoshirvān, two kings of Persia, one legendary and the other historical. They show that as early as this period, a far from negligible portion of the cultural patrimony was correctly recognised as being of Persian origin. Very characteristic, in this context, is the final part of the definition according to which one of the *adab* was prevalent, that of the short stories and conversations which garnished social life. In other words, preference was given, not to serious discussions, but to somewhat casual conversations. [**93**] This was to replace *studium* with *elegantia* – a process which was not without consequences for the evolution of Arabic literature and for which, furthermore, parallels are to be found in other cultural domains. Countless contemporary aphorisms show us to what an extent at this time the prestige of *adab* was enhanced to the detriment of *ʿilm*. "*Adab* is the life of the heart and there is no greater misfortune than to be uncultured," said al-Bayhaqī around the year 300/early tenth century.[13] Or, in the truly Arab style: "*Adab* is something masculine; virile natures love it, the effeminate abhor it."[14] And finally this exuberant anecdote of al-Maʾmūn and of his vizier contemplating from a height the verdant oasis of Damascus. The vizier asks him: "Prince of the Believers, have you ever seen anything more beautiful in the empire of the Arabs?" "Certainly, by God," the caliph replies, "a book of *adab* which clarifies the understanding, inspires the heart and rejoices the soul. What could be a thing more beautiful than that?"[15] etc. Critics speaking out against *adab* are few and far between; they include for example al-Jāḥiẓ who claims that *adab*, when taken to excess, deflects from the obedience owed to God and leads to sin.[16]

Next to be tackled is the question of the princely educators. Their names and the disciplines which they chose enable us to deduce the tenor of the education dispensed and to see to what extent it covers the categories of *ʿilm* and of *adab* mentioned above. We may take as examples the educators

[12] Al-Ḥuṣrī, *Zahr*, i, p.140.
[13] *Kitāb al-Maḥāsin wa-l-masāwī*, ed. F. Schwally, Giessen 1902, p. 428.
[14] *Ibid.*, p. 1.
[15] *Ibid.*, p. 2.
[16] *Ibid.*, p. 452.

of al-Mahdī b. al-Manṣūr, heir to the throne and future caliph. Cited among his mentors are the poet Ḥafṣ b. Abī Jumʿa,[17] the traditionist Abū Saʿīd al-Muʾaddib[18] and his successor Sufyān b. Husayn,[19] – the first mentioned was, later, tutor to the prince al-Hādī. When al-Mahdī came of age and was residing at al-Rayy in the capacity of governor, he was obliged, at the orders of al-Manṣūr, to become acquainted, through the good offices of the historian al-Sharqī b. al-Quṭāmī, with the *ayyām al-ʿarab*, the history of the tribal conflicts of pre-Islamic Arabia.[20] Al-Mufaḍḍal al-Ḍabbī, the philologist of the school of al-Kūfa, imprisoned for his participation [**94**] in an ʿAlid insurrection, was pardoned by al-Manṣūr and taken into the service of al-Mahdī,[21] for whom he later wrote his renowned *Mufaḍḍaliyyāt*. By appointing as companions to al-Mahdī both a representative of the old tradition and a representative of Arab linguistics, al-Manṣūr was no doubt concerned to shield his son, who was very open-minded by nature, from too much exposure, in the exercise of his new activities, to Iranian influences. In any case, we are told that in his early years al-Mahdī enjoyed a good intellectual education (*taʾaddaba*), that he attended meetings of scholars and excelled in these milieux.[22] Jaʿfar, the brother of al-Mahdī, had the poet Muṭīʿ b. Iyās as mentor or intimate companion – no doubt amounting to the same thing: Arabic does not always express such matters with clarity; it is only said: *ḍamma ilayhi fulānan* "the caliph gave (to the prince) such a person for companion." It is true that the poet Muṭiʿ was reputedly a *zindīq* or at least a free-thinker, which induced al-Manṣūr to remove him from the entourage of his son.[23] It is curious to note that in more than one instance heretics of Manichean persuasion appear as the educators of princes, and this from the time of the later Umayyads. These were the precursors of a constantly growing Iranian influence which was soon to prevail over specifically Arab culture.

The entry on the scene of these educators did not always have the effect of exerting over the pupils the best of influences. A case in point, for example, was the quarrel between the poet Ḥammād ʿAjrad and the grammarian Quṭrub, who both applied to al-Mahdī for the post of princely educator. His rival Bashshār b. Burd having shot at him some well expressed satirical

[17] Al-Ṭabarī, *Annales*, iii, p. 441.

[18] Ibn Qutayba, *Kitāb al-Maʿārif*, ed. ʿUkāsha, Cairo 1960, p. 549; al-Khaṭīb, *Taʾrīkh Baghdād*, iii, p. 254.

[19] Ibn Qutayba, *ibid.*; *Taʾrīkh Baghdād*, ix, p. 149.

[20] Al-Masʿūdī, *Murūj al-dhahab* (Fields of Gold), vi, p. 251.

[21] Ibn al-Nadīm, *Fihrist*, ed. Flügel, p. 68.

[22] Al-Suyūṭī, *Taʾrīkh al-Khulafāʾ*, ed. M.M. ʿAbd al-Ḥamīd, Cairo 1371/1952, p. 272.

[23] *Aghānī* (Būlāq), xii, p. 85 (= Cairo 1950, xiii, p. 287); al-Nuwayrī, *Nihāyat al-arab*, iv, p. 61 f; G.E. von Grunebaum, in *Orientalia*, 17 (1948), p. 171 f.

verses, the renown of the poet declined to such a point that his application was denied, whereupon he embarked on a tireless campaign of vilification against his more fortunate competitor, finally accusing him in some of his verses of immorality, thus arousing the suspicions of the caliph who ultimately expelled the grammarian from the palace.[24] Al-Hādī, son of al-Mahdī and later his successor, was an individual of somewhat lax moral standards. The caliph knew [**95**] that he was under the influence of Ibrāhīm al-Mawṣilī, cantor at the court of Baghdad and a notorious toper. He forbade him with the utmost severity to continue organising drinking sessions under the guise of musical education. Having failed to comply, the cantor was subjected to 360 strokes of the birch and made to swear never again to approach the prince.[25] It would be superfluous to continue here the list of princely mentors. For the ʿAbbāsid period, an impressive number could be cited, including such distinguished-sounding names as those of al-Kisāʾī, al-Farrāʾ, al-Jāḥīz, Ibn al-Sikkīt, al-Balādhurī, etc.

It was thus to scholars of all types, especially to philologists and traditionists but also to poets and musicians that the caliphs entrusted their sons. In the court the teachers did not have the status and rank of functionaries; the caliphs appointed masters on recommendation or through a process of candidature and personally supervised, to the best of their ability, the education of their sons. An appointment was regarded as honorific and lucrative, and it was usually accepted. Nevertheless, it sometimes happened that an official was designated. Or indeed the caliph, wanting to attract a scholar to his court, might offer him a choice of assignments, one of which would be the education of the prince. It was thus that al-Mahdī told a *qāḍī*: "You may either practise as a judge, or you may teach my sons tradition, or indeed you may dine at my table." On reflection, the *qāḍī* opted for the last of these offers as being the easiest of the three.[26] Educators were discharged on completion of their assignment, or on the grounds of incapacity, or moral turpitude, or because they nourished hostile (i.e. ʿAlid) attitudes towards the state, or as a result of libellous attacks. Only al-Jāḥiẓ, appointed educator of his son by al-Mutawakkil, was apparently dismissed – not without lavish compensation – on account of his repulsive ugliness.[27]

---

[24] *Aghānī* (Būlāq), xiii, p. 78; O. Rescher, *Abriss der arabischen Literaturgeschichte*, i, Stuttgart 1925, p. 285. It also sometimes happened that rivals quarrelled over the privilege of princely education, cf. al-Ṣūlī, *Akhbār al-Rāḍī billāh wa-l-Muttaqī billāh*, tr. M. Canard, i, Algiers 1946, p. 55, note 7.

[25] *Aghānī* (Būlāq), v, p. 5 (=Cairo 1932, v, p. 160); Rescher, *Abriss* ii, Stuttgart 1933, p. 70.

[26] Al-Masʿūdī, *Murūj*, vi, p. 226; al-Suyūṭī, *Taʾrīkh al-khulafāʾ*, p. 275.

[27] Ibn Khallikān, *Wafayāt*, iii, p. 141.

In general the caliphs allowed the princely educators a right of unlimited punishment. "To educate" (in Arabic *addaba*, meaning to inculcate *adab*) often becomes a synonym of "to chastise" (*ḍaraba*). Even the general supervisory staff could avail themselves of this right. A young ʿAbbāsid, invited by al-Manṣūr to dine, declined this offer on the grounds that he had already eaten. Hearing this, the caliph's doorkeeper seized the prince and thrashed him soundly [**96**] like a child. His father complained indignantly to the caliph who summoned the retainer before him and received the following explanation: "You invited him to dine in your company and he replied that he had already eaten. But you invited him to give him honour and distinction, not so that he could satisfy his hunger. Thus I have corrected him (literally: I have inculcated *adab* in him), because his father has not done so." As the act of declining an invitation from the prince of the believers was a serious impropriety, the caliph could not fault his doorman and the father was ejected.[28] It was al-Mahdī in particular, it seems, who considered correction the very last word in pedagogic matters. His son, the crown prince al-Hādī, infringing a repeated prohibition, indulged in alcoholic excess and was subjected, together with his companions, to exemplary *bastinado*.[29] The educators themselves shared this point of view, and it should come as no surprise to us to know for example that the eminent al-Kisāʾī, tutor to the princes al-Amīn and al-Maʾmūn, on one occasion during his youth was the recipient of a flurry of blows for having recited a false Qurʾānic variant.[30]

Undoubtedly, it was not always because some pedagogic value was attached to them that these corrections were employed: in the event they were practised rather out of pure formality. Otherwise it would be hard to explain the fact, for example, that al-Mahdī, intent on sanctioning two contradictory actions of a poet, addressed him in these terms: "The choice is yours. If you wish, we shall correct you (literally, we shall inculcate you with *adab*), giving you painful blows for daring to do something which I forbade, and at the same time we shall offer you 30,000 dirhams as a reward for composing a hymn of praise in our honour; or indeed, if you prefer, we shall simply award you a pardon" (because punishment and reward cancel out).[31] Quite often these corrections were administered in an excessive manner, with blind frenzy. Al-Bayhaqī for example asserted that in general an educator who set out to give ten strokes of the birch would finally inflict a hundred or more: his self-control would tell him, assuredly, that ten were enough, but once started

[28] Al-Bayhaqī, *al-Maḥāsin wa-l-masāwī*, p. 172 f.
[29] Al-Ṭabarī, *Annales*, iii, p. 583 f.
[30] Yāqūt, *Irshād al-arīb*, ed. Margoliouth, v, p. 187.
[31] Al-Ḥuṣrī, *Zahr*, ii, p. 38.

on the process, his blood would be up and his anger increasing along with the number of blows.[32]

[**97**] What is particularly striking about this right of punishment, and the aspect which has led us to devote some attention to it, is that it enabled educators, most often drawn from inferior social classes, to apply it to the most distinguished members of the ruling family, conscious of their kinship with the Prophet. It is impossible to deal here with a highly interesting sociological question, viz. the position occupied in Islam by the schoolmaster, the *mu'addib* or *muʿallim*. To my knowledge, this question has never been systematically addressed. It may be noted however that the teacher – just like the *paidagogos* [G] or the *skholastikos* [G] in Greek society – did not enjoy high prestige. This attitude, it seems, has its roots in part in the period of conquests: the Arabs, almost invariably unable to read and write, but becoming masters of a vast empire, found themselves obliged for practical reasons to acquire education from those whom they had subjugated, i.e. principally from Christians and Jews. They retaliated by despising them, and this contempt was applied to the whole of the teaching profession. The process also took on a political twist, at times: thus it was found that the best way of casting a slur on the reputation of al-Ḥajjāj b. Yūsuf, a competent and incorruptible governor – and for this reason detested – was to remind him that he had formerly been a minor schoolmaster.[33] Aphorisms and jokes at the expense of schoolmasters are legion, as may be seen in the works, among others, of al-Jāḥīz, *al-Bayān wa-l-tabyīn*, and of al-Bayhaqī, *al-Maḥāsin wa-l-māsāwi*.[34] The mentors of princes, for their part, were not so discredited: the fact that in principle only the most capable were appointed to these posts was considered more important than the issue of whence they came. Their prestige and conditions improved, and their origins were forgotten. Their pupils, on coming of age, treated them with reverence. When Alexander was asked why he respected his tutor more than his father, he is supposed to have replied: "Because my father is the author of my ephemeral days, whereas my tutor has engendered my eternal life".[35]

We thus arrive at the manner in which the cultural patrimony was – in total or in part – transmitted to the ʿAbbāsid princes. The latter in fact seem hardly to have shown a particular congenital disposition [**98**] towards the higher humanities. Thanks to the researches of Henri Lammens on the history of the

[32] Al-Bayhakī, *Maḥāsin*, p. 9.

[33] J. Périer, *Vie d'al-Ḥadjdjâdj ibn Yousof*, Paris 1904, p. 6 f., with references.

[34] Cf. also I. Goldziher, *Muhammedanische Studien*, i, p. 110; A. Mez, *Die Renaissance der Islams*, p. 177 f.

[35] Al-Ḥuṣrī, *Zahr*, i, p. 192 f.

Umayyads, it is already known that this dynasty had been renowned, since the pre-Islamic era, for a particularly pronounced taste for culture, while the Hāshimids (among whom the ʿAbbāsids were included) were often reproached for their intellectual inferiority, real or supposed. We are told in any case that in the course of a plenary assembly of the Hāshimids, al-Manṣūr complained bitterly of the vulgarity and intellectual ineptitude of his family, which had nevertheless been promoted to the Imamate.[36] It was this reason no doubt that he appointed as tutor to his son al-Mahdī a poet of Umayyad origin, the Ḥafṣ b. Abī Jumʿa who has been previously mentioned.[37] This was, at the start of the ʿAbbāsid period, proof of a remarkable openness of spirit towards the ousted dynasty.

Direct testimony regarding the educational curriculum of a young ʿAbbāsid is very sparse. The cantor Isḥāq al-Mawṣilī gives us indications of the way in which the school day proceeded. This man, who for a considerable period of time was in the first rank of the musical life of Baghdad, describes his own schooling to us: "During a certain period, from dawn, I presented myself regularly to Ḥusayn b. Bashīr for classes in tradition; then I called upon al-Kisāʾī or al-Farrāʾ or Ibn Jazāla to read the Qurʾān; then I went to Manṣūr Zulzul who played me two or three pieces of music. Then it was the turn of ʿĀtika bint Shuhda who taught me one or two melodies. Then, it was to the house of al-Aṣmaʿī or the house of Abū ʻUbayda, for an hour dedicated to the recitation of poems or the narration of history. Then I returned to my father with whom I took my breakfast while relating to him everything that I had done and learned during all those hours. After the evening prayer I set out on my way to visit Hārūn al-Rashīd."[38]

This may be taken as an approximation of the daily timetable of a son of the caliph. But it is not enough to have assimilated these subjects. Since – as may be deduced from the extensive definition of *adab* quoted above – the young prince was obliged to practise a large number of athletic and worldly disciplines, to learn the forms of court ceremonial, etiquette and good manners, in other words: *savoir-vivre*. And fundamentally, [**99**] in the strictest sense of the term, *adab* signifies nothing other than *savoir-vivre*. It used to be said of the ʿAbbāsid prince Ibn al-Muʿtazz: "He was distinguished from all his contemporaries through his outstanding qualities, his nobility of heart, his *savoir-vivre* (*adab*), his poetic talent, his elegance and his mastery in the other categories of *adab*."[39] Here the term *adab* is quite correctly used both in its

[36] *Aghānī* (Būlāq), vi, p. 61 (=Cairo 1935, vi, p. 273).
[37] Al-Ṭabarī, iii, p. 441: cf. p. 93, n. 5.
[38] *Aghānī* (Būlāq), v, p. 54 (= Cairo 1932, v, p. 271 ff); Yāqūt, *Irshād*, ii, p. 198.
[39] *Aghānī* (Būlāq), ix, p. 140 (= Cairo 1938, x, p. 274).

most restrained acceptance and its broadest sense; it denotes, in the same phrase, both a part of the whole and the whole itself. As to the nature of these categories of *adab*, this can essentially only be learned by indirect means: primarily, through retroactive deduction, in relying on the sciences and disciplines which we know to have been much in evidence during the reign of a caliph, but which in all probability were acquired in his time as a prince, and secondly, *a posteriori*, examining what we know of education under the Sasanids.

We may mention first the game of chess, which had a number of illustrious enthusiasts in the persons of the caliphs Hārūn al-Rashīd, al-Amīn, al-Maʾmūn, al-Muʿtaṣim, a-Muktafī, al-Muqtadir and al-Rāḍī. Besides chess, there was a whole series of other board-games, ball games, horsemanship, archery, hunting practised in accordance with the rules of venery. Also considered desirable was knowledge of the culinary art. We are often told – notably by al-Masʿūdī,[40] of conversations at the caliph's table on the subject of gastronomy. And Ibrāhīm b. al-Mahdī, known for his poetry, saw nothing discreditable in writing a book about cuisine.[41] Copious information regarding the education of a Sasanid prince may be gleaned from the Pahlevi book, *Khusro ī Kavādhān u redhag-e* "The Book of King Khosrau and of his Page". We are told here that the boy was required first, at the elementary school, to learn by heart the principal parts of the Avesta including the commentaries; then, at what could be called the higher school, he had to familiarise himself with national literature, history, rhetoric, while practising equitation, archery, the handling of the lance and the battle-axe. Also included among his studies were music, singing, astronomy, chess and other games, as well as principles of gastronomy and of sartorial fashion.[42] It is striking to note to what extent this curriculum of studies resembles that of the ʿAbbāsids.

[**100**] As for the innumerable rules of propriety that the young prince was expected to observe, these were not necessarily of Persian provenance, since they could also be considered as belonging to humanity in general. We are told for example that at social events hosted by the caliph al-Muʿtamid it was customary to broach the following topics of conversation: the behaviour of the dinner-guest, the traits of character expected of him, these being moderation in the consumption of wine, the ability to control emotions, to be moderate even in the pursuit of pleasures and to shun frivolities (in other terms: temperance, *sophrosune* [G], *mesotes* [G]). Furthermore there

[40] Al-Masʿūdī, *Murūj*, vi, p. 227–229, 305–308, 349–351, etc.

[41] Ibn al-Nadīm, *Fihrist* (Flügel), p. 116 (*Kitāb al-ṭabīkh*).

[42] *The Pahlavi Text "King Husrau and his Boy"*, pub. J.M. Unvala, Paris 1921, especially pp. 13–17.

was the art of drawing up invitations (using extracts from model-letters), different kinds of reputable drinks, various themes of history and music, questions of precedence at social events, formulas of politeness, etc. Added to this were subjects of the genre, "Speech is silver, silence is golden".[43] The *Kitāb al-Muwashshā* is an inexhaustible mine of information regarding good manners. The author, al-Washshāʾ (fourth/tenth century), made a meagre living as a school-teacher, but as a writer he revived in convincing fashion the image of grand master of the old school.[44] The ruling family was required in principle to submit itself to the whole of this code, even in its dealings with subordinates. The son of the caliph al-Mahdī did not obtain from his master, a traditionist, any response to a scientific question because he asked it leaning against the wall, or rather he only obtained it once he was kneeling.[45] One day when he was personally conducting the prayers in the mosque, al-Mahdī waited, before beginning, until a Bedouin had finished his ritual ablutions.[46]

In view of the precocity of the Orientals, it may be assumed that the ʿAbbāsids began their schooling from their fifth year, a plausible hypothesis if we apply to the ʿAbbāsids too what we know of the young Sasanid prince Bahrām.[47] Much value was placed on early education, having regard to the extra receptivity and good memory of the young as, it used to be said: "To teach [**101**] in infancy, is to engrave a stone with a chisel"[48] This education, of considerable scope as we have just seen, and not in any way superficial, was apparently concluded at the age of maturity. At thirteen years old the prince a-Muqtadir was still attending school and, according to Hilāl al-Ṣābī,ʾ he rejoiced with all his heart when there were no classes.[49] But at fifteen years of age schooling was ended, if we may, once more, deduce from a Sasanid source, the *Pandnāmak i Zarathusht*.[50]

It is true that the end result of this education was nothing more than the acquisition of the obligatory fundamentals of general, intellectual and physical education, entrusted essentially to the tutors of the court. Henceforward it was through the practice of war and in administration that the young prince

[43] All of this according to al-Masʿūdī, *Murūj*, vi, pp. 131–133; viii, p. 102 f. and *passim*.

[44] Al-Washshāʾ, *Kitāb al-Muwashshā*, ed. R. Brünnow. Leiden 1886, repr. Cairo 1327/ 1905.

[45] Al-Samʿānī, *Adab al-imlāʾ wa-l-istimlāʾ*, ed, Weisweiler, p. 133; al-Suyūṭī, *Taʾrīkh al-Khulafāʾ*, p. 275.

[46] Al-Suyūṭī, *Taʾrīkh*, p. 277.

[47] Al-Ṭabarī, *Annales* i, p. 855; cf. Th. Nöldeke, *Geschichte der Perser und Araber zur Zeit der Sasaniden*, Leiden 1879, p. 87 f.; A. Christensen, *L'Iran sous les Sassanides*, 2nd ed., Copenhagen 1944, p. 417.

[48] Al-Bayhaqī, *al-Maḥāsin wa-l-masāwī*, p. 14.

[49] A. Mez, *Renaissance*, p.7.

[50] A. Christensen, *ibid*.

was expected to prove himself, accompanied for some time, admittedly, by an experienced general or a seasoned functionary. It was thus that al-Manṣūr entrusted to his secretary Abū ʿUbayd Allāh, a man of merit and talent, the task of teaching his successor al-Mahdī the rudiments of administration;[51] similarly he sent alongside his son the experienced Khāzim b. Khuzayma in the campaign to subdue the rebellious provinces of Khorāsān and of Ṭabaristān.[52] The union of state and religion, characteristic of the regime of the ʿAbbāsids – as it had previously been for the Sasanids – explains the fact that wherever possible, princes were expected to take on the role of Chief of Pilgrimage (*amīr al-ḥajj*), every year escorting across the desert from Baghdad to Mecca the official government caravan, which could be joined by believers of any social status. This mission was sometimes accomplished by princes at a very early age; one of them, the future caliph Muntaṣir, was at the age of thirteen at the head of the caravan of pilgrims – accompanied, admittedly, by his grandmother,[53] a redoubtable lady who would have acted as his chaperone during the *iḥrām*.

We have just alluded to the training that was given to princes in natters of state administration. Also worthy of mention in this context is a particular educational instrument which was regarded by the caliphs as being of essentially practical and political importance and served them a guideline for the art of [**102**] government: historical science. Here we are concerned not with the genre of the *akhbār*, those traditional accounts of tribal conflicts, but rather with the study of political events and of their interactions. On the basis of table conversations which have been relayed to us, we know that the caliphs had at their disposal a stock of historical knowledge which was very extensive, even astonishing; having acquired the fundamentals during their youth, once in power they undertook to deepen and extend their knowledge still further, and this they did tirelessly. This corresponds manifestly to an old oriental tradition and in this respect the motivation of the caliphs was identical to that of the Hittite, Assyrian and Persian kings: only one who was in possession of notions of history was capable of pursuing politically just actions, in other words – governing. The caliph al-Muʿtaḍid ordered a scholar to assemble in a special library all books dealing with the following subjects: first jurisprudence, then biographies, ancient or recent, the history of kings, the history of wars, the history of the ʿAbbāsid dynasty. These were the matters which the caliph wanted taught to his sons, of whom one, the future

[51] Ibn al-Ṭiqṭaqā, *al-Fakhrī*, Beirut 1386/1966, p. 182; Jahshiyārī, *Kitāb al-wuzarāʾ wa-l-kuttāb*, Cairo 1357/1938, p. 126.
[52] Al-Ṭabarī, iii, p. 355.
[53] Al-Masʿūdī, *Murūj*, ix, p. 72.

al-Muqtadir, was not yet seven years old, while the other was only a few years older.[54] The following generation of princes had for a master the famous vizier al-Ṣūlī who, having discovered the mediocrity of their knowledge of history, was capable of enthusing them for historical studies to such a point that after a certain period of time he thought it preferable to tackle other topics to avoid excessive specialisation on the part of his pupils. He entrusted them to a person who was an authority on matters of tradition and other religious sciences – no doubt to appease influential theologians.[55] Al-Manṣūr asked a historian to write a book about the campaigns of the Prophet; he himself took a particular interest in the reign of the Umayyad caliph Hishām, imitating him in a number of ways;[56] furthermore he sketched out a perfectly adequate portrayal of the Umayyad ruler, conforming even to the modern exigencies of historical science.[57] Hārūn al-Rashīd took up with al-Aṣmaʿī the subject of the Umayyad Sulaymān,[58] and consulted ʿAbd Allāh b. Muṣʿab to find out how he judged the assassination of ʿUthmān and the relations which the first two caliphs maintained with the Prophet.[59] Al-Maʾmūn asked [**103**] a scholar questions about history, and finding that the latter knew nothing, he supplied the answers himself;[60] being aware of the financial policy of the first four caliphs, he rejected it to follow the example of the first Umayyad,[61] etc. It is evident to what extent the caliphs took an interest even in particular problems. This interest was motivated by the practical need for exact political knowledge and without doubt it gave a powerful boost to historiography.

As a final note, we shall try to give slightly more precise contours to the image presented hitherto of ʿAbbasid princely education, by attempting to identity its particular characteristics. The most effective way to proceed, it seems to me, is to establish a comparison with the educational practices of their predecessors, the Umayyads. Structurally, as is well known, the *mulk* of the Umayyads remained attached, to a large extent, to the pre-Islamic Bedouin social organisation, and detached itself from it only gradually. By contrast the *dawla* of the ʿAbbāsids, a supranational imamate claiming credit for the victory of authentic Islam, was obliged to start from different principles. Furthermore, the education of the Umayyads was secular and, in the religious context, rather indifferent, while for the ʿAbbāsids it was

[54] F. Rosenthal, *A History of Muslim Historiography*, Leiden 1952, p. 44.
[55] Rosenthal, *ibid.*
[56] Al-Masʿūdī, *Murūj*, v, p. 479.
[57] Al-Masʿūdī, vi, p. 161.
[58] Ibn al-Ṭiqṭaqā, *Fakhrī*, p. 128.
[59] Al-Ṭabarī, iii, p. 749 f.
[60] Al-Bayhaqī, *Maḥāsin*, p. 160.
[61] Al-Bayhaqī, *Maḥāsin*, p. 528 f.

canonical and orthodox. In the entourage of Muʿāwiya there was discussion of the ancient Arab virtues, generosity, intrepidity, chivalric spirit,[62] while al-Manṣūr, the ʿAbbāsid caliph, recommended to his son the fear of God, compassion, and warfare for the faith.[63] It is quite significant that, in the Bedouin manner, the Umayyads had themselves compared by their panegyrists to "roaring lions" "high mountains" or other symbols of might and majesty,[64] whereas all the ʿAbbāsids – with the exception of the first – adopted nicknames borrowed from the religious sphere. The young Yazīd was obliged simply to familiarise himself with the principal variants of Qurʾānic reading;[65] he had no need to immerse himself in exegesis nor in the science of tradition, although it was in precisely these areas that the young Maʾmūn had his basic education,[66] which perhaps explains in part his interest in the [**104**] subtleties of Muʿtazilite dogma. Bedouins, Christians and poets of worldly knowledge constituted the entourage of the Umayyad princes, who preferred to leave their residence for the desert where they could, at leisure and in total liberty, indulge themselves with the old *kāmil* ideal of the perfect man. In contrast, the ʿAbbāsid prince was placed primarily under the rod of lectors of the Qurʾān, jurists and traditionists. He grew up in the palace, in a sometimes rather stifling scholastic atmosphere, and was introduced at a very early age to the rules of etiquette. In relations with his peers, he did not learn, like the Umayyads, to be, but rather to appear. In the final analysis, the ʿAbbāsid pedagogic maxims are a homage to the Iranian spirit, although exaggeration should be avoided here, since this heritage was transformed structurally into an Islamic context: for the Sasanid prince, conforming to the old Persian tradition, military service was of the highest importance; in the eyes of the ʿAbbāsids, religious and intellectual education was superior to athletic and military training.

The reflections that I have sketched in here, though incomplete in some areas – will they be of use some day to anyone undertaking to write a general history of pedagogy? I do not have an answer to this question. It seems to me that anyone intent on pursuing Islamic princely education through all its subsequent evolutions and ramifications is likely to become lost in a vast morass of material.[67] We may recall only the concrete, unique and precious

[62] Al-Masʿūdī, *Murūj*, v, p. 32 and, analogue, p. 106 f.

[63] Al-Yaʿqūbī, *Historiae*, ed. Houtsma, ii, pp. 472–474; cf. A. Dietrich "Das politische Testament des zweiten ʿAbbāsidenkalifen al-Manṣūr", in *Der Islam*, 30 (1952), pp. 156–158 (133–165).

[64] H. Lammens, in *Mélanges de la Faculté Orientale de Beyrouth*, iii (1908), p. 216 f.

[65] *Ibid.*, p. 210.

[66] F. Gabrieli, in *Riv. Degli Studi Orientali*, ix (1928), p. 354 f.

[67] Other materials, and also an overall view of educators and their ʿAbbāsid pupils may be found in the thesis, presented in Hamburg, by Munir-ud-Din Ahmed, *Muslim education and*

material which is constituted by paintings in miniature. But that is another story. My more modest objective has been to cast a little light on the manner in which the ʿAbbasids perceived their "noblesse oblige".

the scholar's social status up to the 5th century Muslim Era in the light of Ta'rīkh Baghdād, Zurich 1968, pp. 46–51. However this work is based exclusively on the comprehensive biographical work indicated in the title. Cf. also A.S. Tritton, *Materials on Muslim Education in the Middle Ages*, London 1957, pp. 3–12; Khalil A. Totah. *The Contribution of the Arabs to Education*, New York City 1926 (including a very useful chapter on "Arab pedagogical literature", pp. 67–77); Ahmad Shalaby, *History of Muslim Education*, Beirut 1954 (also including, p. 125 f., a brief account of educators and of their pupils); A.L. Tibawi, *Islamic Education, its Traditions and Modernization into the Arab National Sphere*, London 1972 (describing, after a brief historical perspective, the systems of education currently in operation in the Arab states).

4
THE AGE STRUCTURE OF MEDIEVAL ISLAMIC EDUCATION

Richard W. Bulliet

The mental world of the medieval Muslim religious scholar is becoming increasingly well mapped, but the world of education in which he lived his life is still largely unexplored. No comprehensive history of Islamic education covering the pre-*madrasa* period has been written, and much that has been written about the institution of the *madrasa* itself remains problematic. (1) This lacuna in our knowledge is particularly regrettable because it deprives the researcher engaged in the study of a single medieval intellectual figure of a background against which to measure his subject while at the same time it leaves the social historian with a major gap in his understanding of medieval urban society.

The one aspect of medieval education that will be dealt with in this article, namely, the age structure of the educational

(1) Ahmad Shalaby's extensive *History of Muslim Education* (Beirut: Dar al-Kashshaf, 1954) is representative of the existing general works on Islamic education. Its approach is largely anecdotal, and it does not draw necessary distinctions between different periods in the history of education. One specific study of the pre-*madrasa* period, Munir-ud-Din Ahmed's *Muslim Education and the Scholars' Social Status* (Zurich: Der Islam, 1968) discusses the age of students and teachers at some length (pp. 143-52, 187-89), but the lack of a systematic approach to the problem leads to distorted conclusions. On the origin and character of the *madrasa* itself see George Makdisi, "Muslim Institutions of Learning in Eleventh-Century Baghdad," *Bulletin of the School of Oriental and African Studies*, 24 (1961), 1-56; A. Tibawi, "Origin and Character of *al-Madrasah*," BSOAS, 25 (1962), 225-238; R. W. Bulliet, "The Social History of Nishapur in the Eleventh Century," PhD Dissertation, Harvard University (1967), 92-100.

system in the period before the *madrasa* became the dominant institution of learning, is subject to the further restriction that the data derive from a single, though important, educational center, the city of Nishapur in northeastern Iran. Off-setting this narrowness is the breadth afforded by utilization of a quantitative approach in the study. In the absence of any strong evidence that Muslim educational norms differed radically from one city to another, the proposition may be advanced that what was true of the average student/scholar of Nishapur in the tenth and eleventh centuries was probably true of his contemporary counterparts in other cities as well.

The data subjected to quantification in this study come from the biographical dictionary of Nishapur compiled by ʿAbd al-Ghāfir al-Fārisī (d. 1135) entitled *as-Siyāq li-ta'rīkh Naisābūr.* (1) They consist of individual biographies in which evidence of student-teacher relationships is recorded, usually in the form of a list of teachers under whom the individual studied or from whom he transmitted *ḥadīth.* Twelve hundred and fifty-five or almost three quarters of the approximately 1 700 biographies in the compilation contain such information. It is evident, therefore, that education of a type warranting written commemoration was a typical trait of the people whose biographies are preserved.

The laborious procedures for assembling and rearranging the data in useful forms need not be detailed here, but one procedural note is of special importance. The names of teachers are usually given in a brief and unstandardized form. For example, one person may have studied under Abū Bakr al-Baghdādī, another under Sahl al-Ḥāfiẓ, and a third under Abū Bakr Sahl al-Baghdādī al-Ḥāfiẓ—all the same person. Great care was taken to identify the several variants of a teacher's name and then to find out who each teacher was by consulting other biographical and reference materials. Yet in 175 biographies the teachers mentioned proved to be isolated examples or

(1) R. N. Frye, ed., *The Histories of Nishapur* (Cambridge, Mass.: Harvard University Press, 1965), contains facsimiles of the two extant abbreviated versions of al-Fārisī's work.

unidentifiable, thus somewhat reducing the total number of cases available for analysis. In many of these 175 cases, however, it is likely that the teacher or teachers listed are actually known figures, but too little of the name is given to confirm an identification. Hence, these cases need not be considered a totally separate and mysterious category.

The collation of 2 582 instances of student-teacher relationships from 1 080 biographies yielded 189 teachers for whom three or more students can be identified. Of those 189, at least 23 taught elsewhere than in Nishapur, thus the number of active teachers indicated for the city of Nishapur itself is approximately 166. The earliest recorded death date for these 166 is 339 AH. Assuming he died at the end of a teaching career of average length, that is, of 22 years (see below), 317 AH may be taken as the date of initiation for the educational data, and the date of death of the last of the 166 teachers, 514 AH, represents the end of the series. In short, the teaching data cover a period of 197 Muslim lunar years, or approximately 191 Christian solar years, 929-1120 AD.

A good question with which to begin a study of the age structure of education is how old was the typical student when he began his studies? There is a certain ambiguity in the posing of this question since the education to which the available data pertain is primarily, but not always certainly, the study of the *ḥadīth* of the Prophet. Fundamental reading and writing skills were obviously learned as well, but no quantifiable information has been preserved concerning this elementary level of education. Still, an answer to the question with regard to *ḥadīth* studies will of necessity give a good indication of whether the two types of education were pursued simultaneously or in sequence.

The best data available for indicating age at the commencement of studies comes from the lists of students known to have studied under the same teacher. In some instances—well under half—the birth date of the student is known, and the death date of the teacher is usually known. Therefore, it is frequently possible to determine the age of a teacher's youngest known student at the time of the teacher's death. If the teacher had taught for over twenty years, of course, the youngest known student may have been someone from his early teaching days, and the student's age at the time of the teacher's death would be meaningless. But if a great many students are listed for a single teacher, and that teacher taught up until his death, the likelihood becomes fairly great that the youngest student listed was a product of the teacher's final years. This is particularly so in that it was considered very desirable for children to learn *ḥadīth* from very old men and thus shorten the chain of transmission *(isnād)* between them and the Prophet Muhammad. The youngest known student may not have been at the start of his own learning career, of course, but the calculation of an average age for a group of youngest known students should nevertheless provide a maximum age by which studies were normally begun.

The Nishapur data yield 26 cases of teachers with twenty or more known students. Four cases in which the youngest student was over 25 at the time of the teacher's death may be discounted. In one instance, the teacher probably taught in the city of Jurjan instead of Nishapur and therefore would not have had access to juvenile students from the latter city. In two instances the teachers are well known sufis, Abū al-Qāsim al-Qushairī and Abū 'Alī ad-Daqqāq, and it is reasonable to assume that they did not accept small children as candidates for initiation into the path of mystic enlightenment. The fourth case is that of Imām al-Ḥaramain al-Juwainī whose teaching was done as the first professor of the Niẓāmiya *madrasa* of Nishapur. The prototype of a *madrasa* form that was to influence all later Muslim education, the Nishapur Niẓāmiya very probably set a minimum age for its students. [1]

In the remaining 22 cases, the average age of the beginning student was 7.5 years with a standard deviation of 2.7. [2]

(1) Few details are preserved concerning the operation of the Nishapur Niẓāmiya. For information on the later but more famous Baghdad institution see Asad Talas, *L'enseignement chez les arabes*; *la madrasa Niẓāmiya et son histoire* (Paris: Geuthner, 1939).

(2) All figures relating to spans of years have been calculated to represent solar years rather than the shorter lunar years of the Muslim calendar.

In other words, the sample indicates that typical students had begun their education by the time they reached the age range 4.8-10.2. As already mentioned, this should be considered a maximum age range. Hence it is clear that *ḥadīth* study regularly began in childhood and therefore must have been concurrent with elementary training in reading and writing. Anecdotal evidence of fathers and uncles escorting children to class, and probably taking notes for them, supports this conclusion. (1)

The sample involved in this calculation is not very large, but the general validity of the conclusion drawn from it can be measured by comparison with a figure derived from different data. For the 166 teachers mentioned earlier as working in Nishapur, information regarding their own teachers is frequently recorded. Where there are several such teacher's teachers listed, it is often possible to determine the age of the subject teacher at the time of the death of the earliest of his teachers to die. The logic is the same as in the preceding calculation, but the data are entirely different. In 22 instances in which at least three teacher's teachers with known death dates are listed, the average age of the subject teacher at the time of the death of his earliest dying mentor is 11.1 with a standard deviation of 6.7. The age range thus indicated for beginning to study, 4.4-17.8, is somewhat greater than that produced by the earlier calculation, but the general import is the same: *ḥadīth* study usually commenced in childhood. However, the age range determined by the first calculation will be used henceforth in this article since it refers to typical students rather than to those who ultimately achieved great distinction as teachers and who may have discounted their own earliest childhood instruction in determining what they felt competent to teach.

Having determined an age range for the commencement of *ḥadīth* education, we can turn to the question of how long the average student's learning career lasted. The answer to this question should indicate how old a man was when he entered

(1) Ahmed, *Muslim Education*, 144-145.

society as an educated person, if such a concept is appropriate for the society in question. (1)

There are again two ways of inferring from the data average length of learning careers. One method goes back to the subgroup already utilized of teachers whose own teachers are known. In 46 instances death dates are recorded for two or more of a teacher's teachers. If one were to assume that the suject teacher studied under every one of his teachers during the last year of that teacher's life, then the difference between the death of the earliest dying teacher and that of the latest dying teacher should be the duration of the learning career of the subject teacher. This assumption may not be entirely realistic, but the calculation of an average duration for a substantial number of cases should at least provide a good figure for maximum length of learning career. In the 46 instances where a subject teacher had two or more teachers of known date of death, the average difference between the earliest and latest dates is 20.4 years with a standard deviation of 19.4 years.

The other method of approaching the question looks at instances in which two teachers shared the same student. A thorough collation of this type of data yields for any given teacher the death date of both the earliest dying teacher with whom he shared a student and the latest. Again assuming that every teacher taught until his death, the differences between the death date of the subject teacher and that of his earliest dying co-teacher, one the one hand, and between his death and that of his latest dying co-teacher, on the other hand, provide for each subject teacher two time spans for the learning careers of two separate students. Unlike the first method, this approach should yield a minimum figure for span of learning career rather than a maximum figure since the subject teacher cannot be assumed to have been either the first or the last teacher a student had. A total of 94 cases produces an average of 13.4 years with a standard deviation of 7.9.

(1) While there are a number of biographical entries of women in al-Fārisī's dictionary, they are too few to convey the impression that education of women was other than an unusual phenomenon.

Drawing a reasonable conclusion from the figures produced by the two preceding methods is clearly problematic given the large standard deviations. Yet the median point between the hypothesized minimum and maximum learning careers, namely, 16.9 years, seems not too unlikely as long as it is understood that some students may have studied *ḥadīth* for as briefly as a year or two while others may have persevered for several decades. A special value of the median figure of 16.9 is that it makes possible a rough estimate of the age at which a man was expected to have "completed" his education. If he began to attend classes on *ḥadīth* between 5 and 10 years of age, as already suggested, he should have completed his studies sometime in his twenties, roughly between 22 and 27 with a generous additional allowance made for those who dropped out substantially earlier and those who persevered substantially longer.

If a man entered society as an educated person sometime in his mid-twenties, then, at what age did those who were destined to transmit *ḥadīth* to the next generation begin their teaching careers? The first step in answering this question is to determine the average lifespan of the teachers in our sample of 166. In the 47 ascertainable cases, the average age at death was 84.3 years with a standard deviation of 8.9. If we subtract from this figure the length of the average teaching career, we will discover the typical age at which a person's teaching career commenced.

There are two ways of estimating the average length of a teaching career. One is quite straightforward. In 18 instances a specific statement in the teacher's biography gives the inaugural date of his first class. The average length of time between this first class and the teacher's death is 21.6 years with a standard deviation of 18.8.

The second indicator derives from 69 instances in which at least two students with known birthdates are recorded as studying under the same teacher. The average length of time between the birth of the youngest recorded student and the birth of the oldest is 21.3 years (SD 14.4). Although both methods yield high standard deviations, the mean figures for span of teaching career are essentially identical. It thus seems reasonable to adopt 22 years as the length of the typical career even while allowing that some teachers may have taught for less than ten years and others for more than 35.

If the typical teacher died between 75 and 93 at the end of a teaching career of 22 years, then 53-71 should be the age range for the commencement of a career in *ḥadīth* transmission. Taking into account the high standard deviation associated with the estimate of 22 years, a plausible conclusion is that while it was not out of the question for a person to begin transmitting *ḥadīth* when he was as young as forty, it was more likely that he would be over fifty if not over sixty years old.

This conclusion may be tested by two independent estimates. In 34 cases where a teacher with a known birth date has one or more students with known birth dates, it is possible to determine the average age of the teacher at the birth of his earliest known student. The resultant figure is 50.3 (SD 15.4). If 7.5 is added to this figure to represent the average age of a student at the commencement of his studies as earlier determined, the average age of the beginning teacher can be estimated at 57.8 years, well within the range already indicated.

The second test estimate is derived by finding the average difference between the date of death of a teacher and the date of death of the last of his known students. The resultant figure is 60.9 (SD 20.9), again in the middle of the range of ages indicated above.

The overall picture that emerges from the preceding welter of numbers is fairly clear. A typical male inhabitant of Nishapur whose social status permitted him to enter upon a course of learning and ultimately a career of *ḥadīth* transmission began his studies sometime in childhood and had them basically completed by his late twenties. There then passed a period of thirty years or so during which he was not obviously active in educational affairs. In his late fifties or even his sixties his first class was convened, and he pursued a career of reciting *ḥadīth* to children and adolescents until his death at a ripe old age.

But is this picture a reliable one? And if it is reliable, what else may be concluded from it?

The most apparent potential sources of unreliability are those inherent in the character of the biographical dictionary providing the data. It is possible, for example, that only a small and biased fraction of all student-teacher relationships has been preserved in this source. While it is difficult to prove that this is not the case, a reasonable indicator that bias is probably not a major problem comes from the student-teacher data relating to the relatives of the dictionary's compiler. 'Abd al-Ghāfir al-Fārisī's paternal grandfather of the same name was a famous scholar of *ḥadīth* and has the maximum number of 115 students listed in his grandson's dictionary. His maternal grandfather, however, the even more famous sufi scholar Abū al-Qāsim al-Qushairī, has only 55 students listed. By comparison there are eleven *ḥadīth* scholars with whom the author had no noteworthy connection who have between 55 and 80 students listed. The compiler, therefore, seems not to have given special prominence to family and friends.

The same information also suggests that the sample is not unreasonably small in comparison with the total number of recorded teaching events. If the compiler's paternal grandfather, for whom the data can be assumed to be reasonably complete, has only 115 recorded students, then the smaller numbers preserved for other well known scholars are unlikely to be understated by more than fifty percent. In other words, the 2 582 student-teacher relationships indicated by the 1 080 biographies may actually stand for some 5 000 such relationships, but probably not for a great many more.

If the 5 000 figure is a roughly reliable estimate, the conclusion would seem to be inescapable that classes were very small in size. It was established earlier that Nishapur had 166 teachers active over a period of 191 years. With an average teaching career of 22 years, this means 3 652 teacher-years of instruction or 19 teachers actively giving instruction in any given year. If there were 5 000 student-teacher contacts spread out over the same 191 year period, it would appear that each teacher completed instruction of only 1.4 students per year. These calculations do not take into account teachers who had less than three known students or unidentified teachers, but these would surely not affect the broad conclusions very greatly. While there is no way of determining how long a student studied with a single teacher whom he later regarded as his mentor, the indicated rate of student production per teacher seems unrealistically low given any reasonable estimate.

Here it seems highly probable that the character of the biographical dictionary source does produce a distortion. For one thing, the presence in class of visiting scholars from other cities is largely unrecorded even though the practice of travelling to hear *ḥadīth* was widespread. But more importantly, there is substantial evidence that much of the matter of al-Fārisī's compilation, like that of comparable works produced at that time in other cities, came ultimately from notebooks (books of shaikhs=*kutub al-mashā'ikh*) in which students kept a record of who their teachers were and what *ḥadīth* they learned from them. (1) Such notebooks would eventually become useful if the student became himself a teacher later in life.

By the time a student was in his late twenties, however, it must have become evident to him and to everyone else that any *ḥadīth* that he might eventually transmit to the next generation were already in his mental possession. He might still attend classes in *ḥadīth*, but it would be pointless to make the same kind of formal record of the fact since he would probably never teach those *ḥadīth*. The desirability of having a "high" (fewest links) chain of transmission *(isnād)* between oneself and the Prophet would make the following cohort of students a decade younger the logical eventual transmitters of *ḥadīth* heard so late in one's learning career. (2) In other words, what terminated by the age of thirty was not the habit of

(1) For a noteworthy example of such a work see G. Vajda, "La *Mašyaḫa* d'Ibn al-Ḥaṭṭāb al-Rāzī," *Bulletin d'Études Orientales*, 23 (1970), 21-99.

(2) An interesting illustration of this attitude by denial is put into the mouth of the great vizier Niẓām al-Mulk; "My way of proceeding with regard to 'highness' of *ḥadīth* is different from that of my masters. They maintain that the 'high' *ḥadīth* is the one with the fewest intermediate reciters. For me, the 'high' *ḥadīth* is the one that is a soundly reliable recitation from the Messenger of God even though the number of reciters should reach a hundred." S. Zakkar, "Biographie de Niẓām al-Mulk," *Bulletin d'Études Orientales*, 24 (1971), 236.

attending classes on *ḥadīth* so much as the utility of making a formal record of attendance for future use in teaching.

The low rate of student production per teacher, therefore, need not be interpreted as reflecting very small class size. Anecdotal evidence gives numerous instances of adults attending *ḥadīth* sessions, frequently accompanying their children or as a way of honoring the teacher. (1) It is quite likely, in fact, that at least some classes by famous transmitters had only a few people in attendance who were recording the *ḥadīth* for their permanent educational record, including out-of-town visitors. The majority of the class may have been local adults who attended simply as a matter of piety and social convention.

If this is the case, it helps resolve another question raised by the educational cycle summarized earlier. How did people spend the three or four decades between "completing" their education and beginning to teach? Most of the answer, of course, lies in rearing families, making a living, serving in religious or public office, and so forth. But from the educational point of view, the answer is probably that studying continued off and on, in an informal fashion, simply as a natural part of the life of a patrician of that period. Some individuals undoubtedly taught other subjects during their middle decades and only turned to *ḥadīth* late in life. Most probably never taught at all.

The primary reason for the long hiatus between formal *ḥadīth* study and eventual *ḥadīth* teaching was the necessity of waiting for enough time to pass to make the *ḥadīth* one had to transmit valuable in the eyes of young students whose desire for a "high" chain of transmission drew them strongly to the oldest teachers. Yet even then, only a few of those who studied *ḥadīth* in their youth ever taught them in old age. How they were selected or selected themselves for this important social role is unclear, but simple longevity seems not to be involved. (2) An initial

(1) For an example of *ḥadīth* session arranged and attended for the purpose of honoring the teachers, ambassadors from a foreign ruler, see R. W. Bulliet, *The Patricians of Nishapur* (Cambridge, Mass.: Harvard University Press, 1972), 55.

(2) This is contrary to the remarks stressing longevity made by Roy P. Mottahedeh in *Loyalty and Leadership in an Early Islamic Society* (Princeton: Princeton University Press, 1980), 145-146.

class for transmitting *ḥadīth* was usually convened when one was in one's fifties or sixties, as already mentioned, but over two thirds of the population represented in al-Fārisī's biographical dictionary died between 66 and 96. Thus the transmitters of tradition to the generation of grandchildren were not simply the last survivors of the generation of grandfathers.

At this point, a few broad conclusions may be ventured on the basis of the foregoing discussion. First and most obvious is the remarkable stress placed by the system of *ḥadīth* education upon the extreme ends of the age scale. The ideal was to have the very old teach the very young even though people of all ages might be in attendance at the class. Related to this is the apparent fact that a patrician became socialized into the system of *ḥadīth* education as a normal part of childhood. A reverence for the traditions of the Prophet was inculcated at such an early point that their collection, retention, and transmission became an engrained and undisputed societal norm.

Another conclusion relates to the debate over whether acquisition of learning commonly provided a route for social mobility in medieval Islam. With regard to the data available for Nishapur in the tenth and eleventh centuries, it is difficult to conclude that there was much social mobility through education. The student production rate per teacher suggests that the educational system did little more than service the offspring of the patrician class. The estimate made earlier of 1.4 students "graduated" per teacher per year yields 26 such "graduates" per year. If each of these had a normal family life over 35 years, the span of a generation, the cumulative total for the size of the fully educated stratum of society would be 910. (1) Assuming a household size of five, this means a patrician class of 4 550 or 4 % of an urban population conservatively estimated at 110,000. (2) Given the economy of the period, particularly

(1) For the calculation of the length of a generation see R. W. Bulliet, *Conversion to Islam in the Medieval Period* (Cambridge, Mass.: Harvard University Press, 1979), 21.

(2) The estimate of 110,000 is based upon a lower guess as to average household size, but the upper class could be expected to have larger than average households. R. W. Bulliet, "Medieval Nishapur: A Topographic and Demographic Reconstruction," *Studia Iranica*, 5 (1976), 88.

the fact that many of the most common occupations are not found among the family names contained in the biographies, 4 % would seem to be a not unrealistic number. (1) Therefore, even though the individuals whose biographies are preserved come mostly from well established families, thus introducing a circular element into these deductions, there appears to have been little room in the society at large to accomodate a significant upwardly mobile but not yet arrived educated group that might have been deliberately overlooked by the compiler.

A final observation is less a conclusion than a question calling for further study. The reason the age structure of the educational system is so difficult to ascertain with precision is that the system as a whole lacked formal parameters. Matriculation, graduation, set curricula, age limits, degrees, admissions qualifications, the whole panoply of modern educational administration was absent, with the likely exception of a means of controlling who would be allowed to teach. (2) With the gradual introduction over the next several centuries of the *madrasa* system of education, patterned ultimately on the Niẓāmiya of Nishapur, this lack of system gave way to something more familiar to the modern scholar, an institution roughly definable as a college of Muslim religious studies and of religious law in particular. The question that is posed by this educational transition is whether the introduction of the *madrasa* system fundamentally altered the age structure described in this study, and if so, whether in the process it worked changes upon the societal norms and relationships embodied in the previous system?

Richard W. Bulliet
(New York)

(1) Butchers, bakers, and greengrocers are scarcely ever encountered, while names associated with the luxury cloth trades abound.

(2) On the question of the control over who was allowed to teach see R. W. Bulliet, *The Patricians of Nishapur*, 49-55, and the queries raised about parts of the analysis presented therein by Roy P. Mottahedeh in his review in *Journal of the American Oriental Society*, 95 (1975), 492-493. On the practice of certifying teachers in Baghdad during the same period see Ahmed, *Muslim Education*, 190-193.

5
ADVICE FOR TEACHERS: THE 9TH CENTURY MUSLIM SCHOLARS IBN SAḤNŪN AND AL-JĀḤIẒ ON PEDAGOGY AND DIDACTICS*

Sebastian Günther

Dedicated to Professor Michael Marmura,
on the occasion of his 75th birthday, 11 November 2004.

As Islam was spreading among diverse peoples between the 7th and the 9th century C.E., education came to be recognized by the Muslim community as a proper channel through which the universal and cohesive social order—in the way the Quran commanded it—could be established. This resulted in a rapidly increasing need for accessible and effective formal education at both the primary and higher levels. Interestingly enough, the major educational efforts in the formative period of Islam were made by individual scholars, most of them teachers themselves. In other words, these educational activities were individual in nature and intellectual in expression.

1 *The* ādāb al-ʿālim wa-l-mutaʿallim *literature*

By the 9th century, educational thought in Islam started to find its literary expression in Arabic texts devoted to teaching and learning. At this time, educational writing appears to have developed a distinct genre of its own, i.e. the *ādāb al-ʿālim wa-l-mutaʿallim* literature. This subcategory of classical Arabic literature is represented, in its core, by works expressly dealing with "rules of conduct for teachers and students." These texts explain and analyze teaching methods, the ways in which learning takes place, or should take place, the

---

* This chapter presents some of the first results of a long-term research project devoted to educational thought in the classical period of Islam. A monograph on this topic is in progress. Research for this article was partly supported by a grant generously provided by The NIWANO Peace Foundation Tokyo, Japan.

aims of education, as well as the means by which such goals may be achieved. This includes the manner in which teachers and students act and behave, their (moral) characteristics, their relationship with one another in the process of education, the contents of learning, and the means and methods of imparting and absorbing knowledge. In short, this particular type of text can aptly be called pedagogical.

Classical Arabic pedagogical writings provide useful insights into the intellectual culture of Islam in medieval times. They suggest the following: Firstly, the social transfer of knowledge and the intellectual development of individuals and groups were subject to the vivid scholarly interest of Muslims—as witnessed shortly after the rise of Islam in the early 7th century—and became more evident in literary and scholarly writing during subsequent centuries. Secondly, initiated by the translation of classical Greek and Syriac texts into Arabic in the 8th and 9th centuries, the creative adoption of the Hellenistic heritage also left its mark on the Islamic theory of education. This is particularly noticeable in the writings of Muslim authors who deal, from a philosophical-ethical point of view, with the developmental stages in the formation of human character and personality, the early education of the child, and with higher learning. Thirdly, the views on education in Islam benefited from, but also influenced, certain Jewish and Christian ideas on education significant to the Middle East at that time.

Thus far, the *ādāb al-ʿālim wa-l-mutaʿallim* literature as a particular type of scholarly expression in Arabic in medieval times has gained only scant attention in Western studies on Islam,[1] despite the fact that al-Ghazālī's (d. 505 A.H./1111 C.E.) insightful passages on the ethics of education in several of his works are fairly well known.[2]

[1] A classic, so to speak, of Western research on educational thought in medieval Arabic literature is Franz Rosenthal's *The Technique and Approach of Muslim Scholarship* (1947). Furthermore, one would need to mention Khalil Abdallah Totah's *The Contribution of the Arabs to Education* (1926), Ahmad Shalaby's *History of Muslim Education* (1954), and A.S. Tritton's *Materials on Muslim Education* (1957). For more specific aspects of the social history of Islamic education, the transmission of knowledge, and the educational practice and institutions, see, for example, the studies by A. Munir-ud-Din (1968), A. Tibawi, (1979), G. Schoeler (1985–), H. Nashshabe (1989), J. Berkey (1992), A. Gilʿadi (1992), and M. Chamberlain (1994).

[2] Cf. the passages on education included in al-Ghazālī's "The [Re-]Vitalization of Religious Sciences (*Iḥyāʾ ʿulūm al-dīn*)" and "The Criterion of Action (*Mīzān al-ʿamal*)," but also the educational-ethical treatise "O Son (*Ayyuhā l-walad*)" attributed to him.

The originality of the educational ideas in these works, along with the sophisticated way in which they are presented, have caused modern scholarship to appreciate al-Ghazālī as an intellectual mastermind behind classical Islam's philosophy and ethics of education, in addition to his many other celebrated scholarly achievements.

However, a good number of Arabic works from the time before and after al-Ghazalī also deal in a most fascinating way with various aspects of pedagogy and didactics. Unfortunately, only a small portion of these educational texts have been studied and published, and the information about them is rather scattered throughout the primary and secondary sources. The evidence of the *ādāb al-ʿālim wa-l-mutaʿallim* works, however, does provide a clear idea of the impressively long and continuous tradition of medieval Arabic scholarship dealing with pedagogical and didactic issues, regardless of their authors' individual theological and juridical stances, ethnic origins, or geographical affiliations.

* * *

In this chapter, the focus is on two very early and, in many ways, remarkable examples of classical Arabic writings on education. The first treatise is entitled "Rules of Conduct for Teachers (*K. Ādāb al-muʿallimīn*)," and was written by Ibn Saḥnūn, a scholar from the western part of the Islamic empire. The second work bears the title "The Teachers (*K. al-Muʿallimīn*)," and it is the work of ʿAmr ibn Baḥr al-Jāḥiẓ, a famous contemporary of Ibn Saḥnūn's from the eastern lands of Islam.

Like other works of the *ādāb al-ʿālim wa-l-mutaʿallim* literature, these two texts are significant in several regards: firstly, as historical sources, since they provide information on the realities of intellectual life in medieval Islam; secondly, as evidence for the development of the theory of education, since their authors attempt to establish rules for teachers and students; and thirdly, as literary testimonies, since these texts show the distinctive methods used by their authors for presenting their educational ideas in writing.

2 *Ibn Saḥnūn*

2.1 *The scholar's life and academic career*

Muḥammad Ibn Saḥnūn al-Tanūkhī[3] was a prominent expert of Mālikī law, a *ḥadīth* scholar, historian, and biographer.[4] He was born in 202/817 in al-Qayrawān, a city in modern Tunisia. At the beginning of the 9th century, al-Qayrawān was a flourishing economic, administrative, cultural, and intellectual center, as well as a nucleus of the Mālikī school of law for the western lands of Islam.[5]

Ibn Saḥnūn was of Arab descent. His grandfather Saʿīd had arrived in al-Qayrawān in the middle of the 2nd/8th century with a group of people from Ḥimṣ in Syria, sent there by the Umayyad authorities in Damascus to support (militarily) the presence of the Muslims in the Maghrib.[6] Ibn Saḥnūn's father, Saḥnūn,[7] "a man of rigorous and demanding ethics," is known as "one of the great architects of the exclusive supremacy of Sunnism in its Mālikī form throughout the Muslim West."[8] In addition, it is interesting to note that Saḥnūn had begun his academic career as an elementary schoolteacher, teaching the Quran in a simple building rented for this particular purpose.[9]

---

[3] His full name is Abū ʿAbdallāh Muḥammad ibn (Abī Saʿīd) Saḥnūn ibn Saʿīd ibn Ḥabīb ibn Ḥassān ibn Hilāl ibn Bakkār ibn Rabīʿa at-Tanūkhī; see Ibn Saḥnūn's biography in: al-Mālikī, *Riyāḍ al-nufūs*, i, 443–458; and i, 345ff.; and ʿIyāḍ, *Tarājim* 170–188; see furthermore the art. "Muḥammad b. Saḥnūn," in: *EI*² vii, 409 (G. Lecomte); and G. Lecomte, Le Livre 77–82, esp. 79–80.

[4] Al-Mālikī, *Riyāḍ al-nufūs* i, p. 13 of the introduction.

[5] Under the rule of the Aghlabides (r. 184–296/800–909), al-Qayrawān became a stronghold for the study of the Quran and the Sunna, and for Mālikī law. Nonetheless, scholars from al-Qayrawān and other Maghribi cities were in vital academic contact with the east of the ʿAbbāsid caliphate, to which the area ruled by Aghlabides nominally belonged. Scholars made pilgrimages and study trips to Mecca and Medina, and traveled to centers of higher learning such as Baghdad, Basra, and Kufa. See, for example, ʿIyāḍ, *Tarājim* 93; *EI*² viii, 843; and the art. "Mālikiyya" (N. Cottart), in: *EI*² vi, 278–283, esp. 278, 280–281.

[6] Al-Mālikī, *Riyāḍ al-nufūs* i, 346–7; ʿIyāḍ, *Tarājim* 86; al-Qayrawānī, *Ṭabaqāt* 184.

[7] For his biography, see al-Mālikī, *Riyāḍ al-nufūs* i, 345–375; and the art. "Saḥnūn" (M. Talbi), in: *EI*² viii, 843–845. The nickname Saḥnūn—the name of a bird—was given to him because of his sharp eyesight.

[8] *EI*² viii, 845.

[9] Al-Mālikī, *Riyāḍ al-nufūs* i, 343–344; and Ismail 37. Saḥnūn owes much of his scholarly reputation to his *Mudawwana*, one of the great manuals of Mālikī law. Through this work, Saḥnūn played a major role in "the definitive implantation of Mālikism in the Maghrib" (*EI*² vii, 409 and *EI*² viii, 843), although he had—due to the lack of financial resources, as he himself attested—not been able to study himself with Imām Mālik.

Ibn Saḥnūn spent a carefree childhood in al-Qayrawān. He received a traditional primary education at an elementary school (*kuttāb*),[10] including an introduction to the Quran and the basics of writing. It appears that his father, Saḥnūn, cared very much for his son; for example, he is credited with having expressly requested that his son's teacher:

> Educate him with compliments and kind words only. He is not the one to be educated by beating and reprimanding. [When I pass away,] I will leave him [as someone who acts] in accordance with what I believe (*atrukuhū ʿalā niḥlatī*). Hence I hope that he will be unique in his kind and unparalleled among the people of his time.[11]

Already as a young boy, Ibn Saḥnūn frequently attended the classes given by his father for more advanced students.[12] Thus he came to know the academic activities and the pious life-style of scholars participating in these study circles on Mālikī law, along with the topics and teaching methods of higher learning.[13] This exceptional study opportunity at a young age was certainly not an insignificant factor in preparing Ibn Saḥnūn intellectually for his future academic career as a leading Mālikī scholar.

In 235/850, at the age of thirty-three, Ibn Saḥnūn left on pilgrimage. He reached Mecca via Tripolis and Cairo (*miṣr*).[14] He is reported to have taught at the Friday-Mosque, ʿAmr ibn al-ʿĀṣ, in Fusṭāṭ[15] and to have attended lectures by various prominent scholars in Egypt. After fulfilling the obligations of the pilgrimage, he went from Mecca to Medina. An anecdote relates that, upon arriving there, he paid a visit to the Mosque of the Prophet (*al-masjid al-nabawī*) where a study circle (*ḥalqa*) was held by Abū Muṣʿab Aḥmad ibn Abī Bakr al-Zuhrī (d. 242/854), one of Imām Mālik's closest

---

[10] "A primary, or elementary school, . . . [it] introduces the six to seven year old child to the basics of language, and instructs him in Qurʾān, *ḥadīth*, and different religious rituals. The structure and teaching methods of the *kuttāb* . . . were almost certainly inherited from Byzantium and reflect a wide Mediterranean tradition . . .;" cf. Baer, Muslim Teaching Institutions 73.

[11] Al-Mālikī, *Riyāḍ al-nufūs* i, 443–444.

[12] Al-Mālikī, *Riyāḍ al-nufūs* i, 444, 448; ʿIyāḍ, *Tarājim* 171.

[13] His father was his first and most important teacher. Ibn Saḥnūn studied also with some other leading Maghribi scholars such as Mūsā ibn Muʿāwiya al-Ṣumādiḥī (d. 225/840), ʿAbd al-ʿAzīz ibn Yaḥyā al-Madanī (d. 240/854), and ʿAbdallāh ibn Abī Ḥassān al-Ḥimṣī al-Yaḥṣūbī (d. 227/842); see al-Mālikī, *Riyāḍ al-nufūs* i, 444.

[14] Al-Mālikī, *Riyāḍ al-nufūs* i, 444; ʿIyāḍ, *Tarājim* 177.

[15] Al-Mālikī, *Riyāḍ al-nufūs* i, 444; and *EI*[2] vii, 409.

colleagues in Medina. The students at this circle were arguing on the legal issue of *umm al-walad*. When Ibn Saḥnūn told them a joke about the topic of discussion, he attracted Abū Muṣʿab's attention so that Abū Muṣʿab recognized him as *the* Ibn Saḥnūn from al-Qayrawān.[16] It is more important, however, to note that Ibn Saḥnūn's biographers all emphasize the very favorable impression the young scholar left on the intellectual milieu in Egypt and the Ḥijāz.[17]

At some point before the year 239/854–5, Ibn Saḥnūn returned to his hometown, al-Qayrawān. There he established his own study circle (*ḥalqa*) next to his father's.[18] After his father's death in Rajab 240/December 855, Ibn Saḥnūn became the chief *qāḍī* of the Mālikites in the Maghrib. Supported by the Aghlabid regent and *de facto* governor, Emir Ibrāhīm II (r. officially from 875 to 902), Ibn Saḥnūn is said to have led the Mālikī struggle against the Ḥanafites and Muʿtazilites in the Maghrib.[19]

Ibn Saḥnūn died in al-Qayrawān in 256/870 at the age of fifty-four. On the day of his funeral, the stores and schools in al-Qayrawān were closed as an expression of mourning. The funeral prayer for the deceased scholar was led by Emir Ibrāhīm II.[20] Ibn Saḥnūn was buried in al-Qayrawān next to his father's tomb. The memorial shrine (*qubba*) built over his grave shortly became such a popular site that shops opened to accommodate and benefit from the many visitors. The Emir, however, eventually ordered these shops closed and dispersed the people.[21]

Ibn Saḥnūn was a productive scholar. He is reported to have written nearly 200 books and treatises. Twenty-four works have been identified by title, but only three texts have been preserved. Most titles point to *fatwā*s and other short legal documents. Some books, however, are said to have been multi-volume encyclopaedias on Ḥadīth and Islamic history. The preserved book titles indicate that Ibn Saḥnūn had, in general, a vivid interest in the systematic teaching of the Quran and the essentials of Islamic belief.[22] One can imag-

---

[16] Al-Mālikī, *Riyāḍ al-nufūs* i, 184.
[17] See also *EI*² vii, 409.
[18] Al-Mālikī, *Riyāḍ al-nufūs* i, 444.
[19] *EI*² vii, 409.
[20] Al-Mālikī, *Riyāḍ al-nufūs* i, 444.
[21] ʿIyāḍ, *Tarājim* 186–187.
[22] Al-Mālikī, *Riyāḍ al-nufūs* i, 443; ʿIyāḍ, *Tarājim* 173. The other two preserved

ine how important this was especially when taking into consideration the attempts made in the 8th and 9th centuries in the Islamic West to Islamize and Arabicize the Berber population.

2.2 *Ibn Saḥnūn's book on "Rules of Conduct for Teachers"*

2.2.1 *Structure, contents, and style*

In terms of intention, content, and style, Ibn Saḥnūn's *K. Ādāb al-muʿallimīn*[23] is part of the so-called professional *adab*-literature. Like other manuals of this type—compiled for secretaries, clerks, copyists, or judges—Ibn Saḥnūn's work addresses a specific community of people: the teachers at elementary schools, whom he provides with professional and juridical advice.

Ibn Saḥnūn's *K. Ādāb al-muʿallimīn*[24] starts with quotations of prophetic traditions, expressing the "merit" (*faḍl*) and the advantage of teaching and learning the Quran. The book concludes with similar statements by Mālik ibn Anas, which in turn display Ibn Saḥnūn's affiliation to the Mālikī school of law. Ibn Saḥnūn's treatise has ten chapters, as follows:

i. [Traditions] on the teaching of the Quran.	*Mā jāʾa fī taʿlīm al-Qurʾān al-ʿazīz*
ii. [Traditions] on the equity [to be observed in treating school]boys.	*Mā jāʾa fī l-ʿadl bayna l-ṣibyān*

books are: the *K. Masāʾil al-jihād* (ms. Tunis) and the *K. Ajwibat Muḥammad ibn Saḥnūn, riwāyat Muḥammad ibn Sālim al-Qaṭṭān ʿanhu* (ms. Escorial 1162; three copies in Tunis); see *EI*[2] vii, 409; Lecomte 80.

[23] The complete text of the *K. Ādāb al-muʿallimīn* has been preserved in a unique Tunisian manuscript from the 14th or 15th century (National Tunisian Library, ms. Tunis 8787); cf. also Lecomte, Le Livre 78. For a short description of the Tunisian ms., see Ḥijāzī 43. Fragmentary passages of the text have also been preserved in a Rabat manuscript (catalogued as ms. 85*qāf*) consisting of approximately sixty percent of the work; cf. Ḥijāzī 46. While the Tunisian text starts with *qāla Abū ʿAbdallāh Muḥammad ibn Saḥnūn*, the Moroccan text indicates a different transmission by stating: *ḥaddathanī Abū l-ʿAbbās ʿAbdallāh ibn Aḥmad ibn Furāt ibn Muḥammad, qāla: ḥaddathanī Muḥammad ibn Saḥnūn ʿan abīhī* [. . .]. This suggests that Ibn Saḥnūn's treatise for teachers circulated in more than one transmitted version; see also Ḥijāzī 46. A French translation of the *K. Ādāb al-muʿallimīn* was published by G. Lecomte; see his Le Livre 82–105.

[24] This article's references to Ibn Saḥnūn's *K. Ādāb al-muʿallimīn* are based on Muḥammad al-ʿArūsī al-Maṭwī's edition as reprinted in: Ḥijāzī, *al-Madhhab*, 111–128; lower case Roman numerals indicate chapters of Ibn Saḥnūn's work.

iii.	Chapter [of traditions] on the reprehensibility of erasing the Word of God the Exalted [when written on slates], and what should be done [instead] in this regard.	*Bāb mā yukrahu maḥwuhu min dhikr Allāh taʿālā wa-mā yanbaghī an yufʿala min dhālika*
iv.	[Traditions] on disciplining [students], and on what is permissible in this [regard] and what is not.	*Mā jāʾa fī l-adab wa mā yajūzu min dhālika wa-mā lā yajūzu*
v.	[Opinions] on the final exams for the recitation of the Quran [at elementary schools], and what is [to be given] to the teacher on this [occasion]	*Mā jāʾa fī l-khitam wa-mā yajibu fī dhālika li-l-muʿallim*
vi.	[Opinions] on the presentation of gifts [to the teacher] on feast days.	*Mā jāʾa fī l-qaḍāʾ fī ʿaṭiyyat al-ʿīd*
vii.	[Opinions] on [the occasions] when [the teacher] should give days off to the [school]boys	*Mā yanbaghī an yukhallā l-ṣibyān fīhi*
viii.	[Opinions] on the obligation on the teacher to stay all the time with the pupils [under his supervision]	*Mā yajibu ʿalā l-muʿallim min luzūm al-ṣibyān*
ix.	[Opinions] on the wage of the teacher and when it is obligatory	*Mā jāʾa fī ijārat al-muʿallim wa-matā tajibu*
x.	[Opinions] on renting a copy of the Quran, law books, and other such books	*Mā jāʾa fī ijārat al-muṣḥaf wa-kutub al-fiqh wa-mā shābahahā*

Based on criteria such as formal structure and style, the book is divided into two main parts: The first part comprises chapters one to four. Here the fundamentals of teaching pupils at elementary schools are provided. The author deals with the obligation to learn and memorize the Quran and the need for people to teach it. He talks about the practical issues implied when writing exercises are based on the quranic text, about the disciplinary measures to correct the pupils' behavior, and about physical punishment. As indicated above, this first part is almost entirely based on quotations of prophetic traditions. Only occasionally does the author make short comments on these *ḥadīths*, rounding off a particular topic.

The second part of the book is formed by chapters five to ten. These chapters follow a different scheme: they present almost exclusively questions Ibn Saḥnūn asked his father and answers his father gave him. Here the author addresses more specific issues related to the actual process of education. He covers the following topics: hiring a teacher, the various obligations regarding the *khatma* (the final oral exam after the pupil has memorized the Quran),[25] some teacher's obligations (including the rental of the school or classroom at the teachers' expense, and the preparation teachers need before entering the classroom), enforcement of the curriculum (including obligatory and optional topics to be taught, supervision of pupils, and consultation with a pupil's parents on the child's strengths and weaknesses). Furthermore, the author discusses the basic salary, additional payments for teachers (including questions of the permissibility of such additional payments), and the legitimacy of renting books for teaching purposes.

As for the formal structure of this second part, a decisive question-answer pattern is striking in Ibn Saḥnūn's work. This pattern supports the sequence of thesis and antithesis which, in turn, displays the author's legal training in reasoning and arguing.[26] Occasionally, the pros and cons of issues are given. For example, he first provides a statement that may reflect an arguable opinion or circumstance, and then quotes an authoritative tradition or a statement that sets things right.

These characteristics of the text altogether make Ibn Saḥnūn's book read like a legal document: it enumerates rules and precedents

---

[25] *Khatma* (colloquial: *khitma*), pl. *khitam*, is the technical term used in Islamic education for a child's recitation of the entire Quran and his/her graduation. In modern times, "the so-called *iḥlāba* is celebrated when a boy has read through the whole of the sacred book (the ceremony after the half or one-third is called *iṣrāfa*);" cf. Fr. Buhl, in: *EI*[2] iv, 1112.

[26] The use of a question-and-answer pattern in scholarly writing has a long tradition in the Middle East; see U. Pietruschka's contribution to this book and the references given there. It is worth mentioning that this pattern is also evident in the narrative passages of the Quran, used there as a powerful stylistic tool to promote instruction; see my art. "Teaching," in: *Encyclopaedia of the Qur'ān*, ed. J.D. McAuliffe, vol. iv, Leiden: Brill, forthcoming.

and its language is precise and prosaic, as in a *fatwā*. Ibn Saḥnūn's primary concern is to clarify issues; the style in presenting these ideas is secondary to him. This latter observation might explain, to some extent, why the discussion of certain topics does not always correspond to the chapter headings; why subject matters relating to one and the same issue are occasionally scattered throughout different chapters or listed under various rubrics; and why there are some passages which almost lack a logical sequence for the ideas addressed therein. The last chapter may even give the impression to some readers that issues were included there which the author, for some reason, omitted mentioning earlier in his book at a, perhaps, thematically more fitting place.

2.2.2 *Reflections of historical realities*

In terms of historical and cultural information, Ibn Saḥnūn's book has plenty to offer. As G. Lecomte already noted,[27] there are passages that vividly evoke in the reader's mind the diligent world of elementary schools at the beginning of the 9th century. We learn about the medieval teacher who is proud of the ink spots on his clothing; "It is the sign of manliness (*murū'a*) to see ink on a man's clothing or lips" (iii.116). There is also mention of the parents who offer the teacher gifts as a reward for his good work (vi.118). Yet if a father is unhappy with the results of his child's education, he does not hesitate to argue frankly with the teacher (ix.124, 125).

There are passages that allow us to picture situations where young schoolboys take care of each other at school and accompany each other home after class (vii.118; viii.119). We learn about the different ways of cleaning the writing tablet, either using a little dust cloth or even the tongue (iii.115). If one uses the foot to erase quranic text written on the tablet, one commits—as the text states—an act of irreverence toward the Quran and risks receiving punishment (iii.115). The text talks about school holidays and family celebrations taking place when pupils pass the *khatma* exam and graduate (v.117).

Along with these insights into the everyday life at elementary schools at the beginning of the 9th century, the book provides some significant historical information. One can conclude from the text,

[27] Cf. his Le Livre 81–82.

firstly, that the teaching of the Quran and its supplementary disciplines at the primary level was, at that time, already well established in the Muslim West. Secondly, primary education was apparently in need of more systematic regulations and scholars responded to this need by offering professional advice. Within this context, the raising of fees for teaching classes—as Ibn Saḥnūn indicates—and even remuneration for teaching the Quran had become a common practice. The author generally supports this practice, yet he feels it indispensable to discuss it in detail (i.114; ix.124).

Ibn Saḥnūn also deals at length with physical punishment (see chapter iv). This, however, is less surprising when taking the author's legal background into consideration. Hence one can appreciate, for example, why he attempts to cover all *possible* precedents, those which actually occurred and those which might occur. Although the text makes it quite clear that punishment was part of rectifying a child's behavior in Islam in the medieval times, Ibn Saḥnūn leaves no doubt that physical punishment should not cross the line. He stresses that the child should not be seriously harmed. On the contrary, basing himself on prophetic traditions, he emphasizes that modesty, patience, and a passion for working with children are indispensable qualities of teachers (ii.115; iv.116; viii.119).

Moreover, Ibn Saḥnūn also advises the teachers to create situations to challenge pupils intellectually. He mentions, for example, that pupils may dictate to each other (ix.124), or that advanced pupils may profit from writing letters for adults (viii.119). Competition amongst pupils is expressly favored because, as the text says, it contributes to the formation of their personalities and to their general improvement (viii.119).

2.2.3 *The curriculum*

As for the curriculum, Ibn Saḥnūn presents to the teachers a number of rules. Some of them are obligatory; others are recommended. One can conclude from the text the following obligatory rules:

1. Teachers must instruct pupils in the precise articulation of the Quran, along with knowledge of reading, orthography, and grammar (viii.119).
2. Teachers are strongly advised not to teach melodious recitation of the Quran (*alḥān al-Qur'ān*). This is "unlawful" since it leads to singing, which is reprehensible (viii.120).

3. Teachers must teach the duties of worship (such as the ablutions before prayers, the number of inclinations and prostrations in prayer, etc.) (viii.121).
4. Teachers must teach the pupils good manners, since these are obligations towards God (viii.120).

As recommended topics for teaching, Ibn Saḥnūn suggests the following:

5. The basics of Arabic language and linguistics (viii.119).
6. Arithmetic (viii.119).
7. Calligraphy (viii.119).
8. Writing letters (viii.119).
9. Poetry, however, only if the verses are decent (viii.119).
10. Proverbs of the ancient Arabs.
11. Historical reports (*akhbār*) of the ancient Arabs and legends of their battles (viii.120).
12. Sermons (*khuṭab*), if the pupils show interest in them (viii.120).

Given the priority that the Mālikites in the Maghrib generally gave to instructing boys in the Quran, these rather diverse recommendations of Ibn Saḥnūn are significant.

Some other rules concern a variety of matters. For example, teachers are advised not to instruct young girls together with boys, because mixed classes corrupt young people (viii.123). This statement seems to point to the fact that, firstly, education was not restricted to boys, and secondly, that coeducation may have been practiced at elementary schools to some degree. Also, teachers must not teach the Quran to the children of Christians (viii.122). This rule is given on the authority of Ibn Saḥnūn's father. It seems to indicate, on the one hand, that Muslim and Christian children were attending the same classes. On the other hand, it shows that Ibn Saḥnūn took the quranic command "There is no compulsion in matters of faith" (Q 2:256) literally.

2.2.4 *Rules for teachers and how Ibn Saḥnūn presents them to the reader*

The following passages in translation provide a more detailed and immediate idea of Ibn Saḥnūn's text. They highlight some major themes dealt with by Ibn Saḥnūn and the methods used by him for presenting these issues. These texts may also give an impression of the pious tone characteristic of this treatise.

Merit and necessity of learning and teaching the Quran

Abū ʿAbdallāh Ibn Saḥnūn said:
[it has been transmitted . . . that] the Messenger of God—God bless him and grant him peace—said:

قال أبو عبد الله بن سحنون:
[... إنّ] رسول الله، صلّى الله عليه وسلّم، قال:

> "The best of you is the one who learns the Quran and teaches it."
> "Through the Quran God elevates [many] peoples."
> "You must [occupy yourselves with and continually] make use of the Quran, for it eliminates hypocrisy in the same way that fire eliminates rust from iron."
> "He who recites the Quran accurately (lit.: with desinential inflexion) will receive the reward of a martyr."
> "He who learns the Quran in his youth, the Quran will mix with his flesh and blood. [However,] he who learns it in old age, and does not give up on it even when it escapes [his memory], will receive double the reward" (i.113–114).

"أفضلكم من تعلّم القرآن وعلّمه."

"يرفع الله بالقرآن أقواماً."

"عليكم بالقرآن فانّه ينفي النفاق كما تنفي النار خبث الحديد."

"من قرأ القرآن بإعراب فله أجر شهيد."

"من تعلّم القرآن في شبيبته اختلط القرآن بلحمه ودمّه، ومن تعلّمه في كبره وهو يتفلّت منه ولا يتركه فله أجره مرّتين."

* * *

[It has been transmitted] *on the authority of ʿUthmān ibn ʿAffān* (the third Rightly Guided Caliph, d. 35/656)—may God be pleased with him—concerning God's saying—blessed and exalted be He—'*Then We bequeathed the Book on those of our servants we chose* (Q 35:32)' [that] he said, "Everyone who learns the Quran and teaches it is amongst those whom God has chosen from humankind" (i.114).

... **عن عثمان بن عفّان** رضي الله عنه، في قول الله تبارك وتعالى: ﴿ثمّ أورثنا الكتاب الذين اصطفينا من عبادنا﴾، قال: "كلّ من تعلّم القرآن وعلّمه فهو ممن اصطفاه الله من بني آدم."

[It has been transmitted that *ʿAbdallāh*] *Ibn Masʿūd* [d. ca. 32/625] said: "Three [things] are essential for people:

[1.] A ruler who rules amongst them [in justice]; if it were not for that, they would devour each other.

[2.] Buying and selling copies of the Quran; if it were not for that, the Book of God would decrease [in number].

[3.] Teachers who teach their children and who receive a salary for that; if it were not for that, the people would be illiterate" (i.114).

... **قال ابن مسعود:** "ثلاث لا بدّ للناس، منهم: لا بدّ للناس من أمير يحكم بينهم ولولا ذلك لأكل بعضهم بعضاً، ولا بدّ للناس من شراء المصاحف وبيعها ولولا ذلك لقلّ كتاب الله، ولا بدّ للناس من معلّم يعلّم أولادهم ويأخذ على ذلك أجراً ولولا ذلك لكان الناس أميّين."

Further teaching topics

I asked [*Saḥnūn*]: "So, it is permissible for the boy to write letters for someone?"

قلت: فيأذن للصبيّ أن يكتب لأحد كتاباً؟

He answered: "There is no harm [in it]. If he writes letters, this is something that contributes to the boy's education. The teacher should [also] teach the pupils calculation, although this is not obligatory for him to do—unless it is imposed on him as an obligation. Likewise [for] poetry, unfamiliar [words], the Arabic language, calligraphy, and all parts of grammar—[the teaching of] all of this is at his discretion.

قال: لا بأس، وهذا ممّا يخرّج الصبيّ إذا كتب الرسائل. وينبغي أن يعلّمهم الحساب، وليس ذلك بلازم له إلاّ أن يشترط ذلك عليه. وكذلك الشعر، والغريب، والعربية، والخطّ، وجميع النحو. وهو في ذلك متطوّع.

The teacher should teach them the desinential inflexion of the quranic text—this is incumbent upon him. [He should also teach them] vocalization and spelling, good handwriting and to read well, when to pause and when to recite [the quranic text] in a slow, measured rhythmic way—[all] this is incumbent upon him.

وينبغي له أن يعلّمهم إعراب القرآن وذلك لازم له. وبالشكل، والهجاء، والخطّ الحسن، والقراءة الحسنة، والتوقيف، والترتيل، يلزمه ذلك.

[Also,] there is no harm in teaching them poetry—as long as there is nothing indecent in it from the language and the anecdotes of the

ولا بأس أن يعلّمهم الشعر ممّا لا يكون فيه فحش من كلام العرب وأخبارها، وليس ذلك بواجب عليه.

Arabs. This [however] is not an obligation on him" (viii.119–120).

I said [*to Saḥnūn*]: "Some Andalusians related that there was no harm in hiring [someone] to teach Islamic jurisprudence, religious duties, poetry, and grammar. It is similar to [teaching] the Quran.

قلت: روى بعض أهل الأندلس أنّه لا بأس بالإجارة[٢٨] على تعليم الفقه والفرائض،[٢٩] والشعر، والنحو، وهو مثل القرآن.

He replied: "Mālik and our companions (i.e. the experts of our Law School) detested this. How could it be similar to the Quran? [Learning] the Quran has a [specific] goal that can be reached, whereas what (i.e., the topics) you have mentioned has none. So, this [i.e. the idea mentioned by the Andalusians?] is unknown.

فقال: كَرِهَ ذلك مالك وأصحابنا. وكيف يشبه القرآن، والقرآن له غاية ينتهي إليها، وما ذكرت ليس له غاية ينتهي إليها، فهذا مجهول.

Islamic jurisprudence and [religious] knowledge (as studied by the *ʿulamāʾ*) are something about which there has been disagreement, whereas the Quran is the truth about which there is no doubt at all. Islamic jurisprudence is not to be learned by heart like the Quran; hence it is not similar to it, nor does it have a [definite] goal or time in which to reach it" (x.128).

والفقه والعلم أمر قد اختُلِف فيه، والقرآن هو الحقّ الذي لا شكّ فيه. والفقه لا يستظهر مثل القرآن، فهو لا يشبهه، ولا غاية له، ولا أمد ينتهي إليه.

Writing exercises based on quranic text

Anas [ibn Mālik] was asked: "How were the educators during the time of [the first four caliphs,] the Imāms Abū Bakr, ʿUmar, ʿUthmān, and ʿAlī—may God be pleased with them?"

قيل لأنس: كيف كان المؤدّبون على عهد الأئمّة أبي بكر وعمر وعثمان وعليّ - رضي الله عنهم؟

[28] *Ijāra* is a legal term that "refers to the permission granted for a compensation to use a thing owed by, or the service of, another person." Hence the term can also refer "to a book that was 'hired' for the purpose of, and with the right to, copying it." See Rosenthal, *The Technique* 8, fn. 3.

[29] *Farāʾiḍ* is ambiguous; it can refer to Islamic inheritance law but, in the present context, it is more likely to indicate "religious duties."

Anas answered: "The teacher had a basin. Each boy used to come—every day, each in his turn—with some pure water. They would pour it into the basin and use it to erase the writing from their tablets." [Then] *Anas added*: "Afterwards, they used to dig a hole in the ground and pour this water into it and so it was absorbed" (iii.115).

قال أنس: "كان المؤدّب له إجانة.[٣٠] وكلّ صبيّ يأتي كلّ يوم بنوبته ماء طاهراً فيصبونه فيها فيمحون به ألواحهم. **قال أنس:** "ثمّ يحفرون حفرة في الأرض فيصبون ذلك الماء فيها فينشف.[٣١]

Mental challenges for pupils, teaching assistance, and teacher responsibilities

[*Ibn Saḥnūn*] *said that Saḥnūn stated*: ". . . There is no harm in having them dictate to each other, because this is for their benefit. Yet he (the teacher) must review their dictation. [Moreover,] he must not let them move from one sura to another until they have memorized [the first sura] with its desinential inflexion and orthography—unless [the pupils'] fathers give him leeway to do so" (viii.120).

قال: وقال سحنون: ... ولا بأس أن يجعلهم يملي بعضهم على بعض، لأنّ ذلك منفعة لهم، وليتفقّد إملاءهم. ولا يجوز أن ينقلهم من سورة إلى سورة حتّى يحفظوها بإعرابها وكتابتها إلاّ أن يسهّل له الآباء.

[*Saḥnūn*] *stated*: "It is more appropriate for the teacher not to put one of the boys in charge of the beatings nor designate for them a monitor from amongst them, unless it is a boy who has finished [learning] the Quran and knows it, and no longer needs instruction. Hence, there is no harm in it. [Also, there is no harm for] the boy to help the teacher; [for] this is of benefit to the boy.

قال: وأحبّ للمعلّم أن لا يولّي أحداً من الصبيان الضرب، ولا يجعل لهم عريفاً منهم، إلاّ أن يكون الصبيّ الذي قد ختم وعرف القرآن، وهو مستغنٍ عن التعليم، فلا باس بذلك، وأن يعينه؛ فإنّ ذلك منفعة للصبيّ.

---

[30] For *ijjāna* (vulg.) and *ījāna*, see Lane i, 26.

[31] This was done so that the quranic text would be erased from the tablets respectfully.

Yet it is not permissible for him (i.e. the boy assisting the teacher) to give orders to any of the pupils, or to instruct any of them—unless there is benefit in that for the boy's formation, or his father has approved of it. [If this is not the case,] the teacher himself should be in charge of this [teaching] or hire someone to help him, if he is equally qualified" (vii.118).

ولا يحلّ له أن يأمر أحداً، وأن يعلّم أحداً منهم إلاّ أن يكون ذلك منفعة للصبيّ في تخريجه، أو بأذن والده في ذلك. ولْيَلِ هو ذلك بنفسه أو يستأجر من يعينه إذا كان في مثل كفايته.

Supervision of pupils

[*Saḥnūn*] *stated*: The teacher must be committed to working hard. And he must devote himself to the pupils, . . . for he is a hireling and cannot leave his work (viii.119).

قال: وليلزم المعلّم الاجتهاد، وليتفرّغ لهم ...، لأنّه أجير لا يدع عمله.

I asked [*Saḥnūn*]: "Then, can the teacher send the boys to look for each other?"

قلت: أفيرسل الصبيان بعضهم في طلب بعض؟

He replied: "I am not of the opinion that he is allowed to do so—unless their fathers or [their] guardians grant him (the teacher) permission in this regard, or if the places are nearby and the boy is not occupied with it [for too long]. He (the teacher) himself must be mindful of the boys at the time [they] return home, and inform their guardians [if] they did not come [to school]" (vii.118).

قال: لا أرى ذلك يجوز له، إلاّ أن يأذن له آباؤهم أو أولياء الصبيان في ذلك، أو تكون المواضع قريبة لا يشتغل الصبي في ذلك. وليتعاهد الصبيان هو بنفسه في وقت انقلاب الصبيان، ويخبر أولياءهم أنّهم لم يجيؤوا.

I asked [*Saḥnūn*]: "Are you of the opinion that it is [permissible] for the teacher to write *fiqh* books for himself?"

قلت: فهل ترى للمعلّم أن يكتب لنفسه كتب الفقه؟

He replied: "As for the time when he has finished [teaching] the boys, there is no harm in writing [such books] for himself and for others.; for example, [when] he has permitted them to return home. But as long as they are around him, no! That is, it is not permissible for him, for how can he be permitted to deviate from something

قال: أمّا في وقت فراغه من الصبيان فلا بأس أن يكتب لنفسه وللناس، مثل أن يأذن لهم في الانقلاب، وأمّا ما داموا حوله فلا، أي لا يجوز له ذلك، وكيف يجوز له أن يخرج ممّا

that it is incumbent upon him to observe, towards something that is not incumbent upon him? Don't you see that he is [also] not permitted to entrust to some of [the boys] the teaching of others? How, [then,] could he occupy himself with something other than them!" (viii.119).

يلزمه النظر فيه إلى ما لا يلزمه، ألاّ ترى أنّه لا يجوز له أن يوكّل تعليم بعضهم إلى بعض؟ فكيف يشتغل بغيرهم!

Saḥnūn stated: The teacher is not permitted to send the boys [to take care of] his personal matters (viii.121).

قال سحنون: ولا يجوز للمعلّم أن يرسل الصبيان في حوائجه.

Just treatment of pupils

[It has been transmitted] on the authority of Anas ibn Mālik that the Messenger of God—God bless him and grant him peace—stated: "Any teacher who is entrusted with three boys from this community and does not teach them on an equal basis—the poor with the rich, and the rich with the poor—will on the Day of Resurrection be raised up with the treacherous" (ii.115).

[...] **عن أنس بن مالك،** قال: قال رسول الله – صلّى الله عليه وسلّم – : "إيّما مؤدّب ولي ثلاثة صبية من هذه الأمّة فلم يعلّمهم بالسوية فقيرهم مع غنيّهم، وغنيّهم مع فقيرهم حُشر يوم القيامة مع الخائنين."

[It has been transmitted] on the authority of al-Ḥasan (al-Baṣrī?) that he said: "If a teacher has been hired for a fixed salary and does not treat them—i.e. the boys—on an equal basis, he will be deemed to be one of the wrongdoers" (ii.115).

[...] **عن الحسن،** قال: "إذا قوطع المعلّم بالسوية فلم يعدل بينهم – أي الصبيان – كتب من الظلمة."

Handling trouble between pupils

Ibn Saḥnūn said: Saḥnūn was asked about the teacher: "Should he accept the word of boys concerning the harm [done] by others?"

قال: وسئل سحنون عن المعلّم: أيأخذ الصبيان بقول بعضهم عن بعض في الأذى؟

He replied: "I do not consider this [an issue] requiring legal judgment. However, the teacher should discipline them if they have harmed one another. In my view, he should do so if

فقال: ما أرى هذا من ناحية الحكم. وإنّما على المؤدّب أن يؤدّبهم إذا آذى بعضهم بعضاً. وذلك عندي إذا استفاض علم الأذى

knowledge of the harm has been spread by a group of them, or [if] there was admission [of the misdeed]—unless they are boys known to him to be truthful; then, he should accept their word and punish accordingly. The teacher must not be excessive [in his punishment], as I have [already] told you. [Moreover,] he must command them to refrain from harming [one another], and return to them whatever they took from each other—[but] this is not [an issue] requiring a legal ruling; this is [at least] what I heard from more than one of our companions. Their testimony had been granted admission [even] in cases of homicide or injury, so how much more [should it be accepted] in this [matter]! God knows best" (viii.123).

من الجماعة منهم أو كان الاعتراف، إلاّ أن يكونوا صبياناً قد عرفهم بالصدق فيقبل قولهم ويعاقب على ذلك.

ولا يجاوز في الأدب كما أعلمتك، ويأمرهم بالكف عن الأذى، ويردّ ما أخذ بعضهم لبعض، وليس هو من ناحية القضاء.

وكذلك سمعت من غير واحد من أصحابنا. وقد أجيزت شهادتهم في القتل والجراح فكيف بهذا! والله أعلم.

Appointing a teacher

Saḥnūn stated: "Some scholars from the Ḥijāz—including Ibn Dīnār and others—were asked [about] a teacher hired for a group [if then] a due share should be allotted to each of them. *So he answered*: "It is permissible if the fathers come to terms on this matter. [This is so,] because this (i.e., education) is a necessity and something the people simply must have. It is the most suitable [thing to do]" (ix.124).

قال سحنون: وقد سئل بعض علماء الحجاز – منهم ابن دينار وغيره – أن يُستأجر المعلّم لجماعة، وأن يُفرض على كلّ واحد ما ينوبه. **فقال:** يجوز إذا تراضى بذلك الآباء، لأنّ هذا ضرورة ولا بدّ للناس منه، وهو أشبه.

Classroom and teaching equipment

[*Saḥnūn said*:] It is incumbent [upon the teacher]—and not upon the pupils—to rent the shop [to be used as a classroom]. He must inspect [the pupils] by teaching and reviewing

[**قال سحنون:**] وعليه كراء الحانوت، وليس ذلك على الصبيان، وعليه أن يتفقّدهم بالتعليم والعرض، ويجعل لعرض القرآن وقتاً

[with them]. He must schedule a fixed time to review [the children's knowledge] of the Quran, such as Thursdays or Wednesday evenings. Yet he must give them the day off on Fridays. This has been the practice of teachers since there have been teachers, and they have not been faulted for that (iii.120).

معلوماً مثل يوم الخميس، وعشية الأربعاء. ويأذن لهم في يوم الجمعة، وذلك سنّة المعلمين منذ كانوا و لم يُعَبْ ذلك عليهم.

[*Saḥnūn stated*:] Also, the teacher is obliged to obtain [at his own expense] the scourge and the device to hold the legs of the delinquent during the bastinado; this is not to be at the expense of the boys (viii.120).

[قال سحنون:] وعلى المعلّم أن يكسب الدِّرّة والفَلَقة، وليس ذلك على حساب الصبيان.

Mālik was asked about the teaching of the boys in the mosque. *He answered*: "I do not consider this to be permitted, because they are not mindful of impurity. And mosques have not been set up for teaching [children]" (viii.120).

وسئل مالك عن تعليم الصبيان في المسجد. **قال:** لا أرى ذلك يجوز، لأنّهم لا يتحفّظون من النجاسة. و لم يُنصب المسجد للتعليم.

Payment for teaching the Quran

[It has been transmitted] from ʿAṭāʾ [ibn Abī Rabāḥ] that he used to teach the art of writing during the time of Muʿāwiya (the first Umayyad caliph who r. 661–680 C.E.) and that he stipulated [payment for it] (i.114).

... عن عطاء، أنّه كان يعلم الكَتْب على عهد معاوية ويَشترط.

Ibn Jurayj said: I asked ʿAṭāʾ: "Can I take wages for teaching the Book? Do you know of anybody having detested it?" He said: "No, I do not" (i.114).

... عن ابن جريج، قال: قلت لعطاء: أ آخذ أجراً على تعليم الكتاب؟ أعلمت أن أحداً كرهه؟ قال:لا.

[It has been transmitted] on the authority of Ibn Shihāb [al-Zuhrī] that Saʿd ibn Abī Waqqāṣ got a man from Iraq to teach the Book to their children in Medina and that they (the Medinans) gave him wages (i.114).

... عن ابن شهاب أن سعد بن أبي وقّاص قدم برجل من العراق يعلّم أبناءهم الكتاب بالمدينة ويعطونه الأجر.

Mālik [ibn Anas] stated that "there is no harm in a teacher's taking [payment] for teaching the Quran. If he stipulates something [as payment], it is lawful and permissible. So, there is no harm in his stipulating in this regard.

... وقال مالك: لا بأس بما يأخذ المعلّم على تعليم القرآن. وإن اشترط شيئاً كان حلالاً جائزاً. ولا بأس بالاشتراط في ذلك.

[Moreover,] what is due to him when the Quran has been completely recited from memory is obligatory, whether he had stipulated it or not. The scholars of our country [agree] on this as it concerns the teachers (i.114).

وحقّ الختمة له واجب اشترطها أو لم يشترطها.
وعلى ذلك أهل العلم ببلدنا في المعلّمين.

Muḥammad [ibn Saḥnūn] said: There is no harm in a man's hiring a teacher to teach his children the Quran for a predetermined sum for a fixed time, or for each month. Also, [he can teach] half or a quarter of the Quran or any other portion specified by the two [parties].

قال محمد: لا بأس أن يستأجر الرجل المعلم على أن يعلم أولاده القرآن بأجرة معلومة إلى أجل معلوم أو كل شهر. وكذلك نصف القرآن أو ربعه أو ما سميا منه.

He said: If a man hires a teacher to teach certain boys, it is permissible for the teacher to teach others together with them—provided that this does not divert him from teaching those for whom we was hired" (x.126).

قال: وإذا استأجر الرجل معلما على صبيان معلومين جاز للمعلم أن يعلم معهم غيرهم إذا كان لا يشغله ذلك عن تعليم هؤلاء الذين استؤجر لهم.

He said: There is no harm in a man's hiring [an instructor] to teach his child writing and spelling. [In fact,] the Prophet—God bless him and grant him peace—used to free a man who taught writing [to the Muslims] (x.127).

قال: ولا بأس بالرجل يستأجر أن يعلم ولده الخط والهجاء. وقد كان النبي – صلى الله عليه وسلم – "يفادي بالرجل يعلم الخط."

Graduation

I asked him [Saḥnūn]: "When is the time due for the final exam?"
He replied: "[It is due] when he (the pupil) comes near it and has gone beyond [learning] two thirds [of the Quran]."

وسألته متى تجب الختمة، **فقال:** إذا قاربها وجاوز الثلثين.

Then I asked him about [the possibility of having] the final exam [after memorizing only] half [of the Quran].
He replied: "I do not consider it to be compulsory."
Saḥnūn stated: "The final exam on anything other than the entire Quran—be it half, a third, or a quarter [of it]—is not compulsory, unless they volunteer in this regard" (v.117).

فسألت عن ختمة النصف، فقال: لا أرى ذلك يلزم. **قال سحنون:** ولا يلزم ختمة غير القرآن كله، لا نصف ولا ثلث ولا ربع، إلا أن يتطوعوا بذلك.

In conclusion of this part of our study, it is worth noting that Ibn Saḥnūn's *vademecum* for teachers was—already in the Middle Ages—of much interest to Muslim scholars. An example of this is Abū l-Ḥasan al-Qābisī (d. 403/1012), a leading representative of the Mālikī law school from al-Qayrawān who lived about 150 years after Ibn Saḥnūn. Al-Qābisī used Ibn Saḥnūn's text extensively as a source and commented on it when compiling his own "Elaborate Treatise on the Circumstances of Teachers and the Legal Regulations for Teachers and Students (*al-Risāla al-mufaṣṣala fī aḥwāl al-muʿallimīn wa-aḥkām al-muʿallimīn wa-l-mutaʿallimīn*)"[32] Thus, al-Qābisī sets forth Ibn Saḥnūn's educational efforts and, at the same time, affirms that he was one of the earliest Muslim educationalists.

3 *Al-Jaḥiẓ*

3.1 *The scholar: life and academic career*

Due to his masterly compositions in the areas of belles-lettres, Muʿtazili theology, and political-religious polemics, Abū ʿUthmān ʿAmr ibn Baḥr al-Fuqaymī al-Baṣrī al-Jāḥiẓ is well known as one of the most prominent classical Arabic writers. He was born in Basra in about 160/776 and died there in Muḥarram 255/December 868–January 869. He was probably of Abyssinian origin and received his sobriquet due to a malformation of the eyes.[33]

From an early age, al-Jāḥiẓ dedicated himself to learning. He participated in study circles held at mosques and also attended the debates on Arabic philology, lexicography, poetry, and philosophy conducted at the Mirbad, a celebrated public place in Basra, which played an outstanding role in the shaping of Arabic culture in medieval times.

Al-Jāḥiẓ acquainted himself with the works of the ancient Greek philosophers (especially Aristotle) available in Arabic since the great translation movement under the caliph al-Maʾmūn (r. 813–833). He participated frequently in the intellectual conversations taking place in the salons of the upper class, where issues of general concern to

[32] Reprinted in: Shams al-Dīn, *al-Fikr al-tarbawī ʿinda Ibn Saḥnūn and al-Qābisī* 117–196. See also al-Ahwānī, *at-Taʿlīm fī raʾy al-Qābisī*, esp. 39–41.
[33] Art. "al-Djāḥiẓ" (Ch. Pellat), in: *EI*² ii, 385–388.

Islamic society were discussed. One of his favorite activities, however, was to spend a great deal of time in libraries and bookstores. For a small amount of money, he is said to have rented a bookstore overnight to read and copy what was of interest to him.[34]

Only in about 200/815–6, at the age of forty-five, does he seem to have started writing professionally. Writing, and the considerable amounts of money he received for dedicating his works to people of influence and wealth, thus seem to have been his main sources of income. He built up his private library and even employed a copyist (*warrāq*) known by the name of ʿAbd al-Wahhāb ibn ʿĪsā.[35] Nevertheless, al-Jāḥiẓ also had some bitter experiences, for works of his were torn apart by envious colleagues and critics shortly after they were published.[36]

Al-Jāḥiẓ seems to have held no official or regular post in his life. It is known, however, that when he was in Baghdad he worked for some time as a scribe and teacher. Al-Jāḥiẓ himself reports that the caliph al-Mutawakkil (r. 847–861) had apparently endeavored to entrust him with the education of his children. However, the caliph later changed his mind, seemingly because of al-Jāḥiẓ's ugliness.[37]

The circumstances and often unfair treatment of professional teachers al-Jāḥiẓ witnessed, and may have experienced firsthand,[38] seem to have induced him to write a book entitled "The Teachers."[39] This

[34] Yāqūt, *Muʿjam al-udabāʾ* vi, 56.

[35] Shalaby 90.

[36] Cf. al-Jāḥiẓ's own statements in *Risālat Faṣl mā bayna l-ʿadāwa wa-l-ḥasad*, in: *Majmūʿ rasāʾil al-Jāḥiẓ*, ed. Bāwl Krāws [Paul Kraus] and Muḥammad Ṭaha al-Ḥājirī, Cairo: Maṭbaʿat Lajnat al-Taʾlīf wa-l-Tarjama wa-l-Nashr, 1943, 108–109; and Pellat, *The Life* 218–219; see also Rosenthal, *The Technique* 24.

[37] Hirschfeld 202; and Pellat, "al-Djāḥiẓ," in: *EI*² ii, 385.

[38] Hirschfeld 202.

[39] For the theory and practice of Islamic education in medieval times, the encyclopedic work of al-Jāḥiẓ as a whole is an important source. It provides much insightful information on the curriculum for princes, the social status of teachers, the value of books, and even on the etiquette to be observed by people attending literary salons, to mention a few topics. This is also the case for al-Jāḥiẓ's main works: the *K. al-Ḥayawān* ("The Book of Animals," a cerebral anthology on a large variety of subjects, based on animals); the *K. al-Bayān wa-l-tabyīn* ("The Book of Eloquence and Exposition," which Pellat called "an inventory of what have been called the "Arabic humanities," designed to stress the oratorical and poetic ability of Arabs;" cf. *EI*² ii, 386); and the *K. al-Bukhalāʾ* ("The Book of Misers," an entertaining work praising Arab generosity and analyzing non-Arab avarice). Other works dealing in more detail with intellectual refinement and ethics are: (1) The *Risālat al-maʿāsh wa-l-maʿād* ("The Treatise on the Manner of Living [in this World] and the Hereafter," known also as *Risāla fī l-Akhlāq al-maḥmūda wa-l-madhmūma*, "Treatise

provided him with the opportunity not only to defend but also to champion schoolteachers and stress their superiority over all other classes of educators and tutors.[40]

3.2 *Al-Jāḥiẓ's book "The Teachers"*

As is the case for quite a number of al-Jāḥiẓ's writings, no complete text of the book "The Teachers" has been preserved.[41] Various fragments of this work were discovered, however, in four manuscripts in Cairo, Istanbul, London, and Mosul.[42] The text has been published several times.[43] Nonetheless, this work of al-Jāḥiẓ's—which he apparently composed at a late stage of his life[44]—is little known thus far, in either the Arab or the Western world.

---

on Laudable and Blameworthy Morals"); (2) The *Kitāb Kitmān al-sirr wa-ḥifẓ al-lisān* ("The Book on Keeping Secrets and Controlling the Tongue"), and (3) the treatise *Dhamm akhlāq al-kuttāb* ("Censure of the Manners of Scribes").

[40] Pellat remarks that al-Jāḥiẓ's "acute powers of observation, his light-hearted skepticism, his comic sense and satirical turn of mind fit him admirably to portray human types and society." He says also that, at times, "he uses all his skill at the expense of several social groups (schoolmasters, singers, scribes, etc.) [although] generally keeping within the bounds of decency; cf. *EI*² ii, 386. The fact that al-Jāḥiẓ praises the schoolteachers highly in one passage (e.g., *K. al-Bayān wa-l-tabyīn* i, 250–2) and makes rather unflattering jokes about them in another (ibid. 248–49) may therefore be understood as the result of an essentially dialectical intellect—something, however, that was interpreted by his contemporaries (Ibn Qutayba, for example) as a lack of seriousness. G.J. van Gelder suggests that it is precisely this "lack of seriousness" which seems to be one al-Jāḥiẓ's attractive sides: the fact that al-Jāḥiẓ mixes jest and earnestness; see van Gelder's article on this topic in: *Journal of Arabic Literature* 23 (1992), esp. 95–106. In addition, al-Jāḥiẓ's Muʿtazilite views, which eventually aim at tackling the various aspects of a given topic, may also have played a role in this regard.

[41] Al-Jāḥiẓ's works comprise nearly 200 titles. However, only about thirty works—whether authentic or apocryphal—have been preserved in full length. Of about fifty works, only excerpts, quotations, or fragmentary passages have come down to us; see *EI*² ii, 386–388, with further references. The *K. al-Muʿallimīn* belongs to this latter category; cf. Geries 9. C. Brockelmann classified al-Jāḥiẓ's works according to real or assumed subjects; his list provides a good idea of the breadth of al-Jāḥiẓ's literary and scholarly interests (*GAL* Supplement i, 241–247).

[42] Geries 9–17, 25.

[43] (1) In the margin of *Kitāb al-Kāmil fī l-lugha wa-l-adab, taʾlīf* [. . .] *Abī l-ʿAbbās Muḥammad ibn Yazīd al-maʿrūf bi-l-Mubarrad al-Naḥwī,* [. . .] *wa-qad ṭurriza hāmishuhu bi-Kitāb al-Fuṣūl al-mukhtāra min kutub al-Imām Abī Uthmān ʿAmr al-Jāḥiẓ ibn Baḥr ibn Maḥbūb al-Kinānī al-Baṣrī* [. . .], *ikhtiyār al-Imām ʿUbaydallāh ibn Ḥassān*, Cairo: Maṭbaʿat al-Taqaddum al-ʿIlmiyya, 1323 [1905], 17–40; (2) *Rasāʾil al-Jāḥiẓ*, ed. ʿAbd al-Salām Muḥammad Hārūn, ¹Beirut, 1991 (based on the ed. Cairo 1964), vol. iii, 27–51; (3) in: *al-Mawrid* (Baghdad) 7.4 (1978), *ʿAdad Khāṣṣ: Abū ʿUthmān ʿAmr ibn Baḥr al-Jāḥiẓ*, 149–158; and (4) *Kitābān li-l-Jāḥiẓ*, ed. Ibrahim Geries, Tel Aviv: Tel Aviv University, 1980, 57–87. Cf. also Pellat, Nouvel essai 148–149 (no. 143); and Geries 9.—I have

3.2.1 *Intention and literary style*

With regard to al-Jāḥiẓ's literary oeuvre in general, Ibrahim Geries observed that this medieval scholar seems to have believed that "the people's need for one another is a salient characteristic of their nature and an inborn feature of the core of their souls. It is permanent and . . . covers all beings, from the smallest to the greatest."[45] None of God's creatures would be able to reach his goal without the assistance of those deployed to help him; the most respected cannot exist without the least respected; rulers need the lower classes as the lower classes need rulers; rich people need the poor and slaves need masters.[46] This idea, of Greek origin, regarding the interdependence of elements in the universe, influenced al-Jāḥiẓ's general perception of the world. For al-Jāḥiẓ, attempts to comprehend the microcosm lead to an understanding of the macrocosm. This scientific-philosophic approach made al-Jāḥiẓ the sharp observer and analyst he was. Basing himself on deduction and logical reasoning, he unveils to the reader the significance of what is insignificant in the eyes of those relying simply on superficial perceptions and initial sensory impressions. Such a view of the world eventually enabled him to observe and minutely examine various social groups. As a result, his writings reflect, rather objectively and realistically, actual circumstances, opinions, and viewpoints prevalent in his own time, thus providing a spectacular insight into Arabic-Islamic culture and society under the ʿAbbāsids.[47]

The book "The Teachers" reveals in an aesthetic way many of these characteristics of al-Jāḥiẓ's approach as a scholar and as a man of letters. For example, the various digressions and the original sequence of thoughts in this text appeal to the reader through the

consulted Hārūn's and Geries' editions of the *K. al-Muʿallimīn.* All references to al-Jāḥiẓ's *K. al-Muʿallimīn* in this article are based on Geries' edition, if not indicated otherwise. I would like to thank Dr. Khaled Sindawi (Haifa) for drawing my attention to the latter edition.

Passages of al-Jāḥiẓ's essay on "The Teachers" have been translated into English (by H. Hirschfeld, 1922), German (by O. Rescher, 1931), and French (by Ch. Pellat, 1953). In the light of the more recent editions by Hārūn and Geries, some passages in these translations seem to require further thought. Pellat's French translation was later also rendered into English (Pellat, *The Life* 112–114) and German (Pellat, *Arabische Geisteswelt* 181–184).

[44] Geries argues that al-Jāḥiẓ wrote the book "The Teachers" after he had completed the *K. al-Ḥayawān, K. al-Bayān wa-l-tabyīn* and *K. al-Bukhalā'*; cf. Geries 23.

[45] Geries 28–29.

[46] Geries 23–24 (mainly based on al-Jāḥiẓ's *K. al-Ḥayawān*, i, 204–210).

[47] Geries 24.

balanced repetition of similar ideas presented each time in a different way. Hence "what would be pointless repetition" in terms of modern thinking and presentation, arose "in the mind of the 3rd/9th century writer . . . from the desire . . . to give ordinary prose the symmetry of verse," wrote Charles Pellat, one of the best-known experts on al-Jāḥiẓ.[48]

3.2.2 *Structure and contents*

The author of the book "The Teachers" addresses the reader directly in the second person singular. He starts with an appeal to God to protect the people—including the reader of his book—from the rage of anger and to grant them justice and patience in their hearts. Then he sets out to defend the teachers against a (fictitious) critic and to commend them highly. The teachers are described as knowledgeable, diligent, and hardworking people. Moreover, it is said that they are passionate about their profession and suffer with their students when they do not make the progress expected. Parents should not, therefore, blame the teachers when their children are slow in their education, but instead look at the mental capability of their offspring.

Al-Jāḥiẓ starts his book with a particularly appealing chapter. It deals with writing in general and with the fundamental impact writing has had on human civilization. Writing and recording, along with calculation, are "the pillars" on which the present and the future of civilization and "the welfare of this world" rest. Writing and calculation are God-given, as are the teachers themselves, for God "made them available to us" (p. 60).[49]

The next paragraph of the book deals with memory and memorization. Interestingly enough, the author stresses here that independent thinkers and researchers dislike (*kariha*) memorization. He says that depending on it makes "the mind disregard distinction" and causes it to neglect thought (p. 62). People with a good memory are tempted to rely simply on what their predecessors achieved,

---

[48] *EI*² ii, 387.

[49] Such praise of books and writing must have been perceived as being even more polemical and provocative in a society in which people seem to have looked askance at writing down knowledge. It is worth mentioning here that al-Jāḥiẓ's refreshing views in this regard are paralleled in a lengthy passage in his *K. al-Ḥayawān*; see esp. i, 38–102.

without making attempts to reach conclusions of their own. Nevertheless, for the process of studying, a good memory is valuable and necessary; otherwise, the results of study and research would not last.

As for the trust one is to have in teachers, the teachers of princes are mentioned as examples. Rulers entrusted teachers with the education of their children and so should everybody else. However, one is advised to do so only after testing the teacher and being convinced of his pedagogical skills. Attention is also drawn to the many great scholars in all branches of the arts and sciences and to the men renowned in politics and society who were once teachers (p. 63).

At this point of the presentation, the author effectively alerts the reader not to draw conclusions prematurely; instead he advises us to finish reading the entire treatise first (p. 64). He points to the fact that there are teachers for everything one needs to know: writing, arithmetic, law, the religious duties (*farāʾiḍ*), the Quran, grammar, prosody, poetry, and history. This is followed by a list of further subjects that are taught: these include astronomy, music (*luḥūn*), medicine, geometry, polo, archery, and horsemanship, playing musical instruments, chess, and other games. The children of the lower classes are given lessons in farming, shop-keeping,[50] construction, jewelry-making, sewing, weaving, dying, and other handicrafts and occupations. It is noted that even animals can be taught. Yet, schoolteachers, as al-Jāḥiẓ stresses, are superior to all other categories of teachers (pp. 64–66).

Manifold pieces of advice for teachers follow. They focus on the qualifications teachers need for their work, but also deal with the actual process of teaching and the curriculum. The "Chapter on the Instruction of Boys (*Fī riyāḍat al-ṣabī*)," one of only two chapters in the treatise that bears a title, discusses extensively the teaching of grammar (as will be shown below in more detail). Further thoughts relate to literature and scholarship, to writing prose, and to the value of reading good books. Frequently these remarks are interspersed with sayings and anecdotes from Arabic literature (p. 72).

The flow of the presentation is seemingly interrupted here by a chapter entitled "On the Censure of Homosexuality (*Fī dhamm al-liwāṭ*)."

[50] *Tijāra* ("trading") in Geries' edition, p. 66; *nijāra* ("carpentry") in Hārūn's edition, p. 117.

It denounces certain sexual activities among adults, both male and female, and the lust for boys (p. 78).[51]

Then, back to literature, the author praises ʿAbdallāh ibn al-Muqaffaʿ (d. ca. 139/756), who is best known for his translation of the fables of *Kalīla wa-Dimna* into Arabic. As it is said, he is admired not only as a man of letters, an expert on literary style, a poet, and translator, but also as a teacher (p. 79).

The following paragraph warns that too much self-confidence in scholarly matters is a dangerous mistake. To have knowledge and noteworthy achievements in one or two branches of knowledge, for example, does not necessarily indicate an equivalent excellence in other branches. The famous al-Khalīl ibn Aḥmad (d. ca. 175/791) is given as an example; it is said that he gained a fine reputation for his work in Arabic grammar and prosody, but that he failed and made a fool of himself when claiming to be an expert in theology (*kalām*) and the metres of songs (*awzān al-aghānī*; p. 80).

Various fragmentary passages follow: they relate to the importance of the ruler (*sulṭān*) and the administrators of the government. These are praised as most intelligent people and it is said that society is in need of them. Another statement admonishes the teaching of the books of Abū Ḥanīfa. Further remarks then deal with the proper application of analogies (in teaching?). The author uses the history and the merits of the clan of the Quraysh—well known to most Muslims—to show how analogies should or should not be used. The harsh critique of the merchants (which expresses the opposite of what al-Jāḥiẓ said of them in his other writings) and of the money changers seems, again, not to have been initially part of this educational treatise (p. 81).

---

[51] Even if one takes into account the possibility that this passage initially was not part of the book "The Teachers" (Rescher 108–109), some readers may nonetheless wonder why a medieval copyist of this book should have included this passage in a text expressly addressing teachers. However, the appropriateness of addressing such a topic in a book on teachers is understandable given the fact that homoerotic love of young and adolescent boys was rather common in ʿAbbāsid times, and bawdy anecdotes about teachers and their pupils abound. See also the art. "Liwāṭ" (editors), in: *EI*² v, 776–779, which includes more information on al-Jāḥiẓ's concerns in this regard. See furthermore Adam Mez: *Die Renaissance des Islams*, Hildesheim: G. Olms (Repr. Heidelberg 1922), 337–341 (Engl. Tr., Patna: Jubilee Printing and Publishing House, 1937. 364–361). For the meaning of *liwāṭ* in Islamic law, cf. Arno Schmitt: Liwāṭ im Fiqh: Männliche Homosexualität?, in: *Journal of Arabic and Islamic Studies* 4 (2001–2002), 44–110.

The book "The Teachers" concludes with a moving passage on the gentle treatment students merit. In the second person singular, it once again directly addresses the teachers and us readers. It advises us to treat the students with great care, gentleness, and kindness and not to force them so as not to make them dislike good manners, nor to neglect them since students "deserve your care and hard efforts" (p. 87).

3.2.3 *Curricular and non-curricular topics of teaching*
In his book "The Teachers," al-Jāḥiẓ suggests an impressive variety of topics to be taught. He does so, however, without indicating that these topics in fact relate to two very different categories of teaching: (a) the formal, curricular kind of teaching, as conducted by the schoolteachers at the elementary and the more advanced levels (i.e. the kind of instruction which Ibn Saḥnūn is concerned with in his treatise on primary education); and (b) the informal, non-curricular kind of teaching, which could take place at various locations, including "on the shop floor," for example. Since al-Jāḥiẓ was interested in teaching in general terms, a clear-cut distinction between the teaching topics belonging to one or the other category is rather difficult to make. This notion needs to be taken into account when looking at the following list of teaching topics drawn from his book.

Obligatory topics:
1. Reading and Writing
- The essentials of writing (*kitāb*); the focus is on correct spelling (even if the handwriting is at a low level) (p. 64).
- The essentials of grammar needed for correct verbal communication and for writing (p. 73).
- The essentials of stylistics, including the use of easy and precise words, and the clarity of expression (p. 74).
- Correct articulation and basic skills in rhetoric (pp. 74–75).

2. Arithmetic
- Good knowledge of arithmetic (pp. 64, 70); accuracy is important here even more so than for writing. At the beginner's level, the focus is on the basics of calculation; later on one may deal with higher arithmetic, geometry, field measurements etc. (pp. 74–75).

3. The Essentials of Religion
- Religious duties (*farāʾiḍ*, pp. 64, 69).
- The Quran (pp. 64, 69).

4. Literature and Literary Theory
- Poetry: all poems, including those displaying "metrical speech, as used in poems in the metre of *qaṣīd* verse and in poems in *rajaz* metre (*al-mawzūn min qaṣāʾid wa-l-arjāz*; pp. 65, 69).
- Prose: including what is balanced and often rhymed (*min al-muzdawij wa-l-asjāʿ*; p. 69),[52] what provides historical information (*akhbār*), and what is to be found in literary works from former times (*āthār*) (pp. 65, 73).
- Prosody (*ʿarūḍ*, p. 65).

5. Logic and Disputation
- Articulate prose (*al-manṭiq al-manthūr*, p. 68).
- Logical argumentation and debate, i.e. formulating questions and answers (p. 68).

6. Accounting
- What is required of government clerks and registrars (*kuttāb al-dawāwīn*); such as arithmetic and what is related to marketing and promotion, as well as correct spelling (for the knowledge of accounting is more useful and fruitful than the knowledge possessed by editors and scribes; p. 74).

Recommended topics [at a more advanced stage of education]:
7. Hunting.
8. Sports, including the use of light arms.

[52] For *muzdawij* as a technical term of philology, rhetoric, and prosody, see the art. "Muzdawidj," in: *EI*[2] vii, 825 (M. Bencheneb). For the meaning of *muzdawij* as related here, cf. al-Jāḥiẓ, *al-Bayān wa-tabyīn*, ed. Hārūn, ii, 116–117, where al-Jāḥiẓ provides examples of what he calls *muzdawij al-kalām*. See furthermore Abū Hilāl al-ʿAskarī, *K. al-Ṣināʿatayn, al-kitāba wa-l-shiʿr*, ed. ʿAlī Muḥammad al-Bajāwī and Muḥammad Abū l-Faḍl Ibrāhīm, [1]Cairo: Dār Iḥyāʾ al-Kutub al-ʿArabiyya; ʿĪsā al-Bābī al-Ḥalabī, 1371/1952, 260–265 ("*Fī dhikr al-sajʿ wa-l-izdiwāj*"). For this term referring to poetry that has paired rhyme (*aa bb cc* . . .), see Gustav E. von Grunebaum, On the Origin and Early Development of Arabic *Muzdawij* Poetry, in: *Journal of Near Eastern Studies* 3 (1944), 9–13; and Manfred Ullmann, *Untersuchungen zur Rağazpoesie, Ein Beitrag zur arabischen Sprach- und Literaturwissenschaft*, Wiesbaden: Harrasowitz, 1966, 44–60 ("Das Muzdawiğ-Gedicht"). I am grateful to Prof. G.J. van Gelder (Oxford) for drawing my attention to these publications.

9. Music, including how to play various musical instruments.
10. Astronomy, i.e. "the knowledge of the stars."
11. Medicine.
12. Geometry (*handasa*).
13. Teaching (or training) animals, especially those used by people for labor, including camels and horses (pp. 65–66).

Topics recommended specifically for children of people from the lower class: Farming, trading, construction, goldsmithing, sewing, weaving, dyeing, and other crafts (p. 66).

3.2.4 *Advice for teachers*

The text provides numerous pieces of advice for teachers, some of which are given expressly, while others are indicated in a more general way. Some of the more striking examples shall be presented here. They concern:

The process of education

- Take the mental ability of students into account. Use a language understandable to them (p. 74).
- Treat students gently and in a most lovable way. Attempt to reach their hearts when it comes to the subject matters taught (p. 77).

The purpose of reading

- Make the students understand that the purpose of reading books is to learn and to understand and not, simply, the enjoyment of nice words, for: "He who reads the books of eloquent writers and leafs through the collections of sages to acquire ideas pursues the right course. He, [however,] who looks into these books [simply] to learn [more] words pursues the wrong course (*wa-man qaraʾa kutub al-bulaghāʾ wa-taṣaffaḥa dawāwīn al-ḥukamāʾ li-yastafīda l-maʿānī fa-huwa ʿalā sabīl ṣawāb; wa-man naẓara fīhā li-yastafīda l-alfāẓ fa-huwa ʿalā sabīl khaṭaʾ*)" (pp. 75–76).

The means of expression and style

- Make the students familiar with the arguments of writers and their eloquent use of simple and easily understood words. Make them taste "the sweetness of brevity and the comfort of sufficiency [in expression] (*ḥalāwat al-ikhtiṣār wa-rāḥat al-kifāya*)" (p. 74).

- Warn the students against pretentiousness (p. 74).
- Teach them to express themselves in a way understandable to people without the need for any additional interpretation and comment (pp. 74–75).
- Teach them to choose simple words whose semantic fields, or meanings, do not cover "extremes, nor extravagance and unnaturalness;" there are already too many people who do not care about the loss of meaning in words, but concern themselves instead with eloquence and "meaningless elegance" in expression (p. 75).
- Make the students understand that content has priority over style, because the least eloquent person is he "who has prepared the means of conveying meaning before preparing the meaning itself." Enrich their active vocabulary, for one should not just stick to the words one already knows. New vocabulary, however, should be limited to known and distinct meanings, and should not just be created off-hand (p. 75).

Good manners and style in writing

- Warn the students about using bad manners in life and in writing. They should also be warned about slow articulation, inactive performance, extreme arrogance, and the keenness to be counted among the eloquent. Again, make them aware of good style; prepare them to distinguish between a smooth and easy style and a complicated one (p. 75).

3.2.5 *Further pieces of advice and examples of how al-Jāḥiẓ presents them*

Deduction vs. memorization

The leading sages, masters of the art of deductive reasoning and [independent] thinking, have been averse to excellence in memorization, because of [one's] dependence on it and [its rendering] the mind negligent of rational discernment, so [much so] that they said: "Memorization inhibits the intellect."	وكرهت الحكماء الرؤساء، أصحاب الاستنباط والتفكير، جودةَ الحفظ لمكان الاتّكال عليه، وإغفال العقل من التمييز، حتّى قالوا: "الحفظ عِذق الذهن."

[They have been averse to it] because the one engaged in memorization is only an imitator, whereas deductive reasoning is that which brings the one engaged in it to the coolness of certainty and the strength of confidence.

ولأنّ مستعمل الحفظ لا يكون إلاّ مقلّدا، والاستنباط هو الذي يفضي بصاحبه إلى برد اليقين وعزّ الثقة.

The true proposition and the praiseworthy judgment is that, when [a student] perpetuates learning by memorization, this harms deductive reasoning; and when he perpetuates deductive reasoning, this harms learning by memorization—even if memorization has a more honorable rank than [deductive reasoning].

والقضية الصحيحة، والحكم المحمود: أنّه متى أدام التحفّظ أضرّ ذلك بالاستنباط، ومتى أدام الاستنباط أضرّ ذلك بالحفظ، وإن كان التحفّظ أشرف منزلة منه.

So, when he neglects rational reflection, ideas do not come quickly to him, and when he neglects learning by memorization, [these ideas] do not stick in his mind or remain long in his heart.

ومتى أهمل النظر[٥٣] لم تسرع إليه المعاني، ومتى أهمل التحفّظ، لم تَعْلَق بقلبه، وقلّ مكثها في صدره.

The nature of memorization is other than [that] of deductive reasoning. [However,] that which is treated and helped by both [memorization and deductive reasoning] is [something] agreed upon: it is freeing the mind for—and desiring—only one thing. By means of these two (i.e. memorization and deductive reasoning), perfection comes to be and virtue appears.

وطبيعة الحفظ غير طبيعة الاستنباط. والذي يعالجان به ويستعينان [به] متّفق عليه وهو فراغ القلب للشيء والشهوة له، وبهما يكون التمام وتظهر الفضيلة.

The adherent of learning by memorization [and the adherent of deductive reasoning] have another aspect [of learning] on which they agree: this is the location and the time [for studying].

ولصاحب التحفّظ [ولصاحب الاستنباط] سبب[٥٤] آخر يتّفقان عليه، وهو الموضع والوقت.

---

[53] *Nazar* refers here to "inferential knowledge" differentiated from "necessary knowledge," *'ilm ḍarūrī*, i.e. the knowledge known immediately without reflection (such as the knowledge of one's existence and of the self-evident truth of logic).

[54] *Sabab* means "cause, reason, motive, occasion," etc.; it was decided, however, to render it here as "aspect" for the generality of the term.

As for the locations, whatever both of them choose [is appropriate]; if they so wish [however, these locations could be upper] chambers without distractions.

فأمّا المواضع فأيّهما يختاران إذا أرادا ذلك الغرف دون الشغل.[55]

As for the hours, the early mornings [are preferred] above all other times, because that time is before the time of being occupied [with other things,] and [it] follows [the time of] total relaxation and rest;

وأمّا الساعات فالأسحار دون سائر الأوقات، لأنّ ذلك الوقت قبل وقت الاشتغال، وتعقب تمام الراحة والجمام،

[this is so] since there is a certain amount of time for relaxation, which is [for one's] benefit, just as there is a certain amount of time for hard work, which is [also for one's] benefit. (pp. 62–63).

لأنّ للجمام مقداراً هو المصلحة، كما أنّ للكدّ مقداراً هو المصلحة.

The teaching of grammar

About the training of the boy:

في رياضة الصبيّ:

As for grammar, occupy [the boy's] mind with it only to the extent that it would safeguard [him] against the [commission of] excessive grammatical errors and against the measure of [grammatical] ignorance [encountered in the parlance of] the commonality—should he happen to draft a piece of writing, recite poetry, [or] describe something.

وأمّا النحو، فلا تُشغِلْ قلبه منه إلاّ بقدر ما يؤديه إلى السلامة من فاحش اللحن، ومن مقدار جهل العوامّ في كتاب إن كتبه، وشعر إن أنشده، وشيء إن وصفه.

Anything exceeding this is a diversion from what has a higher claim [for the pupil's education] and is a distraction

وما زاد على ذلك فهو مَشغلةٌ عمّا هو أولَى به، ومُذهِلٌ عمّا هو أردُّ عليه منه، من رواية

[55] *Ghurfa*, pl. *ghuraf*, means "an (upper) chamber." It also signifies the highest place(s) in Paradise (see Q 25:75, 29:58, 34:37, 39:20; see also Lane vi, 2249). Furthermore, it is one of the names of Paradise (Lane vi, 2249). *Shughl* means "business, occupation, or employment . . . [and in particular business . . . that diverts one from a thing] or an occurrence that causes a man to forget, or neglect, or be unmindful" (Lane iv, 1567). Hārūn's edition, p. 30, offers a different (and perhaps more likely) reading:

فأمّا الموضع فأيّهما يختاران إذا أرادا ذلك الفوق دون السفل.

As for the location [for studying], both [groups] choose, if they so wish, the [quiter?] upper rather than the lower [levels of a building].

from what is more profitable for him in the way of relating the [pointedly] illustrative proverb, the true informative account, and the [most] outstanding interpretation.

المثل الشاهد [٥٦] والخبر الصادق، والتعبير البارع.

He who desires to reach the utmost limits [of grammar], and to go beyond [studying only] a moderate amount [of it], is someone who does not need to familiarize himself with substantial matters, the deductive unveiling of the obscurities in the [art of] governance, [knowledge of] the welfare of peoples and countries, the pillars [of religion], and the axis around which the [world's] millstone revolves; [that is to say, this is someone] who has no share [of knowledge] nor any livelihood other than [grammar].

وإنّما يرغب في بلوغ غايته ومجاوزة الاقتصاد فيه من لا يحتاج إلى تعرّف جسيمات الأمور، والاستنباط لغوامض التدبير، ولمصالح العباد والبلاد والعلم بالأركان، والقطب الذي تدور عليه الرحى، ومن ليس له حظّ غيره ولا معاش سواه.

The difficulties of grammar do not occur in human transactions and there is nothing compelling [you] to indulge in it.

وعويص النحو، لا يجري في المعاملات، ولا يضطرّ إليه شئ.

It is sound judgment, then, to direct [the pupil] towards finger reckoning, rather than Indian calculus, and rather than geometry and the difficulties belonging to the [science of] measuring surface areas. Concerning all of this, however, you are obliged to teach him what the competent [clerks] of the ruler and secretaries in the chancelleries need [to know].

فمن الرأي أن يصمد به في حساب العقد دون حساب الهند [٥٧] ودون الهندسة وعويص ما يدخل في المساحة، وعليك في ذلك بما يحتاج إليه كفاة السلطان وكتّاب الدواوين.

[56] This seems to be the nuance of what al-Jāḥiẓ means by *al-mathal al-shāhid*. A more literal translation would be something like "the proverb that bears witness," or ". . . provides evidence." Alternatively, if *mathal* is taken to mean "example," it would be translated as "the example that serves as evidence," which therefore would make it relevant for the exegesis of the Quran. Hārūn's edition, p. 38, has *al-mathal wa-l-shāhid*. While this reading would also be possible, the text as given in Geries' edition seems to be rhetorically better with respect to the following pairs of noun plus adjective.

[57] Medieval Arabic scholars were aware of the significance of the decimal numeral system of the Indians. This is shown, for example, by the many books on *al-ḥisāb al-hindī*, as medieval Arabic scholars called the numeral system based on "ten" (see *GAS* v, 195–196). For the Indian calculus as an arithmetic method (and for the classical theory of numbers in medieval Arabic scholarship in general), see al-Hassan

I say that reaching an [adequate] knowledge of accounting, about which [all this] work revolves, and progressing in it and being motivated to do so, is more beneficial for [the pupil] than reaching [the level] of craftsmanship of the skilled copyists and chief calligraphers.

وأنا أقول إنّ البلوغ في معرفة الحساب الذي يدور عليه العمل، والترقي فيه والسبب إليه، أرد عليه من البلوغ في صناعة المحررين ورؤوس الخطاطين؛

[This is] because there is communication at the lowest level of penmanship—as long as the spelling is correct—while this is not the case for calculation (pp. 73–74).

لأن في أدنى طبقات الخط مع صحة الهجاء بلاغا، وليس كذلك حال الحساب.٥٨

The treatment of the student

After that, I am of the opinion that you should not force him [to work] and so make him dislike good manners and education. [Also,] do not neglect him, lest he get used to wasting [time] in amusing activities.

وبعد هذا، فإني أرى أن لا تستكرهه فتبغض إليه الأدب. ولا تهمله فيعتاد اللهو.

Moreover, I know of nothing in the entire world that is more [capable of] attracting complete corruption than bad companions and leisure-time beyond [what is needed for] relaxation.

على أني لا أعلم في جميع الأرض شيئا أجلب لجميع الفساد من قرناء السوء والفراغ الفاضل عن الجمام.

Teach him knowledge as long as he is free from the tasks of men and the demands of those with high-minded ambitions.

درسه العلم ما كان فارغا من أشغال الرجال ومطالب ذوي الهمم.

(ed.), *The Different Aspects of Islamic Culture* iv, 189. Also see Gohlman (ed.), *The Life of Ibn Sina* 20 and 21.

It interesting to note that the word *hind* in classical Arabic also means "a hundred camels," or any hundreds, or higher numbers; or "two hundred [camels or years];" see *Lisān al-ʿArab* iii, 437; and Lane viii, 2903–4. This seems to indicate that the word *hind* in general referred to higher numbers. At any rate, even in this latter case, the first part of the sentence at issue here would refer to "basic" calculation, while the latter would refer to "higher" arithmetic.

[58] In other words: communication is possible even with little knowledge in writing. In calculation, however, the smallest mistake will lead to inaccurate results.

Devise artful means to make yourself more lovable to him than his mother.

واحتل في أن تكون أحب إليه من أمّه.

[However,] you cannot [expect] him to show tender affection and sincere friendship towards you with his dislike for the heavy burden of education you put on him, [that is] on someone who has not [yet] reached the state of somebody who is familiar with erudition.

ولا تستطيع أن يمحضك المقة، ويصفي لك المودة، مع كراهته لما تحمل إليه من ثقل التأديب عند من لم يبلغ حال العارف بفضل.

Therefore, bring out his innate affection with righteous words and the offer of financial [assistance].

فاستخرج مكنون محبّته ببرّ اللسان وبذل المال.

However, there is a limit to this; whoever goes beyond it is excessive, and excessiveness is dissipation; and whoever does not reach it is excessive in neglect, and the one who is neglectful is a wastrel.

ولهذا مقدار، من جازه أفرط، والإفراط سَرَف، ومن قصّر عنه فرّط والمُفرِّط مضياع [...].

The one you attempt [to induce]—by way of benefiting the state of affairs of [this person being] the one in whom you have the hope that he will take your place amongst your people and will take care of [and continue] what you have left behind, in the way you would have done [it],—is worthy of all care and the making of every effort on your part (p. 86).

والذي تحاول من صلاح أمر من تؤمل فيه أن يقوم في أهلك مقامك — وصلاح ما خلّفت كقيامك — لحقيق بالحيطة عليه، وبإعطائه المجهود من نفسك.

4 *Conclusions*

As has become apparent, the two treatises presented in this chapter show in an impressive way the attempts made by two 9th century Muslim scholars to analyze and explain primary education, the objectives of education, and the pedagogical and didactic tools to be applied in achieving such goals.

In terms of the history of ideas, most of the educational rules given by Ibn Saḥnūn and al-Jāḥiẓ can be found—in a more systematic and perhaps more elaborate way—in the writings of the theologian and original thinker al-Ghazālī, who lived 250 years after these predecessors of his in this particular field of scholarship. Nonetheless, it is remarkable that these two early texts should already address many major aspects of educational ethics and philosophy, regardless of the fact that each of them approaches these issues from a different perspective: one from a legal and the other from a literary-philosophical point of view.

In more general terms, the pedagogical advice given in the two classical Arabic texts under discussion may remind us also of similar ideas introduced to Europe in the educational renaissance of the 16th and 17th centuries. In Europe, it was somebody like the Czech educational reformer and religious leader John Amos Comenius (1592–1670) who became known for his innovative teaching methods in his time. Like Ibn Saḥnūn, Comenius emphasized the need for teaching all aspects of language, since good language skills are a basic prerequisite for the intellectual improvement of students. Like Ibn Saḥnūn also, Comenius argued that education should aim at equipping young people with a profound knowledge of the Holy Scripture and religious duties. Comenius, though, stressed as well that teachers should ensure a rapid, pleasant, and thorough education, which follows in "the footsteps of nature."[59] These latter ideas of making teaching and learning a natural and pleasant experience are not yet addressed clearly in Ibn Saḥnūn's book on "Rules of Conduct for Teachers." However, they are present and discussed most insightfully in al-Jāḥiẓ's book "The Teachers."

For these reasons, these two classical Arabic works from the 9th century not only represent some of the very earliest attempts of Muslim scholarship to deal, in an elaborate manner, with pedagogy and didactics,[60] but they also deserve recognition for their contribution to the history of pedagogy in general.

[59] Weimer, *Geschichte der Pädagogik* 81–86.

[60] See my art. "Education: Islamic Education," in: *New Dictionary of the History of Ideas* ii, 640–45, esp. 643–44.

Frequently Quoted References

al-Ahwānī, Aḥmad Fu'ād: *at-Ta'līm fī ra'y al-Qābisī min 'ulamā' al-qarn al-rābi'*, Cairo: Maṭba'at Lajnat al-Ta'līf wa-l-Tarjama wa-l-Nashr, 1364/1945.
al-'Askarī, Abū Hilāl (d. 395/1005): *Dīwān al-ma'ānī*, Cairo: Maktabat al-Qudsī, [1352/1933–34].
Baer, Eva: Muslim Teaching Institutions and their Visual Reflections: The *Kuttāb*, in: *Der Islam* 78 (2001), 73–102.
Buhl, Fr.: art. "Khaṭma, Khiṭma," in: *EI*[2] iv, 1112
EI[1] = *Enzyklopädie des Islam*, hrsg. von Martin Theodoor Houtsma [et al.], Leiden: Brill [et al.], 1913–.
EI[2] = *Encyclopaedia of Islam*, new edition, Leiden: Brill, 1954–.
GAL = Carl Brockelmann, *Geschichte der arabischen Litteratur*, [. . .] *erweitert um ein Vorwort von Jan Just Witkam*, 2 vols. + 3 supplementary vols., Leiden et al.: Brill, 1996.
GAS = Fuat Sezgin: *Geschichte des arabischen Schrifttums* [. . .] bis ca. 430 H, Leiden, Brill 1967–.
Gelder, Geert Jan van: Mixtures of Jest and Ernest in Classical Arabic Literature, in: *Journal of Arabic Literature* 23 (1992), 83–108 (part 1); 169–190 (part 2).
Geries, Ibrahim [Jiryis, Ibrāhīm] (ed.): *Kitābān li-l-Jāḥiẓ. Kitāb al-mu'allimīn wa-kitāb fī l-radd 'alā al-mushabbiha* [the title is also given in English:] *Two Essays by al-Jāḥiẓ: "On Schoolmasters" and "Refutation of Anthropomorphists,"* annotated, with an introductory study, and ed. by Ibrahim Geries, [1]Tel Aviv: Tel Aviv University, Department of Arabic Language and Literature, Srugy-Acco [also: 'Akkā: Maṭba'at al-Surūjī], 1980, 57–87.
Gohlman, William E.: *The Life of Ibn Sina: A Critical Edition and Annotated Translation*, Albany, NY: State University of New York Press, 1974.
Günther, Sebastian: art. "Education: Islamic Education," in: *New Dictionary of the History of Ideas*, ed. Maryanne Cline Horowitz, Detroit: Charles Scribner's Sons, 2005, vol. ii, 640–45.
Hārūn, 'Abd al-Salām Muḥammad (ed.): *Rasā'il al-Jāḥiẓ*, iv parts in two vols., [1]Beirut: Dār al-Jīl, 1411/1991.
al-Hassan, A.Y. (ed.): *The Different Aspects of Islamic Culture*, iv: *Science and Technology in Islam*, Paris, Beirut: Dergham, 2001, 189. (= *UNESCO Publications*).
Ḥijāzī, 'Abd al-Raḥmān 'Uthmān: *al-Madhhab al-tarbawī 'inda Ibn Saḥnūn*, Beirut: Mu'assasat al-Risāla, [1]1406/1986.
Hirschfeld, Hartwig: *A Volume of Essays by al Jahiz, Reprinted from a volume of oriental studies presented to Professor E.G. Browne, February 1922*, Cambridge: University Press, 1922.
Ibn Saḥnūn, Muḥammad: *Ādāb al-mu'allimīn*, ed. Muḥammad al-'Arūsī al-Maṭwī, [reprinted] in: Ḥijāzī, *al-Madhhab*, 111–128.
Ismail, Sha'ban Muftah: Muḥammad ibn Sahnūn [sic]: An educationalist and faqīh, in: *Muslim Education Quarterly* 12.4 (1995), 37–54.
'Iyāḍ, al-Qāḍī Abū l-Faḍl [Ibn Mūsā] (d. 544/1149): *Tarājim aghlabiyya. Mustakhraja min madārik al-Qāḍī 'Iyāḍ*, ed. Muḥammad al-Ṭālibī, Tunis: al-Maṭba'a al-Rasmiyya li-l-Jumhūriyya al-Tūnisiyya, 1968. (= *Biographies aghlabides. Extraits des «Madarik» du Cadi 'Iyad. Édition critique avec introduction et index par M. Talbi*).
al-Jāḥiẓ, 'Amr ibn Baḥr al-Baṣrī, *K. al-Bayān wa-l-tabyīn*, ed. 'Abd al-Salām Hārūn, iv parts in two vols., Cairo: Maktabat al-Khānjī, [5]1405/1985.
——: *K. al-Ḥayawān*, ed. 'Abd al-Salām Hārūn, 7 vols., Cairo: Maktabat Muṣṭafā al-Bābī al-Ḥalabī, 1938.
——: *K. al-Mu'allimīn*, in: Hārūn (ed.), *Rasā'il al-Jāḥiẓ* iii, 27–51; Geries (ed.), *Kitābān li-l-Jāḥiẓ* 57–87.
——: *Majmū' Rasā'il al-Jāḥiẓ, wa-hiya rasā'il lam tunshar li-Abī 'Uthmān 'Amr ibn Baḥr al-Jāḥiẓ*, ed. Bāwl Krāws [Paul Kraus], Muḥammad Ṭaha al-Ḥājirī, Cairo:

Maṭbaʿat Lajnat al-Taʾlīf wa-l-Tarjama wa-l-Nashr, 1943 [it contains: 1. *Risālat al-Maʿāsh wa-l-maʿād*; 2. *Kitāb Kitmān al-sirr wa-ḥifẓ al-lisān*; 3. *Risāla fī l-Jidd wa-l-hazl*; and 4. *Risālat Faṣl mā bayna l-ʿadāwa wa-l-ḥasad*].

Lecomte, Gérard: art. "Muḥammad b. Saḥnūn," in: *EI*[2] vii, 409.

——: Le Livre des Règles de Conduite des Maîtres d'Ecole par Ibn Saḥnūn, in: *Revue des Etudes Islamiques* 21 (1953), 77–105.

Mālikī, *Riyāḍ al-nufūs* = [Ibn Abī ʿAbdallāh al-Mālikī] Abū Bakr ʿAbdallāh ibn Muḥammad al-Mālikī (5th/11th cent.), *Riyāḍ al-nufūs fī ṭabaqāt ʿulamāʾ al-Qayrawān wa-Ifrīqiyā wa-zuhhādihim wa-ʿibādihim wa-nussākihim wa-siyar min akhbārihim wa-faḍāʾili-him wa-awṣāfihim*, ed. Bashīr al-Bakkūsh, rev. by Muḥammad al-ʿArūsī al-Maṭwī, 2 vols., [2]Beirut: Dār al-Gharīb al-Islāmī, 1414/1993.

Pellat, *Arabische Geisteswelt* = Charles Pellat, *Arabische Geisteswelt, ausgewählte und übersetzte Texte von al-Ǧāḥiẓ (777–869), unter Zugrundelegung der arabischen Originaltexte aus dem Französischen übertragen von Walter W. Müller*, Stuttgart: Artemis Verlag, 1967.

Pellat, Charles: art. "al-Djāḥiẓ," in: *EI*[2] ii, 385–388.

Pellat, Nouvel essai = Charles Pellat, Nouvel essai d'inventaire de l'oeuvre Ǧāḥiẓienne, in: *Arabica* 31 (1984), 117–164.

Pellat, *The Life* = Charles Pellat, *The Life and Works of Jāḥiẓ, Translation of selected texts, translated form the French by D.M. Hawke*, London: Routledge & Kegan Paul, 1969.

al-Qayrawānī, Abū l-ʿArab Muḥammad ibn Aḥmad ibn Tamīm (d. 333/945): *Ṭabaqāt ʿulamāʾ Ifrīqiyya* (sic), ed. ʿAlī al-Shābbī, Nuʿaym Ḥasan al-Yāfī, Tunis: al-Dār al-Tūnisiyya li-l-Nashr, 1968.

Rescher, Oskar: *Excerpte und Übersetzungen aus den Schriften des Philologen und Dogmatikers Ǧāḥiẓ aus Baçra (150–250 H.) nebst noch unveröffentlichten Originaltexten*, Teil 1, Stuttgart: [no publisher], 1931.

Rosenthal, Franz: *The Technique and Approach of Muslim Scholarship*, Rome: Pontificium Institutum Biblicum, 1947. (= *Analecta orientalia* 14).

Shalaby, Aḥmad: *History of Muslim Education*, Beirut: Dar al-Kashshaf, 1954.

Shams al-Dīn, ʿAbd al-Amīr Z.: *al-Fikr al-tarbawī ʿinda Ibn Saḥnūn wa-l-Qābisī*, Beirut: Maktabat al-Madrasa; Dār al-Kitāb al-ʿĀlamī, [1]1990. (= *Mawsūʿat at-Tarbiya wa-t-Taʿlīm al-Islāmiyya*).

——: *al-Fikr al-tarbawī ʿinda Ibn al-Muqaffaʿ, al-Jāḥiẓ, ʿAbd al-Ḥamīd al-Kātib*, Beirut: Maktabat al-Madrasa; Dār al-Kitāb al-ʿĀlamī, [1]1991. (= *Mawsūʿat at-Tarbiya wa-t-Taʿlīm al-Islāmiyya*).

Totah, Khalil Abdallah: *The Contribution of the Arabs to Education*, [Ph.D. thesis] New York: Columbia University, Teachers College, 1926 [repr. New York: AMS Press, 1972; [1]Gorgias Press 2002].

Tritton, A.S.: *Materials on Muslim Education in the Middle Ages*, London: Luzac, 1957.

Weimer, Hermann: *Geschichte der Pädagogik, 19., völlig neu bearb. Auflage von Juliane Jacobi*, Berlin: de Gruyter, 1992. (= *Sammlung Göschen* 2080).

al-Yāqūt ibn ʿAbdallāh al-Ḥamawī (d. 626/1229): [*Muʿjam al-udabāʾ*.] *K. al-Irshād al-arīb ilā maʿrifat al-adīb. Dictionary of Learned Men*, ed. D.S. Margoliouth. [Repr.] Cairo: Maṭbaʿa Hindiyya bi-l-Mūsakī bi-Miṣr, [1907–]. (= *E.J.W. Gibb Memorial Series* 6).

Ziriklī = Khayr al-Dīn al-Ziriklī: *al-Aʿlām. Qāmūs tarājim li-ashhar al-rijāl wa-l-nisāʾ min al-ʿarab wa-l-mustaʿribīn wa-l-mustashriqīn*, 8 vols., [8]Beirut: Dār al-ʿIlm li-l-Malāyīn, 1979.

6
THE ISLAMIC PREACHER
WĀʿIẒ, MUDHAKKIR, QĀṢṢ

Johannes Pedersen

With the ancient Arabs the art of the spoken word played an overwhelming role: how strong was the power of the Word had been pointed out by Goldziher. That the verbal art also had been of importance at the appearance of Islam finds its expression in the doctrine that the Qurʾān is *muʿjis*, a view that is not put forth as a dogma, but is claimed to be a comprehension which only presupposes a sufficient knowledge of Arabic. Practitioners of the art of the spoken word in pre-Islamic times were the poet, *shāʿir*, and the rhetorician, *khaṭīb*. In Islam the poet maintained his influence in public life, and as the one who stimulated the Prince; and likewise poetry entered the service of religion. This fact, however, failed to provide the poet with any preferential position within Islam. Otherwise with the rhetorician. He obtained a position as the one who in continuance of the Prophet's function as a leader addressed the congregation from the *minbar* during Friday's service. Besides this official preacher, *al-khaṭīb*, the congregation, however, at an early period got another pulpit orator, who more at his liberty might instil needed teachings and influence people's turn of mind. The term of *wāʿiẓ* is the best to characterize his profession, but the two above mentioned terms are employed also. Even his activity has its roots in the old Arabian community.

The root of *wʿẓ* is well-known from Hebrew and Aramaic. The Hebrew word *ʿēṣā* means 'counsel' i.e. an idea stamped by will and ready for action. To give advice means to induce another to catch a like idea. The Israelitish king had a *yōʿēṣ*, a man with a special gift for backing him up in this way. He stimulated the king by helping him to conceive efficacious plans.[1] In Arabic usage the verb **[227]** *waʿaẓa* is closely related to its use in Hebrew, it being applied to express imparting of knowledge, and through it inducing to the right action. It is often employed in the Qurʾān as characteristic of the activity of the prophets. It refers to the Israelitish prophets (7, 164), the ancient Arabic prophets like Hūd (26, 136) and Luqmān (31, 12): and Muḥammad is called upon to address a *waʿẓ* to the unreliable and to say a penetrating word to them (4, 66). The whole Qurʾān is a *waʿẓ* (*ʿiẓa, mawʿiẓa*) as was the Law of Moses (7, 142) and the Gospel (5, 52).

---

[1] cf. my *Israel*,I–II, pp. 130, 183; III–IV, Index *s.c.* counsellor.

"Remember God's benefactions towards you, and the Book, and the Wisdom by which he admonishes you (*yaʿiẓukum*)" (2, 231). The Qurʾān is for the believers the truthful rule, admonition, and reminding (*al-haqq wa-mawʿiẓa wa-dhikrā*, 11, 121 cf. *mawʿiẓa wa-hudā*, 3, 132). It is pointed out that this *mawʿiẓa* is a cure for the soul, guidance, and mercy from God (10, 58, cf. 2, 276). Thus God directs his *waʿẓ* on to Noah lest he should belong to the witless (11, 48). So in the commentaries on the Qurʾān the word is often rendered as *nuṣḥ* and *irshād* (good advice, and communication of the Right, e.g. Baiḍāwi *ad* 4, 66; 34, 45). What is contained in the good advice is naturally the subordination to Allāh's will and that of the Prophet, and the inducement may be implied in the attractive pictures of Paradise that are called *waʿẓ* (4, 61). The word may be used for a lenient appeal to the believers, e.g. concerning the treatment of their wives (2, 232; 65, 2; cf, 4, 69) and also for a direct order to act righteously and a prohibition against bad deeds (16, 92). It is applied to designate rebuke of the recriminations against ʿĀʾisha, this being administered in order to prevent a recurrence to take place (24, 16), but it also means plain punishment as the penance laid on the one who undertakes *ẓihār*-divorce (58, 4, cf. 4, 38). Accounts of previous acts of punishment are called *mawʿiẓa* (2, 62; 24, 34), as they serve as an example (*ʿibra*). The one who acts according to the prompting, *ittaʿẓa* 'is appropriating the admonition'.

In the same way is used *tadhakkara* (13, 19; 20, 46 etc.), *dhakkara*, 'remind', being employed in much the same meaning as *waʿaẓa*, probably, however, somewhat less forcibly (5, 16, 17; 6, 44; 25, 73; 32, 15; 37, 13 etc.). It is mentioned as a task of the Prophet (50, 45; 51, 55; 52, 29 and elsewhere), and in a singular passage he is characterized **[228]** as a *mudhakkir* 'reminder' (88, 21). Like *dhikre* also *dhikr* can be applied to the admonishing preaching of the Prophet (7, 61, 67), and, corresponding to the mentioned verb, *tadhkira*, which is used both for the preaching of the Qurʾān (69, 48; 73, 19; 74, 50, 54 etc.) and earlier occurrences containing admonishing teachings, as the deliverance from the Deluge (69, 12), the gift of Fire to Man (56, 72) that bears witness to God's might and his benevolence towards him (cf. 36, 80). The most frequent term used as a characterization of the activity of the Prophet is *nadhīr*, admonisher, which is more threatening than those mentioned above, and accordingly is often brought into equilibrium by the corresponding *bashīr*, "messenger of good tidings" (2, 113; 5, 22; 11, 2 and elsewhere).

Naturally this usage is not created by the Qurʾān. Says ʿAbīd b. al-Abras, "Men do not arouse to understanding (*lā yaʿiẓu*) the one whom Time does not arouse to understanding, and it is no good seizing (a man) by his breastfold", i.e. to urge him.[2] It is a characteristic trait with the ancient Arabs to say that "Time", i.e. the

---

[2] ed. Lyall, *Gibb Mem. Ser.*, 1913, I 19.

Fate, "admonishes" Man, that is, to perceive the changeability of everything and to act accordingly. Thus says Labīd, "Tell him (the man), when he settles his plan: Has not Time aroused you to understanding (*a-lammā ya'iẓka 'l-dahru*) – may your mother become childless! – that you know that you cannot grasp what is past, and that you cannot escape of what the soul is afraid",[3] in short once more the same teaching given by the inconstancy of life about the humbleness and destitution of Man. The connection between pre-Islamic and Qur'ānic *wa'ẓ* is to be found in the fact that in his conception of the transitoriness of the world and the humbleness of Man, Muḥammad is on a line with the ancients, but just in this fact he finds an admonition to submit to God's revelation. It is an interesting fact that some verses of a like character as those mentioned are said to have been pronounced by 'Adī b. Zaid to al-Nu'mān b. al-Mundhir as a *maw'iẓa* for Christianity. He makes a tree say, "How many horsemen have halted by us, drinking wine with clear water. Time (*al-dahr*) **[229]** has snatched them away, and they are lost; thus does Time to anon and anon." And a burial place says, "Oh, you horsemen, who eagerly trot over the ground! We have been like you, and you will become like us". Al-Nu'mān declared that he understood that the poet would arouse his understanding (*aradta 'iẓatī*) and asked how one might be delivered, upon which 'Adī pointed to Christianity, and Nu'mān adopted this religion.[4]

We have no evidence that the story about the *wa'ẓ* of 'Adī to al-Nu'mān is historical, but the fact of a poet addressing a chief with *'iẓa* is in concordance with the character of the ancient Arabic poet. 'Abīd b. al-Abraṣ says, "When thou art one who gives no heed to counsel (*ra'y*), nor follows advice (*nuṣḥ*), nor inclines to the voice of him who points out the right way (*murshid*), then art thou not ... one fit for chiefship preeminent, nor near to being a chief", and 'Abīd says that he himself is a man of judiciousness (*ra'y*) through the excellency of which life is created.[5]

Wa'ẓ in the face of sovereigns happened to play a distinct part in Islam, of which fact Goldziher has rendered an account in his edition of al-Ghazzālī's pamphlet against *al-bāṭinīya*.[6] It did not turn upon certain men appointed to that end but people of acknowledged piety and wisdom of life, whom the ruler honoured by asking of them instruction with the word *'iẓnī* "give me an admonition", the continuance of which he demanded with the word *zidnī*, "give me some more". Some specimens of such a *wa'ẓ* is given in *Kitāb al-bayān* of al-Jāḥiẓ, in *Al-'iqd al-farīd* of Ibn 'Abd Rabbihi, and above all in *Sirāj al-mulūk* of al-Ṭurṭūshī. In these speeches to the sovereign the transitoriness of life is figuring

[3] ed. Brockelmann, Leiden 1891, XLI, 4

[4] *Kitāb al-aghānī*, 3[d] ed., 2, 96; v. also Ṭurṭushī, *Sirāj al-mulūk*, Cairo 1919, p. 13 sq.

[5] ed. Lyall, XXX, 10, 14, 21.

[6] Introduction, pp. 97 sqq.

largely. On the death of Alexander a sage is said to have uttered, "Yesterday he was more loquacious than today, but today he is more 'admonishing' than he was yesterday", an utterance that is also employed in a poem of Abu'l-ʿAtāhiya: "From your life I have got *ʿiẓāt* (admonitions), and today you are **[230]** more admonishing than you being alive."[7] Especially this subject is used as a warning against haughtiness due to power. Hārūn al-Rashīd said to Ibn al-Sammāk "*ʿiẓnī*." He just had a drink of water in his hand, and Ibn al-Sammāk asked if he would admit that if this drink was kept from him, he would give his kingdom for it. This having been answered in the affirmative, Ibn al-Sammāk went on asking that if the Khalīfa were prevented from making water of what he had drunk, would he give his kingdom to have it granted? As this also was answered in the affirmative the sage declared that the kingdom was worth less, since it was not worth either a drink or urine.[8] Al-Nuʿmān, the erector of the castle al-Khawarnaq, is blamed by a sage for his delight in it, because he is going to die and to lose it without that.[9] On the whole, the idea is constantly recurrent that nothing in the world has any real worth, because it is gained at the death of a predecessor and is to be given up at the death of oneself. The sage also may give general exhortations to reign according to God's commandments,[10] or propound rules of life often reminding of the logia of the Ṣūfis, or as al-Ḥasan al-Baṣrī they may quote a Qurʾānic text.[11] Al-Baihaqī (circ. 300/912) tells among other things about several pious men who were summoned to al-Manṣūr to give him advice, and who frankly censured his encroachments. In the speeches communicated by him, in which connection also a Bedouin makes his appearance, the contrast between this transitory world and the other world plays a leading part.[12] The corruptibility is found expressed under the following form: Where is Adam, father of the first and the last of men? Where is Noah, chief of the messengers? Where is Idris etc.[13] Becker inquired into this topic of "ubi sunt qui ante **[231]** in mundo fuere" in European and Oriental literatures and made out that the same rhetoric form occurs in Cyril of Alexandria and Efraem Syrus.[14] From that he draws the conclusion that the Islamic penitential sermon is an adage of the corresponding Christian sermon. The connection with the penitential exhortations of Christianity cannot be

---

[7] *Sirāj*, p. 13; *Al-bayān wa 'l-tabyin*, Cairo 1345, I, 255.

[8] *Sirāj*, p. 8.

[9] ibid., p. 9.

[10] e.g. *Bayān*, 2, 236 before al-Mahdī.

[11] *Sirāj*, 24 (Sūra 26, 205–207).

[12] al-Baihaqī, *Kitāb al-maḥāsin wa l-masāwī*, ed. Schwally, Giessen 1902, pp. 364 sqq. (the section on *waʿẓ*). Some of the tales here mentioned are also to be found in al-Jāḥiẓ' work with the same title, ed. v. Vloten, Leiden 1898, p. 172 sq.

[13] *Sirāj*, p. 7 cf. Ibn al-Jawzi, *Al-mudhish*, Baghdad 1348, pp. 222, 256, 343 and elsewhere.

[14] C.H. Becker, *Islamstudien*, I, 1924, pp. 501–519.

denied, but it must not be overlooked that the whole fundamental idea can be traced back to the Qur'ān, and hence to the ancient Arabic poetry.

We have dwelt upon the *wa'ẓ* aimed at the rulers, because in it an aspect of the activity of the monitor is at hand which is also connected with something pre-Islamic, namely the appearance of poets before the sovereign, a tradition that was carried over into Islam. By his *madḥ* the poet gives the sovereign a stimulus which is necessary for his self-assertion, or he gives him good advice. Thus the Islamic *wā'iẓ* gives him a guidance that will keep him in the path of Islam, warn him against arrogance, open his eyes to the frailty of Man, and at the same time strengthen his Muslim mind with good advice.

This activity, however, did not aim exclusively at the sovereign. Already one of the Prophet's companions, Sa'd b. 'Ammāra, was addressed by a man who said, "*'iẓnī*", and Sa'd recommended him punctually to fulfil the purgation before the prayer on the one side, and to avoid having many needs on the other.[15] People would seek guidance by a man who was able to give them advice. In the above mentioned writings similar "admonitions" from 'Umar, 'Alī and others of the Prophet's companions are to be found. But with a view to revival and guidance to the congregation, people who were apt for it were appointed to work for Islam in the spirit of the Prophet alongside with the *qāḍī* and the Qur'ān-teacher. In older times the term used for those preachers of calling was not *wā'iẓ,* but *qāṣṣ*, and alongside with it *mudhakkir,* in accordance with the use made of this word by Muḥammad in the Qur'ān as mentioned above.

Already in Ṭabarī's description of the battle of Yarmūk in the year 13 with Saif as an informer, mention is made **[232]** of Abu 'l Dardā as *qāḍi* and Abū Sufyān b. Ḥarb as *qāṣṣ*, while Miqdād functioned as *qāri',* "reciter of the Qur'ān", figuring in a list of participators of the battle. Abū Sufyān opened the battle with some encouraging words to the army and prayer for victory.[16] From this account we notice that a *qāṣṣ* acts as an official orator in the field to rouse the warriors. The verb *qāṣṣa*, is frequently employed in the Qur'ān concerning God's tales of how people fared in earlier history; moreover it is used in connection with the tale of Joseph and his dreams (12, 5), and the tales of the prophets (6, 130; 7, 33.175). The appellation indicates that the tale was his most important pedagogic means; also the Prophet, when being present at parties, would tell stories, to which effect the tale about Naḍr b. al-Ḥārith bears witness.[17]

At any rate the employment of *quṣṣāṣ* in the war to excite the warriors was no extraordinary feature in the times of old for in the year 65/685, when the 'repentent' Shī'ites under command of Sulaimān b. Ṣurad delivered a fight against the army

[15] *Usd al-ghāba*, II 287, a passage to which Goldziher has drawn the attention.
[16] Ṭabarī, ed. de Goeje, I 2095.
[17] Ibn Hishām, ed. Wüstenfeld, pp. 191, 235.

of Marwān, they had, according to Ṭabarī, three *quṣṣāṣ* with them, and one of these, Rifāʿa b. Shaddād al-Bajalī, incessantly *yaquṣṣu wa-yuḥaḍḍiḍu ʾl-nās*[18] on the right wing. Hence it appears that *al-qāṣṣ* carries on the activity of the Prophet and the poet of former times as one who excites to fight, and that the verb *qaṣṣa* has acquired the corresponding shade of signification.

At an early time preachers were attached to the mosques. As the first is mentioned Tamīm al-Dārī who is said to have attached himself to Muḥammad in Medina and to have influenced him as a former Christian.[19] He is said to have been *qāṣṣ* in Medina, and even if this may be as unlikely as the story of the Prophet giving him Hebron as a fief the statement is of evident interest. After having rejected it at first ʿUmar allowed him to admonish (*yudhakkiru*) in the mosque on Fridays before the arrival of ʿUmar, and under ʿUthmān he got permission to speak [**233**] twice a week.[20] In all this discussion about the lawfulness of *qaṣaṣ* makes itself felt. Another *qāṣṣ* from the times of the Prophet, al-Aswad b. Sarīʿ, was the first at the mosque of Baṣra,[21] in the year 38 or 39 Sulaim b. ʿItr al-Tujībī was appointed the first *qāṣṣ* at the ʿAmr-mosque in Cairo, some time as a *qāḍī*, too. We are told that during the prayer, in connection with the *al-qaṣaṣ*, he raised his hands, a manner introduced later on by ʿAbd al-Malik at the advice of his learned counsellors, imposing it upon all the *quṣṣāṣ*. We come to know about them in the main cities of the East.[22] It is suggestive what is related by al-Maqrīzī (d. 845/1442) on the basis of al-Quḍāʿī (d. 454/1062) about the further history of this institution in Egypt, i. e. in the ʿAmr-mosque. While being governor in Egypt ʿAbd al-ʿAzīz b. Marwān b. al-Ḥakam acquired a precious copy of the Qurʾān that was brought every Friday from his abode to the mosque where a recital was made, upon which a *qaṣaṣ* was held, and, on closing up, the Qurʾān in question was taken back. The then *qāṣṣ* (from the year 76 onwards)[23] was ʿAbd al-Raḥmān b. Ḥujaira al-Khawlānī, being at the same time a *qāḍī*; after him came Abu'l-Khair Marthad b. ʿAbdallāh al-Yazanī, sometime *qāḍī* in Alexandria. Later on followed ʿUqba b. Muslim al-Hamdānī, who in the year 118 was succeeded by Thawba b.

---

[18] Ṭabarī, II, 559, 10 sqq.

[19] G Levi della Vida, *s. v.* in *Encycl. of Islām.*

[20] al-Maqrīzī, *Khiṭaṭ*, Cairo 1326, IV, p. 16 sq. As far as I can see he is not mentioned by al-Jāḥiẓ but by Ibn al-Jawzī.

[21] *Usd al-ghāba*, I 86; Balādhurī, ed. de. Goeje, p. 89 and text p. 346; Ibn Duraid, *Ishtiqāq*, p. 152 infra; al-Jāḥiẓ mentions him as the first one in *Bayān*, I 234.

[22] In his *Essai*, pp. 141 sqq., Massignon has enumerated a series of *quṣṣāṣ*, in particular from al-Jāḥiẓ, *Bayān*, and Ibn al-Jawzi, *K. al-quṣṣāṣ*. Unfortunately, I only know the book mentioned from reports, among others by Goldziher, and summaries in the glossary of the Goeje to Balādhurī, p. 88 sq.

[23] According to al-Kindī, *Governors and Judges*, ed. Guest, pp. 314, 315, 320, he became qāḍī in the year 69, 70 or 71.

Nimr al-Ḥaḍramī who was a *qāḍī*. During his tenure of office the precious copy of the Qur'ān was deposited in the mosque, and the salary of the one who recited from it amounted to three dinars a month. According to al-Kindī (p. 342), he was appointed in 115. Upon him followed Ismā'il Khair b. Nu'aim al-Ḥaḍramī in 120, also being a *qāḍī*. He read aloud from the Qur'ān standing, while seated when [**234**] delivering the *qaṣaṣ*, being the first who acted in this way,[24] and it took place every Friday, until Abū Rajab al-'Alā' b. 'Āṣim al-Khawlāni became *qāṣṣ* in 182 (beginning 22nd of Febr. 798). He spoke on Mondays. Al-Muttalib al-Khuzā'i, al-Ma'mūn's emir for Egypt, had fixed a salary of ten dinars for him. Behind him Muḥammad b. Idris al-Shāfi'ī took part in the prayer during his stay in Egypt, and he declared that he had not partaken in any *ṣalāt* better than that. In 240 'Anbasa b. Isḥāq, the emir of al-Mutawakkil, designated Ḥasan b. al-Rabi' b. Sulaimān as a *qāṣṣ*, and he recited from the magnificent Qur'ān-copy on Mondays, Thursdays and Fridays. In 292 Ḥamza b. Aiyūb b. Ibrāhim al-Hāshimī took over his post by writ from al-Muktafī. He held the *ṣalāt* in the background of the mosque, as it was molested, and he had the Qur'ān brought there in spite of protests against this novelty. He declared, "Bring it me, for the Qur'ān has been descended to us and has come to us." This was not repeated until the 20th of Sha'bān 403 (7 March 1013), when Abū Bakr Muḥammad b. al-Ḥasan al-Sūsī took over *al-ṣalāt wa 'l-qaṣaṣ*, and had the magnificent Qur'ān-copy placed close by *al-fawwāra*. "By that the matter has been at rest until now." It is interposed that Abū Bakr Muḥammad b. 'Abdallāh b. Muslim al-Malaṭī, who became *qāṣṣ* in 301, recited from the Qur'ān daily for some short time.[25]

This information is supplemented by al-Suyūṭī who in his work on Egypt[26] enumerates a few of the *wu''āẓ* and *quṣṣāṣ* of Egypt, above all four, each from his own century, namely Abū 'l-Ḥasan 'Alī b. Muḥammad al-Wā'iz al-Baghdādī, who held a big *majlis wa'ẓ*, and is entitled the first man of his age in regard to *wa'ẓ* by Ibn Khaldūn. He wrote books on *ḥadīth*, *wa'ẓ* and *zuhd*, and al-Dāraquṭnī among others passed on traditions from him (d. 338/949). Moreover Ibn Najā al-Wā'iẓ, a Ḥanbalite from Damascus, who studied *fiqh* in Baghdād and Damascus, and arrived in Egypt under Saladin, who estimated [**235**] him highly (d. 559/1203). Then Zain al-Dīn from Andalus, scholar and poet, being imām for *al-wa'ẓ*. He died in Cairo 684/1285. Lastly Shihāb al-Dīn al-Shādhilī, who made a powerful impression through his *wa'ẓ*-meetings (749/1348).

---

[24] In al-Kindī, *op. cit.*, p. 303 sq., it is said of al-Tujībī that he held his *qaṣaṣ* standing, but was rebuked for this aberration from the practice of the Prophet by one of the Prophet's companions.

[25] al-Maqrīzī, *Khiṭaṭ* IV, pp. 17–19.

[26] *Ḥusn al-muḥāḍara*, Cairo 1321, I, p. 264 sq.

This survey of conditions in Egypt[27] makes the impression of an institution that for centuries remained largely untouched by changing circumstances. The "narrator" is closely connected with the official religion and fills a reputable and influential position. His activity, making up a link in the service of the mosque, consists on the one side in the recital of the Qur'ān, a circumstance that is stressed in some distinct way here in connection with a certain honoured copy of the Qur'ān, on the other side in leading the prayer, and lastly in the succeeding speech. The importance of his position appears from its frequent connection with the office of *qāḍī* and the fact that its incumbent is designated by the governor or even by writ from the far-away Khalifa himself. Of a few we hear that they introduced reforms into the practice of *ṣalāt*. Thus it is said about Ḥasan b. al-Rabīʿ that he forbade pronouncing the *basmalah* at the prayer (of al-Tujībī it is related that he spoke it aloud) and ordered to pray five *tarāwīḥ* instead of the accustomed six. And Abū Rajab al-Khawlānī, whose *ṣalāt* was praised by al-Shāfiʿī, was the first to deliver two *taslīmas* instead of one at the close of the prayer in the mosque in conformity with a letter from al-Ma'mūn.[28] It may therefore cause no surprise that al-Suyūṭī is able to mention several people who were erudite theologians and highly respected orators at the same time. A *qāṣṣ* may discharge his task both as *imām*, as *qāri'*, and as *khaṭīb*. The difference between him and the *khaṭīb* in the proper sense is that his speech is no part of the Friday's service and consequently he is a *khaṭīb al-yaqẓa*,[29] a revivalist preacher. For that reason he might be employed in warfare in older ages, even as Muʿāwiya caused his *quṣṣāṣ* to bless him and the people of Syria after the prayers at sunrise and [**236**] sunset, because he had heard that ʿAlī cursed them after the prayer.[30]

The popular evaluation of this commission finds its expression in the outcry of ʿAbd al-Raḥmān b. Hujaira's father, when he came to know his son's appointment to *qāṣṣ*, "Thank God! My son praises God and admonishes (*dhakara wa-dhakkara*)," and after his appointment to *qāḍī*: "My son has been befallen with a misfortune and leads into misfortune".[31] It is evident that the preacher here ranks above the judge.

Also from ʿIrāq we hear of the high position of the free preacher among the theologians. Al-Nadīm mentions a *qāṣṣ*, Abū ʿUmar Muḥammad al-Bāhilī al-Baṣrī (d. 300/912), who was an influential theologian and among other things

[27] Several distinguished *quṣṣāṣ* are mentioned by al-Jāḥiẓ, *Bayān* I 234 sq.

[28] al-Maqrīzī, IV, p. 18.

[29] Ibn al-Jawzī, *Al-mudhish*, p. 200, 2.

[30] al-Maqrīzī, IV 17 supra. A quotation from Ibn Ḥajar in al-Kindī, *Governors*, p. 304. It is not correct that ʿAlī and Muʿāwiya employed the *quṣṣāṣ* to curse each other according to Maqrīzī, loc. cit., as asserted in my article Masjid C3 in *Enc. of Islam*.

[31] cf. al-Kindī, *Governors*, p. 315. His father lived in Syria.

wrote on *tawḥīd*, following the *madhhab* of the Baṣrians, and whose meetings were attended by many of *al-mutakallimūn*. Both these and ordinary people did he move to tears by the beauty of his narrations (*qiṣaṣ*) and the delicacy of his linguistic style.[32] Al-Maqdisī, who wrote at the same time as al-Nadīm (375/985) likewise mentioning *al-quṣṣāṣ wa 'l-mudhakkirīn* in his writings, refers to Bukhārā (Numujkath) as a principal seat of thorough scholarship where only the student of law and the Qur'ān commentator deliver sermons (*yudhakkiru*).[33] When he declares that in Baṣra the *imām* preached (*yakhṭubu*) and invoked God every morning, this *khuṭba* must fall under the same heading as a sermon delivered by a *qāṣṣ*. They thought it to follow the *sunna* of Ibn ʿAbbās.[33a]

The free preacher continued playing a great part. Ibn Baṭṭūta (d. 779/1377), who travelled some four hundred years later than al-Maqdisī, gives an account of one *faqīh wāʿiẓ* who visited the sultan Shāh b. Ghiyāth al-Din Tughluq in Dihlī and stayed with him a year or so. Before [**237**] he left, the sultan caused a *minbar* of white sandalwood to be erected, covered with gold and precious stone, and he preached for the sultan, his court, and the scholars an eloquent *khuṭba*, *waʿẓ*, and *dhikr*. The sultan embraced him and distinguished him with an honorary gown, presents, and a big pageant in which he was carried on the back of an elephant,[34] a testimony to the importance that was attributed to a man of his standing.

The information about the older *quṣṣāṣ* shows that their activity consisted in interpreting the Qur'ān and *ḥadīth*, enforcing law, and impressing people with fear and hope. This is *tadhkīr* or *waʿẓ*. The preacher is not only expected to scare, but also to encourage. Sufyān b. Habīb said of a *qāṣṣ* in Baṣra, Ṣāliḥ al-Murrī, "He is no *qāṣṣ*, he is a *nadhīr*, "warner, one who scares".[35] Both in *waʿẓ* and *tadhkīr* something positive is involved. Abū ʿUbaida wrote to ʿUmar that Abū Jandal, who had been scourged for wine-bibbing, should become downcast, "if God does not bring him a joy through thee; write to him *wa-dhakkirhu*."[36] As we have seen in connection with the *waʿẓ* to the sovereign he must be a counsellor in possession of experience of life; thus *waʿẓ* becomes identical with *waṣīya*. This word is employed for advice and exhortations given by a father to his son, or on the whole

---

[32] A formerly unknown fragment of the *Fihrist*, ed. Fück, ZDMG, 90, 1936, p. 306 sq.

[33] *Bibl. Geogr. Arab.*, III 2, 13; 281 annot. H.

[33a] *op. cit.*, III 130, 14 sq.

[34] Ibn Baṭṭūta, *Riḥla*, Cairo 1322, II 51 sq.

[35] *Bayān*, I 235; on p. 79 infra is quoted a saying of Ibrāhīm b. Hāni', a paradox-monger, to the effect that a blind *qāṣṣ* spoke best. Naturally such persons turned up, e. g. Ṭabarī, III 560, 2.

[36] Ṭabarī I 2572, 6, cf. *Kāmil*, 100, 20, where *dhakkara* has the meaning of 'inspire and encourage'. As specimens of "bad *mawāʿiẓ*" two tales are adduced in the two above mentioned (annot. 12) works of al-Jāḥiẓ and al-Baihaqī, terminating in the result that the one who solicits a soothing response gets a pessimistic retort instead of it.

from one more experienced or superior to another, and the verb *awṣā* means to give such guidance. It is used both for concrete advice and ordinary rules of life. Al-Jāḥiẓ communicates a whole lot of such pieces of advice from father to son and uses for them either forms of *wṣy*, or *wʿẓ*.[37] It is easily understood how the signification of bequest as a legal notion is developed from it. It is used for **[238]** the admonitions of the Prophet and the early Khalīfas,[38] and of God's biddings to the Prophet.[39] In the same way as one asks *ʿiẓa* of some prominent person, one asks for *waṣīya*.[40] The word is used in the Qurʾān with similar shadings.[41]

Of the greatest import was the fact that the free preachers were subjected to be influenced by the ascetic view of life and the mysticism that made its way into Islam. It is obvious that the free preacher, whose task it was to influence people individually and to act upon the souls, was more fit than anybody else for propagating the new conception of life. It might mean only a slight deviation from the early Islam. This had, as mentioned above, inherited from the ancient Arabs the feeling of the fluctuation of all values in this life. The ancients called for resignation, but their pessimism was counterbalanced by their obligations to the claims of honour maintained by the individual and the tribe. From these facts the conclusion was drawn in Islam that one ought to accept the joys of the ordinary mode of life, but submit to the Almighty in obedience, after which He would grant the believers the joys of ever-lasting durability. The only new thing conveyed by asceticism often consisted in a claim to a more stressed independence from the benefits of this world through a life that was wholly occupied with the beyond, resultant in the resumption of asceticism by Oriental Christianity. Important as the new tinge might be occasioned by this, it did not bring about any fundamental renewal until it was connected with that form of mysticism which placed Man's experience of the unity with God in the centre of life, because in that case one has acquired the full bliss already in this world. His thought is not conditioned upon the **[239]** inferiority of this world, but it is a consequence of his experience. Both of these shades of meaning left its traces deeply on the activity of the preachers.

Some of the older representatives of asceticism are met with among the Khārijites. Ṭabarī tells us about Ṣāliḥ b. Musarriḥ, who lived in Dāra between

---

[37] *Bayān*, I 56 infra, 245; II 94; 153, 3–5; 215, 9–10; III 252 sq., 265.

[38] *op. cit.*, II 32 infra, 36, 48.

[39] *Awṣānī rabbī*, *op. cit*, II 33 medio. *Waṣiya* and *waṣat* generally of commands, Zuhair, 15, 22; *K. al-aghānī*, 3. ed., III 243, 5; al-Qalqashandī, *Ṣubḥ al-aʿshā*, XI 206 infra.

[40] *Bayān*, II 116, 3; III 102, sect. 4.

[41] Sūra 2, 126 *waṣṣā* of Abraham's admonition to his son; 4, 130; 6, 145, 152 sqq.; 29, 7; 31, 13; 42, 11; 46, 14 of God's ordinances for Men, espec. The Prophet, 4, 12; 19, 32 *awṣā* in the same meaning; 51, 53; 90, 17; 103, 3 *tawāṣaw* of the mutual exhortation of people to something; 2, 178 *awṣā* about setting up of a last will; *waṣīya* used for bequest 2, 241, 176; 5, 105.

Nisibis and Mardin in northern Mesopotamia, where the life of monks and anchorets had flourished so vigorously. In the years until 71, when he joined the opposition, he had lived here in ascetic piety (*nāsikan*), with his face sallowed, occupied with worship (*ʿibāda*), teaching people the Qurʾān and *fiqh*, and delivering sermons to them (*yaquṣṣu ʿalaihim*). One man related that he possessed his sermons (*qiṣaṣ or qaṣaṣ*), which consequently must have been committed to writing by then. In a letter that is quoted it runs as follows, "I advise you (*ūṣīkum bi*) fear of God and continence (*zuhd*) from the world and desire for the hereafter, and to be mindful of death, withdrawal from the sinners and love for the believers. For continence from the world arouses the desire of the servant for what is with God and makes free his body for obedience to God. And much mindfulness of death inspires the servant with fear of his master so that he cries out to him and subjects himself to him."[42] This is a typical *qaṣaṣ* from one of the earlier ascetics, not very much different from what the Syriac Christians thought and uttered. Characteristic of these older *nussāk* is an utterance as the following, "Your abodes are before you and your life after your death." It is quoted among a series of utterances collected by al-Jāḥiẓ.[43]

Al-Ḥasan al-Baṣrī (d. 110/728) vented the true mysticism in his sermons. His *mawāʿiẓ* are known through some reproductions, especially as given by al-Jāḥiẓ.[44] In the following time there exists a close connection between *waʿẓ* and *zuhd*. Ibn ʿAbd Rabbihi (ob. 328/940) entitles the section of his book, reproducing some sermons, *al-mawāʿiẓ waʾl-zuhd*. The genuine mystics, however, confined themselves to their own circle, and their influence upon the preachers corresponds to the momentum they gained over the ordinary Islamic piety.

[240] A *wāʿiẓ* of great importance was Jamāl al-Dīn Ibn al-Jawzi (d. 597/1200), the well known Ḥanbalite and opponent of mysticism. He not only wrote a book about *al-quṣṣāṣ* but besides that several books on *waʿẓ*, in which are found collections of the speeches he delivered as a celebrated *wāʿiẓ*, mainly in Baghdād.[45] Ibn Jubair gives an impressive account of his own and others' activity during his visit to Baghdād in the year 580/1184.[46] He extols the teachers of *fiqh* and *ḥadīth* in Baghdād, and the local *wuʿʿāẓ* and *mudhakkirūn*, who all but daily held meetings. He listened to Raḍī al-Dīn al-Qazwīnī, the *raʾīs* of the Shāfiʿites and teacher of *fiqh* at the Niẓāmīya-school, who spoke at a gathering in this *madrasa* on Friday the 5th of Ṣafar after the *ʿaṣr*-prayer. He ascended the *minbar* and placed Qurʾānic

42 Ṭabarī, II 882.

43 *Bayān*, 3, p. 73, *K. al-zuhd*.

44 Espec. *Bayān*, .3, 76 sq; cf. Massignon, *Essai*, pp. 152 sq.

45 Cf. the list of his works in Brockelmann, *Gesch. d. Arab. Litt.* I 504 sq. and Suppl. I 918. Cf. note 22.

46 *The Travels of Ibn Jubayr*, ed. Wright, 2nd ed. de Goeje, *Gibb Mem. Ser.*, 1907, pp. 219–224.

reciters on chairs, *karāsī*, in front of him. After their recital he held a dignified *khuṭba,* in which he interpreted the Qur'ān and sayings from the *ḥadīth.* Next a bunch of written questions was handed over to him, and gathering them in his hand he answered them one by one until evening. Ibn Jubair designates it as a *majlis ʿilm wa-waʿẓ* and declares that his *waʿẓ* induced to humility and tears. The meeting was pervaded with blessings, gentleness, and dignified peace. It was resumed the next Friday in the presence of the *sayyid* of the Khurāsān scholars, and Ṣadr al-Dīn al-Khujanjī, the *ra'īs* of the Shāfiʿite *imāms.*

Ibn al-Jawzī held two meetings a week, one on Saturday morning, opposite his residence on the river in the Eastern district of the city, and the other on Thursday morning in the Caliphal palace. Ibn Jubair heard him in both places and gave a rapturous description of the gatherings and the man, who was no common "ʿAmr or Zaid". At the Saturday's meeting (the 13th of Ṣafar) the arrangement was like that of the meetings just mentioned. More than twenty Qur'ān-reciters recited in chorus, alternately, with an artful delivery, while he stood on the *minbar.* Then he held his *khuṭba,* which was permeated by a challenging *waʿẓ* that called forth groans and moanings from the penitents **[241]** (*al-tā'ibin*), some fainted, and terror took hold of them at his *tadhkīr* on the dreads of the day of the Last Judgement, while at the same time a yearning (*ishtiyāq*) was stirred up in the hearts. After that notes were produced with questions, which he answered unhesitatingly. The Thursday's meeting (the 11th of Ṣafar) had its special flavour being held within the palace, where the Khalīfa (al-Muqtadī) and his mother were present together with people from the court. He showed his deference by taking his *ṭailasān* off his head, and when the Qur'ān-reciters had recited a dozen of verses he interwove his *khuṭba* with a praise of the Khalīfa and a prayer for him and his mother, upon which he went over to the *waʿẓ* that made a violent impression on the listeners. People repented of their sins and showed signs of *tawba*, they revealed their secret yearnings (*shawq*), and their reason (*ʿaql*) was wasted away. Towards the end he recited erotic verses (*ashʿār al-nasīb*) that aroused yearnings, tenderness and passion (*wajd*), and the erotic topic went over into ascetic yearnings (*zuhd*). His recital ended with the following words:

"Where is my heart? Molten by passion (*wajd*)! Where is my heart? It has not known of sobriety (*mā ṣaḥā*) ever since.

Oh, Saʿd, heighten my passion through their remembrance (*dhikr*) of God! Address me with 'Be thou redeemed, oh Saʿd!'"

The tears flowed, and when he left the *minbar*, the audience was shaken by commotion. "We had not imagined that an orator in this world might acquire such a mastery over the souls and play upon them as this man. Praise to Him who distinguishes with perfection such of his servants as He decrees; there is no God but He."

Ibn Jubair listened to other *wu‘‘āẓ* in Baghdād, who surpassed what he knew of theologians (*mutakallimūn*) in the West, but everybody, even in Mekka and Medina, were second to this man. At another Saturday's meeting that Ibn Jubair attended, Ibn al-Jawzī himself was so moved while he quoted some erotic verse of ascetic yearning that he jumped from the pulpit raving (*wālihan*) and the listeners behaved as if intoxicated.

It is a matter of some interest to notice that the pattern of this service is quite the same as in the – by several hundred years older – services of the same kind in [**242**] Egypt mentioned above, but the influence of Ṣūfism is apparent. It appears from the emphasizing of sin and conversion (*tawba*), the stress that is laid upon shunning the world, *zuhd*, the typical Ṣūfic notions of *shawq, wajd,* the conquering of *‘aql*, the abandonment of sobriety, *ṣaḥw*, and not least the erotic poetry and the whole ecstatic behaviour. From Ibn al-Jawzī's *Kitāb al-mudhish* we are able to check the picture drawn by Ibn Jubair. In the first place it contains some remarks on the Qur'ān and some details of names, several linguistic phenomena etc. Next follows *dhikr al-mawā‘iẓ* divided into two sections: *al-qiṣaṣ* and *al-mawā‘iẓ wa 'l-ishārāt*. The first of these communicates tales of pious people in the past, starting with Adam, the second is a collection of sermons, *mawā‘iẓ*. In these the instability of the world is markedly underlined, the ancient Arabic talk about *dahr* and *manāyā* rings out afresh, and we recognize the pre-Islamic turn of phrase; *yā man ya‘iẓuhu 'l-dahru*.[47] The world is a carcass that invites to weeping.[48] Sin and desire are condemned, and claim is made for *zuhd* and *tawba* for the soul,[49] that must be fought with *jihād*;[50] overcome with *wajd*[51] he quotes erotic verses, bewailing that nearness (*qurb*) has been displaced by remoteness (*bu‘d*), and that he in his love cannot bear the veiling, that he is intoxicated and "even if the eye does not see you, the heart is near to you."[52] He avails himself of expressions as *fanā'*, *waṣl* and *hajr*,[53] *shawq* and *ṣabr*,[54] *waḥsha* and *īnās*,[55] he quotes mystics as Ibn Adham, Rābi‘a, Yaḥyā b. Mu‘ādh, al-Shiblī etc. Even if no mystic experience in proper sense is involved, a state of mental sore makes itself felt that originates from mysticism and uses it phraseology, and as a matter of consequence must lead to scenes like those depicted above.

[47] Ibn al-Jawzī, *Al-mudhish*, p. 238 cf. 221, 271, 302, 371, 384 etc.
[48] *op. cit.*, 205, 206, 222.
[49] *op. cit.*, 204, 205, 209, 222, 304.
[50] *op. cit.*, 211.
[51] *op. cit.*, 222.
[52] *op. cit.*, 388.
[53] *op. cit.*, 224.
[54] *op. cit.*, 290.
[55] *op. cit.*, 221.

[**243**] In the account of Ibn Jubair we notice a tendency of drawing a distinction between the more official *khuṭba* and the reviving and crushing *waʿẓ* in the sermon, and Ibn al-Jawzī himself distinguishes between *waʿẓ* and *qiṣaṣ*, the latter, however, becoming a part of the *waʿẓ*. This agrees with what he says in the introduction to his *k. al-quṣṣāṣ*[56] to the effect that *qāṣṣ* is the one who delivers narratives about the past and expounds on matters that give an example and an admonition (*ʿiẓa*) while on the other side *tadhkīr* is a teaching about God's benefactions towards the creatures and an appeal to thankfulness and a warning against opposing God, and *waʿẓ* is the inspiration with fear, by which the heart becomes sensitive; but many use the term of *qāṣṣ* about the *wāʿiẓ* of which he disapproves. The later tendency of supplanting the word *qāṣṣ* with *wāʿiẓ* is obvious here, but at the same time the recognition of the connection with the old usage, as *qaṣaṣ* is employed about the element of narration that goes into the sermon.

The free character of the activity of these preachers and the personal turn in their locution invested them with great influence, but also gave rise to the criticism that was whirled up against them. This was due not only to those "narrators" that entertained people in the streets and exercised all sorts of juggleries as has been described by Goldziher,[57] but also to the real preachers. The main attack came from Ṣūfic circles, as clearly appears from the statements of Abū Ṭālib al-Makkī (d. 386/996) in *Qūt al-qulūb* in several passages. He remarks somewhere that *qaṣaṣ* did not come into existence until after Abū Bakr and ʿUmar at the same time as *al-fitna*. ʿAlī opposed it and turned out *al-quṣṣāṣ* from the mosque of Baṣra, and ʿAbdallāh b. ʿUmar made the police chase out a *qāṣṣ* from the mosque, which shows that it cannot have been reckoned among the *majālis al-dhikr*, since Ibn ʿUmar was well-known for his piety and asceticism. A tradition is mentioned to the effect that al-Ḥasan al-Baṣrī declared it for *bidʿa* and recommended to someone to pay visits to the sick as something better than to listen to a *qāṣṣ*. He also narrates that ʿA'isha being disturbed by a *qāṣṣ* who delivered a sermon outside her abode, made Ibn ʿUmar turn him [**244**] away in which he broke a stick on his back. It is objected to them that men and women gather around them raising their voices and uplifting their hands, which is a *bidʿa*.[58] Al-Makkī also declares that a *qāṣṣ* is a *mutakallij*, 'one who meddles with affairs of others' concern', which presumably means that he functions without any authorization; and he speaks of bygone things, which are not needful at the moment, wherefore

[56] Communicated by de Goeje in Balādhurī, p. 89.

[57] *ZDMG*, 28. 1874. p. 320; *Muh. Studien*. II, pp. 159 sqq.

[58] *Qūt al-qulūb*, Cairo 1310, I, 148 sq. As to uplifting the hands cf. what is stated above of al-Tujībī.

the activity of *al-qāṣṣ* is to be disapproved of (*makrūh*).[59] In earlier generations, he says, the men of knowledge were asked about the permissibility of settling down in a *majlis* with *al-wāʿiẓ wa ʾl-mudhakkir*, and this was answered to the effect that his orthodoxy, his intelligence, and his taste had to be examined beforehand. If he held heretical opinions, he was speaking with Satan's tongue; if he had a bad taste, he was speaking of his own accord; and if he did not possess sound intelligence, he spoiled with his tongue more than he gave of service and people ought to keep away from him.[60]

A similar criticism he puts in a more concentrated shape in connection with a mention of Manṣūr b. ʿAmmār (d. 227/beginning 21st Oct. 841). This personality, being mentioned by al-Nadīm as an *ʿābid zāhid* and the composer of a book on *zuhd*, and by al-Shaʿrānī and al-Dhahabī as one of the best of *al-wāʿiẓūn* who touched the hearts and set the minds astir in Baghdād, Syria and Egypt, is nevertheless the object of no little criticism cited by al-Dhahabī, claiming above all that he used weak *ḥadīths*.[61] Al-Makkī says that he heard many beautiful stories about Manṣūr b. ʿAmmār from Bishr b. al-Ḥārith, and that be belonged to the famous *wāʿiẓūn*, but Bishr and learned people of his contemporaneous equals like Abū Thawr and Aḥmad, did not reckon him among *al-ʿulamāʾ*, but among *al-quṣṣāṣ*, a **[245]** fact that Bishr made known to him in a rather harsh way. Al-Makkī assumes a difference between *ʿālim* and *mutakallim*. The really learned man is silent until he is asked, and then answers according to what God has enjoined on him, but forbears answering, when silence is the best. In this respect he refers to Mālik b. Anas.[62] On the contrary, *al-qāṣṣ* at once betakes himself to tell tales, from which he has got his appellation. Moreover the great saints only spoke to few, for "distinct knowledge (*ʿilm al-khuṣūṣ*) is only for the distinct ones (*al-khuṣūṣ*)". In this there is a difference between the two sorts of *majlis*. *Al-qaṣaṣ* is unlimited and for the multitude, so from the time of Ḥasan to that of al-Makkī the *majālis al-quṣṣāṣ wa ʾl-mudhakkirīn wa ʾl-wāʿiẓīn* gathered hundreds of people. "One of our scholars has said: In Baṣra there were one hundred and twenty who were spokesmen in the service and admonition (*mutakallim fī ʾl-dhikr wa ʾl-waʿẓ*), but there was nobody who was a spokesman in the science of intrinsic knowledge and certainty and stages and states (*yatakallamu fī ʿilm al-maʿrifa wa ʾl-yaqīn wa ʾl-maqāmāt wa ʾl-aḥwāl*) apart from six, among them Abū Muḥammad Sahl and

[59] *op. cit.*,1, 132, 1 sq.

[60] *op. cit.*, 2, 288, 10 sqq.

[61] *Al-fihrist* p. 184; al-Shaʿrānī, *Al-ṭabaqāt al-kubrā*, Cairo 1315, I, p. 71; al-Dhahabī, *Mīzān al-iʿtidāl*, Cairo 1325, III, p. 202 sq. Massignon, *Essai*, p. 208 mentions that according to b. al-Jawzī it was he who introduced *waʿẓ* into Baghdād. It is difficult to suppose this to be understood literally.

[62] By the way, a *Risālat waʿẓ* to Hārūn al-Rashīd and his minister is ascribed to Mālik, see Brockelmann, *Gesch.*, I, p. 176.

al-Ṣubaiḥī and ʿAbd al-Raḥīm". Bishr says that "*ḥaddathanā* and *akhbaranā* is one of the doors to this world."[63]

Thus the criticism centres around general views on the one side, like disorder at the meetings, lack of certainty in the doctrine and abuse of weak *ḥadīths* and in markedly mystic views on the other side: the preachers are destitute of the true knowledge that is given by the mystic experience, and therefore talk superficial nonsense to the multitude. That the Ṣūfis felt prone to advance this criticism was so much more at hand as both they and the preachers wanted to affect the inner spiritual life, and the gatherings of the latter must seem to be a caricature of the Ṣūfic *majālis al-dhikr*, not the least because to a large extent they imitated their style of speech.

The preachers continued retaining their great importance. Hundred odd years after al-Makkī, al-Ghazzālī deals [**246**] thoroughly with them,[64] especially in his principal work *Iḥyāʾ ʿulūm al-dīn*.[65] In al-Ghazzālī's view the preacher is an aid to that impersonation of the religion which is the result he has reaped from the activity of Ṣūfism. The goal is to become one's own admonisher. "When God loves a man he procures him a *wāʿiẓ* out of himself and a reviver of his heart, who gives him command and prohibition" (4, 236, 8sq.). First when Man has carried through the admonition to his worst enemy, that is his own soul, he can admonish others (4, 299, 15–21). For this he must train himself by picking up the *waʿẓ* he gets in considering the flux of time, and he must stand by with vigilance and prayer (4, 303, 11sqq.), just as he must seek *waʿẓ* through God's word, the sunna and study (4, 271, 31; 283, 16).[66] Through instruction and *waʿẓ* he gets aid in approaching to God (4, 308, 34). The one who wants to act as a *wāʿiẓ* must imitate the "master of admonition", that is the Prophet, availing himself cautiously of tales that inspire with fear and hope, according to his need, which he has to ascertain by examining the inner causes (*al-ʿilal al-bāṭina*) of the state of the person concerned. If he does not heed this he causes more mischief than benefit by his *waʿẓ* (4, 107, 6, 10; 109, 17sq.). Reference is made to Ḥanẓala, who related that he had stayed with the Prophet "who admonished us by an admonition, by which the hearts were moved and the eyes overflowed", and edifying in this way he went away, but then entertained himself in wordly wise with his wife

[63] *op. cit.*, I. 153 sq., 156.

[64] One of his tracts, *Risālat al-waʿẓ wa l-iʿtiqād*, in the same impression as *Faiṣal al-tafriqa* etc., Cairo 1325, holds as a main topic that God has given Man a speaking and a silent *wāʿiẓ* namely the Qurʾān and Death. His pamphlet against the Bāṭinites directed to the Khalīfa al-Mustaẓhir contains an appeal to the Khalīfa to submit to the admonition from *mawāʿiẓ mashāʾih al-dīn*, see Goldziher, *Streitschrift des Gazālī*, 1916, pp. 95 sqq.

[65] Cited here from the ed., Cairo 1322.

[66] He compares the "comprehensive perception" with somebody who is mastering both *qaṣaṣ* and books from the different parts of the world (4, 81, 14 sqq.).

and forgot his previous mood. But the Prophet consoled him when he accused himself of hypocrisy (4, 118, 13 sqq.). It is also related how the Prophet gives a *waʿẓ* in the shape of good rules of life (4, 330, 30). Likewise David is mentioned as a great *wāʿiẓ* upon the **[247]** admonition of whom 30,000 out of 40,000 persons met death (4, 131, 34), which of course is meant as an illustration of the willingness to sacrifice oneself.

Al-Ghazzālī gives an indication of what must be the contents of the sermon. He warns earnestly against arousing false hopes and quenching the fear, which reminds of the methods of quacks (4, 13, 8sq.; 37 sq.). He sees the impossibility of solving the individual problems and adapting the *waʿẓ* to every person, so the preacher must say what is needful to a plurality of people, and he recommends the use of the Qurʾān and the *ḥadīth*, tales about the Prophet and the saints of the past, and the demonstration of the punishment of sin in this very life. Such a *waʿẓ al-ʿāmma* is a daily nourishment to the benefit of the public, but he regrets that too many of the *wuʿʿāẓ* display rhymed prose and poems and discourse obtained at second hand, while their talk ought to issue from the heart in order to reach the heart (4, 38–41; 99, 21 sqq.). They must revive and animate, moving those who are indifferent and benumbed in their hearts (3, 58, 24 sq.). The application of extraneous measures is not prohibited to them. The good *wāʿiẓ* is free to recite poems on the *minbar* to tunes that move the hearts, and to weep so as to bring his audience into tears (2, 188, 36 sq.). But several times al-Ghazzālī warns against the dangers that threatened the preachers, ambition, emulation, and self-righteousness, thinking that, when they speak of fear and hope, patience (*ṣabr*) and thankfulness (*shukr*), devotion (*tawakkul*), abstinence (*zuhd*), certainty (*yaqīn*), sincerity (*ikhlāṣ*), truthfulness (*ṣidq*) or the like, they possess these qualities themselves (3, 277, 29 sqq.; 291, 36 sq.; 4, 272, 30 sqq.).

What *al-wuʿʿāẓ* introduced "in these times" of tawdry words and pathetic phrases connected with poems that do not serve the religion, by inspiring the Muslims with fear and on the contrary raising bright hopes and urging to sin by all kind of loose anecdotes, must be cleared away, for they are the agents of Satan (3, 227, 25 sqq.). Those preachers who force their way to the pulpit without any scientific accomplishment, and whose aim it is to delude the hearts of the vulgar and to coax them out of their property, in reality belong to the same category as impostors and jugglers, ḥashīsh-dealers, amulet-sellers and soothsayers (3, 158, 30 sqq.). And al-Ghazzālī describes **[248]** with psychological acumen the *wāʿiẓ* who finds a singular joy in his own *waʿẓ* and the impression it makes upon the hearts of his listeners, being moved to crying and moaning. Thus he is prompted to speak according to the tastes of the multitude to gain a repute in their hearts, and he is led by desire to domineer spiritually, not by joy for knowing the right way (3, 226, 30 sqq.).

It is well-known that al-Ghazzālī availed himself of al-Makkī's work on a large scale. It is of some concern that he (without making mention of his source, however) took over the saying mentioned above that there were one hundred and twenty *mutakallimūn* of *waʿẓ* in Baṣra, but only six who spoke in *ʿilm al-yaqīn*, with the exception that al-Ghazzālī says "three", namely those three mentioned by name (1, 59, 15 sqq.). But al-Ghazzālī's view of *al-wāʿiẓ* is very different from that of al-Makkī, according to whom their activity is objectionable. Al-Ghazzālī has a tale about Abū ʿAbdallāh b. Khalīf (Muhammad b. Khafīf al-Shīrāzī, d. 371/982), who travelled from Egypt to Tyrus to profit from two men who lived there in meditation (*murāqaba*), but when after the lapse of some time he said to one of them, "ʿ*iẓnī,* give me advice", he got the answer that they were in that stage where the hearts are overcome by the Majesty and could not engage in anything else, and he had to look for others who might give him *waʿẓ* with their deeds, not with their tongues (4, 286, 9sqq.). He also has a tale relating how a penetrating *waʿẓ* might have a deadly effect upon a listener (4, 135, 20 sqq.).

But al-Ghazzālī does not apply the standard of pure mysticism to the preacher, he attributes to him his traditional position as a guide and helper for the common Muslims to realize their religion. He testifies to their great influence even in his time, and just for al-Ghazzālī their activity must needs be of great importance. The idealized picture he draws of the preacher is shaped to his own likeness. Nothing tends to show that al-Ghazzālī had mystic experiences properly speaking. But he put himself in possession of the knowledge of the mystics that gave him a foundation for certainty in his own belief and realization of the claims of Islam to the development of the inner life of the soul and refinement of the spiritual foundation for the extraneous acts. So it was immensely important that men with a pure belief and with spiritual tact made useful their [**249**] faculties for educating the multitude and the individual characters, in the same way as he found himself obliged decidedly to warn against preachers who were devoid of these capacities.

One hundred years after al-Ghazzālī we see in Ibn al-Jawẓī how mystic modes of expression are employed by a preacher who was no mystic, mainly in al-Ghazzālī's spirit though in a different style. From the 8th/14th century onwards we still have accounts of the free preachers, among whom the above mentioned *wāʿiẓ* who met so much honour with the sultan of Dihlī. In the West we have the same evidence of the stern social chastener, the Maghribī Ibn al-Ḥājj (d. 737/1336). In particular he inveighs against the partaking of women in the *mawlid*-festivals, on which occasions people make their appearance with tales of the Prophet, wherein they make additions and subtractions, and the women fall into disbelief without anybody to guide them. And they sit among men and youths listening to a *wāʿiẓ* or a *wāʿiẓa*, who speaks from the *minbar* swaying to and fro, with cries and gesticulations, beating the *minbar* or the *kursī* with his hands or feet under hypocritical moaning and weeping. He quotes al-Makkī's criticism and assertion that the whole of it is *bidʿa*, and that older authorities have forbidden to attend *al-quṣṣāṣ*, i.e. *al-wuʿʿāẓ*, in the mosque and elsewhere.[67] He also refers to the fact that Ibn Rushd declared *al-qaṣaṣ* to be *makrūh* according to the *madhhab* of Mālik. It is the duty of the *imām* of the mosque to take care that disciples do not sit listening to a *qāṣṣ*. Utterly revolting it is when also women are present.[68] It is of some interest that also female preachers made their appearance. But from the severe denouncing of Ibn al-Ḥājj we cannot expect to get an objective description of phenomena that he did not acknowledge.

We also get information of them in the works of a more administrative character, thus by Ḍiyāʾ al-Dīn Muḥammad al-Qurashī, nicknamed Ibn al-Ukhuwwa (d. 729/1329), in his book on *al-ḥisba,* as *al-muḥtasib* is also in charge of supervising the visitors to the mosque and **[250]** *al-wuʿʿāẓ*.[69] In this book it is said that the person who wants to be a *wāʿiẓ* must be famous for knowledge of the Qurʾān, the *ḥadith* and tales of the saints. If he passes a test in this, he is to be permitted to the *minbar* in any mosque. If someone professes some knowledge about it and makes himself an income through it, it is allowed but he must not set foot upon the *minbar*. The author says that in "these times of ours" *al-wāʿiẓ* is only resorted to on occasions of burials and weddings or frivolous gatherings, and improper behaviour is said to take place, as men and women associate freely with one another. The exact range of their activity is not stated. He says that the scholars call them *quṣṣāṣ*, and that their gatherings are good when they are conducted decently and they do not tell untrue stories and introduce *bidʿa*. He denounces the fact of their having Qurʾānic reciters before them, who do not recite correctly, and they must not make themselves smart or indulge in poetical quotations, gestures, and movements. At best women ought to keep away, and if they take part in it, there must be a screen between men and women. In short, *al-wāʿiẓ* still acts according to old tradition, but seems to be employed in a new way in private dwellings, and *qāṣṣ* has become an obsolete word.

Half a century later al-Subkī (d. 771/1370) mentions both *al-wāʿiẓ* and *al-qāṣṣ*, but here is no real distinction between *al-wāʿiẓ* and *al-khaṭīb*, while *al-qāṣṣ* is nothing but the street-preacher who is charged with enjoining the keeping of the Islamic law on the public. We perceive a reverberation from al-Ghazzālī when he declares concerning *al-wāʿiẓ* that "if the speech does not come from the heart, it does not reach the heart".[70]

---

[67] *K. al-madkhal*, Cairo 1320, I, p. 158, 160 medio.

[68] *op. cit.*, II, 13, 50.

[69] *Maʿālim al-qurba fī aḥkām al-ḥisba*, ed. R. Levy (Gibb Mem. Ser.), 1938, ch. 48.

[70] *Muʿīd al-niʿam*, ed. Myhrman, 1908, p. 161 sq.

As has been pointed out, the distinction between two kinds of *qāṣṣ* is an old one. Al-Maqrīzī (d. 845/1442) says that the lawyer al-Laith b. Saʿd (d. 175/791) maintained a distinction between *qaṣaṣ al-ʿāmma* and *qaṣaṣ al-khāṣṣa*.[71] Al-Maqrīzī affirms that in his time *majālis al-waʿẓ* took place in the mosque of al-Azhar, and at the solemn consecration of a new minaret in the same mosque [**251**] *al-wuʿʿāẓ* made their appearance together with Qurʾānic reciters.[72]

In the following centuries the approach between *khaṭīb* and *wāʿiẓ* seems to have been in the increase, and in consequence the importance of *al-wāʿiẓ* as an independent official of the mosque has been diminished. Lane does not mention this institution, and he says that the sermon on Fridays is called *khuṭbet al-waʿẓ*.[73] Nevertheless, the institution is still in existence, and from recent times we have got a collection of *mawāʿiẓ* by Nuʿmān b. Muḥammad Alūsī, who was mufti in Baghdād under ʿAbd al-Ḥamīd Il and at the same time occupied himself with *al-waʿẓ* and *tadhkīr al-khawāṣṣ*.[74] His sermons show that the old tradition as to the customary contents of such speeches has been kept alive. Other works of a similar kind may have appeared. It admits of no doubt whatever that the whole of this institution has been of great importance to the religious life in Islam, and its history gives an illustration both of the connection of Islam with its Arabic past and its own religious development.

JOHS. PEDERSEN

University,
Copenhagen, Denmark

[71] *Khiṭaṭ*, IV, 17.
[72] *op. cit.*, IV, 54.
[73] *Manners and Customs* (Everyman's Library), p. 87 (ch. 3).
[74] *Ghāliat al-mawāʿiẓ wa-miṣbāḥ al-muttaʿiẓ wa-qabs al-wāʿiẓ*, Ṭantā I–II, 1329 1911.

7
THE SCHOLARLY FORMATION OF AL-ṬABARĪ (224–310/838–923)

Claude Gilliot

[**203**] *The present article is a modified version of the first chapter of our doctoral thesis: *Aspects de l'imaginaire islamique commun dans le commentaire de Tabari*, University of Paris-III, September 1987, pp. 21–48 with notes, pp. 521–534 [= Gilliot]. To this we have added, in particular, twenty-six names of masters of Abū Jaʿfar, and a complementary index. [Since has been published: Cl. Gilliot, *Exégèse, langue et théologie en islam*. Le commentaire coranique de Tabari (m. 310/923), Paris, 1990, for his formation, pp. 19–37; Fr. Rosenthal (General Introduction and translation by), *The History of al-Ṭabarī*, I, Albany, 1989, pp. 5–134, for his life and works].

The symbol [= ...] with the name of an author or an abridged title indicates an abbreviation used for the references. The symbol: Tr. followed by a figure indicates a number in the order of traditions contained in the *Commentary* of al-Ṭabarī, ed. Shākir, or in his *Tahdhīb al-āthār*.

In the text, the letter "M", followed by a number, introduces the name of one of the masters of al-Ṭabarī.

This study has been supplemented by an article on the works of al-Ṭabarī: Les oeuvres de Tabari, in MIDEO 19 (1989) pp. 49–90.

In July 855 (Rabiʿ I 241) or in the following month, a young man, Muḥammad b. Jarīr b. Ziyād, eighteen years of age at the most, arrived in Baghdad in the hope of attending the lectures on *ḥadīth* and on Islamic law of Aḥmad Ibn Ḥanbal: but on entering the caliphal city, he learned that the master had just died. The Imām Aḥmad had in any case stopped teaching some time before his death. This episode in the life of al-Ṭabarī is typical of the education of scholars in the classical period. They did not hesitate to undertake long journeys to attend the school of a renowned master. The long years of al-Ṭabarī's education are marked by these displacements and these temporary residencies as part of the "quest for knowledge". One wishes it were possible to reconstruct with precision the travels of Abū Jaʿfar which led him from his native town of Āmul in Ṭabaristān, to Iraq, then to

Egypt, by way of Syria, with numerous journeys back and forth in these regions.[1]

[**204**] These journeys are intimately linked to the constitution of his intellectual personality: this is why it is necessary to follow the principal stages, in the primary sense of the term, of his training in the various branches of knowledge. The best written treatment of the subject, in Arabic and in European languages, remains even today the study in Latin by Michael Jan De Goeje, published in 1901 in the introduction to the edition of the *Annales* of which he was the architect and prime mover. Nevertheless, certain important points about the intellectual itinerary of al-Ṭabarī can be clarified through the examination or re-examination of bio-bibliographical notices which the ancient sources devoted to him. Furthermore, in a number of cases the chains of authority most often cited in his *Commentary*, in his *Annales*, in his work on the Divergences of the Scholars (*Ikhtilāf al-ʿulamāʾ/ al-fuqahāʾ*) and in the edited sections of his book intitled the Pruning of Traditions (*Tahdhīb al-āthār*) could be a precious indicator of the intellectual influences which he underwent, the first link of these chains being represented by one or other of his masters.

Besides information concerning his travels and his master's, the biographical notices evoke episodes where he appears in contact with other scholars of the time who did not give him any instruction in the science of traditions, in exegesis or in jurisprudence, but with whom he held conversations, particularly in Iraq and in Egypt, including Abū Ḥātim al-Sijistānī and Abū l-Faraj al-Iṣfahānī who followed his courses. Finally, he also sometimes lived in the entourages of caliphs and of senior functionaries of the ʿAbbāsid dynasty.

Nevertheless, these notices are not in themselves enough to present an intellectual portrait of our author. In fact, they are concerned above all with the mode of oral transmission and insist on *ḥadīth*, Qurʾānic readings and exegesis. Thus, although an excellent grammarian, al-Ṭabarī does not figure in the lists of philologists and grammarians, if we exclude the *Inbāḥ al-ruwāt* of al-Qifṭī. What is known of his philological education, of his literary and poetic training? [**205**] Partial responses to these questions we have provided elsewhere.[2] It is thus that in grammar, for example, al-Ṭabarī quotes whole

[1] Yāqūt, *Muʿjam al-udabāʾ* [= Yāqūt], ed. A.F. al-Rifāʿī, Cairo, Dār al-Maʾmūn, 1936–38, xviii, p. 50. In contradiction to what F. Sezgin has written, al-Ṭabari never attended the classes of Ibn Ḥanbal, *Geschichte des arabischen Schrifttums* [= GAS], i, p. 323; al-Baghdādī, *al-Riḥla fi ṭalab al-ḥadīth*, ed. Nūr al-dīn ʿItr, Beirut 1975, p. 186 ff., gives the names of several traditionists who, having set out to follow the teachings of a master, discovered that he was dead.

[2] Cf. Gilliot, *Aspects*, chap. vii, esp. pp. 297 ff.; Id., *Exégèse*, pp. 189ff.

passages of the *Maʿānī l-Qurʾān* of al-Akhfash or of al-Farrāʾ, or indeed of the *Majāz al-Qurʾān* of Abū ʿUbayda.

Finally the lists of authorities given by the onomastic works which devote an article to our author make no distinction between masters from whom he transmitted many traditions and those from whom he received only a few; we shall in part rectify this omission, in so far as is possible.[3]

I The education of al-Ṭabarī in his native region

Speaking of Abū Jaʿfar himself, his education began at a very early age in his native town, Āmul. From the age of seven years old, he knew the Qurʾān by heart; at nine years old, he was "writing" *ḥadīth*, in other words he took notes during the lessons of a master who subsequently verified and corrected what he had written.[4] Of his masters in this period of his life, only one name has been preserved by the sources:

M1 al-Muthannā b. Ibrāhīm al-Āmulī (al-Ṭabarī): this individual, from whom al-Ṭabarī reports exegetical traditions in his commentary on Suras one to sixteen,[5] does not feature in onomastic collections; what is certain, is that our exegete followed his instruction, either in Ṭabaristān, at Āmul, or in the Jibāl, at Rayy.

Al-Ṭabarī subsequently made his way to Rayy to complete his elementary education. **[206]** More information is available for this second stage. Among the educators for this period, we may mention:

M2 Muḥammad b. Ḥumayd al-Rāzī (d. in Baghdād 248/862) who was his master in *ḥadīth* and in Qurʾānic commentary. Al-Ṭabarī transmitted from him the *Maghāzī* of Ibn Isḥāq in the recension of Salama b. al-Faḍl al-Rāzī (d. 191/806). The latter did not have a good reputation

[3] Cf. on this subject the instructive remarks of G. Lecomte, *Ibn Qutayba. L'homme, son oeuvre et ses idées*, Damascus, Publications de l'Institut Francais de Damas, 1965, pp. 45–49.

[4] Yāqūt, xviii, p. 49.

[5] Cf. Cl. Gilliot, *La sourate al-Baqara dans le Commentaire de Tabari*, 3rd cycle thesis, University of Paris-III, 1982, p. 135 [= Gilliot, *Baqara*]; H. Horst, *Zur Überlieferung im Korankommentar aṭ-Ṭabariṣ*, in *Zeitschrift der Deutschen Morgenlandischen Gesellschaft* [ZDMG], 103 (1953), p. 293 [= Horst]; Idem, *Die Gewährsmänner des Ṭabarī. Ein Beitrag zur Kenntnis des exegetischen Überlieferung im Islam*, (Inaugural Dissertation), Bonn, 1951, pp. 42–43 [=*Gewährsmänner*]. Our very unreliable edition of Yāqūt gives al-Ubullī instead of al-Āmulī, xviii, p. 49.

among critics of traditions; he was accused of changing chains of authority and attributing to traditionists of Rayy traditions emanating in fact from Kūfa and from Baṣra, or even of reversing letters or terms (*maqlūbāt*).[6]

With some of his fellow pupils, al-Ṭabarī travelled to and fro between Rayy, where he attended the lessons of Ibn Ḥumayd, and a village close to this town (perhaps the village of Dūlāb) where he received instruction from:

M3 Aḥmad b. Ḥammād al-Dūlābī. What is quoted by Yāqūt from Ibn Kāmil (= Aḥmad, disciple of al-Ṭabarī, d. 350/960), regarding this traditionist and historiographer, poses a problem. In fact, according to Ibn Kāmil, al-Ṭabarī would have received the instruction of al-Dūlābī on the *Kitāb al-Mubtada' wa-l-Maghāzī* of Ibn Isḥāq, in the recension of Salama b. al-Faḍl, under the mode of writing (*kataba 'an*) and it was on the basis of this *Kitāb* that he constructed his *History*. Now, on the one hand, the *History* of al-Ṭabarī, unless we are mistaken, contains only one tradition traced back to al-Dūlābī. On the other hand, the bio-bibliographical collections which mention the recension of Salama b. al-Faḍl, transmitted by Ibn Ḥumayd, say nothing similar about al-Dūlābī. There must have been therefore an arbitrary deduction, either by Ibn Kāmil or by Yāqūt. In the passage immediately preceding, Ibn Kāmil quotes al-Ṭabarī who says, [**207**] having mentioned his master in Rayy, Ibn Ḥumayd: "We subsequently made our way to Aḥmad b. Ḥammād al-Dūlābī who lived in a village situated some distance from Rayy. Then we would run like lunatics to return to Ibn Ḥumayd and to join his circle". Subsequently it is Ibn Kāmil or Yāqūt who goes on to say: "He (i.e. al-Ṭabarī) wrote as a pupil of Aḥmad b. Ḥammād the *Kitāb al-Mubtada' wa-l-Maghāzī*, which he held from Salama b. al-Faḍl, who held it from Muḥammad b. Isḥāq, and it was on the basis of this (= the *Kitāb*) that he constructed his *History*". What is certain is that al-Ṭabarī owed much to the work of Ibn Isḥāq in the recension of Salama, but there is no evidence for the proposition that

[6] Yāqūt, xviii, 49–50; Ibn Ḥajar, *Tahdhīb al-tahdhīb* [= TT], ix, pp. 127–131; Ibn Ḥibbān, *Kitāb al-Majrūḥīn min al-muḥaddithīn wa l-du'afā' wa l-matrūkīn*, ed. Maḥmūd Ibrāhīm Zāyid, Aleppo, 1976 ii, pp. 303–304 [= *Majrūḥīn*]; al-'Uqaylī (a. Ja'far M. b. 'Amr), *K. al-Ḍu'afā' al-kabīr*, ed. 'Abd al-Mu'ṭī Amīn al-Qal'ajī, Beirut, Dār al-kutub al-'ilmiyya, 1984[1], iv, p. 61, no 1612; al-Dhahabī, *al-Mughnī fī l-ḍu'afā'*, ed. Nūr al-dīn 'Itr, Aleppo 1971, p. 573, no 5449.

he received instruction on this subject from Ibn Ḥammād; it is most likely that there has been confusion with Ibn Ḥumayd.[7]

It was also at Rayy that al-Ṭabarī attended classes which were to be definitive for him, those of:

M4 Abū Zurʿa al-Rāzī (200–264/815–878).[8] He was born in Rayy, and among his other travels he spent two terms in Baghdad, one in 227 and the other in 230, where he attended the courses of Ibn Ḥanbal. He returned to Rayy in 232, and remained there until his death. He was, along with his friend Abū Ḥātim al-Rāzī (195–277/811–890), one of the most prestigious critics of *ḥadīth*, and al-Ṭabarī would thus have acquired the technique of criticism of traditions very early; this explains, in part, how he showed himself to be such an expert in this field, in particular in the *Tahdhīb al-āthār.*

[**208**] Another master of al-Ṭabarī, in jurisprudence this time, is mentioned by Ibn al-Nadīm:

M5 Abū Muqātil, with whom he studied "the *fiqh* of the people of ʿIraq", an expression habitually denoting the jurisconsults of the school of Abū Ḥanīfa, for example, the pupils of Muḥammad b. al-Ḥasan al-Shaybānī (d. 189/805). It has not been possible to identify Abū Muqātil. It is most likely that this individual was in fact Muḥammad b. Muqātil al-Rāzī al-Ḥanafī (d. 242/856), a disciple of al-Shaybānī, in which case, in Ibn al-Nadīm's text, Ibn Muqātil should be read rather than Abū Muqātil.[9]

---

[7] Yāqūt, xviii, pp. 49–50, p. 50, it should read al-Faḍl, and not al-Mufaḍḍal; ʿAlī Jawād, *Mawārid taʾrīkh al-Ṭabarī* in MMʿIʿI 1 (1950), p. 202.

[8] Abū Zurʿa is quoted among the masters of al-Ṭabarī by Ibn ʿAsākir, in De Goeje, *Annales quos scripsit Abu Djafar Mohammed Ibn Djarir at-Tabari, cum aliis edidit M.J. De Goeje, introductio, glossarium, addenda et emendana,* Lugduno Batavorum, E.J. Brill, 1901 [= *Introductio*], p. lxix; on Abū Zurʿa: TT, vii, pp. 30–34; GAS, i, p. 45; al-Rāzī (Ibn a. Ḥātim), *Kitāb al-Jarḥ wa l-taʿdīl,* Hyderabad, 1952; repr. Beirut, i, p. 340 [= *Jarḥ*, same pagination but volume-numbering different from that of the original ed.]; al-Ṭabarī, *Tahdhīb al-āthār. Musnad ʿAlī*, ed. Maḥmūd m. Shākir, Cairo, Maṭbaʿat al-Madanī, distrib. al-Khanjī, 1982 [= TA/A]; Idem, *Tahdhīb al-āthār. Musnad Ibn ʿAbbās*, i–ii, Cairo 1982 [= TA/IA]; Idem, *Tahdhīb al-āthār. Musnad ʿUmar b. al-Khaṭṭāb*, i–iii, Cairo 1983 [= TA/U].

[9] *Fihrist*, p. 234, l. 16 ff./ ed. Tajaddud, Teheran 1971, p.29, 2 [= Ibn al-Nadīm, ed. G. Flügel; when reference is to the Tajaddud edition, this will be indicated]; for Ibn Muqātil al-Rāzī, KZ, vi, col 13; ii, col. 1457 [KZ, i–ii = *Kashf al-ẓunūn*; KZ, iii–iv = *Īḍāḥ al-maknūn*; KZ, v–vi = *Hadiyyat al-ʿārifīn*, respectively, Istanbul, 1941–43, 1945–47, 1951–55; repr.

Having completed this period of elementary and complementary education in his native region and the neighbouring Jibāl, al-Ṭabarī made his way to Baghdad, hoping to attend the classes of Ibn Ḥanbal; we have already seen that fate had decided otherwise. However, he remained for a few months in the capital of the Empire, attending the classes of various scholars, before moving on to Baṣra, Wāsiṭ and Kūfa, always with the object of perfecting his knowledge. These residencies in these three cities took place between 241 and 243. In effect, the *terminus a quo* is marked by the date of the death of Ibn Ḥanbal and the terminus *ad quem* is fixed by the date of one of the masters with whom he studied in Kūfa, Hannād al-Sarī (d. in Rabīʿ II 243/June 857).

M6 Aḥmad b. Thābit b. ʿAttāb al-Rāzī is not mentioned in the lists of authorities of al-Ṭabarī. Little is known of this person. However, he is by far the authority most frequently cited by al-Ṭabarī for the transmission of the *Maghāzī* and of the *History* of the caliphs by Abū Maʿshar, with the following chain: Aḥmad b. Thābit al-Rāzī/ anonymous/ Abū Maʿshar. We assume that al-Ṭabarī attended his classes in Rayy. **[209]** According to Ibn Abī Ḥātim: "No one doubted that he was a liar". As was often the case, the fact that the chain of transmission was interrupted did not prevent al-Ṭabarī citing it extensively, especially for the list of those who led the Pilgrimage.[10]

II Al-Ṭabarī in Baṣra

The only list given by Yāqūt[11] of the Baṣran masters of al-Ṭabarī is only a pale reflection of his activity as a student in the Muslim metropolis. This picture may be complemented by deductions drawn from encounters which he made and from certain episodes mentioned by biographers. Among those masters of his identified by name, the following are to be noted:

Beirut, al-Muthannā]; KAHH, xii, p. 45 [= Kaḥḥāla, *Muʿjam al muʾallifīn*]; al-Laknawī, *Kitāb al-Fawāʾid al-bahiya fi tarājim al-Ḥanafiyya*, 1334/1906, p. 201. It could also be that his *kunyā* was Abū Muqātil, but on this the sources consulted tell us nothing.

[10] Al-Dhahabī, *Mīzān al-iʿtidāl fī naqd al-rijāl*, ed. ʿAli M. al-Bijāwī, Cairo 1963; repr. Beirut, Dar al-Maʿrifa, undated [= *Mizān*], i, p. 86; *Jarḥ*, ii, p. 44. The chain of authorities in the *History* of al-Ṭabarī is the following: Aḥmad b. Thābit/ *ʿamman ḥaddathahu* (or: *dhakarahu*, or: *ḥaddathanā muḥaddith*)/ Isḥāq b. ʿĪsā b. Najīḥ (Ibn al-Ṭabbāʿ al-Baghdādī, d. 215/830; *Jarḥ*, ii, pp. 230–31; TT, i, p. 245)/ Abū Maʿshar (cf. GAS, i, pp. 291–92); cf. al-Ṭabarī, *Taʾrīkh al-rusul wa l-mulūk*, ed. M. Abū l-Faḍl Ibrāhīm, Cairo, 1967² [= *History*, without mention of the author], iv, p. 60, 96, 103, 104, and *passim*.

[11] Yāqūt, xviii, pp. 50–51.

M7 Muḥammad b. Mūsā al-Ḥarashī al-Baṣri (d. 248/862) who transmitted *ḥadīth* to him. He appears once in the fragments of the *Tahdhīb al-āthār* which have been edited, three times in the *History* and numerous times in the *Commentary*. All of which indicates that he did not play a major role in the education of al-Ṭabarī.[12]

M8 The same judgment applies to Abū ʿAmr ʿImrān b. Mūsā al-Qazzāz al-Baṣrī (d. after 240/854) who was also al-Ṭabarī's master in traditions.[13]

[**210**] M9 Abū ʿAbd Allāh Muḥammad b. ʿAbd al-Aʿlā al-Ṣanʿānī al-Baṣrī (d. 254/859) transmitted traditions to him and gave him lessons in exegesis. Al-Ṭabarī also studied with him the *Kitāb al-Maghāzī* by Maʿmar b. Rāshid (d. 153/769).[14]

M10 Yāqūt also lists Bishr b. Muʿādh al-ʿAqadī (d. 245/859) from whom al-Ṭabarī received, by way of a Baṣran chain, numerous traditions of Qatāda. His *isnād* is the one which features most frequently in the Qurʾānic *Commentary*.[15]

M11 Abū l-Ashʿab Aḥmad b. al-Miqdām al-Baṣrī (d. 251/865 or 253) left even fewer traces in the work of Abū Jaʿfar. His name appears only three times in the *Tahdhīb al-āthār* and twice in the *History*. It is interesting to note that he was a humorist of some renown, for which reason Abū Dāwūd al-Sijistānī (d. 275/888) declined to transmit his traditions. The fact that he taught in such a way as to entertain the merry folk who populated Baṣra (*kāna yuʿallimu l-mujjāna l-mujūna*) did not prevent Ibn Ḥibbān from including him among the authorities worthy of trust.[16]

---

[12] TT, ix, p. 482, n° 778; Ibn Ḥibbān, *Kitāb al-Thiqāt*, ix, Hyderabad 1984, p. 108 [= *Thiqāt*]; *History*, i, p. 7; ii, p. 337; iv, pp. 281, 518; TAB iv, p. 439, n° 4382; 444, n° 4458 [TAB = al-Ṭabarī, *Tafsīr*, i–xvi, ed. Ṣakir, Cairo, Dār al-Maʿārif, 1954–1969]; TA/A, p. 114, no 187.

[13] Abū l-Faḍl Ibrāhīm, in *History*, i, p. 7, following the edition of Yāqūt, reads: *ʿImād*, which is an error; it should be read *ʿImrān*; cf. TT, viii, p. 141; *Jarḥ*, vi, pp. 305–306, no 1697; TAB, iii, p. 134, Tr. 2154; TA/A Tr. 186; in both cases, he transmits from ʿAbd al-Wārith b. Saʿīd al-Anbarī.

[14] TT, ix, p. 289; he appears in *isnad* n° 13, according to the numeration of H. Horst, *art. cit.*, pp. 290–307. Horst notes that this chain appears 1080 times in the *Commentary*; cf. Gilliot, *Baqara*, pp. 267–268.

[15] TT. i, p. 458; *Jarḥ*, ii, p. 368; GAS, i, p.32; Horst, "Gewährsmänner", p. 301, chain 14; Gilliot, *Baqara*, pp. 268–270. For his *gentilicium*: al-ʿUqdī or al-ʿAqadi*, in the absence of conclusive proofs, we opt for the choice of Shākir in TAB, I, p. 197, n. 1; cf. Ibn al-Athīr (ʿIzz al-Dīn), *al-Lubāb fī tahdhīb al-ansāb*, Cairo 1357–1369/1938–1949; repr. Beirut undated [= *Lubāb*]; al-Qalqashandī, *Nihāyat al-arab fī maʿrifat ansāb al-ʿArab*, ed. ʿAlī al-Khāqānī, 1958, p. 337.

[16] For Aḥmad b. al-Miqdām, cf. also infra: M50 and note 67; TT, i, pp. 81–83; *Thiqāt*, viii, p. 32; *Mīzān*, i, p. 158; *History*, i, p. 143, 160; ii, p. 380; TA/A n° 221 and 227; TA/IA, n° 706.

M12 Abū Bakr Muḥammad b. Bashshār al-ʿAbdī al-Baṣrī (d. 252/866) was held to be a traditionist worthy of trust. His traditions are related by the "community of scholars" (*al-jamāʿa*), i.e. by the recognised authors of collections of traditions. Al-Ṭabarī received from him, in particular, some exegetical traditions of Mujāhid.[17]

[**211**] M13 Muḥammad b. Muthannā al-Zamin (d. 250/864) is one of those whom al-Ṭabarī cites most often in his *Commentary* and in the *Tahdhīb al-āthār.*[18]

Al-Dāwūdī (Shams al-Dīn M. b. ʿAlī, d. 945/1538) mentions two other Baṣran masters of al-Ṭabarī:

M14 Abū Hafs ʿAmr b. ʿAlī al-Fallās al-Bāhilī al-Sayrafī l-Baṣri (247/861). He was the author of a *Musnad* and of a *History.* Al-Ṭabarī transmitted sixteen of his traditions in the fragment of his *Musnad* of Ibn ʿAbbās which has survived and nine traditions in his *History*; he also features in his Commentary, but not in the most frequently used chains of authority.[19]

M15 Abū ʿAlī (Abū Muḥammad) al-Ḥasan b. Qazʿa al-Khalqānī al-Baṣrī (d. 250/864) is the other traditionist mentioned by al-Dāwūdī; his name does not feature in the *Musnad* of Ibn ʿAbbās nor in that of ʿAlī (in the *Tahdhīb al-āthār*), nor in the *History*; in the *Commentary,* he plays a minor role.[20]

The above is what is essentially to be gleaned from the explicit accounts given in the biographical notices on the masters of al-Ṭabarī in Baṣra. However they also mention a certain number of episodes which make it possible to complete the picture of al-Ṭabarī's scholastic activity in the metropolis of ʿIrāq.

---

[17] GAS, i, pp. 113–114; TT, ix, pp. 70–73; TB, ii, pp. 101–105 [TB = al-Baghdādī, *Taʾrīkh Baghdād*]; Horst, *art. cit.*, p. 296, with a chain which goes back to Mujāhid and which appears 32 times in the *Commentary*; TAB, I, pp. 240, 342, 360, 293, 477, 481, and *passim*; very frequent in TA: TA/A, index, pp. 1052–1053; he is one of the masters of al-Ṭabarī whose name appears most often in TAB and in TA. Abū Dāwūd would have transmitted fifty thousand traditions from him.

[18] TT, ix, pp. 425–427; TB, iii, pp. 283–286; TAB, i, p. 49, 50. 185, 198, 202, 233, 420, 643, 735; v, p. 185, 199, 200, and *passim*, in the whole of the *Commentary*.

[19] al-Dāwūdī, *Ṭabaqāt al-mufassirīn*, Beirut 1983, ii, p.111 [= Dāwūdī]; for ʿAmr b. ʿAlī: TT, viii, pp. 80–82: *min fursāni l-ḥadīth, ṣannafa l-musnada wa l-ʿilala wa l-taʾrīkh*; TA/IA, index, p. 1065, sixteen traditions; TAB, iii, n° 1989 and 2155. He visited Isfahan on a number of occasions and stayed in Baghdad. Cf. also *infra* M51 and note 68.

[20] TT, ii, p. 316, his name appears neither in the *History* nor in TA; TAB, vii, no 8281, v.g.

[**212**] It is thus that we know that he had contacts at least with Abū Ḥātim al-Sijistānī (d. 255/869), philologist, grammarian, specialist in Qurʾānic readings and author of a *Kitāb Iʿrāb al-Qurʾān*. Al-Ṭabarī would have consulted him about a tradition of al-Shaʿbī (ʿĀmir b. Sharāḥīl, d. 103/721), traditionist and judicial scholar, concerning analogy, and would have given him on this occasion the etymology of Ṭabaristān. This information alone is not enough to make al-Ṭabarī a disciple of Abū Ḥātim. However it is known that the latter was a disciple of al-Akhfash al-Awsaṭ (d. 215/830) and that he wrote critical remarks about his works. The same applies to the *Majāz al-Qurʾān* of his master Abū ʿUbayda (d. 207/822 or 213), and it may be wondered whether al-Ṭabarī did not benefit from the knowledge at the disposal of Abū Ḥātim, and from the *Maʿānī l-Qurʾān* of al-Akhfash and from Abū ʿUbayda's book, two works of which he makes considerable use in his Commentary.[21]

Before reaching Kūfa, al-Ṭabarī spent some time in Wāsiṭ, but the biographical collections do not mention any names of scholars whose teaching he would have followed there. Since the majority of the authorities mentioned in his *Commentary*, in the two edited *Musnads* of the *Tahdhīb al-āthār* and in his *History* and bearing the ethnic of al-Wāsiṭī had also spent time in Baghdad, it is impossible to say in which of the two imperial capitals al-Ṭabarī collected their traditions. Furthermore, not one of them holds an important place in these three works.[22]

III Al-Ṭabarī in Kūfa [213]

After a brief stay at Wāsiṭ, al-Ṭabarī reached the cradle of Shiʿism which was already distinguished by great names in various branches of knowledge: Abū Yūsuf (d. 182/798), whom he often mentions in his *K. Ikhtilāf al-fuqahāʾ*, and al-Shaybānī (d. 189/804) in jurisprudence; Hishām b. Muḥammad al-Kalbī (d. 206/821) in various branches of the Arab legacy; al-Suddī l-Kabīr (d.

[21] Yāqūt, xviii, p. 48. For Abū Ḥātim, al-Qifṭī, *Inbāh al-ruwāt ʿalā anbāh al-nuḥāt*, ed. M. Abū l-Faḍl Ibrāhīm, Cairo 1950; repr. Beirut 1986, iii, 58–64, no 282 [= *Inbāh*]; al-Zubaydī, *Ṭabaqāt al-naḥwiyyīn wa l-lughawiyyīn*, ed. M. Abū l-Faḍl Ibrāhīm, Cairo 1954, pp. 100–103; for the manuscript bearing the remarks of Abū Ḥātim, GAS, ix, p. 66. For al-Shaʿbī: GAS, i, p. 277. It may be noted that a co-disciple and friend of al-Ṭabarī who is encountered often in his company, Ibn Khuzayma (M. b. Isḥāq, 223–311/838–923) had Abū Ḥātim as a master; cf. al-Dhahabī, *Tadhkirat al-ḥuffāẓ*, Hyderabad, 1956–58[3]; repr. Beirut, Dār Iḥyāʿ al-turāth al-ʿarabī, undated [= *Tadhkira*], pp. 720–731.

[22] For example, al-Ḥasan b. al-Ṣabbāḥ al-Bazzāz Abū ʿAlī al-Wāsiṭī, d. 249/863, but he also taught in Baghdad, TB, vii, pp. 330–332; Aḥmad b. Sinān Abū Jaʿfar al-Wāsiṭī l-Qaṭṭān, d. 258/872, who appears in the *History*, ii, p. 297; TAB, v, p. 158, n° 5421, seems not to have taught in Baghdad; likewise Isḥāq b. Shāhīn, d. after 250/864, TT, i, pp. 236–237.

128/745), in Qur'ānic exegesis; Abū Mikhnaf (d. 157/773), one of the first historiographers; ʿĀṣim, Ḥamza and al-Kisāʾī, in Qurʾānic readings; al-Farrāʾ, in grammar and in exegesis.[23]

Al-Ṭabarī began by collecting the *ḥadīth*s transmitted by the traditionists of this city:

M16 Abū Kurayb Muḥammad b. ʿAlāʾ al-Hamdānī (d. 247/861, at 87 years of age). He would have transmitted three hundred thousand traditions in Kūfa, and is one of the authorities most often cited by al-Ṭabarī. Despite the variety of the chains of transmission ending with him in the diverse works of al-Ṭabarī, it is noticeable that the latter records especially the exegetical traditions traced back to al-Ḍaḥḥak b. Muzāḥim (d. 105/723) and to Qatāda b. Diʿāma al-Sadūsī (d. 118/736). It was not easy to gain admission to the presence of this master, besieged as he was by students; al-Ṭabarī achieved this after an "examination", in other words, having shown that he knew by heart the traditions of this master, which he had studied in the written form. It is said that he heard a thousand traditions from his lips. Abū Kurayb was also one of the transmitters of the *Kitāb al-Maghāzī* of Ibn Iṣḥaq, through the intermediary of Yūnus b. Bukayr (d. 199/814).[24]

[**214**] M17 Hannād b. al-Sarī b. Muṣʿab (d. 243/857), known for his asceticism (it is noted that he never married) belonged to the line of the "weepers" (*al-bakkāʾūn*); he is the author of a *Kitāb al-Zuhd* of which at least two manuscripts are available to us. Al-Ṭabarī had him as a master in *ḥadīth*; he transmits a few of his traditions in his *Commentary*, five in his *History*, including one with the link Yūnus b. Bukayr, whose *Kitāb al-Maghāzī*[25] was transmitted by Hannād, as well as by Abū Kurayb.

[23] H. Djait, "al-Kūfa" in EI [= *The Encyclopedia of Islam*] v, p. 351a; ʿA. Jawād, *art. cit.*, p. 217, 224.

[24] TK [al-Bukhārī, *al-Taʾrīkh al-kabīr*] i, pp. 205–206; TT, ix, pp. 385–386; he was also a reader, he transmitted the reading of ʿĀṣim (*ʿan* Abī Bakr) but transmitted little of it: *Ghāya* [= Ibn al-Jazarī, *Ghāyat al-nihāya fī ṭabaqāt al-Qurrāʾ*, ed. G. Bergsträsser and O. Pretzl, Leipzig and Cairo, 1933–35], ii, p. 197; cf. also ʿA. Jawād, p. 202 and 222; GAS, i. p. 30. Some examples of chains ending with him in TAB, i, p.113, 135, 233, 371; *History*, x, index, p. 378; TA/A, index, pp. 1067–1069. For Yūnus b. Bukayr, cited below, cf. GAS, i, p. 289; TT, xi, pp. 434–436; Jawād, p. 202; he had as transmitters of the *Maghāzī*: Wakīʿ b. al-Jarrāḥ, Abū Kurayb, and Hannād al-Sarī.

[25] GAS, i, p. 111; TT, xi, pp. 70–71; *Jarḥ*, ix, pp. 119–120; *Thiqāt*, xi, 246–247; *Tadhkira*, pp. 507–508; see the Introduction by Taqī al-dīn al-Nadawī to his edition of al-Bayhaqī, *Kitāb al-Zuhd al-kabīr*, Kuwait 1983², pp. 32–36 and especially nº 5, p. 33; TAB, iii, p. 69, 427, 517, 518; x, p. 542; TA/A: three traditions including one of Yūnus b. Bukayr. The transmitters whose traditions he accepted are essentially, according to al-Ṭabarī: Abū l-Aḥwaṣ (=

The Scholarly Formation of al-Ṭabarī 11

M18 Ismāʿīl b. Mūsā al-Fazārī (d. 245/859) would have been the grandson of al-Suddī (d. 128/755). Some accused him of having Shiʿite tendencies. Al-Ṭabarī transmitted few of his traditions.[26]

M19 ʿAbbād b. Yaʿqūb al-Rawājinī al-Asadī al-Kufī (d. 250/864) was considered a Shiʿite. Ibn Ḥibbān has preserved for us a tradition attributed to the Prophet and transmitted by the following route: Ibn Ḥibbān/ al-Ṭabarī (most likely our man)/ Muḥammad b. Ṣāliḥ/ ʿAbbād.../ the Prophet: "If you see Muʿāwiya on my throne, kill him!" Ibn Khuzayma, co-disciple and friend of al-Ṭabarī, would have refused to transmit traditions of his on account of his Shiʿite opinions. His name appears once in the *History*, three times in the *Tahdhīb al-āthār* and several times in the *Commentary*.[27] The importance of this traditionist in the education of al-Ṭabarī should not be exaggerated, but it is interesting to note that he also attended the classes of Shiʿite traditionists.

[**215**] M20 ʿAbd al-Aʿlā b. Wāṣil al-Asadī (d. 247/861) was reckoned an authority worthy of confidence. Among those who transmitted traditions from him, we note Abū Ḥātim al-Rāzī, al-Tirmidhī and al-Nasāʾī. Al-Ṭabarī mentions him three times in his *History* and several times in his *Commentary*.[28]

M21 From ʿUbayd b. Ismāʿīl al-Habbārī (d. 250/864), al-Ṭabarī transmitted several traditions in his *Commentary* and in the *Tahdhīb*. Also among his transmitters, were al-Bukhārī and Abū Ḥātim.[29]

M22 Abū Hammām al-Walīd b. Shujāʿ (d. 242/856) was not considered an absolutely reliable authority. Al-Ṭabarī transmitted four of his traditions in his *History* and a few others in his *Commentary*.[30]

M23 Finally, and still according to the biographical notices, al-Ṭabarī attended the classes on Qurʾānic readings of Sulaymān b. ʿAbd al-Raḥmān al-Ṭalḥi (d. 252/866) who transmitted the reading of Ḥamza, which he took from Khallād b. Khālid al-Kūfī (d. 220/835). The chain of

Sallām b. Sulaym), Abū Muʿāwiya al-Ḍarīr (= M. b. Khāzim) and Wakīʿ. For the *bakkāʾūn*, cf. Asad b. Mūṣa, *Kitāb al-Zuhd*, ed. R.G. Khoury, Wiesbaden, 1976, p. 39; Massignon, *Passion*, iii, p. 220.

[26] *Fihrist*, p. 234; TT, I, pp. 335–336; two occurrences, in *History*, iv, p. 456; v, p. 156; TA/U, Tr. 926.

[27] *Fihrist*, p. 234, l. 12; TT, v, pp. 109–110: according to Ibn Khuzayma: *fīhi ghuluwwun fī l-tashayyuʿ*; *Majrūḥīn*, ii, p. 172; TA/IA, Tr. 582, 630; TA/IA, Tr. 441; TAB, v, Tr. 5475, p. 216.

[28] Dāwūdī, ii, p. 111, mentions him among the masters of al-Ṭabarī; TT, vi, p. 101; TA/A, once; TA/IA, three times; *History*: twice; TAB, ix, p. 538, n° 11125; M. b. al-Qāsim al-Asadī/ al-Awzāʿī.

[29] *Fihrist*, p. 235, l. 12; TT, vii, p. 59; TAB, iii, n° 2890; TA/A, three times; TA/IA, four times.

[30] TT, xi, pp. 135–136; TB, ii, p. 162; absent from TA; TAB, xii, p. 454, n° 14691; *History*, four traditions *sub nom.* Abū Hammām.

transmission of this reading was the following: Sulaymān/ Khallād/ Sulaym b. ʿĪsā (d. 188/803)/ Ḥamza b. Ḥabīb al-Zayyāt (d. 156/772).[31]

M24 As is known, works of onomastic have not always retained all the names of the most important educators of [**216**] scholars, while those of individuals who played a secondary role are recorded. Thus it is that the biographical notices dedicated to al-Ṭabarī do not mention Abū Muḥammad Sufyān b. Wakīʿ b. al-Jarrāḥ al-Ruʾāsī al-Kūfī. Al-Ṭabarī cites him forty times in the *Musnad* of Ibn ʿAbbās, eleven times in that of ʿAlī, thirty times in the *History*, and he is among those most often mentioned in his *Commentary*, in particular in reference to the route of several chains which, from his father, led to Mujāhid, to Ibn Jubayr and to Ibn ʿAbbās. His renown was such that works were attributed to him which were not of his making. One of his scribes would have been responsible for the poor quality of some of the traditions which he related.[32]

IV Al-Ṭabarī in Baghdad

It was most of all in Baghdad that al-Ṭabarī completed his education, in particular in jurisprudence. The list of masters whose lessons he attended in the ʿAbbāsid city is virtually endless.

M25 One of the major intellectual events which marked al-Ṭabarī was certainly the teaching given to him by al-Ḥasan b. Muḥammad b. al-Ṣabbāḥ al-Zaʿfarānī (d. 260/874) in Shāfiʿite law. It was during his courses that al-Ṭabarī copied the *Book* of al-Shāfiʿī; al-Zaʿfarānī had heard the *Risāla* from the very mouth of the founder of the School. He

[31] *Ghāya*, i, p. 314; al-Dhahabī, *Maʿrifat al-qurrāʾ*, ed. M. Sayyid Jād al-Ḥaqq, Cairo, Dār al-Kutub al-ḥadītha, 19691, i, p. 212 [= *Qurrāʾ*]. A correction is required to Abū l-Faḍl Ibrāhīm in *History*, i, p. 7 who has: Sulaymān b. Khallād. Evidently this should read: Sulaymān b. ʿAbd al-Raḥmān al-Ṭalḥī *ʿan* Khallād. For the transmission of this reading, cf. Gilliot, p. 221.

[32] TT, iv, pp. 123–125; for the episode of the copyist, p. 124, *in fine*; similarly in *Jarḥ*, iv, pp. 231–232: *lahu warrāqun qad afsada ḥadīthahu*. He features in the collections of weak traditionists: *Majrūḥīn*, i, p. 359; al-Nasāʾī. *Kitāb al-Ḍuʿafāʾ wa l-matrūkīn*, ed. Maḥmud Ibrāhīm Zāyid, with the *Kitāb al-Ḍuʿafāʾ al-saghīr*, of al-Bukharī, Aleppo 1396/1976, p. 55 [= *Ḍuʿafāʾ*]; for his position in the *History* of al-Tabarī: Jawād, p. 215; Horst, p. 296: Ibn Wakīʿ/ ʿAbd Allāh b. Numayr/ Warqāʾ b. ʿUmar/ Ibn a. Najīḥ. For the *Tafsīr* of Mujāhid: G. Stauth, *Die Überlieferung des Korankommentars Mujāhid b. Jabrs. Zur Rekonstruktion der in den Sammelwerken des 3. Jh. d. H. benuzten frühislamischen Quellenwerke*, Inaugural-Dissertation, Giessen 1969, pp. 116–117; Gilliot, pp. 252–261; the following chain is to be added here: Ibn Wakīʿ/ Wakīʿ/ Sufyān (b.ʿUyayna)/ unknown or Ibn a. Najīḥ/ Mujāhid.

was considered the most reliable transmitter of "the doctrine of the first period" (*athbat ruwāt al-qadīm*). Al-Ṭabarī was to complete [**217**] this education in Shāfiʿism in Egypt with the doctrine of the second period (*al-jadīd*).[33]

M26 There were also in the caliphal capital masters in Ḥanbalism of whom the biographers tell us nothing, but whose names appear here and there in his works; we may mention, for example, Muḥammad b. ʿAlī al-Ḥasan b. Shaqīq al-Marwazī (d. 250/864).[34]

M27 Still in the context of *fiqh*, worthy of mention is Dāwūd b. ʿAlī b. Khalaf al-Iṣfahānī (d. 270/884), founder of the Ẓāhirite school, which first followed the doctrine of al-Shāfiʿī. Al-Ṭabarī attended his classes in law and in *ḥadīth*; he must have witnessed some of his controversies with the Muʿtazilites over the created/uncreated Qurʾān, in particular the one which Yāqūt mentions between Dāwūd and Abū Mujāhid (= Aḥmad b. al-Ḥusayn al-Ḍarīr al-Muʿtazilī), which took place at Wāsiṭ.[35]

The list of traditionists whose lectures al-Ṭabarī attended in Baghdad would be impressive. Biographical notices cite some of them who are not always the most important:

[**218**] M28 Abū Yaʿqūb Iṣḥāq b. a. Isrāʾīl al-Marwazī (d. 246/860). Some say that he died in 240/854, but since al-Ṭabarī heard him in Baghdad, he must have died after 241, the date of al-Ṭabarī's first residence in Baghdad.

[33] GAS, i, 491–492; TT, ii, pp. 318–319; TB, vii, pp. 407–410; De Goeje, *Introductio*, p. xcix, according to al-Nawawī. This passage has since been printed in al-Nawawī, *Tahdhīb al-asmāʾ wa l-lughāt*, Cairo 1929; repr. Beirut, undated, i, p. 79; *Wafayāt*, ii. pp. 73–74: *huwa aḥadu ruwāti l-aqwāli l-qadīmati ʿani l-Shāfiʿī* [= Ibn Khallikān, *Wafayāt al-aʿyān*, i–viii, ed. I. ʿAbbās, Beirut 1968–1972]. The six transmitters of the doctrine of al-Shāfiʿī in his new state are: al-Muzanī, al-Rabīʿ b. Sulaymān al-Jīzī, al-Rabīʿ b. Sulaymān al-Murādi (master of al-Ṭabarī) al-Buwayṭī, Ḥarmala, Yūnus b. ʿAbd al-Aʿlā (master of al-Ṭabarī).

[34] TT, ix, p. 369; TB, iii, pp. 55–56. His name features four times in TA and also in the "retraction"/ Profession of faith of al-Tabari, in D. Sourdel, *Une profession de foi de l'historien al-Ṭabarī* in REI, 1968/2, p. 191 [= "Profession de foi"]; TAB, ii, p. 372, nº 1591. For the various states of the doctrine of al-Shāfiʿī: J. Schacht, *The Origins of Muhammadan Jurisprudence*, Oxford 1950¹, 1979⁶, p. 120 [= *Origins*].

[35] According to *Fihrist*, p. 234: *qaraʾa l-fiqha ʿalā Dāwūd*; for Dāwūd, refs. will be found in GAS, i, 521ss; al-Ṭabarī and Dāwūd, in Yāqūt, xviii, pp. 72–80; TB, viii, pp. 369–375. He was criticised for his opinions on the Qurʾān. Ibn Ḥanbal refused to meet him because he held the opinion according to which the content of the Qurʾān on "the well guarded Table" is uncreated, but to the extent that it exists in exemplars, it is created (p. 372; cf. J. Schacht, in EI, ii, 188b). On account of this opinion he became associated with al-Nāshī al-Akbar, cf. J. van Ess, *Frühe muʿtazilitische Häresiographie*, Beirut/Wiesbaden, 1971, pp. 6–8 and especially pp. 128–129 [= FMH].

He was reckoned a reliable purveyor of *ḥadīth*, but he drew the denunciation of Aḥmad b. Ḥanbal because he did not take a position on the uncreated nature of the Qur'ān, confining himself to saying it is the Word of God (*wāqifī*). Al-Ṭabarī derived few traditions from him, but it is important to note, as in the case of Dāwūd al-Iṣfahānī, that al-Ṭabarī found himself directly in an ambience where the "conflict over the Qur'ān" gave rise to animated debates.[36]

M29 Abū Ja'far Aḥmad b. Manīʿ al-Aṣamm al-Baghawī al-Baghdādī (d. 244/858) is classed among the authorities of repute. Al-Ṭabarī transmitted few traditions derived from him.[37]

M30 Yaʿqūb b. Ibrāhīm al-Dawraqī enjoyed a good reputation as an authority on traditions. Al-Ṭabarī transmitted many of his traditions, especially those which Yaʿqūb derived from Ibn ʿUlayya (Ismāʿīl b. Ibrāhīm al-Asadī, d. 193/809) or from Ḥushaym b. Bashīr (d. 183/799), exegete, traditionist and jurist who had Ibn Ḥanbal as a disciple. Al-Dawraqī was the author of a *Musnad* which al-Ṭabarī wrote out in two stages, as he himself relates in an episode which perhaps supplies the answer to the scandalised astonishment of the editor of the *Commentary*, A.M. Shākir, when al-Ṭabarī transmitted traditions which could "give orientalists weapons to denigrate the Qur'ān and the Prophet": "A man said to Abū Jaʿfar: 'The people of *ḥadīth* choose'."

We will not write, replied al-Ṭabarī, but I wrote the *Musnad* of Yaʿqūb b. Ibrāhīm al-Dawraqī, and I left a part of it. I did not teach [**219**] the part which I wrote. Then I revised it to include *ḥadīth* and to write it in order (*li-uṣannifahu*), but it remained more than I had written before. That which I omitted held me up for a long time. So I rewrote the *Musnad* in full. People choose, but in doing so, they perhaps omit the greater part of what is useful.

This is the substance of what he said (*aw naḥwa hādhā l-kalām*)."

This episode is richly informative from more than one point of view, not only on the conceptions of al-Ṭabarī himself, but also on the passage from oral to written. On the one hand, even if the master had a *Musnad*, the disciple could take from it and leave parts of it, and reorganise it. On the other hand, the setting into writing, when it was done, was a process of remodelling, omissions

[36] According to TB, ii, p. 162; cf. his notices in TT, i, pp. 223–225; TB, vi, pp. 356–362: *wāqifī maʿṣūm*, according to Ibn Ḥanbal, p. 360. His name appears five times in al-Ṭabarī's *History*.

[37] Like the preceding, he is included in the list of eleven masters given by TB, ii, p. 162/ Yāqūt, xviii, p. 41; TB, v, pp. 160–161; *Thiqāt*, viii, p. 22; he appears, for example, in TAB, v, n° 5432; absent from the *History*, he is mentioned once in TA.

and revivals. This calls into question to some extent the manner in which F. Sezgin, for example, perceives the putting into writing of *ḥadīth*. Finally it should be noted that al-Ṭabarī was animated by the desire to transmit as many traditions as possible for fear lest what was useful to the community might be omitted, reserving the right to rule subsequently on the "health" of these traditions, as he did often in his *musnads* (i.e. in his *Tahdhīb*) and very seldom in his *Commentary*, which aroused the ire of the Shākir brothers![38]

M31 Al-Zubayr b. Bakkār (d. 256/870) is included on the list of masters given by al-Dāwūdī. His name occurs only five times in the *History*. Al-Ṭabarī must have attended his classes on his *Kitāb Nasab Quraysh*, but he may also have borrowed from other works of his as could be suggested by the use of words such as *qāla*, *ruwiya* and *dhakara*. His name features very little in the *Commentary* and four times in the *Musnad* of ʿUmar.[39]

[**220**] M32 Abū Ayyūb Sulaymān b. ʿAbd al-Jabbār al-Khayyāt al-Baghdādī (d. ?) is included in the list of masters provided by al-Dāwūdī. He was a traditionist seldom cited by al-Ṭabarī.[40]

M33 Abū ʿAbd Allāh Aḥmad b. Yūsuf al-Taghlibī (d. 237/886) occupies a distinguished place in the education of Ibn Jarīr, since it was he who transmitted the *Kitāb al-Qirāʾāt* of Abū ʿUbayd al-Qāsim b. Sallām.[41]

M34 Muḥammad b. a. Maʿshar Najīh b. ʿAbd al-Raḥmān al-Sindī al-Madanī al-Baghdādī (d. 244/858 or 247/861, at 99 years of age) would have transmitted to al-Ṭabarī, according to al-Dhahabī, the *Maghāzī* of his father Abū Maʿshar (d. 170/787). In any case, al-Ṭabarī did not make use

[38] Yaʿqūb b. Ibrāhīm is included in the list of the eleven masters: Yāqūt, xviii, p. 52; TT, xi, pp. 381–382; *Tadhkira*, pp. 505–507: *ṣannafa wa jamaʿa*; GAS, i. p. 38; TB, xiv, pp. 277–280. The episode with al-Ṭabarī is found in Yāqūt, xviii, p. 53; v.g. in TAB, i, 237, 283, 338, 548, and *passim*; twenty-six times in TA/A, thirty-three times in TA/IA and seventy-three times in TA/ An index, pp. 1288–89; thirty-three times in the *History*; at least twice in IFK[1] [= Al-Ṭabarī, *Ikhtilāf al-fuqahāʾ*, ed. Fr. Kern, Cairo, 1320/19021; repr. Beirut, Dār al-kutub al-ʿilmiyya, undated]. For Ibn ʿUlayya, GAS, i. p. 112; for Ḥusaym b. Bashīr, GAS, i, p. 38, with other references.

[39] GAS, i, pp. 317–318; he is cited as a master of al-Ṭabarī by Dāwūdī, ii, p. 111. *History*, ii, p. 271, 273; iv, pp. 431–432; viii, p. 62, 71, 88; TAB, vii, p. 222, n° 7855; TA/U, Tr. 93, 223, 958, 989.

[40] TB, IX, pp. 52–53. He is mentioned by Dāwūdī, ii, p. 111; TT, iv. p. 205: he also lived in Samarrāʾ; Ibn Ḥajar, *Taqrīb al-Tahdhīb*, Beirut, Dār al-Maʿrifa, 1975[2], i, p. 327; *Jarḥ*, iv, p. 130. None of the sources consulted gives the date of his death. In TA/A, twice, in TA/IA, three times; TAB, ii. p. 12, no 850.

[41] Dāwūdī, ii. p. 114, where it is said of al-Ṭabarī: *rawā l-ḥurūfa samāʿan ʿan…*; *Ghāya*, pp. 152–153: *rawā l-qirāʾata samāʿan ʿan Abī ʿUbaydi l-Qāsimi bni Sallāmin*. His disciples included, besides al-Ṭabarī, also Ibn Mujāhid, himself a disciple of al-Ṭabarī; cf. TAB, xvi, n° 5919 and 5954; xvi, p. 452, n° 20140, and *passim*. In Yāqūt, xviii, p. 68, there is a misprint to be corrected. It should read al-Taghlibī and not al-Thaʿlabī.

of this edition in his *History*; neither does it feature in his *Commentary* nor in the parts of the *Tahdhīb al-āthār* which have survived.[42]

The above are the masters of al-Ṭabarī mentioned in the biographical notices. But many others could be cited, some of whom played an important part in his education, such as:

M35 Aḥmad b. Abī Khaythama (= A. b. Zuhayr b. Ḥarb, d. 279/892); [**221**] he is the author of a *History* of the caliphal period. He attended the classes of Muṣʿab b. ʿAbd Allāh al-Zubayrī (d. 233/848 or 236/851) on the genealogy of the Arabs. He is mentioned sixty-five times in the *History* for the caliphal period.[43]

M36 Abū l-Ḥasan ʿAlī b. Dāwūd b. Yazīd al-Adamī al-Baghdādī al-Qanṭarī (d. 262/876, or 270, or 272/885) is one of the masters to whom al-Ṭabarī owes much. He derived from him numerous exegetical traditions attributed to Ibn ʿAbbās, via Abū Ṣāliḥ ʿAbd Allāh b. Ṣāliḥ al-Juhanī (d. 223/838).[44]

M37 Al-Ḥārith b. Muḥammad b. Usāma Dāhir al-Tamīmī l-Baghdādī (d. 282/895) transmitted to al-Ṭabarī numerous exegetical traditions attributed to Mujāhid. This traditionist was the author of a *Musnad* and of a *Kitāb al-Khulafāʾ* from which al-Ṭabarī quoted passages in his *History*.[45]

M38 Abū ʿAlī al-Ḥasan b. Yaḥyā al-ʿAbdī al-Jurjānī (d. 263/876) from whom al-Ṭabarī collected, among others, exegetical traditions of ʿAbd al-Razzāq al-Sanʿānī.[46]

M39 Muḥammad b. ʿAmr al-Bāhilī al-Baṣrī (d. 249/863) transmitted to al-Ṭabarī a large number of traditions attributed to Mujāhid.[47]

---

[42] Master of al-Ṭabarī, according to SAN [=Dhahabī, *Siyar aʿlām al-nubalāʾ*, ed. Sh. al-Arnaʾūṭ et al., 25 vols., Beirut, 1981–88], xiv, p. 268. This is confirmed by TT, pp. 467–68; TB, iii, pp. 326–27; *Jarḥ*, viii, p.110, no 487. It is reported that M. b. a. Maʿshar came to Maṣṣīṣa and demanded from Ḥajjāj (= b. M. al-Miṣṣīṣī, d. 206/821 a book which the latter had heard from his father (Abū Maʿshar). He took it and copied it, without having heard from Ḥajjāj (and consequently, not from his own father either). This episode should be understood, according to the traditional criteria of transmission, as illustrating the "weakness" of the traditionist.

[43] GAS, i, pp. 319–320; Jawād, pp. 220–221; Yāqūt, xviii, pp. 35–37; TB, iv, pp. 162–164. [The extant parts of *History* have been edited in 4 vols., Cairo, 2004; v. Gilliot, "Textes arabes anciens ...", *MIDEO*, 27 (2008) no. 175.]

[44] TB, xi, pp. 424–25; SAN, xiii, p. 143; Horst, p. 293, *isnād* 1; Gilliot, *Baqara*, p. 127ff.

[45] GAS, i, p. 160; TB, viii, pp. 218–19; SAN, xiii, pp. 388–90.

[46] Horst, p. 296, n. 2; TB, vii, pp. 453–54; SAN, xii, pp. 356–57.

[47] Horst, p. 287, *isnād* 7a; TB, iii, p. 127. He was also a specialist in readings, cf. *Ghāya*, ii, p. 221, nº 3328.

M40 Muḥammad b. Sa'd b. Muḥammad b. al-Ḥasan b. 'Aṭiyya b. Sa'd b. Junāda al-'Awfī (d. 276/889) is one of the traditionists most often cited in the *Commentary* of al-Ṭabarī. The latter collected from him numerous exegetical traditions attributed to Ibn 'Abbās, through the conduit of a familial chain of authorities.[48]

[**222**] M41 Al-Qāsim b. al-Ḥasan is one of the Baghdadi masters of al-Ṭabarī whose name appears most often in his *Commentary*, in particular for the exegetical traditions dating back to Ibn Jurayj. His identity is uncertain. What is certain, is that al-Ṭabarī followed his courses in Baghdad and that he owed him a great deal.[49]

The education of al-Ṭabarī in the caliphal city was not confined to *ḥadīth*, to exegesis, to law and to Qur'ānic readings; we also see him involved in the literary life of this epoch. Abū l-Faraj al-Iṣfahānī (284–356/897–967) visited him regularly and was one of his assiduous disciples, as is shown by the chains of guarantees ending with him in the *Kitāb al-Aghānī*, especially when it is a question of episodes related by the *Sīra*.[50]

Al-Ṭabarī also acquired the reputation of a good grammarian. According to a tradition related by Yāqūt and deriving from 'Abd al-'Azīz b. Muḥammad al-Tabarī, he established himself near the bridge of Baradān, in the eastern part of Baghdad; this quarter was home to a veritable dynasty of grammarians, including: Abū 'Ubayd al-Qāsim b. Sallām (d. 224/838), 'Allān al-Azdī (?), Abū Bakr Hishām b. Mu'āwiya al-Naḥwī al-Ḍarīr (209/824), Abū 'Abd Allāh Muḥammad b. Yaḥyā al-Kisā'ī (= Kisā'ī l-Ṣaghīr, d. 288/900), and finally Abū Ja'far al-Ṭabarī. As for Ibn Mujāhid, he records a tradition of Abū l-'Abbās (i.e.

---

[48] TB, v, pp. 322–23; Ibn Ḥajar, *Lisān al-mīzān*, v, p.174, no 603; *Ghāya*, ii, p. 142, no 3017; Gilliot, *Baqara*, pp. 136–145, restores the *isnād* 3 of Horst, p. 294 who saw in Muḥammad b. Sa'd: *Kātib* al-Wāqidī, which is impossible, the latter having died in 230/844.

[49] Horst, p. 95, n°1, on the basis of TB, xii, pp. 432–433, identifies him with al-Qāsim b. al-Ḥasan b. Yazīd al-Hamadhānī, d. 272/885. However not one of the names of his masters appears in the chains ending with the al-Qāsim b. al-Ḥasan of al-Ṭabarī's acquaintance. For this reason we share the doubts expressed by A.M. Shākir regarding the feasibility of identifying him, cf. TAB, vii, p. 507, note 1. In the *History*, he appears twenty-eight times in the first volume and twice in the second; he features once in TA/IA, pp. 499–460, Tr. 7450. For al-Ḥusayn b. Dāwūd al-Miṣṣīṣī, called Sunayd (d. 226/840), who had a great Koranic commentary, and one of the masters of al-Qāsim b. al-Ḥasan, cf. TB, viii, pp. 42–44; the name of al-Qāsim does not appear in the list of his masters; cf. GAS, i. p. 31, 91.

[50] Yāqūt, xviii, p. 87; Aghānī, i, 18, 16; xiv, p. 299; xvii, p. 55, l. 5; 65, l. 7; 111, l. 11; 324, l. 16, etc... [= al-Iṣfahānī, *Kitāb al-Aghānī*, ed. Dār al-kutub, then al-Hay'a al-miṣriyya]. Cf. *Richtungen*, p. 86, n. 2 [= I. Goldziher, *Die Richtungen der islamischen Koranauslegung*, Leiden, Brill, 1920[1], 1970[3]]. [See now M. Fleischhammer, *Die Quellen des Kitāb al-Aġānī*, Wiesbaden, 2004, p. 58, nr. 119; 126–127, nr. 68].

Tha'lab, d. 291/903) which makes of al-Ṭabarī the best Kufian of Baghdad in his time. This tradition [**223**] contributed to some extent to placing al-Ṭabarī among the Kufians.[51]

V Al-Ṭabarī between the Shām and Egypt

There are two dates on which al-Ṭabarī arrived in Egypt, which approximately fix those of his periods of residence in the Shām. With one of these dates, the year 253, we encounter a difficulty which has attracted little attention except on the part of Rudi Paret. Yāqūt relates that Abū Ja'far had begun receiving an education in Shāfi'ite jurisprudence from al-Za'farānī in Baghdad, then that in his turn he taught a group which included Abū Sa'īd al-Iṣṭakhrī (= al-Ḥasan b. Aḥmad, 244–310/858–922), and this before his departure for Fusṭāṭ. If this is the journey of 253, Abū Sa'īd would then have been 9 years old. According to Yāqūt, again, it was around this date that he paused in the cities of the Shām before going on to Egypt, then he revisited the Sham and returned to Egypt in 256. We know, in any case, that he was in Baghdad in 258. It is thus around 253 and 256 that his two periods of residence are to be situated.[52]

Abū Sa'īd Ibn Yūnus (= 'Abd al-Raḥmān b. Aḥmad b. Yūnus al-Ṣadafī al-Miṣrī, 281–347/894–958) gives a single date, according to Ibn 'Asākir and according to al-Dāwūdī, who seems to derive it from the latter, for [**224**] al-Ṭabarī's stay in Egypt, that of 263. Are we to suppose that Ibn Yūnus or a copyist confused the dates 253 and 263, or that al-Ṭabarī made a third journey, in which case why does Ibn Yūnus make no mention of the two others? Only

---

[51] Yāqūt, xviii, pp. 60–61; Maḥmūd Shabaka, *al-Naḥw fī Tafsīr al-Ṭabarī* in *Majallat Kulliyat al-lugha al-'arabiyya* (Riyadh), 10 (1980), p. 69. In this line of grammarians, we have been unable to identify 'Allān al-Azdī; for Hisham b. Mu'āwiya, cf. *Bughya*, ii, p. 328 [= al-Suyūṭī, *Bughyat al-wu'āt*... i–ii, ed. M. Abū l-Faḍl Ibrāhīm, Cairo 1964–65]; *Inbāh*, iii, p. 421; *Inbāh*, iii. p. 229. For al-Ṭabarī the grammarian, cf. Gilliot, *Aspects*, chap. vii, pp. 264–323, and especially p. 297ff.

[52] Yāqūt, xviii, p. 52, 23, 55. Cf. Ibn 'Asākir, in De Goeje, *Introductio*, p. lxxii, l. 14–15; Dāwūdī, ii, p.111; For Abū Sa'īd al-Istakhrī: TB, vii, pp. 268–270; al-Shīrāzī (Abu Isḥāq), *Ṭabaqāt al-fuqahā'*, ed. Iḥsān 'Abbās, Beirut 1981², p. 111, l. 3 [= Shīrāzī]; al-Subkī, *Tabaqāt* [ed. 1326], ii, pp. 193–205; al-Ḥusaynī (Hidāyat Allāh), *Tabaqāt al-Shāfi'iyya*, ed. Ādil Nuwayḥid, Beirut 1971, 1979², p. 62 [= Ḥusaynī]; al-'Abbādī, *Tabaqāt al-fuqahā' al-Shāfi'iyya*, ed. G. Vitestam, Leiden 1964, p. 66 [= 'Abbādī]. Ibn Yunus divided his History of Egypt into two parts: *Kitāb Miṣr* and *Kitāb al-Ghurabā'*; it was in the latter book that he wrote about al-Ṭabarī. Cf. *Geschichte der arabischen Literatur* [= GAL], SI, p. 229; al-Ṣuyūṭī, *Ḥusn al-muḥāḍara fī ta'rīkh Miṣr wa l-Qāhira*, ed. M. Abū l-Faḍl Ibrāhīm, Cairo 1967, I, p. 351. Al-Ṭabarī was in Baghdad in 258, cf. *History*, iii¹/ ix, p. 492. [See Fr. Rosenthal, Introduction to *The History of al-Ṭabarī*, I, op. cit., 27–28].

Rudi Paret has drawn attention to this contradiction which went unnoticed by both ancient and modern, by Muḥammad Abū l-Faḍl Ibrāhīm as well as by A.M. al-Ḥūfī, who furthermore do not mention the date given by Ibn Yūnus. This problem of dating has yet to be resolved.

Of the masters of Damascus, no names are cited by the biographical sources. The chains of authorities given by al-Ṭabarī nonetheless enable us to mention some of them.

M42 Ibrāhīm b. Yaʿqūb al-Saʿdī al-Jūzajānī (d. 259/873 or 256). Fr. Kern has written that he was the master and disciple of al-Ṭabarī in *fiqh*. In fact, he was not the disciple of Abū Jaʿfar, but only his master.[53] The error seems to derive from al-Samʿānī who calls Ibrāhīm b. Yaʿqūb "al-Jarīrī", giving the impression thereby that he was following the madhhab of Ibn Jarīr. In fact, the correct reading is "al-Ḥarīzī", which signifies that he followed the doctrine of Ḥarīz b. ʿUthmān al-Raḥabī who professed the *naṣb*; in other words he declared his hostility to ʿAlī b. al-Ṭālib; he was a disciple of the Nāṣibiyya. It is said furthermore of Ibrāhīm b. Yaʿqūb that he was Ḥarūrī, attacking ʿAlī and declaring: "I do not like ʿAlī, he massacred my ancestors (i.e. at the time of the massacre of Nahrawān).

This Jūzajānī should not be confused with the one who is often cited in the *Kitāb Ikhtilāf al-fuqahā'*, who is Abū Sulaymān Mūsā b. Sulaymān (d. 200/815).[54] Al-Ṭabarī borrowed from his works of *fiqh*, **[225]** *al-Nawādir*. He was a disciple of Abū Yūsuf and of Muḥammad b. al-Ḥasan al-Shaybānī.

---

[53] GAS, i, p. 135; TT, i, pp. 181–183; IFK[1], p. 20 of Introduction/IFK[2] [second repr. Beirut, Dār al-kutub al-ʿilmiyya, undated (between 1980 and 1984), with another pagination], p. 68, n. 7; *Thiqāt*, viii, pp. 81–82, with the important note 7 of page 81. For Ḥarīz b. al-Mishraqī: TT, ii, pp. 237–241. Ḥarīz died in 163/779; cf. Ibn Mākūla, *al-Ikmāl fī rafʿ al-irtiyāb ʿan muʾtalif wa l-mukhtalif fī l-asmāʾ wa l-kunā wa l-ansāb*, Hyderabad 1962ss, repr. Beirut undated, ii, p. 212 [= *Ikmāl*]. For *ahl al-naṣb*: Lane, col. 2800c; *Qāmūs*, I, p. 138, l. 4–5; *Taj*, iv, 277b; H. Laoust, *Schismes*, p. 114. It is said of Ibrāhīm b. Yaʿqub that he was known for his hostility towards ʿAli: *maʿrūf bi-naṣb* or *shadīd al-mayl ilā madhhab ahl Dimashq fī mayl ʿalā ʿAlī*: Ibn ʿAsakir, TTD, ii, pp. 313–314 [= *Tahdhīb Taʾrīkh Dimashq*; Id., TD, vii, pp. 278–85]; *Jarḥ*, ii, pp. 148–149. [TG, I, p. 70; II, p. 436.] [TG = Van Ess, J., Theologie und Gesellschaft im 2. und 3. Jahrhundert Hidschra, 6 vols., Berlin, 1991–97].

[54] GAS, i. p. 433. Fr. Kern is unsure of the identity of the al-Jūzajānī who appears often in IFK. Al-Ṭabarī never mentions him there in connection with a chain; on the other hand J. Schlacht has clearly identified him in IFS [= *Ikhtilāf al-fuqahā'*, ed. J. Schlacht, Leiden 1933], p. 262. Either al-Ṭabarī did not receive licence for transmission, or he utilised a work in the absence of a master who possessed this licence.

M43 It was in Ramla that al-Ṭabarī attended the lessons in *ḥadīth* of ʿAlī b. Sahl al-Ramlī (d. 261/874).[55] The latter transmitted the traditions of al-Awzāʿī, but he was also the author of *Maghāzī* and of *Sunan*. His name appears thirty-two times in *Tahdhīb al-āthār*, eight times in the *History*, once in his profession of faith where he cites a tradition of al-Awzāʿī via al-Walīd b. Muslim al-Dimashqī (d. 195/810). He is also present in the *K. Ikhtilāf al-fuqahāʾ*. Through him, al-Ṭabarī had access to the doctrine of al-Awzāʿī.

The notices have also preserved for us the name of one of his masters in Beirut:

M44 Al-ʿAbbās b. al-Walīd b. Mazyad al-Āmulī al-Bayrūtī (d. 266/879).[56] Al-Ṭabarī attended his classes on Qurʾānic readings. He also benefited from his teaching in jurisprudence according to the doctrine of al-Awzāʿī, as is shown by certain passages of his book on the controversies of scholars.

The time spent by al-Ṭabarī in the Shām was of great importance in the domain of readings, in that of exegesis and of traditions, or finally in that of the *fiqh* of al-Awzāʿī.

VI Al-Ṭabarī in Egypt [226]

In Egypt, as elsewhere, al-Ṭabarī had masters in diverse branches of Islamic scholarship. However it may be supposed that he went there essentially to perfect his education in Shāfiʿism, and specifically, to study the doctrine of the second period (*al-jadīd*). In fact, the diverse biographical notices draw a degree of attention to this point.

On the one hand, they tell us, as we have already seen, that al-Ṭabarī was initiated into the doctrine of the first period (*al-aqwāl al-qadīma* or *al-qadīm*) as a student of al-Zaʿfarānī in Baghdad; he subsequently studied it before his departure for Fusṭāṭ, where he had as his master al-Rabīʿ b. Sulaymān

[55] TT, vii. p. 329; *Mīzān*, iii, p. 130, n° 5852; Yāqūt, *Buldān*, iii, 70a; TA/A, seven traditions; TA/IA, twenty-five traditions; Sourdel, "Profession de foi", p. 191; TAB, ii. p. 268, Tr 1384.

[56] Ibn ʿAsākir, TTD, vii, p. 275; Id., TD (Damascus 1982), pp. 278–283 [= *Taʾrīkh Dimashq*]; ID., in De Goeje, *Introductio*, p. lxii; *Ghāya*, i, p. 355; TT, v. pp. 131–133. On ʿAbd al-Ḥamīd b. Bakkār: *Ghāya*, ii. p. 106; in *fiqh* cf. IFS, p. xx, 163, 172, 181 etc...; IFK², p. 27, 36, 43 etc...; TAB, ii, p. 42, Tr. 891.

al-Murādī, and where he knew al-Muzanī, transmitters of the doctrine of the second period.[57]

On the other hand, al-Ṭabarī was happy to recall that one of the masters of Shāfiʿism in Baghdad, alongside Abū Saʿīd al-Iṣṭakhrī, Ibn Surayj (d. 306/918), had received the doctrine of the first period from one of his own disciples, Ibn Bashshār al-Aḥwal (= ʿUthmān b. Saʿīd al-Anmāṭī, d. 288/900): "It was I (al-Ṭabarī) who introduced and practised the rite of al-Shāfiʿī in Baghdad over a period of ten years. It was I who educated Ibn Bashshār al-Aḥwal, the master of Abū l-ʿAbbās Ibn Surayj...".[58] In this text there are various points raised; one of them relates to the precedence of Shāfiʿism in Baghdad and to the priority of the leaders of this school. Ibn Surayj is considered one of the greatest after Abu Saʿīd. With these assertions, al-Ṭabarī "claimed his place" in the line of masters of this school.

A second point may also be seen in this declaration; it concerns his purpose in making his way to Egypt. Just like al-Ṭabarī, Ibn [**227**] Surayj spent time in Egypt where he was initiated into the doctrine of the second period as a student of al-Rabīʿ b. Sulaymān and of al-Muzanī; competition between masters was vigorous!

M45 It was thus in Egypt that al-Ṭabarī attended the classes of al-Rabīʿ b. Sulaymān al-Murādī (d. 270/883). The latter transmitted the greater part of the works of al-Shāfiʿī, and in particular the *Kitāb al-Umm* and the other works of the second period. It is he who is denoted in the *Kitāb Ikhtilāf al-fuqahāʾ*, when al-Ṭabarī, after quoting a passage from al-Shāfiʿī, says: *ḥaddathanī bi-dhālika ʿanhu l-Rabīʿ*; he should not be confused with another disciple of al-Shāfiʿī, al-Rabīʿ b. Sulaymān al-Jīzī (d. 256/869).[59]

---

[57] Yāqūt, xviii, p. 53. Al-Ṭabarī was in dispute with al-Muzanī, but we do not know what the point at issue was. It is not said that he had him as a master.

[58] Ibn ʿAsākir, in De Goeje, *Introductio*, p. lxxxiv. We shall correct the translation of Massignon, in *Passion*, i, p. 420, who furthermore read Bashshār al-Aḥwal when it should have been Ibn Bashshār; cf. TB, xi, pp. 292–293; *Wafayāt*, ii, p. 241; Subkī, ii, p. 52. For Ibn Surayj, cf. J. Schlacht, in EI, iii, p. 974; GAS, i, p. 495; TB, iv, pp. 287–290; Ḥusaynī, pp. 41–42; *Passion*, i, p. 420ss. For the two states or the two periods of the doctrine of al-Shāfiʿī, cf. J. Schlacht, *Introduction*, pp. 46–48; ID., *Origins*, p. 120: distinguishes "the earliest period" and "the middle period". In the second period he was reconciled with the traditionists, so well, in fact, that it was the first period which was the more "innovative".

[59] According to al-Nawawī, *Tahdhīb*, i, p. 79 in De Goeje, *Introductio*, p. xcix. For al-Rabīʿ b. Sulaymān: GAS, i, p. 487; *Wafayāt*, ii, pp. 291–292; *Ḥusn*, i, p. 387; there is an error to be corrected – he was not born in 274, but in 174; Shīrāzī, p. 98; Ḥusaynī, p. 24: *rawā l-Ummata wa ghayrahā mina l-jadīdi*; IFK^2, p. 25, 26, 27, 31, 39, and *passim*; IFS, p. xiii, xxi, 19, 24, 37, and *passim*. Cf. M. Khadduri, Introduction to his English translation,

M46 It was as a pupil of Yūnus b. ʿAbd al-Aʿlā (d. 264/877), another disciple of al-Shāfiʿī, that al-Ṭabarī also studied the doctrine of Mālik. Yūnus had for masters Ibn Wahb (= ʿAbd Allāh, d. 197/812) and Ashhab b. ʿAbd al-ʿAzīz (d. 204/819); al-Ṭabarī also owed him a great deal in exegesis. In fact, via the same conduit that appears eighteen hundred times in his *Commentary*, he transmits to him the *Tafsīr* of ʿAbd al-Raḥmān b. Zayd b. Aslam al-Madanī (d. 182/798), from whom al-Thaʿlabī also borrowed extensively in his *Kashf al-bayān*. Finally, it was courtesy of the same Yūnus that al-Ṭabarī received the reading of Ḥamza, with the following chain: Yūnus/ ʿAlī b. Kīsa al-Miṣrī al-Muqriʾ/ Sulaym b. ʿĪsā al-Kufi (d. 188/803)/ Ḥamza.[60]

[**228**] M47 He also perfected his education in Mālikite *fiqh* as a pupil of the sons of ʿAbd Allāh b. ʿAbd al-Ḥakam (d. 214/869), these being Muḥammad, ʿAbd al-Raḥmān and Saʿd, as well as a pupil of Ibn Akhī Wahb (= Aḥmad b. ʿAbd al-Raḥmān b. Wahb, Baḥshal, d. 264/877). We may note that Ibn Wahb himself (= ʿAbd Allāh, d. 197/812) was the author of *al-Muwaṭṭaʾ al-Kabīr*.[61]

Al-Ṭabarī also met in Egypt one of the most important disciples of al-Shāfiʿī, Ismāʿīl b.Yaḥyā al-Muzanī (d. 264/877). He also quarrelled with him over an issue of law, but al-Ṭabarī declined to reveal the point of contention, we are told, out of respect for al-Muzanī; Yāqūt suggests that the substance of the debate centred on the notion of consensus.[62]

Islamic Jurisprudence. Shāfiʿīs Risāla, Baltimore 1961, p. 15; for al-Jīzī: Subkī, *Ṭabaqāt al-Shāfiʿiyya*, ii, p. 132.

[60] According to *Fihrist*, p. 234, l. 9; Ibn ʿAsākir, in De Goeje, *Introductio*, p. xc; Yāqūt, xviii, pp. 66–67; *Ghāya*, ii, p. 107; Horst, *Gewährsmänner*, p. 105, with *isnād* n° 20 in his numeration. For Yūnus himself: TT, xi, pp. 440–441; *Tadhkira*, pp. 527–528; ʿAbbādī, p. 18; *Ghāya*, pp. 406–407; IFK², p. 27, 28, 34. For Sulaym b. ʿIsa: *Ghāya*, i, p. 318; Dhahabī, *Qurrāʾ*, i, p. 115; for Ashhab: GAS, i, p. 466; IFK², p. 45, 48; IFS, p. 133, and *passim*. ʿAlī b. Kīsa does not figure either in *Ghāya* or in *Qurrāʾ*; on the other hand, he is mentioned by *Taj*, xvi, 462b and 463a.

[61] *Fihrist*, p. 234; for ʿAbd Allāh b. ʿAbd al-Ḥakam: GAS, i, p. 467; his son ʿAbd Allāh: TT, ix, pp. 260–262; GAS, I, p. 474; TA/IA, index, p. 1072. For ʿAbd al-Raḥmān: TT, vi, p. 208; TA/IA, index, p. 1062; *History*, i, p. 113, 114, 325; ii, p. 316, 389, 391, 453; iv, p. 197, 384. For Ibn Wahb: GAS, i, p. 466. [Now above all: M. Muranyi, *ʿAbd Allāh b. Wahb. Leben und Werk*. Al-Muwaṭṭaʾ Kitāb al-muḥāraba, Wiesbaden, 1992]. For his nephew Aḥmad: TT, i, pp. 54–56; SAN, xii, pp. 317–23; TA/A, Tr. 12, 343, 398; TA/IA, Tr. 156, 405, etc..., cf. index, p. 1051: TA/U, eighteen times, cf. index, p. 1258.

[62] GAS, i, p. 492; Yāqūt, xviiii, pp. 54–55 and p. 53. J. Schacht, *Introduction*, p. 57, writes: "While Shāfiʿī had called the Qurʾān and the *sunna* 'the two principles' and considered *idjmāʿ* and *qiyās* as being subordinate to them, al-Ṭabarī recognised three *uṣūl*: the Qurʾan,

The sources also supply us with certain information about the time spent by al-Ṭabarī in Egypt; this has the effect of completing the picture of his intellectual training in this country. As happened on a number of occasions in the course of his life, al-Ṭabarī found himself at one time in a state of utter destitution, in the company of three other Muḥammads, his fellow students: Muḥammad b. Naṣr al-Marwazī (d. 294/906) who, born in Baghdad, lived in Nīsābūr and studied in Iraq, in the Ḥijāz and in Egypt. He was a leading traditionist and a Shāfiʿite jurist; he acquired certain renown for his analysis of the divergent views of the Companions (*ikhtilāf al-Ṣaḥāba*). His *Kitāb Ikhtilāf al-ʿulamāʾ* has been edited by al-Sayyid Ṣubḥī al-Sāmarrāʾī (Beirut, 1985). The second Muḥammad was Ibn Hārūn al-Rūyānī (d. 306/919), he too a traditionist and jurist, author of a *Musnad* which has survived into the present day. As for Muḥammad b. Isḥāq Ibn Khuzayma (d. 311/923), the celebrated theologian of Nīsābūr, [**229**] he was a fellow pupil of al-Ṭabarī and his longstanding companion. They had many things in common. Ibn Khuzayma was the author of a large number of works including the *Kitāb al-Tawḥīd wa ithbāt ṣifāt al-Rabb*, in which he campaigns against the Jahmites and the Muʿtazilites; al-Ṭabarī did the same in his *Commentary*. We also possess a *Ṣaḥīḥ* composed by him.[63]

It was also in Egypt that al-Ṭabarī showed his expertise in poetry and in metrics. Among those he encountered there was the traditionist and man of letters, Abū l-Ḥasan ʿAlī b. Sirāj al-Baṣrī l-Miṣrī (d. 308/920), who asked him questions about poetry; al-Ṭabarī dictated to him some *rara* of al-Ṭirimmāḥ, a poet whom al-Ṭabarī often cites in his *Commentary* and in his *Tahdhīb*.[64]

---

the *sunna* as expressed in traditions derived from the Prophet and *idjmāʿ*, which for him was absolutely decisive..." Was this the subject of the debate with al-Muzanī?

[63] The episode regarding the poverty of al-Ṭabarī and of his co-disciples is related in TB, ii, pp. 164–65 and repeated by Yāqūt, xviii, pp. 46–47. For M. b. Naṣr: GAS, i, p. 494; Ḥusaynī, pp. 34–35; TB, iii, p. 415. His *Ikhtilāf al-ʿulamāʾ*, ed. al-Sayyid Ṣubḥī l-Badrī l-Sāmarrāʾī, Beirut, Ālam al-kutub, 1985, 308 p. For M. b. Ḥārūn, GAS, i, p. 171; *Tadhkira*, pp. 752–754, which also relates the episode between the four Muḥammads. For Ibn Khuzayma: GAS, i, p. 601; J. van Ess, *Ibn Kullāb und die Miḥna* in *Oriens*, 18–19 (1965–66), p. 101ss. p. 124; *Tadhkira*, pp. 730–731: among other common masters: M. b. Ḥumayd; Aḥmad b. Manīʿ; Bishr b. Muʿādh, al-Rabī b. Sulaymān al-Murādī, etc...Ibn Khuzayma had eulogised the *Commentary* of al-Tabari, in Yāqūt, xviii, p. 42. His *Kitāb al-Tawḥīd wa ithbāt ṣifāt al-Rabb*, Cairo 1937; ed. M. Khalīl Harrās, Beirut 1978[2] (1968[1]); *Ṣaḥīḥ Ibn Khuzayma*, i–iv, ed. M. Muṣṭafā al-Aʿẓamī, Beirut-Damascus, al-Maktab al-islāmī, 1970–1979. This ed. is based on a single incomplete manuscript. This work is an abridgment of the author's great *Musnad*.

[64] Yāqūt, xviii, p. 56, pp. 52–53; TB, xi, pp. 431–433; *Tadhkira*, pp. 756–757; he was addicted to strong liquor, *kāna yashrabu l-muskira*. For al-Ṭirimmāḥ: GAS, ii, pp. 351–352; *Tāj*, vi, p. 351 [= al-Zabīdī, *Tāj al-ʿarūs*, Kuwait edition].

VII Other masters of al-Ṭabarī

We refer under this heading to twenty individuals mentioned by al-Dhahabī, though it is not always possible to know where al-Ṭabarī received their instruction. What is certain, is that he met none of them in Egypt.

M48 Abū Sahl ʿAbda b. ʿAbdallāh al-Khuzāʿī al-Baṣrī al-Ṣaffār [**230**] (d. 257/870 or in 258, in Baṣra or al-Ahwāz). Al-Ṭabarī transmitted few of his traditions.[65]

M49 ʿAbd al-Ḥamīd b. Bayān al-Sukkarī al-Wāsiṭī al-Qannād (d. 244/858). Al-Ṭabarī transmitted few of his traditions.[66]

M50 Abū l-Ashʿab Aḥmad b. al-Miqdām b. Sulaymān al-ʿIjlī al-Baṣrī (d. 253/867). Al-Ṭabarī must have attended his classes in Baṣra, but he retained few of his traditions in the works which have survived. The fact that this traditionist lectured in comical style to the jocular types who abounded in Baṣra (*kāna yuʿallimu l-mujūn*) does not prevent him being considered worthy of confidence; only Abū Dāwūd refused to transmit his traditions.[67]

M51 Abū Ḥafṣ ʿAmr b. ʿAlī b. Baḥr al-Bāhilī al-Baṣrī al-Ṣayrafī al-Fallās (d. 249/863) is one of the authorities used by the authors of six books. Al-Ṭabarī attended his classes in Baṣra or in Baghdad. He has already been mentioned above (M14).[68]

M52 Abū ʿAlī al-Ḥasan b. ʿArafa b. Yazīd al-ʿAbdī al-Baghdādī al-muʾaddib (d. 257/870). Al-Ṭabarī attended his lessons in Baghdad. He was born in 150/767, the year of the birth of al-Shāfiʿī and died in Sāmarrāʾ. His longevity is underlined in symbolic fashion: he would have died at 110 years old and would have had ten sons, giving each of them the name of one of the Ten (to whom Muhammad promised Paradise).[69]

---

[65] TT, vi, pp. 460–61; *Jarḥ*, vi, p. 90, n° 362: *History*, x (index), p. 326; TA/U, Tr. 102, 182. M48 to M66 are mentioned among the masters of al-Ṭabarī in SAN, xiv, pp. 268–69.

[66] TT, vi, p. 11; al-Dhahabī, *al-ʿIbar fī khabar man ghabar*, ed. Abū Hājir M. al-Saʿīd b. Basyūnī Zaghlūl, Beirut, Dār al-kutub al-ʿilmiyya, 1985[1], p. 348. ʿAbd al-Ḥamīd is mentioned four times in the index of *History*, twice in TA/U.

[67] Cf. also supra: M11 and note 16; TB, v, pp. 162–66; SAN, xii, pp. 219–21: in the two works the episode of the "drawn purse" game is related. Cf. the traditions relayed in TA/U, Tr. 333, 463.

[68] TB, xii, pp. 207–212; SAN, xi, pp. 470–72; TA/U, thirteen times, Tr. 677, 768, 855, 1223, etc… *History*, x (index), p. 354, eight times. Cf. *supra* M14 and note 19.

[69] al-Ḥasan b.ʿArafa: GAS. i, p. 134; TB, vii, pp. 394–96; SAN, xi, pp. 547–51; *History*, i, p. 11, 188, 260; TA/U: six times.

[231] M53 Abū l-Qāsim Hārūn b. Isḥāq al-Hamdānī al-Kūfī al-muʿammar would also have died as a centenarian. He was born around 160/776 and died in 258/871. Al-Ṭabarī quoted few of his traditions.[70]

M54 Abū ʿAlī al-Ḥasan b. al-Ṣabbāḥ al-Wāsiṭī al-Baghdādī al-Bazzār (d. 249/863). This traditionist whom al-Ṭabarī seldom mentions was summoned on two occasions before al-Maʾmūn; he was accused, among other things, of insulting the memory of ʿAlī.[71]

M55 Abū ʿAmmār al-Ḥusayn b. Ḥurayth al-Khuzāʿī l-Marwazī (d. 244/858) has left few traces in the works of al-Ṭabarī.[72]

M56 Ibrāhīm b. Saʿīd al-Jawharī al-Baghdādī (d. 247/861 or 244, or 249), originally from Ṭabaristān, is the author of a major *Musnad*.[73]

M57 Abū ʿAlī Muḥammad b. ʿAbd Allāh b. Bazīʿ al-Baṣrī (d. 247/861).[74]

M58 Abū ʿAbd Allāh Muḥammad b. Maʿmar al-Qaysī al-Baṣrī al-Baḥrānī (d. after 250/864).[75]

M59 Muhannā b. Yaḥyā al-Shāmī (d. ?) has left very few traces in the works of al-Ṭabarī. He was one of the disciples of Ibn Ḥanbal.[76]

[232] M60 Mūsā b. Mujāhid Abū ʿAlī al-Khwārizmī (d. 244/858) lived in Baghdad.[77]

M61 Naṣr b. ʿAbd al-Raḥmān al-Awdī l-Kūfī al-Washshāʾ (d. 248/862).[78]

M61A Abū ʿAmr Naṣr b. ʿAlī al-Jahḍamī al-ṣaghīr al-Azdī al-Baṣrī (d. 250/864). The authors of six books transmitted traditions from him. Al-Mutawakkil had him flogged for having transmitted a tradition favourable to ʿAlī and to his family. He owed his survival to his friends who attested to his Sunnism.[79]

---

[70] Hārūn b. Isḥ: TT, xi, pp. 2–3; SAN, xii, pp. 126–27.

[71] al-Ḥasan b. al-Ṣabbāḥ: TB, vii, pp. 330–32; SAN, xii, pp. 192–95; TA/IA, once.

[72] al-Ḥusayn b. Ḥurayth: TB, vii, pp. 36–37; SAN, xi, pp. 400–1; TA/U, once. His name does not appear in the index of the *History*; eight times in TA/U.

[73] Ibrāhīm b. Saʿīd: TB, vi, pp. 93–96; SAN, xii, pp. 149–51, six times in the index of the *History*, eight times in TA/U.

[74] Muḥammad b. ʿAl: TT, ix, pp. 248–49; *History*, twice; TA/U, twelve times; TA/IA, twice.

[75] Muḥammad b. Maʿmar: TT, ix, pp. 466–67.

[76] See TB, xiii, 266–67; Ibn ʿAsākir, TD, li, 310–13; *Lisān al-mīzān*, vi, pp. 108–9; does not feature in the *History*; TA/U, once.

[77] Mūsā b. Mujāhid resided in Baghdad (*nazīl Baghdād*); SAN, xi, pp. 495–6. He features neither in the *History* nor in TA.

[78] Naṣr b. ʿAr.: TT, x, p. 428, which gives: al-Azdī; *History*, twice; TA/U, twice, TA/IA, four times.

[79] Naṣr b. ʿAlī: TB, xiii, pp. 287–89; SAN, xii, pp. 133–35. The tradition related before al-Mutawakkil is the following: "Who would love me, as well as these two children (i.e. Ḥasan and Ḥusayn) their father (i.e. ʿAlī) and their mother (i.e. Fāṭima) will be with me in my rank on the Day of Resurrection."

M62 Abū ʿUthmān Saʿīd b. ʿAmr al-Sakūnī al-Ḥimṣī (d. ca. 260/873).[80]
M63 Abū ʿUthmān Saʿīd b. Yaḥyā al-Umawī al-Baghdādī (d. 249/863).[81]
M64 Abū l-Faḍl Ṣāliḥ b. Mismār al-Marwazī al-Sulamī (al-Rāzī, according to some, d. 246/860).[82]
M65 Sawwār b. ʿAbd Allāh al-ʿAnbarī l-Tamīmī al-Baṣrī (d. 245/859).[83]
M66 Tamīm b. al-Muntaṣir al-Wāsiṭī (d. 244/858 or 240/854). [**233**] Al-Ṭabarī transmitted numerous traditions of his in his *Tahdhīb al-aṭhār*.[84]

This list, in itself, gives us little information regarding the education of al-Ṭabarī. It will be noted however, even if we have not drawn attention to it in every instance, that the authors of six books also transmitted the traditions of these masters, according to the expressions which recur in their biographical notices: *rawā ʿanhu aṣḥāb al-kutub al-sitta*, or more often: *rawā ʿanhu l-jamāʿa siwā...* Furthermore, almost all of them were also the masters of the disciple and friend of al-Ṭabarī, Ibn Khuzayma.

VIII Al-Ṭabarī the Baghdadian

In the survey of al-Ṭabarī's masters in Baghdad, no distinction has been made between his periods of residence in the capital. It could be considered that he installed himself there definitively after his return from Egypt, thus after 256. What is certain, is that he was there in 258/871. He revisited Ṭabaristān on two occasions, the second time in 290/902; on his return from this journey, we know that he stopped at Dīnawar.[85]

In Baghdad he was often in contact with leading functionaries of the dynasty, sometimes even with the caliph, whether the intention was to offer him material assistance, commission a report from him or ask him to perform a service. There were even occasions when an employee of the state attended his classes or was witness to one of the disputes which he had with his enemies, the Ḥanbalites in particular.

---

[80] See Dhahabī, *Taʾrīkh al-islām*, ed. B. ʿA. Maʿarūf, 17 vols., Beyrouth, 2003, vi, p. 337; TT, iv, pp. 67–68; he does not figure in the *History*; TA/U, twice; TA/IA, once.

[81] Saʿiḍ b. Yaḥyā: TT, iv, pp. 97–98; *History*, seven times; TA/U, three times.

[82] Ṣāliḥ b. Mismār: TT, iv, p. 403; *History*, once; TA/U, four times; TA/IA, three times.

[83] Sawwār b. ʿAbd Allāh: SAN, xi, pp. 543–45; *History*, ix. 189, 213; TA/IA, Tr. 42, 215, 503; TA/A, Tr. 154, 161.

[84] Tamīm: TT, i, pp. 514–15; *History*, i, seven times; TA/U, seventeen times; TA/IA, eight times.

[85] al-Ṭabarī in Ṭabaristān: Yāqūt, xviii, p. 56; *History*, iii1, 1862/ix, p. 492: in 258 in Baghdād.

From the time of his first contact with the capital of the empire, he made the acquaintance of al-Mutawakkil's vizier, Abū l-Ḥasan ʿUbayd Allāh b. Yaḥyā b. Khāqān (during his first vizierate: 236–247 850–861), in other words from his arrival in 241, or after his return from Kūfa in 243.[86] **[234]** Al-Ṭabarī had brought commodities which, sold in Baghdad, would have guaranteed him a reasonable standard of living, but bandits on the highway deprived him of them, and he found himself in the most abject poverty. He was introduced to the vizier who appointed him tutor to one of his sons, Abū Yaḥyā. For this work al-Ṭabarī refused all the gifts that were offered him in addition to the stipulated fees. The family of the vizier remained close to him and persisted in trying to offer him money on numerous occasions, without any more success. It was thus that Abū ʿAlī Muḥammad b.ʿUbayd Allāh, appointed vizier in his turn (299-301/911-913), in an attempt to persuade him to accept the ten thousand dirhams offered to him, was obliged to propose that they be shared with his companions.[87]

It was yet another vizier who was witness to his disputes with the Ḥanbalites, ʿAlī b. ʿĪsā b. al-Jarrāḥ.[88] The episode took place, according to Ibn al-Jawzī, in 309/921; ʿAlī b. ʿĪsā was no longer vizier but it was he, in fact, who still took the important decisions under the vizierate of Ḥamīd b. al-ʿAbbās (309–311). Al-Ṭabarī presented himself at the palace of ʿAlī b. ʿĪsā for a debate with the Ḥanbalites, but they did not reply to the invitation. It was the same vizier who had a doctor sent to him some time before his death.

Al-Ṭabarī was equally adamant in refusing fees and honours. When al-Khāqānī[89] (ʿUbayd Allāh, at the time of his second vizierate, in 256/869, or his son Muḥammad in 299/911?) succeeded to the vizierate, he sent a substantial sum of money to al-Ṭabarī; the latter sent it back. He then offered him the opportunity to supervise the *qaḍāʾ* or criminal affairs (*al-maẓālim*), but al-Ṭabarī refused both these propositions.

The high esteem which these individuals accorded to al-Ṭabarī is also illustrated by numerous instances in which they sought instruction from him or looked to his knowledge for justification. Thus the caliph al-Muktafī (289–295/902–908), wanting to establish a pious foundation on judicial principles which would be accepted unanimously by scholars, instructed al-ʿAbbās b. al-Ḥasan (= al-Jarjarāʾī), his vizier, to summon Abū Jaʿfar. The

[86] Ibn ʿAsākir, in De Goeje, *Introductio*, p. lxxv/ Latin text, p.11. On ʿUbayd Allāh: Sourdel, *Vizirat*, pp. 274–286, 305–309.

[87] Yāqūt, xviii, pp. 87–88. For M. b.ʿUbayd Allāh: *Vizirat*, *op. cit.*, pp. 394–399.

[88] According to Ibn al-Jawzī, in De Goeje, *Introductio* [= Muntaẓam, vi, p. 159], p. xcviii. For the role of ʿAlī b. ʿĪsā under the vizierate of Ḥamīd b. al-ʿAbbās: *Vizirat*, pp. 414–424; H. Bowen, in EI, i, pp. 397–399. For the sickness episode: Yāqūt, xviii, p. 94.

[89] Ibn ʿAsākir, in De Goeje, *Introductio*, p. lxxxv.

latter dictated [**235**] a report on this subject, in the presence of the caliph, and refused the reward which he was offered. Since it would have been inappropriate to refuse the caliph's largesse and leave empty-handed, he made a request to which the caliph responded favourably: henceforward the police prevented access to the *maqṣūra* before the end of the sermon.[90]

As for the vizier al-Faḍl b. Jaʿfar b. Furāt, he had occasion to attend the classes of al-Ṭabarī. One day, he came to hear him in his circle; Abū Jaʿfar asked a man to read a text but he, on account of the presence of the vizier, declined to do so (the vizier was regarded as taking precedence in this respect). Al-Ṭabarī said to him: "If it is your turn, you should pay no attention either to the Tigris or to the Euphrates (*al-Furāt*)".[91]

Furthermore it was al-ʿAbbās b. al-Ḥasan who asked him to compose for his use a compendium of his *madhhab*, to which al-Ṭabarī gave the title of: *al-Khafīf fī l-fiqh* or *al-Khafīf fī aḥkām sharāʾiʿ al-Islām*.[92]

Finally, Abū Bakr Aḥmad b. Kāmil (d. 350/961), a disciple of al-Ṭabarī and *Qāḍī* of Kūfa, has preserved for us an exchange of verses between Aḥmad b. ʿĪsā al-ʿAlawī and al-Ṭabarī on the question of authorities worthy of confidence.[93]

This fragmentary picture, drawn from the vicissitudes of transmission, from al-Ṭabarī's contacts with certain of the greatest individuals of the time, shows that his help was sought by the major institutions of the dynasty, even that he was courted. This is only one example among many of the interworking between the machinery of power and the various clerical processes.

The biographical notices are interested primarily in the direct masters and [**236**] in particular those whose lessons in *ḥadīth* and in Qurʾānic readings, supplemented by grammar and poetry, were attended by scholars. They pay little attention to their indirect education. We can nevertheless form an idea of it on the basis of reported anecdotes or of the deductions that we can make.

---

[90] *Ibid.*, p. lxxvi; Subkī, iii (Cairo 1965), p. 24. For al-ʿAbbās b. al-Ḥasan: *Vizirat*, pp. 360–368.

[91] Ibn ʿAsākir, in De Goeje, *Introductio*, p. lxxxvi, p. vii. The episode took place before al-Faḍl became vizier. He acceded to the vizierate in 320.

[92] Ibn ʿAsākir, *ibid.*, p.lxxvi; Subkī, ii (1965), p. 124. For al-ʿAbbās: *Vizirat*, p. 359ss.

[93] Yāqūt, xviii, p. 43. He has been putatively identified with Aḥmad b. ʿĪsā b. Zayd, the Shiʿite leader and scholar, but he died in 247/861; cf. W. Madelung, in EI^2, Suppl., pp. 48–49 (here: French edn.). Ṣalāḥ al-dīn al-Munajjid confuses him with Aḥmad b. ʿĪsā b. ʿAlī b. Ḥusayn al-Ṣaghīr (according to *Bidāya*, xi, p. 6) in his edition of al-Dhahabī, *Asmāʾ alladhīna ramaw l-khilāfa*, Beirut 1982, p. 13, note 18. We believe it is likely to be the above-mentioned Aḥmad b. ʿĪsā b. ʿAlī b. Ḥusayn al-Ṣaghīr. We may discount the possibility that this could be Aḥmad b. ʿĪsā b. M. al-Muhājir, too young in the lifetime of al-Tabarī, he died, in fact, in 354/956: cf. O. Löfgren, in EI, i, p. 278.

IX Indirect Education

This picture of the education of al-Ṭabarī remains very incomplete. On the one hand, biographical notices concentrate essentially on direct education, that which he received from teachers with whom he was in a disciple to master relationship. Even in this domain, the list is partial since it is limited to those from whom he collected traditions (*ḥadīth*, exegetical and historiographical traditions, Qurʾānic readings, etc.). In view of these data, on the whole quite material, it could be concluded that our author had an education without manifest intellectual confrontations. This would be doing an injustice to what is perhaps the most profound reality of all education, i.e. indirect education. In ancient societies in particular, children and adolescents are mainly socialised by family and community structures. Education begins within the family circle, but it is also pursued through the influences which the individual experiences, under the effects of the meetings, readings, debates and controversies which animate the lives of the groups which surround him. This evidently includes a movement of circulation of ideas which come to him outside the channels of direct education.[94]

Of al-Ṭabarī's childhood, we know virtually nothing. However an anecdote reported by the *Qāḍī* Abū Bakr Ibn Kāmil shows that his father was intent on making a sage of him at a very early age. [**237**] Al-Ṭabarī declares: "At seven years old, I knew the Qurʾān by heart; I led the prayers (*ṣallaytu bi-l-nāsi*) at eight years old; I received instruction on *ḥadīth* under the mode of writing (*katabtu l-ḥadītha*) at nine years old. My father saw me in a dream; I was before the Messenger of God and I had a sack filled with stones and I threw them towards him. The interpreter of dreams told him that when I am grown up, I shall be a faithful counsellor in my religion and I shall defend its Law. My father therefore sought to help me acquire knowledge, although I was only a very young child."[95] This anecdote, which has all the appearance of a formulaic trope of the kind found in the "childhoods" of many a Companion, of numerous pious and scholarly men, rests, there can be no doubt, on a basis of historical veracity: the precocity of al-Ṭabarī in the acquisition of the fundamental elements necessary for the education of a Muslim scholar at this

[94] On the distinction between direct and indirect education, cf. M. Arkoun, *Contribution a l'étude de l'humanisme arabe au IVe/Xe siècle, Miskawayh philosophe et historien*, Paris 1970, pp. 57–80. On this subject, reference may be made to the pioneering book of Ph. Aries, *L'enfant et la vie familiale de l'Ancien Régime*, Paris 1960; D. Julia, "Education" in A. Burguière, *Dictionnaire des sciences historiques*, Paris 1986, p. 233; J. Revel "Education" in J. Le Goff (under the direction of), *La nouvelle Histoire*, Paris 1978, pp. 157–158.

[95] Yāqūt, xviii, p. 49; for the *topos*, cf. Cl. Gilliot, "Portrait 'mythique' d'Ibn ʿAbbās", *Arabica*, xxx (1983), pp. 145–146, 180–181.

time. Al-Ṭabarī could have acquired the prodigious knowledge which he is known to have had of prophetic traditions and of the criticism of traditions except by means of early training of the memory. We have no reason to doubt that his father, whether he had a dream or not, induced him to study. This insistence on the Qurʾān and on *ḥadīth*, from his early childhood, marked him for life.

We have also seen that al-Ṭabarī achieved renown in the study of poetry and of metrics, having studied *al-Shiʿr wa l-shuʿarāʾ* under the direction of Thaʿlab.[96]

However he was not initiated into all branches of knowledge by masters. He also acquired basic knowledge through the solitary study of specialised works. This is what is indicated by the following anecdote which, although not devoid of the kind of hyperbole typical of scholars intent on showing their pupils that only determined work is profitable, is nevertheless instructive about a kind of indirect education through books. One day when he was in Egypt, someone asked him a question on the subject of metrics, an area in which he had little expertise at that time. Al-Ṭabarī deferred his answer [**238**] to the following day and borrowed from a friend a book of Khalīl Ibn Aḥmad: "I spent, he said, the night studying, and thus, although I was not a metrician in the evening, I became one by the morning."[97]

Whole sections of this education remain obscure because they are not illustrated through the channels normally used by biographical notices when the subject is the education of a scholar of religious sciences of al-Ṭabarī's stature. This is the case in particular with branches of knowledge which are not directly religious, not historiographical and not literary or poetic. We are thinking most of all of logic, philosophy, cosmology and the natural sciences. An episode which we have mentioned elsewhere suggests that al-Ṭabarī did not live outside certain philosophical currents which flourished in his native region and in the caliphal capital, even if his work shows few echoes of them. One evening, the *Qāḍī* Abū Bakr Ibn Kāmil came to pay him a visit, and he noticed under his oratory the Paradise of Wisdom (*Firdaws al-ḥikma*) by ʿAlī b. Sahl Rabban al-Ṭabarī (d. after 240/855), one of the first medical compendia written in Arabic. When Ibn Kāmil wanted to reach out and take it, al-Ṭabarī had it taken away by a servant. This work bore a certificate of audition by ʿAlī b. Sahl. It is known that the latter completed it in 238/850, and thus al-Ṭabarī must have attended the lessons of the master, although he was only sixteen

[96] Yāqūt, xviii, p. 60. The reference is probably to *Muʿjam al-shuʿarāʾ*, cf. GAS, ii, p. 95, no 46; Thaʿlab also had a *Kitāb Maʿānī l-shiʿr*, GAS, ii, p. 59, n° 20 and a *Kitāb Qawāʿid al-shiʿr* which has been edited, GAS, ii, p. 10 and 105, n° 5.

[97] Yāqūt, xviii, p. 56.

years old.[98] Ibn Kāmil also associates al-Ṭabarī's good table manners and his culinary and dietary practices with the work of this doctor, probably of Christian origin who did not [**239**] convert to Islam until late in life and at the insistence of al-Mutawakkil. Abū Ja'far himself possessed medical knowledge, and he had occasion to prescribe remedies to the sick.

This insistence of Ibn Kāmil on the profound knowledge which al-Ṭabarī had of the *Firdaws al-ḥikma* and the fact that its author had been his master suggests to us that he also lived in a milieu of sages by virtue of whom he was subjected to diverse philosophical and cultural influences. It is known in fact that 'Ali b. Sahl was versed in Indian medicine, that he had been in the service of Māziyar b. Qārin, prince of Ṭabaristān, who had returned to the Mazdakian faith. It was in Rayy, the second city in which al-Ṭabarī studied, that Abū Bakr Muḥammad Ibn Zakariyyā al-Rāzī was born, in 251/865. Certain sources make him a disciple of 'Alī b. Sahl al-Ṭabarī, which is chronologically impossible.[99] But what is important for us to note, is that there was in Rayy a milieu propitious to the study of ancient philosophy and wisdom. Ibn Jarīr must at least have been familiar with the fringes of it during his adolescence.

In Baghdad, similarly, al-Ṭabarī cannot have remained in ignorance of certain philosophical debates. We may recall that al-Kindī was the tutor of Aḥmad, the son of al-Mu'taṣim (reg. 218–227). He enjoyed great prestige in the

[98] Yāqūt, xviii, p. 49, 92. For 'Alī b. Sahl Rabban al-Ṭabarī, cf. al-Qifṭī, *Kitāb Ikhbār al-'ulamā' bi-akhbār al-ḥukamā'*, ed. M.Amīn al-Khanjī, Cairo 1326/1909; repr., Beirut, undated, p. 155; KAHH, vii, 156a; GAL, i, p. 231, SI, pp. 414–415. His *Firdaws al-ḥikma* was edited in 1928 in Berlin by M.Z. Ṣiddiqī, cf. M. Ullman, *Die Natur- und Geheimwissenschaften im Islam*, Leiden 1972, p. 82, 406ss; GAS, iii, pp. 236–240. For his apologetic and polemical output, references will be found in R. Caspar, et alii, *Bibliographie du dialogue islamo-chrétien* in *Islamo-christiana*, I (1975), pp. 144–145, no 11–10. The translation made by A. Mingana of his *K. al-Dīn wa l-dawla*, under the title: *The Book of Religion and Empire*, Manchester 1922, has been reprinted in New Delhi, Kitab Bhavan, 1986, vii+174p. The best inquiry into the name and the controversial origins of 'Alī b. Sahl Rabban al-Ṭabarī is that of Ṣiddīqī, pp. 4–9 of the introduction to his edition of the *Firdaws al-ḥikma*. According to 'Alī b. Sahl himself, his father received the title of Rabban on account of his great wisdom. Thus there is no need to see here a Jewish or Christian religious title. Cf. *Firdaws al-ḥikma*, p. 1, l. 15, and introduction, p. 6.

[99] For Abū Bakr al-Rāzī, an exhaustive bibliography will be found in 'Abd al-Raḥmān Badawī, *Histoire de la philosophie en Islam*, Paris 1972, ii, pp. 578–594, especially p. 594, n. 1. Following al-Qifṭī and Ibn a. Uṣaybi'a, this author makes Abū Bakr a disciple of 'Alī b. Sahl Rabban al-Ṭabarī; for chronological reasons, we prefer to adopt the opinion of P. Kraus, in EI[1], iii, 1213a, 2nd para. This does not mean that Abū Bakr could not have fallen under the influence of Rabban, cf S. Pines, *Beitrage zur islamischen Atomenlehre*, Berlin 1936, p. 43, 45, notes. This study remains an excellent presentation of the thought of al-Rāzī, from which Badawī seems to have borrowed extensively. See also 'A. Badawī, *Min Ta'rīkh al-ilḥād fī islām*, Cairo 1945; Beirut 19802, pp. 163–186; 'A. Badawī in M.M. Sharif, *A History of Muslim Philosophy*, Wiesbaden 1963, i, pp. 434–449.

caliphal court until there was a conspiracy against him under al-Mutawakkil (232–247/847–861). He died probably in 256/870, when al-Ṭabarī was thirty-two years old.[100] A celebrated disciple of al-Kindī, Abū l-ʿAbbās Aḥmad b. M. b. Marwān al-Sarakhsī (Aḥmad al-Ṭayyib, d. 286/899), tutor of al-Muʿtaḍid (279–289/892–902), [**240**] then his close confidant, until the latter had him put to death, had formulated criticisms against the necessity of prophecy, just like Abū Bakr al-Rāzī.[101] Even if al-Ṭabarī did not necessarily belong to these philosophical circles, he was a witness to these debates. All of this also contributed, if only in terms of reaction, to the elaboration of his intellectual personality. We have spoken elsewhere of the *Kitāb Ādāb al-nufūs* of al-Ṭabarī;[102] the description of it does not indicate any direct influence from the *De Anima* of Aristotle. Nevertheless the intellectual milieu of Baghdad in the period of al-Ṭabarī articulated theories and ideas of Greek influence, especially in the domain of ethics and moral philosophy. Al-Kindī, in particular, wrote a *Risāla fī l-qawl fī l-nafs al-mukhtaṣar min kitāb Arisṭū wa Flāṭin wa sāʾir al-falāsifa*. His disciple, al-Sarakhsī, had a *Kitāb al-Nafs*, probably modelled on its Aristotelian counterpart. Al-Ṭabarī, disciple of Ibn Rabban and assiduous reader of the *Firdaws al-ḥikma*, cannot have been indifferent to these trends, even if they did not correspond to his primary interests as a traditionist.[103]

In this society, the "indirect channels" of knowledge, in other words those following routes other than the ones recognised by the science of transmission (*ʿilm al-riwāya*), were no less important than the "direct channels", but the knowledge that we have of them is only partial, and is only available to us, in general, in the form of anecdotes, the interpretation of which in most cases is nothing more than hypothetical.

---

[100] On al-Kindī, cf. Badawī, *Histoire*, II, p. 385sqq; A.F. El-Ehwany, "Al-Kindi" in M.M. Sharif, *op. cit.*, i, pp. 421–434, is barely interested except in the Islamic religious aspect of his work.

[101] On al-Sarakhsī, cf. Badawī, *op. cit.*, ii, 394–395; Yāqūt, iii, pp. 98–102, and other refs. in KAHH, ii, 157a–b. The episode of the disgrace of al-Sarakhsī is translated in Fr. Rosenthal, *Aḥmad b. aṭ-Ṭayyib as-Sarakhsī*, New Haven, Connecticut, AOS, 1943, pp. 28–31; on the basis of the *Muntaẓam*. This study remains the fundamental reference for the personality and thought of al-Sarakhsī against the necessity of prophecy: van Ess, *Erkenntnislehre*, p. 328.

[102] On this work, cf. Gilliot, *Aspects*, pp. 68–72; Id., *Les oeuvres de Tabari*, in MIDEO, 19 (1989), pp. 61–63 ; Id., *Exégèse*, pp. 51–54.

[103] For the *Risāla* of al-Kindī: Badawī, *Histoire*, ii, p. 389, no 8, with references to the edition and Italian translation of G. Furlani. On the *De Anima* and *L'Ethique a Nicomaque* in Arab circles: ʿA. Badawī, *La transmission de la philosophie grecque au monde arabe*, Paris 1968, p. 80 and 83. For the work of al-Sarakhsī: Ibn a.Uṣaybiʿa, *ʿUyūn al-anbāʾ fī ṭabaqāt al-aṭibbāʾ*, ed. N. Riḍā, Beirut 1965, p. 294; Fr. Rosenthal, op. cit., p., nº 7.

This sketch of the influences experienced by al-Ṭabarī and of his indirect education [**241**] will be completed in a study which we shall devote to his attitude towards "sectarian" groups.[104]

If we follow the gallery of portraits of the direct masters of al-Ṭabarī as painted by the biographical notices, it is suggested to us, in the final analysis, that the message of Muḥammad and the Companions has been faithfully transmitted by masters to disciples from generation to generation. From this point of view, the education of al-Ṭabarī is exemplary for the group. In fact, one of the essential functions of the lists of authorities and works of onomastics is to entrench the group in one of its fundamental ideologies which is the uninterrupted and faithful transmission of the stock of revelation which includes the revealed Law (*al-sharʿ*) and the prophetic traditions.

As for indirect education, that which does not pass through the channels which have become traditional, in particular from the third century onward, it is illustrated only from the angle of anecdotes or of various episodes. The "profane wisdom": philosophy, natural sciences, etc... is left in shadow, although it exercised a real influence, especially over the milieu of Baghdad. Moreover, it is excluded. The same apparently applies to *kalām*, which had an influence on al-Ṭabarī as we shall show elsewhere.[105] It was also the role of the *kutub al-rijāl* to disseminate a certain image of the intellectual milieu of their period, not only through what they say but also through that which they pass over in silence. With this "classical" picture, we could contrast the misfortunes of Aḥmad b. al-Ṭayyib al-Sarakhsī (d. 286/899) of whom we are told that his knowledge (*ʿilm*) was greater than his intelligence (*ʿaql*), an expression customarily applied to heretics.[106] The knowledge of al-Ṭabarī, on the other hand was conveyed through the received channels, or at least this is the view that we are persuaded to take.

Alphabetical list of al-Tabari's masters

[Since the publication of this article in French three indexes of the authorities of Ṭabarī have been published: Fālūjī, Badrī M., *al-Muʿjam al-ṣaghīr li-ruwāt al-imām Ibn Jarīr al-Ṭabarī*, 2 vols., Amman, al-Dār al-athāriyya, 2005; Ḥallāq, Ṣubḥī b. Hasan, *Rijāl al-Ṭabarī jarḥan wa taʿdīlan min taḥqīq Jāmiʿ al-bayān ʿan taʾwīl āy al-Qurʾan*, Beirut, Dār Ibn Ḥazm, 1999; Saqqāf, ʿAlawī, *Rijāl Tafsīr*

---

104 Cf. now Gilliot, *Aspects*, chap. viii, pp. 322–418; [Id., *Exégèse*, pp. 207–278].
105 *Ibid.*
106 Fr. Rosenthal, *op. cit.*, p.33.

Imām al-muffassirīn Ibn Jarīr al-Ṭabarī llaḏīn tarjama lahum A. wa Maḥmūd Shākir, Riyad, Dār al Hiğra, 1991.]

(The 'M' numbers give the order in which the names are listed in the text. Numbers in square brackets refer to the pagination of the original article.)

ʿAbbād b Yaʿqūb	M19	[214]
al-ʿAbbās b. al-Walīd al-Bayrūtī	M44	[225]
ʿAbda b. ʿAbd Allāh al-Khuzāʿī	M48	[229]
ʿAbd al-Aʿlā b. Wāṣil	M20	[215]
ʿAbd al-Ḥamīd b. Bayān al-Sukkarī	M4	[230]
Abū Kurayb	M16	[214]
Abū Zurʿa al-Rāzī	M4	[207]
Aḥmad b. Ḥammād al-Dūlābī	M3	[206]
Aḥmad b. a. Khaythama	M35	[220]
Aḥmad b. Manīʿ al-Baghawī	M29	[218]
Aḥmad b. al-Miqdām al-ʿIjlī l-Baṣrī	M11	[210]
Ditto	M50	[230]
Aḥmad b. Thābit al-RāzĪ	M6	[208]
Aḥmad b. Yūsuf al-Taghlibī	M33	[220]
ʿAlī b. Dāwūd al-Qanṭarī	M36	[221]
ʿAlī b. Sahl al-Ramlī	M43	[225]
ʿAmr b. ʿAlī l-Fallās	M14	[211]
Ditto	M51	[230]
Bishr b. Muʿādh al-ʿAqadī	M10	[210]
Hannād b. Sarī	M17	[214]
al-Ḥārith b. Muḥammad al-Tamīmī	M37	[221]
Hārūn b. Isḥāq al-Hamdānī	M53	[231]
al-Ḥasan b. ʿArafa	M52	[230]
al-Ḥasan b. Muḥammad al-Zaʿfarānī	M25	[216]
al-Ḥasan b. Qazʿa	M15	[211]
al-Ḥasan b. al-Ṣabbāḥ al-Bazzāz	M54	[231]
al-Ḥasan b. Yaḥyā l-Jurjānī	M38	[221]
Ḥusayn b. Ḥurayth	M55	[231]
Ibrāhīm b. Saʿīd al-Jawharī	M56	[231]
Ibrāhīm b. Yaʿkūb al-Juzajānī	M42	[224]
ʿImrān b. Mūsā l-Qazzāz	M8	[209]
Isḥāq b. Isrāʾīl al-Marwazī	M28	[218]
Ismāʿīl b. Mūsā l-Fazārī	M18	[214]
Muḥammad b. ʿAbd al-Aʿlā l-Ṣanʿanī	M9	[210]

Muḥammad b. ʿAbd Allāh b. Bazīʿ	M57	[231]
Muḥammad b. ʿAlī l-Marwazī	M26	[217]
Muḥammad b. ʿAmr al-Bāhilī	M39	[221]
Muḥammad b. Bashshār Bundār	M12	[210]
Muḥammad b. Ḥumayd al-Rāzī	M2	[206]
Muḥammad b. Maʿmar al-Qaysī	M58	[231]
Muḥammad b. a. Maʿshar Najīḥ	M34	[220]
Muḥammad b. Muqātil al-Rāzī	M5	[208]
Muḥammad b. Mūsā l-Ḥarashī	M7	[209]
Muḥammad b. al-Muthannaʾ l-Zamin	M13	[211]
Muḥammad b. Saʿd al-ʿAwfī	M40	[221]
Muhannā b. Yaḥyā al-Sāmī	M59	[231]
Mūsā b. Mujāhid al-Khawārizmī	M60	[232]
al-Muthannā b. Ibrāhīm al-Āmuli	M1	[205]
Naṣr b. ʿAbd al-Raḥmān al-Awdī	M61	[232]
Naṣr b ʿAlī l-Jahḍam* l-saghīr	M61a	[232]
al-Qāsim b. al-Ḥasan	M41	[222]
al-Rabīʿ b. Sulaymān al-Murādī	M45	[227]
Saʿīd b. ʿAmr al-Sakūnī	M62	[232]
Saʿīd b. Yaḥyā l-Umawī	M63	[233]
Ṣāliḥ b. Mismār al-Marwazī	M64	[232]
Sawwār b. ʿAbd Allāh al-ʿAnbarī	M65	[232]
Sufyān b. Wakīʿ al-Ruʾāsī	M24	[216]
Sulaymān b. ʿAbd al-Jabbār al-Khayyāṭ	M32	[229]
Sulaymān b. ʿAbd al-Raḥmān al-Ṭalḥī	M23	[215]
Tamīm b. al-Muntaṣir al-Wāsiṭī	M66	[232]
ʿUbayd b. Ismāʿīl al-Habbārī	M21	[215]
al-Walīd b. Shujāʿ al-Sakūnī	M22	[215]
Yaʿqūb b. Ibrāhīm al-Dawraqī	M30	[218]
Yūnus b. ʿAbd al-Aʿlā l-Miṣrī	M46	[227]
al-Zubayr b. Bakkār	M31	[219]

8
THE HUMAN ELEMENT BETWEEN TEXT AND READER: THE *IJĀZA* IN ARABIC MANUSCRIPTS

Jan Just Witkam

The *ijāza* is the certificate of reading or hearing which is sometimes written on manuscripts, usually near the colophon or on the title page. It confers upon the recipient the right to transmit a text, or to teach, or to issue legal opinions. It also bears witness to attendance at a reading session. The *ijāzat al-tadrīs*, the licence to teach, and the *ijāzat al-samā'*, the certificate of attendance at a reading session and hence the licence to transmit the text read, should not be confused. Our attention here will be focused on the *ijāzat al-samā'*, the protocols of reading sessions which were often added to a text, as these in particular provide us with ample information on the human element in the transmission of texts.

The *ijāza* is a conspicuous feature of Arabic manuscripts and it illustrates how a text functions in an educational, scientific or cultural environment. Studying *ijāzas* increases our knowledge of the human element in the use of texts and manuscripts. For a better understanding of the *ijāza* it is also important also to be aware of the individual and personal element in the transmission of Muslim scholarship: we, therefore, deal with this subject briefly in the following section. Finally, we suggest a proposal for collecting and analysing *ijāzāt al-samā'* in Arabic manuscripts.[1]

---

[1] There is no monograph devoted to the *ijāza*, nor is there a published corpus of texts. Some useful sources which provide a wealth of material on the subject are: 'Abd Allāh Fayyāḍ, *al-Ijāzāt al-'ilmiyya 'inda al-muslimīn* (Baghdad, 1967) (with emphasis on the Shi'a); P.A. MacKay, *Certificates of Transmission on a Manuscript of the* Maqāmāt *of Ḥarīrī, MS.* Cairo, Adab 105, Transactions of the American Philosophical Society, New Series, LXI/4

Personal approach and continuity in Islamic scholarship

It has often been stated that in Islam there is no hierarchic structure comparable with the church-like organisation of the Christians. Strictly speaking, this is true. Islam does not have an infallible pope nor does it have a clergy with an intricately differentiated hierarchic structure who claim to occupy a position between God and the believer and dispense sacraments and pretend to possess the monopoly of doctrine. This does not, of course, mean that clerical organisation is totally lacking in Islam. It is only that the dynamics of continuity — since organisation produces continuity — in Islam have developed in a different way. In Islam no intermediary between God and man is necessary. And just as a Muslim's relationship with God is direct and personal, so too is a man's way of procuring religious knowledge. In Islam it is the personal relationship between teacher and pupil that, through the generations of scholars, has produced a powerful driving force that ensures a continuity of its own.

Several genres of Islamic literature have developed in the course of time, which reflect this individual and personal attitude. It started very early indeed, with the emergence of Islamic tradition, *ḥadīth.* As important as the content of the Tradition is the chain of authorities, the *isnād*, which precedes each tradition. The early collections are even organised not according to subject matter but to their authorities, and hence referred to by the name *Musnad.* Half of Islamic Tradition is *'ilm al-rijāl*, the "knowledge of the transmitters". Only an authentic chain of trustworthy authorities validates the text of a *ḥadīth.* Without it a *ḥadīth* is suspended in space and is incomplete — at least that is the

---

(Philadelphia, 1971); Ṣalāḥ al-Dīn al-Munajjid, "Ijāzāt al-samā' fī al-makhṭūṭāt al-qadīma", *Majallat Ma'had al-Makhṭūṭāt al-'Arabiyya (MMMA),* I (1375/1955), 232-51; J. Pedersen, *The Arabic Book* (Princeton, 1984), esp. 31-4; Qāsim Aḥmad al-Sāmarrā'ī, "Al-ijāza wa-taṭawwuruhā al-tārīkhī", *'Ālam al-Kutub,* II (1981), 278-85. Many illustrations of *ijāzāt* are found in A. J. Arberry, *A Handlist of the Arabic Manuscripts of the Chester Beatty Library* (8 vols., Dublin, 1955-66). The use of the *ijāza* in the Islamic educational system has been treated by George Makdisi, *The Rise of Colleges. Institutions of Learning in Islam and the West* (Edinburgh, 1981), while Georges Vajda, *Les certificats de lecture et de transmission dans les manuscrits arabes de la Bibliothèque Nationale de Paris* (Paris, 1956), gives an analysis of the contents of a great number of *ijāzāt* in 72 manuscripts. I also wish to thank Léon Buskens for putting at my disposal a number of published *ijāzāt* or *ijāza*-related texts from his private library.

opinion of the early Muslim scholars. For practical reasons these Tradition texts and chains of authorities were written down, but, according to the old ideals, religious knowledge was best disseminated orally. The *isnads* can thus be read as protocols of successive instances and sessions in which learning was transmitted. The written form of *ḥadīth* is thus but one dimension of the Tradition: the human factor in the transmission and continuity of knowledge is as important as the recorded message itself . The saying that "knowledge is in the breasts [of men], not in the lines [of books]" (*al-ʿilm fī al-ṣudūr lā fī al-suṭūr*) aptly summarises this idea.[2]

The rapid expansion of Islam and the enormous diversification of the different disciplines of learning made it impossible to maintain oral transmission as the only vehicle for passing on knowledge. The Word of God, the divine revelation, had to be written down, since the early carriers of the Holy Word died on the battlefields of the expansion wars. At a later stage, historical and Tradition texts were written down as well, initially in all sorts of personal notebooks[3] of transmitters, later in more organised collections that were intended for a wider audience. Though, in the end, books became accepted as the ordinary medium, the individual and personal approach nevertheless remained intact. Just reading a book in order to grasp its contents, as we do nowadays, was not enough. In the classical period, it was thought, a book should be read with a teacher, preferably the author himself, or else it should be studied with an authoritative and respected professor. Reading, or rather studying, was not a solitary affair. It was also a social event, as we shall see.

Biographical literature emerged in Islam as one of the consequences of this individual and personal approach. The genre was not new around the Mediterranean. In classical antiquity biographical literature such as the "Parallel Lives" of Plutarch served historical, didactic, moralistic and sometimes ideological purposes. Some of the Islamic biographical literature had a similar purpose but there was an extra dimension. The "science of men", or *ʿilm al-rijāl*, developed into a critical method

2 See Ibn al-Akfānī, *Irshād al-qāṣid ilā asnā al-maqāṣid*, ed. J. J. Witkam (Leiden, 1989), 446, no. 191.

3 For their use, and the distrust they evoked, see al-Balkhī (d. ca. 319/913), *Kitāb Qabūl al-akhbār wa-maʿrifat al-rijāl*, MS Cairo, Dār al-Kutub al-Miṣriyya, *Muṣṭalaḥ* 14M, *passim*. An edition of this text by myself is in an advanced stage of preparation.

for the assessment of scholarly authority. Many biographical works were concerned with describing networks of scholarship and chains of transmission. A clear example of this is the *Tahdhīb al-tahdhīb* by Ibn Ḥajar al-ʿAsqalānī (d. 852/1449), which is a biographical dictionary of trustworthy transmitters of Islamic Tradition.[4] The usual structure of a biography in this work breaks down into three parts: firstly the full name and some other pertinent life data of the subject are given, then follow enumerations of earlier authorities from whom he transmits Tradition, and then of those later authorities who in turn transmit from him. The biographee is thereby presented in the centre of an activity of transmission of knowledge. This particular work by Ibn Ḥajar is exclusively concerned with traditionists and this particular approach can, therefore, be observed here very clearly. Other biographical works, even those that are not so exclusively concerned with traditionists, often contain similar bits of network information.

Literary genres of an individual and personal nature

Other individual and personal genres evolved. The *fahrasa*,[5] which developed in al-Andalus and the Maghreb, is one of these. This genre, in which a scholar enumerates his shaykhs and the works he read with them, can be read as a scholarly curriculum vitae. The *thabat*, which is not confined to the Maghreb, is a list compiled by a relater of traditions in which he mentions his shaykhs and the scope of his transmissions on their authority. Likewise, in the *riḥla*, or travel account, attention shifted from geography and ethnography in the classical period to the personal relationships of scholars. Especially in later times it became much more than just a travel account. In it, the itinerant author has ample opportunity to enumerate the scholars he has met, the lessons he has taken and the authorisations he has received during his travels. And the purpose of his travels was, of course, not touristic but of a much more edifying nature, namely the pilgrimage to Makka.[6] Yet another type of personalised text is

---

4 Published in 12 volumes in Hyderabad, 1325-7 [1907-9].

5 See Ch. Pellat, s.v. "Fahrasa", *Encyclopaedia of Islam*, 2nd ed (*EI*²), (Leiden and London, 1960-), II, 743-4.

6 This genre of travel accounts became specially developed in the Western part of the Islamic world. The great distance from the Arabian Peninsula must have contributed to this development.

the *silsila*, the spiritual or scholarly genealogy.[7] The *barnāmaj*[8] and the *mashyakha* have a function very similar to that of the *fahrasa*, and sometimes contain accounts of travels in search of knowledge, the *ṭalab al-ʿilm*, just as in the *riḥla*. One of the most conspicuous types of compilation of biographical data are the works describing the *ṭabaqāt* ("the layers") of scholars, which list the successive generations of persons active in a certain field. This treatment "by generation" kept intact both the synchronic and diachronic connections in the history of a field of scholarship.

Especially in later times, such enumerations were compiled as a sort of scholarly autobiography. Sometimes the main attention is directed to the texts which were read with teachers, as in the *barnāmaj*, and sometimes the shaykhs themselves are the main object of attention, as in the *mashyakha*. Often these texts were compiled by the subjects themselves and were written in the first person, although the third person is used in the autobiography as well. When others took care of the compilation of such a list of subjects taught or authorities met by their shaykh, such a survey could simply be called *al-Taʿrīf bi-...*, followed by the name of the shaykh in question. The same applies to works which are entitled *Tarjamat ...*, followed by the name of the biographee. Titles such as *al-Sanad al-muttaṣil ilā ...*, followed by the name of an early authority, occur as well. Compilations with the word *asānīd* in the title serve a similar purpose in describing the chains of authorities by which a certain scholar is connected to the great imams of an earlier period. At a much later stage, probably only as late as the 12th/18th century, separate booklets with titles including the word *ijāza* began to appear. At first sight these seem to belong to the category of educational *ijāzāt* rather than that of readers' certificates but there are also connections between the two types of texts since the later diplomas frequently contain a *silsila* of learned predecessors, often putting the Prophet Muḥammad at the beginning of the *silsila* and the student to whom the booklet was issued at its end. Elaborately adorned, impressively calligraphed and elegantly worded, these diplomas can be considered to constitute the final stage of the *ijāza* and its

---

7 Many *silsila*s are known. The Sufis have their own sets of *silsila*s. I have published and analysed the *silsila* of the Bosnian Ḥanafī scholar Ḥasan Kāfī al-Aqḥiṣārī (d. 1025/1616) in *Manuscripts of the Middle East (MME)*, IV (1989), 85-114.

8 For this type of book, see ʿAbd al-ʿAzīz al-Ahwānī, "Kutub barāmij al-ʿulamāʾ fī al-Andalus", *MMMA*, I (1955), 91-120, 252-71.

finest artistic expression. Because of them, the *ijāza* has become an independent literary genre.[9]

Yet another special literary genre that developed from this practice is the *juz'*, a short text usually consisting of not much more than one quire, and often small enough for it to be easily carried. It could happen that only a very small part of a scholar's work was read and taught in a session in which an *ijāza* was going to be granted. In that case the issuer of the *ijāza* had the choice between two options. He could confer upon his pupil, or a visiting scholar, the right to transmit the whole of a book by him, or his transmissions (*marwiyyāt*), or his own orally received knowledge (*masmū'āt*), or the works for which he himself had already acquired certificates (*mustajāzāt*), or of any other of his works even if they had only been partially read or not read at all. Such *ijāzāt 'āmma* abound.

The other option was that the short text or the specific collection of transmissions which had been read could be written out separately. Such shorter collections of part of the repertoire of a shaykh often bear the title *juz'*.[10] Sometimes these *ajzā'* are provided with a more detailed specification and a more meaningful title.[11]

---

9 Such booklets are available in numerous libraries. The MS Montreal, McGill University Library, No. AC 156 is such a separate diploma. Its content was analysed and published by Adam Gacek, "The Diploma of the Egyptian Calligrapher Ḥasan al-Rushdī", *MME*, IV (1989), 44–55. Another one is MS Leiden, University Library, Or. 11.121. This thin volume, which probably originates from Istanbul, contains an *ijāza* in the readings of the Qur'ān conferred upon Abū Bakr Luṭfī Afandī b. al-Sayyid 'Umar al-Sanūbī by his teacher Ismā'īl Ḥaqqī b. 'Alī in *Muḥarram* 1260/1844.

10 It is not impossible that the *juz'* as an independent genre developed from the old practice of writing *ijāzāt*, *samā'āt* and the like on each *juz'*, here more or less meaning quire, or gathering, of a manuscript. Such manuscripts are referred to as *mujazza'*, divided into *ajzā'*. This feature is by no means rare. It can be attested by the Leiden manuscripts Or. 122 (*Makārim al-Akhlāq)* and Or. 12.644 (*Tārīkh Madīnat Dimashq*). These manuscripts contain on each gathering a number of almost identical certificates. The gatherings have title pages of their own and break up the text into parts of more or less equal length which have no connection with any division into chapters and sections that the text may also have. This latter characteristic is shared, of course, with the Qur'ān, which has a formal division into *ajzā'* and, at the same time, a division into chapters, or *sūras*.

11 *Ajzā'* with *samā'āt* are mentioned by Ṣalāḥ al-Dīn al-Munajjid, "Ijāzāt al-samā'", nos. 10 and 11.

When a scholar's trust in his colleague or student was great, it could happen that he conferred upon him the right to transmit all his works, even if they had not been the subject of a teaching session. In such a case the *ijāza* may contain the titles of most or all of the teacher's works and be, in effect, an autobibliography. Such lists of titles of books in the *ijāza*, or elsewhere in a manuscript for that matter, are have hardly been explored as yet.[12] There are many more works, often with more flowery titles, which serve the same purpose, namely to record and assess a scholar's authority. When one starts searching for this type of book the supply is seemingly endless. The common features that may be observed in all of them are the enumerations of scholars visited, of books read, and of authorisations (*ijāzāt*) received. In this context the *ijāza* is the conclusion of a meeting between two scholars which simultaneously contains an account of their scholarly antecedents. By virtue of it, the recipient is invested with the authority to transmit or teach part or whole of the work of the scholar who has issued the *ijāza.* The whole process is not unlike the diplomas which students of present day universities consider as the culmination of their study, the difference being that these *ijāzāt* reflect the relationship between two natural persons, rather than between a student and his institution of education.

Finally, we may note that the alphabetical arrangement of biographical material, such as in Ibn Ḥajar's *Tahdhīb al-tahdhīb*, encompassed all previous developments. This type of arrangement was, of course, the only organisational answer to an ever increasing corpus of material, although we do also find limitations of a chronological or geographical nature within alphabetically arranged biographical dictionaries.

12 See my "Lists of Books in Arabic Manuscripts", *MME,* V (1990-1), 121–36, especially the section on '*Ijāzāt and autobibliography*' on pp. 126–30 where I discuss an 8/14th century document of such a nature. Another autobibliography which takes the shape of an *ijāza*, dated Damascus, 1169/1756, is found in MS Dublin, Chester Beatty Library, no. 3488 (cf. Arberry, *Handlist*, II, plate 63).

Codicology and the ijāza in Arabic manuscripts

What, one might ask, has all this to do with manuscripts and, more particularly, with codicology? The latter science is sometimes described as the specialism that devotes attention to all aspects of a manuscript other than the contents of the text it contains. In more positive wording, it is sometimes designated as the science that focusses exclusively on the physical features of the handwritten book. These are useful definitions but as summarised here they are too simplified. Indeed, there are often more things to be learned from a manuscript volume than the philological aspects of the text which is contained in it. One cannot, however, make such a simple schematic distinction between immaterial text and physical manuscript, between soul and body, so to speak. There is always an interaction between the two aspects, as is illustrated by, for example, the occurrence of a great variety of indications of personal use that can be found in many manuscripts. Each manuscript is, of course, a personally made artefact and contains information — always implicitly and sometimes explicitly — on the maker and sometimes on the users of the manuscript as well. On the whole, features such as the colophon, copyist's verses, owner's marks and reader's certificates enable us to gain an idea of the functioning of a certain text in general and the use of a certain manuscript volume in particular. Therefore, the study of these features, which belongs to the field of codicology in as much as the study of writing materials and script are part of it, gives a text an extra dimension and places it in its cultural context. Only this overall and integrated approach to the manuscript does justice to its features in coherence with one another. It is philology in the widest sense of the word, involving all these aspects and also the interaction between the text and the environment in which it was launched.

One usually finds *ijāzāt*, or copies of them,[13] added at the end of a text or written on the title page preceding the text for which the authorisation is granted. Sometimes the *ijāza* consists of a few lines only but sometimes they can be quite elaborate. They may be combined with readers' certificates. To add *ijāzāt* to texts was a time honoured practice in Arabic manuscripts which remained in use for a number of centuries. By looking at the manuscripts in which they are written, one can gain an idea of how this system of authorisation to teach operated. In addition to this, an *ijāza* can

13 Copies (*mithāl* or *ṣūra*) are often not recognised as such.

reveal much about the way a certain text or manuscript was used. Quite surprisingly, as yet very little has been done by way of a systematic collection of the data contained in the *ijāzāt* in Arabic manuscripts.[14] A corpus of such texts with an analysis of both their formulaic peculiarities and their content would be highly desirable. The fact that such a corpus would indeed be useful is illustrated by the discovery by Ebied and Young of the etymology of the term "baccalaureate": by scrutinising the Arabic wording of the *ijāzāt* in a number of manuscripts they found evidence for their thesis that the well known European academic term is in fact derived from the Arabic term *bi-ḥaqq al-riwāya.*[15]

Examples of some important ijāzāt

The *ijāza* originated within the Islamic educational system in which the Islamic religious sciences were taught. Its use, however, has by no means remained restricted to that field. Of the 72 manuscripts listed by Vajda, 59 have a "traditional Islamic" content, that is disciplines that are part of the *madrasa* curriculum, whereas 13 do not have a directly religious content but deal with such topics as medicine, literature and the sciences. This is still a high proportion in view of the fact that there are so many more manuscripts of the first category. Vajda's geographical register reveals that Damascus and Cairo are the places from where most manuscripts with *ijāzāt* on them originate. Baghdad, Makka and Aleppo are the runners up as places where *ijāzāt* were most frequently issued. Most other places are also situated in the Mashreq. Eighty percent of Vajda's corpus dates from the 6–9th/12–15th centuries, with a more or less even distribution over this period.[16]

One of the most outstanding sets of *ijāzāt* is found not in an Islamic scholarly text, but in what is probably the most prestigious text of Arabic imaginative literature, the *Maqāmāt* of

[14] MacKay's extensive analysis of the *ijāzāt* in MS Cairo, Dār al-Kutub al-Miṣriyya, *Adab* 105 (see n. 1 above), which contains a contemporary copy of the *Maqāmāt* of al-Ḥarīrī (d. 512/1122), makes ample reference to secondary manuscripts and is exemplary both in this respect and from the methodological point of view. Vajda's collection of certificates (see n. 1 above) also provides a wealth of information.

[15] R. Y. Ebied & M. J. L. Young, "New Light on the Origin of the Term 'Baccalaureate'", *The Islamic Quarterly*, XVIII (1974), 3-7.

[16] See Vajda, *Certificats de lecture*, 65–6.

al-Ḥarīrī. This becomes clear from the *ijāzāt* found on the authoritative manuscript of the text, copied from al-Ḥarīrī's own copy. In the principal and contemporaneous *ijāza* on this manuscript the names of some 38 scholars, a number of whom are identified as distinguished notables of Baghdad, are mentioned as having been present at the reading of the entire work, which took more than a month of intermittent sessions to complete.[17] MacKay's meticulous analysis of the numerous *ijāzāt* in this manuscript has, in fact, reconstructed a period of almost two centuries of cultural life in Baghdad, Aleppo and Damascus. It all started in Baghdad in the year 504/1111, when the first reading of a copy of the author's autograph took place. That reading was followed by a number of subsequent readings, all in Baghdad. In the 60 or so years since the first reading, the manuscript had become quite heavy with *samā'* notes. After a period of 40 years, which remains unaccounted for, it came into the possession of the Aleppan historian Kamāl al-Dīn Ibn al-'Adīm (d. 660/1262). The manuscript then remained for more than 30 years in Aleppo, and bears numerous names of members of the best Aleppan families as auditors at sessions at which the manuscript was read. Finally, the manuscript bears certificates of reading sessions held in Damascus in the course of the year 683/1284. The manuscript then fades from view until, almost exactly six centuries later, it was acquired in 1875 by Dār al-Kutub al-Miṣriyya, where it still is.

When one looks at the more than 200 names of those involved in reading and listening to the manuscript, one is struck by the fact that many of them are related by family ties. The history of the transmission of the text in this manuscript often goes hand in hand with the history of generations of scholars and literary men who occupied themselves with it.

One of the earliest known *ijāzāt* is that found in the unique manuscript of *al-Nāsikh wa-l-mansūkh fī al-Qur'ān* by Abū 'Ubayd al-Qāsim b. Sallām (d. 223/837).[18] Here we do indeed

---

[17] See MacKay, *Certificates of Transmission*, 9.

[18] MS Istanbul, Topkapı Sarayı Library, Ahmet III A 143. The *ijāza* itself appears to be a copy (*mithāl*). A facsimile edition of the manuscript was published by Fuat Sezgin, Publications of the Institute for the History of Arabic-Islamic Science, Series C, XII (Frankfurt am Main, 1985). Pp. 418-9 of the facsimile edition contain the *ijāzāt*. The text was edited by John Burton, *Abū 'Ubaid al-Qāsim b. Sallām's* K. al-nāsikh wa-l-mansūkh *(MS. Istanbul, Topkapı, Ahmet III A 143)*, E. J. W. Gibb Memorial Series, New Series, XXX (Cambridge, 1987). Burton gives the readers' certificates

have a work which belongs to the core of Islamic sciences, the knowledge of the abrogating and abrogated verses of the Qur'an. The earliest *samā'* in it dates from 392/1001-2, while the latest dates from 587/1191. In one of *samā'āt* in this manuscript a place is mentioned: al-Jāmi' al-'Atīq bi-Miṣr.[19] Here, too, several members of the same family are mentioned, including a father, his sons, and several brothers. Just as in the previously mentioned example of al-Ḥarīrī's *Maqāmāt*, it becomes clear that transmitting a text was a social event and sometimes also a family affair. In either case the personal element is clearly present. Comparison of the *ijāzāt* at the end of the Istanbul manuscript of Abū 'Ubayd's *al-Nāsikh wa-l-mansūkh* with the list of *riwāyāt* on the title page of another Istanbul manuscript, the *Kitāb al-Mujālasa* by Abū Bakr al-Dīnawarī,[20] reveals the occurrence of the same person in both manuscripts, namely, the otherwise unknown scholar Abū 'Abd Allāh M. b. Ḥamd b. Ḥāmid b. Mufarraj b. Ghiyāth al-Artājī. In the very old manuscript of Abū 'Ubayd's *al-Nāsikh wa-l-mansukh,* he is active as *musmi'* in 587/1191, while in the copy of al-Dīnawarī's *Kitāb al-Mujālasa,* copied in 671/1272, he is one of the transmitters of the text preceding the manufacture of the manuscript. This shows that it is rewarding to accumulate the data of *ijāzāt, samā'āt, riwāyāt* and the like, with the present example, for instance, revealing the beginning of a scholarly network.

The *ijāzāt* given by Ibn al-Jawālīqī (d. 539/1144), one of the foremost philologists in Baghdad,[21] can be found in a number of manuscripts. A manuscript in Dublin contains on its title page a certificate of reading signed by Ibn al-Jawālīqī in 514/1120.[22] A

---

of the Topkapı manuscript on pp. 101-3 of his edition, with an analysis of their contents and an identification of most persons mentioned in them on pp. 52-3 of his introduction.

19 This must be the manuscript to which Ṣalāḥ al-Dīn al-Munajjid refers ("Ijāzāt al-samā'", 233, n. 1). The date which he gives there, 372 AH, is apparently a misreading for the clearly written date of 392 AH.

20 MS Istanbul, Topkapı Sarayı Library, Ahmet III, No. 618. Facsimile edition by Fuat Sezgin, Publications of the Institute of the History of Arabic-Islamic Science, Series C, XXXVIII (Frankfurt am Main, 1986).

21 See C. Brockelmann, *Geschichte der arabischen Litteratur,* I (Weimar, 1898), 280.

22 Chester Beatty Library, No. 3009 (Arberry, *Handlist,* I, plate 1). See also S. A. Bonebakker, "Notes on Some Old Manuscripts of the *Adab al-kātib* of Ibn Qutayba, the *Kitāb aṣ-ṣinā'atayn* of Abu Hilāl al-'Askarī and the *Mathal as-sā'ir* of Ḍiyā' ad-Dīn ibn al-Athīr", *Oriens,* XIII-XIV (1960–

Leiden manuscript containing Abū al-ʿAlāʾ al-Maʿarrī's *Luzūm mā lā yalzam* was copied by Ibn al-Jawālīqī before 496/1102-3.[23] His handwriting is easily identified and the date can be established from an autograph note by his teacher and predecessor at the Niẓāmiyya school in Baghdad, al-Khaṭīb al-Tabrīzī (d. 502/1108).[24] Other reading notes in the same manuscript reveal the reading by a pupil, Ibn al-Khashshāb, in the course of the year 519/1125. The manuscript then travelled from Baghdad to Cairo, as is borne out by notes about its new owner, the grammarian Ibn al-Naḥḥās (d. 698/1299).[25] Another Leiden manuscript containing the philological work *Kitāb al-Alfāẓ* by ʿAbd al-Raḥmān b. ʿĪsá al-Hamadhānī (d. 320/932), was copied in 522/1128.[26] It, too, contains an autograph *qirāʾa* note by Ibn al-Jawālīqī on the title page. The manuscript itself contains notes of *bulūgh* and *muqābala* at fairly regular intervals and from these the length of the reading sessions can be approximately measured, each probably lasting around one or two hours. A late copy (11th/17th century?) of a *qirāʾa* note by Ibn al-Jawālīqī, dated *Ṣafar* 501/1107, is available in MS Leiden Or. 403, f. 430b, which contains the *Dīwān* of Abū Tammām with a commentary by al-Khaṭīb al-Tabrīzī.[27] The impression one gets from Ibn al-Jawālīqī's notes is that his transmissions were probably not as much of a social event as were the previous cases. It would appear that he had a predilection for a smaller group to whom he taught the important texts of his time. His copy of al-Maʿarrī's *Luzūmiyyāt*, with only his teacher al-Khaṭīb al-Tabrīzī between the author and himself, is an eloquent witness of this.

1), 159-94. The note in the Dublin manuscript is edited by Bonebakker on p. 165.

23 University Library, Or. 100. See also S. M. Stern, "Some Noteworthy Manuscripts of the Poems of Abu'l-ʿAlāʾ al-Maʿarrī", *Oriens*, VII (1954), 322-47, especially 339-44.

24 The *qirāʾa* note was published by me in *Seven Specimens of Arabic Manuscripts* (Leiden, 1978), 11.

25 See Stern, "Some Noteworthy Manuscripts", 343–4.

26 MS Leiden Or. 1070 (P. Voorhoeve, *Handlist of Arabic Manuscripts in the Library of the University of Leiden and Other Collections in the Netherlands* [Leiden, 1957], 10).

27 Voorhoeve, *Handlist*, 62.

Conclusions and perspectives

Two aspects of the *ijāza* have been dealt with, one from the point of view of cultural history, the other with codicological considerations taken into account. Both are necessary and the two complement one another by interaction. The *ijāza* itself is a good example for proving that these two orientations cannot be isolated from one another. The *ijāza* is an important source for the history of scholarly and cultural networks and gives the details by which an entire cultural environment can be reconstructed.

The *ijāza* as a mechanism in the distribution of learning deserves to be studied on a much wider scale than has hitherto been the case. Librarians should collect the *ijāzāt* in their manuscripts and publish them. Such publications should not only consist of an analysis of the data of the certificates, as Vajda and MacKay have done, but should also contain as complete a transcript as possible of the Arabic texts themselves. Only then can the most important work begin, namely, the compilation of a cumulative index of all the bio-bibliographical information contained in such certificates, which would be a valuable addition to existing bio-bibliographical reference works. The publication of a large corpus of *ijāzāt* will enable us to make a survey of the technical terminology employed which, in turn, will deepen our knowledge of the function of the *ijāza* in Arabic manuscripts.

The minimal requirements for such a corpus are, firstly, the full texts, with good photographs, of a great number of *ijāzāt*. These would constitute the main body of the work. Secondly, such a corpus should also contain a number of research aids: summary descriptions of the manuscripts in question, an index of persons with their functions in the process of the issuing of the *ijāzāt*, an index of the places to where the manuscripts in which the *ijāzāt* are found peregrinated in the course of time, and a glossary of the technical terminology employed.

This is not an easy task to perform, since the scholarly certificates are often written in the least legible of scripts. The study of the *ijāza* will only be fruitful if the student of the *ijāzāt* is well acquainted with the formal requirements of these certificates[28] and the educational environment from which they stem, and if at the same time he has a wide experience in working with manuscripts. In the ongoing development towards an increased

[28] As sketched by Ṣalāḥ al-Dīn al-Munajjid, "Ijāzāt al-samāʿ", 234–41.

professionalisation of the science of manuscripts, it is only natural that such a corpus of *ijāzāt* should be compiled by a professional codicologist.

9

THE ORAL TRANSMISSION OF KNOWLEDGE IN TRADITIONAL ISLAM

Georges Vajda

(Paper delivered on 8 November 1974 at the Instituto Per l'Oriente of the University of Rome, in the context of the annual congress of Onamasticon Arabicum. Only a few adjustments have been made to the colloquial style of the original.)

Attachment to the oral transmission of knowledge, entrenched in the mentality of traditional scholars of Islam, remained active and is still active today, long after the commitment to writing of the materials to be transmitted and the determination – according to the criteria of the appropriate discipline, *ʿilm al-ḥadīth* – of chains of authenticity (*isnād*).

Consequently, it could not be said that the repetitive reading of texts, reading certified by authorisations of transmission (*ijāza*) established for the benefit of hearers, should be a procedure aimed towards the conservation of the works concerned, or even necessarily, in the first instance at least, towards formative education; it is in some respects a meritorious work, perpetuating a state of affairs which found its full *raison d'etre* only in the crystallisation of the major collections of *ḥadīth*; it is known furthermore that a transmitter as prolific and committed as the *imām* Aḥmad Ibn Ḥanbal (d. 241/855) was scrupulous to transmit otherwise than on the basis of written texts which his hearers were obliged to take under his dictation; on the contrary, it did not prevent the procedure of oral transmission being indefinitely and ultimately fictitiously maintained: this also extends to disciplines and literary genres other than *ḥadīth*: to give only one example which could serve as "sounding", a currently fashionable process in all contexts – in the classification of the seventy certificates which I have encountered in the Arabic archives of the Bibliotheque Nationale of Paris, manuscripts of *ḥadīth* represent precisely a third (twenty-four), the remainder being divided among no fewer than twenty-one rubrics, *fiqh*, *tafsīr* and history being the best represented.

[2] Furthermore, another specific product of Muslim science responds to the desire to be located in the mainstream of a tradition which is hopefully

to be kept alive: the lists of their transmitters and of the latter's authorities compiled by numerous scholars: they are called *mashyakha* (*muʿjam al-mashāyikh*) in the East and *barnāmaj* (curiously, this is a Persian term) in the West; *ijāza* and *mashyakha* in Shīʿite circles (although only transmission in a Sunni context will be considered here).

Interest in the deciphering and analysis of these two types of documents, certificates of audition born in the margin and on the available sheets of manuscripts and "dictionaries of authorities" resides in the fact that "It is their nature to supply information of the highest order on many aspects of intellectual and religious, and indeed social and political life of a given milieu at a given date, often extending over several generations. It is here that we come into contact with the transmitters, scribes and listeners, in other words with the entire scholarly and enthusiastic population of the *madrasas*, and that we find for ourselves a plethora of information [...] about all these individuals and their activities. In short, this is the realm of living historical material [...] where austere narration exists in close proximity to descriptions of customs, often amusing to the outside observer" (according to G. Lecomte, *A propos de la résurgence des ouvrages d'Ibn Qutayba sur le ḥadīth*, in *Bulletin d'Etudes Orientales*, xxi, 1968, intro).

I shall begin by reviewing the principal modalities of tradition codified by the theoreticians of the science of *ḥadīth*; subsequently I shall trace the regular structure, more or less followed in reality, of certificates of transmission; finally I shall illustrate, very schematically, with a few examples, the material which the historian can draw from the analysis, either of certificates, or of lists of authorities.

I *Taḥammul al-ʿilm (al-ḥadīth)*: reception of transmission

Transmission may be effected according to eight modalities which the theoreticians list in descending order of worth (*aqsām ṭuruq al-ḥadīth*).

1) *Samāʿ*: the disciple or the auditor hears traditions recited from memory or read in the book (or the *juzʾ* notebook) of the *shaykh*. The terms (*alfāẓ*) which denote this mode of reception are: *samiʿtu* or *ḥaddathanī*.
2) *Qirāʾa* (most often *ʿarḍ*): the disciple or another person reads aloud from the book (notebook) or even recites by heart one or several *ḥadīths* before the *shaykh*; the latter listens and compares what is recited with his examplar or with what he has conserved in his memory. Terms: *akhbaranī* (*-nā*) or *qaraʾtu ʿalā* (less frequently, *anbaʾanā* or *nabbaʾanā*).

These two procedures are characterised as *riwāya ʿalā l-wajh*.

[3] 3) *Ijāza* "licence": it can be of two kinds (with subdivisions of which the special works supply the detail:

• the *shaykh* or an authorised transmitter gives permission to transmit one or several texts;

• he delivers to a certain person authority to transmit works which he does not specify; he will say for example: "I permit you to transmit (in your turn) everything which I am authorised to transmit."

Terms: *akhbaranī* and sometimes *ajāzanī*.

4) *Munāwala* (hanging over). The *shaykh* gives to the disciple either the original where the traditions heard by him are written or a comparative exemplar of this original, while reciting a formula such as: "this is what I have collected" or "that which I have been given by such and such a person, pass on in your turn on my authority". He can hand the pupil the written document either in definitive form or on the stipulation that once copied the exemplar be returned to him. Term generally employed, *akhbaranī*, less often *nāwala*.

Also recognised as *munāwala* is the presentation of a book or notebook by the disciple to the master who authorises its transmission only after verifying the text (this is known as *ʿarḍ munāwala*).

5) *Kitāba* or *mukātaba*. The *shaykh* personally executes a copy of his book or of his transmissions (he may however entrust this task to another person, usually to the disciple who is the direct recipient of the transmission. In these circumstances, the transmitter is not obliged to declare explicitly to the recipient (whose effective presence is furthermore not required): "I entrust to you the right to transmit". Terms: *akhbaranī* or *min kitāb*.

6) *Iʿlām* (declaration). This procedure, the validity of which has been disputed by some theoreticians, consists in the declaration by the *shaykh* that a certain text has been heard by him, without necessarily specifying that he has received licence to transmit it or that he gives the auditor authorisation to do so. Terms: *akhbaranī* or simply *ʿan*.

7) *Waṣiyya* (testament). Close to death or to setting out on a journey, the master bequeaths to some individual a casebook of traditions reported by him. The best authors reject the validity of this procedure. Terms: *akhbaranī waṣiyyatan ʿan* or *waṣṣānī*.

8) *Wijāda* (invention). On coming into possession of the manuscript of the last transmitter, one acquires the right to make use of the document thus "found", whether the latter be contemporary or ancient. In fact, the validity of a transmission operated in these conditions is not recognised and the worth of the *ḥadīth* thus transmitted depends on its credibility,

guaranteed or otherwise by the "criticism" of the chain of transmission or the plausibility of the text. Terms: *wajadtu*, *qāla*, *ukhbirtu*, *ḥuddithtu*.

[**4**] [See Bibliography I]

II Nature and structure of certificates of audition

It may be noted from the outset that the origin of documents of this type is linked to the institution of establishments for the teaching of religious sciences, the *madrasas*; thus they are only encountered very rarely before the fifth century of the Hegira (eleventh of the Christian era). It was as a supplement to the courses given in the *madrasa* that the practice began of inscribing the attestations of successive readings on the manuscripts used; this method of certifying the study or the reading of a text was subsequently extended to literary productions other than *ḥadīth* and *fiqh*, the study of which was not relevant to the *cursus* of the *madrasa* and was not necessarily effected within its precincts (furthermore, even for *ḥadīth* there was no constraining rule in this respect).

According to formal criteria, two types of authorisation of transmission (*ijāza*) are distinguished and three of attestation of reading (*samāʿ*): *ijāzat al-qirāʾa*, authorisation delivered following a reading made by a master to a pupil or – which is the more frequent case – following a reading made by the pupil under the supervision of the master; use of the expression *ijāzat al-samāʿ* implies the presence of auditors (or recipients) other than the reader. As for *samāʿ*, the distinctions are as follows;

- the author of the work attests with his own hand that a student has heard the text from him;
- the student affirms that he has read the work before the author (*qaraʾa ʿalā*);
- attestation of reading made before a master who is not the author of the work read.

This third type of *samāʿ* is, by the nature of things, the most frequently encountered.

A *samāʿ* presented according to the rules comprises ten elements (in fact, they are not always found in their totality, especially when it is a case of summaries or simple mentions of certified auditions of manuscripts anterior to the one which we have before us).

1) The name of the transmitter (*musmiʿ*); if he is not the author of the text transmitted, it is appropriate to specify in addition the authority whereby he has received the text (*sanad*); sometimes, the whole chain of transmitters (*riwāya*) linking the reader to the author is given in detail. It is not very unusual to find certificates [**5**] which avail themselves of two or even three *musmiʿ*, which can function according to the authority either of the same *riwāya*, or of distinct *riwāyāt* (to signify that someone is authorised to transmit on behalf of another, a formula such as *bi-ḥaqqi samāʿih ʿan*).
2) The names of auditors: men, women, children, with indication of the age of the latter (for example *fī l-rābiʿa*, in other words, *fī l-sanati l-rābiʿa min ʿumrih*), freemen and slaves. Personal names and those of fathers are not considered enough; supplementary indications are added, starting with the *kunya*; these customs of precision prove, it may be noted in passing, extremely useful for the identification of individuals, and thus for the collection of the materials of the Onomasticon Arabicum.
3) Precise account of what such and such an auditor actually heard (where necessary, it is stated quite bluntly that he slept during the reading) and of the sessions which he may possibly have missed (formulas used: *samiʿa maʿa fawt, fātahu l-juzʾ*).
4) Name of the reader.
5) Type of manuscript (original, copy belonging to a certain person) which has been used in the reading.
6) Identity of the registrar of the names of participants in the audition (*ḍābit al-asmāʾ*); this is usually the reader of the transmitted text or the writer of the certificate, these two functions being assumed in the majority of cases by the same person. The term denoting the writer is *kātib al-ṭabaqa* (pl. *ṭibāq*); in some instances forgers (*muzawwir*) are also encountered.
7) The formula *ṣaḥḥa wa-thabata* following the names of the auditors (this is why the term *thabat*, pl. *athbāt*, "certificates" of any kind, comes to be employed in the restricted sense of a document attesting to the didactic transmission of a text); moreover we have here a judicial formula of which the exact equivalent in Jewish Aramaic, *sharīr waqīm*, is anterior to Islam and to the Arab conquest.
8) Place of the audition (lessons did not take place only in the *madrasa* or the mosque, but almost anywhere: at the lodgings of the transmitter, who often lived in the building of a pious foundation serving, among other purposes, as a place of education (and naturally this was always the case when the transmitter was a woman), in a garden, even on the back of a mule during a journey.

9) Date of the audition; possibly the number of sessions or the initial and final date of the readings (*fī mudda(tin) ākhiruhā*, *fī majālis ākhiruhā*, *fī nawbatayn*).

[**6**] 10) The signature of the *musmi'*.

If there is a need to specify that the reading is not the simple recitation of a text but a study in the strict sense, with analysis and explanation, this character is underlined by formulas such as *qirā'at taṣḥīh wa-tafahham* (or *baḥth*).

[See Bibliography II]

III. The documentary importance of certificates of audition and of lists of authorities

Finally, we shall show, through various examples, the contribution that can be made to our knowledge of Islam and of Muslim civilisation by the analysis and decipherment, an irksome task in its own right, of authorisations of transmissions, certificates of reading and of lists of authorities.

In the first place, surveys bearing on these materials allow us, to a certain extent, to evaluate the intensity of interest taken, over the course of time, in the religious disciplines. This interest can be twofold, and often its [**7**] two aspects are inseparable one from the other: it is either the issue of ensuring the training, professional training it could be called, of experts in *ḥadīth* and in *fiqh* (the same may be said of the disciplines of *'arabiyya*, philology, poetry and even, more rarely, of other branches of knowledge) or, more specifically but not exclusively, in the case of recitation of the traditions of the Prophet, the issue of the edification of believers and the education of the young, in other words of a public provisionally or definitively incapable of penetrating the sense of the material presented to it. From this point of view, information collected regarding the nature of texts read, the frequency and timing of meetings, the composition of the audience, throws light on an aspect of daily Muslim life, which would be less easily discerned with the same precision, by any other means.

It happens that the chronology and the geographical distribution of auditions recorded on manuscripts give us the opportunity to gauge the decline or the renewal of interest in a certain text or a certain author; the very discontinuity of a series of reading, which in many cases we are capable of following over the centuries, is extremely instructive and apt to encourage reflection on the survival of works or of the reputation of the authors concerned. See for example Gérard Lecomte, study cited above.

The Oral Transmission of Knowledge in Traditional Islam 7

The topographical distribution of the *samāʿ* and the information supplied by lists of authorities give us first-hand documentary evidence on the mobility of scholars (they could, at the same time, be merchants) who undertook long journeys in search of long traditions (*fī ṭalab al-ʿilm*) or to receive the lessons of a renowned master. Examples are innumerable, but study of the available material is only in its early stages: thus the work of al-Silafī, probably the most interesting of all from this point of view, has barely been touched on; besides my article, recourse is needed to the book by M. Iḥsān ʿAbbās, *Akhbār wa-tarājim andalusiyya min Muʿjam al-safar li-l-Silafī*, Beirut 1963 [Now published: al-Silafī, *Muʿjam al-safar*, ed. Sher M. Zaman, Islamabad 1988; ed. ʿA. al-Bārūdī, Beirut 1993]. Among the travellers *fī ṭalab al-ʿilm*, three texts may be seen analysed in easily accessible publications: they emanate from two Egyptians, Manṣūr Ibn Salīm al-Hamdānī (607–673/ 1210–1275) and ʿAbd al-Muʾmin b. Khalaf al-Dimyāṭī (613–705/ 1217–1306), and from an Indian Ṣūfī, Isḥāq b. ʿAlī al-Multānī al-Bakkarī, whose wanderings we can follow, from his home-territory in the subcontinent to Cairo, by way of Baghdad and Mecca, over a period of some forty years, from 702/1302 to around 745/1344. They are published under the titles:

[G. Vajda] *Le Dictionnaire des Autorités* [...] *de ʿAbd al-Muʾmin al-Dimyāṭī*, Paris 1962 (Publications de l'Institut de Recherche et d'Histoire des Textes, Documents, Etudes et Répertoires, vii); Id., "De Multān au Caire", *Journal Asiatique*, 1962, p. 218–233; Id., "La liste d'autorités de Manṣūr Ibn Salim Wajiḥ al-Dīn al-Hamdānī", *Journal Asiatique*, 1965, p. 341–406.

[8] The Islamic metropolises such as Baghdad, Cairo or Damascus naturally witnessed the passage of a large number of itinerant scholars, which enabled certain local masters to compile lists of authorities, without having to travel too far to find them. A good example of documents of this type is the collection established in Cairo by Muḥammad b. Aḥmad Ibn al-Ḥaṭṭab al-Rāzī (434–525/ 1042–1131). This *mashyakha* which I was able to study on the basis of two manuscripts of the Ẓāhiriyya is also eloquent testimony to the freedom with which Sunni education was practised in Egypt at the height of the Fāṭimid period, at a time when the decline of the Shīʿite dynasty was still far from an advanced stage. The *Mashyakha of Ibn al-Ḥaṭṭab al-Rāzī* (extract from *BEO*, 1970, p. 21–99, 79 pages). [Gilliot, Cl., "Prosopography in Islam. An essay of classification", *Medieval Prosopography*, 23 (2002), p. 47–8 (19–54).]

Among later works which have been the object of thorough analysis, I shall mention only the compilation of Aḥmad b. Muḥammad Ibn Ḥajar al-ʿAsqalānī (773–852/ 1371–1449) *al-Mashyakha al-Bāsima li-l-Qibābī wa Fāṭima*, set out in the thesis by Mlle Jacqueline Sublet, *Les maîtres et les études de deux traditionnistes de l'époque mamelouke*, BEO, xx (1967), p. 9–99.

These works, to which should be added those concerning the *barnāmaj* of the West given to us recently by Egyptian and Spanish researchers (cf. art. *Idjāza*, in *Encyclopedia of Islam* [2]) and including Jose Mª Forneas, "El Barnamay de Muḥammad Ibn Yābir al-Wādī Āsī, Materiales para su studio y edicion critica (Primera Parte)", *Al-Andalus* 38 (1973), p. 1-67, authorise conclusions here and now which are not at all unexpected, regarding the field of interest of traditional intellectuals in search of knowledge; they also teach us that differences of *madhhab* (of the four Sunni schools certainly, but not excluding the Ẓāhirites) did not influence the choice of texts and of transmitters retained; it may however be observed, especially in Damascus, though it would be unwise to extrapolate to excess the facts already established, a certain concentration of transmissions in Ḥanbalite circles.

Before all this, we remain within the precincts of the *madrasa*, of the *dār al-ḥadīth* and sometimes of the *khānqāh*, the Ṣūfī convent. But the *ijāza* could also serve as a political instrument, as was the case with the zeal shown by the caliph al-Nāṣir (reigned from 575/ 1180 to 622/ 1225) with a view to the obtaining of licences to transmit on the part of scholars belonging to each of the four *madhhabs*, as may be observed from the piece which I analysed under the title: "Une liste d'autorités du calife al-Nāṣir li-dīn Allāh", *Arabica* vi, 1959, p. 173–177; this quest for authorisations clearly responded to the policy of this sovereign, noted by the historians, of re-establishing the internal unity of Islam.

Finally, a word about the certificates accompanying philological and literary texts; their analysis is also instructive for the knowledge of the milieux of grammarians or of simple aficionados of literature [**9**] – the function exercised for the transmission of religious knowledge by the information drawn from the documents of which we have spoken hitherto.

In this order of research, I shall commend to you three works, the first of which I evoke here, in the precincts of the University of Rome, with some emotion: the study of the certificates attached to the *Nasab al-khayl* of Ibn al-Kalbī in the introduction to the edition of this work provided by the unforgettable master Giorgio Levi della Vida (*Les "Livres des chevaux"* de Hišām ibn al-Kalbī et Muḥammad ibn al-Aʿrābī, publiés d'après le manuscrit de l'Escorial ar. 1705, Leiden, 1928), who introduces us into the circle of the Baghdadi philologist Mawhūb b. Aḥmad Ibn al-Jawālīqī (466–539/ 1073–1144).

The second is owed to one of the best Arabists and Islamologists of our generation, unfortunately taken from us by an untimely death: Samuel M. Stern who, regrettably, published only a short sample of the work which he had in hand: "Some Noteworthy Manuscripts of the Poems of Abū l-ʿAlā al-Maʿarrī", *Oriens* 7 (1954), p. 322–347, where there are analyses of *samāʿ*

relating to the *Siqt al-zand*, a work of notorious difficulty studied in the circle of the grammarian al-Khaṭīb al-Tibrīzī (421–502/ 1130–1109).

The third, which is distinguished by its detail and the excellent reproductions of documents which may thus be utilised with profit for practical exercises, is the thesis of the young American scholar Pierre A. MacKay, *Certificates of Transmission on a Manuscript of the Maqāmāt of Ḥarīrī* (Transactions of the American Philosophical Society n.s.61, 4) Philadelphia 1971.

An immense amount of work remains to be done in the area of research which I have attempted to describe to you in very summary fashion. But I hope I have shown you that the pioneering work has been seriously undertaken and that progress is being made.

I conclude by expressing the hope that our topic of discussion this morning will contribute to the encouragement or consolidation of enthusiasms among my audience, and as a result some of you may be inspired one day to take up the illustrious mantle of *taḥammul al-ʿilm*.

Bibliography I

William Marçais, *Le Taqrīb de En-Nawawi*, traduit et annoté, Paris 1902, p.101–140 (*JA* 1901, no 3, 193–232); F. Sezgin, *Geschichte des Arabischen Schrifttums*, i, Leiden 1967, 58–60. The best (or most manageable) traditional commentary on the *Taqrīb* is that of Jalāl al-Dīn al-Suyūṭī: *Tadrīb al-rawī fi sharḥ Taqrīb al-Nawāwī*, recent edition, with a very useful annotation by ʿAbd al-Wahhāb ʿAbd al-Laṭīf, second imp., two vols., Cairo 1385/1966 (analytical table of contents, covering the text and the editor's notes; no index); *taḥammul* is dealt with there in vol. ii, p. 4–63.

Bibliography II

Ṣalāh al-dīn al-Munajjid, "Ijāzāt al-samāʿ fī l-makhṭūṭāt al-ʿarabiyya", *Revue de l'Institut des Manuscrits Arabes* i, 2, 1955, p. 232–251 (with 16 facsimile transcripts of *ijāzāt*; a practical publication for the novice reader of this kind of document). Rules for the editing of *samāʿ* are summarised in *Tadrīb* ii, 89–92. More generally, the rules for the setting into writing of *ḥadīth* and consequently the precautions to be observed during the collection of texts, form the object of the twenty-fifth section *nawʿ* of the *Taqrīb* (tr. Marçais, p. 140–156; *Tadrīb* ii, 64–92); sections 48 to 59, as well as 65 (Marçais, *Le Taqrīb de En-Nawawi*, 222–236, 242, *Tadrīb* ii, 268–349, 384–385) deal with the establishing of the names of transmitters. On the organisation of meetings of transmission (dictated courses), we have at our disposal the monograph of ʿAbd al-Karīm b. Muḥammad al-Samʿānī (d. 562/1167), *K. adab al-imlāʾ wa-l-istimlāʾ*, ed. Max Weisweiler, Leiden 1952, under the title of *Die Methodik des Diktatskollegs* (more briefly in sections 26–28 of the Taqrīb ii, 125 ff.). In the fundamental work of Khaṭīb Baghdad (Aḥmad b. ʿAlī b. Thābit, d. 463/1071) al-*Kifāya fī ʿilm al-riwaya*, Hyderabad 1357/1938, p. 314–325, there is an important survey of the question of *ijāza* (see also his *Taqyīd al-ʿilm*, a monograph on "the transmission of *ḥadīth*" (ed. Youssef Eche [Yūsuf al-ʿIshsh], Damascus 1949). An unpublished pamphlet of the very eminent expert in *ḥadīth*, Aḥmad b. Muḥammad al-Silafī (478–576/ 1085–1180 [art. Cl. Gilliot, in EI², IX]) on the question (*al-Wajīz fī dhikr al-mujāz wa l-mujīz*, "Brief account of the master who gives licence and the one who receives it" [Now published: ed. M. Kh. al-Biqāʿī, Beirut 1991]), has been analysed by G. Vajda, "Un opuscule inedit d'as-Silafī", *Bulletin de l'Institut de Recherche et d'Histoire des Textes*, 14 (1966), p. 85–92, where there will be found, notably, indications of the divergent opinions held by Muslim scholars regarding the credibility of the practice of *ijāza*.

[Among the numerous Dictionaries of Authorities and Masters edited since the publication of this study, we may mention: al-Ismāʿīlī, Abū Bakr (d. 371/981), *K. al-Muʿjam [fī asāmī shuyūḥ Abī Bakr al-Ismāʿīlī]*, 3 vols. in 2, ed. Z. M. Manṣūr, Medina, 1990; Ibn Ḥajar al-ʿAsqalānī (d. 852/1449), *al-Majmaʿal-muʾassas li-l-muʿjam al-mufahras*, 4 vols., ed. Y. ʿA. al-Marʿashlī, Beirut, 1994.]

[Bibliography III]

[Since the publication of this article the following studies and translations have been published: E. Dickinson, *The Development of Early Sunnite ḥadīth criticism*. The Taqdina of Ibn Abī Ḥātim al-Rāzī (240/854–327/938), Leiden, 2003; E. Dickinson (translated by), *An Introduction to the Science of the Ḥadīth*. Kitāb Maʿrifat anwāʿ ʿilm al-ḥadīth of Ibn al-Ṣalāḥ al-Shahrazūrī, reviewed by Muneer Fareed. Reading, Garnet, 2005; S. Leder et al., *Muʿjam al-samāʿāt al-dimashqiyya*. Les certificats d'audition à Damas – 570–750h/1155–1349, 2 vols., Damascus, IFEAD, 1996; *Introduction au ḥadith*, Special issue of *Etudes Arabes* (Roma, P.I.S.A/I.), 90 (1996/1).]

10
THE OFFICE OF THE *MUSTAMLĪ* IN ARABIC SCHOLARSHIP

Max Weisweiler

[Remarks of Claude Gilliot: The references of Weisweiler were in the text, they are here in the footnotes. We have also modified the abbreviations of his references to render them clearer. Our additions to these notes are in square brackets. The bibliography at the end of the text has been completed. Our additions to this bibliography, our corrections and additions to the chronological list are also in square brackets].

We are generally accustomed to imagining the creation of a work of literature in the old days in such a way that the scholar or writer would have penned his brainchild in the quiet of his study. The more unusual case, in which the original manuscript would have been the result of dictation, was frequent among the Arabs. [Adam] Mez recounts an instructive instance of this, after Ibn al-Nadīm (Mez, *Renaissance*, p. 171–3 [/178–81]; Ibn al-Nadīm, *Fihrist*, p. 76). In this case, there were several copyists present at the original dictation, the copies were supplemented and revised several times, and consequently the text entered the world, as it were in several original versions and editions at the same time. We can be sure that this and similar ways of recording original texts were not at all rare. Still more frequent, however, was the other way, where the scholar or man of letters, in a word: the sheikh, would have had a person on hand, who was working for him more or less permanently and would have written down his works or the traditions transmitted by him. While anyone who copied texts from dictation could be called '*mustamlī*', the title more specifically referred to this deputy; and if we read '*mustamlī* of NN', this usually refers to this dictation secretary of the sheikh's who, as we shall see below, had another important duty.

[Meaning and construction of the term *istamlā*]

As the meaning and the construction of the term *istamlā* are not described exhaustively in either the European or the Arabic dictionaries, a necessary condition for a definitive interpretation will be a lexicological discussion based on numerous instances from the relevant literature.

The basic meaning of *istamlā* is 'to ask for dictation; to take dictation; to write from dictation'. Thus Ibn Manẓūr:[1] *istamlaytuhū l-kitāba: sa'altuhu an yumliyahu 'alayya.* Likewise al-Fīrūzābādī,[2] or Ibn 'Asākir: *irtaḥaltu min waṭanī li-ṭalabi l-'ilmi wa-stimlā'i l-ḥadīthi.*[3] 'I left home in order to [**28**] search for *'ilm* and write hadiths from dictation'. We find also: *ḥaddathanā Abu l-Qāsimi ... imlā'an min lafẓihi bi-Iṣbahna stimlā'ī 'alayhi*[4] 'Abū l-Qāsim told me, himself dictating in Isfahan while I wrote from his dictation'. Or: *qad jathā 'alā rukbatayhi yas'alu Ḥammāda bna Zaydin 'an hādha l-ḥadīthi wa-yastamlī*[5] 'he went down on his knees asking Ḥammād b. Zayd for this hadith and writing from his dictation'. Or: *lammā amlā Manāqiba Abī Ḥanīfata kāna yastamlī 'alayhi arba'u mi'ati mustamlin*[6] 'When he dictated the Manāqib Abī Ḥanīfa, four hundred were writing from his dictation'. *Qara'a 'alayya jamī'a Fatḥi l-bāri'i wa-talaqqāhu minnī stimlā'an fī l-mabādi'i thumma 'arḍan wa-taḥrīran*[7] 'He read the complete *Fatḥ al-bāri'* with me, taking it down from my dictation at first, and later as *'arḍ* and *taḥrīr*'.

In a narrower sense the word means 'to perform the duties of a professional *mustamlī*', which may refer either of the two duties discussed in the following.

Examples for the absolute use of the verb can be found: *Kuntu 'inda Māliki bni Anasin aktubu wa-Ismā'īlu bnu 'Ulayyata qā'imun 'alā rijlayhi yastamlī*[8] 'I was with Mālik b. Anas, where I was writing while Ismā'īl b. 'Ulayya was standing on his feet officiating as *mustamlī*'. *Ma kānū yuqaddimūna li-l-istimlā'i illā khayrahum wa-afḍalahum*[9] 'only the best and most excellent among them were usually chosen to officiate as *mustamlī*'. *Wa-l-yastamli 'alā mawḍī'in murtafi'in*[10] 'his office as *mustamlī* he should perform from a raised place'.

When the verb governs an object, it takes the meaning 'pass on something in one's position as *mustamlī*'. *Yastamlī li-l-nāsi: Ḥammādu bnu-Salamata*[11]

---

[1] LA, XX, p. 161 [cf. Tāj, XXXIX, p. 555].
[2] Fīrūzābādī, *Qāmūs*, IV, p. 455.
[3] Ibn 'Asākir, IV, p. 180 [/IV, p. 183].
[4] *Adab*, p. 68.
[5] *Adab*, p. 87.
[6] Ibn a. l-Wafā', *Jawāhir*, I, p. 289.
[7] Sakhāwī, *Ḍaw'*, I, p. 146.
[8] *Adab*, p. 89.
[9] *Adab*, p. 91.
[10] Ibn Ṣalāḥ, *Ulūm*, p. 206 [/p. 364].
[11] *Adab*, p. 92.

'He transmitted to the people as a *mustamlī*, Hāmmād b. Salama'. *Fa-stamlā: Ḥaddathanā Bishrun*[12] 'And he transmitted as a *mustamlī*: Bishr told us'.

The most frequent usage is with the preposition *ʿalā* in the meaning 'occupy the position of *mustamlī* with (a sheikh)'. *Kāna lahū arbaʿatu mustamlīna yastamlūna ʿalayhi*[13] 'He had four *mustamlī*s occupying the position of *mustamlī* with him'. *Kāna yastamlī ʿalayhi Hārūn al-Dīk wa-Hārūn Mukḥula*[14] 'Hārūn al-Dīk and Hārūn Mukḥula used to occupy the position of *mustamlī* with him'. *Yaʾmuru ḥājibahū an yanqaṭiʿa mustamlīhi ʿani l-stimlāʾi ʿalayhi*[15] 'he ordered his chamberlain that his *mustamlī* should be interrupted in his occupation as *mustamlī* with him'. *Qaddamahū li-l-istimlāʾi ʿalayhi*[16] 'He had him appear as his *mustamlī*'.

[**29**] Besides this construction with *ʿalā* there is another with *li*, with only a slight shift in meaning 'to work as *mustamlī* for (a sheikh)'. *Kuntu astamlī lahu*[17] 'I used to work as *mustamlī* for him'. *Raʾaytu Sufyāna l-Thawriyya yumlī ʿalā ṣabīyin wa-yastamlī lahu*[18] 'I saw Sufyān al-Thawrī dictating to a boy who was working as *mustamlī* for him'. *Kāna Abū Ḥafṣini l-mustamlī yastamlī lahū huwa wa-l-ḥuffāẓu l-kibāru mina l-ghurabāʾi*[19] 'Abū Ḥafṣ *al-Mustamlī* and the great *Ḥuffāẓ* from among the strangers used to work as *mustamlī* for him'.

Both constructions, i.e. with *ʿalā* and with *li* can be found side by side.[20]

The construction with *ʿinda* (and *li*) meaning 'work as *mustamlī* with (a sheikh) for (or on behalf of) (a pupil)' is rare: *Kāna Bilālun yastamlī ʿinda Fuḍayli bni ʿIyāḍin*[21] 'Bilāl used to work as *mustamlī* with Fuḍayl b. ʿIyāḍ'; *kāna Muḥammadu bnu Abāna yastamlī lanā ʿinda Wakīʿin*[22] 'Muḥammad b. Abān used to work on our behalf as *mustamlī* with Wakīʿ'.

Occasionally there are passages in the literature where it is not certain whether *istamlā* is used in the basic meaning 'ask for dictation; take dictation; write from dictation' or in the more restricted meaning 'work as a professional *mustamlī*': *anna Sībawayhi kāna yastamlī ʿalā Ḥammādi bni Salamata*[23] '... that Sībawayh used to write (?) from Ḥammād b. Salama's dictation (as his pupil)'.

---

[12] Ibid.
[13] TB, XIV, p. 326.
[14] TB, XII, p. 248.
[15] Ibn ʿAsākir, III, p. 283 [/III, p. 286].
[16] Sakhāwī, *Ḍawʾ*, I, p. 13; III, p. 228.
[17] TB, II, p. 20.
[18] *Adab*, p. 86.
[19] Ibn ʿAsākir, II, 205 [/p. 208].
[20] TB, V, p. 225f., X, 258f.; Dhahabī, *Tadhkira*, III, p. 218.
[21] *Adab*, p. 87.
[22] Ibid.
[23] *Adab*, p. 105; TB, XII, p. 195.

Samʿānī defines the participle in its use as an epithet in the following way: *ikhtaṣṣa bi-hādhihi l-nisbati jamāʿatun kathīratun kānū yastamlūna li-l-akābiri wa-l-ʿulamāʾi*[24] 'Many people were called by this *nisba*, who occupied the position of *mustamlī* for great and learned men'. It is, however, doubtful whether the term '*mustamlī*' conveys anything to the author of *Tāj al-ʿarūs* when he says: *minhu l-mustamlī li-lladhī yaṭlubu imlāʾa l-ḥadīthi ʿan shaykhin wa-shtahara bihi Abū Bakrin Muḥammadu bnu Abāna bni Wazīri l-Balkhiyyu ... li-annahū stamlā ʿalā Wakīʿin*[25] 'Derived from this, *al-mustamlī* is a name for him who requests the dictation of hadith from a sheikh. Abū Bakr Muḥammad b. Abān b. Wazīr l-Balkhī is known by this epithet ... because he was *mustamlī* with Wakīʿ'. In accordance with the above, even in the case of the simple participle when it is not used as an epithet, the question often remains unanswered of whether it refers to a *mustamlī* in the narrower, professional sense or to a pupil simply taking dictation, particularly as occasionally the two terms might well overlap.

[The activities of the *mustamlī*]

[**30**] In the following we will attempt to define the activities of a *mustamlī* more closely and in the end to conclude with a list of *mustamlī*s together with their respective sheikhs as well as one of sheikhs whose *mustamlī*s are not known to us by name. However, neither the definition nor the list can claim to be complete. While a large amount of material has been perused for the purposes of this article, it should not be difficult to adduce more material. What matters is to paint a picture that outlines the essential aspects of an office that was not without relevance in the scholarly world of the Arab Middle Ages. Additional material might then give more depth and detail to such a picture.

The main source on offer is the extensive biographical literature, together with later works on the principles of the study of traditions (*uṣūl al-ḥadīth*). The earliest of these, Rāmhurmuzī's (d. 360/971) *al-Muḥaddith al-fāṣil* appears to touch upon the subject only briefly,[26] while al-Ḥākim al-Nīsābūrī does not mention it at all in his *Maʿrifāt ʿulūm al-ḥadīth*. Being forced to do without al-Khaṭīb al-Baghdādī's works, which only exist in manuscript form [since

[24] Samʿānī, *Ansāb*, f. 529a (*sub al-Mustamlī*)/V, p. 287.

[25] *Tāj*, X, p. 347; [XXXIX, p. 555].

[26] V. Weisweiler, *Istanbuler Handschriftenstudien zur arabischen Traditionsliteratur*, Leipzig, 1937, p. 5 [Now edited: Rāmhurmuzī, *al-Muḥaddith al-fāṣil bayna al-rāwī wa-l-wāʿī*, ed. M. ʿAjjāj al-Khaṭīb, Beirut 1971].

several works of al-Khaṭīb al-Baghdādī have been edited[27]], is bitter, although those texts are replaced approximately by the later works based on it them. Among these, Ibn al-Ṣalāḥ's book, which puts all others in the shade, and Suyūṭī's exhaustive commentary (*Tadrīb al-rāwī*) on Nawawī's excerpt are of particular importance even beyond the limits of the present essay. Valuable enrichment of these sources is provided by *Adab al-imlā' wa-l-istimlā'*, written by ʿAbd al-Karīm b. Muḥammad al-Samʿānī (d. 562/1166);[28] the author of the famous text on nisbas. It survives in a unique copy in the manuscript Feyzullah 1557 of Millet Kūtūphanesi in Istanbul, my edition of which is printing [now edited]. As the title states, the text discusses the correct conduct of the person dictating, the *mustamlī* and the pupil taking dictation. In addition we find a long description, supported by many instances in the literature, which is devoted to the *mustamlī*'s task and code of honour. This confirms and completes the observations found in the general texts on *Uṣūl al-ḥadīth* and the information in the biographical literature in a most valuable way.

We have already seen that Samʿānī defined the term '*mustamlī*' in such a way that it is an epithet of many people who used to work as *mustamlī* for prominent people and scholars. Thus we hear about al-Rabīʿ b. Sulaymān al-Murādī (d. 270)[29] that he was the *mustamlī* of everyone who transmitted from ʿAbd Allāh b. Wahb (d. 177)[30] in Egypt. [**31**] About Aḥmad b. al-Mubārak (d. 284), who bears the epithet *al-Mustamlī*, we hear that he was a *mustamlī* from 28 years of age until the end of his life;[31] and about others still we hear that they worked for the teachers in Bukhara or Nishapur, or indeed for all the sheikhs in Bukhara.[32] All this goes to prove that the work of a *mustamlī* was a professional occupation. It is proved further by the use of '*al-Mustamlī*' as an epithet, as it is hardly likely that an ordinary traditionist – who simply received traditions and other teachings by taking dictation as well as through other methods of transmission such as simple *samāʿ*, *qirā'a* and *ijāza* – would have been awarded the title '*al-Mustamli*'. And while dictation as a method of transmission enjoyed favoured status among scholars, there is no mention anywhere in the literature of people who, when they were pupils, received knowledge generally or mainly in this way. Consequently the epithet or title *Mustamlī* in connection with a proper name does not refer to one of many

[27] [*V. infra* bibliography.]
[28] GAL, I, pp. 329–30; S I, p. 564.
[29] *Adab*, p. 87; Dhahabī, *Tadhkira*, II, p. 149; Nawawī, *Tahdhīb*, p. 243.
[30] GAL S I, p. 257, 948.
[31] Dhahabī, *Tadhkira*, II, p. 196 [/p. 644, no. 666].
[32] Samʿānī, *Ansāb*, f. 529a [/V, p. 288–90].

pupils who took dictation, but the one person with the specific office of working on a more or less permanent basis as a sheikh's scribe taking dictation. The essential difference does not lie in the degree of continuity only, but also in the fact that the ordinary pupil who writes from dictation does so for himself, whereas the *mustamlī* writes for the sheikh, or at least on his behalf or according to his wishes.

We frequently read in the literature about sheikhs from the earlier days that no book was ever seen in their hands. At first it seems strange to find that they did have *mustamlī*s who were not simply pupils taking dictation, unless we want to assume in these instances that their activities were restricted to the second duty of the *mustamlī*, which will be discussed below. We have to bear in mind, however, that the statement that no book was ever seen in his hands does not necessarily mean that the sheikh did not own any books. On the contrary, many teachers did own books, but when teaching and transmitting they would draw on the rich stores of their extensive and reliable memories.

It is in the nature of the situation that the office of *istimlā*ʾ was a position of trust. Consequently it says in the biographies of many a *mustamlī* that he was a pupil of the teacher whom he served as *mustamlī* and whose works he transmitted. ʿAbd al-Wahhāb b. ʿAṭāʾ (d. ca. 204), the *mustamlī* of Saʿīd b. Abī ʿArūba (d. ca. 154), was the best authority on Saʿīd's hadiths,[33] and ʿAlī b. Sālim (d. 852) maintained a close relationship with his teacher Ibn Ḥajar al-[**32**]ʿAsqalānī (d. 852) whom he served as *mustamlī*.[34] The sheikh would dictate to the *mustamlī* his own literary creations or traditions he had received from others and committed to memory, with the aim of preserving them and creating a definitive and reliable version. In particular in the earlier years, when people relied more on their memory, many a sheikh bearing the honorary title *ḥāfiẓ* will in the end have felt that the treasures he had been preserving only or mostly in his memory needed to be saved from oblivion by being written down. The copyist's reward was, if the sheikh did not insist on keeping the written version, the text itself or a further copy. This meant personal ownership of the teacher's literary creations or his traditions, a reward that cannot be valued too highly if the teacher was an important scholar. Thus we may be able to understand that vast numbers of people aspired to this profession and that Shuʿba b. al-Ḥajjāj (d. 160) had as many as six or seven men working at copying his hadiths out for him.[35] As late as the ninth century, Yaḥyā b. Muḥammad al-Qabbānī (d. after 894), who was interested in acquiring valuable books, served ʿAbd al-Raḥmān b.

---

[33] TB, XI, p. 22.

[34] Sakhāwī, *Ḍaw*ʾ, V, p. 222f.

[35] TB, VII, p. 28; Dhahabī, *Tadhkira*, I, p. 369 [/409].

Aḥmad al-Qalqashandī (d. 871) as *mustamlī*, because he considered him to be knowledgeable.[36] Because of the close personal link to the sheikh, the *mustamlī*'s copies acquired a great philological value according to the will of the sheikh as well as the *mustamlī*. They became *uṣūl*, and their owner became a personality sought out by all those people who were interested in his teacher's works or traditions. The monetary value of the manuscript may have played a not unimportant part here, too. It is evident that under these circumstances the boundaries between a dictation secretary employed permanently and a mere pupil occasionally writing from dictation could on occasion be fluid.

In cases where the *mustamlī* was a copyist (*warrāq*) working for payment, economic considerations played a decisive part. A well-off scholar would usually have his works copied by a *warrāq*; the presence of the scholar was not even required. If, however, the copying or duplication was done by a professional copyist according to the scholar's dictation, the copyist would be *warrāq* and *mustamlī* in one person. The sources are not sufficiently eloquent to show us to what extent the *mustamlī*s were merely a specialist group of *warrāq*s, but we will have to expect it in many cases. Ādam b. Abī Iyās (d. 220), Shuʿba b. al-Ḥajjāj's (d. 160) *mustamlī*, was a *warrāq*,[37] and it was just the same [**33**] in the case of those people who bore the epithet al-Warrāq together with the epithet al-Mustamlī, for instance Isḥāq b. Yaʿqūb al-Kafarsūsī (ca. 270) and Muḥammad b. Ismāʿīl (d. 378). The latter's questionable methods when it came to tradition scholarship may well have been causally related to his work as a commercial scribe. Muḥammad b. Maʿmar al-Jayyānī (d. 377), the *mustamlī* of Ismāʿīl b. al-Qāsim al-Qālī (d. 355), and al-Qālī's *warrāq* together prepared an improved edition of al-Qālī's *al-Bāriʿ fi-l-lugha* from the autograph as well as the copies both of them took from al-Qālī's dictation.[38] We may safely assume that the delight they thus excited in al-Ḥakam al-Mustanṣir bi-Llāh, an Umayyad favouring scholarship, found its expression in hard cash. Abu'l-ʿAlāʾ al-Maʿarrī (d. 449), who employed several *mustamlī*s, expressed his surprise when one of them, apparently, did not ask to be paid for his work.[39] ʿAmr b. ʿAwn al-Wāsiṭī (d. 225) was not so lucky. He replaced his *mustamlī*, who was a warrāq but made many mistakes when speaking, with another warrāq who studied adab and poetry but did not have any understanding of hadith; in the end al-Wāsiṭī returned, contrite, to his first *mustamlī*.[40] Muḥammad b. ʿAlī

[36] Sakhāwī, *Ḍaw*ʾ, X, p. 247; Id., *Tibr*, p. 256.
[37] Ibn Saʿd, VII/2, p. 186 [/VII, p. 490].
[38] Ibn al-Abbār, *Muʿjam*, no. 360, 362.
[39] Yāqūt, *Irshād*, I, p. 179f.
[40] Adab, p. 95.

b. Qamar (d. 876), one of Ibn Ḥajar al-ʿAsqalānī's (d. 852) *mustamlīs*, wrote much, especially Ibn Ḥajar's works. Thus he made two copies of his *Fatḥ al-barī* which he sold.[41]

Although the great teachers had their own personal *mustamlī*, this does not have to rule out the possibility that they could have been more or less dedicated copyists themselves. Thus Ibrāhīm b. al-Ḥusayn b. Dīzīl (d. 281) had *mustamlīs*, but we still hear about him that one night he sat down to do some copying. He became so completely engrossed in this work that he wrote until the end of the following night. He received the epithet Sīfanna after an Egyptian bird that strips the leaves off the trees, because whenever he left another traditionist, he would refuse to leave him before he had copied all the other's hadiths.[42] Muḥammad b. Yaʿqūb al-Aṣamm (d. 346) did have a *mustamlī*, but remained a *warrāq* like his father before him. In times of need he supported himself by means of this profession and refused to take money for his work as a transmitter of traditions. To his great regret his own *warrāq* – he must have employed one at times – who may have been one and the same man as his *mustamlī*, together with Muḥammad's own son, asked for money from people.[43]

The *mustamlī*'s activities discussed so far referred only to [**34**] his service as a sheikh's dictation secretary. However, in addition he had a further duty within the dictation lecture, a discussion of which must be prefaced with a brief sketch of this kind of lecture.

Of the various methods of transmitting and teaching, the most highly valued one among those who preferred fixing texts in writing to committing texts to memory was dictation.[44] It was especially commended for its greater reliability as compared to simple *samāʿ* and *qirāʾa ʿalā l-shaykh*. The relevance attributed to dictation can be deduced from Abū Bakr b. Abī Shayba (d. 235/849),[45] according to whom nobody could be counted as *ṣāḥib ḥadīth* unless they had copied at least 20,000 hadiths from dictation.[46] However exaggerated the large numbers of participants named in the original sources as having taken part in the events of mass dictation, to be discussed below, may have been, they show the importance dictation possessed at one time. Samʿānī[47]

---

[41] Sakhāwī, *Ḍaw*ʾ, VIII, p. 176.

[42] Dhahabī, *Tadhkira*, II, p. 167; [p. 608–9, no. 633]; Ḥākim, *Maʿrifa*, p. 213; Ibn al-Jazarī, I, p. 12.

[43] Dhahabī, *Tadhkira*, III, p. 74f. [p. 860–3, no. 835].

[44] *Adab*, p. 8; Ibn al-Ṣalāḥ, p. 206 [/p. 364–5]; Suyūṭī, *Tadrīb*, p. 173 [II, p. 132f.; Marçais, 182–6].

[45] GAL S I, p. 215.

[46] *Adab*, p. 11.

[47] *Adab*, p. 15.

mentions the hosts of dictation lectures among the great traditionists of the second and third centuries, in particular Shuʿba b. al-Ḥajjāj (d. 160), Waqīʿ b. al-Jarrāḥ (d. 197), Yazīd b. Hārūn (d. 260), ʿĀṣim b. ʿAlī (d. 221), ʿAmr b. Marzūq (d. 224),[48] Bukhārī (d. 256), Abū Muslim Ibrāhīm al-Kajjī (d. 292) and Jaʿfar b. Muḥammad al-Firyābī (d. 301). In rare cases, people even received traditions in the form of dictation only, e. g. Zuhayr b. Muʿāwiya (d. 173),[49] and ʿAffān b. Muslim (d. ca. 220).[50] Listeners and copyists collected not only in the mosques, but also in streets and squares. A town crier announced that the great Bukhārī had arrived in Basra and would hold a dictation lecture,[51] and before a similar mass lecture, Firyābī was received in a grand triumph in Baghdad.[52] The preferred time for such a lecture was on a Friday, after the main prayer;[53] if it was not held on a Friday, it would still take place on a specific day of the week, while the other days were devoted to *qirāʾa*.[54] As with most customs of religious and private life, this was sanctioned by a fabricated saying of the Prophet: 'He who says the afternoon prayer and then sits down in order to dictate good words till the evening is a better man than he who releases eight of Ismāʿīl's children'.[55] Although the dictation lecture was cultivated particularly in tradition scholarship, other scholars did use it **[35]** to a great extent too. Suyūṭī has some instructive examples from the field of lexicology.[56]

In the fourth century, as Mez[57] already pointed out, the dictation lectures became less frequent, especially in the secular subjects, without, however, ever being replaced completely by other methods of transmitting. The last philologist to have dictated is said to have been [Abū l-Qāsim] Yūsuf b. ʿAbd Allāh al-Zujājī (d. 415).[58] The *qirāʾa ʿalā l-shaykh* – to say nothing of other methods of transmitting – was, after all, much easier for the student as it

[48] Ibn Saʿd, VII/2, p. 55 [/VII, p. 305].

[49] Ibn Saʿd, VI, p. 262 [/VI, p. 372]; Dhahabī, *Tadhkira*, I, p. 214 [/233, no. 219]; *Adab*, p. 11.

[50] Ibn Saʿd, VII/2, p. 51, 78 [/VII, p. 298, 336]; Dhahabī, *Tadhkira*, I, p. 344 [/p. 379–81, no. 378]; *Adab*, p. 11.

[51] TB, II, p. 15.

[52] TB, VII, p. 201; *Adab*, p. 17.

[53] TB, III, p. 182; Ibn Khallikān, no. 653 [/IV, p. 341, no. 642]; Ibn Abī Yaʿlā, *Ṭabaqāt*, p. 382 [/II, p. 69, no. 604]; Yāqūt, *Muʿjam al-Buldān*, I, p. 616; Id., *Irshād*, VII, p. 74; *Adab*, 46; Suyūṭī, *Tadrīb*, p. 176 [II, /p. 139–40].

[54] *Adab*, p. 23.

[55] Suyūṭī, *Tadrīb*, p. 176 [II, 140; taken up from Bayhaqī, *Shuʿab*, I, 410, nr. 563].

[56] Suyūṭī, *Muzhir*, I, 30 [cf. *Muzhir*, I, p. 92, 94 (towards the end of chap. I), 145–6 (chap. VI), 159–60 (chap. VII); all on Thaʿlab, Ibn Durayd, al-Qālī]

[57] Mez, *Renaissance*, p. 171 [/178–9].

[58] Dhahabī, *Mushtabih*, p. 239 [/p. 335]; Yāqūt, *Irshād*, VII, p. 308; Suyūṭī, *Bughya*, p. 422 [/II, 357–8, no. 2183]; Id., *Muzhir*, I, 30. The form of his name and the date given by Mez are wrong [Marçais, p. 182, n. 1, *ubi leg.* Zujājī, *non* al-Zajjājī]

transferred the main workload from the lecture itself to the quiet of one's own study. The decline of dictation becomes quite apparent when we hear about a sheikh who was living at the turn of the fourth and fifth centuries that he dictated one single lecture each year, on the 1st Muḥarram.[59] All the same, even in Samʿānī's day there were teachers who specialised in dictation,[60] as well as sheikhs who taught their pupils the verses:

> "Be diligent in writing dictation after the words of the *ḥuffāẓ* and the *fuḍalāʾ*!
> For the best kind of *samāʿ* is that which you write down from dictation"[61]
> [two verses said by Abū Ṭāhir al-Silafī, d. 576/1180][62]

On the other hand, Samʿānī[63] had to lament the fact that in his day the fire of religious knowledge had died down, its sparks were few in number and its market but little visited, and that consequently, after a dictation lecture, not even one inkwell was to be found with which the names of the participants could have been written down. And this despite the fact that in the classical heyday of dictation the preferred way of estimating the number of participants had been by counting the number of inkwells!.[64]

While we have seen that Ibn al-Ṣalāḥ (d. 643) still had a very high opinion of the dictation lecture, after his death it was practised less and less, but later experienced a second flowering in the field of hadith, dating from the last years of ʿAbd al-Raḥīm b. al-Ḥusayn al-ʿIrāqī's life (d. 806). The latter resumed the practice in 795 or 796 and delivered 416 dictation lectures until his death, dictating at first various texts, then the *Takhrīj* of Nawāwī's *Arbaʿūn* and finally a *Mustakhraj* of Ḥākim al-Nīshābūrī's *Mustadrak* during ca. 300 lectures. If we spread these 416 dictation lectures over the ten years during which they are said to have taken place we find that he dictated a lecture less frequently than once a week. After [**36**] this time the custom petered out again, until his son Aḥmad b. ʿAbd al-Raḥīm al-ʿIrāqī (d. 826) revived it and dictated 600 lectures until his death; Ibn Ḥajar al-ʿAsqalānī (d. 852) even more than 1000. These lectures by the two ʿIrāqīs and Ibn Ḥajar were devoted to the study of tradition. After Ibn Ḥajar's death, there was no dictation for about 20 years, until, early in 872, Suyūṭī once again began dictating traditions and dictated 80 lectures at first, and later another 50. When, however, he intended to deliver a

59 TB, V, p. 67.
60 *Shadharāt*, IV, p. 102; *Adab*, p. 24.
61 *Adab*, 11–12 [. Ibn Daqīq al-ʿĪd, *Iqtirāḥ*, p. 275].
62 [Op. cit., p. 276; Sakhāwī, *Fatḥ al-mughīth*, 5 vols., Riyadh, 2005, III, p. 249].
63 *Adab*, p. 18.
64 TB, VI, p. 122; *Adab*, 17, 18, 96; Subkī, *Ṭabaqāt*, II, p. 150; Suyūṭī, *Tadrīb*, p. 173.

lecture devoted to the subject of lexicology, he found no students and had to abandon this intention.[65]

As for their size, the lectures changed from a small circle of students listening to their sheikh to the great mass lecture which attracted thousands and was an important event in town. From the earlier days in particular we have numerous references to similar mass lectures. To give but a few examples from the wealth of traditions: Abū Zakariyyā' al-ʿĀ'idhī's lecture in Cordoba in 369 was attended by thousands of people,[66] Bukhārī's (d. 256) lecture in Baghdad had 20,000 students.[67] ʿAlī b. ʿĀṣim (d. 201) had more than 30,000 listeners,[68] and Sulaymān b. Ḥarb (d. ca. 224) in Baghdād, 40,000.[69] Ibrāhīm b. ʿAbd Allāh al-Kajjī (d. 292) attracted the same number of students, and as Baghdād's Ghassān Square was not large enough, they had to write standing up.[70] The presumably highest reported number of students attending a single lecture is attributed to ʿĀṣim b. ʿAlī al-Wāsiṭī (d. 221) with more than 100,000.[71] These figures may well be exaggerated many times over the actual numbers, and we may well have to deduct – as, indeed, some Arab historians have done – a substantial number of onlookers who were not interested in the subject at all. However, even so there would have been many people who genuinely wished to hear the sheikh, people who, without the aids of modern technology or, depending on the situation, other possible support, had to go away empty-handed because of the great space and the large number of listeners.

The remedy for this predicament was to employ, when needed, one or more intermediaries between the sheikh and his students, who would repeat the sheikh's words to the students with increased volume. Where necessary this repetition was organised in such a way that the sheikh was speaking to the people [37] nearest to him and a first intermediary, who repeated his words to the second one standing a certain distance away, and so forth, and the text of the dictation could thus reach even the furthest corners of the lecture hall. It is easy to imagine to what extent the philological faithfulness must have suffered from this system of transmission, and the misgivings, to be discussed below, in studying tradition are only too understandable. Someone employed in this

---

[65] Sakhāwī, *Ḍaw'*, I, p. 339–41: IV, p. 174; Suyuṭī, *Tadrīb*, p. 176 [/II, p. 139]; Id. *Muzhir*, I, p. 30: Goldziher, 'Zur Charakteristik', p. 20–1 [Silvestre de Sacy, *Anthologie*, p. 137]; Ibn Kathīr, *Ikhtiṣār*, p. 182.

[66] Ibn al-Abbār, no. 1536.

[67] TB, II, p. 20; *Adab*, p. 17.

[68] TB, XI, p. 454; *Adab*, p. 17.

[69] TB, IX, p. 33; Ibn Bashkuwāl, *Ṣila*, no. 449.

[70] TB, VI, 121–2; *Adab*, p. 96.

[71] TB, XII, p. 248; *Adab*, p. 17.

way was at first called *muballigh* 'intermediary' and his work *tablīgh*.[72] The synonym *mulqī* is also found. While Samʿānī[73] defines the latter term as someone entrusted with *al-ilqā' wa-l-iʿāda* during the lecture, it is not a term with which Subkī is familiar, and he appears to be unsure whether to equate a *mulqī* with the *muʿīd* of his day, or the *qāri'* of a *mudarris*, or a *muʿallim*'s *mustamlī*.[74] Occasionally we also find the term *muktib* 'someone who dictates'. Thus we read about Ādam b. Abī Iyās (d. 220) that he worked as a *muktib* for Shuʿba b. al-Ḥajjāj (d. 160).[75] This occupation, which consisted in immediate and word-by-word repetition confined to the dictation lecture, was entirely different from the work of the *muʿīd* (tutor), who could have been employed in any kind of teaching. Generally, during a lecture there would be one on each side of the sheikh. Unlike the intermediary in the dictation lecture, they only started their work *after* the actual lecture, as they were explicitly coaching tutors.[76]

As we saw above, some sheikhs had *mustamlīs* as their assistants to write the sheikhs' works and collections of traditions from dictation. We may safely assume that especially famous and sought-after teachers would employ a *mustamlī*. These, however, were the same teachers who gave great dictation lectures which suffered from the difficulty that the sheikh's voice could not reach the furthest corners. In most cases the obvious solution was for the *mustamlī* to be in charge of transmitting the sheikh's words to those listeners who were too far away to hear. The *mustamlī*'s known ability in his job of taking dictation ensured his reliable and competent performance of this duty as well. Consequently the word *mustamlī* became the term for someone who transmitted the sheikh's words during the dictation lecture, and replaced the other terms mentioned above.[77] Indeed, it was used to describe the

[72] Ibn Abī Yaʿlā, *Ṭabaqāt*, p. 382 [/II, p. 69f., no. 604]; *Adab*, p. 18, 105; Ibn Ṣalāḥ, *ʿUlūm*, 149 [Marçais, p. 183, n. 2]; Suyūṭī, *Tadrīb*, 136; Dozy, *Supplément*, p. 113a, *sub b-l-gh*, second verbal form.

[73] Samʿānī, *Ansāb*, f. 542a [/V, p. 381].

[74] Subkī, *Ṭabaqāt*, II, p. 314: where we read *al-muʿallim* rather than *al-mʿly*.

[75] Dhahabī, *Tadhkira*, I, p. 369 [/p. 409, no. 414].

[76] Ibn Jamāʿa, *Tadhkira*, p. 151, 201, 204; Ibn Baṭṭūṭa, *Riḥla*, II, p. 109; Qalqashandī, V, p. 464; EI[1], III, p. 425.

[77] Because of the dearth of source texts available to him, A. von Kremer (in Sitzungsberichte der Akademie der Wissenschaften zu Wien, phil.-hist. Klasse, 98, p. 580) fails to appreciate the function of the *mustamlī* when he says: **[38]** 'We find combined information very early on in the transmission of traditions: through writing and oral recital at the same time. The teacher of traditions recited the texts by heart, but he had a secretary (*mustamlin*) who followed the recitation minutely from a written text, and could correct every mistake in the recitation ... He was the prompter for the professor talking from memory.' If one has to use the term 'prompter' for a man whose basic job requirement was a

intermediary even [**38**] in cases where he could not have been a *mustamlī*, i.e. a secretary writing from dictation, but might well have been employed for general or individual external reasons. (In this context it is interesting that Mālik b. Anas (d. 179) had a secretary (*kātib*) named Ḥabīb who had copied his works. The latter read them to the students during the lecture and Mālik corrected him if he made mistakes.)[78] Thus when Abū Ḥātim b. Ḥibbān al-Bustī (d. 354) came to Nishabur and, when requested, prepared to give a dictation lecture, he looked around him and of the all his listeners addressed the youngest, saying: 'You act as *mustamlī*!'.[79]

Consequently, while the *mustamlī* as the sheikh's secretary did also have the job of intermediary during a dictation lecture, not every intermediary in a dictation lecture must also have been a *mustamlī*. Maybe we even need this distinction in order to explain the terms *muballigh*, *mulqī* and *muktib* mentioned above. In individual cases it will only rarely be possible to determine with certainty whether a *mustamlī* performed both duties, although Ādam b. Abī Iyās (d. 220), mentioned several times before, is someone about whom we do have explicit statements to this effect.[80] Rather, in the case of a *mustamlī* with great vocal powers it is to be expected that he will be used exclusively as intermediary in a dictation lecture because of his special physiological ability. One such *mustamlī* was Hārūn *al-Mustamlī* who was called because three other *mustamlī*s had failed, and whose voice then proved equal even to the thunder.[81] This may also be apply to some extent to those *mustamlī*s about whose lack of education and attention as well as their general unpleasantness we sometimes find complaints. In his *Adab al-imlā' wa-l-istimlā'* Sam'ānī has a chapter about the *mustamlī*, and in the theoretical exposition he mentions only the *mustamlī*'s role as intermediary in the dictation lecture. His examples, on the other hand, are often stories which obviously or probably refer to the *mustamlī*s' work as secretary writing from dictation. Sam'ānī's approach shows most clearly how closely the two were linked in practice, [**39**] and that we may regard this twofold employment as the rule for *mustamlī*s. When the dictation lectures came to an end, the term disappeared and both the *mustamlī*'s duties fell into oblivion. While Muḥammad Murtaḍā [al-Zabīdī][82] explains *istamlā* correctly as meaning 'to request dictation', he

powerful voice as he had to carry out his duties shouting rather than talking, it should at least be understood that he did not 'prompt' the professor but the students.

[78] Dhahabī, *Tadhkira*, I, p. 197 [/p. 211].

[79] Yāqūt, *Mu'jam al-buldān*, I, p. 616.

[80] Dhahabī, *Tadhkira*, I, p. 369 [/409].

[81] TB, IX, p. 33.

[82] *Tāj*, X, p. 347 [/XXXIX, p. 555].

then gives the example that Muḥammad b. Abān al-Balkhī (d. 244) practised *istimlā'* under Wakī' b. al-Jarrāḥ (d. 197), thus proving that in his (i.e., Muḥammad Murtaḍā's) day, the *mustamlī*'s twofold office was not known any more.

The true domain of a *mustamlī* working as intermediary in a dictation lecture was, of course, a mass lecture. However, *mustamlī*s were not employed for all big dictation lectures. Sulaymān b. Mihrān al-A'māsh (d. 148)[83] reports[84] that Ibrāhīm al-Nakha'ī's (d. ca. 95)[85] audience used to be so numerous that those sitting further away were obliged to enquire from one another the words of the sheikh. In another instance, 'Āṣim b. 'Alī al-Wāsiṭī's (d. 221) gigantic dictation lecture did not from the beginning have a *mustamlī*.[86] In Sulaymān b. Ḥarb (d. ca. 224) and Abū Zakariyyā' al-'Ā'idhī's (d. ca. 369) dictation lectures, only one *mustamlī* was employed despite the fact that thousands of people attended.[87] In general, however, several *mustamlī*s would be employed in the larger dictation lectures. In Baghdad 'Āṣim b. 'Alī al-Wāsiṭī (d. 221) had the two Hārūn who were famous *mustamlī*s.[88] 'Alī b. 'Āṣim (d. 201),[89] Sulaymān b. Ḥarb (d. 224),[90] Bukhārī (d. 256),[91] and Ibn al-Farrā' (d. 458)[92] employed three *mustamlī*s at the same time, al-Ḥasan b. Ismā'īl al-Mahāmilī (d. 330)[93] four, and the learned vizier Ismā'īl b. 'Abbād (d. 385)[94] six or seven.[95] At Ibrāhīm b. 'Abd Allāh al-Kajjī's (d. 292) dictation lectures seven *mustamlī*s were present,[96] at Muḥammad b. Muslim b. Wāra's (d. ca. 270) twenty,[97] and at Ja'far b. Muḥammad al-Firyābī's (d. 301) is said to have had as many as 316 *mustamlī*s.[98] While there is some information as to the number of participants, it is not possible to determine with any certainty the ratio between *mustamlī*s and students in general or, indeed, whether there was any kind of rule, as we

---

[83] Ibn Khallikān, 270 [p. 400–3, no. 271]; Dhahabī, *Tadhkira*, I, 145 [/p. 154, no. 149].

[84] Ibn Ṣalāḥ, *'Ulūm*, p.150; Suyūṭī, *Tadrīb*, p. 136.

[85] Nawawī, *Tahdhīb*, p. 135; Dhahabī, *Tadhkira*, I, 69 [/p. 73–5, no. 70].

[86] TB, XII, p. 248; *Adab*, p. 16–7.

[87] TB, IX, p. 33; Ibn Bashkuwāl, *Ṣila*, no. 449; Ibn al-Abbār, *Mu'jam*, no. 1536.

[88] TB, XII, p. 248; *Adab*, p. 96.

[89] TB, XI, p. 454.

[90] TB, IX, p. 33.

[91] TB, II, p. 20.

[92] Ibn Abī Ya'lā, *Ṭabaqāt*, p. 382.

[93] TB, XIV, p. 326; Ibn Abī Ya'lā, *Ṭabaqāt*, p. 345

[94] Yāqūt, *Irshād*, II, p. 312; Suyūṭī, *Bughya*, p. 196 [/I, p. 449–51, no. 918].

[95] Mez, *Renaissance*, p. 171 [/p. 179], misunderstood the passage in Yāqūt as regards the *mustamlī*'s technique and consequently arrived at an erroneous interpretation of the passage.

[96] TB, VI, p. 122; *Adab*, p. 96.

[97] *Adab*, p. 96.

[98] *Adab*, p. 18.

are obliged to note that, conversely, there are instances of a *mustamlī* having been present even in relatively small dictation lectures.[99]

In any case the *mustamlī*'s work was an important part [**40**] of dictation lectures, especially those by traditionists. The degree to which had merged into the general consciousness is shown by the fact that the Abbasids al-Manṣūr and al-Ma'mūn were reported to have said[100] that the only delights of the world they were lacking were for the traditionists to gather round them and for the *mustamlī* to ask them: 'Of whom did you narrate?' The mischievous cynic Abū l-ʿIbar Muḥammad b. Aḥmad [al-Hāshimī] (d. 250) used to parody learned style by occasionally dictating a lecture, where he would sit on a ladder, a length of pipe in his hand, a slipper on his head, and a cap on each foot. If anyone should laugh, he would be doused with water from the sewer in front of the sheikh. Of course he also had a *mustamlī*, whom, in a true reversal of conditions, he put inside a well, whence his voice would in vain attempt to penetrate the noise made by three people clattering with mortars.[101] How important a part the *mustamlī* was can also be seen in a passage by Sakhāwī,[102] where in a brief description of a dictation lecture in the year 853 he mentions explicitly who was employed as *mustamlī*.

It is obvious that under these circumstances the *post* of *mustamlī* was valued and sought after. Occasionally the sheikh would mention this to his *mustamlī*.[103] There was a great struggle for the position with Ibn Ḥajar al-ʿAsqalānī (d. 852) which led to jealousies among the scholars.[104] The rank of a *mustamlī* compared to the sheikh could not be shown more clearly than by the dream in which Yaʿqūb b. Sufyān al-Fasawī (d. ca. 277) is alleged to report from the afterlife that God has forgiven him and ordered him to continue transmitting in Heaven as he did on earth, whereupon Gabriel served as his *mustamlī* and the angels wrote with golden quills.[105] Occasional disparaging remarks, more of which will have to be said below, by some sheikhs have done nothing to diminish this esteem. Besides sociological reasons of a more general nature, the esteem enjoyed by this position should be assumed to have been the main reason why there are some instances of hereditary *mustamlīs*. It seems that not only Ṭāhir b. Muḥammad al-Shaḥḥāmī (d. 479) was a *mustamlī*, but also his son Zāhir (d. 533) and in turn his son ʿAbd

[99] Sakhāwī, *Tibr*, p. 256.
[100] *Adab*, p. 18–20.
[101] *Aghānī*, XX, p. 89; Kutubī, *Fawāt*, II, p. 217–8 [/III, p. 299–300]; Ṣafadī, *Wāfī*, II, p. 42–3.
[102] Sakhāwī, *Tibr*, p. 256.
[103] TB, V, p. 228; *Adab*, p. 89.
[104] Sakhāwī, *Ḍaw'*, VIII, p. 178; Id., *Tibr*, p. 215.
[105] *Adab*, p. 14; Suyūṭī, *Tadrīb*, p. 214

al-Khāliq (d. 549); and ʿAbd al-Waḥḥāb b. Aḥmad al-ʿIrāqī (d. 818) stepped as *mustamlī* into his father Aḥmad b. ʿAbd al-Raḥmān's (d. 826) footsteps. Other family relations can also be found; for instance two brothers in the same profession.[106]

[Change in office]

Before we consider in more detail the requirements a *mustamlī* had to fulfil, [**41**] let us briefly mention the change in office. The list at the end of this article shows us that it was not unusual for one *mustamlī* to serve several sheikhs, although we cannot say with certainty whether this was at one time or consecutively. Some more examples we have already given above, when discussing the professional nature of this office. Conversely, a sheikh, who (as we have seen) might well in the past have been a *mustamlī* himself, frequently employed more than one *mustamlī* later, and that not always simultaneously as for the great dictation lectures of the earlier days. Death,[107] change of place[108] and other reasons could prompt this change of person. We do not, however, gain a clear picture in all the individual cases. Consequently it is of no little interest to follow the changes of *mustamlī* under Ibn Ḥajar al-ʿAsqalānī (d. 852), of which we have knowledge, albeit not complete, thanks to the more detailed writings of his pupil Sakhāwī (d. 902). At first Ibn Ḥajar himself worked as a *mustamlī* for ʿAbd al-Raḥīm al-ʿIrāqī (d. 806),[109] whom we mentioned above because of his services to the revival of the dictation lecture. Once he was a sheikh and dictated his own lectures, Riḍwān b. Muḥammad al-ʿUqbī (d. 3th Rajab 852) was his preferred and permanent *mustamlī*,[110] and after his faithful assistant's death we find Ibn Ḥajar in prayer by his graveside.[111] For a time, in Damascus he occasionally employed Ibrāhīm b. Aḥmad al-ʿAjlūnī (d. 888),[112] who had been warmly recommended to him but proved to be imperfect all the same. While in Aleppo he employed his travelling companion ʿAlī b. Sālim (d. 852),[113] and a further temporary *mustamlī* mentioned is Ibrāhīm b. Khiḍr (d. 852).[114] After the death of his

[106] TB, XIV, p. 406.
[107] Sakhāwī, *Tibr*, p. 215.
[108] Ibn Abī l-Wafāʾ, *Jawāhir*, I, p. 298.
[109] Sakhāwī, *Ḍawʾ*, IV, p. 175.
[110] Sakhāwī, *Ḍawʾ*, III, p. 228; Id., *Tibr*, p. 241.
[111] Sakhāwī, *Tibr*, p. 214.
[112] Sakhāwī, *Ḍawʾ*, I, p. 13.
[113] Sakhāwī, *Ḍawʾ*, V, p. 222; Id., *Tibr*, p. 244.
[114] Sakhāwī, *Ḍawʾ*, I, p. 45.

long-term *mustamlī* Riḍwān al-ʿUqbī, Ibn Ḥajar entrusted the position, much coveted by several rivals, to Muḥammad b. Qamar (d. 876),[115] who held it until Ibn Ḥajar's own early death.

[Requirements for the office of *mustamlī*]

It is obvious that for a serious conception of tradition scholarship and its rules, and for attempting philological precision, certain requirements would have to be made of the person who was *mustamlī*, requirements which would be essential in establishing his suitability.

Physically, the first requirement was a strong voice, which would enable him to broadcast the teacher's words as far as even the most distant listener to a dictation lecture. The size of the lectures, the fact that they frequently took place in the open air, and the need for absolutely faithful rendering of words and even individual letters give us an indication of what volume of voice would often be required. Consequently it is not astonishing to find Bashīr b. ʿUqba al-Dawraqī[116] saying: 'In a dictation lecture the *mustamlī* is what a drummer (or: the drum) is in the army'.[117] **[42]** It is for the same reason that the first quality Samʿānī[118] asks for in a *mustamlī* is that he should be possessed of a strong voice. When Ismāʿīl b. ʿUlayya (d. 193) was asked by his *mustamlī* to speak louder because of the large crowd assembled for his dictation lecture, he pointed out to the *mustamlī* that, unlike a *muḥaddith*, it was in fact the *mustamlī*'s professional duty to raise his voice.[119] When we already read about Abū Zakariyyāʾ al-ʿĀʾidī's (ca. 369) *mustamlī* in Cordoba[120] that he raised his voice to reach the loudest possible volume, one of the two *mustamlī*s known as Hārūn *al-Mustamlī* must indeed have been unsurpassed in this respect. When Sūlaymān b. Ḥarb (d. 224) dictated a great lecture in front of the caliphs' palace, attended by the caliph al-Maʾmūn himself, three *mustamlī*s were not enough to make the sheikh's words audible throughout the audience. The universal consensus was that Hārūn would have to be fetched. When he arrived and began 'Of whom are you narrating?' his voice was equal to the thunder, and the other *mustamlī*s were silent.[121]

---

[115] Sakhāwī, *Ḍaw'*, VIII, p. 176–8; Id., *Tibr*, p. 215.
[116] Samʿānī, *Ansāb*, f. 231a [/III, p. 501]; Yāqūt, *Muʿjam al-buldān*, II, p. 619; TT, I, p. 465–6.
[117] *Adab*, p. 89.
[118] Ibid.
[119] Ibid.; Suyūṭī, *Tadrīb*, p. 136; [Azami, *Studies*, p. 194].
[120] Ibn al-Abbār, *Muʿjam*, no. 1536.
[121] TB, IX, p. 33.

Great vocal volume was of only dubious value, however, if the *mustamlī* lacked the necessary intellectual qualities. Consequently Samʿānī (Ad f. 76b, 79b) asks of a *mustamlī* that he must be attentive and interested in scholarship, and not half-witted and careless. His speech should be pure and his choice of words lucid and elegant. Similar demands are made by Ibn al-Ṣalāḥ[122] and Suyūṭī.[123] It was particularly important that the candidate should have a certain measure of education in tradition scholarship.[124] Ibrāhīm b. Muḥammad al-Fazārī (d. ca. 185)[125] considered himself justified in stating[126] that usually the most excellent men were selected for the position. Despite certain deficiencies in his tradition scholarship, Muḥammad b. Ismāʿīl *al-Mustamlī* (d. 378) was awarded the title *ḥāfiẓ*,[127] and 'the great *ḥuffāẓ* from among the foreigners' used to serve Ibrāhīm al-Ḥusayn al-Hamadhāṇī al-Kattānī (d. 281) as *mustamlī*.[128]

It appears that everyday practice, however, did not always conform to these theoretical requirements. Otherwise Shuʿba b. al-Ḥajjāj (d. 160) would not already have stated,[129] albeit only occasionally, that only a low person would serve as *mustamlī*, and Sufyān b. ʿUyayna (d. 198) would not have been driven to saying[130] that 'every group of people has some riffraff. *Mustamlī*s are the riffraff among the traditionists'. And Sakhāwī laments[131] the writing, intelligence, choice of words, half-wittedness and meanness about books [**43**] of a man who was Ibn Ḥajar al-ʿAsqalānīs favourite *mustamlī* for his dictation lectures in Damascus. A typical example of a *mustamlī*'s stupidity is the following anecdote:[132] Yazīd b. Hārūn (d. 206) once said during a dictation lecture, 'Several (*ʿidda* = a number of) narrated to us'. When his *mustamlī* called 'Whose son is ʿIdda?', Yazīd replied with a sigh "Idda, the son of Oh-would-that-I-were-rid-of-you (*faqadtuka*).' When Khālid b. al-Ḥārith (d. 186) said during the explanation of a hadith, ʿAbū ʿUthmān had doubts concerning (the correctness of the word) "God"', his inattentive *mustamlī* called angrily: 'You are lying, enemy of God! I have never doubted God!'.[133]

---

122 Ibn al-Ṣalāḥ, *ʿUlūm*, p. 206.
123 Suyūṭī, *Tadrīb*, p. 173.
124 *Adab*, p. 93.
125 Dhahbī, *Tadhkira*, I, p. 251 [/p. 273–4, no. 259]; TT, I, p. 151.
126 *Adab*, p. 91.
127 TB, II, p. 54
128 Ibn ʿAsākir, II, p. 205 [/II, p. 208].
129 *Adab*, p. 91.
130 *Adab*, p. 91.
131 Sakhāwī, *Ḍaw*ʾ, I, p. 13.
132 *Adab*, p. 90; Ibn Ṣalāḥ, *ʿUlūm*, p. 206 [/p. 364]; Suyūṭī, *Tadrīb*, p. 174 [/II, p. 134].
133 *Adab*, p. 90.

Samʿānī[134] also narrates two amusing examples of insurmountable obtuseness or deafness on the part of the *mustamlī*, one from a lecture dictated by Niẓām al-Mulk (d. 485) and one from his own experience.

What was required of the *mustamlī* as regards proper demeanour was probably on the whole similar to what was generally expected of scholars and discussed in adab writings of all kinds. When a stranger who was serving him as a *mustamlī* (or dictation student) spat during his work, Yazīd b. Hārūn (d. 206) reproached him with two verses.[135] Al-Fuḍayl b. ʿIyād (d. 187) criticised an old failing of his *mustamlī*'s, walking off during a lecture.[136] Similar experiences may have been the reason why Abū Usāma Ḥammād b. Usāma (d. 201) asked to 'Bring me a *mustamlī* who is agreeable to the heart. Off with the obnoxious ones!' as well as for Yazīd b. Hārūn's (d. 206) words to his *mustamlī* 'O God, let us not become obnoxious!'.[137]

Despite all these demands even important traditionists occasionally employed boys as *mustamlī*s. An early instance of this practice is Sufyān al-Thawrī's (d. 161)[138] dictation lecture. We have already mentioned that Abū Ḥātim b. Ḥibbān al-Bustī (d. 354) after a Friday prayer in 334 in Nishabur chose as his *mustamlī* al-Ḥākim al-Nīshābūrī (321–405) as he was the youngest of those present.[139]

While a sheikh was not able to choose his students, he did chose his own *mustamlī*,[140] often not without critical examination. When al-Zubayr b. Bakkār (d. 256) came to Baghdad, he asked to be introduced to the *mustamlī* recommended by his students. When, in the first lecture, the *mustamlī* addressed him with the customary question: 'Of whom are you narrating, o son of the disciples (ḥawāri) of God's messenger?', al-Zubayr was so pleased about the form of address, unusual in its elegant [**44**] courteousness, that he continued to employ this *mustamlī*.[141] The relationship of personal trust existing between teacher and *mustamlī* occasionally allowed the teacher to joke with the *mustamlī*,[142] just as it allowed the *mustamlī* to point out the sheikh's mistakes.[143] Even so, Shuʿba b. al-Ḥajjāj (d. 160) was incensed with his

[134] *Adab*, p. 93.
[135] *Adab*, p. 86.
[136] *Adab*, p. 87.
[137] *Adab*, p. 85.
[138] *Adab*, p. 86.
[139] Yāqūt, *Muʿjam al-buldān*, I, p. 616.
[140] *Adab*, p. 84.
[141] TB, VIII, p. 468.
[142] Ibn ʿAsākir, II, p. 31
[143] TB, III, p. 182–3; Yāqūt, *Irshād*, VII, p. 174; Ibn Khallikān, no. 653.

mustamlī for contradicting him,[144] and the Qāḍī Ḥayyān b. Bishr (d. 237) even had his *mustamlī* thrown into gaol for correcting him.[145]

If the *mustamlī* was to perform his duties during the dictation lecture efficiently, he had to sit on a raised seat, such as a bench or a chair, which would of course have to be directly next to the sheikh.[146] During a great lecture dictated by ʿĀsim b. ʿAlī (d. 221) in the palm courtyard of the main mosque in al-Ruṣāfa, the *mustamlī* was sitting on a bent palm tree.[147] If the sheikh himself is sitting on a raised seat,[148] this will determine the *mustamlī*'s position. If he does not have a raised seat at his disposal, he will perform his duties standing up, which, indeed, appears to have been the customary position. When he was Mālik b. Anas's *mustamlī*, Ismāʿīl b. Ibrāhīm b. ʿUlayya (d. 193)[149] stood before him,[150] Ādam b. Abī Iyās (d. 220) stood before Shuʿba b. al-Ḥajjāj.[151] When Abū l-ʿIbar Muḥammad b. Aḥmad al-Hāshimī (d. ca. 250) dictated a lecture in the front part of a house in Baghdad, his *mustamlī* was standing in the courtyard.[152] Correspondingly, he positioned his *mustamlī* inside a well in his parody of a dictation lecture mentioned above.

His position of trust with the sheikh allows the *mustamlī* to influence the time at which the dictation lecture starts, and, for instance, a sheikh who arrived for the dictation was asked by his *mustamlī* to wait until Sulaymān b. Aḥmad al-Ṭabarānī (d. 360)[153] was present.[154] The *mustamlī* begins his actual duties by requesting, if necessary, the students to be silent, and then reciting a sura from the Koran followed by the *basmalah*, the *ḥamdalah* and the *taṣliyyah*, unless the sheikh does all this himself.[155] The fact that any participant may recite the sura and that it is permitted to recite it before asking for silence shows how much these words have become formulae.[156] Then the *mustamlī* prays for the sheikh in the following words: 'May God be well pleased with

---

[144] *Adab*, p. 91.

[145] TB, VIII, p. 285; *Adab*, p. 105–6.

[146] Adab, p. 88; Ibn Ṣalāḥ, *ʿUlūm*, p. 206 [/p. 364]; Suyūṭī, *Tadrīb*, p. 174 [/II, p. 134]; Ibn Kathīr, *Ikhtiṣār*, p. 133 [Marçais, p. 183: as the *muballigh* for the prayer, on a *dakka*].

[147] TB, XII, p. 248; *Adab*, p. 17; Dhahabī, *Tadhkira*, I, p. 359 [/p. 397, no. 397]

[148] TB, IX, p. 33; Ibn a. Yʿalā, *Ṭabaqāt*, p. 345; *Adab*, 50–1; Ibn Jamāʿa, *Tadhkira*, p. 147–8.

[149] Dhahabī, *Tadhkira*, I, p. 296.

[150] [*Adab*, p. 89, l. 2–3].

[151] Ibn a. Yʿalā, *Ṭabaqāt*, p. 280; *Adab*, p. 15, 89.

[152] Ibn ʿAsākir, II, p. 118.

[153] GAL S I, p. 279.

[154] Ibn ʿAsākir, p. 241 [/p. 243].

[155] *Adab*, 48–9, 51–2, 96–8; Ibn Ṣalāḥ, *ʿUlūm*, p. 207 [/p. 365]; Suyūṭī, *Tadrīb*, p. 174 [/II, p. 135].

[156] *Adab*, 48–9; Ibn Ṣalāḥ, *ʿUlūm*, p. 207 [/p. 365]; *Tadrīb*, p. 174 [/II, p. 135].

the sheikh, his parents and all Muslims';[157] and if the sheikh is aware of the conditional nature of his own worth, the *mustamlī* may use the words 'with our lord' (*ʿan sayyidinā*) instead of 'the sheikh'.[158] **[45]** This choice of words, however, is disapproved of by some,[159] and Abū Bakr b. Ḥāmid, for instance, forbade Ismāʿīl b. Muḥammad *al-Mustamlī* (d. 434) to call him 'imām' during the dictation lecture.[160] The *mustamlī* is also forbidden, at least according to the example of Ibn Ḥanbal and other ancient authorities, to pray for a long life for the sheikh.[161] Sensible people have never valued all those prayers traditionists said for their sheikh any higher than the watchman's call 'Allāhu akbar', although Ibn ʿUyayna (d. 198) is said to have attributed, jokingly, one assumes, his long life to all the good wishes he received from his hadith students.[162]

The *mustamlī* begins his actual duties by dictating to the students in the dictation lecture the sheikh's *ism*, *kunya* and *nisba*. Should he not know these constituents of the sheikh's name, as may happen if strangers or listeners who do not know the sheikh personally are employed as *mustamlī*, he will first ask the sheikh.[163] Afterwards he turns towards the sheikh and requests him to start dictation, with the formula typical of a *mustamlī*: 'Of whom have you narrated?' (*man dhakarta*) or 'Who narrated to you?' (*man ḥaddathaka*) or 'What have you narrated?' (*mā dhakarta*), adding the benediction 'God have mercy on you' or 'May God be well pleased with you'.[164] Of these questions, 'Of whom have you narrated?' appears to have been the most frequently used formula. Exactly how characteristic it must have been for the start of a great dictation lecture can be seen not only from its reiteration in many individual accounts, but also from the statement attributed to the chief judge Yaḥyā b. Aktham (d. ca. 243), who said that despite his position as vizier and chief judge, nothing seemed to him to be more delightful than the *mustamlī*'s question 'Of whom have you narrated?'.[165] Similar statements are attributed to the Abbasid caliphs al-Manṣūr and al-Maʾmūn.[166]

The sheikh then replies to this question by giving the exact name of his authority: 'X narrated to us', and recites the relevant hadith. The *mustamlī*

---

[157] Ibn Jamāʿa, *Tadhkira*, p. 162.
[158] *Adab*, p. 98.
[159] *Adab*, p. 99.
[160] *Adab*, p. 99–100.
[161] *Adab*, p. 100.
[162] *Adab*, p. 102.
[163] *Adab*, 103–4.
[164] TB, VIII, p. 468; IX, p. 33; *Adab*, p. 53, 103, 104–5; Ibn Ṣalāḥ, *ʿUlūm*, p. 207 [/p. 365]; Suyūṭī, *Tadrīb*, p. 174 [/II, p. 136; Ibn Daqīq al-ʿĪd, *Iqtirāḥ*, p. 276–7].
[165] *Adab*, p. 104; Suyūṭī, *Tadrīb*, p. 174 [/II, p. 135].
[166] *Adab*, p. 19–21; Cf. Goldziher, *Muhammedanische Studien* II 66, n. 5.

repeats it, raising his voice. If there is only one *mustamlī*, his repetition addresses all the listeners. In the great dictation lectures, where more than one *mustamlī* is working, he always calls the words for his nearest colleague to hear, so that in the end all the listeners would be included. However, according to the description we have of a great dictation lecture in 369 in the main mosque in Cordoba, [**46**] this deviated from this plan.[167] According to this account, Abū Zakariyyā' al-ʿĀ'idhī began by dictating to those listeners sitting closest to him, who would pass the subject matter on to the *mustamlī* word by word, and the *mustamlī* then dictated it with raised voice to the rest of those present. It is the *mustamlī*'s duty to repeat the sheikh's words in exact detail, especially if the sheikh is knowledgeable and well versed in the rules of hadith scholarship. In this case, his words command more reverence than if his technique of hadith was characterised by negligence of method. Many complaints in the relevant texts show, however, to which extent the *mustamlī*s offended against this basic law of their profession, be it through incompetence or through negligence. The philologist Abū ʿUbayda Maʿmar b. al-Muthannā (d. 207–13) complained about his *mustamlī* Kaysān: 'He hears something different from what I say, he says something different from what he hears, he writes something different from what he says, he reads something different from what he writes and he remembers something different from what he reads'.[168] According to Yāqūt,[169] however, this rebuke was directed at his slipshod collection of Bedouin poetry. We have already reported Ḥayyān b. Bishr's (d. 237) rough treatment of his *mustamlī*. While the abovementioned complaints may well have been levelled against the *mustamlī*'s work as dictation secretary, the following one refers unmistakably to his duties during the dictation lecture. For when Dāwūd b. Rushayd (d. 239) dictated to his *mustamlī* Hārūn b. Sufyān b. Bashīr al-Dīk (d. ca. 250): 'Ḥammād b. Khālid told us', he would write in his book 'Ḥammād b. Zayd told us' and then dictate to people 'Ḥammād b. Salama told us'. When he came home, he was so furious about his own faulty copying that he beat his wife until she called the sheikh to help.[170] When the sheikh can pause while the *mustamlī* repeats his words and the pupils copy them, he is to use the time by praying God for forgiveness.[171]

The duties of a *mustamlī* during the lecture do not end with repeating the words of the dictation for the students, as he also has to copy the text down

[167] Ibn al-Abbār, *Muʿjam*, no. 1536; [Dhahabīi, *Siyar*, xvi, p. 421]; *Adab*, p. 53, 105.
[168] *Adab*, p. 92.
[169] Yāqūt, *Irshād*, VI, p. 215.
[170] *Adab*, p. 92.
[171] *Adab*, p. 73.

himself, either for his own use or for the sheikh.[172] If he is employed long-term by one sheikh in the same lecture, it is to be assumed that frequently he would confine himself to repeating the text, dispensing with copying for his own use. In between, he has to be available to the students in case of queries, as his duty is to repeat to them words they might not have heard. If they are in doubt, they discuss with him until all doubt is removed.[173] In Sulaymān b. Dāwūd al-Shādhakūnī's (d. 234) dictation lecture, one student [47] drew the *mustamlī*'s attention to a mistake within the isnad of one hadith, whereupon the *mustamlī* consulted the sheikh and then corrected his mistake.[174] When al-Dāraquṭnī (d. 385)[175] heard in one of Ibn al-Anbārī's dictation lectures that a name was dictated wrongly, he was too shy to point out the mistake during the lecture. Consequently he consulted the *mustamlī* after the dictation was finished, and during the lecture on the next Friday, the *mustamlī* corrected the mistake at al-Anbārī's request.[176] It depended on the *mustamlī*s knowledge and attention, as well as on the sheikh's own, to what extent the former was required to assist the students. Once, when Aḥmad b. Yazīd al-Riyāḥī was employed as *mustamlī* by Ismāʿīl b. ʿUlayya (d. 193), he was annoyed at the frequency with which listeners contradicted him, and Ismāʿīl had to point out to him that no office is without troubles.[177] If the *mustamlī* is himself in doubt concerning the text, he consults the sheikh, as we can see from one example of Samʿānī's own experiences in dictation lectures.

He has to be most careful to add the blessing in a raised voice after every mention of the Prophet, and to follow the names of Companions and their sons with the prayer for God's pleasure (this is also the sheikh's duty[178]), while he prays for God to have mercy on famous imams.[179] (The question of apposite and desired eulogies has been discussed much in the relevant literature, being a question of religious and literary propriety[180]).

The great value ascribed to the collation of the finished manuscript is proved not only by the customary statements in the surviving manuscripts to the effect that the collation had taken place. We also find the attempt at founding the practice on prophetic sayings,[181] or on true or alleged sayings of

[172] Ibn Abī Yaʿlā, *Ṭabaqāt*, p. 280; *Adab*, p. 15, 91–3; Dhahabī, *Tadhkira*, III, p. 75.
[173] *Adab*, p. 106.
[174] TB, X, p. 329.
[175] GAL, I, p. 165; S I, p. 275 [Robson, J., in EI^2, s. v.].
[176] TB, III, p. 182–3; Yāqūt, *Irshād*, VII, p. 74; Dhahabī, *Tadhkira*, III, p. 58.
[177] TB, V, p. 227–8; *Adab*, 89.
[178] *Adab*, p. 63–4, 65; Ibn Ṣalāḥ, *ʿUlūm*, p. 207 [/p. 365]; Suyūṭī, *Tadrīb*, p. 174 [/II, p. 135–6].
[179] TB, VI, p. 61–2; Suyūṭī, *Tadrīb*, p. 174 [/II, p. 135].
[180] Ibn Jamāʿa, *Tadhkira*, p. 162; *Tadrīb*, p. 174 [/II, p. 135–6; Marçais, p. 184].
[181] *Adab*, p. 77–8.

other eminent personalities, the most frequently quoted of which is Yaḥyā b. Abī Kathīr's (d. 129)[182] or al-Awzāʿī's (d. 157)[183] graphic statement that he who does not collate what he has written is like someone who has relieved himself and does not clean himself afterwards.[184] Once the students have finished writing, the *mustamlī*'s duty during the collation is to read out the dictated text once more, in order that the students should proofread their own copies.[185] He concludes his work by praying for mercy and forgiveness for himself, the dictation students and all those present during the lecture, naming himself first.[186]

[**48**] Hearing and receiving individual traditions and complete works of literature, and then recording them in writing was subject to definite rules which had to be followed; otherwise further transmission would have to be considered faulty. Works about the *uṣūl al-ḥadīth* contain more or less detailed descriptions of these rules, and some of them establish a frame of reference for the different kinds of literary transmission and reception. We have already seen that writing from a teacher's dictation was unanimously considered the highest form of reception. Because the *mustamlī* was an intermediary between the teacher and the pupil, the question, discussed in later *uṣūl* texts, was raised whether it was permissible to transmit traditions according to the sheikh if they were actually received through the intermediary *mustamlī*.

Samʿānī (d. 562) does not mention the question in his *Adab al-imlāʾ wa-l-istamlāʾ*. In his discussion of the layout of the copied text, however, he insists[187] that the pupil should write the basmalah on a separate line, and to name on the next line the sheikh's *ism*, *kunya* and *nisbas* 'whose dictation he hears, or whose dictation he takes (through an intermediary)', followed by the dictated text. Thus it appears that he does not insist on the explicit statement that the text was transmitted by a *mustamlī*. This does not, however, rule out the possibility that he would have ascribed higher value to the dictation heard directly from the sheikh's lips than to that transmitted by a *mustamlī*, for immediately afterwards he quotes a statement by Muḥammad b. ʿAbdallāh b. ʿAmmār (d. 242)[188] without personal comment: 'I have never copied from the lips of the *mustamlī* and never turned towards him. I do not know what he says. I have only ever copied from the lips of the *muḥaddith*.' Subsequently

---

[182] Ibn Saʿd, *Ṭabaqāt*, V, p. 404 [/V, p. 505]; Dhahabī, *Tadhkira*, I, p. 120 [/p. 128–9, no. 115].
[183] GAL S, I, p. 308 [; GAS, I, p. 516–7].
[184] Ibn ʿAbd al-Barr, *Jāmiʿ*, I, p. 77–8; *Adab*, p. 78–9; Ibn Ṣalāḥ, *ʿUlūm*, p. 176; Suyūṭī, *Tadrīb*, p. 154.
[185] *Adab*, p. 174.
[186] *Adab*, p. 107–8.
[187] *Adab*, p. 170–1.
[188] Dhahabī, *Tadhkira*, II, p. 71 [/p. 494–5, no. 510]; Ibn Ḥajar, *Lisān*, II, p. 272.

he explains that it is best to write immediately from the sheikh's dictation, and add the necessary diacritics and vowels to the copied text, before the *mustamlī* begins. All the same, it appears that the nature of the literary reception is not changed by the intermediary *mustamlī*. In accordance with this tolerant view he then[189] makes it a moral duty for the participants of the dictation lecture to exchange their notebooks in order to be able to fill in possible gaps in the dictation, but he does not demand that these additions must be marked as such.

Ibn al-Ṣalāḥ (d. 643) and his successors discuss this question in more detail. Ibn al-Ṣalāḥ states[190] that in similar cases more than one authority permitted transmission directly from [**49**] the sheikh. As proof he quotes Sulaymān b. Mihrān al-Aʿmāsh's (d. 148)[191] abovementioned narrative, according to which he and others sometimes sat in a lecture dictated by Ibrāhīm al-Nakhaʿī (d. ca. 95)[192] which was so crowded that those further away could not hear the sheikh at all. Consequently they consulted one another concerning the text, and later transmitted after all, without ever actually having heard the sheikh's words. Similarly, when one of his students consulted Ḥammād b. Zayd (d. 179),[193] Ḥammād referred him to his neighbour in the lecture; and when Sufyān b. ʿUyayna's (d. 198) *mustamlī* Abū Muslim ʿAbd al-Raḥmān (d. 224) pointed out the size of the audience and the impossibility of hearing the sheikh's words, Sufyān pointed out that after all it was his, the *mustamlī*'s, job to ensure that the students could hear the text.[194] While these examples are not necessarily conclusive, some hadith authorities' relaxed attitude as stated by Ibn al-Ṣalāḥ should be considered the rule rather than the exception.

There is evidence to show that the opposite opinion existed as well. He tells us that Khalaf b. Tamīn (d. ca. 213)[195] discarded ca. 100,000 hadiths he had heard during a lecture dictated by Sufyān al-Thawrī (d. 161), and concerning which he had consulted his fellow students, as Zāʾida b. Qudāma (d. ca. 161)[196] bidden him to transmit only words his heart remembered and his ear heard.[197] Similarly, if Abū Nuʿaym al-Faḍl b. Dukayn (d. 219)[198] missed details

[189] *Adab*, p. 174.
[190] Salāḥ, *ʿUlūm*, p. 149ff., 207.
[191] In Khallikān, no. 270; Dhahabī, *Tadhkira*, I, p. 145.
[192] Nawawī, *Tahdhīb*, p. 135; Dhahabī, *Tadhkira*, I, p. 69.
[193] Nawawī, *Tahdhīb*, p. 217; Dhahabī, *Tadhkira*, I, p. 211.
[194] [Irāqi, *Fatḥ al-mughīth*, 198].
[195] Ibn Saʿd, *Ṭabāqṭ*, VII/2, p. 187; Dhahabī, *Tadhkira*, I, p. 344.
[196] Ibn Saʿd, *Ṭabāqṭ*, VI, p. 263; Dhahabī, *Tadhkira*, I, p. 200.
[197] [ʿIrāqī, *Fatḥ al-mughīth*, p. 197].
[198] Dhahabī, *Tadhkira*, I, p. 338.

during the dictations of Sufyān al-Thawrī (d. 161) and Sulaymān b. Mihrān al-Aʿmāsh (d. 148) and had to ascertain these from his fellow students, he later transmitted them according to these fellow students only.[199] A similar story says that when the Hanbalite Yūsuf b. ʿUmar al-Qawwās (d. 385) attended a dictation lecture, he only ever wrote down what he heard from the sheikh's own lips, and consequently pushed past the four *mustamlī*s until he was very close to the sheikh himself. The more rigid attitude among certain circles is illustrated by the account of how one of his fellow students once said to him that he had heard the Prophet tell him in his sleep: 'If you want to hear hadith as if you heard it from me, you should hear as Abu l-Fatḥ al-Qawwās does'.[200] Ibn al-Ṣalāḥ himself is a supporter of the strict opinion and declares the other attitude to be astonishing laxity. According to him, a transmission according to a sheikh is only permitted if the circumstances under which it took place are presented in full.

Nawāwī (d. 676) supports the same opinion.[201] He quotes Aḥmad b. Ḥanbal (d. 241) as having said he hoped it was not forbidden to transmit according to the sheikh a letter **[50]** the sheikh omitted accidentally during dictation.[202] He also hoped it was permitted to transmit according to the sheikh a single word which had to be ascertained from the *mustamlī*, as long as there was agreement concerning the word. However, Khalaf b. Sālim al-Mukharramī (d. 231)[203] forbade this, as he knew that Sufyān b. ʿUyayna (d. 198) once transmitted only part of a sentence: of *ḥaddathanā ʿAmr b. Dīnār* he only transmitted ʿAmr b. Dīnār, as he missed all but the suffix of the word *ḥaddathanā* because of the crowd.

In comparison with this unequivocal rejection, ʿAbd al-Raḥīm b. al-Ḥusayn al-ʿIrāqī (d. 806) occupies a mediating position.[204] While he does believe it to be safest if the pupil refers to reception through a *mustamlī*, such as 'N.N. narrated to me through an intermediary (*tablīgh*)', as Muḥammad b. Isḥāq b. Khuzayma (d. 311) and others did, the determining question for him his whether the sheikh was listening in to the *mustamlī*'s words. If he was listening, in his opinion it should be permitted to the students of a dictation lecture to transmit the text directly from the sheikh, without mentioning the intermediary *mustamlī*. He says, with justification, that according to the technicalities of hadith scholarship, the situation would be comparable to the

199 [ʿIrāqī, *Fatḥ al-mughīth*, p. 197].
200 TB, XIV, p. 326; Ibn a. Yaʿlā, *Ṭabaqt*, p. 345.
201 Suyūṭī, *Tadrīb*, p. 136, 174.
202 [ʿIrāqī, *Fatḥ al-mughīth*, p. 197].
203 Ibn Saʿd, Ṭabaqt, VII/2, p. 92; Dhahabī, *Tadhkira*, II, p. 59.
204 Ibn Ṣalāḥ, *ʿUlūm*, p. 149–50, 207; Suyūṭī, *Tadrīb*, 136 [ʿIrāqī, *Fatḥ al-mughīth*, p. 198].

case of a student reading his copy to the sheikh for authorisation, and that accordingly the text spoken by the *mustamlī* while the sheikh is listening is of equal value to a *Qirā'a 'alā l-shaykh*.[205] Under different circumstances, e.g. when the sheikh is hard of hearing, it would be the student's duty, if were to transmit the text, to point out the fact that he received it from someone other than the sheikh. As an example for the correct attitude he quotes one of Jābir b. Samura's hadiths, containing a saying of the Prophet about the twelve emirs or caliphs descended from the Quraysh.[206] Jābir distinguishes precisely between the parts of the saying he heard for himself and parts about which he had to consult with his father, who was also present. However, even in the case that the sheikh was indeed listening to the *mustamlī*'s repetition, 'Irāqī is of the opinion that a student is not permitted to transmit this text with the words 'I heard this from N.N.'s dictation' or 'N.N. dictated this to me', but rather has to use a more general expression, such as 'N.N. told me'. The two formulae quoted first are only allowable to someone who has actually heard the words from his teacher's lips. As we have seen, when it comes to the technique of tradition, 'Irāqī considers hearing through a *mustamlī* to be equivalent to a *qirā'a 'ala l-shaykh*, and consequently inclines to the opinion that the student may use the formula '(N.N. told me) during one of his lectures' (*qirā'atan 'alayhi*). He does add, however, that it could be argued that the *mustamlī*, **[51]** whose duty is only to pass on the sheikh's words, does not intend to present a *qirā'a 'ala l-shaykh*.

Unlike Ibn al-Ṣalāḥ and 'Irāqī, Ibn Kathīr (d. 774) defends the unconditional transmission according to the sheikh,[207] while among the younger authorities Suyūṭī (d. 911) explains the opposing points of view represented by Nawawī (Ibn al-Ṣalāḥ) and 'Irāqī, respectively, without committing himself to his own view on the question.

While the sources available to us do not allow a clear nor complete view of the development of the attitudes towards the subject, it does appear that the liberal and the rigid opinions have existed side by side ever since the question was recognised as such, and it is not surprising that here, too, we find Hanbalites among the strict judges. Following the general trend towards more liberal rules for the study of tradition, the question appears to have been judged less strictly in the later years.

---

205 Cf. Ibn Ṣalāḥ, *'Ulūm*, p. 145, 207; Suyūṭī, *Tadrīb*, 130ff.

206 Wensinck, *Concordance*, I, p. 103; II, p. 70.

207 Ibn Kathīr, *Ikhtiṣār*, p. 133 [/p. 98].

[Chronological list of *mustamlīs* and teachers who employed them]

In the following we shall present a chronologically arranged list of *mustamlīs* and teachers who employed them. In cases where the name of either the *mustamlī* or the sheikh is unknown it has been replaced by a question mark. In the sources quoted for each name, we find, firstly, the instances mentioning the *istimlā'* and in addition, as far as it can be traced, biographical information. A glance at the chronological distribution confirms the picture of the history of dictation we have sketched above. During the centuries in which it flourished we are able to state an increase in the numbers of *mustamlīs*, then a fast and severe decrease, and finally, during the renaissance of dictation in the ninth century, an increase once more. Although the number of source texts used is much larger than would appear from this list, it is of course necessary to admit that the date, number and type of the sources available will have imparted to the picture a hue diverging from that of reality. This is probably also the explanation of the fact that the second half of the sixth and the whole seventh and eighth centuries are represented by one single *mustamlī*. The geographical distribution conveys the impression that Western Islam knew very few *mustamlīs*, but this conclusion would be problematical, to say the least. Still, it should be pointed out that Muqaddasī stated[208] that the Hanafite scholars in Marv, Sharakhs and Bukhara used to employ a *mustamlī*; and we should furthermore draw attention to the fact that Samʿānī, the chief authority for *istimlā'*, did indeed live in Marv. It is certain, however, that the second flowering of the ninth century was confined to Egypt and Syria.

Translated by Gwendolin Goldbloom

[208] Muqaddasī, *Aḥsan al-taqāsīm fī ma ʿrifat al-aqālīm* ed. M.J. De Goeje, Leiden, 1906, p. 327.

The Office of the Mustamlī *in Arab Scholarship* 29

Chronological List

[New references and corrections are included in square brackets.]

Mustamlī	**Master (Sheikh)**
1. Sībawayh (d. ca. 180) : TB, XII, 195 ; *Adab*, 105 ; GAL, I, 100 ; S I, 160 ; [GAS, IX, 51]	1. Hammād b. Salama (d. 167) : IS, VII/2, 39 ; *Tadhkira*, [Hyderabad, 1333–34] I, 189
2. ?	2. Sufyān al-Thawrī (d. 161) : *Adab*, 87 ; EI, IV, 540 [EI², IX, *s.v.* ; GAS, I, 519]
3. ?	3. Mālik b. Anas (d. 179) : Ibn Ṣalāḥ, 206 ; *Tadrīb*, 173 ; GAL, I, 175, S I, 297 ; [GAS, I, 457]
4. Abū Kināna b. Yūnus b. Hāshim [brother of no. 16] : TB, XIV, 406, 87, l. 18	4. Hushaym b. Bashīr (d. ca. 183) : IS, VII/2, 70 ; TB, XIX, 85 ; *Tadhkira*, I, 229 ; [GAS, I, 38
5. al-Jammāz : *Adab*, 90	5. Khālid b. al-Ḥārith (d. 186) : IS, VII/2, 46 ; *Tadhkira*, I, 284
6. Bilāl (?) : *Adab*, 87	6. Fuḍayl b. ʿIyāḍ (d. 187) : IS, V, 366 ; *Tadhkira*, I, 225
7. Ism. b. ʿUlayya (d. 193) : Adab, 89 ; *Tadhkira*, I, 296	7. Mālik b. Anas (d. 179) : v. no. 3
8. A. b. Yazīd al-Riyāḥī : TB, V, 227 ; Adab, 89	8. Ism. b. ʿUlayya (d. 193) : supra col. 1, no. 7
9. ?	9. ʿA. b. ʿĀṣim (m. 201) : TB, XI, 454 ; IS, VII/2, 61 ; *Tadhkira*, I, 291
10. ?	10. Ḥammād b. Usāma Abū Usāma (m. 201) : *Adab*, 85 ; *Tadhkira*, I, 295 ; TT, III, 2
11. ʿAbd al-Wahhāb b. ʿAṭāʾ (d. ca. 204) : *Adab*, 86 ; TB, XI, 21 ; IS, VII/2, 76 ; *Tadhkira*, I, 309	11. Saʿīd b. a. ʿArūba (d. 156) : IS, VII/2, 33 ; *Tadkkira*, I, 167 ; [GAS, I, 91]
12. Barbakh [Muḥammad b. ʿAmr] : *Adab*, 90	12. Yazīd b. Hārūn (d. 206) : Ibn al-Ṣalāḥ, 206 ; *Tadrīb*, 174 ; [*Siyar*, IX, 358] ; GAL S I, 332
13. Kaysān b. Muʿarrif al-Hujaymī : *Adab*, 62 ; *Irshād*, VI, 215 ; *Bughya*, 382	13. Abū ʿUbayda Maʿmar b. al-Muthannā (d. ca. 208) : GAL, I, 102, S I, 332 ; [GAS, VIII, 67, IX, 65]
14. Yaḥyā b. Rāshid (d. 211) : *Ansāb*, f. 592a ; *Adab*, 87 ; TT, XI, 207	14. Abū ʿĀṣim al-Ḍaḥḥāk b. Makhlad (d. ca. 212) : Ibn al-Ṣalāḥ, 206 ; *Tadhlira*, I, 333 ; TT, IV, 450
15. Ādam b. a. Iyās (d. 220) : TB, VII, 28 ; THan, 280; *Tadhkira*, I, 369; *Adab*, 15, 88, 91 ; IS, VII/2, 186 ; TT, I, 196	15. Shuʿba b. al-Ḥajjāj (d. 160) : Ibn al-Ṣalāḥ, 106 ; *Tadrīb*, 173 ; IS, VII/2, 38 ; TB, IX, 255 ; *Tadhkira*, I, 181

16. ʿAr. b. Yūnus [brother of no. 4] (d. 224) : TB, X, 258, XIV, 406 ; *Ansāb*, f. 529a [/V, 288, l. 18sqq.] ; Ibn al-Ṣalāḥ, 150 ; *Tadrīb*, 136 ; *Tadhkira*, I, 183	16/a. Sufyān b. ʿUyayna (d. 198) : *Tadhkira*, I, 242 [GAS, I, 93] 16/b. Yazīd b. Hārūn (d. 206), v. no. 12
17. ?	17. ʿAmr b. ʿAwn al-Wāsiṭī (d. 225) : *Adab*, 65 ; *Tadhkira*, II, 13 ; *Shadharāt*, II, 52
18. ?	18. Sul. b. Dāwūd al-Shādhakūnī (d. 234) : TB, X, 329,l. 7, IX, 40 ; *Ansāb*, f. 324b ; *Tadhkira*, II, 65
19. Kajja : *Adab*, 106	19. Ḥayyān b. Bishr (d. 237) : TB, VIII, 285
20. M. b. Yazīd al-Ṭarsūsī (before 240) : THan, 240	20. ?
21. Abū Yaḥyā : TB, XIII, 446, l. 6	21. al-Walīd b. Shujāʿ al-Sakūnī (d. 243), TB, XIII, 446 ; *Ansāb*. F. 301 b
22. ?	22. Yaḥyā b. Aktham (d. ca. 243) : *Adab*, 104 ; TB, XIV, 191 ; IKhal, no. 803 ; Nawawī, *Tahdhīb*, 621
23. ʿAbd Allāh b. M. b. Rustam : TT, X, 81 ; Ibn Khayr, 329, [l. 19]	23. Yaʿqūb b. al-Sikkīt (d. ca. 243) : GAL ; I, 118 S I, 180 [EI², III, s.v. ; GAS, VIII, 129, IX, 137]
24. M. b. Abān al-Balkhī [Ḥamdawayh] (d. 244) : TB, II, 78 ; *Ansāb*, f. 529a [/V, 287, l. 9sqq.] ; *Adab*, 87 ; Kutubī, I, 240 ; *Tadhkira*, II, 74 ; Ṣafadī, I, 334 ; *Tāj*, X, 347 [Siyar, XI, 115]	24. Wakīʿ b. al-Jarrāḥ (d. 197) : Ibn al-Ṣalāḥ, 206 ; *Tadrīb*, 173 ; IS, VI, 275 ; *Tadhkira*, I, 282
25. ?	25. Hishām b. ʿAmmār (d. 245) : *Adab*, 105 ; *Tadhkira*, II, 34 ; TT, XI, 51 [GAS, I, 111]
26. Maslama b. Shabīb al-Nīsābūrī (d. 247) : *Ansāb*, f. 592a	26. ?
27. Hārūn b. Sufyān b. Rāshid Mukḥula (m. 247) : TB, XIV, 24, XII, 248, l. 1 ; *Ansāb*, f. 529a [/V, 288, l. 24sqq. ; *Adab*, 17, 96 ; THan, 261	27/a. Abū Nuʿaym al-Faḍl b. Dukayn (d. ca. 219) : TB, XII, 346 ; *Tadhkira*, I, 338 27/b. ʿĀṣim b. ʿAlī al-Wāsiṭī (d. 221) : TB, XII, 247 ; *Tadkira*, I, 359
28. Hārūn b. Sufyān b. Bashīr al-Dīk (d. ca. 250) : TB, XIV, 25, XII, 248, l. 1 ; *Ansāb*, f. 529 a [/V, 289, l. 2sqq.] ; *Adab*, 17, 85, 96 ; THan, 261	28/a. Yazīd b. Hārūn (m. 206), v. no. 12 28/b. ʿĀṣim b. ʿAlī al-Wāsiṭī (d. 221) : *Tadhkira*, I, 359, v. no. 27b 28/c. Dāwūd b. Rushayd (d. 239) : TT, III, 184
29. Hārūn al-Mustamlī : identical to no. 27 ou 28	29. Sul. b. Ḥarb (d. ca. 239) : TB, IX, 33 : Ibn Bashkuwāl, no. 449 ; IKhal, no. 277 ; *Tadhkira*, I, 355

30. ?	30. Abū al-ʿIbar M. b. A. (d. 250) : *Aghānī*, XX, 91 ; Kutubī, II, 218 ; Ibn ʿAsākir, II, 118 ; Ṣafaḍī, II, 42 ; ; TB, V, 40 ; *Irshād*, VI, 271
31. Abū Yāsir ʿAmmār b. Hārūn (ca. 250) : TB, XII, 255 ; TT, VII, 407 ; Mīzān, II, 245	31. ?
32. Ḥamdawayh b. al-Khaṭṭāb : *Tadhkira*, II, 221	32. al-Bukhārī (d. 256) : GAL, I, 157, S I, 260 ; [GAS, I, 115]
33. Abū Ḥāmid : TB, VIII, 468, l. 14	33. al-Zubayr b. Bakkār (d. 256) : GAL, I, 141, S I, 215 ; Tadhkira, II, 99 [GAS, I, 317]
34.	34. al-Jāḥiẓ ? (d. 259) : *Adab*, 93 ; GAL, I, 153, S I, 239
35. Ismāʿīl b. al-Ṣalt (ca. 266) : TB, X, 247, [l. 14–15], VI, 280	35. ʿA. b. ʿAl. al-Madīnī (d. 234) : *Tadhkira*, II, 15 [GAS, I, 108]
36. al-Rabīʿ b. Sul. al-Murādī (d. 270), *Adab*, 78, l. 31 ; *Tadhkira*, II, 149 ; Nawawī, *Tahdhīb*, 243	36. ?
37. ?	37. Bakkār b. Qutayba al-Thaqafī (d. 270) : Ibn ʿAsākir, III, 283 ; IKhal, no. 115 ; *Jawāhir*, I, 168
38. ?	38. M. b. Muslim b. Wāra (d. ca. 270) : *Adab*, 96–97 ; TB, III, 256 ; *Tadhkira*, II, 139
39. ʿA. b. Yūsuf al-Baghdādī (ca. 270) : TB, XII, 123	39. ?
40. Isḥāq b. Yaʿqūb al-Kafarsūsī (ca. 270) : Ibn ʿAsākir, II, 456 [/II, 459]	40. ?
41. ?	41. Yaʿqūb b. Suyān al-Fasawī (d. ca. 277) : *Adab*, 14 ; *Tadrīb*, 174 ; *Tadhkira*, II, 145 [GAS, I, 319]
42. Ibr. b. ʿAlī al-Wāsiṭī (ca. 280) : TB, VI, 131	42. ?
43. Abū Ḥafṣ	43. Ibr. b. al-Ḥus. Ibn Dīzīl [Dābbat ʿAffān or Ibn Sīfanna] (d. 281) : Ibn ʿAsākir, II, 205 [/II, 203 ; *Tadhkira*, II, 166 ; GAS, I, 321]
44. Abū ʿAmr A. b. al-Mubārak (d. 284) : Tadhkira, II, 196, III, 75 ; Shadharāt, II, 186	44. ?
45. ʿAl. b. M. Mukhawwal (d. 288) : TB, X, 91 ; *Adab*, 91	45. ?
46. M. b. Hishām b. a. al-Dumayk (d. 289) : TB, III, 361	46. al-Ḥ. b. ʿArafa (m. 257) : *Shadharāt*, II, 136 [GAS, I, 134]
47. ʿAl. b. ʿĀmir b. Asad (ca. 291) : TB, IX, 325 [l. 13sqq.] ; *Buldān*, I, 845	47. Ṣāliḥ b. M. b. ʿAmr Jazara (d. ca. 293) : TB, VI, 122, IX, 325 ; *Tadhkira*, II, 194

48. ?	48. Abū Muslim Ibr. b. ʿAl. al-Kajjī (d. 292) : TB, VI, 122, IX, 325 ; *Adab*, 96 ; *Tadhkira*, II, 177 ; *Ansāb*, f. 475b [GAS, I, 162]
49. Ṣāliḥ b. M. b. ʿAmr Jazara (d. ca. 293) : v. supra no. 47 ; TB, II, 20 [l. 5sqq.] ; *Adab*, 17	49. al-Bukhārī (d. 256) : v. no. 32
50. ?	50. Jaʿfar b. M. al-Firyābī (d. 301) : TB, VII, 202 ; *Adab*, 17 ; *Tadhkira*, II, 237 ; [GAS, I, 166]
51. Abū Ghānim ʿU. b. M. b. Masʿūd : Subkī, II, 314 [/III, 471]	51. A. b. ʿU. b. Surayj (d. ca. 305) : GAL S I, 306 ; *Tadhkira*, III, 30 [GAS, I, 495]
52. ?	52. ʿAl. b. A. ʿAbdān (d. 306) : Ibn ʿAsākir, VI, 241 ; TB, IX, 378 ; *Tadhkira*, II, 232
53. ?	53. ʿAl. b. M. al-Nīsābūrī (d. 324) : TB, VI, 61 [l. 32sqq.], X, 120 ; *Shadharāt*, II, 302
54. M. b. Ism. al-Jurjānī (d. 324) : Ṣafadī, II, 212	54/a. M. b. Isḥāq Ibn Khuzayma (d. 311) : GAL, I, 193, S I, 345 [GAS, I, 601] ; *Tadhkira*, II, 259 54/b. A. b. M. b. al-Sharqī (d. 325) : TB, IV, 426 ; *Tadhkira*, III, 39 ; *Shadharāt*, II, 306
55. M. b. Mazyad Ibn Abī al-Azhar (d. 325) : Bughya, 104 ; GAL S I, 250 ; TB, III, 288	55. al-Mubarrad (d. ca. 285) ; GAL, I, 109, S 168 ; [GAS, IX, 78]
56. ʿAl. b. Zayd Zurayq (d. 326) : TB, IX, 459	56. ?
57. ?	57. M. b. al-Qāsim al-Anbārī (d. 328) : TB, XIII, 182 ; *Irshād*, VII, 74 ; IKhal., no. 656 ; GAL, I, 119, S I, 182 ; [GAS, IX, 144]
58. ?	58. al-Ḥ. b. Ism. al-Maḥāmilī (dd. 330) :
59. A. b. Ibr. al-ʿAmmī : *Fihrist*, 197 ; *Irshād*, I, 376 ; Ṭūsī, *Fihris*, no. 37	59. ʿAbd al-ʿAzīz b. Yaḥyā al-Julūdī (d. 332) : *Fihrist*, 196 ; GAL S I, 85
60. ?	60. M. b. Yaʿqūb al-Nīsābūrī (d. 346) : *Tadhkira*, III, 75 ; *Shadharāt*, II, 373
61. [Abū Saʿd] Wajīh b. a. al-Ṭayyib (d. ca. 350) : *Ansāb*, f. 529a [/V, 289, l. 21–2]]	61. ?
62. ?	62. Ibr. b. ʿA. al-Hujaymī (d. 351) : *Adab*, 18, *Shadharāt*, III, 8
63. ʿA. b. Ibr. al-Najjād (d. 353) : TB, XI, 338	63. ?
64. M. b. al-Faḍl al-Mudhakkir (d. 362) : *Jawāhir*, II, 109 [/III, 303]	64. ʿAr. b. al-Ḥus. al-Nisābūrī (d. 309) : *Jawāhir*, I, 300 [/II, 378]

65. ?	65. Abū Zakariyyā' al-'Ā'idhī (ca. 369) : Ibn al-Abbār, *Mu'jam*, no. 1536 ; *Buldān*, IV, 27, l. 5
66. al-Ḥ. b. Isḥāq al-Burjī (d. after 370) : Abū Nu'aym, Dhikr, 274 ; Ibn 'Asākir, IV, 153	66/a. Sul. b. A. al-Ṭabarānī (d. 360) : GAL S I, 279 ; [GAS, I, 195] 66/b. M. b. 'U. al-Ji'ābī (d. 355) : TB, III, 26 ; *Tadhkira*, III, 130 66/c. Others
67. [Abū Isḥāq] Ibr. b. M. (or A.) al-Balkhī (m. 376) : TB, II, 9, l. 15 ; *Ansāb*, f. 422a, 529a [/V, 287, l. 22sqq.] ; *Shadharāt*, III, 86	67. Abū Bakr al-Ṭawsānī al-Ḥāfiẓ (*nisba* not sure) [*Ansāb*, IV, 79 : al-Ṭūsānī]
68. M. b. Ma'mar al-Jayyānī (d. 377) : Ibn al-Abbār, Mu'jam, no. 360, 362	68. Ism. b. al-Qāsim al-Qālī (d. 355) : GAL S I, 202
69. M. b. Ism. al-Warrāq (d. 378) : TB, II, 53, 55 ; *Ansāb*, f. 529a [/V, 288, l. 6sqq.]	69. ?
70. ?	70. al-Ṣāḥib Ism. b. 'Abbād (d. 385) : Bughya, 196 ; GAL, I, 130, S I, 198 [GAS, VIII, 206 ; IX, 192]
71. 'Uth. b. A. al-'Ijlī : TB, XI, 309	71. [Abū Ḥafṣ] 'U. b. A. Shāhīn (d. 385) : GAL, I, 165, S I, 276 [GAS, I, 209] ; *Tadhkira*, III, 183
72. al-Ḥ. b. 'Abd al-Malik al-Yashkūrī (d. 393) : *Ansāb*, f. 529a [/V, 288, l.1sqq.]	72. ?
73. A. b. M. al-Ḍarīr al-Rāzī (d. 399) : TB, IV, 435 ; *Tadhkira*, III, 218 ; *Shadharāt*, III, 153	73. [Ibn Abī Ḥātim al-Rāzī] 'Ar. b. a. Ḥātim (d. 327) : GAL S I, 278 ; [GAS, I, 178]
74. Ṣāliḥ b. M. al-Jijārī al-Muṭawwi'ī (d. 404) : Ibn 'Asākir, VI, 380 [/VI, 382] ; *Ansāb*, 123a [/II, 25] ; Dhahabī, *Mushtabih*, 93 ; Buldān, II, 35, III, 40	74. ?
75. M. b. 'Al. al-Ḥākim al-Nīsābūrī (d. 405) : *Buldān*, I, 616 ; GAL, I, 166, S I, 276 ; [GAS, I, 221]	75. Abū Ḥātim M. b. Ḥibbān al-Bustī (m. 354) : GAL, I, 164, S I, 273 ; [GAS, I, 189]
76. Makkī b. M. al-Dimashqī [al-Mu'addib] (d. 418) : *Shadharāt*, III, 211	76. al-Qāḍī al-Mayānijī [al-Mayānajī in *Tāj*[2], VI, 223 ; Yūsuf b. al-Qāsim (d. 375)] : *Ansāb*, f. 547a and b [/V, 425 ; *Shadharāt*, III, 86]
77. [Abū Ṭāhir Ibr. b. A. b. [b. Sa'īd] M. al-Bukhārī (ca. 420) : *Ansāb*, f. 529a [/V, 289]	77. ?
78. Ism. b. M. al-Āmilī [*leg*. al-Āmulī, from Āmul of the Oxus] al-Mudhakkir [al-Bukhārī] (d. 434) : *Ansāb*, f. 529a [/V, 289]	78. ?

79. Aḥmad ?: *Irshād*, I, 179	79. Abū al-ʿAlāʾ al-Maʿarrī (d. 449) : GAL, I, 254, S I, 449
80. ʿA. b. ʿAl. b. a. Hāshim : *Irshād*, I, 179	80. Abū al-ʿAlāʾ al-Maʿarrī (d. 449)
81. M. b. Ibr. al-ʿAṭṭār al-Iṣbahānī (d. 466) : TB, I, 417 ; *Tadhkira*, III, 333 ; *Shadharāt*, III, 325	81. Abū Nuʿaym al-Iṣbahānī (d. 430) : GAL, I, 362, S I, 616 ; *Tadhkira*, III, 275
82. Ṭāhir b. M. al-Shaḥḥāmī (d. 479) : Shadharāt, III, 363	82. ?
83. ʿAbd al-Khāliq b. M. al-Sakānī [*leg.* al-Shikānī] al-Ḥākim (d. before 480) : *Jawāhir*, I, 298 [/II, 371 ; *Ansāb*, III, 448]	83. ⌊Shams al-Aʾimma] ʿAbd al-ʿAzīz b. A. al-Ḥalwānī (d. 449) : *Jawāhir*, I, 318 [/II, 429]
84. Sul. b. Ibr. al-Ḥāfiẓ (d. 486) : *Adab*, 93 ; *Tadhkira*, III, 365 ; *Shadharāt*, 377	84. Niẓām al-Mulk al-Wazīr (d. 485), EI^{1}, III, 1007 [/VIII^{2}, s.v.]
85. ʿAl. b. Jābir b. Yāsīn (d. 493) : THan, 404, 382 ; *Shadharāt*, III, 399	85. Abū Yaʿlā M. b. al-Farrāʾ (d. 458) : GAL, I, 398, S I, 686 ; THan, 377
86. A. b. M. [Ibn] al-Baradānī (d. 498) : THan, 405, 382 ; *Ansāb*, f. 72b [/], *Tadhkira*, IV, 29 ; *Shadharāt*, III, 408	86. Abū Yaʿlā M. b. al-Farrāʾ (d. 458)
87. ʿA. b. M. al-Anbārī (d. 507) ; THan, 382, 408 ; *Shadharāt*, IV, 17	87. Abū Yaʿlā M. b. al-Farrāʾ (d. 458)
88. M. b. ʿAr. b. A. (d. 519) ; *Jawāhir*, II 80 [?]	88. Qāḍī al-Quḍāt Abū Saʿīd M. b. A. b. Saʿīd [?]
89. Zāhir b. Ṭāhir al-Shaḥḥāmī (d. 533) : *Shadharāt*, IV, 102 ; *Buldān*, VI, 434 ; *Mīzān*, I, 345	89. ?
90. ʿAbd al-Khāliq b. Zāhir al-Shaḥḥāmī (d. 549) : *Shadharāt*, IV, 153	90. ?
91. M. b. ʿAbd al-Wāḥid al-Fusārānī (c. 550) : Adab,	91. ?
92. M. b. ʿU. al-Bukhārī (d. 554) : *Jawāhir*, II, 103	92. Bakr b. M. al-Zaranjarī (d. 512) : *Jawāhir*, I, 172 [/I, 465] : *Ansāb*, f. 273b ; Ibn al-Athīr, *Kāmil*, X, 383
93. Ism. b. Yūsuf b. Ḥulā al-Qūṣī : Udfuwī, 89	93. M. b. ʿA. b. Daqīq al-ʿĪd (d. 702) : GAL, II, 63, S II, 69
94. ʿUth. b. Ibr. al-Birmānī (d. 816) : Sakhāwī, IV, 175, V, 123	94. ʿAbd al-Raḥīm b. al-Hus. al-ʿIrāqī (d. 806) : GAL, II, 65, S II, 69
95. ʿAbd al-Wahhāb b. A. al-ʿIrāqī (d. 818) ; Sakhāwī, V, 97	95. A. b. ʿAbd al-Raḥīm [al-Wazīr] al-ʿIrāqī (d. 826) : GAL, II, 66, S II, 71
96. A. b. ʿAbd al-Raḥīm al-ʿIrāqī (d. 826) : Sakhāwī, IV, 175 ; v. no. 95	96. ʿAbd al-Raḥīm b. al-Ḥus. al-ʿIrāqī (d. 806) : v. no. 94
97. ʿAbd al-Raḥīm b. M. al-Haythamī (d. after 830) : Sakhāwī, IV, 185, X, 255	97. A. b. ʿAbd al-Raḥīm al-ʿIrāqī (d. 826) : s. no. 95

98. Ibr. b. M. Sibṭ Ibn al-ʿAjamī (m. 841) : Sakhāwī, IV, 175 ; GAL, II, 67, S II, 72	98. ʿAbd al-Raḥīm b. al-Ḥus. al-ʿIrāqī (d. 806) : v. no. 94
99. Ibr. b. Khiḍr (d. 852) : Sakhāwī, I, 45	99. Ibn Ḥajar al-ʿAsqalānī (d. 852) : GAL, II, 67, S II, 72
100. Riḍwān b. M. al-ʿUqbī (m. 852) : Sakhāwī, I, 339, III, 227, VIII, 176 ; *Tibr*, 239–41 ; GAL, II, 77, S II, 84	100. Ibn Ḥajar al-ʿAsqalānī (d. 852) : v. no. 99
101. ʿA. b. Sālim (s. 852) : Sakhāwī, V, 222 ; *Tibr*, 244	101. Ibn Ḥajar al-ʿAsqalānī (d. 852)
102. Ibn Ḥajar al-ʿAsqalānī (d. 852) : Sakhāwī, IV, 175 ; v. no. 99	102. ʿAbd al-Raḥīm b. al-Ḥus. al-ʿIrāqī (d. 806) : v. no. 94
103. Yaḥyā b. Muḥammad al-Munāwī (d. 871) : Sakhāwī, X, 255 ; GAL, II, 77, S II, 84	103. A. b. ʿAbd al-Raḥīm al-ʿIrāqī (d. 826) : s. no. 95
104. M. b. ʿA... b. Qamar (d. 876) : Sakhāwī, VIII, 176–8 ; *Tibr*, 215	104. Ibn Ḥajar al-ʿAsqalānī (d. 852) : v. no. 99
105. Ibr. b. A. al-ʿAjlūnī (d. 888)	105. Ibn Ḥajar al-ʿAsqalānī (d. 852) : v. no. 99
106. Yaḥyā b. M. al-Qabbānī al-Tājir (d. after 894) : Sakhāwī, X, 247 ; Tibr, 256	106. ʿAr. b. A. al-Qalqashandī (d. 871) : Sakhāwī, IV, 46
107. A. b. Dāwūd al-Bījūrī (d. 897) : Sakhāwī, I, 298	107. M. b. ʿAr. al-Sakhāwī (d. 902) : GAL, II, 34, S II, 31

References and abbreviations

Abū Nuaym al-Iṣfahānī, *Dhikr Akhbār Iṣbahān* [*Geschichte Iṣbahāns*], 2 vols., ed. S. Dedering, Leiden, 1931–4

Adab, *v.* Samʿānī

Aghānī=Abū l-Faraj al-Iṣfahānī, *K. al- Aghānī*, 20 vol., Cairo, 1285/1868 [24 vols., Cairo, 1927–74]

[Azami, M. M., *Studies in early hadith literature*, Indianapolis, 1978, 192–9]

al-Baghdādī, al-Khaṭīb, [*al-Faṣl li-l-waṣl al-mudraj fī l-naql*, 2 vols., ed. M. Nashshār, Beirut 1424/2003]

Id., [*al-Jāmiʿ li-akhlāq al-rāwī wa adab al-Sāmiʿ*, 2 vols., ed. M. ʿAjjāj al-Khaṭīb, Beirut 1414/1994^{2} (1410/1989^{1})]

Id., [*al-Kifāya fī ʿilm al-riwāya*, Hyderabad, 1357/1938; 1390/1970^{2}]

Id., [*al-Riḥla fī ṭalab al-ḥadīth*, ed. Nūr al-Dīn ʿIṭr, Beirut 1395/1975]

Id., [*Sharaf aṣḥāb al-ḥadīth*, ed. M. S. Hatiboğlu, Ankara 1971]

Id., *Taʾrīkh Baghdād*, 14 vols., ed. M.S al-Irāqī, Cairo, 1931–49

[Bayhaqī, Abū Bakr, *al-Jāmiʿ li-shuʿab al-īmān*, 9 vols., ed. Abū Hājir M. al-Saʿīd b. Basyūnī Zaghlūl, Beirut, 1410/1990]

Id., [*al-Madkhal ilā l-Sunan al-kubrā*, 2 vols., ed. al-Aʿẓamī, Kuwayt, 1404/1983[1]; Riyad, 1420/1999[2]]

Dhahabī, Shams al-Dīn, *Mīzān al-iʿtidāl*, 3 vols. Cairo, 1325/1907

Id., *Mushtabih=al-Moschtabih* auctore Schamsoʾddin Abu Abdallah Mohammed bin Ahmed ad-dhahabi, e codd. mss. editus a P. de Jong, Lugduni Batavorum [Leiden], 1881

Id., *Siyar=Siyar a ʿlām al-nubalāʾ*, 25 vols., ed. Sh. al-Amaʾūṭ et alii., Beirut, 1981–8

Id., *Tadhkira=Tadhkirat al-ḥuffāẓ*, 4 vols. Hyderabad, 1333–4 [4 vols. in 2, ed. ʿA. b. Y. al-Muʿallimī, Hyderabad, 1956–83]

al-Fīrūzābādī, Majd al-Dīn, *al-Qāmūs*, Cairo, 4 vols., 1289/1872

GAL=Brockelmann, *Geschichte der arabischen Literatur*, I-II; *Supplement* I-III, Leiden, 1937–49

[GAS, I=Sezgin, F., *Geschichte des arabischen Schrifttums*, I, Leiden, 1967]

Goldziher, I., *Muhammedanische Studien*, 2 vols., Halle, 1889–90; repr. Hildesheim, 2004

Id., Zur Charakteristik Gelāl ud-Dīn us-Sujūṭī und seiner literarischen Thätigkeit, in *Sitzungsberichte Kaiserl. Ak. Wiss. Wien*, phil. hist. Classe, LXIX (1871), p. 7–28; reprint in Gesammelte Schriften, 6 vols., ed. J. de Somogyi, Hildesheim, 1967–73, I, p. 52–73

al-Ḥākim al-Nīṣābūrī, *Maʿrifat ulūm al-ḥadīth* [ed. S. Muʿaẓẓam Ḥusayn], Cairo, 1937 ; [repr. Beirut 1979]

[Ḥākim-Robson=al-Ḥākim al-Nīṣābūrī, *An Introduction to the science of tradition*, being *al-Madkhal ilā maʿrifat al-Iklīl*, introduction, translation, and notes by J. Robson, London, 1953]

Ibn al-Abbār, *al-Muʿjam fī aṣḥāb al-qāḍī Abī ʿAlī al-Ṣadafī* (Almôcham Dictionarium ordine alphabetico de discipulis Abu Ali Assadafi ab Aben al-Abbar), ed. Fr. Codera y Zaidin, Madrid, 1886

Ibn ʿAbd al-Barr, *Jāmiʿ bayān al-ʿilm wa faḍlih*, 2 vols. in 1, Cairo, 1346/1927

Ibn Abī l-Wafāʾ, ʿAbd al-Qādir, *al-Jawāhir al-muḍīʾa fī ṭabaqāt al-ḥanafiyya*, [/5 vols., ed. M. A. al-Ḥulū, Cairo and Riyad, 1978–88, Cairo, 1993[2]]

Ibn Abī Yaʿlā, *Ṭabaqāt al-Ḥanābila*, ed. A. ʿUbayd, Damascus, 1350/1931 [/2 vols., ed. M. Ḥ. al-Fiqī, Cairo, 1371/1952]

Ibn ʿAsākir, Thiqat al-Dīn, *al-Taʾrīkh al-kabīr*, 7 vols., ed. and abridged by ʿA. Badrān, 1329–51/1911–32 [*s.t. Tahdhib Taʾrikh Dimashq*, revised ed., Beirut, 1979]

Ibn al-Athīr, Izz al-Dīn *al-Kāmil fī l-taʾrīkh* [Ibn el-Athiri Chronicon quod perfectissimum inscribitur], 13 vols., ed. K.J. Tornberg, Leiden, 1851–71

Ibn Bashkuwāl, *K. al-Ṣila fī taʾrīkh aʾimmat al-Andalus* [Aben-Pascualis Assila, Dictionarium biographicum], 2 vols., ed. F. Codera, Madrid, 1882–86

Ibn Baṭṭūṭa, *al-Riḥla*, 4 vols., ed. C. Defrémy and B.R. Sanguinetti, Paris, 1874–8
[Ibn Daqīq al-ʿĪd, *al-Iqtirāḥ fī bayān, al-iṣṭilāḥ*, ed. Q. ʿA. al-Dūrī, Baghdad, 1402/1982]
Ibn Ḥajar al-ʿAsqalānī, *Lisān al-Mīzān*, 7 vols., Hyderabad, 1911–3; [repr. Beirut, 1986]
Ibn al-ʿImād al-Ḥanbalī, *Shadharāt al-dhahab fī akhbār man dhahab*, 8 vols., Cairo, 1350–1/1931–2
Ibn Jamāʿa, Badr al-Dīn, *Tadhkirat al-sāmiʿ wa l-mutakallim*, Hyderabad, 1353/1934
Ibn al-Jazarī, *Ghāyat al-nihāya fī Ṭabaqāt al-qurrāʾ* [Das Biographische Lexikon der Koranleser], 3 vols. in 2, ed. G. Bergsträsser and O. Pretzl, Leipzig 1933–5
Ibn Kathīr, Abū l-Fidāʾ, *Ikhtiṣār ʿulūm al-ḥadīth*, Cairo, 1937
IKhal=Ibn Khallikān, *Wafayāt al-aʿyān wa anbāʾ abnāʾ al-zamān*, 2 vols., ed. F. Wüstenfeld, Göttingen, 1835–50/8 vols., ed. I. ʿAbbās, Beirut, 1968–77
Ibn Khayr, Abū Bakr, *Fahrasat... [Index librorum...]*, 2 vols., ed. Fr. Codera et R. Tarrago, Caesaraugustae (Zaragossa), 1894–95; repr. Baghdad, 1963
Ibn al-Nadīm, *al-Fihrist*, ed. G. Flügel (J. Rödiger and A. Müller), Leipzig, 1872; repr. Beirut, 1964
IS=Ibn Saʿd, Muḥammad, *K. al-Ṭabaqāt al-kabir* [*Biographien Muhammeds, seiner Gefährten end der späteren Träger des Islams bis zum Jahre 230 der Flucht*], E. Sachau et alii, 9 vols., Leiden, Brill, 1905–40
Ibn al-Ṣalāḥ, *Muqaddimat ʿUlūm al-ḥadīth*, Aleppo, 1931 [Muqaddimat Ibn al-Ṣalāḥ, ed Bint al-Shāṭiʾ Cairo 1974]
[al-ʿIrāqī, al-Ḥāfiẓ Zayn al-Dīn ʿAbd al-Raḥīm, *Fatḥ al-mughīth bi-sharḥ Alfiyyat muṣṭalaḥ al-ḥadīth*, ed. Rabīʿ, Cairo, 1408/1988² (1355/1936¹)]
Irshād = Yāqūt, *Irshād* ...
[ʿIyāḍ, al-Qāḍī, *al-Ilmāʿ ilā maʿrifat uṣūl al-riwāya wa taqyīd al-samāʿ*, ed. S.A. Ṣaqr, Cairo and Tunis, 1389/1970]
Jawāhir, v. Ibn Abī l-Wafāʾ
Kutubī, Ibn shākir, *Fawāt al-wafāyṭ*, 2 vol., Cairo, 1283/1866 [5 vols., ed. I. Abbās, Beirut, 1973–4]
LA=Ibn Manẓūr, *Lisan al-ʿArab*, 20 vols., Cairo, 1882–1889
[Marçais, W., trans. and annotated by, *Le Taqrīb de en-Nawawī*, Paris, 1902]
Mez, A., *Die Renaissance des Islams*, Heidelberg, 1922 [/The Renaissance of Islam, translated by S. Kh. Bukhsh and D.S. Margoliouth, London, 1937]
Qalqashandī, *Ṣubḥ al-aʿshā*, 14 vol., Cairo, 1913–9
Ṣafadī, *al-Wāfī bi-l-wafāyāt*, I-II, ed. H. Ritter, Leipzig, 1931–44

Sakhāwī, Shams al-Dīn Muḥammad, *al-Ḍawʾ al-lāmiʿ li-ahl al-qarn al-tāsiʿ*, 12 vols., ed. Ḥusām al-Din al-Qudsī, Cairo, Maktabat al-Qudsī, 1353–5/1936–8; reprint Beirut, Maktabat al-Ḥayāt, n.d.

Id., *al-Tibr al-masbūk fī dhayl al-Sulūk*, Cairo, 1896 [reprint, Cairo, Maktabat al-Kulliyyāt al-azhariyya, 1972]

Samʿānī, *Adab al-imlāʾ wa l-istimlāʾ* [*Die Methodk des Diktatkollegs*], ed. Max Weiweiler, Leiden, E.J. Brill, 1952

Id., *The Kitāb al-Ansāb* of ʿAbd al-Karīm ibn Muḥammad al-Samʿānī. Reproduced in facsimile from the ms. in the British Museum, add. 23355, with an introd. by D.S. Margoliouth. Leyden, 1912 [5 vols., ed. ʿA. ʿU. al-Bārūdī, Beirut, 1988]

Shadharāt, v. Ibn al-ʿImād

[Silvestre de Sacy, A.I., *Anthologie grammaticale arabe*, Paris, 1829]

Siyar, v. Dhahabī

Subkī, Tāj al-Dīn, *Ṭabaqāt al-shāfiʿiyya*, 6 vols., Cairo, 1324/1906: ed. Maḥmūd M. al-Ṭināḥī and ʿAbd al-Fattāḥ al-Ḥulw, Cairo, 1964–76

Suyūṭī, [*Bughyat al-wuʿāt fī ṭabaqāt al-lughawiyyīn wa l-naḥwiyyīn*, 2 vols., ed. M. Abū l-Faḍl Ibrāhīm, Cairo, al-Khānjī, 1384/1964]

Id., *al-Muzhir fī ʿulūm al-lugha wa anwāʿihā*, 2 vols., Būlāq 1282/1865 [2 vols., ed. M. A. Jād al-Mawlā, *et al.*, Cairo 1958]

Id., *Tadrīb al-rāwī*, Cairo, 1326/1908 [2 vols. ed. ʿA. ʿAbd al-Laṭīf, Cairo, 1399/1979[2]]

Tadhkira, v. Dhahabī

Tadrīb, v. Suyūṭī

Tāj=Zabīdī, al-Sayyid Murtaḍā M., *Tāj al-ʿarūs*, 40 vols., ed. ʿAbd al-Sattār Aḥmad Farāj *et al.*, Kuwayt, 1965–2001

TB, v. al-Baghdādī, al-Khaṭīb

THan, v. Ibn Abī Ya ʿlā

Tibr, v. Sakhāwī

TT=Ibn Ḥajar al-ʿAsqalānī, *Tahdhīb al-tahdhīb*, 12 vols., Hyderabad, 1325–7

al-Ṭusī, Abū Jaʿfar, *Fihris* [Tūsys list of Shyʾah books], ed. A. Sprenger and Mawlawy ʿAbd al-Haqq, Calcutta, 1853–5

al-Udfuwī, Jaʿfar b. Thaʿlab, *al-Ṭāliʿ al-saʿīd*, Cairo, 1914

Yāqūt al-Rūmī, *Irshād al-arīb ilā maʿrifat al-adīb* [*Muʿjam al-udabāʾ*], 7 vols., éd. D.S. Margoliouth, Leiden and London, 1907–27

Id., *Muʿjam al-buldān* [Jacut's Geographisches Wörterbuch], 6 vols., ed. F. Wüstenfeld, Leipzig, 1866–73, 1924[2]

Wensinck, A.J., et al., *Concordance et indices de la tradition musulmane*, 8 vols., Leiden, 1936–69

11
THE USE OF WRITING FOR THE PRESERVATION OF ANCIENT ARABIC POETRY

F. Krenkow

We rely for our more intimate knowledge of Ancient Arabian civilisation upon two main sources, the traditions of the prophet collected by a host of men who made it their special profession, and in a higher degree the poems of the poets who flourished before the time of Muhammed and for about a century later. The interest in the latter died away at a fairly early date and became the field of labour for a rather limited number of philologists who collected and commented the poems. These commentaries together with the biographical literature connected with the life of the Prophet and the traditionists form the second basis for our knowledge of this civilisation which finally played such an important part in the history of the human race.

While it became a practice for the traditionists to establish an unbroken chain of authorities down to the Prophet himself, this was not done for poetry, except in a few cases, to judge from the collections of poems handed down to us, and we generally have to be content with the assertion that certain readings were those of al-Aṣma'ī, Abū 'Amr ash-Shaibānī, Ibn al-A'rābī, Muḥammad ibn Ḥabīb, al-Mufaḍḍal, Abū 'Ubaida and a few other grammarians. These grammarians, though cited as final authorities, are frequently said to have collected the Dīwān or collection of poems of a certain poet; very seldom, however, we learn whence they collected these poems. At the time the grammarians took the older poets in hand, the taste for poetry had already changed considerably; we can ascertain this with a fair amount of certainty from the style employed by the poets contemporary with them of whom I need mention only Abū Nuwās, Abū Tammām and al-Buḥturī; in addition anthologies had come into fashion. The ancient poetry was at the turn of the 2nd century of the Hijra the field for word-hunters which laid the foundation for the Arabic dictionaries of the 3rd and 4th centuries, and it was the merit of these grammarians to have preserved so many ancient collections of poems which would otherwise have perished, as the interest which evoked this early poetry had faded away with the memory of those times. Had not these grammarians and their pupils put these dīwāns on paper, practically the whole of this poetry would have perished within a further fifty years.

If we accept this assertion as substantially true, we must enquire how much of the older poetry had been preserved up to the time when the grammarians took in hand the work of *collecting* and commenting. The general character of the older Arabic poetry is such that the poems were composed for some specific purpose, in general the praise of the tribe of the poet; in the later periods also of individuals. However, we find among the most ancient poems already some which apparently were composed to display the poet's art in composing works of a literary style in which he employed high-sounding words and difficult rhymes, which no doubt met with applause as this style in certain directions grew into a mania for cramming a poem with so many unusual words that it became almost unintelligible to an ordinary audience; the poets who might be cited as examples are Ṭirimmāh, al-'Ajjāj and Ru'ba.

The method for making a poem widely known was the recital of the poem by the poet himself or by one of his followers or pupils, called the carrier (Rāwī); the poet himself being "the one endowed with knowledge" (Shā'ir). We find frequent references in Arabic literature to the recital of the poems by the poets themselves, and I refer only to the account given in the Kitāb al-Aghānī[1] of the recital of the Mu'allaqa by al-Ḥārith ibn Ḥilliza before King an-Nu'mān and that of the Burdah by Ka'b ibn Zuhair before the Prophet. I have, however, to go to later times to get a further glimpse into the activity of the poets and their manner of reciting. In the Kitāb al-Faraj ba'd ash-Shidda of Tanūkhī[2] the poet al-Buḥturī relates that he recited to the caliph al-Mu'tazz some verses while the latter was in prison. These verses the poet had originally dedicated to Muḥammad ibn Yūsuf ath-Thaghrī, then in prison, and

[1] Agh. IX, 178. [2] Vol. 1, 89–90.

now made al-Mu'tazz believe that they were composed for him. Al-Mu'tazz took *the sheet of paper* (الرقعة) *on which the poem was written* and handed it to a servant who was present for him to keep in safety. Later, when he had obtained his freedom and become caliph, al-Mu'tazz was reminded of the poem and counting the verses rewarded the poet with one thousand dīnārs for each verse; 6000 dīnārs for the six verses.

The poetess Lailā al-Akhyaliyya[1] had a poetical quarrel with the poet an-Nābigha of the tribe of Ja'da and after the customary practice she attacked the tribe of the poet with her lampoons. They, therefore, held a public council and decided to lodge complaint against the offender with the ruler of al-Madina, by which probably the caliph 'Omar or 'Othmān is meant. This being reported to Lailā she composed further verses as a complement to her satire in which she says:

> News has reached me that a tribe at Shaurān is urging forward jaded riding camels.
>
> Night and morning is their embassy journeying with a sheet of writing to get me flogged. What a bad piece of work (on their part)!

It appears that the people who were to lodge the complaint brought the offending piece of poetry with them in *writing*.

Qaisaba ibn Kulthūm as-Sakūnī[2], a South Arabian chief, while intending to perform the pilgrimage to the Ka'ba in the time before Islam, fell into captivity amongst the tribe of 'Āmir b. 'Uqail where he pined for several years. The poet Abuṭ-Ṭamaḥān al-Qainī happened to pass one day the place where Qaisaba was kept in fetters, who learning that Abuṭ-Ṭamaḥān was about to journey to Yaman, made him undo the covering of his saddle and wrote in Musnad or Yamanite script verses which finally led to his rescue and liberation.

It may be considered that these instances are isolated, and that after all the poetry of the desert was handed down by oral tradition and that the poems were composed and remembered first by the poet himself and finally transmitted by his Rāwī and, when the latter had died, by his tribesmen

[1] Agh. IV, 134^{7-11}. Goldziher, *Ḥuṭai'a*, p. 19.
[2] Agh. XI, 130–131.

who had either an interest in the preservation of the poem or admired it for the beauty of the diction.

But we can get a further insight that writing was not so uncommon in Arabia as is generally assumed; if we read the verses of poets come down to us, we find there very frequent references to writing and I give in the following only a few typical examples; also that the art of writing had already attained a certain degree of perfection and that the poets had a sense for the beauty of ornamental writing. We find also that the older poets are not unacquainted with the use of writing and shape of letters.

The Rajaz poet Abun-Najm says[1]:

> I came from Ziyād like one who is bereft of reason,
> My legs tracing different characters,
> Writing on the road a Lām-Alif.

The author of the Khizāna tells us that the poet was blamed for revealing the fact that he knew writing, by whom he does not say, but probably by the grammarians who had put up the thesis that poets did not possess the knowledge of writing.

Very frequently in the earlier verses of a long poem the poet describing the deserted homestead compares the traces with writing or even with illuminated title-pages such as he may have seen in copies executed for wealthy lovers of literature.

Abū Du'ād al-Kilābi says[2]:

> To whom belong the remains of a dwelling like the title-page of a book, in the low ground of Ufāq or the low ground of aḏ-Ḏuhāb?

Al-Akhṭal has seen old manuscripts[3]:

> Just as if they were, through the length of time which has passed, decayed leaves of a book which are spread out.

[1] Khiz. I, 48, Shawāhid Mughnī

أَقْبَلْتُ من عِنْدِ زِيَادٍ كَالخَرِفْ
يَخُطُّ رِجْلَاىَ بِخَطٍّ مُخْتَلِفْ
تُكَتِّبَانِ فى الطَّرِيقِ لَامَ آلِفْ

[2] Bekrī 115[14]

لِمَنْ طَلَلٌ كَعُنْوَانِ الكِتَابِ * بِبَطْنِ أُفَاقٍ أَوْ بَطْنِ الذُّهَابِ

[3] Dīwān, p. 156. 4

فَكَأَنَّمَا هِىَ مِنْ تَقَادُمِ عَهْدِهَا * وَرَقٌ نُشِرْنَ مِنَ الكِتَابِ بَوَالِى

Qais ibn al-Khaṭīm says[1]:

Do you know the traces (of a dwelling) like the lines of gilded (parchments)?

the word *madāhib* being explained as skins on which are lines of writing in gold.

Here we have one kind of material used for writing upon, while in the following verse of Imru'ul-Qais we get acquainted with another kind. He says[2]:

To whom belong the traces of a dwelling-place which I saw and which filled me with sorrow, resembling the hand-writing of a book upon South Arabian palm-bast?

Al-Baṭalyōsī[3] in his commentary informs us that the *'asīb* is the bast of the date palm stripped off the leaves and he adds that the Muslims at the time of the Prophet were using palm-bast and flat stones for writing, while Imru'ul-Qais specially mentions palm-bast because the people of Yaman were accustomed to write their deeds and agreements upon this material.

Ḥātim of Ṭayyi'[4] puts it even plainer that he himself and his audience were acquainted with writing and mentions another writing material in the following verse:

Do you know the traces of dwellings and a dilapidated camp-trench which is like *thy* handwriting upon thin leather scribed in lines?

Frequently we find, however, reference made to writing in another script than Arabic, a fact which has been interpreted as an admission of the poet's inability to read or write. The comparison, however, in these cases is more subtle; the poet cannot make out the meaning of the traces of the dwelling just as he is unable to read a *foreign* script. Instances of this manner of allusion to writing are the following.

Ash-Shammākh a poet of early Islam says[5]:

Just as a Jewish Rabbi in Taimā' writes Hebrew with his right hand, then draws lines (for further writing).

[1] Dīwān, ed. Kowalskī, No. 4, *v.* 1.
[2] Dīwān, ed. Ahlwardt, 63, *v.* 1.
[3] Ed. Cairo, p. 100.
[4] Dīwān, ed. Schulthess, 42, *v.* 1

أَتَعْرِفُ أَطْلَالاً وَنُؤْيًا مُهَدَّمَا * كَخَطِّكَ فِى رِقٍّ كِتَابًا مُنَمْنَمَا

[5] Dīwān, ed. Cairo, p. 26. 7

كَمَا خَطَّ عِبْرَانِيَّةً بِيَمِينِهِ * بِتَيْمَاءَ حَبْرٌ ثُمَّ عَرَّضَ أَسْطُرَا

But much earlier al-Ḥārith ibn Ḥilliza refers to another type of writing[1]:

> Whose were those homesteads at al-Ḥabs which are effaced till their visible traces look like parchment-deeds of the Persians?

But if I could above refer to the poet al-Buḥturī reciting his poem from the written sheet, we are also told that the poet ʿUqaila ibn Hubaira al-Asadī[2] who lived to the time of Muʿāwiya handed the caliph a sheet (رقعة) on which he had written his verses, which probably were too emphatic in their expression to be recited publicly.

The poet Ḏur-Rumma when reciting his poems asks the listener to *write* them down, for he says:

> A book does not forget or alter words or phrases which have taken the poet a long time to compose.

The text of his Dīwān in the oldest manuscript goes back to the poet himself.

We are further told[3] that an-Nuʿmān ibn al-Munḏir, king of al-Ḥīra possessed a collection (Dīwān) of the poems by celebrated poets in his praise and that of his family and that this collection finally got into possession of the Omayyad kings, or at least partly.

In Sukkarī's commentary to the poems of Zuhair ibn Abī Sulmā and his son Kaʿb we are told that the collected poems of the family of Zuhair were preserved among the Banū Ghaṭafān because they resided among this tribe, though belonging to the tribe of Muzaina.

We get, however, more information in other quarters. Zubair ibn Bakkār relates[4] on the authority of a son of Jamʿa the daughter of al-Kuthayyir, who said that among the *books* of his father containing the poems of Kuthayyir a certain poem was found.

Finally Farazdaq[5] tells us clearly that he possessed a copy of the Dīwān of the poet Labīd; that is, at a time before the oldest grammarians who are credited with the collecting of the ancient poems.

Still more important, however, is the fact that for all ancient poems we have a large number of various readings.

[1] Mufaḍḍaliyyāt, ed. Thorbecke, 26, *v.* 1. [2] Khizāna I, 343.
[3] Jumaḥī, *Ṭabaqāt*, ed. Hell, 10[18] ff. [4] Agh. VIII, 30 bottom.
[5] *Naqāʾiḍ*, p. 200. 1.

A great number of these variants are no doubt due to carelessness in handing down, whether caused by errors of hearing or writing, but there are quite a number of readings which can only be due to different interpretation of the unpointed letters of the very defective older Arabic script. Unfortunately only very few of the ancient collections of poems so far published contain really old glosses at first hand to enable us to point out to students these very important readings. I do not refer to the variants caused by careless writing at later periods, but the variants quoted by the earlier grammarians in the commentaries to the poems edited. As examples I cite only the following, which could be increased considerably by systematically going through the Dīwāns edited up to the present.

Dīwān ʿĀmir, ed. Lyall, 4, *v.* 2 أَبَدْنَا and أَبَرْنَا
7, *v.* 12 الخَمْشِ and الجِبْسِ
Hudalī poems, ed. Kosegarten, 20, *v.* 2 بالمَرْفِضِ and بالمِرْبَضِ
21, *v.* 8 سَفْعَاء and سَقْفَاء and سَقْعَاء
21, *v.* 16 ذَايِبْ and رَايِبْ
21, *v.* 21 المُقَرَّنَة and المُقَرَّبَة
22, *v.* 2 اسْتِلَال and انْسِلَال
22, *v.* 12 وَسُطَانَ and وَسْطَانَ and شَوْطَانَ
Dīwān ʿAmr b. Qamīʾa, 1, *v.* 10 أَخْمَدَا and أَجْمَدَا
Dīwān Mutalammis, 1, *v.* 4 مُنْتَقِلاً and مُنْتَفِلاً

I have taken these passages at random, but in all cases it is impossible that the variants can be anything but different interpretations of the unpointed *written* text of the poems at a time before the commentators began to explain the poems.

I might even go further to suggest that the composition of poems and the art of writing were clearly connected, and probably the poet was also the person who wielded the magic art of writing. In addition, the very rhymes of most Arabic poems are more evident to the eye than to the ear. Some poets took a pride in composing poems rhyming upon a letter which occurs only rarely at the end of words, as poems rhyming upon the letters ص ط and ز.

The Dīwān of Abul-Aswad ad-Du'alī contains a small poem, No. 20 in Rescher's edition[1], rhyming upon the letter ذ; against the poet Abul-Jārūd who, we are told, was unable to answer with a poem upon the same rhyme. As Abul-Aswad's life extended well into the time before Islam, we must assume that his striving after unusual rhymes was nothing new. It also seems to me to prove that letters and not sounds played a great part in the art of poetry, and I consider the subject important enough to be followed up further, as we may get more insight into the civilisation of Arabia before Islam.

I need hardly point out that frequent reference is made in ancient poems to deeds and treaties being drawn up in writing, also that from several poets we know that they were Rāwīs of older poets and, we might add, their pupils in this art. With the art of writing the pupil, if gifted, was also initiated in the art of poetry. This might also account to a great extent for the schematic trend of thought with its recurring comparisons of the same subjects. Ancient Arabic poetry as preserved to us was not the free effusion of the soul, it was practically without exception an artificial utterance of the mind, expressed more or less skilfully in accordance with the talent of the poet.

[1] W. Z. K. M. 1913, p. 382.

F. KRENKOW.

12
AUTHORSHIP AND TRANSMISSION IN UNAUTHORED LITERATURE: THE AKHBĀR ATTRIBUTED TO AL-HAYTHAM IBN 'ADĪ*

Stefan Leder

Frankfurt am Main

Transmission, much more than authorship, seems to shape large parts of Arabic literature, since the author himself, rather than expressing his views with his own words, hands down materials quoted from earlier authorities. This aspect of literature is not only found in historical writing—quite naturally, where the quotation of eye-witnesses is concerned—but in most other fields as well, especially in the refined literature of the adab-type, characterized by a didactic intention or attitude which impregnates the narration. With the exception of the Prophetic tradition (*ḥadīth*), most of the material this literature consists of can eventually be defined as self-contained narrative units which we will designate here by the term *akhbār*. Such texts differ widely in theme and structure, and they range from simple statements or utterances to complex stories.

The concept of adab, the works subsumed under it, and the style associated with adab will continue to generate many questions. "Literature of the adab-type" is here understood in its widest acceptation as given by C.A. Nallino, *La littérature arabe des origines à l'époque de la dynastie umayyade*, trad. par Ch. Pellat, Paris 1950, pp. 7-28. Concerning akhbār as a term not limited to factual information, see my article: *Prosa-Dichtung in der aḫbār-Überlieferung*, in: Der Islam 64/1987/6 sqq.

The works containing akhbār—whether or not the material is systematically arranged—are compilations drawing on a multitude of sources, most of which are themselves compilations. These sources are not transmitted in their entirety; instead, single akhbār are taken out and woven into a new context consisting of material from different sources. Within the compilation, the khabar forms a mobile element which may be described as a module; it is not a constituent part of an integrated overall-composition. Its absence would not necessarily imply incompleteness or change the character of the compilation.

---

* This contribution is based on a paper presented at the XIIIe Congrès de l'Union Européenne d'Arabisants et d'Islamisants, Venice 1986.

Although it is not always evident from a given text, the single khabar may have undergone a long process of transmission, having been successively detached from and introduced into a series of works before it appears in the source that one is considering. As a result of this process akhbār are dispersed, and naturally the single element is more apt to be preserved than the work which from it was excerpted. Parallelism between single elements of different works constitutes a characteristic of akhbār literature. Due to the process of repeated reproduction, such parallel versions often show variances of different kinds. Akhbār of a distinctly narrative character, in particular, frequently appear under different forms that may hardly be reduced to a common model. To sum up this preliminary perspective, the khabar is described as a mobile component which may appear at different stages of a complex process of reproduction and be characterized by its own idiosyncrasy.

Many readers familiar with this kind of literature will be familiar with these traits. Taken seriously, this would imply that it is very problematic to make direct use of such material, because any conclusion based on their origin or wording and composition may be misleading. Firstly, their value as self-contained elements favours the spread of akhbār falsely attributed to some authority or author. Indeed, when reproduced in later texts, their attribution, once coined, is transmitted along with the khabar. Since the author of a given source, being a compiler, may have taken his material from an earlier compilation, we cannot be sure that any original text of the authority quoted was known to him. Secondly, even where no doubt concerning authenticity exists, the prevalence of numerous variants may inhibit any subsequent assessment of the author's original wording. Under the circumstances, a detailed description of the process through which reproduction and reshaping of akhbār occurs is indispensable. It would thus be of particular interest to analyze the material of the great akhbārīyūn whose material is so predominant in the later compilations.

Previous attempts in this direction have concentrated on the reconstruction of the akhbārī's works, and have neglected to consider the wording and composition of their material more closely. Cf. Mohamed A. Yagi, *Sahl ibn Hārūn (mort en 215/830), édition des fragments avec traduction* (unpublished dissertation), Paris (Sorbonne) 1955; R. Blachère, *Un auteur d'adab oublié: al-ʿUtbī, mort en 228*, in: Mélanges d'Orientalisme offerts à Henri Massé, Teheran 1963; Badri M. Fahd, *Shaikh al-akhbārīyīn: al-Madā'inī*, Nadjaf 1972. For a study of the diachronical and synchronical aspects of the material related to al-Haytham ibn ʿAdī, see my forthcoming study: Frühe aḫbār-Literatur—Urheber und Gestaltung in Texten nach al-Haiṯam ibn ʿAdī (st. 207/822).

In the following, some observations concerning akhbār transmitted on the authority of al-Haytham ibn ʿAdī (d. 207/822) are set forth in order to prepare the way for a critical evaluation of his authorship. The selection of the material discussed here is based on a comprehensive examination of Haytham's corpus which include, to date, about one thousand akhbār. Except for some fragments, no works by Haytham have been found so far. The material attributed to him is gathered from scattered quotations. Disregarding many of the questions that should be raised in this context, we will concentrate on the fundamental problems of authenticity and originality of form.

The study of a corpus like that of Haytham has to be regarded as a fruitless undertaking if one assumes that these materials do not reflect Haytham's own literary work but were mainly produced by later authors who, according to the rules of literary practice, attributed these materials to him. On the contrary, if one hopes to achieve positive results, one must assume that these quotations are based on a text of which Haytham is either the author or the transmitter, if he refers to a prior authority. In the case of Haytham, as with many akhbārīyūn, proofs to this are very scarce, because there are only few texts or text-fragments that could be attributed to him beyond reasonable doubt. Furthermore, any mere arrangement of the collected materials according to the titles which are ascribed to him in bibliographical literature would not enable us to establish a dependable reconstruction of his opera. Any attempt to assign certain materials to these titles by reason of subject matter would necessarily be vague and arbitrary. Apart from this, it becomes clear, if we compare the titles with the materials collected, that only a small part may be ascribed with some certainty to the alleged titles.

Some of the material is obviously related to the titles mentioned by Ibn an-Nadīm, *K. al-Fihrist*, ed. R. Tadjaddud, Teheran 1391/1971, p. 112 sq., on whom rely Yāqūt ar-Rūmī, *Mu'djam al-udabā'*, ed. A.F. Rifā'ī, 1-20, Cairo 1355/1936-1357/1938, 19/309 sq., as well as Ibn Khallikān, *Wafayāt al-a'yān wa-anbā' az-zamān*, ed. Iḥsān Abbās, 1-8, Beirut 1969-72, 6/106 sq, and Ismā'īl Pasha al-Baghdādī, *Hadīyat al-'ārifīn*, ed. K. Rifat Bilge et al., 1-2, Istanbul 1951-55, 2/511. Valuable references may also be found in other bibliographic sources such as Paul Sbath, *Choix de livres qui se trouvaient dans les bibliothèques d'Alep au XIIIe siècle*, Cairo 1946, nos. 208, 879, and al-Mālikī, *Tasmiyat mā warada bihī al-Khaṭīb al-Baghdādī Dimashqa min riwāyātihī*, in: Yūsuf al-'Ushsh, *Al-Khaṭīb al-Baghdādī, Mu'arrikh Baghdād wa-muḥaddithuhā*, Damascus 1364/1945, nos. 362, 386, 406. Some titles of Haytham are even quoted, e.g. *K. al-Mathālib*: by Abū l-Faradj al-Iṣfahānī, *K. al-Aghānī*, 1-24, Cairo 1345/1927-1394/1974, 1/12; or his *K. al-Khawāridj*: by Ibn Kathīr, *al-Bidāya wan-nihāya fī t-ta'rīkh*, 1-14, Cairo 1348/1929-1358/1939, 7/273. For the evaluation of these and other data, not mentioned here, I can at this point only refer to my forthcoming study on Haytham.

The Haytham corpus has to be regarded as a mass of dispersed elements, which in most cases may not be attributed to the works of which he is purported to be the author. Hence the only way remaining to establish Haytham's authorship is through the proofs which can be derived from the texts themselves. If one hopes to find a criterion for authenticity, the most obvious way to proceed would be—by analogy with the study of different manuscripts reproducing one text—to collate parallel versions, i.e. different reproductions of a khabar attributed to Haytham.

Akhbār which are identical in wording but ascribed to several different authorities would require further investigation. As in the field of poetry, when a *dīwān* has to be reconstructed from the dispersed verses found all through the literature, doubts as to the correctness of the attribution are justified in these cases. If identically parallel versions do not go back to a common informant (or source), they cannot both be of correct attribution. The limitations of this method are defined by what has already been alluded to. In contrast to poetry, no well-defined rules underly the composition of akhbār. The frequency of variances between parallel texts must limit the number of reproductions which, while identical in form, are attributed to two or several different authorities. False attribution can hence only be ascertained in a limited number of cases.

Our perception of identical reproductions must, however, take into account the fact that any reproduction of texts on the base of manuscripts quite naturally generates variants: these have to be distinguished from divergency, which is of greater significance. Non-intentional interferences, such as copyists' errors, small omissions, orthographic particularities, as well as minor adaptations — intentional or not — such as inversion of word order, change of prepositions according to linguistic usage, etc., should be understood as iterative variants. They do not exclude convergency between parallel texts.

Even if one extends the concept of convergency in this manner, the number of parallels, where the identification of false attribution is possible, does not significantly increase. The relations among texts have to be examined in detail, as will be shown below, in view of their partial convergency.

Firstly, it should be mentioned that convergent parallels among the akhbār attributed to Haytham refer to an antetypus that they — provided that there is no interdependency—are independently based on. The older these parallels and the closer they are to the lifetime of Haytham, the more they suggest a link to an original text of his or his direct disciples and exclude the use of intermediate sources. Only few results gained in this fashion can be considered fully reliable, since we often cannot exclude certain interdependencies among the sources. But they provide us, even if they are not numerous compared to the number of akhbār contained in the corpus, with some evidence to Haytham's authorship.

In this context it may, for example, be pointed out that the khabar which appears identically in al-Djāḥiẓ, *al-Bayān wat-tabyīn*, ed. ʿAbdassalām M. Hārūn, 1-4, Cairo 1388/1968, 2/263 sq., and Ibn Qutayba, *ʿUyūn al-akhbār*, 1-4, Cairo 1345/1925-1349/1930, 1/311, could find its place in his *Khiṭaṭ al-Kūfa* (cf. Ibn an-Nadīm, p. 112). It is not a certainly established fact that these sources are independent, but there are good reasons to suppose (see G. Lecomte, *Ibn Qutaiba*, Damascus 1965, pp. 194-98). Also, the identical reproductions of a khabar in al-Qālī, *K. al-Amālī*, 1-3, Beirut n.d. (Cairo 1344 1926) 3/214 sq. and ar-Raqqām, *K. al-ʿAfw wal-iʿtidhār*, ed. ʿAbdalquddūs Abū Ṣāliḥ, 1-2, Riyadh 1401/1981, p. 472 sqq., could refer equally to *Wulāt al-Kūfa*, attributed to Haytham (Ibn an-Nadīm, p. 112), as to the *ʿUmarāʾ al-Kūfa* by ʿUmar ibn Shabba (d. around 263/876; cf. Ibn an-Nadīm, p. 125), who appears in the isnāds of both texts.

Other results obtained through comparison of parallel texts, however, tend to render the question of authenticity irrelevant. Variances which exclude convergency, and thus go beyond our definition given above, cannot be regarded as a mere failure of the copyist. They are so numerous in the Haytham corpus that the process of transmission must be considered as endowed with a literary identity of its own. Divergency of this order may jeopardize the assumption of a common basis. The quest for the original author becomes meaningless, when the parallel reproductions vary to such an extent that the original wording seems to be disguised by the adaptations of later authors.

The analogy with the free adaptation prevailing in oral transmission is obvious, but in the present context its does not offer an adequate explanation. Divergency may very well result from a textual transmission as may be deduced from the comparison of parallel texts which refer to each other through quotation.

E.g. Ibn ʿAbdalbarr, *al-Istīʿāb fī maʿrifat al-aṣḥāb*, ed. ʿAlī M. al-Bidjāwī, 1-4, Cairo n.d., 3/1211 quoted by adh-Dhahabī, *Taʾrīkh al-Islām*, 1-6, Cairo 1367-69, 4/218 sq.

Divergency may also occur when akhbār are repeated either in one book (e.g. Ibn Ḥadjar al-ʿAsqalāni, *al-Iṣāba fī tamyīz aṣ-ṣaḥāba*, 1-8, Cairo 1322-25, 1/10, 181), or in different places by the same author. An example of the latter is given by al-Djāḥiẓ. The utterance of a young boy who, when asked, designates his father, named *kalb* (dog), by the onomatopoeia *wāw-wāw*, is quoted twice on the authority of Haytham. In his *Bayān* (1/64: *qāla l-Haytham*), only the boy's answer is reported, and, by way of explanation, the name of the boy's father. In his *K. al-Ḥayawān* (ed. ʿAbdassalām M. Hārūn, 1-7, Cairo 1356/1938-1364/1945), 2/168: *zaʿama l-Haytham*), we find a narrative elaboration; here the event and its circumstances are reported: "A man called *kalb* (dog) had a little son, who was once playing in the street ...".

The difference between both versions is not just one of wording. Although the plot is the same, the narrative structures differ to a degree that denotes an intentional adaptation. This short example already marks the extent of what adaptation may do to an original text. One hesitates to attribute both versions to Haytham. If he was the author of both, he would have furnished two different versions of this khabar. A more obvious conclusion would be that the later adaptor, in this case al-Djāḥiẓ, concealed the liberties he took by maintaining the attribution to Haytham. This process must, of course, not be misunderstood as falsification. Any rebuke of this sort would here be inappropriate. By making this charge, we would only lend credit to the assertion that the reproduction of texts is generally faithful. It is clear that we in no way subscribe to this view point. The fact that adaptation designates itself as transmission may only be perceived as a reproach by those who claim that faithful reproduction is the norm.

Another example of two structurally different versions ascribed to Haytham is a tale about the young ʿUmar ibn al-Khaṭṭāb. During a visit to Damascus he loses his companions and goes astray. He comes across a Christian monk, who takes advantage of his weakness, but manages to free himself. A second monk, however, offers him hospitality: recognizing him as the future conqueror of Syria the monk implores his protection.

Both versions point to the same source, because Haytham is quoted as referring to Aslam, a maulā of ʿUmar (cf. Ibn Ḥadjar, *al-Iṣāba*, 1/37, 107) as the ultimate authority. Yet, they differ greatly in respect to the representation of the dialogues and the narrator's point of view. Az-Zadjdjādjī (*al-Amālī*, ed. ʿAbdassālam M. Hārūn, Cairo 1382, pp. 39-41) offers a narration in the first person, i.e. allegedly the account of ʿUmar himself, as he told it to his maulā Aslam. In contrast, Ibn Kathīr (*al-Bidāya wan-nihāya*, 7/58 sq.) first quotes Aslam's report about the journey of his patron ʿUmar (i.e. a narration in the third person), and then changes suddenly to a narration in the first person which is roughly the same as that of az-Zadjdjādjī. The abrupt change to another point of view corresponds with the introduction of a substantial element which can hardly be reported by Aslam, since from his "observer's" point of view, he does not have access to it: By the words "I sat down to think about it" (*djalastu mufakkiran*), an aspect of introspection is introduced. Since this passage finds a parallel in az-Zadjdjādjī's version, we conclude that it is the text itself, his source, which induced Ibn Kathīr to change the point of view of his narration. The presumption that the version preserved in this work might have been reshaped from a text close to the version of az-Zadjdjādjī is simply a consequence of our observation concerning the dominant traits of the narration which Ibn Kathīr found in his source. Confirmation of this assumption is gained from further comparison. The introspective momentum is more circumstantial in az-Zadjdjādjī's text, where ʿUmar is engaged in an inner monologue. In addition, Ibn Kathīr gives much shorter dialogues and shows a tendency to avoid direct speech (e.g.: *sa'alanī ʿani l-amri*, Bidāya; *mā yuqʿiduka hāhunā*?, Amālī). The legendary element, according to which the monk was able to foresee the later role of ʿUmar, appears to be better elaborated in az-Zadjdjādjī's text because the monk here formulates his presentiment subtly. Ibn Kathīr, however, presents what seems to be an awkward simplification (*la-adjidu ṣifataka ṣifata llatī tukhridjunā min hādhā d-dairi*, Amālī; *innī la-arāka lladhī tukhridjunā* (sic!) *min bilādinā*, Bidāya). Most probably, the adaptation found in Bidāya was undertaken in order to make a more complex narration compatible with a historical report. This transformation was interrupted and impeded by specific traits of the narrative itself.

Neither Ibn Kathīr nor az-Zadjdjādjī—if we suppose that there had been an "editorial" interference in the elaboration of this text—can be singled out as responsible for the shape of the text as it appears in their works. Az-Zadjdjādjī quotes (*akhbaranī*) Ibn Durayd (d. 321/933; EI[2] 3/757), and Ibn Kathīr refers to (*rawā*) Aḥmad ibn Marwān ad-Dīnawarī (d. 310/922; GAL[2] 1/160 sq. S 1/249). Both are well-known authors in the akhbār field. Ad-Dīnawarī's *al-Muǧālasa wa-ǧawāhir al-ʿilm* (Publications of the Institute for the History of Arabic-Islamic Science, Series C Facsimile Editions 38, Frankfurt 1986, p. 301 sq.) contains a version of Haytham's narrative. Many differences in wording which distinguish his version from az-Zadjdjādjī's Text are faithfully reproduced by Ibn Kathīr. Doubtlessly ad-Dīnawarī's reproduction is the source of his own version. But comparison makes clear, that Ibn Kathīr himself reshaped the text by reductions and simplifications and thus brought it close to the form of a historical report. Adaptation concerning the wording (style) and narrative structure is to be observed in the work of Ibn Kathīr in other instances as well.

The comparison between Ibn Kathīr, *Bidāya* 8.100 sq. and at-Tanūkhī, *al-Mustadjād min faʿalāt al-adjwād*, ed. M. Kurd ʿAlī, Damascus 1365/1946, 125 sq., offers an obvious example.

The data gained from the collation of other parallels show that in many cases wording and composition of akhbār quoted on the authority of Haytham result from a process of repeated adaptation. Reshaping therefore may not be a unique operation but may occur several times within the long chain of transmission from the archetype to the text that reaches us. Intermediate sources may be of importance as lost links within this chain.

Normally, adaptations do not give rise to versions of distinct narrative structure. Divergency is mostly limited to differences in wording, omissions, abridgements, comments, explanations of the motives of the protagonists, and amplifications through the addition of adequate descriptive elements. A story about the Caliph al-Hādī's (d. 170/786) invitation to praise the sword of the famous poet ʿAmr ibn Maʿdīkarib (*mukhaḍram*, cf. GAS 2/306 sq.) will be discussed here. It serves as an example of differential change at different levels of the transmission process which does not entail changes in the narrative structure.

Aṣ-Ṣamṣāma, the sword of the legendary warrior and poet ʿAmr ibn Maʿdīkarib, comes into the hands of al-Hādī. He lays it down in front of him, the blade bare, and invites the poets to praise it. One of them, Ibn Yamīn al-Baṣrī (al-Masʿūdī, *Murūdj*, see below, § 2491 and Index) is the first to pronounce verses that satisfy the Caliph. He is rewarded with a gift of money and the precious sword. After he has offered to share the gift with his colleagues, the Caliph buys back the sword from him.

This story is cited on the authority of Haytham by: Ibn ʿAbdrabbih, *al-ʿIqd al-farīd*, ed. Aḥmad Amīn et al., 1-7, Cairo 1359/1940-1372/1953, 1/210 sq.; al-Masʿūdi, *Murūdj adh-dhahab wa-maʿādin al-djauhar*, ed. Ch. Pellat, 1-7, Beirut 1965-79, §§ 2490 sq.; Abū Hilāl al-ʿAskarī, *Dīwān al-maʿānī*, 1-2, Cairo 1352, 2/52 sq.; Ibn Khallikān, *Wafayāt*. 6/108 sq.; Ibn Hudhayl al-Andalusī, *Ḥilyat al-fursān wa-shiʿār ash-shudjʿān*, ed. M. ʿAbdalghanī Ḥasan, Cairo 1387/1951, p. 189 sq. Two reproductions which are not attributed, neither to Haytham nor to any other authority, but have many traits in common with the renderings already mentioned, are found in al-Ḥuṣrī, *Zahr al-ādāb wa-thamar al-albāb*, ed. ʿAlī M. al-Bidjāwī, 1-2, Cairo ²1384/1969, p. 780 sq., and ath-Thaʿālibī, *Thimār al-qulūb fī l-muḍāf wal-mansūb*, ed. M. Abū l-Faḍl Ibrāhīm, Cairo 1384/1965, p. 622 sq. Finally, we must also mention the text of al-Khafādjī, *Ṭirāz al-madjālis*, Cairo 1284, p. 135 sq., who quotes six of the verses on the sword, but ascribes them to an "Ibn Iyās". Preceding the verses there is a very short description of the scene at the court of al-Hādī, corresponding to that found in al-Masʿūdī. His "Ibn Iyās", therefore, is probably merely an incorrect rendering of Ibn Yamīn. Including his text, altogether eight versions of the khabar, all related to Haytham, can be analyzed here.

The reproductions of the khabar quoted on the authority of Haytham and those related to them may be divided into two families. The texts of Abū Hilāl and Ibn Khallikān are similar to one another. In both, the scene at the Caliph's court is preceded by a sketch of the history of this sword; it passed through the hands of various owners after the death of ʿAmr ibn Maʿdīkarib. When the account reaches the Caliph al-Hādī, the occasion is taken to praise him for the generosity he showed by spending a large sum to acquire it. This madīḥ is likely to confirm Haytham's authorship. Haytham who is here represented as an eye-witness of the event—for this reason, Ibn Khallikān quotes this story in his biographical chapter on Haytham—was once one of the Caliph's intimates (*nudamāʾ*).

The biographies report Haytham's intimacy with several caliphs up to Hārūn ar-Rashīd (e.g. al-Qifṭī, *Inbāh ar-ruwāt ʿalā anbāh an-nuḥāt*, ed. M. Abū l-Faḍl Ibrāhīm, 1-4, Cairo 1369/1950-[1393]/1973, 3/365). A reminiscence of Haytham concerning a meeting (*madjlis*) at the palace of al-Mahdī is quoted by al-Masʿūdī, Murūdj, § 2464.

The two texts of Abū Hilāl and Ibn Khallikān confirm the rendering of al-Ḥuṣrī, although his version shows abridgements and, as regards the Caliph's invitation, inconsistency; these factors denote textual corruption. Al-Ḥuṣrī and Ibn Khallikān have some wordings in common which contrast with Abū Hilāl: e.g. *kāna awsaʿa banī l-ʿAbbās kaffan* instead of *khuluqan*; *miktal fīhi badratun* instead of *danānīru*. This points either to a specific wording shaped by Abū Hilāl himself, or to interference by a copyist. We are inclined to believe the second possibility. Ibn Khallikān's text is so close to that of Abū Hilāl that he has probably drawn his rendering from a version based on Abū Hilāl's text. Yet al-Ḥuṣrī who, on chronological grounds, can hardly have drawn on the work of Abū Hilāl, must have taken the model of his rendering from a source that Abū Hilāl also used.

Only Abū Hilāl gives the chain of transmitters which connects him with Haytham. He quotes (*qāla*) Muḥammad ibn Dāwūd ibn al-Djarrāḥ (d. 296/908; GAL S 1/224 sq.) who refers to (*ʿan*) Abū Hiffān (d. 255/869; GAS 1/372) (*ʿani l-Iyās al-Qāḍī ʿani l-Haytham*). By mentioning these two well-known men of letters and authors of works entitled "What is known about poets" (*akhbār ash-shuʿarāʾ*), we are led to a possible link between Abū Hilāl and al-Ḥuṣrī. Of course this must, due to the lack of textual proof, remain a presumption. Confirmation is found, however, in a remark of ath-Tha'ālibī, who, following his rendering of the story, mentions a version of Abū Hiffān, which he does not reproduce (see below).

Al-Mas'ūdī's and ath-Tha'ālibī's renderings belong to the second family of texts. At first glance, the differences between both seem to outweigh any convergency. Yet, the fact that there are identical passages in these two texts —in contrast to the parallels of the first family—attracts our attention. The end of the story, relating the poet's honest attitude towards his colleagues, appears in both texts in identical form as far as structure and wording are concerned. Also the account of the Caliph's invitation corresponds in both texts: here he addresses his chamberlain (*ḥādjib*). Apart from this, convergencies with corresponding parts of the other texts occur independently at different points. Al-Mas'ūdī cites only three verses, their sequence being in concordance with ath-Tha'ālibī and Abū Hilāl. Also al-Mas'ūdī hints to his source by quoting (*ḥaddathanā*) from 'Abdallāh ibn aḍ-Ḍaḥḥāk (al-Miṣrī; cf. Ibn Ḥibbān al-Bustī, *K. al-Madjrūḥīn min al-muḥaddithīn*, ed. Maḥmūd Ibrāhīm Zāyid, 1-3, Aleppo 1395/1975-1396/1976, 3/91: al-Hadādī). 'Abdallāh ibn aḍ-Ḍaḥḥāk appears several times as a direct transmitter of Haytham in his corpus, mostly as an informant of the well-known historian Muḥammad ibn Zakarīyā' al-Ghallābī.

Mu'āfā ibn Zakarīyā' an-Nahrawānī, *K. al-Djalīs aṣ-ṣāliḥ al-kāfī*, ed. M. Mursī al-Khūlī, 1-2, Beirut 1401/1981-1403/1983, 1/240, 251, 2/36, and id., ms. Seray Ahmet III 2321, p. 385; aṣ-Ṣūlī, *Ash'ār awlād al-khulafā'*, ed. J. Heyworth-Dune, London 1936, pp. 297, 298, 313. For al-Ghallābī (d. 298/910) see Khayraddīn az-Ziriklī, *al-A'lām*, 1-8, Beirut 1980, 6/130, and F. Rosenthal, *A History of Muslim Historiography*, Leiden ²1968, pp. 429, 509.

Al-Ghallābī is not mentioned by al-Mas'ūdī in this context, but his *K. al-Adjwād*, which would be thematically appropriate for this story, belongs to his sources, as al-Mas'ūdī declares elsewhere (*Murūdj*, § 8). Since 'Abdallāh ibn aḍ-Ḍaḥḥāk cannot be a direct informant of al-Mas'ūdī, in spite of what the term *ḥaddathanā* seems to imply, we suppose that the name of al-Ghallābī has been omitted.

Ibn 'Abdrabbih offers an abridged version concentrating on the scene between the Caliph and the poets. The verses quoted by him differ from Abū Hilāl's rendering only in their order and in some details. But his narrative corresponds to the text of al-Mas'ūdī (e.g. when the Caliph addresses his *ḥādjib*) and must be connected with al-Ghallābī's version. Ibn 'Abdrabbih, who does not allude to his source here, quotes al-Ghallābī several times elsewhere in his work (cf. Walter Werkmeister, *Quellenuntersuchungen zum Kitāb al-'Iqd al-farīd des Andalusiers Ibn 'Abdrabbih*, Berlin 1983, S. 320). He receives most of the material from Abū Yusr ash-Shaibānī (d. 298/911; U.R. Kaḥḥāla, *Mu'djam al-mu'allifīn*, 1-15, Damascus 1376/1957-1381/1961, 1/5,

97), whose lost adab-work probably was Ibn ʿAbdrabbih's direct source also in this case. A faithful reproduction of Ibn ʿAbdrabbih's rendering is given by Ibn Hudhayl. But he also reports, in accordance with the texts mentioned above, the end of the story (the poet's reward), which does not appear in the ʿIqd as we now have it. Ibn Hudhayl must have had a more complete copy of this text, at least as far as this detail is concerned, than we do.

Ath-Thaʿālibī also depends on al-Ghallābī in those parts which are parallel to al-Masʿūdī's text. Those passages of their texts which converge with the renderings of the first family would then point back to an original version of Haytham. The parts which appear exclusively in the texts of al-Masʿūdī, ath-Thaʿālibī and Ibn ʿAbdrabbih would consequently reflect a version of al-Ghallābī. Finally, these texts also show individual traits shaped by the authors of the compilations that we use as our sources.

Of course, ath-Thaʿālibī is in part substantially different from the other versions attributed to Haytham. Two elements must here be discussed. Ath-Thaʿālibī deals more with the historical aspect than the parallel texts. He quotes the verses of ʿAmr ibn Maʿdīkarib pronounced when he left the sword to Ibn al-ʿĀṣ, enumerates the Umayyad caliphs who owned it, and mentions its final transfer to al-Hādī. Secondly, according to ath-Thaʿālibī, the poet who is rewarded for his verses—roughly the same as in the parallel texts—is not Ibn Yamīn but Abūl-Haul al-Ḥimyarī (who lived until the reign of the Caliph al-Amīn; cf. GAS 2/599). Both these elements are to be found in a text given by al-Balādhurī (*Futūḥ al-buldān*, ed. Ṣalāḥaddīn al-Munadjdjid, Cairo 1956-58, p. 142 sq.) who quotes (*wa-qāla*) Haytham's colleague Hishām ibn Muḥammad al-Kalbī (d. 204/819 or 206/821; cf. EI² 4/495). The main part of his text relates what could be called a "genealogy of the sword". Ath-Thaʿālibī's shorter version is parallel to it in content—he abridges a long list of owners—and divergent in some details. It does not seem too hazardous to suggest that ath-Thaʿālibī's version is a combination of two strains of adaptation, one leading over al-Ghallābī, a common link to al-Masʿūdī, and the other being of unknown provenance but in some way connected with Ibn al-Kalbī. The attribution of the verses to Abū l-Haul, however, must not necessarily be borrowed from this unknown source. Al-Balādhurī names Abū l-Haul just as do al-Djāḥiẓ (*K. al-Ḥayawān*, 5/87 sq.) and Ibn ash-Shadjarī (*al-Ḥamāsa*, ed. ʿAbdalmuʿīn al-Mulūḥī and Asmāʾ al-Ḥimṣī, 1-2, Damascus 1970, p. 796 sq.). Moreover, one may gather that ath-Thaʿālibī was aware of the opinion of scholars who voted for Abū l-Haul as the poet in question; this is suggested by his quotation (*Thimār*, p. 623) of a commentary from al-Djāḥiẓ, who, in the corresponding text (*Ḥayawān*, 5/87), just quotes the verses from Abū l-Haul without inserting them into a narrative framework. It is possible that ath-Thaʿālibī, from his position of superior insight into the matter, and influenced by authorities like al-Djāḥiẓ, felt obliged and free to change the name of the poet he found in his source. The importance he gave to this question is manifest in his remark subsequent to this story, according to which Abū Hiffān held Ibn Yamīn to be the author (*ṣāḥib*) of the poem (see above).

Nothwithstanding our conclusion concerning the text of ath-Tha'ālibī, it remains that adaptation occurred at different levels of the chain of transmission. Successive adaptations by Abū Hiffān resp. Ibn al-Djarrāḥ and al-Ghallābī could be identified. We have shown further that the authors of the compilations we use also introduced identifiable changes into the text.

A story of quite different character about the Ṣamṣāma sword and the Caliph al-Hādī is given by al-Mu'āfā ibn Zakarīyā', *al-Djalīs*, 1/566-68. Here, the narrator is Abū Muḥammad al-Yazīdī (d. 202/817-18; al-Khaṭīb al-Baghdādī, *Ta'rīkh Baghdād*, 1-14, Cairo 1349/1931, 14/146 sq.; az-Zubaidī, *Ṭabaqāt an-naḥwīyīn wal-lughawīyīn*, ed. M. Abū l-Faḍl Ibrāhīm, Cairo 1373/1954, pp. 60-65). He was present when the Caliph ordered the sword to be struck against a stone, and when the poet's verses then praised the sword that split through the rock without being damaged. Al-Mu'āfā cites al-Ghallābī, who thus appears to be the authority for two different—indeed opposed—stories about al-Hādī and the sword. They differ not only in content (action), but also in their narrative features. The story that al-Mu'āfā quotes from al-Ghallābī includes distinct narrations in the first person: Al-Yazīdī tells about his intimate relation with the Caliph and his attempt to prevent the sword from being put to the test. Within this story appears the account of the Caliph; he tells of his quest for the sword, and why he wanted to test it. This composition has no equivalent among the akhbār of the Haytham corpus, except in the texts found in al-Mu'āfā's book. This adds to my suspicion that, while outwardly claiming to be a faithful traditionist, he has taken great liberties in reshaping the material.

The fact that the material underwent successive modification does not mean that Haytham's akhbār lie buried under an uncontrolled multiplication of variants. In many instances, as in the example presented here, the reproductions of akhbār referred to Haytham reveal, in their convergent parts, a clear outline of "his" version, which can be clearly distinguished from substantially similar akhbār not attributed to Haytham. In these cases, the data given in the isnād may be a reliable indication of the origin of the single khabar.

Our consideration of divergency has made it clear that the isnād does not necessarily ensure the preservation of the original form, as set down by the authority purported to be the primary source in the chain of the isnād. Moreover, the validity of isnāds, thus defined, does not warrant generalization. When two texts are of identical appearance but are not related according to the indications given in the isnāds, doubts naturally arise as to the trustworthiness of these indications. This does not only apply to completely identical texts. If we firstly consider that akhbār may undergo repeated adaptation, the question must be raised in respect to convergent parts of parallel texts: this may indicate a non-explicit relationship. We secondly have to consider that several narrators to whom different versions of a khabar are referred, may relate a story which was common knowledge to many. In this case, the convergency between texts of independent transmissions does not establish false attribution. In this light, what was said in the beginning may be specified: We must insist on a careful evaluation of the convergent and divergent parts of parallel texts.

An evaluation of this kind may bring forth results that do not confirm the indications of the isnāds. The "stemma" derived from the comparison of parallel texts is not always concordant with the isnāds. When one is dealing with several versions, the convergency between texts quoted from different authorities may override the convergency between those parallels which are attributed to a single authority. The distinct versions of a love-story attributed to different authorities serves as an illustration of such a case. Its plot is not without implicit meaning as it is common in stories of this type: A young man is roaming about with his companions and meets a girl. Having fallen in love, he stays alone near her camp and succeeds in contacting and visiting her several times at night. When her family becomes suspicious, she leaves the camp. The young man, taking her to be one of his enemies, kills her with a shot from his bow. When he discovers his tragic error, he recites two verses and then kills himself. Her family arrives on the scene, and both are buried in one grave.

Ibn ʿAbdrabbih, *al-ʿIqd*, 6/470 sq., quotes (*qāla*) two authorities, Hishām ibn Muḥammad al-Kalbī (see above) and Haytham. As-Sarrādj, *Maṣāriʿ al-ʿushshāq*. 1-2, Beirut 1378/1958, 2/143 sq., gives two insnāds leading to Haytham and to Ibn al-Kalbī, who refers to the rāwī Abū Miskīn. Ibn Qutayba, *ʿUyūn al-akhbār*, 4/133 sq., also gives a version of this story on the authority of Abū Miskīn. Al-Kharāʾiṭī, *Iʿtilāl al-Qulūb*, ms. Ulu Cami 1535, foll. 61a-62a, also refers to him. He is quoted by Ibn al-Djauzī, *Dhamm al-hawā*, ed. Muṣṭafā ʿAbdalwāḥid, Cairo 1381/1962, p. 572 sq.

The two texts which mention Haytham in their isnād show much less convergency among each other than each of them does with the rendering of Ibn Qutayba. All parts of this text are spread over all the other versions in literally identical form. His version thus appears closest to an archetype which all texts are drawn from. One element common only to Ibn ʿAbdrabbih and as-Sarrādj is—apart from a few common textual specificities—that both lovers are buried together. Haytham, according to as-Sarrādj, is referring to another informant than Ibn al-Kalbī's Abū Miskīn. We expect therefore to find at least traces of a specific wording which could be considered as a substrate of the Haytham version. But no such text is discernable. The texts, as we have them, do not confirm the isnāds' claim that there were two independently composed versions.

The identification of these three texts with an Ibn al-Kalbī version is not possible either. The fact that they all are, at least in part, attributed to Ibn al-Kalbī / Abū Miskīn may imply a convergence between parts of the texts ascribed to Haytham (ʿIqd; Maṣāriʿ) and the version of Ibn Qutayba. Yet, the ʿIqd shows many wordings of its own, so that there is little common ground between these texts.

Of course, the claim of the isnāds could be supported by other arguments. In this vein, the basic assumption would be that quoting two authorities (or giving two isnāds) does not necessarily establish that the subsequent text is a melange of two versions. In other words, the text of as-Sarrādj would be closer to that of Ibn Qutayba than is Ibn ʿAbdrabbih's, since the former renders more of Ibn al-Kalbī's/Abū Miskīn's wording. The isolated parts of the ʿIqd which do not concord with any other parallel text would then reflect the substrate of a Haytham version. Even if this cannot be decided with full certainty, a close examination of the passages in question reveals that they function as commentaries and explanations of the protagonists' motives. They do not seem to be original.

Al-Kharāʾiṭī's version has been styled into a great love-story and includes some of its most important topics, such as the marvellous beauty of the girl, the passion that drives the young man out of his mind, and the glance at the beloved which is meant to relieve his suffering. Al-Kharāʾiṭī's text therefore documents a thorough adaptation.

The presumption derived from the occurrence of a double isnād does not disprove that there is no text which, in view of its discernable features, could be regarded as the work of Haytham. Two conclusions have to be drawn. The first concerns the attribution to two different authorities and their informants; they cannot both be right. The second concerns the generation of attributions. Theoretically, we can conceive this either as a silent appropriation by the akhbārī (i.e. Haytham) himself, or as an additional incorporation into his repertoire by later scholars. The alternative possibilities cannot be discussed here at length. It will suffice to observe that unavowed appropriation on the part of the akhbārī would reasonably entail a specific shaping of the khabar. If we retain the second hypothesis, we have to ask why the attribution of a love-story like this should be introduced subsequently. In this case, the answer may lie in the grave. Even if it does not seem important to us, the motif of a common grave for the lovers is of great relevance for the story's moral. It seems to denote a reconciliation between the lovers and their antagonists on the one hand, and, on the other, is a sign of forgiveness for what they have done. This unexpected turn in the course of the story might have required, when it was made, the attribution to an authority whose name would endow it with "factual" value.

The study of Haytham's akhbār suggests, as we may advance here, that the activity of the scholars (compilers) who dealt with the material brought about a new literary production. The attribution of entirely new material to prior authorities seems, in the light of these results, rather exceptional. But the arrangement of "drifting" materials through imputation to well-known akhbārīyūn, as well as the attribution of transformed materials to appropriate authorities, are discernable. It is not surprising that this process, due to its decentral character, would not exclude ambiguities.

This does not, however, affect the Haytham corpus as a whole to the extent that it should be considered to be entirely the result of a later production. From the generation of Haytham's disciples onwards, the transmission of thematically defined sets of texts can be traced.

Naturally, many texts ascribed to different authorities are parallel to the akhbār transmitted on the authority of Haytham. These include cases where no indication of a common source is given in the isnāds (e.g. al-Kharā'iṭī, *I'tilāl*, foll. 78a-79b; Abū l-Faradj, *al-Aghānī* 9/133 sq.; Ibn al-Djauzī, *Dhamm al-hawā*, p. 612 sq.). Others go back to an authority prior to Haytham. Often akhbār that Haytham quotes on the authority of ash-Sha'bī (d. 103/721; GAS 1/277), for instance, do not differ remarkably from parallel versions on the authority of other transmitters (*ruwāt*) than Haytham, nor do they show any particular features. An example for this is the statement of ash-Sha'bī on the rhetorical mastery of the famous Ziyād ibn Abīhi (d. 53/674).

We have encountered this statement in six versions, all of which—with one exception—represent variants in the wording of single parts of it: Haytham is quoted by al-Balādhurī only, *Ansāb al-ashrāf*, vol. 4,1, ed. Iḥsān 'Abbās, Wiesbaden/Beirut 1979, p. 203. Close to the wording of this version is the text of az-Zubayr ibn Bakkār, *al-Akhbār al-muwaffaqīyāt*, ed. Sāmī al-'Ānī, Baghdad 1972, p. 310. Here, as in the Ansāb al-ashrāf, ash-Sha'bī is cited by his disciple Mudjālid ibn Sa'īd (d. 143/761 or 144/762; Ibn Ḥibbān, *k. al-Madjrūhīn*, 3/10 sq.). The name of Haytham, who refers to Mudjālid in al-Balādhurī's rendering also, might therefore have been omitted in the text of the Muwaffaqīyāt. Parallel renderings are to be found in al-Djāḥiẓ, *al-Bayān*, 2/65 sq. (*qāla sh-Sha'bī*) and, perfectly concordant with this text, in aṭ-Ṭabarī, *Ta'rīkh ar-rusul wal-mulūk*, ed. de Goeje et al., series I-III, Leiden 1879-1901, II/76 (*ḥaddathanā 'Umar* [*ibn Shabba*], *anba'anā Khallād ibn Yazīd, sami'tu man yukhbi/aru 'ani sh-Sha'bī*). Ibn 'Asākir, *Tahdhīb Ta'rīkh Ibn 'Asākir*, Damascus 1329-1351, 5/414 (*qāla sh-Sha'bī*) and ar-Rāghib al-Iṣfahānī, *Muḥāḍarāt al-udabā'* 1-4, Beirut 1961, 1/59 sq. are related as can be deduced from common wordings. The only word common to the two texts related to Haytham as opposed to other versions is *tamannaitu* (versus *aḥbabtu*). The saying runs in the version of al-Balādhurī: *mā sami'tu mutakalliman qaṭṭu yukthiru wa-yuṭīlu illā tamannaitu an yaskuta makhāfatan an yusī'a illā Ziyādan kāna lā yazdādu kalāman illā-zdāda iḥsānan.*

The only common feature of the two texts related to Haytham is minor, and the coherence of all the texts is obvious from the parts they have in common. This example manifests the preservation of the basic elements of the wording and represents Haytham as one transmitter among others. Even material such as the example dealt with above, which does not raise any question with respect to its provenance and preservation of form, cannot be considered irrelevant to the perspective developed here. The assumption of a growth of the akhbārī's repertoire, resulting from the activity of later scholars, may shed doubt on its seemingly flawless attribution. The establishment, however, of correlations in addition or in contrast to those declared by the isnāds, remains dependent on several conditions and will thereby always be restricted to single cases.

Coming back to our starting point, we may conclude that in unauthored literature, as in the field of akhbār, authorship mingles with transmission in a twofold manner: firstly through the process of adaptation and the reshaping of akhbār, and, secondly, through the arrangement of materials which fashion the akhbārī's repertoire over time.

13
ON THE LEGACY OF THE CLASSICS IN THE ISLAMIC WORLD

Richard Walzer

The main purpose of the following remarks is to remind the reader of a neglected outpost of classical scholarship. Though it is becoming better known, it still lacks recognition and its defenders remain more isolated than is good for them: there are too few cooperators and there is too little discussion and criticism. The days of Scaliger and Reiske who were both classicists and accomplished Arabists seem to have gone for ever, and hence most of the work which is based on Arabic texts is ignored outside the orientalist circle. It may, then, not be useless to mention a few questions connected with the importance which the study of Arabic philosophical texts may have at the present day for classical scholarship.

It is commonly realized that the tradition of philosophy (and science) of which the Arabs got hold between A.D. 800 and 1000 was richer than the Greek-Byzantine tradition of philosophy which reached the West in the days of the great Schoolmen and of Marsilio Ficino. Philosophical and scientific texts less favoured in the later centuries of the Byzantine Empire were still in comparatively easy reach and the Arabic translators made good use of this opportunity.

Only a comparatively small part of the Arabic versions of Greek philosophical texts has survived; not all of those extant have been traced; not all of those traced have been edited and translated into a Western language. A complete survey would be the subject of a monograph. But some recent progress may be indicated. The Arabic text of Aristotle's *Categories* has been known for about 100 years, the *De interpretatione* for more than 40, the *Poetics* for almost 70 years. We have now, in addition, first editions of the *Prior* and *Posterior Analytics*, the *Topics* and the *Sophistici Elenchi* [1], [the *Rhetorics* [2]], the *De anima* [3], the *Metaphysics* [4] and the pseudo-aristotelian work *De plantis* by Nicolaus of Damascus [5]. Manuscripts of the *Physics*, the *De caelo*, the *History of animals*, the works *On the parts of animals* and *On the generation of animals* are in

---

[1] By 'Abd-ar-Raḥmān Badawī, *Manṭiq Arisṭū* I–III (Cairo 1948–52).

[[2] By the same editor (Cairo 1959).]

[3] By the same editor (Cairo 1954).

[4] By M. Bouyges S. J. (Beyrouth 1938–52).

[5] By A. J. Arberry (Cairo 1933/4).

easy reach [1]. Editions of all these treatises are being planned; the editions of the *Meteorology* and of the last four books of the *Nicomachean Ethics* [2] are expected in the not too distant future. The translation of Themistius' paraphrase of the *De anima* is being prepared for publication. The Arabic text of Ps. Plutarch's *Placita Philosophorum* can now be compared with the badly preserved Greek text [3]. To compile a comparative index of philosophical terminology—Greek, Arabic, and Latin—thus appears less difficult now than it did still twenty years ago.

There is no reason to embark on a list of philosophical texts which have survived only in Arabic versions and thus, together with the Egyptian papyri, increase our present knowledge of Greek literature: they are quite well known [4]. I may, however, mention the recent discoveries of lost works by Alexander of Aphrodisias, the founder of the medieval tradition of Aristotle reading, on whose commentaries and monographs both Arabic and medieval philosophers so largely depend. They are partly available in print [5] (but not translated into a European language), partly have been very recently traced in Istanbul; they are of great interest for the history of Greek and later philosophy [6].

There exists a group of Arabic philosophical texts which are evidently based on lost Greek works without reproducing them in every detail but which follow the original argument very closely, as far as can be made out by probable guesses. Apart from the few original Greek texts of the great authors who interest us all—a chapter based on Posidonius [7], fragments of Aristotle's *Dialogues* [8], a line of Democritus embedded in an Arabic Galen [9], etc.—the interpretation of this kind of text is most fascinating and attractive. I refer only to a few examples. A Consolatio

---

[1] Cf. *Orientalia* 20, 1951, pp. 334 ff.; *Philosophical Quart.* 1953, p. 175 ff.

[2] Cf. A. J. Arberry, *Bulletin of the School of Oriental and African Studies* 1955, p. 1 ff.

[3] Ed. Badawī (Cairo 1954).

[4] Cf. e.g. *Philosophical Quart.* 1953, p. 175 ff. and *Oriens* 6, 1953, p. 93 ff. [see below, pp.60–113].

[5] Cf. Badawī, *Aristū 'inda-l-'Arab* (Cairo 1947), pp. 251–308 [cf. below p. 62].

[6] F. Rosenthal, From Arabic Books and Manuscripts V, *Journal of the American Oriental Society* 75, 1955, pp. 16–18. [Cf. S. Pines, *Archives d'histoire doctrinale et littéraire du moyen âge*, 1959, pp. 295–99.]

[7] Cf. my New Light on Galen's Moral Philosophy, *Class. Quart.* 1949, pp. 82–96 [below, pp. 142–163], A Diatribe of Galen, *Harvard Theological Review* 47, 1954, pp. 243–54 [below, pp. 164–174]. K. Reinhardt, RE. s. v. *Poseidonios* col. 745.

[8] Un frammento nuovo di Aristotele, *Stud. Ital. Filol. Class.*, *N. S.* 14, 1937, pp. 125–37 [below, pp. 38–47]. Fragmenta Graeca in litteris Arabicis I, *Journal of the Royal Asiatic Society* 1939, pp. 407–22 [below, pp. 48–59]. Sir David Ross, *The works of Aristotle* XII, 1952, pp. 23–6. S. van den Bergh, *Tahafut al-Tahafut* (London 1954) I p. 90; II p. 65.

[9] *Galen on Medical Experience* (London 1944) IX 5. *Vorsokrat.* 3^5 (Berlin 1938), p. 653.

by Al-Kindī can be proved, argument by argument, to reproduce a late Greek original whose author we cannot identify. It was imitated and used by many later Islamic writers [1]. Of greater importance is Al-Fārābī's small work *On Plato's philosophy* [2], although it does not reproduce the Greek original in full and omits the ideal doctrine and the immortality of the soul. It gives an account of all the Platonic dialogues, arranged in an order both systematically and chronologically different from every arrangement hitherto known: starting with the *Major Alcibiades* and finishing with the *Letters*. With the exception of the *Minos*, all the dialogues to be found in the Alexandrian tetralogical edition are mentioned and characterized. The systematic arrangement is, from a historical point of view, certainly, to say the least, naive. The author looks at Plato's thought with the eyes of an average late Greek professor of philosophy and assumes that Plato had planned a closed philosophical system in the same way as he himself would have done it. In a similar way, the Greek historians of mathematics restored the sequence of events according to the requirements of their own time and did not hesitate to assume that facts which had to be first established on logical grounds should also come first chronologically [3]. What is important in this survey of Plato's thought is that it is utterly independent of the late Neoplatonic view and refrains from interpreting the *Parmenides* as a compendium of Plato's Metaphysics and making the *Timaeus* Plato's most outstanding work. On the contrary, it gives Plato's so-called political thought its due position, by emphasizing the conception of the philosopher-king and even appreciating Plato's attempts to realize it here and now. Such interpretations of Plato must have been still alive, or at least available, when the Arabs came in contact with Greek philosophy, and will have inspired Al-Fārābī in his attempt to proclaim the ideal calif as the platonic philosopher-king [4]. He was helped in the impressive revival of Plato's conception of the philosopher-king which he established in Islamic lands by commentaries of the *Republic* [5] and the *Laws* [6] which are also free from Neoplatonic accretions.

[1] H. Ritter and R. Walzer, Studi su al-Kindī II, *Acc. dei Lincei*, Roma 1938, and the additions and corrections by M. Pohlenz (*GGAnz.* 200, 1938, p. 409 ff.).

[2] F. Rosenthal and R. Walzer, Alfarabius De Platonis philosophia, *Plato Arabus II* (London 1943).

[3] Cf. O. Neugebauer, *The Exact Sciences in Antiquity* (Princeton 1952), p. 142.

[4] Cf. also my contribution to the "Entretiens sur l'antiquité classique" of 1955, to be published by the Fondation Hardt, Vandœuvres (Genève) [below, pp. 236–252] and the article Aflāṭūn in the second edition of the *Encyclopedia of Islam* (Leiden 1955).

[5] Cf. E. Rosenthal's forthcoming edition of Averroes' Commentary on Plato's *Republic* (Cambridge University Press) [published in 1958].

[6] Cf. F. Gabrieli, Alfarabius Compendium Legum Platonis, *Plato Arabus* III (London 1952).

It is obvious that Greek evidence of the teaching of Ethics in the late Greek philosophical schools is rather scanty. Our information about this rather important subject is not at all satisfactory. We know something but not very much from Arius Didymus', the emperor Augustus' court-philosopher's account of Stoic and Peripatetic ethics, as reproduced in the 4th century compiler's Stobaeus work [1]. Plutarch, e.g., obviously presupposed a tradition of this kind but does not reproduce it in any detail when writing his entertaining essays on ethical topics. The Greek commentaries of the *Nicomachean Ethics* which we can read cannot be compared with the learned and well-informed commentaries on the logical, physical and metaphysical treatises which we possess. Strange as it may appear to us, it does not seem that the *Nicomachean Ethics* was a very popular work in late antiquity. Philosophical ethics, we learn from Arabic works, were generally based on the three parts of the soul, the rational, the spirited and the appetitive element. This platonic tripartition of the soul had again been made the basis of ethical thought by men like Posidonius and Galen, and had evidently been generally accepted in average works on ethics in later antiquity. This could be worked out as a system of four main excellences and a large number of subordinate ἀρεταί, as the Stoics had done it, but in a manner more akin to Plato's *Republic*. The Aristotelian definition of excellence as the mean between two extremes could be connected with this scheme, but we also find an Arabic treatise in which long lists of virtues and vices (or rather of bad and good ἤθη) are given without any detailed reference to the afore-mentioned parts of the soul in which they are somehow domiciled. Some sections of these systems certainly go back to the time before Plotinus, and so add to our knowledge of hellenistic ethics, but it requires peculiar discretion to make a clear cut distinction between the different strata [2]. One of the Arabic authors, Miskawaih [3], gives a lively and detailed analysis of human relations based on the φιλία books of the *Nicomachean Ethics*, with two significant additions, due probably to the philosophical climate or the Greek author on which Miskawaih drew. The platonic ἔρως, which Aristotle disowned, is re-established in its dignity, and a new type of relation, the friendship between the philosophical teacher and his pupil, is introduced. It is situated between the friendship of God and the philosopher who is able

---

[1] Ecl. 2, 7 (vol. 2, pp. 37–152 Wachsmuth).

[2] Cf. the article Akhlāq in the second edition of the *Encyclopedia of Islam*.

[3] An older contemporary of Ibn Sīnā (Avicenna); he died A.D. 1030. I refer to his ethical treatise *Tahdhīb-al-akhlāq*; an English translation of this text, by A. F. M. Craig, will be published in the near future. [Cf. below p. 220 ff.]

to know him and the friendship between parents and children. The teacher is the spiritual father of the disciple, who may consider him as a mortal god. I can find no exact parallel to these expressions in extant Greek texts, although it corresponds well to what we know of Proclus' school, e.g., who refers to his teacher Syrianus as his father, to Syrianus' teacher Plutarch as his grandfather, and who is called child (τέκνον) by his master. But the expression 'spiritual, πνευματικός', father or child, which becomes so common in the Middle Ages, in the language of Christian holy orders as in politics, and which can be applied to the Pope, seems not to be found in pagan Greek texts, and is due to a Christian, Greek, Syriac or Arabic alteration. The idea itself is ultimately pythagorean, and a beautiful passage from Seneca *De brev. vitae* 15 comes to mind. It is interesting that this concept of the spiritual relationship between teacher and disciple is then made part of the traditional reading of the Aristotelian ethics [1]. To give some other aspect of the quality of these texts, I quote a passage from an ethical treatise by an Arabic Christian Yaḥyā ibn 'Adī [2], in which the Greek colouring is equally unmistakable: Whoever strives to become perfect must also train himself to love every man, to give him his affection, his compassion, his tenderness and his mercy. For mankind is one race, united by the fact that they all are human beings and that the mark of the divine power is in all of them and in each of them, namely the intellectual soul. Man becomes man on the strength of this soul, which is the most noble part in man. Man *is* in reality the intellectual soul, and that intellectual soul is one and the same substance in all men, and all men are in reality one and the same thing, and many only in their individual existence [3]. This is stoic and neoplatonic language in one.

I have hitherto, emphasized the importance of the Arabs for gaining a fuller picture of Greek philosophy. But before I come to say a few words about Classical and Islamic studies in general, I have to consider, though very briefly, a subject which seems to me to be of some relevance in this context: I mean the importance of the Arabic translations for the history of the Greek texts of the works translated and for the text itself. Very little, comparatively, to emphasize this again, has been done for establishing a

---

[1] A more detailed appreciation of Miskawaih's moral thought and its importance for late Greek ethics is to be found in my article "Some Aspects of Miskawaih's Tahdhīb al-Akhlāq" to be published in *Scritti in onore di G. Levi della Vida* (Rome 1956) [below, pp. 220–235].

[2] Who lived in Baghdād in the tenth century, cf. the article Akhlāq in the second edition of the *Encyclopedia of Islam*.

[3] *Rasā'il al-bulaghā'*, 3rd edition, Cairo 1946, p. 518. [Cf. below, p. 222].

Greek-Arabic vocabulary based on the well known texts, say of Aristotle and Galen, and neoplatonic writings [1]. It would be of interest for the classical scholar, the medievalist and the general historian of philosophy and of the greatest importance for the student of Arabic philosophy. For the time being, no more can be expected than that no text translated from a Greek original still in existence should be published without a full glossary. This is by no means always done. As for the history of the texts it may first be kept in mind that a good translator like Ḥunain ibn Isḥāq established his own Greek text from several MSS first before he started translating [2]. The Arabic texts are certainly as revealing for the text of Greek philosophers or Galen, e.g., as the textual variants provided by the commentators [3]. Like the papyri, they help us to get a more common-sense view of the history of texts in general. Before the importance of the so-called *codices recentiores* was recognized, the study of the translation of the *Poetics*, e.g., was revealing. Similarly, most of the readings to be found in the apparatus of Bekker's edition of Aristotle's *Categories* and *De interpretatione* and rightly put into the text in the most recent Oxford edition [4] are independently attested as old readings by the Syriac and Arabic versions. The comparison of the readings of the Arabic versions in the case of unsatisfactorily edited works of Aristotle like the *Topics* and *Sophistici Elenchi*, e.g., may still sometimes be helpful, if only to get out of the quasi-hypnotizing power of the printed word and printed version. On the whole I make bold to say that the text presupposed by the Arabic versions of a Greek text deserves the same attention as an old MS or a variant recorded in a Greek commentator (this applies, I believe, to texts

---

[1] Cf. for Aristotle's *Categories* : Khalil Georr, *Les Catégories d'Aristote dans leurs versions syro-arabes* (Beyrouth 1948), pp. 205–50 ; the *De interpretatione* : J. Pollak, *Die Hermeneutik des Aristoteles in der arabischen Übersetzung* (Leipzig 1913), pp. 35–64 ; the *Metaphysics* : M. Bouyges, *Bibliotheca Arabica Scholasticorum, Série Arabe* 5, 1 (Beyrouth 1952), p. CXCV–CCVII and *Tome* 7 (Beyrouth 1948), pp. 39–305. For Galen's summary of Plato's *Timaeus* P. Kraus and R. Walzer, *Plato Arabus* I (London 1951), pp. 102–18 ; 41–68.

[2] Cf. G. Bergsträsser, *Ḥunain ibn Isḥāq, Über die syrischen und arabischen Galen-übersetzungen* (Leipzig 1925), p. 4 of the German translation. This is a text with which everybody interested in the history of classical scholarship should be acquainted.

[3] Cf. e.g. the readings presupposed in the Greek text used by the translators of Aristotle's *Metaphysics*, listed by M. Bouyges in *Bibliotheca Arabica Scholasticorum* (cf. above) p. CLXI–CLXXX. For the *Prior* and *Posterior Analytics* cf. New Light on the Arabic Translation of Aristotle, *Oriens* 6, 1953, pp. 115 ff. 134 ff. [below, pp. 77–141]. As for Galen, most of this kind of work remains to be done, and it appears to be promising, especially wherever the Greek text is bad. The Arabic version of Ps. Plutarch's *Placita Philosophorum* appears very worth studying.

[4] Ed. L. Minio-Paluello (Oxford 1949).

of Galen as well). This is by no means an established practice. Theophrastus' metaphysical fragment was re-edited, in Oxford, about 25 years ago, by two of the most distinguished workers in this field [1]. Both of them were unaware of the fact that the Arabic text exists in the Bodleian library and had been treated by the late Laudian professor of Arabic, in a paper published in 1892 [2].

It would, perhaps, be a good thing to stop here and to fill in the rest of this paper with the recital of some examples of Greek texts recovered from the Arabic. But I think it may be more to the point to abandon this aspect of Arabic-Greek relations in philosophy altogether and to turn our attention in a different direction.

Islamic philosophy is Greek philosophy, but it is not Greek philosophy studied for scholarly reasons nor for the satisfaction of scholarly curiosity. It is meant primarily to serve the needs of the new religion of Islam: it is an attempt at a Muslim natural theology, and the greatest representatives of this theistic Islamic philosophy went so far as to see the only valid interpretation of Islam in following the ways of the philosophers. This implies that we may also arrive at a modified view of Greek thought by looking at it from a territory which is very near to it, both in time and in space, and yet sufficiently different to make it appear in a new light and to see certain aspects of it, and also certain limitations, better than we are able to do by looking at the Greeks alone or by comparing their achievements with contemporary 20th century thought. Further: it has always been the classical scholar's concern to look not exclusively at the great outstanding works of the Greeks but also to consider their impact on other civilizations, not to speak of the modern world in which our ancestors have lived and in which we live ourselves. It is one of the outstanding features of the great works of the Greeks that they can live also when separated from their native soil, and be assimilated by different nations in different times and widen their outlook on life and their power to master it. This applies to poetry as well, as to philosophy with which we are concerned here. Classical scholars are used to comparing Greece and Rome and to understanding the limitations and the greatness of Greece better while considering the life of the Romans, so intimately connected with and at the same time so different from the Greeks. It has recently become less unusual to find scholars who are prepared to look with equal interest at the Jewish and Christian tradition and at the Greek way of life, and to understand the prophets as well as Plato. They are still

[1] Theophrastus' *Metaphysics*, edd. W. D. Ross and F. H. Fobes (Oxford 1929).

[2] D. S. Margoliouth, Remarks on the Arabic Version of the Metaphysics of Theophrastus *Journ. of the R. Asiatic Society*, 1892, pp. 192 ff.

too rare, if one has in mind the immense task of trying to understand, in historical terms, the double root of our way of life and to find our feet in the troubled times in which we live. Further: the times have passed, I believe, when classical scholars were inclined to look, say, at Cicero as a quarry for lost hellenistic philosophy alone and when they belittled with contempt the philosophical personality of the great Roman humanist, who did not happen to be a Plato but only a πλατωνίζων. We are aware of the difference between Horace and the Lesbian poets, between Vergil and Homer, but nobody in his senses will deny that Horace and Vergil are great poets in their own right. As for the Fathers of the Church, too much has still to be done to ascertain their debt to Greek and Roman pagan philosophers, and the danger of not appreciating their own achievement appears to be less real than the risk of overlooking what they owe to their non-Christian predecessors. Nobody, not even an inveterate classical man, has ever confessed to studying, say, Hippolytus only for the considerable number of fragments of Heraclitus in one of the sections of his work. Hence after having dwelt so long on the importance of the Arab philosophers for a better material understanding of Greek philosophy, I should now be at pains to emphasize that the Arabic thinkers have a just and deserved claim to be understood in their own right, like the Romans and the Greek and Roman Christians of Antiquity. Indeed they have. They may be a quarry for ancient thought, but not only he who loves the Islamic world should raise his voice in protest. The classicist would betray his best interest if he did not wish to see how Islamic philosophers used Greek thought of varying provenience and different quality in an honest and intense effort to come to a deeper understanding of the problems of their own days and their own and different world; in an effort to analyse the problems of religious truth and philosophical understanding; in an attempt to find a synthesis between a religion based on the reason of the heart and making God an immortal man, and the Greek religion of the mind which can ask man to become a mortal God but sees in God a dehumanized principle; in an attempt to give reasons for something which could only appear foolish to the Greeks and the Muslims eventual failure to accomplish it. All this demands not only our respect: because what is valid in human society, that "homo homini res sacra", applies also to our understanding of other ways of human life, and accordingly to civilizations near to our own like Islam and yet so different in many ways [1]. It throws

[1] Cf. e.g. *Averroes' Tahafut al-Tahafut, translated from the Arabic with Introduction and Notes*, by S. v. d. Bergh, 2 volls., London 1954.—The History of Philosophy, East and West, ch. 32 : *Islamic Philosophy* (London 1953) [above, pp. 1–28].

new light on the achievements of the Greeks also, not only on the intermediaries whom we have mainly considered in this paper but on the great philosophers who dominate the Greek scene as well, on Plato, Aristotle, and Plotinus.

From: *Festschrift Bruno Snell* (C. H. Beck, Munich), 1956, pp. 189-96.

14
ON THE TRANSMISSION OF BUKHĀRĪ'S COLLECTION OF TRADITIONS

Johann Fück

Halle

Next to the Koran there is no book which is as highly esteemed by orthodox Islam as Bukhārī's collection of traditions, known as *al-Ṣaḥīḥ*.[1] Studying it occupies a dominant position in the curriculum of the *madāris* and is surrounded by a halo similar to that surrounding the study of the Koran itself. Completing the perusal of the book is celebrated; in times of need, passages from it are read; and in particular in the Maghreb it is seen as a book that can perform miracles.[2] This deep reverence is explained initially by the fact that the *Ṣaḥīḥ* contains remarks made by the Prophet which are considered to be authentic and whose role for the way of living of the faithful is just as important as the word of God in the Koran. There are, however, more reasons why of the vast number of similar works, the consensus of the Islamic world should have recognised Bukhārī's collection in particular to be the best representation of the Sunna. Even among the six canonical collections (*al-kutub al-sitta*) it occupies a wholly unique position because of the critical selection of the content, its exceptional wealth of information and its clear structure. The strict and critical examination Bukhārī applies to every single transmitter is unequalled; **[61]** not even Muslim attains the same level. The idea that all the traditions in his collection must be proof against criticism consequently gained ground, always more firmly with the passage of time, even though educated circles never ceased to be aware that every scholar of

---

[1] On the subject of Bukhārī and his oeuvre see C. Brockelmann, (*Geschichte der arabischen Literatur*, 2 vols., and *Supplement*, 3 vols., Leiden, 1937–49) GAL 1, 157–60 and Supplement 1, 260–65.

[2] Examples can be found in Brockelmann, Suppl. 1, 261. Like the Koran, the *Ṣaḥīḥ* would be learned by heart, see e.g. Ibn Bashkuwāl, *Ṣila* (*al-Ṣila fī akhbār a'immat al-Andalus*. Aben-Pascualis Assila, *Dictionarium biographicum*, Nunc primum ed. F. Codera, Madrid, Bibliotheca Arabico-Hispana, 2, 1883) 63 penultimate, and Ibn Abbār, *Takmila* (*K. al-Takmila li-Kitāb al-Ṣila*, ed. F. Codera, Madrid, Bibliotheca Arabico-Hispana; 5–6, 1887) 271:6; 696:18; 751:8.

tradition has the right to scrutinise every single instance. The variety of topics discussed in the *Ṣaḥīḥ* is unsurpassed as well. Besides canonical law which, as is only fair, occupies the largest space, dogmatics is dealt with at length. Comprehensive chapters are devoted to the legends of the Prophet, the story of Muhammad and his companions, their campaigns and their 'virtues'; other parts go into individual aspects of popular beliefs such as the interpretation of dreams and eschatology, manners and morals, or devotional exercises. Finally this collection contains an extensive commentary on the Koran. This wealth of material is arranged clearly within a frame whose headings, together with explanatory notes, additional remarks and verses from the Koran, are meant to facilitate the reader's understanding of the traditions presented. If the same tradition is instructive in more than one context, it is (in contrast to Muslim's collection) repeated in all the relevant places, if only in excerpts in some cases. All along the reader sense the solicitous hand of the theologian intent on presenting immaculate traditions, which have stood up to the most critical scrutiny, in the most efficient way for future use.

Of course, the history of the text shows that it was only over the course of the centuries that the *Ṣaḥīḥ* attained the heights of uncontested authority. The book did not immediately find general recognition but had to prove its usefulness in a contest with other collections, such as the more practically oriented works of Abū Dāwūd and Tirmidhī. In disbelief, later generations would tell with pious hyperbole [**62**] of the 90,000 disciples sitting at the feet of the master and copying his words,[3] but the chains of transmitters which precede in particular the great commentaries of Ibn Ḥajar,[4] ʿAynī[5] and Qasṭallānī[6] prove that only very few of Bukhārī's disciples endeavoured to pass his work on. The most important by far among these first-generation traditionists is:

1. al-Firabrī Abū ʿAbd Allāh Muḥammad b. Yūsuf b. Maṭar b. Ṣāliḥ b. Bishr, 231–320 H. In his youth he heard the *Ṣaḥīḥ* twice from Bukhārī himself; the first time in 248 in his home town of Fīrabr, a small place on the Amu-Darya opposite Amul,[7] and the second time in 252 in Bukhārā, four

---

[3] *Taʾrīkh Baghdād* (al-Khaṭīb al-Baghdādī, *Taʾrīkh Baghdād*, 14 vols., Cairo, 1931) 2, 9, $_{15}$, et passim.

[4] *Fatḥ al-bārī*, Bulaq 1300–1/1882–3, 3 vols.

[5] *ʿUmdat al-Qārī*, Istanbul 1308–11/1890–3, 11 vols.

[6] *Irshād al-sārī*, Bulaq 1304/1886, 10 vols.

[7] See Yāqūt, *Geogr. Wörterb.* (*Jacut's Geographisches Wörterbuch*, ed. F. Wüstenfeld, Leipzig, 1866–73) 1, 69; 3, 867.

years before the author's death.[8] According to Dāraquṭnī, however, he was staying with Bukhārī from 253 to 255 H.[9]

Another pupil of Bukhārī's was

2. al-Nasawī Ḥammād b. Shākir who died possibly around 390 H, if Ibn Ḥajar's assumption is justified.[10] For some reason he did not personally attend all of Bukhārī's lectures; consequently his text was not founded on 'hearing' (*samāʿ*) from beginning to end and was thus much less esteemed than that of al-Firabrī, who had never missed a single lecture. His recension may not have vanished quite without trace - thus the famous Muḥammad b. ʿAbd Allāh al-Ḥākim (321–405 H, GAL 1, 166) heard it from Nasawī's pupil Aḥmad b. Muḥammad Ibn Rumayḥ (d. 357 H)[11] - but it did not play an important part later; Ibn Ḥajar (*Fatḥ al-bārī* 1, 3, $_2$, 5, $_4$) could access it only indirectly.

[**63**] The same is true of the third traditionist of the first generation:

3. al-Nasafī Ibrāhīm b. Maʿqīl (210–295 H).[12] He had not heard the whole text; for the last part of the collection beginning with the *Kitāb al-Aḥkām* Bukhārī had granted him a teaching license (*ijāza*). Furthermore, there was a piece missing from his text, as compared with al-Firabrī's, which Ibn Khayr estimated to be about nine pages long.[13] His recension was well known in Spain; it was from Jayyānī's (d. 498 H; GAL 1, 368) *Kitāb Taqyīd al-muhmal* that Ibn Hajar obtained his knowledge of this tradition.

Muslim scholars always endeavour to establish a chain of transmitters between themselves and the author of the text they are studying, and the

---

[8] Ibn Ḥajar, *Fatḥ al-bārī* 1, 2; Ibn Khayr, *Fihrista* (ed. F. Codera and J. Ribera Tarrago, Madrid, Bibliotheca Arabico-Hispana, 9–10, 1894–95) 95.

[9] Samʿānī, *Ansāb* (The Kitab al-ansab, reproduced in facsimile from the MS. in the British Museum, Add. 23355, ed. Ellis, A.G., and Margoliouth, D.S., Leiden, E.J.W. Gibb Memorial Series, 20, 1912) fol. 422a.

[10] *Fatḥ al-bārī* 1, 3, $_2$.

[11] Dhahabī, *Tadhkirat al-ḥuffāẓ*, Hyderabad 1333/34 H, 3, 134.

[12] Samʿānī, *Ansāb*, fol. 559b; Dhahabī, *Tadhkirat al-ḥuffāẓ* 2, 231; Yāqūt, *Geogr. Wörterb.* 3, 23; 4, 782.

[13] *Fihrista* 97f.

fewer links this chain has, the better and 'higher' the *isnād*. Consequently it was important to find out who was Bukhārī's last disciple, who was named as[14]

4. al-Bazdawī Abū Ṭalḥa Manṣūr b. Muḥammad b. ʿAlī b. Qarīna (d. 329) from Bazda[15] near Nasaf, whose recension is used by a traditionist of the third generation, al-Mustaghfirī. However, as the latter also uses a version traced back to al-Firabrī, it is no longer possible to determine al-Bazdawī's contribution. No independent traces of his text appear to have survived.

These are the four names with whom the oldest tradition of the *Ṣaḥīḥ* is closely linked. We may safely conclude that the text did not enjoy universal recognition during its author's life and throughout the third century. (In comparison there is the biography of the Prophet by Muḥammad b. Isḥāq (d. 151 H), who lived a hundred years before Bukhārī and for whose work there are at least sixteen [**64**] scholars known to have transmitted it directly from the author.) One of the reasons for this remarkable phenomenon was the fact that in the third century the collecting and studying of traditions was still an individual task and that no scholar of any importance would have been inclined to accept unseen any collection beside his own. Then, the more this independence dwindled, the greater grew the importance of collections such as Bukhārī's. Consequently the second generation of traditionists, namely those men who studied the collection under the master's immediate disciples, is already noticeably stronger. Al-Firabrī in particular recited the *Ṣaḥīḥ* to an apparently quite considerable number of students; we know of no fewer than ten men who travelled to Firabr during the last years of his life in order to hear the *Ṣaḥīḥ* from him. These traditionists of the second generation are:

5. al-Mustamlī Abū Isḥāq Ibrāhīm b. Aḥmad from Balkh[16] (d. 376 H). He studied in Firabr in 314 H.[17] His text is the basis for the versions of Abū Dharr and Hamadhānī.
6. al-Ḥammawī al-Sarakhsī Abū Muḥammad ʿAbd Allāh b. Aḥmad Ibn Ḥammawayh from Būshang in the far West of Afghanistan, 293–381 H.[18]

---

[14] Ibn Ḥajar, *Fatḥ al-bārī* 1, 3, $_2$.

[15] See W. Barthold, *Turkestan* (*Turkestan down to the mongol invasion*. Transl. from the original russian and rev. by the author with the assistance of H.A.R. Gibb, London, E.J.W. Gibb memorial series, N.S.,5, 1928) (GMS N.S.V) 236f.

[16] Samʿānī, *Ansāb*, fol. 529a.

[17] Ibn Khayr, *Fihrista* 94 ult.

[18] Samʿānī, *Ansāb*, fol. 177a; Dhahabī, *Mushtabih* (*al-Mushtabih fī asmāʾ al-rijāl*, e codd. mss. editus P. de Jong, Leiden, 1863) 174; concerning Būshang see EI s. v.

He studied in Firabr in 315 H.[19] His text is the basis for the version of Abū al-Waqt (*ʿan Dāwūdī ʿanhu*) and was also used by Abū Dharr.

7. al-Kushmēhanī Abū al-Haytham Muḥammad b. Makkī b. Muḥammad b. Zurāʿ (d. 389 H)[20] He studied in Firabr in [**65**] 316 H[21] or, according to one account which is, however, unlikely, not until 320 H, half a year before Firabrī's death.[22] His text is transmitted by Ḥafṣī and Karīma and is also extant in Abū Dharr's version.
8. al-Marwazī Abū Zayd Muḥammad b. Aḥmad b. ʿAbd Allāh.[23] He studied in Firabr in 318 H[24] and taught in Mecca and Baghdad. His version, described by the Khaṭīb as the most revered, is extant (though only for the books *Zakāt, Ṣawm* and *Ḥajj*) in a manuscript owned by A. Mingana who made it the subject of a most detailed study.[25] It was transmitted by by Abū Nuʿaym, Aṣīlī and Qābisī.
9. al-Kushānī al-Ḥājibī Abū ʿAlī Ismāʿīl b. Muḥammad, who died only 391 H, is supposed to have been the last one to hear the *Ṣaḥīḥ* from Firabrī.[26] His father had taken him to hear Firabrī's lectures in 316, although the boy was hardly able at the time to follow the recitation of the difficult text. Consequently one of his pupils, Abū Naṣr al-Dāwūdī, who had read it first with him and later with Istīkhānī, states that Kushānī was 'feeble when he heard it and feeble when he taught'.[27] Nevertheless, his version stood its ground. Thus the Spaniard ʿAṭiyya b. Saʿīd (d. 403 or 408/9 H in Mecca[28]) who had visited Kushānī in Transoxania[29] supported it. In our present-day [**66**] text of Bukhārī it is represented by al-Mustaghfirī's version.

---

[19] Ibn Khayr, *Fihrista* 95, $_{1}$.

[20] Samʿānī, *Ansāb*, fol. 484a; concerning the nisba see Qasṭallānī 1, 49; the 'e' is sometimes transcribed as *ā*, sometimes as *ay* and even as *ī*. According to Yāqūt, *Geogr. Wörterb.* 4, 623, Kushmēhan was situated on the way from Marv to Āmul.

[21] Qurashī, *Al-Gawāhir al-muḍīʿa* (Hyderabad 1332 H) 2, 77, $_{2}$.

[22] Ibn Khayr, *Fihrista* 95, $_{6}$.

[23] *Taʾrīkh Baghdād* 1, 314; Ibn ʿAsākir, *Tabyīn Kadhib al-muftarī* (ed. Al-Qudsī, Damascus 1347/1928) 188f.

[24] Ibn Khayr, *Fihrista* 96, $_{12}$.

[25] A. Mingana, *An Important Manucript of the Traditions of Bukhāri*. With nine Facsimile Reproductions, Cambridge 1936. See also my article "Eine wichtige Handschrift der Traditionssammlung Bukhārīs", *OLZ*, XLI (1938), 401–7.

[26] Ibn Ḥajar op. cit. 1, 3; Samʿānī, *Ansāb*, forl. 149a and 483b. Concerning Kushānīya, Northwest of Samarqand, see Barthold, *Turkestan* 95.

[27] Samʿānī, *Ansāb*, fol. 38a. Samʿānī tried in vain to interpret the sharp criticism as harmless.

[28] *Taʾrīkh Baghdād* 12, 322.

[29] Dhahabī, *Tadhkirat al-ḥuffāẓ* 3, 271; Ibn Bashkuwāl, *Ṣila* 2, 401.

It is not certain during which years the following pupils of Firabrī were in Firabr.

10. Ibn al-Sakan Abū ʿAlī Saʿīd b. ʿUthmān b. Saʿīd from Baghdad (294–353 H),[30] known for his work on the Prophet's Companions. His study trips took him to Firabr where he heard the *Ṣaḥīḥ*. Later he settled in Miṣr where the Spaniard Ibn Asad al-Juhanī heard the text from him, and then introduced it into his home country.[31]
11. al-Shabbawī Abū ʿAlī Muḥammad b. ʿUmar b. Shabbawayh from Marv,[32] from whom al-Hamadhānī and al-ʿAyyār received Bukhārī's text.
12. al-Jurjānī Abū Aḥmad Muḥammad b. Muḥammad b. Makkī b. Yūsuf (d. 373 H) is not unchallenged as a transmitter.[33] He recited the *Ṣaḥīḥ* in Iṣfahān, Shīrāz, Baṣra and Baghdād. Abū Nuʿaym and Aṣīlī studied the text under him.
13. al-Akhsīkathī[34] Abū Naṣr Aḥmad b. Muḥammad b. Aḥmad. His version was continued by his pupil al-Ṣaffār.
14. The Shafiʿite al-Istīkhanī Abū Bakr Muḥammad b. Aḥmad b. Matt (d. 381 H) studied the *Ṣaḥīḥ* under Firabrī at a more mature age.[35] The later commentators do not know him, and his version does not seem to have left any traces in our text of Bukhārī.

With the exception of Ibn al-Sakan from Baghdad, the traditionists of the second generation all came from the Eastern provinces of Islam. With their teaching activities, which took place approximately in the years 320–380 H (the youngest among them, [**67**] Kushānī, died 391 H) [Plate I, The commentaries of Bukhārī's text] they made the *Ṣaḥīḥ* generally known. The picture presented by their pupils, the traditionists of the third generation, however, is remarkably different from that seen in the second generation. While the latter saw Firabrī as the highest authority for Bukhārī's text and flocked to him in order to receive the authentic text without showing any interest in the traditions of other disciples of Bukhārī's, the former did not give preference to one of Firabrī's pupils over the others. On the contrary, the twelve traditionists in this generation who gained influence on our Bukhārī

[30] Dhahabī, *Tadhkirat al-ḥuffāẓ* 3, 140.
[31] Ibn Khayr, *Fihrista* 95.
[32] Samʿānī, *Ansāb*, fol. 329a.
[33] Ibn Ḥajar, *Lisān al-Mīzān* (Hyderabad, 1911–13, 6 vols.) 5, 363.
[34] Concerning Akhsīkath, the capital of Ferghana, see Barthold, *Turkestan* 161.
[35] Samʿānī, fol. 38a; Istīkhān was situated Northwest of Samarqand, see Barthold, *Turkestan*.

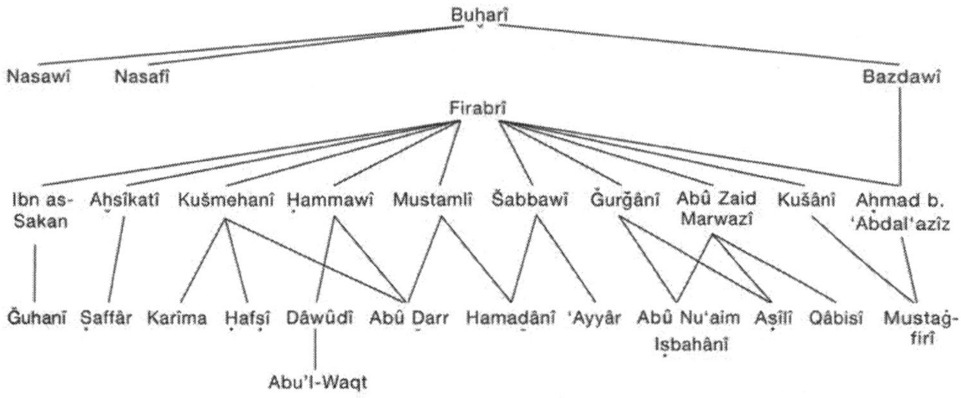

Table I *Die Rezensionen des Buhârî - Textes*

text are distributed fairly evenly among those of Firabrī's pupils mentioned above. It is even more remarkable that of this dozen only half were content with the text in the form in which they received it from their respective teachers, while the other half studied the *Ṣaḥīḥ* under a second of Firabrī's pupils (only Mustaghfirī used a text going back to Bukhārī through Bazdawī instead). Indeed, one of them, Abū Dharr, based his text on the tradition by three of Firabrī's pupils. This shows that they considered those variants worth writing down which had already insinuated themselves into the text in the second generation. This is the first burgeoning of critical feelings in the textual history of the *Ṣaḥīḥ*; the texts created by these men can be seen as the first proper versions. Thus it is justified when Ibn Ḥajar, in the chains of traditions preceding his commentary on Bukhārī, treats the *riwāyāt* of the traditionists of the third generation as those witnesses who form the basis of Bukhārī tradition as such.

In the following overview of these traditionists of the third generation I shall first discuss those who transmitted the text of one single of Firabrī's pupils.

15. Ibn Asad al-Juhanī ʿAbd Allāh b. Muḥammad learnt the text of the *Ṣaḥīḥ* in Cairo in 343 H from al-Sakān (no. 10) and introduced it into Spain. He passed it on to his pupils, e. g. Ibn ʿAbd al-Barr Abū ʿUmar Yūsuf b. ʿAbd Allāh (368–463 H; GAL 1, 367), [**68**] in those days the greatest authority on tradition in the West; also Ibn al-Ḥadhdhāʾ Abū ʿUmar Aḥmad b.

Muḥammad b. Yaḥyā (370–467 H)[36] who studied under Juhanī in 394 H;[37] and also Ibn al-Mukawwī Abū Muḥammad ʿAbd Allāh b. Aḥmad (d. 448 H).[38] Among Ibn al-Ḥadhdhā's pupils, Ibn Mughīth Abū al-Ḥasan Yūnus b. Muḥammad (447–531 H) in particular appears to have supported the *riwāyat Ibn al-Sakan*: it was through him that Ibn Khayr (*Fihrista* 95) and other Spaniards learnt about it.[39] Ibn Ḥajar (*Fatḥ al-bārī* 1, 3, $_{8.\ 22}$), however, appears to have known it from Jayyānī's *Taqyīd al-muhmal*.

16. al-Ṣaffār Ismāʿīl b. Isḥāq b. Ismāʿīl heard the collection from Akhsīkatī; his pupil was Abū Sulaymān Dāwūd b. Muḥammad b. Ḥasan al-Khālidī. I have no further information on both these men. This recension, together with that of Hamadhānī, was later used by the well-known Spanish theologian Abū Ḥayyān (654–745 H; GAL 2, 109).

17. al-Ḥafṣī Abū Sahl Muḥammad b. Aḥmad (d. 466 H) was a pupil of al-Kushmēhanī. The Seljuk vizier Niẓām al-Mulk called him to the newly founded academy al-Niẓāmiyya in Nīshābūr, where he developed extensive activity as professor of tradition. Through him, Kushmēhanī's text became prevalent in the East. Among his pupils were e.g. al-Shādiyākhī Abū al-Futūḥ ʿAbd al-Wahhāb b. Shāh,[40] also al-Shaḥḥāmī Wajīh b. Ṭāhir (d. 541 H)[41] and, above all, Furāwī (441–530 H), whom we will have to mention later. Samʿānī (506–562 H), who read the *Ṣaḥīḥ* under these three teachers, says about Ḥafṣī that while he studied under Kushmēhanī according to the rules, he nevertheless lacked all deeper understanding.[42]

[**69**] 18. There was also a lady who studied the *Ṣaḥīḥ* under Kushmēhanī, the famous Karīma bint Aḥmad al-Marwaziyya (d. 463 H). She later moved to Mecca and there recited the text to a wide circle of students from all parts of the Islamic world. Among her students were e. g. Khaṭīb Baghdādī (392–463 H; GAL 1, 329),[43] at the time the greatest scholar of tradition in

[36] Ibn Bashkuwāl, *Ṣila* 1, 65. Ibn al-Ḥadhdhāʾ also plays a role as transmitter of the *Ṣaḥīḥ Muslim*; see *Centenario M. Amari* (*Centenario della nascita di Michele Amari*, ed. Enrico Besta, et al., Palermo, 1910, 2 vols.), 1, 395.

[37] Ibn Khayr, *Fihrista* 95, $_{18}$.

[38] Ibn Bashkuwāl, *Ṣila* 1, 272 n.

[39] Ibn Abbār, *Takmila* 465, 476.

[40] Samʿānī, *Ansāb*, fol. 324b.

[41] Yāqūt, *Geogr. Wörterb.* 4, 111.

[42] Samʿānī, *Ansāb*, fol. 172a.

[43] Yāqūt, *Irshād al-Arīb* (or *Dictionary of learned men*, ed. D.S. Margoliouth, Leiden and London, E.J.W. Gibb Memorial Series, 1907–27, 7 vols.), 1, 247.

the East; also Muḥammad b. Barakāt from Upper Egypt (c. 420–520 H)[44] and Ibn al-Farrā' from Mosul.[45] In Mecca itself her tradition was perpetuated by Abū al-Fatḥ Sulṭān b. Ibrāhīm.[46]

Two further pupils of Kushmēhanī's should be mentioned here as well, although their recension have had no influence on our text of Bukhārī:

19. The Ashʿarite al-Khabbāzī Muḥammad b. ʿAlī b. Muḥammad (372–447 H)[47] lived at the court of Maḥmūd of Ghazna. Later he returned to Nīshābūr and died there during the persecution of the Ashʿarites staged by Kundurī, the first Seljuk vizier. Ibn ʿAsākir said about the text of his recension that it was the most reliable of its time (*Tabyīn kadhib al-muftarī* 264).
20. Abū al-Khayr Muḥammad b. Mūsā studied under Kushmēhanī in 388 H and was consequently one of his last students. His recension was used by the great Hanafite Burhān al-Dīn al-Marghinānī,[48] the author of the *Hidāya* (d. 593 H; GAL 1, 376).
21. al-Dāwūdī Abū al-Ḥasan ʿAbd al-Raḥmān b. Muḥammad b. Muẓaffar from Būshang (374–467 H)[49] must have been of tender years when he was taken to hear the *Ṣaḥīḥ* from Ḥammawī, as the latter died in 381 H. His text was widely [**70**] disseminated in the commentary of his pupil Abū al-Waqt.
22. al-ʿAyyār Saʿīd Aḥmad b. Muḥammad (d. 457 H) was a pupil of Shabbawī. He was not unchallenged as a transmitter,[50] but gained importance for the textual history through his pupil Furāwī's commentary.

As opposed to the preceding transmitters who perpetuated the recension of one of Firabrī's pupils, the following traditionists heard the text from two (and in one case even three) authorities.

---

[44] Yāqūt, *Irshād al-Arīb* 3, 422; Suyūṭī, *Bughyat al-wuʿāh* (Cairo, 1326/1908) 24.

[45] ʿAynī, *ʿUmdat al-qārī* 1, 7, $_{15}$.

[46] Maqqarī, *Analectes* (*Analectes sur l'histoire et la littérature des Arabes d'Espagne*, par al-Makkari, publié par R. Dozy, et al., Leyde, 1855–61, 2 vols.) 1, 876.

[47] Jazarī, *Ghāyat al-Nihāya* (Ibn al-Jazarī, *Ghāyat al-Nihāya*, *Das Biographische Lexikon der Koranlehrer*, ed. G. Bergträsser, L.eipzig, 1933–5, 2 vols.), 2, 207.

[48] Qurāshī, *al-Jawāhir al-muḍīʿa* 2, 76.

[49] Samʿānī, *Ansāb*, fol. 220a; Kutubī, *Fawāt al-Wafayāt* 1, 262 Bulaq 1299/1881, 2 vols.

[50] See Dhahabī, *Mīzān al-iʿtidāl* (Cairo, 1327/1905, 3vols.) 1, 382 and Ibn Ḥajar, *Lisān al-Mīzān* 3, 30.

23. al-Aṣīlī Abū Muḥammad ʿAbd Allāh b. Ibrāhīm (314–392 H),[51] embarked upon a journey to the Orient in 361 H and heard the *Ṣaḥīḥ* in Mecca from Abū Zayd al-Marwazī in 352 H, and in 359 he heard it in Baghdad a second time from the same teacher. He furthermore heard it from Abū Aḥmad al-Jurjānī, apparently in Baghdad as well.[52] Soon afterwards he was called home by al-Hakam II and landed in Almeria on the day the Caliph died (3 Safar 366H). Soon he found favour with the omnipotent vizier Ibn Abī ʿĀmir who appointed him counsellor and later judge of Zaragoza. His recension enjoyed a wide diffusion in Spain. Three scholars who studied the *Ṣaḥīḥ* under Aṣīlī are known to us from Ibn Bashkuwāl's work (*Ṣila* p. 184, 225, 560); a fourth, Muḥammad b. ʿAbd Allāh b. Saʿīd b. ʿĀbid (d. 439 H),[53] is mentioned by Ibn Khayr who heard this recension through three different channels. A fifth scholar, Ibn al-Qabrī Abū Shākir ʿAbd al-Wāḥid b. Muḥammad b. Mawhib (d. 456 H) passed it on to Jayyānī. We also find it in the writings of [71] the Qāḍī ʿIyād and Yūnīnī used it in his critical edition. It is uncertain whether it is, as Mingana assumes, the recension found in the abovementioned manuscript: the latter belongs to Marwazi's recension, but the question of which one among his pupils was responsible for this text has to remain unanswered.
24. Al-Qābisī Abū al-Ḥasan ʿAlī b. Muḥammad (324–403 H)[54] studied at the same time as Aṣīlī, in the year 353 H under Abū Zayd al-Marwazī in Mecca. It is for this reason that he is included here, although he belongs to the group of scholars who taught the text from only one *riwāya*. As he was blind, he had Aṣīlī correct his own personal copy.[55] This explains the similarities between the two recensions which Ibn Ḥajar (*Fatḥ al-bārī* 1, 4, $_7$), in fact, treats as twins. This does not, however, mean that the blind man submitted to the authority of his helpful fellow pupil; he did indeed preserve his independent judgment and in controversial passages sometimes decided in favour of the reading opposed to that favoured

[51] Ibn Faraḍī, *Taʾrīkh ʿulamāʾ al-Andalus* (ed. F. Codera, Madrid, Bibliotheca Arabico-Hispana, 7–8, 1891–2) 208; Ḍabbī *Bughyat al-multamis* (ed. F. Codera and J. Ribera, Madrid, Bibliotheca Arabico-Hispana, 3, 1885) 327; Yāqūt, *Geogr. Wörterb.* 1, 302; Dhahabī, *Tadhkirat al-ḥuffāẓ* 3, 214; Ibn Farḥūn, *al-Dībāj al-mudhahhab* (Cairo 1347 H) 138.

[52] Ibn Farḥūn op. cit. and Ibn Khayr, *Fihrista* 95 f.

[53] Ḍabbī op. cit. 82.

[54] Ibn Khallikān (*Ibn Challikani Vitae illustrium virorum*, e pluribus codicibus manuscriptis inter se collatis, nunc primum Arabice ed., variis lectionibus, indicibusque locupletissimis instruxit Ferdinandus Wüstenfeld, 2 vols., Göttigen, 1835–50), no. 457; Dhahabī, *Tadhkirat al-ḥuffāẓ* 3, 263; GAL Suppl. 1, 277; Mingana op.cit.

[55] Dhahabī, *Tadhkirat al-ḥuffāẓ* 3, 264; Ibn Farḥūn, *al-Dībāj al-mudhahhab* 200.

by Aṣīlī.[56] Qābisī returned to North Africa in 359 H[57] and settled in Qayrawān where he died in 403 H. The Cordovan Ḥātim b. Muḥammad al-Ṭarābulusī (378–469 H),[58] whose family came from Syrian Tripoli, heard al-Qābisī in the last year of his life. This recension was disseminated in Spain through him; thus e.g. Jayyānī and Ibn ʿAttāb (433–520 H)[59] heard it from him; [**72**] dependent on these are in turn Ibn Khayr, Ibn Bashkuwāl and others. Ibn Khayr (*Fihrista* 98) says that this recension was very similar to Abū Dharr's.

25. Abū Nuʿaym al-Iṣfahānī Aḥmad b. ʿAbd al-Wāḥid b. Aḥmad (336–430 H, GAL 1, 362) studied Bukhārī's *Ṣaḥīḥ* under the same teachers as Aṣīlī: he started with Jurjānī in Isfahan and finished it with him in Baghdad (*Taʾrīkh Baghdād* 3, 222f.). In addition he heard it from Abū Zayd al-Marwazī. Together with e.g. Mustaghfirī's this recension was used by Abū Mūsā al-Madīnī (501–581 H),[60] Isfahan's foremost teacher of tradition in the fourth century.
26. Al-Hamadhānī[61] ʿAbd al-Raḥmān b. ʿAbd Allāh read the *Ṣaḥīḥ* under Shabbawī and Mustamlī. His pupil was Shurayḥ b. ʿAlī. I have no further information on either of these two traditionists. This recension is found in the works of the abovementioned Abū Ḥayyān al-Gharnāṭī.
27. The most important traditionist of the third generation is Abū Dharr al-Harawī ʿAbd b. Aḥmad (355–434 H). He studied Bukhārī's *Ṣaḥīḥ* under three of Firabrī's pupils: first in 373 H in his home town Herāt in Afghanistan with Sarakhsī, the next year with Mustamlī in Balkh, and finally in 387 H in Kushmēhan with Kushmēhanī.[62] After long travels, during which he also came to Baghdad, he betook himself to Mecca, married into a Bedouin family soon afterwards and settled in Sarawān.[63] Every year he went on the pilgrimage and taught in Mecca during the festive months.[64] He followed the *madhhab Mālik* in matters of Fiqh; in

---

[56] I discussed one example (Bu., *Ḥajj*, § 41; see Yāqūt, *Geogr. Wörterb.* 4, 243) in the OLZ.

[57] If Ibn Ḥajar, *Fatḥ al-bārī* 1, 3, $_{19}$ and, following him, Qasṭallānī, *Irshād al-sārī* 1, 40, $_{3}$ name Qābisī rather than Aṣīlī as the transmitter of the riwāyat al-Jurjānī, this is due to confusion of the two, as shown by e. g. Ibn Khayr, *Fihrista* 95f.

[58] Ibn Bashkuwāl, *Ṣila* 158–60.

[59] Ibn Bashkuwāl, *Ṣila* 342; Ḍabbī 344.

[60] Dhahabī, *Tadhkirat al-ḥuffāẓ* 4, 123.

[61] The editions (*Fatḥ al-bārī* 1, 3, $_{23}$; *Irshād al-sārī* 1, 39 antepenultimate etc.) always print *al-Hamdānī*.

[62] Ibn Khayr, *Fihrista* 94.

[63] Yāqūt, *Geogr. Wörterb.* 3, 85.

[64] *Taʾrīkh Baghdād* 11, 141.

Kalām he followed the Ashʿarites, in particular al-Bāqillānī.[65] There is a wealth of information in the writings of Ibn **[73]** Ḥajar and other Bukhārī commentators which gives us a considerably clearer idea of his way of structuring the text than we have for other versions. Abū Dharr was not satisfied to compose a text on the basis of the three witnesses he used, but in more important cases he also provided the variants if his witnesses differed. He furthermore improved the clarity of the text by counting sections (e. g. in the *Kitāb al-Tafsīr* and the *Kitāb al-Tawḥīd*) as individual chapters even where Bukhārī had just strung them together loosely. To aid elucidation further he added explanations in some cases; these were, of course, separated clearly from the actual text, but are nevertheless occasionally quoted by later commentators. His work is, therefore, the oldest attempt at producing a critical edition of the text which is still comprehensible today. This, together with the fact that at least since 415 H[66] Abū Dharr recited the text to a large audience every year, was the reason why his recension was much more widely disseminated than any other. It was by far the preferred version in Spain, about whose scholarly history we are much better informed than that of any other country of Islam, thanks to the masses of information stored in the *Bibliotheca Arabo-Hispana*. Many Spaniards travelling to Mecca used the opportunity to visit Abū Dharr's lectures. Some stayed with him for several years, e.g. Ibn al-Dalāʾī Abū al-ʿAbbās al-ʿUdhrī Aḥmad b. Anas (393–478 H).[67] Another of these was Abū al-Walīd al-Bājī Sulaymān b. Khalaf (403–474 H; GAL 1, 419), later known as an opponent of Ibn Ḥazm, whose Bukhārī lectures in **[74]** Zaragoza gained great fame.[68] Maqqarī says about Bājī's text[69] that it was the most frequently found in Spanish Bukhārī manuscripts, together with that of his pupil Ibn Sukkara. A third Spaniard, Ibn Manẓūr Abū ʿAbd Allāh Muḥammad b. Aḥmad (d. 464 H),[70] heard the *Ṣaḥīḥ* twice from Abū Dharr in 431 – the second time the

---

[65] Dhahabī, *Tadhkira* 3, 285.

[66] That year Ibn al-Saqqāṭ Muḥammad b. Khalaf b. Masʿūd (395–485 H); cf. Ibn Bashkuwāl, *Ṣila* 510 (=Yāqūt, *Geogr. Wörterb.* 3, 924) and 103 (=Yāqūt, op. cit. 4, 204).

[67] Ibn Bashkuwāl, *Ṣila* 69; Yāqūt, *Geogr. Wörterb.* 2, 582; 4, 517. He also distinguished himself as transmitter of the *Ṣaḥīḥ Muslim*, see *Centenario M. Amari* 1, 392. See also Ibn Abbār, *Takmila* 466, 4; 719; 11.

[68] We know about such lectures in the years 463 H (Ibn Abbār, *Takmila* 535, 3; 551, 9; 623, 6), 468 H (ibid. 48, 4 from the bottom), 470 H (ibid. 624, 2). See also Ibn Abbār, *Takmila* 466, 4; 629, 14.

[69] *Analectes* 1, 507 Dozy.

[70] Ibn Bashkuwāl, *Ṣila* 489 no. 1080; Ḍabbī, *Bughyat al-multamis* 41 no. 28 (giving 469 H as the year of his death).

latter had his own manuscript in front of him and the pupil was able to check his own Bukhārī copy against it[71] – and disseminated this text in Spain.[72] A fourth Spaniard, finally, who became important for the textual history of the *Ṣaḥīḥ* was Muḥammad b. Shurayḥ (392–476 H), who studied in Mecca in 433.[73] His son Shurayḥ b. Muḥammad (451–537 H)[74] received the text from him as well as from the abovementioned Ibn Manẓūr, and every year during Ramaḍān he had one specially nominated pupil recite it before his students. Because of his 'high' isnad these lectures attracted students from all over the Iberian Peninsula until in the year 535 H, two years before his death, he had as many as two hundred students.[75] The lecture of 534 H became particularly famous, as the bearers of most illustrious names found themselves among his audience in that year.[76] Ibn Khayr, too, studied the *Ṣaḥīḥ* **[75]** under him.[77] Finally it must be mentioned that just before 500 H, one Spaniard paid a tidy sum to acquire from Abū Maktūm, Abū Dharr's son, the copy of Bukhārī's *Ṣaḥīḥ* Abū Dharr was said to have written at the time he was studying under Mustamlī.[78]

In Mecca, Abū Dharr's tradition was perpetuated by his son, the Abū Maktūm ʿĪsā mentioned in the previous paragraph. His last student was the Meccan Abū al-Ḥasan ʿAlī b. Ḥumayd al-Ṭarābulusī.[79] Through both these men Ibn Ḥajar received the text from an uninterrupted chain of Meccan scholars. On the whole Ibn Ḥajar follows Abū Dharr's recension,[80] which enjoyed great popularity generally. Sometimes it was used as the standard version to revise manuscripts of Bukhārī's text[81] and Yūnīnī used it for his critical edition.

---

[71] Ibn Khayr, *Fihrista* 94.

[72] See e. g. Ibn Abbār, *Takmila* 559, 16= 645, 3; Ibn Bashkuwāl, *Ṣila* 287 antpenultimate; 509, 6; Yāqūt, *Geogr. Wörterb.* 3, 312 (1. *Ibn ʿAbd Allāh*).

[73] Ibn Khayr, *Fihrista* 94, has *403*; however, according to Ibn Bashkuwāl 495 no. 1095 and Jazarī, *Ghāyat al-Nihāya* 2, 153 this must be changed to *433*.

[74] Jazarī, *Ghāyat al-Nihāya* 1, 324.

[75] Ibn Abbār, *Takmila* 496, 8 (see also 421, 6).

[76] See the description given by Ibn Abbār, *Takmila* 495f. and cf. ibid. pp. 244, 11; 267, 6; 488 antepenultimate; 583, 3 (and 520, 1; 682, 17); 673, 11. The lecture of the year 431 H is also mentioned ibid. p. 472, 14. See also pp. 239, 2; 283, 15; 284, 14; 491, 13; 726, 8.

[77] *Fihrista* 94. Several other of Abū Dharr's pupils are mentioned by Ibn Bashkuwāl, *Ṣila* 63 penultimate; 153, 11 (also 290, 8); 635, 7.

[78] Ibn Abbār, *Takmila* 396.

[79] Dhahabī, *Tadhkirat al-ḥuffāẓ* 3, 286, 6; cf. also Ibn Abbār, *Takmila* 18, 15; 274, 12; 677, 2. We meet other listeners of Abū Maktūm's in Ibn Abbār's *Takmila* 395, 2 and 685, 12, and in the *Muʿjam* (BAH IV) 283, 6.

[80] *Fatḥ al-bārī* 1, 5, 7.

[81] E.g. Mingana's manuscript (see Mingana, *An Important Manuscript* p. 3).

28. Al-Mustaghfirī Abū al-ʿAbbās Ghaʿfar b. Muḥammad (d. 432 H)[82] from Nasaf worked differently from all the other third-generation traditionists mentioned so far. While he did use a recension going back to Firabrī, the text of which he received from Firabrī's last pupil al-Kushānī, he also consulted a secondary tradition by studying the *Ṣaḥīḥ* as transmitted by Bukhārī's last pupil al-Bazdawī under a certain Aḥmad b. ʿAbd al-ʿAzīz. In the absence of exact data it is difficult to estimate how far Bazdawī's recension deviated from Firabrī's. Al-Mustaghfirī's recension has not left many traces in the surviving texts; together with Abū Nuʿaym's it is found in Abū Mūsā al-Madīnī.

[**76**] The teaching activities of the traditionists of the third generation took place towards the end of the fourth and then through the first half of the fifth century (as far as it has been possible to determine the dates, the oldest among them, Aṣīlī, died as early as 392 H, whereas the youngest, Dāwūdī, lived until 467 H). It is owing to them that knowledge of the *Ṣaḥīḥ* spread through the whole Muslim world during that time. A particularly important contribution was made by Abū Dharr and Karīma in Mecca, with whom many pilgrims studied the *Ṣaḥīḥ* each year. Here we find confirmation of the fact, provable also in other ways, that around the year 400 H Bukhārī's collection of traditions had acquired canonical status by virtue of the *consensus doctorum*. At this point the history of the transmission of the text undergoes a change. While the textual history had so far presented the picture of a vast stream whose lower reaches spread out into just a few major branches, now we observe a welter of traditions running, disconcertingly manifold, through all the lands of the Muslim world; criss-crossing and converging, only to separate again. Only once all the riches and treasures hidden in glosses to older Bukhārī manuscripts, in textbooks, diplomas and other documents have been raised will it be possible to give an exact picture of this intricate history. Until then we have to rely on the aid of, in particular, chains of witnesses surviving in Ibn Ḥajar, ʿAynī and Qasṭallānī's works, and on more general considerations. Thus we may assume that insofar as leading scholars of Islamic tradition made Bukhārī's collection the subject of their own studies, they would have composed an eclectic text based also on the various recensions they received from their respective teachers. This text would in turn have become the standard work for their pupils and students and would have found recognition in whichever field their authority was predominant.

[82] GAL Suppl. 1, 617; Dhahabī, *Tadhkirat al-ḥuffāẓ* 3, 253; Qurashī, *Al-Jawāhir al-muḍīʿa* 1, 180.

29. Thus, al-Jayyānī Abū ʿAlī Ḥusayn b. Muḥammad al-Ghassānī (437–493 H) in Cordova, [**77**] one of the most critical scholars of his time, based his text on the recensions of Aṣīlī, Qābisī, Ibn al-Sakan and Nasafī, and made use of them in his *Taqyīd al-muhmal wa-tamyīz al-mushkil*. This is a study of those authorities who appear in Bukhārī's and Muslim's collections and whose names look the same when written but would be pronounced differently[83] (e.g. *Asīd: Usayd*). Ibn Ḥajar would draw on this text later.[84]
30. His younger fellow countryman Abū ʿAlī al-Ṣadafī Ḥusayn b. Muḥammad Ibn Firroh Ibn Sukkara in Murcia (b. ca. 454 H, died in the battle of Cutanda in 514 H)[85] recited Bukhārī's *Ṣaḥīḥ* around sixty times and could boast of knowing the isnad to every single of its traditions, and vice versa.[86] Ibn Abbār compiled a list of his pupils, and this text occurs repeatedly among the texts they studied under him.[87] According to Maqqarī's testimony referred to above, his text was found most frequently in Spanish Bukhārī manuscripts, as was Abū al-Walīd al-Bājī's.
31. Ṣadafī's pupil, the Qāḍī ʿIyāḍ b. Mūsā (476–544 H; GAL 1, 369), had exact knowledge of the differing recensions of Bukhārī's text.[88]
32. At the same time in the East, a text of similarly eclectic character was that by al-Furāwī Muḥammad [**78**] b. al-Faḍl (441–530 H),[89] esteemed for his 'high' isnad. This Bukhārī text was based on the recensions by Ḥafṣī and ʿAyyār. Two in particular of his pupils did great service to Bukhārī's collection, namely al-Samʿānī Abū Saʿd ʿAbd al-Karīm b. Muḥammad (506–562 H; GAL 1, 329) who later studied the text under Abū Dharr, and the chronicler of Damascus, Ibn ʿAsākir Abū al-Qāsim ʿAlī b. Ḥasan (506–581 H; GAL 1, 331), about whose sources nothing more appears to be known, and whose edition was later used by Yūnīnī.
33. The case of Ibn Khayr Abū Bakr Muḥammad (502–575 H; GAL 1, 499) is a good example of how intricate tradition had become by the sixth century

---

[83] Preserved in Berlin, Ahlwardt no. 10161 and in Istanbul, see M. Weisweiler, *Istanbuler Handschriftenstudien z. arab. Traditionsliteratur* (*Bibl. Isl. 10*) no. 96. [al-Jayyānī, *Taqyīd al-muhmal wa-tamyīz al-mushkal*, 2 vols., ed. M. Abū al-Faḍl, Rabat, 1997.]

[84] *Fatḥ al-bārī* 1, 3, 1. 25; 4, 8; 5, 2.

[85] Ibn Bashkuwāl 1, 145–48; Ḍabbī, *Bughyat al-multamis* 253; Yāqūt, *Geogr. Wörterb.* 4, 37; Dhahabī, *Tadhkirat al-ḥuffāẓ* 4, 48.

[86] Maqqarī, *Analectes* 1, 521; 607.

[87] Ibn Abbār, *Al-muʿjam fī aṣḥāb al-qāḍī al-imām Abī ʿAlī al-Ṣadafī* (*BAH IV*) pp. 39, 63, 68, 80, 94, 128, 145, 160, 170, 173, 174, 190, 241, 247, 280, 286, 295, 298, 303.

[88] See e. g. the quotations in Yāqūt, *Geogr. Wörterb.* 670, 10; 750, 17; 3, 554, 2; 4, 41, 15; 242, 15 from the *Kitāb Maṭālī al-anwār*, according to GAL, Suppl. 1, 632 published in Cairo in 1332 H.

[89] Yāqūt, *Geogr. Wörterb.* 3, 866; Ibn Khallikān no. 633.

H: in his *Fihrista* pp. 94–98 he lists the exact chains of witnesses linking him to Bukhārī. According to these chains, he studied the *Ṣaḥīḥ* in the following six versions: according to Abū Dharr, Ibn al-Sakan, Marwazī, Aṣīlī, Qābiṣī and Nasafī.

34. In contrast to this eclecticism in the composition of texts, one scholar of this time argued the privileged position of one individual version: Abū al-Waqt ʿAbd al-Awwal b. ʿĪsā, 458–553 H),[90] who presented a critically expurgated text of the recension by Dāwūdī *ʿan Sarakhsī*. Like Abū Dharr, Abū al-Waqt came from Herat and later taught at the Niẓāmiiya in Baghdad. His commentary was soon widely disseminated. Old manuscripts of Bukhārī's text were revised using this text.[91] In the 'genealogies' with which Ibn Ḥajar, ʿAynī and Qasṭallānī preface their texts, this commentary is represented by half a dozen branches interwoven in manifold ways; in ʿAynī's version in particular it stands out to such an extent that the assumption that he mostly followed Abū al-Waqt's text is not without justification.[92]

[**79**] 35. When Abū al-Waqt went to his grave, with him died the last of Bukhārī's editors who was still within the live tradition of the teaching of theology as it flourished in mosques and *madāris* of mediaeval Islam. Already during his time, instruction had become formalised and ossified; then, step by step, desolation spread her shroud over the onetime wealth of all the fields of Islamic academic life. While the ancient forms of lecture recitation (*ismāʿ*) and the teaching licence (*ijāza*) were retained, perceptive observers could hardly fail to notice that the soul of traditional teaching was becoming increasingly hollow and eventually replaced by nothingness, and that no true understanding of the texts could be achieved anymore. Ibn al-Ṣalāḥ Abū ʿAmr ʿUthmān b. ʿAbd al-Raḥmān (577–643 H; GAL 1, 358), whose classic work on the principles of the study of tradition enjoys widespread esteem to this day, confesses in plain words that in his day, and even generations earlier, an uninterrupted chain of authorities was no guarantee of a reliable text anymore. Among the authorities quoted, he said, could be men who did not understand the text and the isnad was only retained because it was an peculiarly Islamic characteristic. Ibn al-Ṣalāḥ draws the conclusion that the only way of arriving at a reliable text was to collate as many correct originals of the

---

[90] Ibn Khallikān no. 414; Mingana op. cit. 18.

[91] An example is Mingana's manuscript, see Mingana op. cit. 3.

[92] Ibn Khallikān (op. cit.) also heard the *Ṣaḥīḥ* in this commentary, also Maqqarī (*Analectes* 1, 746f.); for other examples see Ibn Abbār's *Takmila* 345; 516; 656.

various recensions and, by discovering correspondences, recover the genuine text.[93]

36. In the case of Bukhārī's text, this task, as defined by Ibn al-Ṣalāḥ, was accomplished by al-Yūnīnī Sharaf al-Dīn Abū al-Ḥasan ʿAlī b. Muḥammad (d. 701 H). According to Qasṭallānī's account in the introduction to his commentary of Yūnīnī's work (*Irshād al-sārī* 1, 40f.), Yūnīnī collated the following four textual witnesses:

[**80**] 1. H, a manuscript read to Abū Dharr al-Harawī (abbreviated [*h*]);
2. Ṣ, a manuscript read to Aṣīlī (abbreviated [*ṣ*]);
3. Sh, a manuscript written by Ibn ʿAsākir al-Dimashqī (abbreviated [*sh*]);
4. Ẓ, a manuscript read by Samʿānī[94] to Abū al-Waqt (abbreviated [*ẓ*]).

He used the following abbreviations for Abū Dharr's three authorities:

ḥ ([ح]) = Ḥammawī
st ([ست]) = Mustamlī
h ([ه]) = Kushmēhanī.

In the frequent cases where Ḥammawī cooperated with one of the other two, Yūnīnī used the following grammalogues:

ḥs ([حس]) = Ḥammawī and Mustamlī
ḥh ([حه]) = Ḥammawī and Kushmēhanī.

Besides the four textual witnesses mentioned, Yūnīnī referred to two further manuscripts:

5. A manuscript which ʿAbd al-Ghanī b. ʿAbd al-wāḥid al-Maqdisī al-Jammāʿīlī (541–600 H; GAL 1, 356) had read with al-Artāḥī Abū ʿAbd Allāh Muḥammad b. Aḥmad b. Ḥāmid (d. 601 H),[95] who for his own part had received a teaching licence (*ijāza*) from Ibn ʿUmar al-Farrāʾ for Karīma's text.
6. A manuscript written by Abū Ṣādiq Murshid b. Yaḥyā al-Madīnī (d. 517 H[96]).

It is to be assumed that the copy Yūnīnī had for his own use and in which he recorded his collations presented Bukhārī's text as he [**81**] [Table II al-ʿAynī's version of Bukhārī's text] [Table III Al-Qasṭallānī's version of Bukhārī's text]

---

[93] See Nawawī, *Sharḥ Muslim*, in the margin of Qasṭallānī 1, 20.

[94] In the *Ansāb*, fol. 291f., Samʿānī relates that he heard the *Ṣaḥīḥ al-Bukhārī* from Abū al-Waqt.

[95] Yāqūt, *Geogr. Wörterb.* 1, 290, 23. He was the last one who transmitted from Ibn ʿUmar al-Farrāʾ.

[96] Jazarī, *Ghāyat al-Nihāya* 2, 293, no. 3587; Suyūṭī, *Ḥusn al-Muḥāḍara* (Cairo, 1299 H) 1, 172; Yāqūt, *Geogr. Wörterb.* 4, 454, 19. Yaḥyā b. Saʿdun heard the text from him 513 H, see Ibn Abbār, *Takmila* 724.

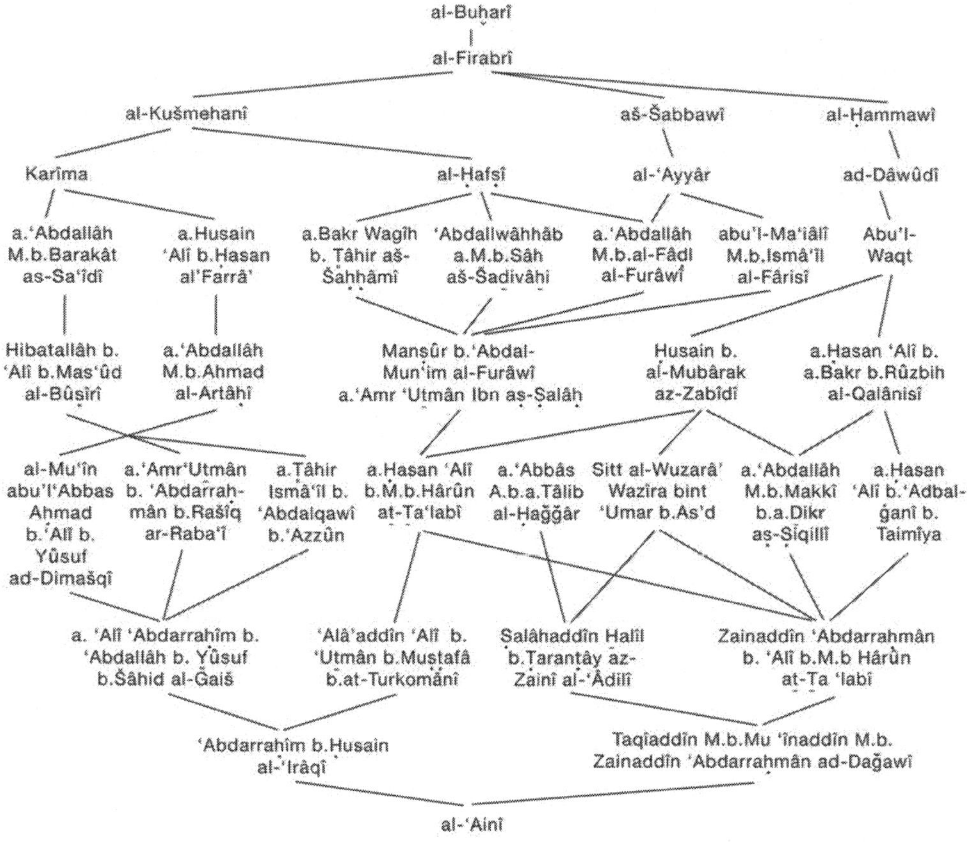

Table II *Die Buḫârî - Text al-'Ainî's*

had learnt it from his teachers.[97] If a reading in his personal copy was confirmed by the four textual witnesses, he wrote the grammalogues [*h ṣ sh ẓ*] above it. If the respective word was missing in the other texts, he wrote [*lā*] in front of those marks. If the reading was found in only one version of the text, he only wrote the relevant letter above it; if it was missing in one version, he wrote [*lā*] in front of the relevant grammalogue. Where he himself considered a reading important that was contrary to those of all three authorities for Abū

[97] According to the isnad found in Qasṭallānī, *Irshād al-sārī* 1, 49, 31, Yūnīnī studied Abu'l-Waqt's recension with Zabīdī Abū ʿAbd Allāh Ḥusayn b. Mūbārak (d. 631 H). This does not, however, make it impossible for him to have 'heard' other recensions as well. On the subject of Zabīdī's role as a transmitter of the *Ṣaḥīḥ*, see Qurashī, *Al-Jawāhir al-muḍīʿa* 1, 216, as well as the comments on Ibn Fahd's *Laḥẓ al-alḥāẓ* (Damascus 1347 H), p. 258f. and 322ff.

Dharr, he wrote [*ṣḥ*] and [*h*] above it; if only one of Abū Dharr's authorities contradicted such a reading, he wrote [*ṣḥ*] together with the relevant mark above it. If the two manuscripts consulted additionally, Jammāʿīlī's and Abū Ṣādiq's, corresponded with one of the four authorities, Yūnīnī would write the relevant reading in read ink. While Yūnīnī was thus establishing the text, Ibn Mālik Jamāladdīn Muḥammad b. ʿAbd Allāh (600–672 H: GAL 1, 298), the greatest grammarian of his time, was present.[98] This is reported by a gloss written in Ibn Mālik's own had on the first page of Yūnīnī's manuscript and quoted word for word by Qasṭallānī,[99] where we read that Yūnīnī read this volume in the presence of a few students who followed the text of the lecture in standardised manuscripts. Whenever a grammatical difficulty appeared, Ibn Mālik pronounced judgement; the discussion of a number of especially difficult cases he reserved for a separate publication.[100] In addition, the concluding note [**82**] in Yūnīnī's own hand at the end of the volume, the words of which survive in Qasṭallānī's book as well, refer to Ibn Mālik's cooperation. It states that he supervised Yūnīnī's recitation and observed his pronunciation, and it was under his direction that Yūnīnī revised the text and added the vocalisation. From this concluding note we learn furthermore that the collation (*muqābala*), correction (*taṣḥīḥ*) and recitation (*ismāʿ*) of the first volume was completed in Ibn Mālik's presence after 71 sessions. Thus we may say with certainty that Yūnīnī would have eliminated obvious mistakes. What we do not, of course, know, is to what extent beyond the elimination of obvious mistakes he was striving to produce a critical edition. Still, the example from one of the first traditions of the *Ṣaḥīḥ* given by Qasṭallānī,[101] shows that Yūnīnī retained in his text a word that was missing from all his four witnesses; thus he tolerated readings which were not covered by the four witnesses and mentioned the variants only in the critical apparatus. What he composed was a critical apparatus rather than a genuine critical edition in the sense of text recension based on reliable manuscript documentation. This may be the reason why his work, however conscientious, painstaking and exhaustive it may have been, did not at first find the appreciation one would have been justified to expect for such a pre-eminent achievement of Islamic scholarship. While Qasṭallānī mentions manuscripts which were compared to Yūnīnī's

[98] As he died in 672 H, it is not possible for his assistance to have taken place in the year 676 H, as stated in the 1304 H Cairo imprint of the *Irshād al-sārī*, 1, 40.

[99] Qasṭallānī 1, 41.

[100] This refers to the *K. Shawāhid al-tawḍīḥ wa'l-taṣḥīḥ li-mushkilat al-Ṣaḥīḥ*, of which Brockelmann, GAL, Suppl. 1, 262, lists several manuscripts and one printed version Allahabad 1319 H (now ed. M. ʿAbd al-Bāqī, Cairo, 1957; and ed. Ṭāhā Muḥsin, Baghdad, 1985).

[101] *Irshād al-sārī*, 1, 40. 70.

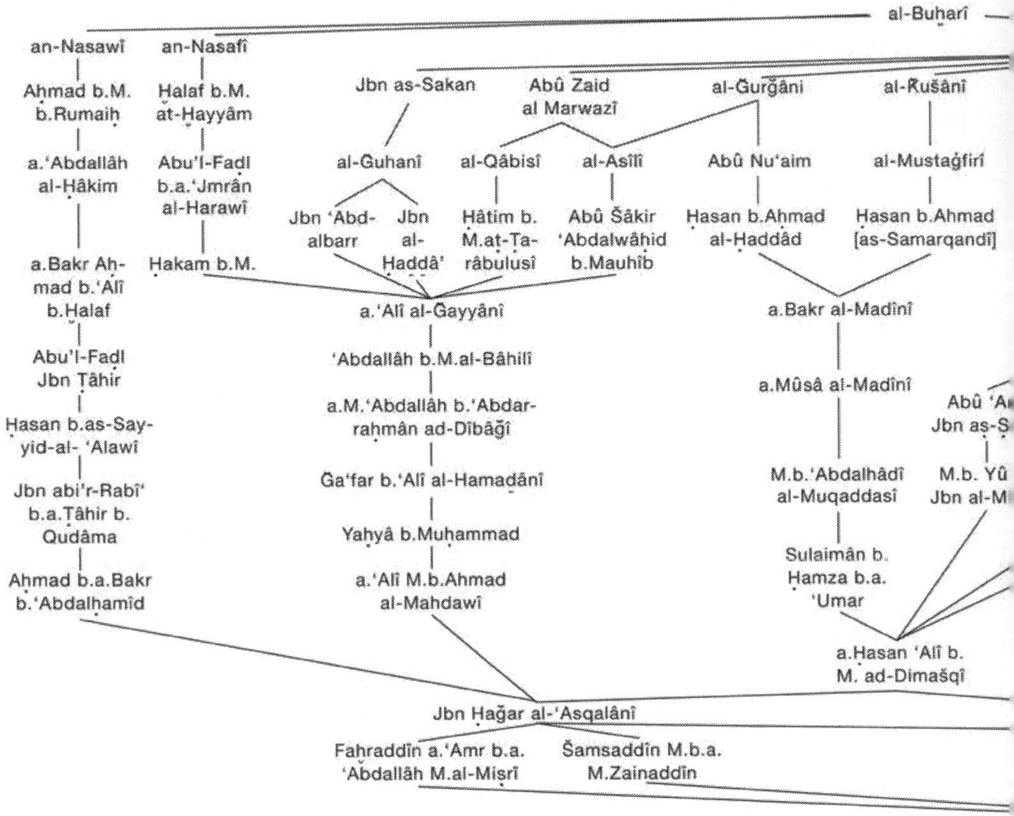

Table III *Die Buhârî - Text al-Qastallânî's*

manuscript,[102] a search for traces of his influence in contemporary Bukhārī literature is in vain. Neither Ibn Ḥajar nor ʿAynī mention his name, despite the fact that their many volumes of commentaries on the *Ṣaḥīḥ* combine the results of half a century's Islamic scholarship of Bukhārī's work. It was due to Qasṭallānī that Yūnīnī received the honour due to him.

37. Ibn Ḥajar al-ʿAsqalānī Abū al-Faḍl Aḥmad b. ʿAlī's (773–852 H; GAL 2, 67) commentary, entitled *Fatḥ al-barī bi-sharkh Ṣaḥīḥ al-Bukhārī*, appeared in print in 13 volumes in Būlāq in 1300/01 H. [**83**] In the preface, the

[102] *Irshād al-sārī*, 1, 41.

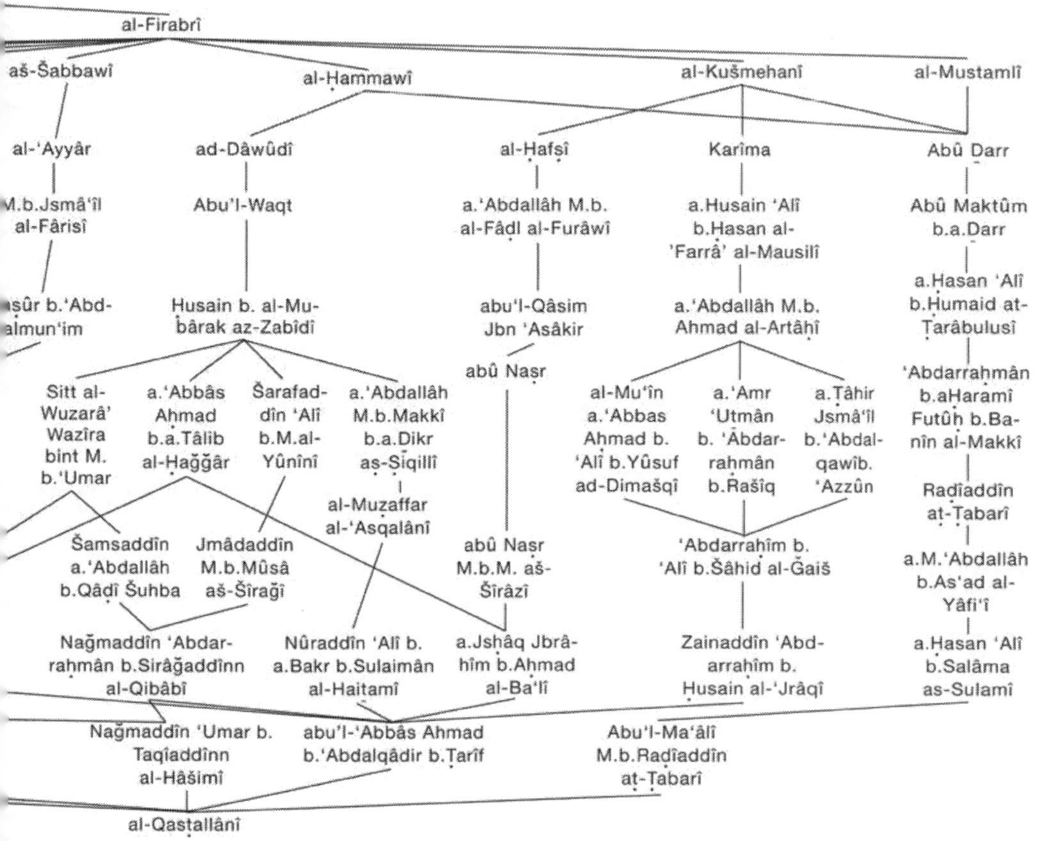

author lists the various recensions and lists the chains of witnesses (*asānīd*) linking him to Bukhārī.[103] At the end (1, 59) he remarks that his commentary refers to Abū Dharr's recension; he does not, however, provide a pure version of this text but in many cases deviates from it. In some instances he notes Abū Dharr's reading, in others the difference is obvious from Qasṭallānī's data. It is obvious that Ibn Ḥajar established his own text recension close to Abū Dharr's text. What makes it more difficult for the reader is that Ibn Ḥajar did not integrate Bukhārī's complete text into his commentary, but instead focussed on individual

[103] A. Mingana op. cit. displays these chains of witnesses in a clear table.

lemmas which do not always correspond with the Bukhārī text found in the margin in the Būlāq edition. I have already mentioned that Ibn Ḥajar did not know Yūnīnī's edition.[104] He would probably have gleaned the readings, which he quotes on an average scale, partly from scholastic traditions, but mainly out of older commentaries and similar works.

38. Even more extensive than the *Fatḥ al-barī*, Maḥmūd b. Aḥmad al-ʿAynī's (762–855 H; GAL 2, 52) *ʿUmdat al-qārī li-sharkh Ṣaḥīḥ al- Bukhārī* only rarely refers to variant readings. According to his own account (1, 7) ʿAynī read the *Ṣaḥīḥ* 788 H with his teacher ʿAbd al-Raḥmān b. Ḥusayn al-ʿIrāqī (GAL 2, 65) and then again in 805 H with Taqī al-Dīn b. Muʿīn al-Dīn Ibn Ḥaydara; he does not mention whether he favours one particular recension. It is remarkable, however, that the name of Abū Dharr does not appear at all in his *asānīd*; indeed, his whole text appears to be completely free from readings peculiar to Abū Dharr. He does not mention Yūnīnī either, and nowhere betrays any knowledge of the latter's edition. It may be assumed that the comparatively rare [**84**] data on different readings would have been drawn from sources similar to those used by Ibn Ḥajar (see Table II).

39. The text on which al-Qasṭallānī Aḥmad b. Muḥammad (851–923 H; GAL 2, 73) based his *Irshād al-sarī ilā sharkh Ṣaḥīḥ al-Bukhārī* is a different matter altogether. It is true that he lists numerous chains of witnesses (*asānīd*) and himself received the text from no fewer than six scholars among whose authorities are Ibn Ḥajar, also ʿIrāqī (al-ʿAynī's teacher mentioned above) and even Yūnīnī. What is much more important, however, is that he consulted Yūnīnī's edition. Yūnīnī's autograph manuscript had been a pious donation to the *madrasa* founded by Aqbogha ʿAbd al-Wāḥid in 740 H,[105] but by Qasṭallānī's time it was nowhere to be found. Consequently he was using a copy made by one Shams al-Dīn Muḥammad b. Aḥmad al-Mizzī al-Ghazūlī, who had used Yūnīnī's original but also consulted a second manuscript. Only after he had finished his work did he happen upon the second volume of Yūnīnī's original manuscript in 916 H and subsequently compared his text with it twice. Finally the first volume appeared at a bookseller's where he could acquire it and thus collate the first half of the text as well. This does not, however, mean that his Bukhārī text is a faithful rendering of Yūnīnī's text: the example quoted above[106] already shows a deviation. Qasṭallānī

[104] Thus e.g. in *Fatḥ al-barī* 4, 397, margin, third line from the bottom we find [*yqrbk*]; whereas Yūnīnī, according to Qasṭallānī 4, 164, penultimate, reads [*yqrbnk*].

[105] ʿAlī Mubārak, *al-Khiṭaṭ al-Tawfīqīya* (Bulaq, 1304–6/1886–8, 20 vols. in 10) 4, 18.

[106] Qasṭallānī 1, 40 compared to 1, 70.

also occasionally notes readings from the Yūnīnīya which he himself did not integrate into his text. He did not relinquish the right to compose his own commentary of the text any more than any of his predecessors, but it is Yūnīnī's original which is Qasṭallānī's source for the extensive information about readings in the older commentaries. He provides a much wider range of variant readings than 'Aynī and Ibn Ḥajar, and it is this that makes his commentary especially valuable (see Table III).

40. Thus the history of Bukhārī's collection of traditions shows [**85**] that the text was originally transmitted by four of the master's disciples and subsequently circulated in only very few commentaries out of which more and more hybrid versions developed, and finally sank into neglect and disregard. In the seventh century H this state of things called onto the scene some men of critical inclination and philological training who went back to the old commentaries and attempted to present a critically expurgated version. While they were not successful in bringing a *textus receptus*, a received text, to universal recognition, the wealth of variant readings surviving in the extensive commentaries of the seventh century is still a lasting monument to their never failing industriousness. Their criticism may not be that of the present day, their data may sometimes be inexact, contradictory or indeed wrong (to say nothing of printing errors in the Oriental editions), but it is true that to this day anyone looking for a critically reliable Bukhārī text will depend on them. Only old and reliable manuscripts could take us beyond this level; one such manuscript being that which recently surfaced in Mingana's fragment, while many others must still be slumbering in the libraries of the Orient. People who expect radical changes to the text, however, would most likely be disappointed. The majority of readings available to us refers to differences which hardly affect the meaning at all. Differences are indeed much wider in the surrounding material which does not actually touch the wording of individual traditions, in the way traditions are organised into books and chapters, under titles and headings. Less numerous are variants in the *asānīd*, and least frequent, and only rarely touching on the actual meaning, are variant readings in the traditions themselves. Thus maybe a critical editor of Bukhārī's text, even if he had at his disposition all the old recensions in good manuscripts, would arrive at the same result with which Ibn Khayr concluded his list of all the Bukhārī editions he studied (*Fihrista* 98), nearly eight centuries ago: 'All these recensions are close to each other.'

Translated by Gwendolin Goldbloom

Index

All the people who have transmitted the *Ṣaḥīḥ* of Bukhārī and who appear above are included in this index. The numbers refer to the paragraphs. Bold type means that a special paragraph has been devoted to the person.

Contributions to the History of Bukhārī's Collection of Traditions 25

26 *Johann Fück*

15
THE INTRODUCTION OF *ḤADITH* IN AL-ANDALUS*

Isabel Fierro

Introduction

Western scholars like Goldziher, Schacht and more recently Juynboll, among others, maintain that *ḥadīth* literature originated at a later stage than that accepted by the classical Muslim tradition. One of the evidences adduced by Juynboll to support this hypothesis is that provided by the *awā'il* and, among them, by the *awā'il* "dealing with those people who were credited with having been the first to introduce *ḥadīth*, specified in genre as well as unspecified, into certain areas of the Islamic world".[1]) On his part, Schacht has studied the impact of *ḥadīth* in the field of law, on the assumption that the origins of Islamic jurisprudence were not based on *ḥadīth*. Al-Shāfi'ī (d. 204/820) was the first to formulate the theory of the *uṣūl al-fiqh* which was to become classical and the attempts to incorporate *ḥadīth* into the field of *fiqh* had to overcome the resistance of the "ancient schools of law". In this process a confrontation took place between the groups called by the sources *ahl al-ra'y* and *ahl al-ḥadīth*.[2])

My aim in this article is to study when the *ḥadīth* literature and the *'ilm al-ḥadīth* were first introduced into al-Andalus, who the protagonists of this

---

*This article is a paper read in the 4th International Colloquium "From Jāhiliyya to Islam" held in Jerusalem 7–13 July 1987. I wish to thank Prof. M. Cook and Dr. M. Lecker for their comments.

[1]) *Muslim Tradition*, p. 22.

[2]) See particularly *Origins . . .*, *Part I* and *Part II*. Schacht's theories have been recently attacked by M. M. Azmi (*On Schacht's "Origins of Muhammadan Jurisprudence"*, Riad 1986) from a classical Muslim point of view. Schacht's method for the dating of traditions has been put to the test and opened to doubt by M. A. Cook ("Eschatology, history and the dating of traditions", paper presented to the *Third International Colloquium "From Jāhiliyya to Islam"*, 1985). I shall come back in thc conclusions to Schacht's theories.

introduction were and what the relationship between the Andalusian *ahl al-ra'y* and *ahl al-ḥadīth* was. This study is organised in the following way:

I. *Awā'il* dealing with the introduction of *ḥadīth* into al-Andalus

1. First phase

1.1 Mu'āwiya b. Ṣāliḥ and Ṣa'ṣa'a b. Sallām (c. second half 2nd/8th century)

1.2 'Abd al-Malik b. Ḥabīb (first half 3rd/9th century)

2. Second phase

2.1 Baqī b. Makhlad (d. 276/889)

2.2 Muḥammad b. Waḍḍāḥ (d. 287/900)

II. The confrontation between the *ahl al-ra'y* and the *ahl al-ḥadīth*

1. The persecution of the traditionists

2. The controversy on *raf' al-yadayn fī l-ṣalāt*

3. The coexistence of the *ahl al-ra'y* and the *ahl al-ḥadīth*

Conclusions

I. *Awā'il* dealing with the introduction of *ḥadīth* into al-Andalus

The scholars credited with having been the first to introduce *ḥadīth* into al-Andalus are the following:
– Mu'āwiya b. Ṣāliḥ al-Ḥaḍramī al-Ḥimṣī,[3]) who left Ḥimṣ in the year 125/742, entered al-Andalus before the year 138/755 and after this date was made *qāḍī* by the first Umayyad *amīr*. According to some sources he died in the year 158/774 and according to others at a later date;

[3]) See *Quḍāt*, p. 31/40, with the following Andalusian *isnād*: Ibn Ḥārith al-Khushanī < Aḥmad b. Ziyād (d. 326/937) < Muḥammad b. Waḍḍāḥ (d. 287/900) < Yaḥyà b. Yaḥyà al-Laythī (d. 234/848).

– Ṣaʿṣaʿa b. Sallām al-Dimashqī,[4]) of Syrian origin like Muʿāwiya. He was a *muftī* of the two first Umayyad *amīrs* and died towards the end of the 2nd/8th century (180/796, 192/807 or 202/817);
– ʿAbd al-Malik b. Ḥabīb al-Sulamī (d. 238/852),[5]) one of the leading Malikite scholars of his age.

On the other hand, two scholars who died in the second half of the 3rd/9th century are credited with having been the first to introduce the *ʿilm al-ḥadīth* into al-Andalus. They are Baqī b. Makhlad (d. 276/889) and Muḥammad b. Waḍḍāḥ (d. 287/900), both of them *mawlàs* from Qurṭuba; thanks to their teachings *ṣārat al-Andalus dār al-ḥadīth.*[6])

According to these *awāʾil*, there were two phases in the introduction of *ḥadīth*:

1. the first phase took place in the last three quarters of the 2nd/8th century (Muʿāwiya and Ṣaʿṣaʿa) or in the first half of the 3rd/9th century (Ibn Ḥabīb) and in it *ḥadīth* literature (in general) was introduced;
2. the second phase took place in the second half of the 3rd/9th century (Baqī and Ibn Waḍḍāḥ) and in it the *ʿilm al-ḥadīth* was introduced.

Before undertaking the study of these two phases, it must be pointed out that the information about the presence of Companions and Successors in al-Andalus lacks in general any historical background. The *tābiʿūn* who actually entered al-Andalus are either not recorded as having been engaged in the transmission of *ḥadīth* or, if they did, had no Andalusian pupils.[7]) The case of Muʿāwiya b. Ṣāliḥ, quoted by later sources as a *tābiʿī*, will be dealt with in the next section.

---

[4]) See *Taʾrīkh*, n. 608; *Jadhwa*, n. 510; *Bughya*, n. 853; Ibn Saʿīd, *Mughrib*, I, 44. The date of his arrival in al-Andalus (coming from Egypt) is unknown. He was *muftī* of Abd al-Raḥmān I and Hishām I and as a follower of al-Awzāʿī's *madhhab* established the practice of growing trees in mosques which was later considered a peculiarity of the Andalusian Malikites: see Fierro, "Los mālikíes de al-Andalus . . .", p. 79.

[5]) See *Siyar*, XII, 106. Al-Dhahabī's source is the Andalusian Abū ʿAbd al-Malik b. ʿAbd al-Barr (d. 338/950), author of a lost *Taʾrīkh* on which see Viguera's article. Al-Shiblī (d. 769/1367) also quotes Ibn ʿAbd al-Barr in his book on *awāʾil.* I thank Prof. M. J. Kister for this information.

[6]) *Taʾrīkh*, I, 318; *Madārik*, IV, 436; *Dībāj*, II, 180; *Tadhkira*, II, 647.

[7]) See Marín, "*Ṣaḥāba* . . .", especially, p. 22. The Egyptian sources from which the Andalusians took their information on those Companions and Successors have been studied in Makki's article.

1. *First phase*

1.1 Mu‘āwiya b. Ṣāliḥ and Ṣa‘ṣa‘a b. Sallām (c. second half of the 2nd/8th century)

As regards the *awā'il* that deal with the introduction of *ḥadīth* by Mu‘āwiya and Ṣa‘ṣa‘a, the information they provide is not supported by external evidence: no *isnād* is recorded in which their names appear as informants of Andalusian transmitters.

In the case of Ṣa‘ṣa‘a b. Sallām, it is the Egyptian traditionist Ibn Yūnus (d. 347/958) that names him as the first to introduce *ḥadīth* into al-Andalus, without any mention as to where he took this information from or whether his source was Andalusian or Oriental.[8]) Apart from this mention, Ṣa‘ṣa‘a is a scholar unknown outside al-Andalus. Ibn ‘Asākir had to rely on Ibn Yūnus and on Andalusian sources for the biography included in his *Ta'rīkh Dimashq*[9]) and I have not found the name of Ṣa‘ṣa‘a in the most important Oriental *rijāl* works. Ṣa‘ṣa‘a is also credited with having been the first to introduce the *madhhab* of al-Awzā‘ī into the Iberian Peninsula.

Mu‘āwiya b. Ṣāliḥ, on the other hand, is a well known traditionist in Eastern Islam. His name appears in the *isnāds* of the six books (with the exclusion of al-Bukhārī's *Ṣaḥīḥ*). He is mentioned as the teacher of famous traditionists like ‘Abd Allāh b. Wahb (d. 197/912), ‘Abd al-Raḥmān b. Mahdī (d. 198/813), Abū Ṣāliḥ (d. 223/838), Asad b. Mūsà (d. 212/827), al-Layth b. Sa‘d (d. 175/791), al-Wāqidī (d. 207/823), Sufyān al-Thawrī (d. 161/778), Sufyān b. ‘Uyayna (d. 198/813), Yaḥyà b. Sa‘īd al-Qaṭṭān (d. 198/813). His transmission of Ibn ‘Abbās's *Tafsīr* was quoted by al-Ṭabarī. No trace, however, is left of his alleged transmissions in al-Andalus.

When the aforementioned Ibn Waḍḍāḥ made his first *riḥla* to the East (between the years 218/833 and 230/844), he studied with the ‘Irāqī Yaḥyà b. Ma‘īn and was asked by him whether Mu‘āwiya's transmissions had been collected in al-Andalus. Ibn Waḍḍāḥ's answer was that they had not, explaining that in those days the Andalusians were not interested in knowledge (*lam yakun ahlu-hā yawmā'idh ahl al-‘ilm*). Muḥammad b. ‘Abd

---

[8]) The problem of the Andalusian sources used by Ibn Yūnus is far from being solved. See Fierro, "Ibn Yūnus, fuente de Ibn al-Faraḍī", *Homenaje a D. Cabanelas O. F. M.*, 2 vols. Granada 1987 I, 297–313.

[9]) I have consulted a ms. in the Sulaymānīya Library (Damat Ibrahim Pasa n. 875, f. 422 b, 6–22). Ibn ‘Asākir quotes Ṣa‘ṣa‘a's biography by Ibn Yūnus, but the text looks defective: where it should appear *kāna awwal man adkhala l-Andalus al-ḥadīth*, this last word is missing and without it the sentence does not make much sense.

al-Malik b. Ayman (d. after 300/912), one of Ibn Waḍḍāḥ's pupils, had a similar experience during his *riḥla* (started in the year 274/879). He realized then that the transmissions by Mu'āwiya were highly valued in 'Irāq and his teacher Ibn Abī Khaythama (d. 279/892) went so far as to mention his desire of visiting al-Andalus in order to examine the *uṣūl* of Mu'āwiya's books.[10]) When Ibn Ayman came back to the Peninsula, he unsuccesfully looked for those books and, at the end, he was forced to conclude (like Ibn Waḍḍāḥ had been before him) that the transmissions by Mu'āwiya had been lost because of the lack of interest and knowledge of the Andalusians.[11])

In my monograph on Mu'āwiya,[12]) I have pointed out how difficult it is to establish what is legend and what is history in the different and often contradictory versions of his biography. Concerning the Andalusian version of his life and activity as a traditionist, my opinion is that it was created in the first half of the 3rd/9th century and that its starting point was the curiosity aroused in the Andalusian travellers when asked in the East about the transmissions of Mu'āwiya. I therefore assume that, before those travels took place, the Andalusians ignored the importance of Mu'āwiya in the transmission of *ḥadīth*: it was only after being informed of his activities in that field through Oriental sources that they reached the conclusion that Mu'āwiya must have been the first to introduce *ḥadīth* in al-Andalus.[13]) As they could not find any evidence of this, they explained the loss of his transmissions through the lack of interest in *ḥadīth* existing in those days. This

---

10) On Mu'āwiya's "books", see Abbott, *Studies* . . ., II, 103. Maybe one of them was Ibn 'Abbās's *Tafsīr*, taught by Mu'āwiya to his Egyptian disciple Abū Ṣāliḥ. Abbott suggests that those "books" probably remained in Egypt, especially taking into account the version that places Mu'āwiya's death there and not in al-Andalus.

11) See these stories in *Quḍāt*, pp. 30–1/38–9 and *Tahdhīb*, X, 211, as well as *Ta'rīkh*, II, 14, where Ibn Ayman says that after his return to the Peninsula he found that all the Andalusian transmitters from Mu'āwiya were dead. According to these sources, there were only two of them: Shabṭūn (whom we shall meet again) and Dāwūd b. Ja'far b. al-Ṣaghīr, both Malikites. Ibn Ayman studied Mu'āwiya's *ḥadīths* with an Andalusian, but his teacher ('Abd Allāh b. Muḥammad b. Ibrāhīm b. 'Āṣim, d. after 300/912) had learnt them from an Egyptian, Abū l-Ṭāhir Aḥmad b. 'Amr b. al-Sarḥ (d. 249/863 or 255/869).

12) The outline of Mu'āwiya's life and career given here can be filled with the details collected in that study.

13) It is worth noting that the information on Mu'āwiya as the first to introduce *ḥadīth* was received by the traditionist Ibn Waḍḍāḥ from his teacher Yaḥyà b. Yaḥyà (see note 3). This last is presented in the sources as a Malikite *faqīh* not interested in *ḥadīth*. However, he could have heard of Mu'āwiya as a *muḥaddith* during his *riḥla*, as 'Abd al-Malik b. Ḥabīb probably did.

"lack of interest" is in fact supported by what we know about the first *qāḍīs* of al-Andalus, in the sense that none of them is recorded as having been engaged in the transmission of *ḥadīth.*[14]) In the case of Muʿāwiya, the few stories preserved about his activities as a *qāḍī* and as a *faqīh* in al-Andalus do not mention any prophetic tradition. From this one can only conclude that the presence of Muʿāwiya in al-Andalus was of no consequence for the actual introduction of *ḥadīth* and that the role ascribed to both Ṣaʿṣaʿa and Muʿāwiya in it is fictitious.

At the same time, the introduction and early history of the law-schools in al-Andalus is never associated in the sources with the study of *ḥadīth*, despite the fact that, at least in the case of Malikism, this meant the reception of a certain corpus of *ḥadīth*.

The legal doctrines of al-Awzāʿī (d. 157/774)[15]) and of Mālik b. Anas (d. 179/795)[16]) were introduced into al-Andalus in the second half of the 2nd/8th century. One of Mālik's pupils, Ziyād b. ʿAbd al-Raḥmān al-Lakhmī, known as Shabṭūn (d. 193/809 or 199/815), is credited with having been the first to introduce *fiqh* and *al-ḥalāl wa-l-ḥarām*[17]) and he is not recorded as having been engaged in the transmission of *ḥadīth.*[18]).

Shabṭūn was one of the first Andalusians to introduce Mālik's *Muwaṭṭa*', together with al-Ghāzī b. Qays (d. 199/815)[19]) and Yaḥyà b. Yaḥyà al-Laythī (d. 234/848), whose *riwāya* attained the highest authority in Western Islam.[20]) As in the case of Shabṭūn, none of the Andalusian

---

[14]) See Juynboll's study on the judges's activity in the transmission of *ḥadīth: Muslim Tradition*, pp. 77–95 and particularly p. 232 on the judges of Qurṭuba.

[15]) See Makki, *Ensayo . . .*, pp. 64–7. Al-Awzāʿī's doctrine dealt with the law of war, including references to the Prophet's *maghāzī* (Schacht, *Origins . . .*, p. 34). This prophetic material could have played some part in the ascription to his disciple Ṣaʿṣaʿa of the role of being the first to introduce *ḥadīth* in al-Andalus.

[16]) See López Ortiz, *Recepción . . .*, and Makki, *Ensayo . . .*, pp. 99–110, with a critical study of the alleged Andalusian disciples of Mālik.

[17]) *Quḍāt*, p. 50/61–2; his biography in *Ta'rīkh*, n. 456; *Bughya*, n. 751; *Madārik*, III, 116–22; *Nafḥ*, II, 45–6.

[18]) The *matn* dealing with him as the first to introduce *fiqh* has the same *isnād* recorded in note 3, which means that *fiqh* and *ḥadīth* were considered as separate entities: see Juynboll, *Muslim Tradition*, p. 23. I have already pointed out (note 11) that Shabṭūn was considered one of Muʿāwiya's disciples, but there is no external evidence of this relationship.

[19]) According to Ibn al-Qūṭīya (pp. 34–5/27), he was the first to introduce the *Muwaṭṭa*' under ʿAbd al-Raḥmān I (138/756–172/788).

[20]) Yaḥyà was also Shabṭūn's disciple, and transmitted from him part of his recension of the *Muwaṭṭa*', that dealing with *iʿtikāf*. For his biography, see *Ta'rīkh*,

pupils of Mālik is associated in the sources with the transmission of *ḥadīth* and, as I have already mentioned, that is so in spite of the *ḥadīth* material collected in the *Muwaṭṭa'*.[21]) One can then conclude that the *Muwaṭṭa'* was not regarded in that period as a representative work of *ḥadīth* literature.[22])

In the first half of the 3rd/9th century, the Malikite *madhhab* was clearly established in al-Andalus as the predominant law-school,[23]) having replaced that of al-Awzāʿī. Its reception went together with the veneration of Mālik b. Anas,[24]) even though the Andalusians were not strict followers of his teachings as compiled in the *Muwaṭṭa'*. As a matter of fact, they often gave preference to the teachings of his pupils[25]) and especially to the *ra'y* of Ibn al-Qāsim.[26]) The inclination of each *faqīh* towards the teachings of one or other of Mālik's pupils aroused discrepancies and controversies among them,[27]) so that there was not a "monolithic" Malikism. However, it is worth pointing out that in those discrepancies, the degree of adequacy to *ḥadīth* of those teachings does not seem to have been adduced as the ultimate authoritative argument. There is no evidence that in the first half of the 3rd/9th century any attempt was made to discuss the role to be played by prophetic traditions as one of the sources of the law.[28])

---

n. 1554; *Jadhwa*, n. 909; *Bughya*, n. 1497; *Madārik*, III, 397-94; *Dībāj*, II, 352-3; *Nafḥ*, II, 9-12; J. López Ortiz, "Figuras de jurisconsultos hispano-musulmanes. Yahya b. Yahya", *Religión y cultura*, XVI (1931), pp. 94-104.

21) See on its number and importance *MS*, II, 202, note 7 and Schacht, *Origins* . . ., p. 22. After the 5th/11th century, the *Muwaṭṭa'* was included among the canonical "six books": see *MS*, II, 243-4.

22) See *MS*, II, 198-204.

23) On the reason for this predominance and for the absence of Ḥanafism, see Idris's article and Aguadé, "Some remarks . . .", pp. 58-62.

24) See Turki's article.

25) See Makki, *Ensayo* . . ., pp. 124-140 and Fierro, "Los mālikíes de al-Andalus . . .".

26) His influence increased after the introduction of Saḥnūn's *Mudawwana*: see Fórneas's article. According to Ibn Shuhayd, the inhabitants of Qurṭuba only accepted as judges those who followed the *ra'y* of Ibn al-Qāsim: E. García Gómez, *Andalucía contra Berbería* (Barcelona 1979), p. 127.

27) One of the best known enmities was that existing between Yaḥyà b. Yaḥyà and ʿAbd al-Malik b. Ḥabīb, because of the latter's introduction of the teachings of the Mālikite Aṣbagh b. al-Faraj: see Fierro, *La heterodoxia* . . ., appendix 2.

28) See Brunschvig's article and Turki's *Polémiques* . . . The role played by *ḥadīth* in early Andalusian Malikite *fiqh* can now be studied in texts like the *ʿUtbīya*, preserved in the commentary by Ibn Rushd al-Jadd, *K. al-bayān*.

1.2. ʿAbd al-Malik b. Ḥabīb (first half of the 3rd/9th century)

With ʿAbd al-Malik b. Ḥabīb we are on firmer ground. He was very likely of *mawlà* origin[29]) and stands out as one of the most important Andalusian scholars of the first half of the 3rd/9th century, especially due to the role he played in the introduction into al-Andalus of Oriental transmissions. His informants were Medinese and Egyptians, as Ibn Ḥabīb did not visit ʿIrāq during his *riḥla*, started in the year 208/823. What we know about his production allows us to consider him a polygraph in the style of Ibn Qutayba or Ibn Abī l-Dunyā.[30]) His activity was mainly focussed on three fields: history, *fiqh* and ascetism. As a historian, he was the compiler of one of the oldest universal histories that have been preserved; in his *Taʾrīkh*, he quotes transmissions from Wahb b. Munabbih and from al-Wāqidī.[31]) In the field of *fiqh* he was the author of a legal work, *al-Wāḍiḥa fī l-sunan wa-l-fiqh*, in which he collected transmissions from Medinese Malikites like Muṭarrif b. ʿAbd Allāh (d. 214/829) and Ibn al-Mājishūn (d. 212/827 or 214/829); at the same time he included transmissions from the Egyptian traditionists al-Layth b. Saʿd (d. 175/791), Ibn Lahīʿa (d. 174/790) and Asad b. Mūsà (d. 212/827).[32]) In the field of ascetism he wrote works on *al-targhīb wa-l-tarhīb*, a *K. fasād al-zamān*, a *K. makārim al-akhlāq* and a *K. al-waraʿ*, which is greatly indebted to the transmissions from Asad b. Mūsà and in all likelihood to his *K. al-zuhd wa-l-ʿibāda wa-l-waraʿ*.[33]) All these works were studied and transmitted in al-Andalus.

Turning to the role of *ḥadīth* in his works, those that have survived do contain *ḥadīth* material. This aspect was underlined by Schacht in the case

---

[29]) His life and works have been studied by Aguadé in various articles and especially in his Ph. D., "*El Taʾrīj* de ʿAbdalmalik b. Ḥabīb", Universidad Autónoma de Madrid 1986 forthcoming.

[30]) He was described as *faqīh, shāʿir, ṭabīb, khaṭīb* (*Madārik*, IV, 125); *naḥwī, ʿarūḍī, ḥāfiẓ li-l-akhbār wa-l-ansāb wa-l-ashʿār, mutaṣarrif fī funūn al-ʿilm* (*Taʾrīkh*, n. 814). He was also called *ʿālim al-Andalus*, while Yaḥyà b. Yaḥyà was *ʿaqīlu-hā* and ʿĪsà b. Dīnār *faqīhu-hā*. Ibn Ḥabīb's works are listed in *Taʾrīkh*, n. 814 and *Madārik*, IV, 127–9 (see the study by López Ortiz in *Recepción*. . ., p. 88): they deal with *fiqh*, *ṭabaqāt*, history, medicine, astrology, Qurʾān and *Muwaṭṭaʾ* commentaries . . . For references of those preserved see GAS, I, 362; III, 230; VII, 346, 374; VIII, 251; IX, 220.

[31]) See Aguadé, "De nuevo sobre ʿAbd al-Malik b. Ḥabīb", p. 13. His *Taʾrīkh* has been edited in the Ph. D. mentioned in note 29.

[32]) See Muranyi, *Materialien*. . ., pp. 14–29. The existing fragments are not yet published; there are also manuscripts of other legal works.

[33]) See Aguadé, "*El libro del escrúpulo religioso* . . ."; an edition of this *K. al-waraʿ* has been prepared by Aguadé.

of the *Wāḍiḥa*.[34]) However, the predominant role still played in this work by the *ra'y* of Mālik's pupils does not allow us to consider it a *muṣannaf* like, for example, the one collected in the same period by al-Bukhārī (d. 256/870).[35]) Ibn Ḥabīb is said to have written works dealing exclusively with *ḥadīth*, but these works have been lost.[36])

On the other hand, it is worth pointing out that his Andalusian biographers did not consider him a good traditionist and criticised the numerous faults to be found in his transmissions. For instance, Abū 'Abd al-Malik b. 'Abd al-Barr, even though he credited him with having been the first to introduce *ḥadīth* in al-Andalus (see note 5), remarked: "he did not know its methods, made many mistakes in the names, used objectionable *ḥadīths* as arguments, the people of his age (*ahl zamāni-hi*) accused him of mendacity and they were not satisfied with him".[37]) "*Ahl zamāni-hi*" must not be understood as referring to "the scholars of his generation", all of them more ignorant than Ibn Ḥabīb in the field of *ḥadīth*,[38]) it seems to refer to the traditionists belonging to the generation of Ibn Ḥabīb's pupils: they had studied in 'Irāq with experts on *'ilm al-rijāl* and *'ilm al-ḥadīth*, learning the techniques of *ḥadīth* criticism; after their return to al-Andalus, they were

[34]) See Muranyi, *Materialien* . . ., p. 23. It would be interesting to establish the percentage of *ḥadīths* in Ibn Ḥabīb's works and their function in his legal thinking. Ibn Ḥabīb made use of *ḥadīth* material in the *fatwàs* given in favour of his brother Hārūn, accused of blasphemy: see Fierro, *La heterodoxia* . . ., 5.5.

[35]) See *MS*, II, 216–26.

[36]) Ibn al-Faraḍī says that Ibn Ḥabīb collected *ḥadīth al-nabī wa-l-ṣaḥāba wa-l-tābi'īn*. Ibn Ḥabīb also wrote a book entitled *Gharīb al-ḥadīth* in order to emulate the homonymous work by Abū 'Ubayd (d. 223/837): see Makki, *Ensayo* . . ., p. 266.

[37]) *wa-kāna lā yafhamu ṭuruqa-hu wa-yuṣaḥḥifu l-asmā' wa-yaḥtaŷŷu bi-l-manākīr wa-kāna ahl zamāni-hi yansubūna-hu ilà l-kadhib wa-lā yarḍawna-hu*. See also *Madārik*, IV, 129–31 for more critical remarks, referring mainly to his carelessness in the formal aspects of learning (*kāna yatasāhalu fī samā' i-hi wa-yaḥmilu 'alà ṭarīq al-ijāza akthar riwāyati-hi*).

[38]) Almost all of Ibn Ḥabīb's contemporaries are described in this way: *lā 'ilm la-hu bi-l-ḥadīth*; they were however experts in *fiqh, masā'il, shurūṭ* . . . The exceptions are: Muḥammad b. 'Īsà al-A'shà (d. c. 221/835) who studied with Ibn 'Uyayna and Wakī' (*Ta'rīkh*, n. 1100; *Bughya*, n. 212; *Madārik*, IV, 114–6); 'Abbās al-Mu'allim, who transmitted from Abū Ṣāliḥ (*Ta'rīkh*, n. 877); Dāwūd b. Ja'far b. al-Ṣaghīr, already mentioned (see note 11 and *Ta'rīkh*, n. 423; *Jadhwa*, n. 430; *Bughya*, n. 735; *Madārik*, III, 346; *Dībāj*, I, 359). Two people are remembered specifically for their transmission of a *ḥadīth*: Duḥaym, who studied with Ādam b. Abī Iyās al-'Asqalānī (d. 220/835) and who taught Ibn Waḍḍāḥ a *ḥadīth* on the excelences of the *ribāṭ* of 'Asqalān (*Ta'rīkh*, n. 429); and Yaḥyà b. Yazīd al-Azdi, who taught the same Ibn Waḍḍāḥ a *ḥadīth al-wara'* (*Ta'rīkh*, n. 1552).

able to compare what they had learnt to Ibn Ḥabīb's transmissions and the latter's weaknesses were then noticed. For example, Ibn Waḍḍāḥ, one of Ibn Ḥabīb's pupils, criticised the latter's way of transmitting from Asad b. Mūsà, way that implied that *qirā'a or samā'* had taken place, when Asad had not even granted the *ijāza* to Ibn Ḥabīb.[39]) It seems that Ibn Waḍḍāḥ did not transmit from his teacher on account of this and similar faults.[40])

Despite the fact that Ibn Ḥabīb fell short of the standards of classical *ḥadīth* criticism, he must be recognized as the actual introducer of *ḥadīth* literature into al-Andalus. Thanks to his activity, by the end of the first half of the 3rd/9th century a good amount of prophetic traditions were known in al-Andalus. This *ḥadīth* material was of a not strictly legal nature unlike that found in the *Muwaṭṭa'*.[41])

2. *Second phase*

The *corpus* of *ḥadīth* introduced in the first half of the 3rd/9th century came from Egyptian and Medinese traditionists. There is no evidence that in this period direct contact with 'Irāq took place, which is worth pointing out as 'Irāq was the most active centre in the *'ilm al-ḥadīth*.[42]) Ibn Ḥabīb and his contemporaries, as well as the previous generations, limited their *riḥla* to Egypt and the Ḥijāz. The reason might be sought in the hostile relationship between the Umayyad emirate in al-Andalus and the 'Abbāside caliphate,[43]) a situation that started to change in the days of 'Abd al-Raḥmān

---

[39]) See *Ta'rīkh*, I, 226–7; *Madārik*, IV 129–31; *MS*, II, 177. Ibn Waḍḍāḥ's criticism was not directed to the contents but to the "form" of the transmission: in al-Shāṭibī's *al-I'tiṣām* (2 vols., Beirut s. d.), II, 16, there is a transmission Ibn Ḥabīb < Asad, which corresponds exactly to Ibn Waḍḍāḥ's *K. al-bida'*, III, 1, with the *isnād* Ibn Waḍḍāḥ < Ibn Abī Maryam < Asad b. Mūsà.

[40]) See *Madārik*, IV, 129 and cf. *Tahdhīb*, VI, 390. Only three of Ibn Ḥabīb's works are mentioned by Ibn Khayr in his *Fahrasa*, I, 202, 265, 290.

[41]) It is worth noting that al-Andalus seems to have lacked the *quṣṣāṣ* who were so active in other parts of the Islamic world. This fact struck al-Muqaddasī in the 4th/10th century. It would seem that legal works were the first to be introduced in al-Andalus to judge by the research started by M. Marín and myself on intellectual activity in al-Andalus during the Umayyad period: see a preview in our "La production intellectuelle dans al-Andalus: ouvrages et transmissions (ss. II/VIII–IV/X)", forthcoming.

[42]) Juynboll, *Muslim Tradition*, pp. 45–66.

[43]) I wonder if the importance of Asad b. Mūsà's teachings during this period in al-Andalus was due to his Umayyad genealogy (he was a descendant of the caliph al-Walīd b. 'Abd al-Malik). His transmissions seem to have dealt mainly with ascetic and eschatological matters: were some of the latter related to the fall of the

II when al-Andalus was opened to ʿIrāqī influences.[44]) It was in fact under ʿAbd al-Raḥmān II that Baqī b. Makhlad and Ibn Waḍḍāḥ (contemporaries of the authors of the six books) made their *riḥla* to the East and met the ʿIrāqī traditionists.

2.1. Baqī b. Makhlad (d. 276/889)[45])

Baqī b. Makhlad (a *mawlà* from Qurṭuba) travelled twice to the East, staying away from al-Andalus for thirty five years (from 218/833 to 253/867). During this period, he studied with about 284 teachers, half of them ʿIrāqīs[46]) and among them the great names of the *ʿilm al-ḥadīth* like Aḥmad b. Ḥanbal, Yaḥyà b. Maʿīn, Abū Bakr b. Abī Shayba . . . When he returned to al-Andalus in the days of the *amīr* Muḥammad (238/852–273/886), Baqī brought with him several Eastern works: al-Shāfiʿī's writings (the *Risāla* and the *K. al-fiqh al-kabīr*, probably including the *K. ikhtilāf Mālik wa-l-Shāfiʿī*[47]), Ibn Abī Shayba's *Muṣannaf*,[48]) the *Sīrat ʿUmar b. ʿAbd al-ʿAzīz* written by Aḥmad b. Ibrāhīm al-Dawraqī (d. 246/860) and Khalīfa b. Khayyāṭ's *Taʾrīkh* and *Ṭabaqāt*. Baqī also transmitted Mālik's *Muwaṭṭaʾ*, but he gave preference to the Eastern *riwāyas* by Abū Muṣʿab (d. 242/856) and Yaḥyà b. ʿAbd Allāh b. Bukayr (d. 231/845), disregarding the *riwāya* by Yaḥyà b. Yaḥyà al-Laythī. Al-Laythī's sons, ʿUbayd Allāh and Yaḥyà, who were among the leading Malikite *fuqahāʾ*, resented Baqī's attitude and became his enemies.

Baqī was more than a mere transmitter. Among the works he wrote, Ibn Ḥazm, in his *Risāla*,[49]), particularly praised the *Tafsīr al-Qurʾān* and the *Musnad*. This latter work was actually a *Musnad/Muṣannaf*: the traditions

---

Umayyads and their future uprising? Traditions in this sense seem to have been used by ʿAbd al-Raḥmān III in order to give support to his adoption of the caliphal title; unfortunately, they are not preserved: see Fierro, "Sobre la adopción del título califal por ʿAbd al-Raḥmān III", *Sharq al-Andalus*, forthcoming.

[44]) See HEM, I, 254–78 and Makki, *Ensayo* . . ., pp. 172 and 178–208.

[45]) His life and works have been recently studied by Marín, al-ʿUmarī and Avila.

[46]) See the list of these teachers in Avila, "Nuevos datos . . .", pp. 339–67, data obtained from the ms. of Ibn Ḥārith al-Khushanī's *Akhbār*. Ibn Ḥabīb is not mentioned.

[47]) See Brunschvig, "Polémiques . . .", pp. 75–82.

[48]) The quotations of Baqī by Ibn Ḥazm seem to come all of them from this *Muṣannaf*: see those quotations in al-ʿUmarī's work, pp. 169–78. Baqī's *riwāya* is preserved in some mss. of Ibn Abī Shayba's *Muṣannaf* like, for instance, the ms. Laleli n. 626 in Sulaymāniya Library.

[49]) *Nafḥ*, III. 168–9, trans., pp. 75–6.

were arranged both according to the Companions who transmitted them (*'alà l-rijāl*) and according to the chapters of the law (*'alà l-abwāb*). Ibn Ḥazm states that Baqī was the first to use this system, which does not seem very useful for practical purposes: maybe this was one of the reasons accounting for its lack of success even among the Andalusians.[50]) Apparently, only the index of the *Musnad* has been preserved. It contains the names of the Companions quoted by Baqī, as well as the number of their transmissions.[51]) The scope of this work can be valued through the following figures:

1,013 Companions quoted (according to Ibn Ḥazm they were more than 1,300) with a total amount of 30,969 *ḥadīths*; as examples, one can mention that the transmissions from Abū Hurayra were 5,374, 2,210 from 'Ā'isha, 142 from Abū Bakr, 537 from 'Umar b. al-Khaṭṭāb, 164 from 'Uthmān, 586 from 'Alī, 163 from Mu'āwiya b. Abī Sufyān.

It was therefore on a sound basis that Ibn al-Faraḍī could say that Baqī *mala'a l-Andalus ḥadīthan wa-riwāyatan.* On his part, Abū 'Abd al-Malik b. 'Abd al-Barr pointed out: *kāna Baqī awwal man kaththara l-ḥadīth bi-l-Andalus wa-nashara-hu.*[52]) Baqī was in fact considered, more than any other of his contemporary traditionists, the foremost representative of the *ahl al-ḥadīth* of his age; his *Musnad/Muṣannaf* shows that his aim was to build the legal system on *ḥadīth,* in the same way that the Shāfi'ites and the Ḥanbalites had started to do. It is thus not surprising that Baqī's name was included in the Shāfi'ite and Ḥanbalite *ṭabaqāt,* whilst being absent from the Malikite *ṭabaqāt.*

2.2. Muḥammad b. Waḍḍāḥ (d. 287/900)[53])

The biography of Ibn Waḍḍāḥ, the other scholar credited with having introduced the *'ilm al-ḥadīth* into al-Andalus, has several points of coincidence with Baqī's. Like him, he was of *mawlà* origin (his grandfather was a *mawlà mu'taq* of the first Umayyad *amīr*) and travelled twice to the East.

---

[50]) According to Ibn Khayr's *Fahrasa,* I, 140, the only disciple of Baqī who transmitted this work was 'Abd Allāh b. Yūnus (d. 330/941). Another one, 'Abd Allāh b. Muḥammad b. Ḥusayn, known as Ibn Akhī Rabī' (d. 318/930), wrote its *Mukhtaṣar.*

[51]) See Marín, "Baqī . . .", pp. 204–8 for a list of the extant mss. and al-'Umarī's edition, with a comparison between Baqī's and Ibn Ḥanbal's works.

[52]) *Siyar,* XIII, 291.

[53]) His life and work have been studied by Mu'ammar in his monograph (see my review in *Sharq al-Andalus* III (1986), pp. 261–5) and by myself as an introduction to a new edition of his *K. al-bida'.*

The aim of his first *riḥla* was to collect information about the ascetics and in its course he became interested in *ḥadīth*. His second *riḥla* had the only aim of learning *ḥadīth* and he took it seriously, as we are told that he studied with 265 teachers, sharing many of them with Baqī; unlike the latter, however, Ibn Waḍḍāḥ did not visit Baṣra. After his return to al-Andalus (towards the year 245/859), Ibn Waḍḍāḥ, like Baqī, transmitted many Oriental works, the most important being the *Muṣannaf* by Wakī' b. al-Jarrāḥ (d. 197/812), *al-Jāmi' al-kabīr* by Sufyān al-Thawrī (d. 161/778), the *Musnad* by Ibn Abī Shayba (d. 235/849),[54]) the *K. al-siyar* by al-Fazārī,[55]) the *K. faḍl al-jihād* by Ibn al-Mubārak (d. 181/797).

But the importance of Ibn Waḍḍāḥ as a transmitter lies (and in this respect the similarity with Baqī stops) in his *riwāyas* of Malikite works, especially Mālik's *Muwaṭṭa'* (in the recension by Yaḥyà b. Yaḥyà) and Saḥnūn's *Mudawwana*. His *riwāya* of the latter was crucial in the spreading of Saḥnūn's work in al-Andalus.[56]) As opposed to Baqī, Ibn Waḍḍāḥ has an outstanding place in the Malikite *ṭabaqāt*; his training as a traditionist enabled him to correct the faults found in the *isnāds* of Yaḥyà b. Yaḥyà's *riwāya* of the *Muwaṭṭa'*.[57]) It is in fact in the field of the *'ilm al-rijāl* that Ibn Waḍḍāḥ seems to have excelled, being quoted as an expert by Ibn Ḥajar al-'Asqalānī. Also, as opposed to Baqī, he is not remembered as the compiler of a *Musnad* or a *Muṣannaf*; he wrote mainly biographical works like the *K. al-'ubbād wa-l-'awābid*, the *Tasmiyat rijāl 'Abd Allāh b. Wahb*, the *Manāqib Mālik b. Anas* and the *Sīrat 'Umar b. 'Abd al-'Azīz*, all of them lost. His only works preserved are his *K. al-bida'*, where he collected transmissions from the Umayyad traditionist settled in Egypt Asad b. Mūsà (d. 212/827), and his *K. al-naẓar ilà Allāh ta'ālà*.[58])

As opposed again to Baqī, his knowledge of *ḥadīth* was considered suspect, especially by his pupil Aḥmad b. Khālid (d. 322/934), who accused Ibn Waḍḍāḥ of rejecting many *ḥadīths* in cases where their authenticity was well established; he was also accused of making many mistakes which spread under his authority (*wa-kāna Ibn Waḍḍāḥ kathīran mā yaqūlu*

[54]) This *Musnad* is preserved in Topkapi Library, ms. M. 290; in the *riwāya*, Ibn Waḍḍāḥ does not appear.

[55]) See M. Muranyi, "Das *Kitāb al-Siyar* von Abū Isḥāq al-Fazārī", *JSAI* VI (1985), pp. 63–97: the ms. studied contains Ibn Waḍḍāḥ's *riwāya*.

[56]) See Fórneas's article.

[57]) These corrections have been preserved in the ms. of Ibn Ḥārith al-Khushanī's *Akhbār*: see Mu'ammar, *Muḥammad b. Waḍḍāḥ* . . ., pp. 347–8.

[58]) See on the extant ms. M. Muranyi, "Fragmente aus der Bibliothek des Abū l-'Arab al-Tamīmī (st. 333/944–5) in der Handschriftensammlung von Qairawān. Qairawāner miscellaneen I", *ZDMG* 136 (1986), pp. 512–35.

laysa hādhā min kalām al-nabī fī shay' huwa thābit min kalāmi-hi wa-la-hu khaṭa' kathīr maḥfūẓ 'an-hu). This criticism may be associated with the ambiguity of Ibn Waḍḍāḥ's position among the *ahl al-ḥadīth* and with his conciliatory attitude towards the Malikite *ahl al-ra'y*. As we shall see, this position influenced his behaviour during the process carried out by the Malikites against Baqī. This ambiguity is also evident in the fact that, although a traditionist, Ibn Waḍḍāḥ was against al-Shāfi'ī, having transmitted in al-Andalus that he was *ghayr thiqa*.

In spite of all the differences between Baqī and Ibn Waḍḍāḥ, both of them appear to have been the first scholars to introduce the *'ilm al-ḥadīth* into al-Andalus and, as in the case of 'Abd al-Malik b. Ḥabīb, the *awā'il* granting them this pioneering role must be accepted as true statements.

II. The confrontation between the *ahl al-ra'y* and the *ahl al-ḥadīth*

1. The persecution of the traditionists

The Malikite *fuqahā'* contemporaries of Baqī and Ibn Waḍḍāḥ are described in the following ways:

– "people of the *ra'y* and of the imitation who refused to have anything to do with *ḥadīth*, did not use the sciences of the verification and were against the enlargement of knowledge";[59])
– "among the Andalusians the *ra'y* of Mālik and his pupils prevailed, together with the study of the *responsa* found in the *Mudawwana*; they displayed enmity against the traditionists and did not accept them";[60])
– "the imitation became their religion and the emulation their conviction. Whenever someone came from the East with (new) knowledge, they prevented him from spreading it and humiliated him, unless he went into hiding among them acting as a Malikite and put his knowledge in a position of subordination".[61])

---

[59]) *"aṣḥāb al-ra'y wa-l-taqlīd al-zāhidūn fī l-ḥadīth al-fārrūn an 'ulūm al-taḥqīq al-muqṣirūn 'an al-tawassu' fī l-ma'rifa"*: Ibn Ḥayyān, *Muqtabas*, p. 248 and Ibn 'Idhārī, *Bayān*, II, 109–10; cf. *Siyar*, XIII, 290–1: *kāna'ilmu-hum bi-l-masā'il wa-madhhab Mālik wa-kāna Baqī yuftī bi-l-athar.*

[60]) *"wa-innamā kāna l-ghālib 'alà ahli-hā . . . ra'y Mālik wa-aṣḥābi-hi wa-l-tafaqquh fī l-masā'il al-mudawwaniya wa-kānū yanṣubūna li-ahl al-ḥadīth wa-lā yarḍawna-hum"*: Ibn Ḥayyān, *Muqtabas*, p. 264 and cf. Turki, *Polémiques . . .*, pp. 14–8 and 48–9.

[61]) *"fa-ṣāra l-taqlīd dīna-hum wa-l-iqtidā' yaqīna-hum wa-kullamā jā'a aḥad min al-Mashriq bi-'ilm dafa'ū fī ṣadri-hi wa-ḥaqqaru min amri-hi illā an yastatira 'inda-*

One of the scholars who aroused the antagonism of the Malikites was Baqī b. Makhlad, because of his introduction of "transmissions in disagreement with the (Malikite) *ra'y*" (*al-riwāyāt al-mukhtalifa li-ra'yi-him*),[62]) because of his loathing of *taqlīd* (*lā yuqallidu aḥadan min ahl al-'ilm*)[63]) and because of his adherence to the *madhhab al-ḥadīth wa-l-naẓar.*[64]) None of these attitudes is ascribed to Ibn Waḍḍāḥ. Among the transmissions introduced by Baqī that won him the hostility of the Malikites, the sources emphasized al-Shāfi'ī's *Risāla* and Ibn Abī Shayba's *Muṣannaf*. The reaction against this latter work was very strong: one of the leading Malikites of Qurṭuba, Aṣbagh b. Khalīl (d. 273/886), went so far as to say that he had rather be buried with a pig head than with Ibn Abī Shayba's *Muṣannaf*. This Aṣbagh b. Khalīl was a staunch follower of Ibn al-Qāsim's *ra'y* (*kāna muta'aṣṣiban li-ra'y aṣḥāb Mālik wa-li-bn al-Qāsim min bayni-him*). He was without doubt one of the Malikites who started the persecution against Baqī presenting charges of *bid'a, ilḥād* and *zandaqa* and asking for the death penalty. Several witnesses supported these accusations and, among them, Ibn Waḍḍāḥ accused Baqī of transmitting *manākīr*. In fear for his life, Baqī went into hiding and planned to escape from al-Andalus. Eventually, however, the support given to him by the *amīr* Muḥammad saved his life and he remained in Qurṭuba.[65])

Baqī was not the only persecuted traditionist. A friend of his, Muḥammad b. 'Abd al-Salām al-Khushanī (d. 286/899), a descendant from the Companion Abū Tha'laba al-Khushanī, went through a similar experience. He had studied in the East with pupils of al-Aṣma'ī (d. 213/829) and Abū 'Ubayd al-Qāsim b. Sallām (d. 224/838) and he introduced several works into al-Andalus like the *Muṣannaf* by Sufyān b. 'Uyayna, the *Sīra* by Ibn Hishām, the *Ta'rīkh* by al-Fallās and the *K. nāsikh al-Qur'ān wa-mansūkhi-hi* by Abū 'Ubayd. He was imprisoned because of this latter work:[66]) accused of stating that some Qur'ānic verses had been abrogated by other verses and some *ḥadīths* had also been abrogated by other *ḥadīths*, al-Khushanī tried to make the *ṣāḥib al-sūq* understand that this doctrine was

---

hum bi-l-mālikīya wa-yaj'ala mā 'inda-hu min 'ulūm 'alà rasm al-taba'īya": Ibn al-'Arabī, *'Awāṣim*, II, 490–1.

[62]) Avila, "Nuevos datos . . .", p. 333.

[63]) Ibid., p. 331.

[64]) Ibid. The followers of al-Shāfi'ī are described in the Andalusian biographical dictionaries as followers of the *madhhab al-ḥujja wa-l-naẓar*.

[65]) See a detailed account of this trial in my *La heterodoxia* . . ., 6.2.

[66]) It looks as if the Andalusian *'ulamā'* were not yet acquainted with the doctrine of *al-nāsikh wa-l-mansūkh*; however, 'Abd al-Malik b. Ḥabīb is said to have written a *K. al-nāsikh wa-l-mansūkh*.

found in the same Qur'ān, quoting the verse II, 100/106, but without success. Again it was only through the *amīr* Muḥammad's support that he was set free after spending three days in jail.[67])

2. The controversy on *rafʿ al-yadayn fī l-ṣalāt*

The persecution against Baqī and Ibn ʿAbd al-Salām al-Khushanī shows that the introduction of the works and the doctrine of the *ahl al-ḥadīth* was held to be a threat to the Malikite doctrine predominant in al-Andalus and it was so because of the divergences between both of them. We have information on a specific case of *ikhtilāf* between the Andalusian *ahl al-ra'y* and *ahl al-ḥadīth* and it concerns the raising of one's hands during the prayer (*rafʿ al-yadayn fī l-ṣalāt*). The practice adopted in al-Andalus was based on the doctrine of Ibn al-Qāsim: according to him, it was lawful to raise one's hands only at the beginning of prayer (in the *takbīrat al-iḥrām*); he based this doctrine on the authority of Mālik without adducing any *ḥadīth* in its support. The same doctrine of Ibn al-Qāsim is held by the Ḥanafites and it can be backed by some *ḥadīths* (with Kūfan *isnāds*) that were quoted by Saḥnūn in his *Mudawwana* as transmissions from Ibn Wahb and Wakīʿ. The traditionists from Qurṭuba Baqī b. Makhlad, Ibn ʿAbd al-Salām al-Khushanī and Qāsim b. Muḥammad (d. 277/890),[68]) however, used to raise their hands in each *takbīr* of the *rukūʿ*, as the Shāfiʿites and the Ḥanbalites do on the authority of a *ḥadīth* transmitted by the Companion ʿAbd Allāh b. ʿUmar, according to which the Prophet raised his hands in those moments as well as in the *takbīrat al-iḥrām*. This *ḥadīth* was quoted, among others, by Sufyān b. ʿUyayna and by Mālik in his *Muwaṭṭa'*. This latter fact, no doubt, must have been emphasized by the aforementioned traditionists, together with the fact that many Companions were known to have acted according to Ibn ʿUmar's *ḥadīth*; on the other hand, this *ḥadīth* was considered the abrogant of the *ḥadīths* with Kūfan *isnāds* in which the Prophet did not raise his hands in the prayer except once (*illā marra*).

The polemic between the *ahl al-ḥadīth* and the Malikites seems to have been very harsh. One of the latter, the already mentioned Aṣbagh b. Khalīl, went so far as to forge a *ḥadīth* which ascribed the limitation of the raising of the hands to the *takbīrat al-iḥrām* not only to the Prophet but also to the first four caliphs. Both *matn* and *isnād* of this forgery were very defective and Aṣbagh was mocked without mercy.

It is worth remarking the fact that both the position of the *ahl al-ra'y* and that of the *ahl al-ḥadīth* could be supported by *ḥadīth*. It is therefore

[67]) See a detailed account of this trial in my *La heterodoxia* . . ., 6.3.

[68]) On this descendant of a *mawlà* of al-Walīd b. ʿAbd al-Malik see note 75.

more striking that Aṣbagh felt the need to forge one in order to give strength to the doctrine of Ibn al-Qāsim, of whom he was a convinced follower. This fact seems to point out that Aṣbagh knew that doctrine only as an opinion (*ra'y*) of the Egyptian Malikite, unaware of the *ḥadīths* collected in the *Mudawwana*, and as a matter of fact Aṣbagh is not credited with its transmission. Having realized how difficult it was to oppose the Prophet's authority with the authority of a Malikite scholar, he tried to reinforce the latter's doctrine ascribing it to the Prophet. As Aṣbagh knew nothing of the *standards* of the *'ilm al-ḥadīth*, his forgery could not escape the criticism of the experts. Despite this failure, the doctrine of Ibn al-Qāsim was not abandoned: it lasted in al-Andalus until the Naṣrite period with occasional reappearances of the polemic that did not succeed in putting an end to the Andalusian Malikite practice.[69])

3. The coexistence of the *ahl al-ra'y* and the *ahl al-ḥadīth*

From the moment in which the *amīr* Muḥammad decided to support Baqī and al-Khushanī onwards, there is no evidence that the Malikites tried to persecute the traditionists again. The reasons of the *amīr*'s decision are not clear. It is possible to understand it as a means to weaken the power of the Malikite *fuqahā'*, which had been increasing since the days of 'Abd al-Raḥmān II.[70]) Some sources tend to present the *amīr* Muḥammad as being in favour of the doctrine of the *ahl al-ḥadīth*; however, he did not make any attempt at replacing the Malikites by the traditionists, neither as *ḥukkām* nor as *fuqahā' mushāwarūn*. The same situation can be observed during the rule of the *amīrs* 'Abd Allāh and 'Abd al-Raḥmān III[71]) with only two exceptions: a *ṣāḥib al-wathā'iq* and a *qāḍī*, both of them Shāfi'ites, though acting as Malikites in their offices.[72]) This duality appears very neatly in the activity of two scholars of this period.

One of them is Ibn Waḍḍāḥ. We have already seen that in spite of his training as a tradidionist and notwithstanding the similarity of his back-

[69]) See Fierro, "La polémique a propos de *raf' al-yadayn fī l-ṣalāt* . . .".

[70]) See Monés's article.

[71]) The *fuqahā' mushāwarūn* during the Umayyad emirate were Malikites: see M. Marín, "*Šrà* et *ahl al-šūrà* dans al-Andalus", *Studia Islamica* LXII (1985), pp. 25–51.

[72]) The former will be dealt with in the following pages; for the latter, Aslam b. 'Abd al-'Azīz (d. 319/931), see *Ta'rīkh*, n. 278; *Jadhwa*, n. 322; *Bughya*, n. 571; *Quḍāt*, pp. 155–60/225–37. The case of Mundhir b. Sa'īd al-Ballūṭī, judge of Qurṭuba in the days of the caliph 'Abd al-Raḥmān III and credited with having been a Ẓāhirite and a Mu'tazilite, even a Shī'ite, is worth being studied in a monograph.

ground with Baqī's he was ready to witness against him during his trial. This attitude could be explained as originating from the fear of being himself prosecuted or from a likely rivalry or envy towards Baqī. But it can also be explained as the attitude of a "moderate" traditionist who was at the same time a Malikite and who did not want to put an end to the legal practice predominant in al-Andalus. This latter explanation seems to be supported by the following portrait of Ibn Waḍḍāḥ made by one of his pupils: "I can not think of a better comparison for Ibn Waḍḍāḥ than this: he was like the good doctor who faces every disease with the best treatment in each case. In fact, when the *ahl al-ra'y* came to Ibn Waḍḍāḥ, he gave them an answer in agreement with the *ra'y*, but if it was the *ahl al-ḥadīth* who came to him, he gave them an answer in agreement with the *ḥadīth*".[73])

The second example concerns Qāsim b. Muḥammad b. Qāsim b. Sayyār, already mentioned as having taken part in the polemic on *raf' al-yadayn fī l-ṣalāt* as a member of the *ahl al-ḥadīth*. An Umayyad *mawlà* from Qurṭuba, he travelled twice to the East, being absent from al-Andalus for eighteen years. During this period, he studied, among others, with the Egyptian pupils of al-Shāfi'ī, al-Muzanī and al-Rabī' b. Sulaymān. He was considered a Shāfi'ite by his biographers, but Ibn Abī Dulaym (d. 351/962) included his name in his Malikite *ṭabaqāt*,[74]) explaining this decision on the grounds that Qāsim delivered his legal opinions in agreement with the Malikite *madhhab* and only acted otherwise when asked for a legal opinion in agreement with the Shāfi' ite *madhhab*. Qāsim justified this attitude, stating that he felt obliged to follow the *madhhab* predominant in al-Andalus.[75]) Thus, for instance, being *ṣāḥib al-wathā'iq*, the *amīr* 'Abd Allāh asked his advice on the penalty of the heretic (*qatl al-zindīq*); two other scholars were also asked, Baqī b. Makhlad and the Malikite Muḥammad b. Sa'īd b. al-Mulawwan. Baqī delivered an opinion in favour of granting the *zindīq* the possibility of repentance (*istitāba*), an opinion that was against the doctrine of Mālik in the *Muwaṭṭa'*. The Malikite Ibn al-Mulawwan agreed with

---

[73]) *"mā kuntu ushabbihu Muḥammad b. Waḍḍāḥ . . . illā bi-l-ṭabīb al-'ayn alladhī yuqābilu kull dā' bi-mā yuṣliḥu-hu min al-dawā' kāna ya'tī-hi ahl al-ra'y fa-yufīdu-hum fī bāb al-ra'y wa-ya'tīhi ahl al-ḥadīth fa-yufīdu-hum fī bāb al-ḥadīth"*: Ibn Ḥārith al-Khushanī, *Akhbār*, fs. 154a–154b; cf. Mu'ammar, *Muḥammad b. Waḍḍāḥ . . .*, p. 93.

[74]) This work is lost: see Pons, *Ensayo . . .*, p. 391.

[75]) See *Ta'rīkh*, n. 1047; *Jadhwa*, n. 1293; *Madārik*, IV, 446–8, particularly p. 447: *kāna yuftī bi-madhhab Mālik . . . qāla Aḥmad b. Khālid qultu la-hu arā-ka tuftī l-nās bi-mā lā ta'taqidu hādhā lā yaḥillu la-ka qāla innamā yas'alūna-nī bi-madhhab jarà fī l-balad fa-'araftu fa-aftaytu-hum bi-hi wa-law sa'alū-nī 'an madhhabī akhbartu-hum bi-hi.*

Baqī. Qāsim, on the contrary, delivered an opinion against the *istitāba*, agreeing therefore with Mālik and disagreeing with al-Shāfi'ī.[76]) Baqī strongly disapproved of this behaviour, even though a similar compromising attitude is ascribed to him by some sources.[77])

These examples show that there was a sort of compromise between theory and practice on the part of the traditionists.[78]) There is no evidence however that attempts were made to reconcile the doctrines of the *ahl al-ra'y* and the *ahl al-ḥadīth*.[79]) The traditionists found themselves forced to accept their inability to change the predominant *'amal* based on the doctrines of Mālik's pupils, not always in agreement with those of the teacher. The Malikites, on the other hand, stopped persecuting the traditionists once they had abandoned any attempt to change the legal practice. This compromise was perhaps helped by the fact that it seems that in the field of dogma there were not discrepancies between them: for example, Baqī b. Makhlad and the Malikite 'Ubayd Allāh b. Yaḥyà b. Yaḥyà al-Laythī fought the Mu'tazilite doctrines that had started to flourish in the days of the *amīr* Muḥammad.[80])

The presence of Shāfi'ites towards the end of the 3rd/9th century did not stimulate any noticeable activity in the field of the refutation of al-Shāfi'ī's doctrine by the Malikites.[81]) This can be explained by the scarcity of those Shāfi'ites and by the sparse spreading of al-Shāfi'ī's works in al-Andalus.[82]) On the other hand, the Malikites could not avoid recognising the increasing authority won by the traditions of the Prophet: the case of Aṣbagh b. Khalīl and his failed attempt at forging a *ḥadīth* must be remembered in this context. So, we find the Andalusian Malikites getting interested in the *ḥadīth* material of the *Muwaṭṭa'* and writing books like these: one

---

[76]) See a detailed account of this *mushāwara* in my *La heterodoxia* . . ., 7.1.

[77]) See Avila, "Nuevos datos . . .", pp. 331 and 323.

[78]) The *fatwà* of the Malikite Ibn al-Mulawwan in favour of the *istitāba* shows that some of the Malikites too were predisposed to the compromise.

[79]) No effort was made by the Malikites in the field of *uṣūl al-fiqh* till the end of the 4th/10th century: see Turki's study in his *Polémiques* . . .

[80]) See Fierro, *La heterodoxia* . . ., 6.4.

[81]) We only know of a *radd 'alà l-Shāfi'ī* written by Yūsuf b. Yaḥyà al-Maghāmī (d. 288/900), the most important transmitter of Ibn Ḥabīb's *Wāḍiḥa*, and he wrote it during his stay in North Africa, as did another Andalusian, Yaḥyà b. 'Umar (died in the same year), who lived in Qayrawān. The *'ulamā'* of Ifrīqiya were more active writing against al-Shāfi'ī: see the recent edition of Muḥammad b. al-Labbād al-Qayrawānī's (d. 333/944) *K. al-radd 'alà l-Shāfi'ī*, Tunis 1404/1986.

[82]) Ibn Khayr only knows one of al-Shāfi'ī's works, his *K. mukhtalif al-ḥadīth*: *Fahrasa*, I, 196. It was transmitted by Aslam b. 'Abd al-'Azīz (see note 72).

K. rijāl al-Muwaṭṭa',[83]) two *Musnad ḥadīth al-Muwaṭṭa'*,[84]) one *K. gharā'ib ḥadīth Mālik b. Anas mimmā laysa fī l-Muwaṭṭa'*,[85]) titles all of them absent in the previous production.

Neither do the Andalusian traditionists appear very active in writing refutations of their opponents. We only know of a work written by Qāsim b. Muḥammad, entitled *al-Īḍāḥ fī l-radd alà l-muqallidīn*; he also wrote a tract on the *khabar al-wāḥid*, a polemical issue between the Shāfi'ites and the Malikites.

If the polemical activity does not seem very important, there was, conversely, a great activity in the introduction of *ḥadīth* literature. The works of Abū Dāwūd and al-Nasā'ī were already known in the beginning of the 4th/10th century. The *Sunan* of the former was very much appreciated[86]) and was used as a model by Muḥammad b. 'Abd al-Malik b. Ayman (d. 330/941) and by Qāsim b. Aṣbagh (d. 340/951) when they wrote their *Muṣannafs*, now lost.[87]) Two Andalusians studied directly from al-Nasā'ī his *Sunan*, the Umayyad Ibn al-Aḥmar (d. 358/968) and Muḥammad b. Qāsim b. Muḥammad b. Sayyār (d. 328/939). In one of Ibn al-Aḥmar's *riwāyas*, the *Faḍā'il 'Alī b. Abī Ṭālib* were missing and maybe this omission should be related not only to his being an Umayyad, but also to the fact that in the same year in which he studied the *Sunan* (297/909) in Egypt, the Fāṭimides became the new masters of Ifrīqiya.[88]) The works of al-Bukhārī, Muslim and al-Tirmidhī were not introduced until the second half of the 4th/10th century. Al-Tirmidhī's *Sunan* were not so much appreciated as the other works: Ibn Ḥazm, in his *Risāla*, only mentions the collections of al-Bukhārī, Muslim, Abū Dāwūd and al-Nasā'ī, stating that the *Musnad/Muṣannaf* of Baqī could well compete with them.

We have seen that in the second half of the 3rd/9th century the *Muṣannafs* of Wakī' b. al-Jarrāḥ, Ibn Abī Shayba and Sufyān b. 'Uyayna had already been introduced. Later on, those of 'Abd al-Razzāq,[89]) Ḥammād b.

---

[83]) Written by Yaḥyà b. Ibrāhīm b. Muzayn (d. 259/873): see *Fahrasa*, I, 92–3; Makki, *Ensayo* . . ., p. 137; GAS, I, 473.

[84]) Written by Aḥmad b. Khālid (d. 322/934) and Muḥammad b. 'Abd Allāh b. 'Ayshūn (d. 341/952): see *Madārik*, IV, 174–8 and VI, 172–3, also Makki, *Ensayo* . . ., pp. 200–1.

[85]) Written by Qāsim b. Aṣbagh (d. 340/951): see Ibn Ḥazm, *Risāla* in *Nafḥ*, III, 169, trans., pp. 77–8.

[86]) See *Fahrasa*, I, 103–7 and Makki, *Ensayo* . . ., p. 204, note 1.

[87]) See Ibn Ḥazm, *Risāla* in *Nafḥ*, III, 169, trans., pp. 77–8.

[88]) See *Fahrasa*, I, 110–7.

[89]) It was introduced by Aḥmad b. Khālid: see *Fahrasa*, I, 127–31.

Salama[90]) and Sa'īd b. Manṣūr[91]) followed. As regards the *Musnads*, the first to be introduced were those of Ibn Abī Shayba (already mentioned) and Asad b. Mūsà.[92]) Ibn Ḥanbal's work was not introduced until the end of the 4th/10th century.[93]) Among the *Musnads* devoted to collecting the transmissions of a single traditionist, the case of the *mu'ammar* Abū l-Dunyā 'Alī b. 'Uthmān b. Khaṭṭāb is interesting:[94]) in the year 311/923, he taught *ḥadīth* in Qayrawān to an Andalusian, Tamīm b. Muḥammad b. Aḥmad b. Tamīm (d. 369/979), pretending to be 365 years old then, so that he could easily transmit directly from Abū Bakr, 'Umar, 'Uthmān and 'Alī. Tamīm does not seem to have found any problem in accepting this claim and after his return to al-Andalus he transmitted the traditions studied with such a long-lived teacher without hesitation.[95])

The works on *gharīb al-ḥadīth* by Ibn Qutayba (d. 276/889) and Abū 'Ubayd were introduced into al-Andalus by two pupils of Ibn Waḍḍāḥ.[96]) Among the Andalusians who wrote works of this genre we may count Muḥammad b. 'Abd al-Salām al-Khushanī[97]) as well as Qāsim b. Thābit and his father Thābit b. Ḥazm (d. 313/925), from Saraqusṭa, who wrote a much praised *K. al-dalā'il.*[98])

In the first half of the 4th/10th century, the *Ṭabaqāt* of Ibn Sa'd,[99]) the *K. ḍa'īf al-rijāl* of al-Fallās[100]) and the *Ta'rīkhs* of Ibn Abī Khaythama[101])

---

[90]) It was also introduced by Aḥmad b. Khālid: see *Fahrasa*, I, 134.

[91]) It was introduced by Muḥammad b. Aḥmad b. Muḥammad b. Yaḥyà b. Mufarrij (d. 380/990): see *Fahrasa*, I, 135–6. He also introduced the transmissions of Wahb b. Munabbih: see M. J. Hermosilla, "Una versión inédita del *Kitāb bad' al-jalq wa-qiṣaṣ al-anbiyā'* en el Ms. LXIII de la Junta", *Al-Qanṭara* VI (1985), pp. 43–77, especially pp. 63–7.

[92]) It was introduced by Sa'īd b. 'Uthmān al-A'nāqī (d. 305/917): see *Fahrasa*, I, 141–2, and the study by R. G. Khoury in his edition of Asad b. Mūsa's *K. al-zuhd*, Wiesbaden 1976.

[93]) See *Fahrasa*, I, 139–40; there is no evidence of an earlier introduction.

[94]) On him see *MS*, II, 161.

[95]) See *Fahrasa*, I, 169–72.

[96]) The former was introduced by Qāsim b. Aṣbagh, and the latter by Aḥmad b. Khālid: see *Fahrasa*, I, 187–8 and 186.

[97]) See *Fahrasa*, I, 195.

[98]) See *Madārik*, V, 248 and *Fahrasa*, I, 191–4. There is still no edition of this work.

[99]) This work was introduced by Aḥmad b. Khālid: see *Fahrasa*, I, 224–5.

[100]) It was introduced by Muḥammad b. Qāsim b. Muḥammad b. Sayyār (d. 328/939): see *Fahrasa*, I, 212.

[101]) It was introduced by Qāsim b. Aṣbagh and Muḥammad b. 'Abd al-Malik b. Ayman: see *Fahrasa*, I, 206.

and Yaḥyà b. Maʿīn[102]) were also introduced. One of the scholars who introduced the latter's *Ta'rīkh*, Aḥmad b. Saʿīd b. Ḥazm (d. 350/961), wrote on his turn one of the first biographical dictionaries of Andalusian traditionists.[103]) Before him, Abū ʿAbd al-Malik b. ʿAbd al-Barr had paid attention to them in his lost *Ta'rīkh*; we have already met him as the transmitter of *awā'il* concerning the introduction of *ḥadīth* into al-Andalus. Abū ʿAbd al-Malik b. ʿAbd al-Barr was suspected to be a Shāfiʿite, which accounts for his interest in *ḥadīth*. He was a close friend of one of the sons of the caliph ʿAbd al-Raḥmān III, called ʿAbd Allāh, who is also said to have been a Shāfiʿite. This ʿAbd Allāh was accused of plotting against his father the caliph and against the latter's heir, the future al-Ḥakam II. After being imprisoned, he was beheaded in the year 338/950. In the same year, Abū ʿAbd al-Malik b. ʿAbd al-Barr, imprisoned under the same charges, died.[104]) Taking into account the few available data, it is difficult to ascertain the role played by their Shāfiʿism in these events and whether one of the aims of the plot was to change the legal *madhhab* of al-Andalus. If so, their failure goes together with the failure of Shāfiʿism in al-Andalus: its followers were always a minority and a few years after ʿAbd Allāh's death, ʿAbd al-Raḥmān III openly proclaimed Malikism as the "official" doctrine of the Peninsula; afterwards, the caliph al-Ḥakam II thought it worthwhile doing the same.[105])

ʿAbd Allāh was the author of a work entitled *al-Muskita fī faḍā'il Baqī b. Makhlad wa-l-radd ʿalà Muḥammad b. Waḍḍāḥ*. His refutation of the latter was as unsuccesful as his plot. The biographies of the scholars active between the end of the 3rd/9th century and the beginning of the 4th/10th century show that the majority of them were the pupils of Ibn Waḍḍāḥ, while the number of Baqī's pupils is considerably smaller.[106]) These figures were without doubt influenced by the fact that the Malikite scholars forbade their pupils to study with Baqī. In my study on the activities of 145 out of the 216 pupils of Ibn Waḍḍāḥ, it appears that 50% devoted themselves to *fiqh* and only 13% to *ḥadīth*. It then follows that it was not Baqī, a

---

[102]) It was introduced by Muḥammad b. ʿAbd Allāh b. ʿAyshūn and Aḥmad b. Saʿīd b. Ḥazm: see *Madārik*, VI, 172–4 and *Fahrasa*, I, 228–9.

[103]) See Pons, *Ensayo* . . ., pp. 67–8 and Ibn Ḥazm, *Risāla* in *Nafḥ*, III, 170, trans., p. 79.

[104]) See Viguera's article with a detailed account of these events.

[105]) See Fierro, *La heterodoxia* . . ., 8.4. and 9.1.

[106]) Ibn Waḍḍāḥ had 216 disciples and Baqī only 85: both of them appear as the top teachers of their age: see my study on Ibn Waḍḍāḥ, pp. 44–57 and M. Marín, "La transmisión del saber en al-Andalus (hasta 300/912)", *Al-Qanṭara* VIII (1987), pp. 87–97.

"pure" traditionist, but Ibn Waḍḍāḥ, more a Malikite than a traditionist, who eventually led the way in the introduction of the *'ilm al-ḥadīth* into al-Andalus.

Conclusions

The Iberian Peninsula was conquered towards the end of the 1st century (year 93/711) and it is only a century later when we have evidence of the actual introduction of *ḥadīth* literature into it. Claims relating to its earlier introduction are, as we have seen, to be disregarded. The material introduced by 'Abd al-Malik b. Ḥabīb was far from meeting the requirements of classical *'ilm al-ḥadīth*, especially as regards the formal aspects of the transmission. He was for this reason criticised by the protagonists of the second phase of the reception of *ḥadīth* (second half of the 3rd/9th century), Baqī b. Makhlad and Ibn Waḍḍāḥ, who, trained with 'Irāqī teachers, introduced into al-Andalus not only new material but also its science. Until that moment, *fiqh* (introduced in the second half of the 2nd/8th century) and *ḥadīth* were seen as separate and different entities: the scholars who introduced *fiqh* (mainly Malikite *fiqh*) are not mentioned in the sources as traditionists. The reception of *ḥadīth* as a structured *corpus* of legal material, over and above the limited amount of *ḥadīth* embedded in Malikite works, aroused the opposition of the Andalusian Malikites because of the threat it represented to their doctrinal teachings and to the legal practice established in al-Andalus. If the persecution of Baqī did not lead to his execution, that must be attributed to the intervention of the *amīr*, who played the role of umpire between the two groups of the *ahl al-ra'y* and the *ahl al-ḥadīth*, without replacing the former with the latter. Between the end of the 3rd/9th century and the first half of the 4th/10th century, the Shāfi'ites had a certain weight in the intellectual milieu; nevertheless, they did not succeed either in establishing their doctrine or in replacing the Malikites. The latter were, in turn, forced to pay more attention to *ḥadīth*, but they did so without introducing any substantial change in their doctrine and practice. It is only from the end of the 4th/10th century onwards that we have evidence of Malikite activity in the field of the *uṣūl al-fiqh*.

The picture drawn fits quite neatly in Schacht's study on the secondary role played by *ḥadīth* in the law-schools prior to al-Shāfi'ī, on the tensions aroused in them by the growing importance attached to prophetic traditions as the second source of law and on their final acceptance of this principle without it implying a change of their already established doctrine and practice.

Sources and Bibliography

ABBOTT, N., *Studies in Arabic literary papyri*, vol. II: Quranic commentary and tradition, Chicago 1967.

AGUADE, J., "Some remarks about sectarian movements in al-Andalus", *Studia Islamica* LXIV (1986), pp. 53–77.

– "De nuevo sobre ʿAbd al-Malik b. Ḥabīb", *Actas de las II Jornadas de Cultura Arabe e Islámica (1980)*, Madrid 1985, pp. 9–16.

– "El *Libro del escrúpulo religioso* (*Kitāb al-waraʿ*) de ʿAbdalmalik b. Ḥabīb", *Actas del XII Congreso de la UEAI* (*Málaga 1984*), Madrid 1986, pp. 17–34.

AVILA, M. L., "Nuevos datos para la biografía de Baqī b. Majlad", *Al-Qanṭara* VI (1985), pp. 321–68.

BRUNSCHVIG, R., "Polémiques médiévales autour du rite de Mālik", *Al-Andalus* XV (1950), pp. 377–435.

Bughya: see AL-ḌABBĪ

AL-ḌABBĪ (d. 599/1202), *Bughyat al-multamis fī ta'rīkh rijāl al-Andalus*, ed. F. Codera and J. Ribera, Madrid 1884–5, *BAH*, t. III.

AL-DHAHABĪ (d. 748/1348 or 753/1352), *Siyar aʿlām al-nubalā'*, 23 vols., Beirut 1401/1981–1405/1985.

– *Tadhkirat al-ḥuffāẓ*, 2 vols., Beirut s.d.

Dībāj: see IBN FARḤŪN

Fahrasa: see IBN KHAYR

FIERRO, M. I., "Los mālikíes de al-Andalus y los dos árbitros (*al-ḥakamān*)", *Al-Qanṭara* VI (1985), pp. 79–102.

– "Muʿāwiya b. Ṣāliḥ al-Ḥaḍramī al-Ḥimṣī: historia y leyenda", *Estudios onomástico-biográficos de al-Andalus*, Madrid 1988, pp. 281–411.

– "La polémique à propos de *rafʿ al-yadayn fī l-ṣalāt* dans al-Andalus", *Studia Islamica* LXV (1987), pp. 69–90.

– *La heterodoxia en al-Andalus durante el período omeya*, Madrid 1987.

FORNEAS, J. M., "Datos para un estudio de la *Mudawwana* de Saḥnūn en al-Andalus", *Actas des IV Coloquio Hispano-Tunecino* (*Palma de Mallorca 1979*), Madrid 1983, pp. 93–118.

Jadhwa: see AL-ḤUMAYDĪ.

GOLDZIHER, I., *Muslim Studies*, English trans., London 1967–71.

HEM: see LÉVI-PROVENÇAL.

AL-ḤUMAYDĪ (d. 488/1095), *Jadhwat al-muqtabis fī dhikr wulāt al-Andalus*, ed. Muḥammad b. Ṭāwīt, Cairo 1372/1952.

IBN AL-ʿARABĪ (d. 543/1148), *al-ʿAwāṣim min al-qawāṣim*, ed. ʿAmmār Ṭālibī in *Ārā' Abī Bakr b. al-ʿArabī al-kalāmiya*, 2 vols., Alger s.d.

IBN AL-FARAḌĪ (d. 403/1012), *Ta'rīkh ʿulamā' al-Andalus*, ed. F. Codera, 2 vols., Madrid 1891–2, *BAH*, t. VII–VIII.

IBN FARḤŪN (d. 799/1397), *Kitāb al-dībāj al-mudhhab fī maʿrifat aʿyān ʿulamā' al-madhhab*, 2 vols., Cairo s.d.

IBN ḤĀRITH AL-KHUSHANĪ (d. 361/971), *Kitāb al-quḍāt bi-Qurṭuba*, ed. and trans. by J. Ribera, Madrid 1914.

– *Akhbār al-fuqahā' wa-l-muḥaddithīn*, Ms. of the Royal Library of Rabat, n° 6916; ed. by M. L. Avila and L. Molina, forthcoming.

Ibn Ḥajar (d. 852/1449), *Tahdhīb al-tahdhīb*, 12 vols., Hyderabad 1325–7.

Ibn Khayr (d. 575/1179), *Fahrasa*, ed. F. Codera and J. Ribera, 2 vols., Zaragoza 1893, *BAH*, t. IX–X.

Ibn Ḥayyān (d. 469/1076), *al-Muqtabas min anbā' ahl al-Andalus*, ed. M. A. Makki, Beirut 1393/1973.

Ibn Ḥazm (d. 456/1064), *Risālat faḍā'il al-Andalus*, text in al-Maqqarī, *Nafḥ al-ṭīb*, vol. III, pp. 156–179; trans. by Ch. Pellat, "Ibn Ḥazm, bibliographe et apologiste de l'Espagne musulmane", *Al-Andalus* XIX (1954), pp. 53–102.

Ibn 'Idhārī (d. 695/1295), *Kitāb al-bayān al-mughrib fī akhbār mulūk al-Andalus wa-l-Maghrib*, ed. G. S. Colin and E. Lévi-Provençal, 2 vols., Leiden 1948–51.

Ibn al-Qūṭīya (d. 367/977), *Ta'rīkh iftitāḥ al-Andalus*, ed. and trans. by J. Ribera, Madrid 1926.

Ibn Rušd al-Jadd (d. 520/1126), *al-Bayān wa-l-taḥṣīl* (a commentary of the '*Utbiyya*), 18 vols., Beirut 1404/1984.

Ibn Sa'īd (d. 685/1286), *al-Mughrib fī ḥulà l-Maghrib* ed. S. Ḍayf, 2 vols., Cairo 1964.

Ibn Waḍḍāḥ al-Qurṭubī (d. 287/900), *Kitāb al-bida'*, nueva edición, traducción, estudio e índices por M. I. Fierro, Madrid 1988

Idris, H. R., "Réflexions sur le Malikisme sous les Omayyades d'Espagne", *Atti del 3° Congresso di Studi Arabi e Islamici (Ravello 1966)*, Naples 1967, pp. 397–414.

'Iyāḍ (d. 544/1149), *Tartīb al-madārik wa-taqrīb al-masālik li-ma'rifat a'lām madhhab Mālik*, 8 vols., Rabat s.d.

Juynboll, G. H. A., *Muslim Tradition. Studies in chronology, provenance and authorship of early "ḥadīth"*, Cambridge 1983.

Lévi-Provençal, E., *Histoire de l'Espagne musulmane*, 3 vols., Paris/Leiden 1950–3.

Lopez Ortiz, J., *La recepción de la escuela malequí en España*, Madrid 1931.

Madārik: see 'Iyāḍ.

Makki, M. A., *Ensayo sobre las aportaciones orientales en la España musulmana y su influencia en la formación de la cultura hispano-árabe*, Madrid 1968.

– "Egipto y los orígenes de la historiografía arábigo-española", *Revista del Instituto Egipcio de Estudios Islámicos* V (1957), pp. 158–248.

al-Maqqarī (d. 1041/1631), *Nafḥ al-ṭīb*, 8 vols., ed. Iḥsān 'Abbās, Beirut 1398/1968.

Marin, M., "Baqī b. Majlad y la introducción del estudio del *Ḥadīṯ* en al-Andalus", *Al-Qanṭara* I (1981), pp. 165–208.

– "*Ṣaḥāba* et *Tābi'ūn* dans al-Andalus: histoire et légende", *Studia Islamica* LIV (1981), pp. 5–49.

Mones, H., "Le rôle des hommes de religion dans l'histoire de l'Espagne musulmane jusqu'à la fin du califat", *Studia Islamica* XX (1964), pp. 47–88.

MS: see Goldziher.

Mu'ammar, N., *Muḥammad b. Waḍḍāḥ al-Qurṭubī, mu'assis madrasat al-ḥadīth bi-l-Andalus ma'a Baqī b. Makhlad*, Rabat 1983.

al-Muqaddasī (d. after 375/985), *Aḥsan al-taqāsīm*, parcial ed. and trans. by Ch. Pellat, *Description de l'Occident musulman au IVe/Xe siècle*, Alger 1950.

MURANYI, M., *Materialien zur mālikitischen Rechtsliteratur*, Wiesbaden 1984.
Nafḥ: see AL-MAQQARĪ.
PONS BOIGUES, F., *Ensayo bio-bibliográfico sobre los historiadores y geógrafos arábigo-españoles*, Madrid 1898.
Quḍāt: see IBN ḤĀRITH AL-KHUSHANĪ.
SCHACHT, J., *The Origins of Muhammadan Jurisprudence*, Oxford 1979.
SEZGIN, F., *Geschichte des Arabischen Schrifttums* (GAS), vol. I, Leiden 1967.
Siyar: see AL-DHAHABĪ.
Tadkhira: see AL-DHAHABĪ.
Tahdhīb: see IBN ḤAJAR.
Ta'rīkh: see IBN AL-FARAḌĪ.
TURKI, A. M., "La vénération pour Mālik et la physionomie du malikisme andalou", *Studia Islamica* XXXIII (1971), pp. 41–65.
— *Polémiques entre Ibn Ḥazm et Bāǧī sur les principes de la loi musulmane*, Alger s. d.
AL-'UMARĪ, A. D. (ed.), *Baqī b. Makhlad al-Qurṭubī wa-muqaddimat Musnadi-hi* (*'Adad mā li-kull wāḥid min al-Ṣaḥāba min al-ḥadīth*), Beirut 1404/1984.
VIGUERA, M. J., "La *Historia de alfaquíes y jueces* de Aḥmad b. 'Abd al-Barr", *Revista del Instituto Egipcio de Estudios Islámicos* XXIII (1985–6), pp. 49–61.

16
THE TRANSMISSION OF KNOWLEDGE IN AL-ANDALUS (UP TO 300/912)

Manuela Marín

Preparing a list of the savants of al-Andalus who died before the year 350/961[1] has allowed me to study quite a sizeable amount of biographical data, from which a number of conclusions may be drawn regarding the cultural and social life of the period in question. One of these aspects, and not the least important, is the relationship between masters and disciples, and the spread of teachings and knowledge during this first era of Islam in Spain.

Studying the list of masters with whom the savants of al-Andalus studied shows, upon an initial assessment of the data, a significant increase in the number of Middle-Eastern masters. There is nothing surprising in this, given that during this period, and above all during the beginning of the spread of Islam in Spain, it was logical to study at centres of scientific learning in other regions of the Islamic world that were already well-established. Without neglecting this first aspect of the theme, which I hope to study in more detail in the near future, my aim here is to outline the relationships between the masters of al-Andalus and their disciples. This issue has already been studied in connection with later periods[2] and, in part, has also been dealt with in relation to the earliest period of Spanish Islam: for example, the work of J. López Ortiz, *The Reception of the Maliki School in Spain*,[3] which brings together information about many of the disciples who studied with the most important figures of the maliki *madhhab* in al-Andalus.

[1] Marín, Manuela, "Nómina de sabios de al-Andalus", in Id. (ed.), *Estudios Onomástico-biográficos de al-Andalus (EOBA)*, Madrid, Consejo Superior de Investigaciones Científicas, 1988, 23–182; from here on referred to as "*List*". Both this article and the above work form part of the results obtained in the Research Project, *Biographical Groupings of al-Andalus. Onomasticon Arabicum* (funded by C.A.I.C.Y.T., Comisión Asesora para la Investigación Científica y Ténica).

[2] In particular by Urvoy, D., *Le monde des ulémas andalous du V/XIe au VII/XIIIe siècle* (Geneva, 1978).

[3] [López Ortiz, José, "La Recepción de la escuela maleguí en España", *Anuario de historia del derecho español*, 7 (1930), 1–167.]

The procedure followed for this study is based on reconstructing the groups of disciples who corresponded to each master, by means of the biographies in which the latter are mentioned. In this way, it is possible to amplify considerably the number of disciples named in the biographies of each figure. The number of disciples mentioned tends to be much smaller than that of their masters.[4]

Of a total of 1,631 savants and men of science who died before 350/961, a group of personalities stands out, who were, in effect, the men who contributed to the spread of knowledge in Islamic Spain, and who had at least one disciple each. This group is made up of a total of 279 personalities. However, in weighing up this purely quantitative data, one has to take into account two important factors. The first is that, of the total number of 1,631 names collected in *List*, one part—although small—corresponds to men of letters or poets whose activities with regard to the transmission of scientific knowledge were unimportant, or indeed non-existent. The same can be said of figures who held public positions—that of judge in particular—who, because of their character merited a biography, but who rarely had an impact on other intellectual fields. The second factor, which is much more difficult to evaluate, relates to the characteristics of the sources used in this study. The selection of the personalities to be written about by the authors of *kutub al-tarājim*, depends, essentially, on the sources which they had to hand;[5] similarly, the selection of the names of their masters was in the hands of these same authors, who many times must have tended to summarise this kind of information.

Nevertheless, it is true that one of the factors that the authors of the biographical sources take into account in gauging the importance of a personality is the amount of disciples he had, or the amount of sources which quote him as an authority. However, the majority of these disciples do not mention themselves in detail in the biographies of each master, instead limiting themselves to mentioning the names of the most prominent disciples.

[4] This same system is followed by Urvoy, *op. cit.*, and by Gilbert, J.E., *The 'Ulamā' of Medieval Damascus and the International World of Islamic Scholarship* (PhD., University of California, Berkeley, 1977) and "Institutionalization of Muslim Scholarship and Professionalization of the 'Ulamā' in Medieval Damascus", *Studia Islamica*, LII (1980), pp. 105-134 (summary of thesis mentioned, in which the theme of the master-disciple relationship is not dealt with). Abiad, M., *Culture et éducation arabo-islamiques au Šam pendant les trois premiers siècles de l'Islam* (Damasacus, 1981), catalogues savants by the number of their masters (pp. 200–1).

[5] See, in this respect, the work of Avila, M.L., "El Metódo historiográfico de Ibn al-Abbār" (on the sources of the *Takmila* of Ibn al-Abbār), in *Estudios Onomástico-biográficos de al-Andalus*, op. cit., pp. 555–583.

In significant cases a master's importance is emphasised by means of the number of anecdotes and stories about him.[6]

Among the 279 masters who correspond to the period being studied, several groups can be established according to the number of disciples that correspond to each master. It is important to note that with the personalities that died after 290/902–3 (approximately), a considerable numerical distortion takes place: many of their disciples died after 350/961 and therefore are not included in calculations. As a consequence, in this study we can only have a clear idea of the masters' importance by means of the number of their disciples in the period ending in the III/IX century. Confining ourselves, therefore, to those personalities who died in 300/912, we obtain the following results:

	1–2 disciples	3–10 disciples	More than 10 disciples
II/VIII centuries	1	4	—
III/IX centuries	29	24	22

Due to the nature of the sources that deal with this period, the above table has been produced only on the basis of the masters whose date of death is known to us. To this, one must add a group of 69 personalities whose exact date of death is unknown, but who are very likely to have lived during the II–III/VIII–IX centuries, and perhaps at the beginning of the IX/X century. The figures regarding their disciples is as follows:

1 to 2 disciples: 60 masters.
3 to 10 disciples: 9 masters.
More than 10 disciples: —

The group that holds the greatest interest is, logically, that of those masters who had an important number of disciples. We saw in the previous table that the nucleus of personalities whose teachings had a notable effect is reduced to 22 in the period studied. This figure might seen insignificant, above all if we compare it with the total of biographies studied for the same period. Essentially, it attracts our notice that the result of this investigation is not too far from the conclusions reached by Bulliet for Nīsābūr.[7] If we look at the era

[6] See, for example, the biography of Yaḥyā b. ʿUmar in ʿIyāḍ, *Tartīb al-madārik* (8 vols., Rabat, ed. M. Tāwīt al-Óanjī *et al.*, Rabat, Wizārat al-Awqāf, 1965–1983), IV, pp. 357–364.

[7] Bulliet, Richard W., "The Age Structure of Medieval Islamic Education", *Studia Islamica*, LVII (1983), pp. 15–117, in particular p. 107.

immediately after the one studied here, with a slightly wider time frame (317–514/929–1120) the number of biographies is considerably similar (1080) and the conclusions do not overly differ. The "masters" of Nīsābūr do not exceed 192 and only 26 have 20 or more disciples.[8] Faced with this parallel, one could ask oneself if this might not be due to the fact that, geographically-speaking, in both cases we are dealing with areas situated on the periphery of the Islamic world; in any case, the fact remains significant, and allows us to draw nearer to a more accurate assessment of the information contained in the biographical dictionaries.[9]

Chronologically one can observe in this period a process of progressive growth in the number of masters, parallel to the introduction of the Islamic sciences to al-Andalus, a process which intensified from the first years of the III/IX century on. The following list maps, according to date of death, the names of the masters of al-Andalus of this period; in cases where the biographical sources provide more than one date, for practical reasons only one is indicated. The number which follows each name indicates its inclusion number in *List*, where the corresponding biographical references may be consulted.

Date of Death	*Master*
158/774–5	Mu'āwiya b. Ṣāliḥ (1409)
180/796	Ṣa'ṣa' b. Sallām (635)
189/804–5	Yaḥyā b. Muḍar (1572)
198/813–4	'Abd al-Khāliq b. 'Abd al-Jabbār (686)
199/814	al-Ghāzī b. Qays (1008)
204/819	Ziyād b. 'Abd al-Raḥmān Shabṭūn (504)
206/821	Muḥammad b. Yaḥyā al-Sibā'ī (1353)
207/822	Ḥusayn b. 'Āṣim (407)
210/825	Qar'awūs b. al-'Abbās (1076).
212/827	'Īsā b. Dīnār (993)
220/835	Wahb b. Akhṭal (1509)

[8] Although Bulliet's study only deals with the city of Nīsābūr, the comparison with al-Andalus can be sustained if we take into account that during the era studied here, the great majority of the masters of al-Andalus lived in Cordoba and taught there, in particular those with the greater number of disciples.

[9] Regarding the significance of Arabic biographical literature, there is a bibliography which is becoming more and more important in size and quality. To the titles quoted, for example, in Avila, M.L., *Hispano-Muslim Society at the End of the Caliphate* (Madrid, 1985), pp. 13–14, one can add Goiten, S.D.'s suggestive evaluation in "Individualism and Conformity in Classical Islam", *Fifth Giorgio Della Vida Biennial Conference* (ed. A. Banani and S. Vryonis) (Wiesbaden, 1977), pp. 3–17.

221/835–6	al-Ḥārith b. Abī Sa'īd (363)
222/836–7	Muḥammad b. 'Īsā al-A'shā (1291)
224/838–9	Muḥammad b. Khālid b. Martanīl (1174)
233/846	'Abd al-Malik b. al-Ḥasan Zawnān (862)
234/848	Yaḥyā b. Yaḥyā (1576)
235/849	Sa'īd b. Ḥassān (537)
237/851	'Āmir b. Mu'āwiya (659)
	Qāsim b. Hilāl (1075)
238/852	'Abd al-Malik b. Ḥabīb (861)
	Hārūn b. Sālim (1475)
246/860	'Uthmān b. Ayyūb (901)
254/868	'Umar b. Mūsā al-Kinānī (965).
255/868–9	Muḥammad b. Aḥmad al-'Utbī (1125)
256/869–70	'Abd Allāh b. Muḥammad b. Khālid (810)
258/871	'Abd al-Rahmān b. Ibrāhīm (691)
259/872–3	Yaḥyā b. Ibrāhīm b. Muzayn (1523)
260/873–4	Sulaymān b. Naṣr (602)
261/874	Muḥammad b. Yusūf b. Maṭrūḥ (1368)
262/875	Abān b. Īsā b. Dīnār (3)
265/878	'Abd al-Raḥmān b. Sa'īd (700)
	al-Faḍl b. al-Faḍl b. 'Amīra (1041)
	Ibrāhīm b. Shu'ayb (31)
268/881	Ibrāhīm b. Yazīd b. Qulzum (55)
	Mālik b. 'Alī (1088)
269/882	Sa'īd b. al-Namir (573)
270/883	'Abd al-Raḥmān b. 'Īsā b. Dīnār (709)
	Ibrāhīm b. Khālid (23)
272/885	'Abd Allāh b. Muḥammad b. Qāsīm b. Hilāl (823)
273/886	Yaḥyā b. Qāsim b. Hilāl (1564)
273/886	Aṣbagh b. Khalīl (267)
	Ibrāhīm b. Muḥammad b. Bāz (46)
	Wahb b. Nāfi' (1518)
275/888	'Abd Allāh b. Sawwār (776)
	Ibrāhīm b. 'Ajannas (36)
	Muḥammad b. Idrīs (1135)
276/889	Baqī b. Makhlad (315)
278/891	Ibrāhīm b. Labīb (42)
	Qāsim b. Muḥammad (1066)
280/893	Ḥāmid b. Akhṭal (365)
282/895	Ibrāhīm b. Qāsim b. Hilāl (40)

	Muṭarrif b. ʿAbd al-Raḥmān (1397)
283/896	Ibrāhīm b. al-Nuʿmān (51)
	Yūsuf b. Yaḥyā al-Maghāmī (1607)
285/898	Muḥammad b. al-Rabīʿ (1179)
286/899	ʿAbd Allāh b. Masarra (826)
	Aḥmad b. Ibrāhīm al-Faraḍī (94)
	Muḥammad b. ʿAbd al-Salām al-Khushanī (1225)
287/900	ʿAbd al-Malik b. Ayman (858)
	Aḥmad b. Sulaymān b. Abī Rabīʿ (129)
	Ibrāhīm b. Naṣr (49)
	Muḥammad b Waḍḍāḥ (1351)
293/905–6	Muḥammad b. Abī Ḥujayra (1110)
	Qāsim b. ʿAbd al Wāḥid (1059)
294/906–7	Muḥammad b. Abī al-ʿAbbās b. al-Walīd (1215)
	al-Ṣabāḥ b. ʿAbd al-Raḥmān (634)
295/907	Muḥammad b. Ghālib (1294)
	Yaḥyā b. ʿAbd al-ʿAzīz (155)
296/908–9	Aḥmad b. Sulaymān al-Qarawī (128)
	Muḥammad b. ʿAbd Allāh b. al-Ghāzī (1251)
	Muḥammad b. ʿAbd al-Jabbār (1217)
	Muḥammad b. Junāda (1157)
297/909–10	ʿUbayd Allāh b. Yaḥyā (896)
298–910	ʿAttāb b. Bishr (899)
	Hāshim b. Khālid (1478)
299/911	Aṣbagh b. Mālik (276)
300/912	Hishām b. Muḥammad b. Hishām (1488)
	Ibrāhīm b. Mūsā b. Jamīl (48)
	Muḥammad b. ʿAbd Allāh b. Suwayd (1246)
	Qāsim b. ʿĀṣim (1055)

We will now look at a group of 22 masters who had more than ten disciples each, placed in descending order according to importance:

Muḥammad b. Waḍḍāḥ: 216 disciples[10]

[10] Ibn Waḍḍāh's disciples have been studied in detail by Fierro, M.L, in her Doctoral Thesis *The Kitāb al-bidaʿ wa-l-nahy ʿanhā of Muḥammad b. Waḍḍāh* (died 287/900), Madrid [Now published: *Kitāb al-Bidaʿ* (*Tratado contra las innovaciones*), nueva edición, traducción, estudio e indices por M.ª Isabel Fierro, Madrid, Consejo Superior de Investigaciones científicas, 1988; review of Gilliot, Cl., in *Studia Islamica*, LXXVII (1993), 198–199.]

Baqī b. Makhlad:	85
ʿUbayd Allāh b. Yaḥyā:	79[11]
Muḥammad b. ʿAbd al-Salām al-Khushanī:	75
Ibrāhīm b. Muḥammad b. Bāz:	61
Yaḥyā b. Yaḥyā:	58
Muḥammad b. Aḥmad al-ʿUtbī:	46
Yaḥyā b. Ibrāhīm b. Muzayn:	43
Saʿīd b. Ḥassān:	2
Ibrāhīm b. Qāsim b. Hilāl:	23
Muḥammad b. Yusūf b. Matrūḥ:	23
Muṭarrif b. ʿAbd al-Raḥmān:	22
Abān b. Īsā b. Dīnār:	18
Qāsim b. Muḥammad:	18
ʿAbd al-Raḥman b. Ibrāhīm Abū Zayd:	16
Yūsuf b. Yaḥyā al-Maghāmī:	15
Aṣbagh b. Khalīl:	13
ʿAbd Allāh b. Masarra:	13
Aḥmad b. Ibrāhīm al-Faraḍī:	13
ʿAbd Allāh b. Muḥammad b. Khālid:	13
Īsā b. Dīnār:	13

If we consider this to be the most important group among the savants of al-Andalus before 300/912, it is also evident that the figure among them with the greatest influence was Muḥammad b. Waḍḍāh, followed after a certain distance by Baqī b. Makhlad; but if we unite this data with a diachronic study of the influence of the masters of al-Andalus, we will be able to better understand the evolution of transmission of the Islamic sciences in al-Andalus.

The first group of savants of al-Andalus which appears to have been important according to the number of their disciples, is made up of Yaḥyā b. Muḍar and al-Ghāzī b. Qays. Yaḥyā b. Yaḥyā, Aṣbagh b. Khalīl, ʿAbd al-Raḥmān b al-Faḍl b. ʿAmīra and al-Faḍl b. ʿAmīra all learnt from Yaḥyā b. Muḍar. Aṣbagh b. Khalīl was also a disciple of al-Ghāzī b. Qays; the other disciples of Ibn Qays were, at the same time, disciples of al-Ṣaʿṣaʿ b. Sallām (in both cases) or of ʿĪsā b. Dīnār, who already had a more considerable number of followers.

[11] In this case, the disciples of ʿUbayd Allāh b. Yaḥyā who died after 350/961 have also been factored into the calculations; see Marín, M., "A Family of Cordovan ʿulamās: the Banū Abī ʿĪsā", *Al-Qanṭara*, VI (1985), pp. 291–320.

Ten of ʿĪsā b. Dīnār's 13 disciples were also disciples of Yaḥyā b. Yaḥyā, who, for his part, was the master in common of many of them together with ʿAbd al-Malik b Ḥabīb and Saʿīd b. Ḥassān apart from being the most important figure of his era with regard to number of disciples:

Disciples in common of Yaḥyā b. Yaḥyā, ʿAbd al-Malik b Ḥabīb and Saʿīd b. Ḥassān:	9
Disciples in common of Yaḥyā b. Yaḥyā and Saʿīd b. Ḥassān:	12
Disciples in common of Yaḥyā b. Yaḥyā and ʿAbd al-Malik b Ḥabīb:	7.

Muḥammad b. Aḥmad al-ʿUtbī, who died twenty years after Yaḥyā b. Yaḥyā, together with Yaḥyā b. Ibrāhīm b. Muzayn dominated the teaching of the period immediately subsequent to the period under study: both were masters in common to 22 disciples. Some disciples of Ibn Waḍḍāḥ studied with Muḥammad b. Aḥmad al-ʿUtbī and Yaḥyā b. Ibrāhīm b. Muzayn, a practice that had took place throughout the whole second half of the III/IX century, an era in which the overwhelming majority of savants of al-Andalus shared their teaching with Muḥammad b. Waḍḍāḥ.[12]

The group of 22 masters reveals in this way a strong internal cohesion, as the majority of their disciples were not followers of one single master, but of groups of two or three (and sometimes more) masters. This same phenomenon was pointed out by Urvoy regarding the final era of the caliphate, in which the nucleus of Islamic culture in al-Andalus was concentrated in some eleven people.[13] We are before the veritable ruling caste of the intellectual life of al-Andalus, those whose teaching was sufficiently important to attract a number of disciples who would only sporadically attend the lessons of other masters. The groups of secondary importance are so, very often, for a number of reasons: in the first place, it was common for many masters of one or two disciples to belong to the same family circle: this took place, for example, with savants who received their scientific initiation from their fathers, to later attend the lessons of other, better-known masters. On the other hand, one can see in this era the formation of small poles of attraction in the provinces, of which the most important was Elvira, and which represented a similar function: those interested in acquiring knowledge first sought out the local masters, later to gather in the Umayyad capital of Cordoba, where the most important figures in intellectual life were concentrated.

---

[12] For example, with the exception of two, all of Baqī b. Makhlad's disciples were also students of Ibn Waḍḍāḥ; the latter and al-Khushanī shared 64 disciples, etc.

[13] See Urvoy, *Le Monde des ulémas*, p. 87.

The qualification of a master as such was, therefore, the axis around which the transmission of knowledge rotated,[14] and his recognition as a bearer and transmitter of knowledge was made within the ʿulamāʾ community itself, without outside intervention. Among the names we have emphasised as the "leaders" of intellectual life in al-Andalus, the recognition of their importance by means of the number of their disciples coincides with their personal influence, based on the quality of their transmission of Middle-Eastern masters (as in the case of Yaḥyā b. Yaḥyā and Saʿīd b. Ḥassān); their activity as authors of works that circulated widely (for example, Ibn Ḥabīb's *Wāḍiha*[15] or *Mustakhraja*[16] by al-ʿUtbī); or on their introduction of new fields of knowledge (the cases of Baqī b. Makhlad and Muḥammad b. Waḍḍāḥ). It was not political power that determined the authority of a master,[17] but the fact that he bore the stamp of recognition from the members of the scientific community. But up to what point this intellectual authority had total social recognition in the era under study is a question I have avoided exploring here, as it would need to be studied in greater depth.[18]

---

[14] See Bulliet, R.W., *The Patricians of Nishapur* (Cambridge, Mass., 1972) pp. 54–5.

[15] [See Muranyi, Miklos, *Beiträge zur Geschichte der Ḥadīṯ- und Rechtsgelehrsamkeit der Mālikiyya in Nordafrika bis zum 5. Jh. d. H.* Bio-bibliographische Notizen aus der Moscheebibliothek von Qairawān, Wiesbaden, Harrassowitz, 1997, 325–355 (*Kitāb al-Ḥajj*), 472–473, et passim; Ossendorf-Conrad, Beatrix, *Das "K. al-Wāḍiḥa" des ʿAbd al-Malik b. Ḥabīb*, Edition und Kommentar zu Ms. Qarawiyyīn 809/40 (*Abwāb al-ṭahāra*), Beirut, Orient-Institut der DMG, Stuttgart, in Kommission bie Franz Steiner Verlag (Beiruter Texte und Studien, 43), 1994, X+574 p.]

[16] [*Op. cit.*, 356–365 (*Kitāb al-Ḥajj*), 453, et passim; al-ʿUtbī, *Kitāb al-Ḥajj*. Min al-masāʾil al-mustakhraja min al-asmiʿa mimmā laysa fī al-Mudawwana (pp. 49–160), followed by Ibn Mājishūn, *Kitāb al-Ḥajj* (pp. 174–191), ed. M. Muranyi, n.p. (Beirut, Dār Ibn Ḥazm), 2007.]

[17] For an example when the Caliph appoints the teachers of a *madrasa*; see Mottahedeh, R., *Loyalty and Leadership in an Early Islamic Society* (Princeton, 1980).

[18] The majority of studies carried out using the middle-eastern dictionaries of biography as their basis focus their interest on the ʿulamāʾ as a social group. Regarding al-Andalus, Urvoy's work is above all a cultural-sociological study, while Avila, in her *Hispanic-Muslim Society*, insists on analysing the savants outside their cultural context for his demographical study. An approach towards the theme of the ʿulamā's social role can be seen in Mones, H., "Le rôle des hommes de religion dans l'histoire de l'Espagne musulmane jusqu'à la fin du Califat", *Studia Islamica*, XX (1964), pp. 47–88. It continues to be useful to consult Ribera y Tarragó, Julián, *La enseñanza entre los musulmanes españoles* (Saragossa, 1893) [reprint Córdoba, 1925[3], and in *Disertaciones y opusculos*, I, 1928, with other texts; Arabic trans. in Makkī, al-Ṭāhir A., *al-Tarbiyya al-islāmiyya fī al-Andalus*, Cairo, Dār al-Maʿārif, 1981, with other texts]. Regarding the authority of the ʿulamāʾ and lawyers, see Makdisi, G., "Authority in the Islamic Community" in *La notion d'autorité au Moyen-Age. Colloques Internationaux de la Napoule* (Paris, 1982), pp. 117–126.

Abstract

This article examines the spread of knowledge in al-Andalus by reconstructing the most important groups of masters according to the number of their disciples. In studying the period in question, in which a total of 1,631 savants—or individuals related to the intellectual life—have been registered, a group of 279 personalities stands out, with at least one disciple each. Within this group, 22 masters are notable as having had more than 10 disciples each. This group may, therefore, be considered the veritable elite among the transmitters of knowledge in al-Andalus. This article also indicates the most important masters of each generation and the relationships that existed between them, by means of the groups of disciples they had in common.

17
LIBRARIES AND BIBLIOPHILES IN THE ISLAMIC EAST

Adolph Grohmann

[Remark: In the footnotes, the passages between square brackets have been added by Cl. Gilliot]

ṭalab al-ʿilm farīḍa ʿalā kull muslim
'Pursuing knowledge is every Muslim's duty'[1]

These words, which I have put at the beginning of my contribution, are the opening words of the inscription above the entrance gate into the library in Constantinople; built by Sultan Muḥammad II the Conqueror (1451–1481 AD), it was later destroyed by an earthquake and rebuilt by Muṣṭafā III in 1771 AD.[2] The duty demanded here had long since become a necessity for large groups of those professing Islam. The tremendous advance of intellectual work began under the influence of Hellenistic and Persian scholarship in the second Islamic century and embraced many groups of the Arab people, in particular among those who had settled. Of course, this was an impetus that also considerably advanced the development of books and all that pertained to them. Consequently it was not by chance that most of the great libraries were created at the time that also saw the greatest flourishing of so-called Arab culture, namely during the third to fifth centuries AH.[3] The increased demand for books – which were, as in the Classical world, disseminated as copies only – furthermore encouraged the book trade to prosper, and the historian al-Yaʿqūbī for instance tells us that in his day (the second half of the third century AH) there were more than a hundred booksellers in Baghdad.[4] These

[1] [Fr. Rosenthal, *Knowledge triumphant*. The concept of knowledge in medieval Islam, Leiden, 1970, p. 89: Among the six authoritative books of Hadith in Sunni Islam, Ibn Māja is the only one to quote this hadith attributed to Muḥammad. It should be noted that «science» here refers to religious knowledge and above all Hadith].

[2] G. Flügel, *Die arabischen persischen und türkishen Handschriften der kaiserlich-königlichen Hofbibliothek zu Wien*, Vienna, 1865, p. 58.

[3] A. von Kremer, *Culturgeschichte des Orients unter den Chalifen*, II, Vienna 1877, p. 409, 413.

[4] Op. cit., p. 310.

booksellers frequently were bookbinders as well as copyists, made their own paper and sold not only books but pens, ink and paper,[5] and in addition many of them were men with a literary education who would occasionally put pen to paper themselves. [**432**] In any case many a literary product would pass through their hands, and consequently they possessed extensive knowledge in the fields of biography and history of literature. One of the best-known representatives of this guild is Abū al-Faraj Muḥammad b. Isḥāq al-Warrāq al-Baghdādī Ibn Abī Ya'qūb al-Nadīm, who in 987 AD compiled a catalogue of all the works that had passed through his hands or had come to his attention in any other way, together with biographical notes about the authors; a book that is known under the title of *Kitāb al-Fihrist*. The shops of these booksellers who, like all the trades, had their own district in the bazaars, were favourite meeting points of learned people,[6] just as the taverns of the *librarii* had been in Ancient Rome. We are able to form an idea of the book production in those days if we hear that a scribe was able to copy a hundred pages in one day and one night.[7]

Not only did the increase in literary production advance the book trade; the constantly expanding academic activity required the establishment of great libraries, accessible to everyone, where everything worth knowing would be stacked. A number of rulers met this requirement in the most liberal fashion. It was a matter of course that Baghdad, as the centre of the 'Abbāsid Empire, soon became a major centre of learning. Not the least of the contributing factors was the ruling dynasty's sympathetic support of science. First and foremost it is al-Ma'mūn (813–833 AD) who must be mentioned, as he founded a court library in the capital which bore the name 'House of Wisdom' or 'Treasury of Wisdom' (*dār* [*bayt*] *al-ḥikma* or *khizāna al-ḥikma*), and which had three Persian directors. It contained not only books, but also old autograph manuscripts.[8] Numerous scholars enjoyed working there; thus the author of the *Fihrist* used many rare works in this library. The Caliph al-Mu'taḍid (892–902 AD) also had a collection of books, about which we unfortunately have no more detailed information.[9] At any rate the 'Abbāsids'

---

[5] J. Karabacek, 'Das arabische Papier', *Mitteilungen aus der Sammlung der Papyrus Erzherzog Rainer*, II/III (1886), p. 124.

[6] Ibn 'Abd Rabbihi, *al-'Iqd al-farīd*, Būlāq 1293, II, p. 223.

[7] Ibn al-Nadīm, *Fihrist*, edited and annotated by G. Flügel, Leipzig 1871, I, p. 264. Cf. A. Mez, *Die Renaissance des Islâms*, Heidelberg 1922, p. 176 [/*The Renaissance of Islam*, translated by S.Kh. Bukhsh and D.S. Margoliouth, London, 1937, p. 183–4].

[8] Ibn al-Nadīm, *al-Fihrist*, I, p. 5, 19, 120, 274; von Kremer, *Culturgeschichtliche Streifzüge auf dem Gebiet des Islam*, Leipzig, 1873, p. 32, n. 2.

[9] *Fihrist*, op. cit., I, p. 61

Plate 1. Miniature from the Codex Arabe 5847 of the Bibliothèque Nationale in Paris, depicting the library in Ḥulwān.

library, which was destroyed under Hūlāgū, must have been most remarkable, for al-Qalqashandī[10] mentions it in first place among the greatest libraries of Islam. In second place al-Qalqashandī names the library of the Fāṭimid Caliphs in Cairo which embraced all the sciences and about whose fortunes we have more detailed knowledge.[11] This library was particularly

[10] al-Qalqashandī, *Ṣubḥ al-Aʿshā*, Cairo 1903, I, p. 278 [ed. M.Ḥ. Shams al-Dīn, Beyrouth, 1407/1987, I, p. 537].

[11] [Ibid.]; al-Maqrīzī, *Khiṭaṭ*, Būlāq, 1270/1853, I, p. 408, l. 28ff., 458, l.29ff.

4 *Adolf Grohmann*

rich in autograph manuscripts. Thus, for instance, among its thirty-odd copies of [**433**] the comparatively valuable *Kitāb al-ʿAyn* by Abū ʿAbd al-Raḥmān al-Khalīl b. Aḥmad – one copy, allegedly from the Ṭāhirid library and offered in Baṣra by a bookseller from Khorāsān, sold for fifty gold dinars[12] – one was the author's own manuscript. The Caliph al-ʿAzīz bi-Llāh (975–996 AD) was offered a copy of al-Ṭabarī's Chronicle which he had bought for a hundred dinars. However, the library already possessed twenty-odd copies, among them once again an autograph manuscript. Of Ibn Durayd's *Jamhara*, there were even a hundred copies. [**434**] Among the various fields of knowledge represented there were: jurisprudence, according to the individual schools of law, grammar, rhetoric, tradition scholarship, history, rulers' biographies, astronomy, spiritualist lore and chemistry. Ibn al-Ṭuwayr tells us that the library was housed in one of the halls in the Māristān, which was called the Old Māristān in al-Maqrīzī's time. We do not know when it had been taken there. It was arranged on a number of book cabinets all along the walls of the great hall, the cabinets were divided into shelves and every shelf fitted with a hinged door with a lock. Manuscripts from every field of knowledge were recorded, and if something was missing or not complete, this would be noted as well, all on a piece of paper stuck to each of the doors in the hall. We also hear that Qurʾān manuscripts – the library owned no fewer than 2400, some by famous calligraphers and illuminated with gold, silver, etc. – were housed in a room above this hall, and that furthermore there were booklets in the hand of the calligrapher Ibn Muqla and those emulating his work, such as Ibn al-Bawwāb and others. We may be able to form an idea of this arrangement if we look at the picture of the library in Ḥulwān at Plate 1. This is from the precious codex of Ḥarīrī's *Maqāmāt* written in 1237 AD which forms part of the Collection Ch. Schefer in Paris and is now kept in the Bibliothèque Nationale.[13]

The library, which comprised 200,000 bound volumes alone – there was only a small number of stitched booklets – or, according to other sources, even 601,000 volumes,[14] had a varied fate. It is certain that in 1005 AD a large part of its collection was moved from the library quarters in the Fāṭimid palaces into the 'House of Science' – called 'House of Wisdom' by al-Musabbiḥī – founded

---

[12] *Fihrist*, I, p. 42; von Kremer, *Culturgeschichte*, op. cit., II p. 311.

[13] F.R. Martin, *The Miniature painting and painters of Persia, India and Turkey from the 8th to the 18th Century*, London, 1912, II, Plate 11 (bottom).

[14] Ibn Abī Wāṣil's statement that it contained no more than 120,000 volumes cannot be valid for its heyday. Presumably this is meant to refer to the its size at the time it was sold by Saladin; Abū Shāma al-Maqdisī, *Kitāb al-Rawḍatayn fī akhbār al-dawlatayn*, Cairo, 1287/1870, p. 200.

by al-Ḥākim bi-amr Allāh. This was situated near the West palace and was entered from the gate of the straw sellers. In al-Maqrīzī's day it was called Dār al-Ḥaḍīrī (Greengrocers' House) and was situated in the street of the same name opposite the Aqmar mosque. The library established here was open to general use and it was possible, on request, to copy anything one liked; furthermore it was used for lectures. As soon as the new library was furnished and decorated, its doors and doorways covered with curtains, and doormen, servants, ushers etc. had taken up their jobs, it naturally became a meeting place for jurists, astronomers, grammarians, rhetoricians and physicians. Here al-Ḥākim bi-amr Allāh had stacked works from all fields of knowledge, in particular [**435**] precious autograph manuscripts, a collection no other ruler's could equal. All these treasures he made available to the public, guaranteeing in addition a certain yearly budget to pay for the people working for the library, and also provided ink, pens, paper and inkwells. In the year 403 AH (1012–13 AD) al-Ḥākim received a delegation of scholars from a similar academy, including mathematicians, rhetoricians, jurists, physicians, all of whom were admitted according to their guilds to an extraordinary audience. They were invited to a disputation and then dismissed with gifts of garments of honour. On this occasion al-Ḥākim also donated some real estate in Old-Cairo (al-Fusṭāṭ) for his academy. 257 dinars were allocated for the yearly budget of the library, distributed among the following items:

For rush mats from ʿAbbadān etc. – 10 dinars
For writing paper – 90 dinars
For the librarian's salary – 48 dinars
For drinking water – 12 dinars
For the servant's salary – 15 dinars
For the salary of the administrator of paper, ink and pens – 12 dinars
For repairing the curtains – 1 dinar
For repairing torn books and damaged papers – 12 dinars
For felt rugs for winter – 5 dinars
For winter blankets – 4 dinars

As an addition of these items results in only 209 dinars, it may be assumed that the remaining 48 dinars were distributed either among such expenses as are not mentioned specifically in the library's budget or, which is much more probable, among the salaries of other servants. After all it is wholly improbable that only one single servant was employed, as might be inferred from the relevant entry in the library's budget. We will come to know a number of institutions related to this foundation of al-Ḥākim, which ceased to exist only after more than 120 years. It was closed by al-Afḍal b. Amīr al-Juyūsh, allegedly because it had become a seat of sectarianism and religious unrest.[15]

Perhaps it was a good thing that thanks to this foundation of al-Ḥākim the major part of the magnificent library of the Fāṭimids was housed elsewhere, as in 1068 a terrible fate befell it. In the month of October of that year, 25 camel loads of books had been transported from the palace of the Fāṭimid al-Mustanṣir bi-Llāh to the palace of the vizier Abū al-Faraj Muḥammad b. Jaʿfar al-Maghribī. The vizier had removed these books, whose value was estimated by eye witnesses to have been around 100,000 dinars – from the palace stacks [**436**] in order to provide collateral for the requirements of the grasping, undisciplined soldiery. After the defeat of the Ḥamdānid Nāṣir al-Dawla in November of that year, this great treasure of books was ransacked and dragged from his palace during the great pillage by the Turkish guards, who did not spare his two travelling companions either. The books that were spared were those in the 'House of Science' and those that had been moved to ʿImād al-Dawla Abū al-Faḍl b. al-Muḥtariq in Alexandria; after his murder they passed to the Maghrib. However, this unprecedented book looting was by no means all. Those precious, beautiful and matchless manuscripts that had survived and not been sold off were now maltreated in the most cruel manner. Their magnificent leather bindings were ripped off in order to be made into footwear for negro slaves, and the pages of the manuscripts were simply burnt. Whatever escaped this auto-da-fé was covered with dust by the winds and heaped up into hills which could still be seen near the ruins in al-Maqrīzī's day and which were popularly called 'book hills'.

Of course, such a great library, regarded as one of the wonders of the world, and the greatest library in the Islamic Empires, could not be destroyed completely even by a catastrophe of this order. After the death of the last Fāṭimid al-ʿĀḍid (d. 1171 AD), al-Malik al-Nāṣir Ṣalāḥ al-Dīn entrusted Ibn Ṣūra with selling the remaining library treasures. The Qāḍī al-Fāḍil ʿAbd al-Raḥmān b. ʿAlī, who had built a madrasa in Cairo, endowed it with a library of 100,000 volumes and succeeded in acquiring from Ibn Ṣūra a large part of the Fāṭimid library.

Another declared booklover was the Spanish Umayyad Caliph al-Ḥakam II (d. 976 AD) who had precious and rare books bought at any cost in Cairo, Baghdad, Damascus and Alexandria. In his palace in Cordova he had a workshop for copyists, bookbinders and miniaturists. His library's catalogue comprised 44 booklets of 20 or even 50 sheets which contained only the titles of the books without further specification, and the library is indeed said to

[15] Mez, *Renaissance*, p. 169–70 [/p. 177–8].

have contained 400,000 volumes. Most of them the learned Caliph himself had read and annotated with biographical information about the author of the respective work: al-Ḥakam II was also the greatest authority of his day on Arabic literary history.[16]

Rulers of smaller states felt impelled to emulate the fame and munificence of the ʿAbbāsids, Fāṭimids and Umayyads. Thus the Būyid ʿAḍud al-Dawla (d. 982 AD), in his spacious palace in Shirāz, had a separate library building erected which was in the charge of an administrator (*wakīl*), a librarian (*khāzin*) and an inspector (*mushrif*), dignitaries selected from among the best society of the city. Here the founder had collected the entire academic literature published until his day. [**437**] The library consisted of a long columned hall with a large vestibule all sides of which were connected to the book rooms. Along the walls of the great hall as well as the book rooms there were bookcases made from decorated wood, as tall as a man and three cubits wide, fitted with doors which could be lowered from above. The booklets were laid on top of each other on shelves, as we can see on Plate 1. This arrangement had already been used in the ancient world and was retained in Europe for a long time too. For each field of knowledge there were designated bookcases and catalogues listing the titles of the books.[17] The Būyid Majd al-Dawla was a great booklover too, and spent a considerable part of his free time reading and copying books.[18] This, however, did not prevent him staging a large-scale auto-da-fé when the Muʿtazilites were expelled to Khorāsān. On this occasion, the works of philosophers and sectarians were burnt; the remaining confiscated books – which still amounted to 100 camel loads – he kept.[19] Of course there were libraries of greater or lesser importance in the residences of other princes as well. Thus in Alamut, the residence of the Grand Master of the Assassins, there was a great library which was used by the learned vizier Juwaynī but went up in flames in 1257 AD,[20] and crusaders are said to have burnt a library of some 3,000,000 volumes in Tripoli, although that number of books is sure to be greatly exaggerated.[21]

The generosity shown by princes when furnishing and founding libraries often encouraged their highest dignitaries to emulate them. Thus the Caliph

[16] R. Dozy, *Histoire des Musulmans d'Espagne*, Leiden, 1861, III, p. 107–8.

[17] Al-Muqaddasī, *Aḥsan al-taqāsīm fī marifat al-aqālīm*, ed. M.J. De Goeje, Leiden (Bibliotheca Geographorum Arabicorum, III), 1906, p. 449; cf. von Kremer, *Culturgeschichte*, op. cit., II, p. 483–4; Mez, *Renaissance*, p. 165 [/p. 172].

[18] Ibn al-Athīr, *al-Kāmil fī l-Taʾrīkh*, ed. C. J. Tornberg, Leiden 1863, IX, p. 261.

[19] Op. cit., IX, p. 262.

[20] J. von Hammer-Purgstall, *Geschichte der goldenen Horde von Kiptschak*, Pesth, 1840, p. 156, 157.

[21] J. von Hammer-Purgstall, *Geschichte der Ilchane*, Darmstadt, 1842, I, p. 233.

al-Mutawakkil's vizier al-Fatḥ b. Khāqān (murdered in 861 AD) owned a library which the astronomer ʿAlī b. Yaḥyā had collected for him. The author of the *Fihrist* cannot praise this library enough and states that he never saw a more beautiful or more extensive one. The palace of this vizier, who was an enthusiastic patron of men of letters, was frequented by philologists and scholars from al-Kūfa and al-Baṣra. Al-Fatḥ b. Khāqān was considered to be the greatest booklover apart from the scholar al-Jāḥiẓ and the Qāḍī Ismāʿīl b. Isḥāq.[22] Another close friend of scholars, men of letters and books was the Baghdad Jew Abū al-Faraj Yaʿqūb b. Yūsuf b. Killis, an exceedingly intelligent and well-read man. He had been the merchants' wakīl in al-Ramla in Syria, had fled after various malversations under the Ikhshīd Kāfūr to Egypt, had known to insinuate himself into his service where he had soon [**438**] achieved a high position and was appointed *wazīr ajall* to the Fāṭimid Caliph Muʿizz li-dīn Allāh in April 979. In his palace in Cairo he employed several copyists who had to copy the Qurʾān, legal and medical works, books of Adab literature etc. for him. After completion the copies were collated and corrected. He also employed Qurʾān readers and imāms in his palace who would say prayers in the palace mosque; and for himself and his friends as well as servants and page-boys he had a number of kitchens installed. A special table was prepared for his personal use, where he would dine with favoured scholars, noble copyists, select page-boys and invited guests. For the remaining chamberlains, secretaries and servants there were numerous other tables. As soon as he had seated himself, he would read a legal treatise he had composed after hearing it from al-Muʿizz and al-ʿAzīz, and nobody would dare interrupt him. According to the account of his compatriot and contemporary Yaḥyā b. Saʿd, Yaʿqūb spared no expense when it came to these enthusiasms: he spent no less than a thousand dinars a month on the scholars, copyists and bookbinders, which was a gigantic sum, in particular if we bear in mind the value money had at that time.[23] Muʿizz al-Dawla's son in Baṣra owned a library of around 15,000 volumes, which also contained numerous fascicles and unbound works, which were confiscated in 357 AH (967/968 AD).[24] The Būyid vizier Ibn ʿAbbād (d. 995 AD) owned a library in al-Rayy whose catalogue filled ten volumes. Of theological writings alone he owned 400 camel loads. He had started as a village schoolmaster and worked his way up until he was the chancellor of the Iranian Būyid empire. His library went up in flames under

[22] *Fihrist*, I, p. 116; cf. Mez, *Renaissance*, p. 165 [/p. 173].
[23] Maqrīzī, *Khiṭaṭ*, II, p. 6, l.31 ff. Cf. Mez, op. cit. p. 169 [/p. 176].
[24] Ibn al-Athīr, *Kāmil*, VIII, p. 431; Cf. Mez, op. cit. p. 166 [/p. 173–4].

Shāh Maḥmūd of Ghazna.[25] In Baghdad Sābūr b. Ardeshīr (d. 416 AH = 1025/25 AD), the vizier of the Būyid Bahā' al-Dawla, owned a library in 381 AH (991/92 AD) which contained more than 10,000 volumes (*dār al-kutub*) and which burned down when Ṭughril Beg took Baghdad in 450 AH (1058/59 AD).[26] The vizier Bahrām (d. 433 AH = 1041/42 AD) built a library (*dār al-kutub*) in Fīrūzābād and furnished it with 7000 volumes.[27] Al-ʿAlqamī, the last ʿAbbāsid vizier (d. 1258 AD), possessed a library of 10,000 volumes many of which had been dedicated to him. Together with the other libraries of Baghdad – there were no fewer than 36 – his library was destroyed when the Mongols [**439**] took the city by storm; some were burnt, some thrown into the water.[28] Indeed there were numerous libraries in other cities as well. In 613 AH (1216/17 AD) the geographer al-Yāqūt found no fewer than ten in Marv, unequalled in the wealth and preciousness of their collections. Two collections of books were in the great mosque; one of them, called ʿAzīziyya, contained 12,000 volumes and was named after one of Sultan Sanjar's wine suppliers who had founded it, the other collections were housed in various colleges (madrasas). The administration was very liberal. Yāqūt always had more than twenty volumes at his home, each of which had a value of about one dinar (this appears to have been the average value of a book in almost all the Islamic countries), without having to give any security.[29] The library in Ḥulwān cannot have been without importance, either – we have seen its picture at p. 433 above. According to the flowery language of the famous al-Ḥarīrī, whose *Maqāmāt* were translated into German by Friedrich Rückert, it was a

> Treasury of wisdom,
> meeting place and playground too
> of learned men and chosen,
> native as well as foreign.[30]

---

[25] Von Hammer-Purgstall, *Geschichte der Ilchane*, I, p. 124; also Mez, op. cit. p. 95, 167 [/p. 104, 175].

[26] Ibn al-Athīr, *Kāmil*, IX, p. 246–7; Cf. von. Kremer, *Culturgeschichte*, II, p. 483; Mez, *Renaissance*, p. 168 [/p. 176]

[27] Ibn al-Athīr, *Kāmil*, IX, p. 344

[28] Von Hammer-Purgstall, *Geschichte der Ilchane*, I, p. 157.

[29] Yāqūt, *Muʿjam al-buldān* [Jacut's Geographisches Wörterbuch], 6 vols., ed. F. Wüstenfeld, Leipzig, 1866–73, 1924², IV, p. 509–10; cf. von Kremer, *Culturgeschichte*, II, p. 434–5; Mez, op. cit., p. 164 n. 4 [p. 176, n. 1].

[30] [Gilliot: V. on Internet: http://gutenberg.spiegel.de/rueckert/makamen/maka01.htm: Hareth Ben Hemmam erzählt (...): «(...) besuchte ich ihre Bibliothek, den Weisheitsschatz, – den Sammel- und Tummelplatz – gebildeter Männer, auserkorner, – fremder und eingeborner»; Friedrich Rückert, *Die Makamen des Hariri*, Halle, 1897]

It was as good as a matter of course for all mosques to have had a library attached to them; it would be futile to give examples. Often private people, especially scholars, owned quite important book collections. The Arab historian al-Wāqidī (d. 823 AD) left no fewer than six hundred chests of books. He employed at all times two slaves whose duty it was to copy books for him day and night, and even before that he had bought books for 2000 dinars.[31] A courtier of the name of ʿAlī Yaḥyā al-Munajjim had a beautiful collection of books in his country estate and called it proudly, after the foundation of the Caliph al-Maʾmūn, 'Treasury of Wisdom' (*khizānat al-ḥikma*). Anyone who came to study there received free meals.[32] Abū l-Ḥusayn ʿAbd al-ʿAzīz b. Ibrāhīm Ibn Ḥājib al-Nuʿmān was another one who owned a beautiful library. In the days of Muʿizz al-Dawla he was director of the audit office of the Sawād. His library contained mostly valuable original manuscripts with glosses by the respective scholars.[33] The book collection of Muḥammad b. al-Ḥusayn, who was acquainted with the author of the *Kitāb al-Fihrist*, in al-Ḥadītha was even more outstanding. There were Arabic works [**440**] on the subjects of grammar, rhetoric, Adab, and, particularly, very old manuscripts. From fear of the Ḥamdānids the man was most timorous and cautious with his book treasures, but occasionally he would show al-Nadīm a large chest of books containing some 300 pounds of vellum, diplomas, papyri, Chinese and Khorāsānī and Tihāma paper, as well as (rolls of) leather. Among these were manuscripts of the ʿArab, and Qaṣīdas of their poetry which survived in one copy only; furthermore grammatical treatises, anecdotes, history, onomastic and genealogical works as well as other writings from the scholarly literature of the Arabs. The lucky owner of these treasures narrated that a man from al-Kūfa, whose name escaped the author of the Fihrist, and who was not much interested in the old writings, left these things to Muḥammad al-Ḥusayn because of the friendship between them as well as the kindness he had shown to him and the sect (he too was Shīʿite). In this way, al-Nadīm came to see them as well; and he found among them some wondrous things which suffered only from the ravages of time. He mentions, as being particularly interesting, that each fascicle, sheet or roll had a personal inscription by the scholar in question, stating whose work it was, and under each inscription there was an authentication by five or six more scholars. Among these treasures, the author of the *Fihrist* found, among others, a copy of the Qurʾān by the famous calligrapher Khālid b. Abī al-Hayyāj (1st century AH = 7th century AD), the companion of the Caliph ʿAlī. He also found autograph manuscripts by the two

[31] *Fihrist*, I, p. 98.
[32] A. Mez, op. cit., p. 166 [/p. 173]
[33] *Fihrist*, I, p. 134.

imāms al-Ḥasan and al-Ḥusayn, defence treaties and deeds by the Caliph ʿAlī and others of the Prophet's secretaries. Furthermore there were scholars' manuscripts on grammar and rhetoric by, for instance, Abū ʿAmr b. al-ʿAlāʾ and Abū ʿAmr al-Shaybānī, al-Aṣmāʿī, Ibn al-ʿArabī, Sībawayhi, al-Farrāʾ, al-Kisāʾī; autograph manuscripts by traditionists such as Sufyān b. ʿUyayna and Sufyān al-Thawrī, al-Awzāʿī and others. There also was a grammatical treatise by Abū al-Aswad, the originator of Arabic grammar, on four sheets of Chinese paper in the hand of Yaḥyā b. Yaʿfur with old inscriptions. After the death of this man, al-Nadīm made every effort to obtain this chest and its contents, but he did not succeed in finding out anything about its fate. Of all the beautiful things he had seen inside it, he never saw any again, except for the copy of the Qurʾān mentioned above.[34]

Another great collector of books was the judge Abū al-Muṭarrif [Ibn Fuṭays] in Cordova (d. 1011 AD), who employed six copyists who were continually working for him. Whenever he heard about a beautiful book, he sought to acquire it and made exaggerated offers. He never lent a book; he preferred to have a copy made and gave that away, without even asking for it back. [**441**] After his death his library was sold by auction in his mosque, fetching 40,000 dinars over the course of one whole year.[35] The library of the physician Abū al-Ḥasan Saʿīd al-Sāmirī, who was executed in 1251 AD, was a companion piece to Abū al-Muṭarrif's library. Al-Sāmirī owned 10,000 volumes, mainly precious works and masterpieces of calligraphy; he employed several copyists, as did the physician Ibn Matrān who also possessed a library of many volumes.[36]

Foundations similar to the Dār-al-Ḥikma of the Fāṭimid al-Hākim about which we heard above were also established by private individuals. Thus the poet and scholar Ibn Ḥamdān (d. 995 AD), who was a member of the nobility of Mosul, founded a house of science there to which was attached a library with volumes on every subject. It was open to anyone searching for instruction, and poor people got the writing paper for free. The founder himself had a seat there where he would recite his own and other poets' verses and dictate on the subjects of history and jurisprudence. The [traditionist and] judge Ibn Ḥibbān (d. 965 AD) left to the city of Nīshāpūr a house containing a library and living quarters for foreign scholars as well as an allowance for their support. The books were not to be lent outside of the library. One of ʿAḍud al-Dawla's courtiers built a library in Rām Hormuz on the Persian Sea as well as in

[34] *Fihrist*, I, p. 40–1.

[35] Mez, op. cit., p. 167 [/p. 174–5].

[36] F. Wüstenfeld, *Geschichte der arabischen Ärzte und Naturforscher*, Göttingen 1840, p. 101, 122.

Baṣra, where those who came to read and copy received an allowance. The former, which was attended by the geographer al-Muqaddasī, was under the administration of a scholar who lectured on dogmatics according to the Muʿtazilite creed.[37]

Of course, as everywhere there were bibliophiles of questionable character in the East who were not guided by any scholarly or artistic interests but bought books merely in order to paper their bare walls and attract attention as owners of a wealthy library at the same time. Thus a scholar visiting Cordoba, the foremost book market in Spain, had the following experience which I am quoting here in his own words:[38] 'I was spending some time in Cordova and kept visiting the book bazaar there, as I was looking for a book for which I had been searching for a long time. In the end a copy of this book in magnificent script appeared for sale, and joyfully I began bidding for the book. However, the crier always came back with a higher offer, until the price far exceeded the actual value of the book. Then I asked the crier to show me the competitor who was offering so much for the book, and he led me to a gentleman in magnificent attire. I addressed him as 'doctor', and said to him that I was willing to let him have the book if he really [**442**] required it so urgently, as it would be futile to force the price up any further. He, however, replied in the following way: I am neither a scholar nor do I know what the book is about, but I am just by way of furnishing my library and sparing no expense on it in order to distinguish myself among the dignitaries of the city. It so happens that I have a space which this book would fill nicely, and as it is expertly calligraphed and prettily bound it took my fancy. How much it costs is of no importance to me, for God has given me a large income.'

It is impossible to overcome a feeling of sadness when we remind ourselves of how little of all these collections of books, some of which were exceedingly valuable, has come down to us. Occasionally old and precious manuscripts surface in one or the other library in the East. Only recently Ernst Herzfeld [1879–1948] has acquainted us with a number of wondrous treasures from Persian libraries[39] which are most welcome to the philologist as much as to the art historian. There is to this day a sufficient number of educated men in the East, who collect books with true passion. However, the loss of the great libraries of, e.g., the Fāṭimids and the ʿAbbāsids cannot, of course, ever be repaired. A few fragments of magnificent codices survive from the era of the Ṭulūnids and Fāṭimids in the collection of papyri Erzherzog

[37] Mez, op. cit., p. 168 [/p. 176]; von Kremer, *Culturgeschichte*, II, p. 483.

[38] Von Kremer, *Culturgeschichte*, II, p. 312–14.

[39] E. Herzfeld, 'Einige Bücherschätze in Persien', *Ephemerides Orientales*, 28 (1926), (Leipzig, O. Harrassowitz), pp. 1–8.

Rainer which I am going to publish shortly.[40] These fragments show us all the more clearly what a terrible blow was dealt us with the loss of the greatest libraries of the Islamic East and their treasures from the early days of the Islamic Era.

Translated by Gwendolin Goldbloom

[40] A. Grohmann and Th. W. Arnold (ed. and illustrated by), *Denkmäler islamischer Buchkunst*, Munich, Kurt Wolff-Verlag 1927, with 22 illustrations in the text and 150 phototypic plates [Gilliot: It seems to be: Firenze, Pantheon/Leipzig, H. Schmidt and C. Günther, Munich, 1929].

18
ARABIC BOOKS AND LIBRARIES IN THE UMAIYAD PERIOD

Ruth Stellhorn Mackensen

With the murder of ᶜAlī, the fourth caliph, and the establishment of the Umaiyads at Damascus, the capital of Islam moved into a country which had been predominantly Christian for centuries. This fact was to have an influence both in the development of life and religion at the court and in the homeland. Despite prejudices against the Umaiyads on the part of many of the devout, Medina was not cut off entirely from the political capital. Some would have no dealings with the caliphs of Damascus, whom they regarded as godless impostors, and accordingly the interests and studies of this party had a backward look. Others, however, accepted the Umaiyads as the legitimate heads of Islam, asking only that the rulers pay outward homage to the religion of the Prophet; this group was willing to serve them. An intermediate position held it to be the duty of every Moslem to support the head of the state, however unworthy he might be, for the unity of Islam must be preserved at all costs.[1] Hence scholars and poets passed back and forth between the Hijāz and Syria, to some extent bridging the gap between the uncompromising position of the devout of Medina and the freer ways and outlook of those attached to the court at Damascus.

It is exceedingly difficult to deal justly with the Umaiyads, for most of the extant Arabic literature comes from a day when their names were anathema. The Abbasids not only sought to exterminate every surviving member of the previous dynasty but were determined to destroy their very memory. When that was impossible they were portrayed in a most unfavorable light. Their inscriptions were defaced, and those who dared to speak a word in their praise were subject to persecution. The scheme succeeded all too well, for it is impossible to write anything approaching an adequate history of the Umaiyad period. Except for ᶜUmar II (caliph from 99–101/717–20),

[1] A. Guillaume, *The Traditions of Islam* (Oxford, 1924), pp. 44 ff.

Arabic writers have seen little to praise in the personal lives of these caliphs. Their military and political achievements are acknowledged, for they left obvious results which are to the glory of Islam, but in general the Umaiyads are represented as irreligious, loose-living, and uncultivated. Poets flourished at their courts, but otherwise the arts and learning languished. On the whole, Islam has accepted this picture of the dark days preceding the glorious era of the early Abbasids.

Shiites have agreed with the orthodox estimate of the Umaiyads, or rather gone one better, for they look upon ᶜAlī as the first scholar of Islam and on his brief caliphate as witnessing the beginning of true Moslem learning. Hence a modern Moslem writer, the late Amīr ᶜAlī, who spoke of the fourth caliph as the "beloved disciple" and the "scholar," referred to the accession of the Umaiyads as a "blow to the progress of knowledge and liberalism."[2]

To the orthodox as well as to many Occidentals, Moslem learning and the arts of civilization begin with the Abbasids. But recently there has been some tendency to discount the prejudices of most Arabic authors and to give attention to any fragmentary evidence which presents the Umaiyads in a more favorable light. Fortunately, not all Arabic writers fell in line with the official policy. Aḥmad ibn Hanbal, founder of one of the four great schools of Moslem law, impartially reported traditions favorable to the claims of the Umaiyads and the house of ᶜAlī as well as to the Abbasids. However, except for slight traces, the Syrian tradition is lost to us. Wellhausen held that the best acquaintance with the spirit of the Syrian tradition was to be gained from Christian chronicles, particularly the *Continuatio* of Isidor of Seville, where the Umaiyads appear in a very different and more favorable light than that in which they are customarily presented.[3] Furthermore, the anecdotal character of much Arabic writing and the tendency to quote earlier authors extensively have preserved fragmentary evidence which often contradicts the general point of view.

On the literary side the Umaiyad period, except for a widespread love of poetry, is poor compared to the one which followed. Neverthe-

[2] *Spirit of Islam* (rev.; London, 1922), p. 363.

[3] J. Wellhausen, *The Arab Kingdom and Its Fall*, trans. M. G. Weir (Calcutta, 1927), pp. xiv f.

less, it was not as utterly barren as would appear both from the small number of works which have survived and from the remarks of historians. The lack of literary remains from the early days of Islam is to be accounted for in part by the prevalent use of papyrus following the conquest of Egypt. Climatic conditions in Syria, Iraq, and Persia are not conducive to the preservation of that fragile material, and the earliest Arabic papyri from Egypt are chiefly documents, private letters, and accounts.[4] Becker says that the earliest book manuscript which survives is a twenty-seven-page papyrus book dated 229/844. It is interesting that this is in codex rather than roll form.[5] At any time, of course, earlier material may be found, for literary papyri have not yet received as much attention as non-literary. It is difficult, however, to account for the imposing lists of authors from the end of the second century on, unless one supposes modest beginnings in preceding years.

One must use allusions to early authorities with caution, for it is often difficult to distinguish between quotations of oral traditions and those taken from books. It is very likely, however, that some were taken from written sources. I believe there is sufficient evidence for the existence, in Umaiyad times, both of the beginnings of a prose literature and of an interest in books and book-collecting.

First of all, what precisely is meant by a book at this time? According to all reports, Zaid's first edition of the Koran consisted of leaves (*ṣaḥīfa;* pl. *ṣuḥuf*) kept together in some fashion, which were intrusted to the safekeeping of Ḥafṣa, ʿUmar I's daughter. It is uncertain how precise the order was in which they were kept, for at the time of the preparation of the ʿUthmānic Koran there was some disagreement on the arrangement of the *sūra*'s. After that the order was fixed. Both *ṣaḥīfa* and the more common word for book (*kitāb;* pl. *kutub*) refer primarily to pieces of paper, skin, or other materials on which are or may be writing. The terms often refer merely to loose sheets, documents, or letters, but they may also apply to books in the ordinary sense of the word. The Koran was considered a book, the record of separate revelations which are united by common authorship and ultimate purpose. Mohammed himself was aware of the

[4] D. S. Margoliouth, *Catalogue of Arabic Papyri in the John Rylands Library, Manchester* (Manchester, 1933), p. xiv.

[5] C. H. Becker, *Papyri Schott-Reinhardt* (Heidelberg, 1906), I, 8 f., MS P.S.R. 22–49.

existence of books. The last verse of *sūra* 87 refers to the books (*ṣuḥuf*) of Abraham and Moses, and any religious group possessed of sacred books was called the people of Scripture, or "book-people" (*ahl al-kitāb*).

Accordingly it is often impossible to tell whether *ṣuḥuf* and *kutub* are to be understood as books or merely as loose sheets or pages of writing. For example, suppose for the moment the historicity of a tradition to the effect that Anas ibn Mālik (d. 92 A.H.) handed his students writings (*kutub*), containing sayings of the Prophet. Did he have formally published books, or merely loose leaves of notes? Probably the latter. The great canonical compilations of traditions, prepared in the Abbasid period, appear to have been preceded by informal private collections for the use of scholars and their disciples. These are more akin to the notes of a lecturer or the notebooks of his students than to books, as the term is usually understood. But they indicate an appreciation of the value of written records and the tendency to fix oral tradition in a permanent form. According to a report, which occurs in but one version of the *Muwaṭṭa*ᵓ of Mālik ibn Anas, the Umaiyad caliph ᶜUmar II feared that valuable traditions might be lost and ordered one who had known the prophet to gather and commit them to writing. Guillaume and others doubt the trustworthiness of the report on the ground that none of the later writers on tradition refers to such a compilation, and the occurrence of the report in but one version of the *Muwaṭṭa*ᵓ.[6]

There are many reports of learned men in the early days of Islam who committed their collections of traditions to writing, often merely for their own use. Some, having memorized them, destroyed them or ordered this to be done after their death. Years ago Sprenger collected a number of such anecdotes, some of which are probably apocryphal, but in general they represent a prevalent custom. Al-Ḥasan

[6] Guillaume, *op. cit.*, p. 19; al-Shaibanī's version of the *Muwaṭṭa*ᵓ, p. 389; see Sprenger, "Origin and Progress of Writing Down Historical Facts," *Journal of the Asiatic Society of Bengal*, XXV (1856), 303 ff. and cont. 375 ff.; Khuda Bukhsh's translation of von Kremer's *Kultur-Geschichte des Orients*, under the title of *The Orient under the Caliphs* (Calcutta, 1920), pp. 373 ff.; I. Goldziher, *Mohammedanische Studien* (Halle, 1888–90), II, 210. Horovitz, on the other hand, apparently accepted this as authentic; see "The Earliest Biographies of the Prophet and Their Authors," *Islamic Culture*, January, 1928, pp. 24 f., citing Ibn Saᶜd, *Biographien Muhammeds, etc.* (Leyden, 1905–28), II*b*, 134, and Ibn Hajar, *Fatḥ al-Bari bi Sharḥ Ṣaḥīḥ al-Bukhari* (Cairo, 1901–11), XII, 39, as saying that Abū Bakr ibn Mohammed ibn ᶜAmr, judge at Medina (d. *ca.* 120), was so requested by ᶜUmar II. If such a book was written, it was short-lived, for, when asked concerning it, Abū Bakr's son ᶜAbd Allāh admitted it was lost (Ibn Hajar, *ibid.*).

of Baṣra (d. 110/728) had a great mass of notes which he directed to be burned after his death, and he was accused of passing off as oral traditions information which he had really drawn from books.[7] Mūsā ibn ᶜUḳba said that a client of Ibn ᶜAbbās, Kuraib (d. 98 A.H.), possessed a camel-load of the writings (*kutub;* again probably the notes) of Ibn ᶜAbbās (d. 68), a companion of the Prophet. Whenever his grandson ᶜAlī ibn ᶜAbd Allāh (d. 113) wished to refer to any of them, he wrote for such-and-such a page (*ṣaḥīfa*) to the owner, who would send him a copy.[8] Kuraib left these *books* to Ibn ᶜUḳba, and both he and ᶜIkrima utilized them. There are numerous references to students who wrote down the words of their teachers on pages, rolls, tablets, or even on their shoes. Saᶜīd ibn Jubair (d. 95 A.H.) is reported to have said, "In the lectures of Ibn ᶜAbbās, I used to write on my page [or roll: *ṣaḥīfa*]; when it was filled, I wrote on the upper leather of my shoes, and then on my hand." Of the same student it is said that he used to write on his shoes, literally feet, and the next morning copied his notes.[9] Two other sayings seem to indicate that such books or notes had market value. "My father wrote to me when I was at Kūfa, 'Buy books [*kutub*] and write down knowledge, for wealth is transitory, but knowledge is lasting' "; and another: "My father used to say to me, 'Learn by heart, but attend above all to writing, when you come home [probably from lectures] write, and if you fall into need or your memory fails you, you have your books.' "[10]

Ibn Khallikān's remarks on Abū ᶜAmr ibn al-ᶜAlāᵓ (d. 154/770) are suggestive as to the nature of books collected by early scholars.

> The books [*kutub*] containing the expressions he had written down from the lips of the purest speakers among the Arabs of the desert nearly filled one of his rooms [or his house] up to the ceiling, but when he took to reading [the Koran], that is, when he commenced the practice of devotion, he threw them away; and when he returned to the study of his old science, he possessed nothing of it except what he had learned by heart.[11]

[7] De Goeje, art. "Tabari and Early Arabic Historians," *Encyc. Brit.* (9th ed.), p. 2.

[8] Sprenger, "Origin and Progress, etc.," *op. cit.*, p. 325; and *Das Leben und die Lehre des Mohammed* (Berlin, 1861–65), I, xciv; Horovitz, *op. cit.*, p. 167; Ibn Saᶜd, V, 216 (quoting Ibn ᶜUḳba).

[9] Sprenger, "Origin and Progress, etc.," *op. cit.*, p. 321.

[10] *Ibid.*, p. 324. These sayings may be genuine, although they smack of controversy.

[11] *Biographical Dictionary*, trans. De Slane (Paris, 1843), I 400=Arabic text (Cairo, 1310 A.H.), I, 387. Margoliouth's remarks in *Lectures on Arabian Historians* (Calcutta, 1930), p. 97, on Abū ᶜAun ibn al-ᶜAṭaᵓ, sound like a confusion of names, for the dates and details are the same.

Abū ᶜAmr was a philologist and Koran reader, but it is probable that the books (*kutub* or *ṣuḥuf*) of traditionalists were similar collections of notes they had taken down.

As late as 400 A.H. an eccentric scholar of Bagdad, Abū Ḥaiyān al-Ṭawḥīdī, destroyed his books, and, being reproved by the judge Abū Sahl ᶜAlī ibn Mohammed, wrote a letter of apology which Yāḳūt preserves in full. He defends his act by citing the example of men of the past who had done likewise. He says Abū ᶜAmr and Dāūd al-Ṭāʾī burned their books, Tāj al-Amma flung his into the sea, Yūsuf ibn Asbāṭ hid his books in a cavern in the mountains (the entrance to which he blocked), Sulaimān-al-Dārānī put his into an earthen oven and baked them, Sufyān tore up a tremendous number of pages and tossed them to the wind, and, finally, Abū Ḥaiyān's own teacher, Abū Saᶜīd al-Sīrāfī, bequeathed books to his son, with the stipulation that they be burned "if they betray you."[12]

Although it appears that such notes and books were intended merely for the private use of their owners, some crystallized into more formal books and were in a sense published either by repeated dictation to students who thereby multiplied copies or by permitting them to be read and copied. These methods of publication of manuscript books continued in Islam, being augmented later by the custom of having copies multiplied by professional scribes. Many who could not afford the services of a copyist borrowed books or used copies in libraries and made copies for their own use.

We shall never know the extent of the publication of formal works on traditions produced in pre-Abbasid days: only one such work has survived, a small collection known as the *Book of Asceticism* (*Kitāb al-Zuhd*) by Asad ibn Mūsā (d. 133/749).[13] It is curious that although no work on tradition from the pen of Mohammed ibn Sīrīn (d. 110/728), an authority on the subject, has remained, his work on divination of dreams (*Kitāb al-Ghawāmiᶜ*) is still extant.[14]

Traditions of a distinctly Shiite complexion were circulating and perhaps had begun to be gathered in this period, although the canonical Shiite texts came into being even later than the orthodox. ᶜAlī

[12] Yāḳūt, *Biographical Dictionary* ("Gibbs Series" [Leyden, 1907–27]), V, 389.

[13] This work is not yet published (Berlin MS 1553). See Brockelmann, *Geschichte der arabischen Literatur* (Weimar, 1898, 1902), I, 66; Nicholson, *A Literary History of the Arabs* (London, 1907), p. 247.

[14] Brockelmann (*op. cit.*) mentions another work by Ibn Sīrīn. On his reputation as a legalist and interpreter of dreams see Ibn Khallikān (De S.), II, 586 ff.

is frequently spoken of as "the scholar of God in this [Moslem] community,"[15] and he is said to have been one of the few of the Ḳuraish who could write in the earliest days of Islam. The Prophet is reported to have declared that "if all the learning of thc Arabs were destroyed it might be found again in ᶜAlī as in a living library."[16] There are traditions to the effect that ᶜAlī had a special copy of the Koran on which were marginal notes of his own, preserving explanations he had received from Mohammed in conversation. This has grown in Shiite tradition to a mysterious book, the *Jafr*. But al-Bukharī and others say that ᶜAlī disclaimed having a special book, rather that the writings consisted merely of simple regulations for the community. "In it are instructions about the wounded, what to do with the older camels, and the extent of the sacred territory about Medina."[17]

It is not improbable that ᶜAlī had a written record of some instructions given him personally by the Prophet. However, its growth into a document "seventy cubits long as measured by the arm of the Prophet," containing everything "permitted and forbidden" and "everything necessary for mankind," "the knowledge of the prophets and the reports of the prophets and the scholars of the Beni Israel," is typical of the tendencies of traditional literature.[18] The same Shiite writer who describes the *Jafr* in such glowing terms reports that before his death ᶜAlī gave the sacred books and his armor to his son Ḥasan with regulations as to their subsequent disposal.[19]

Popular story-tellers and poets who sympathized with the house of ᶜAlī made so much of the tragedy of Kerbela and other episodes in the history of the blessed family that the caliphs of Damascus were forced to deal with them, either courting their favor and thereby rendering them harmless or, when this failed, silencing them by imprisonment or death. Apparently Shiite tradition had become sufficiently widespread and dangerous to call for official censorship. Al-

[15] D. M. Donaldson, *The Shiᵓite Religion* (London, 1933), p. 46, from al-Ḥasan of Baṣra as preserved by al-Ḳālī, *Kitāb al-Amālī* (Bulaḳ, 1324/1906), III, 173 and 198.

[16] L. Twells, *Life of Dr. Edward Pococke*, Preface to *Theological Works of the Learned Dr. Pococke* (London, 1740), I, 9.

[17] Al-Bukharī, *Ṣaḥiḥ* (Leyden, 1862–68, 1908), II, chap. lviii, §§ 10 and 17; Donaldson, *op. cit.*, pp. 47 f. The author of the *Fihrist* (written 987 A.D., see pp. 40–41) says he saw autographs of ᶜAlī and other of Mohammed's scribes, and of ᶜAlī's sons, Ḥasan and Ḥusain in the library of a devout Shiite bibliophile.

[18] Al-Kulainī (d. 328 or 329/939) *Kāfi fi ᶜIlm al-Dīn* (Teheran, 1889), p. 85, as translated by Donaldson, *op. cit.*, p. 48; see the following pages for other elaborate descriptions of the supposed writings of ᶜAlī; also art. "Djafr," by Macdonald, in *Encyc. Islam.*

[19] Al-Kulainī, *op. cit.*, p. 110; Donaldson, *op. cit.*, pp. 67 f.

Ṭabarī says that Muᶜāwīya ordered the suppression of all traditions favorable to the house of ᶜAlī to be replaced by declarations of the glory of the family of ᶜUthmān, the third caliph and ᶜAlī's predecessor.[20] This would indicate that the caliphs recognized the value of traditions for propaganda purposes. It also falls in line with other indications that a body of distinctly Umaiyad traditions once existed. Remnants of the Syrian tradition are to be found especially in statements which emphasize the sanctity of Jerusalem as a place of pilgrimage at least equal to Mecca and Medina.[21] Al-Zuhrī, of whom more will be said presently, is reported to have confessed "these princes [the Umaiyads] have compelled us to write *ḥadīth*,"[22] and there is every reason to suppose that he was among those who felt no scruples against serving the "godless caliphs."[23]

A most interesting character who flourished under the Umaiyads was the learned lawyer and traditionalist, al-ᵓAᶜmash abū Mohammed Sulaimān ibn Mihrān, who was born in 60 or 61/680 and died in 148/765. The caliph of the time, Hishām ibn ᶜAbd Allāh, wrote a letter to him requiring that he compose a book[24] on the virtues of ᶜUthmān and the crimes of ᶜAlī. Al-ᵓAᶜmash, after reading the note, thrust it into the mouth of a sheep, which ate it up, and said to the messenger, "Tell him I answer it thus." The latter, terrified because he had been told that his life would be forfeited if he returned without a written answer, solicited the aid of the friends of al-ᵓAᶜmash, who finally prevailed on him to send a written reply, which was couched in the following terms: "In the name of God, the Merciful, the Clement! Commander of the Faithful! Had ᶜUthmān possessed all the virtues in the world they had been of no utility to you; and if ᶜAlī committed all the crimes of which the human race is guilty, they had done you no injury. Mind the qualities of your own little self, and adieu!" Ibn Khallikān's sketch of this man bespeaks a vigorous and refreshing personality in whom the independent spirit of the desert Arab was still alive, possessed of a salty wit and a sharp tongue,

[20] Al-Ṭabarī, *Annales*, ed. De Goeje (Leyden, 1879–1901), II, 112; Guillaume, *op. cit.*, p. 47.

[21] Guillaume, *loc. cit.*

[22] *Ibid.*, p. 50; Muir, *Life of Mahomet* (ed. 1861), I, xxxiii, as from Ibn Saᶜd, II, 135.

[23] Cl. Huart, *History of Arabic Literature* (New York, 1903), pp. 61 f.; Nicholson, *op. cit.*, p. 247.

[24] So trans. by De Slane, Ibn Khallikān, I, 588 = Arabic text (Cairo ed.), I, 213, lit.: "Write for me the virtues." The letter devoured by the sheep was on papyrus (*ḳirṭās*).

a lack of awe for position and authority, and a sense of justice. The caliph apparently appreciated this exhibition of the ancient virtues which the Umaiyads admired, for there is no mention that he punished the audacity of al-ʾAʿmash. One may perhaps be pardoned a digression to recount two other anecdotes concerning this interesting character. Some students went to him one day to learn traditions. Greeting them, he announced, "Were there not in the house a person [meaning his wife] whom I detest more than I do you, I should not have come out to you." On another occasion a man followed him as he took a walk and saw him enter a cemetery and lie down in a newly dug grave. As he came out he shook the earth from his head and exclaimed, "Oh, how narrow the dwelling!"[25]

Among the devout there seems to have been a quite sincere feeling that the desire to write books was based on sinful pride, and they sought to avoid the appearance of producing anything which might detract from the unique position of the Koran. This applied to the writing of traditions more than to any other type of literature, probably owing in part to the fact that traditions contained words of the Prophet, which might easily be regarded as of equal interest and authority with those of the sacred book. This attitude continued far down in the history of Moslem literature.

As late as the middle of the fifth century after the Hijra a learned Shāfiʿīte doctor of Bagdad, al-Māwardī (d. 450/1058), refused to publish any of his works, which, however, he kept together in a safe place. As death approached he said to his confidant:

> The books in such a place were composed by me, but I abstained from publishing them because I suspected that, although my intention in writing them was to work in God's service, that feeling, instead of being pure, was sullied by baser motives. Therefore when you perceive me on the point of death and falling into agony, take my hand in yours, and if I press it, you will know thereby that none of these works have been accepted by me; in this case you must take them all and throw them by night into the Tigris, but if I open my hand and close it not, that is the sign of their having been accepted and that my hope in the admission of my intention as sincere and pure has been fulfilled. "When al-Māwardī's death drew near," said the person, "I took him by the hand and he opened it without closing it on mine, whence I knew his labors had been accepted and I then published his works."[26]

[25] *Ibid.*

[26] *Ibid.*, II, 225.

[*To be continued*]

ARABIC BOOKS AND LIBRARIES IN THE UMAIYAD PERIOD—*Continued*

RUTH STELLHORN MACKENSEN

Moslem traditions are valuable not only in themselves, but also because they are the roots from which grew the more important legal, historical, and biographical studies and literature. However formless and temporary the written collections of traditions remained in the Umaiyad period, there was a real beginning in the writing of books on these allied subjects. The celebrated handbook for lawyers, the *Muwaṭṭa*ᵓ, of Mālik ibn Anas, a jurist of Medina (d. 179/759–6), was preceded by similar works, none of which has survived, for instance, by Mohammed ibn ᶜAbd al-Raḥmān al-ᶜĀmirī (d. 120/737), Saᶜīd ibn Abī ᶜArūba (d. 156/773), and ᶜAbd al-Mālik ibn Juraij (d. 150/767). The first of them, al-ᶜĀmirī, was, like Mālik ibn Anas, a pupil of al-Zuhrī, and his work, which bore the same title, *Al-Muwaṭṭa*ᵓ, was considered by some Arabic critics as superior to the later one which has survived.[27] Although this type of book incidentally preserves traditions, that is not its primary purpose, which is rather to establish a system of law based on the customary procedure of Medina. Although Mālik's book was written in the early days of the Abbasids, it is the fruit of earlier legal studies and practice, and furnishes some evidence of the activities during the Umaiyad period. We see in the writings of Mālik and his predecessors the rise of Moslem canon law, which is a long step from the mere recounting and collecting of tradition.[28]

Another legal compendium which purports to come from this period is that attributed to Zaid ibn ᶜAlī (d. about 122/740), an ᶜAlid who led an unsuccessful revolt against the caliphs of Damascus. Although there is evidence that Zaid possessed some learning, it is exceedingly doubtful if this work and others also bearing his name are actually

[27] Brockelmann, *op. cit.*, I, 65 f.; Goldziher, *op. cit.*, II, 220; Guillaume, *op. cit.*, pp. 19 f.

[28] *Encyc. Islam*, art. "Mālik ibn Anas"; Guillaume, *op. cit.*, pp. 20 ff.; D. B. Macdonald, *Development of Muslim Theology, Jurisprudence, and Constitutional Theory* (New York, 1903), pp. 99–103.

from his hand, at least in their present form. It is more likely that they were fathered on him by the sect which bears his name—the *Zaidīya*—and which regards him as one of the martyrs of the Prophet's family.[29]

Moslem traditions consist of unconnected anecdotes purporting to record the words and deeds of the Prophet and events of the early days of Islam. Moslem history arose with the first attempts to put these sources into a more connected narrative form. This takes the shape of biographies of the Prophet and accounts of his military exploits. Hence we have two types of literature dealing with Mohammed's life and work—the biography (*sīra*), and the records of conquest (*maghāzī*). The oldest biography which survives is that of Ibn Isḥāḳ (d. 150/768), in the recension of Ibn Hishām (d. 833 A.D.), and the earliest example of *maghāzī* literature is the *Book of the Wars*, by al-Wāḳidī (d. 822 A.D.). Both were written under the first Abbasids. Behind them lay earlier and perhaps cruder works of similar types.

ᶜUrwa ibn al-Zubair (d. about 94/712–13) was the first so to utilize traditions. He was unusually well situated to gather traditions, for both of his parents were early converts. His paternal grandfather was a brother of Khadīja, Mohammed's first wife and his maternal aunt, ᶜĀʾisha, was the Prophet's favorite wife. ᶜUrwa made good use of his opportunities, and recited numerous traditions on their authority, although it is probable that the inclusion of his name in the genealogies of many traditions purporting to come from ᶜĀʾisha is spurious. He took little part in the political and military escapades of his brother, ᶜAbd Allāh, but lived in studious retirement at Medina, broken only by visits to Egypt and the Umaiyad court at Damascus. ᶜUrwa is considered one of the seven outstanding divines of Medina and is frequently quoted as a most reliable authority. Ḥājji Khalīfa credits him with having written a biography of the Prophet.[30] Of such a work nothing else is known, and it is more likely that the quotations from him in the writings of Ibn Isḥāḳ, al-Wāḳidī, Ibn Saᶜd, al-Balādhurī, al-

[29] Macdonald, *op. cit.*, pp. 36 f.; *Encyc. Islam*, art. "Zaid Ibn ᶜAlī."

[30] *Kashf al-Zunūm* (Leipzig and London, 1835–58), V, 646, § 12464; others say a *maghāzī* work. Horovitz credits Abān, son of ᶜUthmān, the third caliph, with having been the first to put into writing a special collection dealing with *maghāzī*; of his writing nothing has survived. See "The Earliest Biographies of the Prophet and Their Authors," *Islamic Culture*, October, 1927, p. 539.

Ṭabarī, al-Bukharī, and others are either from oral traditions or the brief tractates which are the characteristic form of his writing. Unfortunately at one time in his life ᶜUrwa was influenced by the current prejudice against books other than the Koran and destroyed his writings. His son, Hishām, stated that in 63 A.H. he burned his books of law (*kutub fiḳh*) and subsequently regretted their loss,[31] for he said his books would have been useful to his children. Whether he rewrote them is uncertain, but he took pains to teach traditions to his children and pupils.[32]

There is evidence that with ᶜUrwa we have a genuine beginning of Arabic prose literature. Al-Ṭabarī, in his great history, preserves several fragments of ᶜUrwa's writings in the form of little treatises written to elucidate various points on early Moslem history in response to inquiries made by the caliph ᶜAbd al-Malik,[33] and in one case also by al-Walīd.[34] All of them are preserved on the authority of ᶜUrwa's son, Hishām. One of these is prefaced by the remark, "Thou hast written to me concerning Abū Sufyān and his sortie, and askest me how he then conducted himself."[35] Horovitz has shown that the fragments addressed to ᶜAbd al-Malik connect and are pieces of the same dissertation.[36] Another answer preserved by al-Zuhrī, his pupil, was addressed to Ibn Abī Hunaida, who lived at the court of al-Walīd.[37] It is apparent that these brief expositions, of which there were doubtless others, preceded the writing of longer and more formal books. As has been observed before, the word "books" must be interpreted with caution, and it may be that the only writings of ᶜUrwa were of this sort—short tracts of a page or two each, with little or no effort to connect them. As Caetani has pointed out, although they are mere fragments, the style of which is awkward, they are of great significance

[31] Ibn Saᶜd, V, 113; al-Dhahabī, *Tahdbih*, ed. by Fischer as *Biographien von Gewährsmännern, etc.* (Leyden, 1890), p. 41.

[32] Sprenger, "Von Kremer's Edition of Wāḳidī," *Journal of the Asiatic Society of Bengal*, 1856, p. 208, as from al-Khatīb al-Baghdādī.

[33] Al-Ṭabarī, I, 1180, 1224, 1234, 1284, 1634; probably also 1654, 1636, 1670, 1770.

[34] *Ibid.*, III, 2458.

[35] *Ibid.*, I, 1284, trans. Horovitz, *op. cit.*, p. 549; for a translation of several of the longer sections see Sprenger, *Das Leben, etc.*, I, 356; II, 42; III, 142 ff. For a discussion of ᶜUrwa's significance see *ibid.*, pp. lxii f., and Horovitz's excellent and detailed sketch, *op. cit.*, pp. 542–52; Wüstenfeld, *Die Familie el-Zubeir* (Göttingen, 1878), pp. 51–56.

[36] Horovitz, *op. cit.*, pp. 548 f.

[37] Ibn Hishām, p. 754; al-Ṭabarī, *Tafsīr*, XXVIII, 42; see Horovitz, *op. cit.*, pp. 549 f.

in the development of historical writing.[38] A characteristic of ᶜUrwa's style is the inclusion of bits of poetry of which he is said to have known a great deal.[39] Ibn Isḥāḳ, later, was also fond of quoting verses.

The remark of V. Vacca in his article on ᶜUrwa in the *Encyclopedia of Islam*, "He had collected an *important library* bearing upon many subjects both historical and juridical," is somewhat misleading unless one is reminded that this collection probably consisted of notes taken down by himself and perhaps by others. The same may be said of Sachau's reference to the books ᶜUrwa possessed.[40] It seems very likely that ᶜUrwa at times used documents; for instance, he quotes from Mohammed's letter written to the people of Hajar.[41] Sprenger's remarks on the library of the historian al-Wāḳidī (d. 207/823) apply as well to the libraries of ᶜUrwa and other early historians:

> Al-Wāḳidī's patron spent some 2,000 dinars on books for him, and in addition the historian kept two slaves busy copying others for him, and thereby amassed 600 chests of books, each of which was so heavy that it required two men to carry it. It is evident from his "Book of the Wars" that al-Wāḳidī had gathered thousands of traditions, often the same one in several versions. These he sifted and arranged to make a fairly continuous narrative. There is no reason to doubt that he had some real books, but most of his material consisted of lecture notes [*Kollegien Hefte*] taken down by numerous students.[42]

We are also told that ᶜUrwa's pupil, al-Zuhrī (d. 124/742), owned many books (*kutub*) which filled his house; the study of them so occupied all his time that his wife complained, "By Allāh! These books [*kutub*] annoy me more than three other wives would [if you had them]."[43] At one time he shared the general disapproval of writing but later saw that its use was not incompatible with piety—in fact, his friends jested about his habit of writing down everything he heard. At first his notes were merely for his own convenience, for

[38] *Annali dell'Islām* (Milan, 1905), I, Introd. §§ 11, 269, and 340; Caetani, *Chronographia Islamica*, Fasc. V, pp. 1154 f., lists all the references to ᶜUrwa.

[39] Horovitz, *op. cit.*, pp. 551 f.

[40] E. Sachau, *Ibn Saᶜd's Biography of Mohammed* (Leyden, 1904), III, Part I, Introd., p. xix.

[41] Al-Balādhurī, *Kitāb al-Futuḥ al-Buldān*, ed. De Goeje (Leyden, 1866), p. 79; Ibn Hishām, *Das Leben Muhammeds*, ed. Wüstenfeld (Göttingen, 1858–60), p. 961. Other scholars also had access to copies or originals of the Prophet's official communications; see al-Ṭabarī, *op. cit.*, I, 1717, and Ibn Hishām, p. 961.

[42] *Das Leben, etc.*, III, lxxxi.

[43] Ibn Khallikān (De S.), II, 582 = Arabic text (Cairo ed.), I, 451 f.

after having memorized their contents he tore them up.[44] Later he permitted his writings and the material he dictated to be used by others. He is accused of having permitted a volume of traditions transmitted by him to be circulated without having read it through, although the volume had been submitted to him.[45]

Several of the Umaiyad caliphs thought highly of him, and he is supposed to have admitted that he forged traditions in their favor. The evidence for this charge is of dubious veracity. One would rather agree with Horovitz that whereas at the behest of the caliphs he departed from his former reticence and dictated traditions, this innovation does not prove that he invented *ḥadīth* in their interests. There is even a report, of which there are several versions, that he once engaged in a heated verbal battle with either Hishām or al-Walīd, who tried to force him to change a statement so that it would reflect adversely on ᶜAlī. If true, the story does credit to al-Zuhrī's veracity and personal courage.[46] Whatever the facts may be, nothing has detracted from his reputation as a dependable jurist, traditionalist, and historian. The caliph ᶜUmar II is reported to have sent letters to the various provinces recommending that al-Zuhrī be consulted in all legal difficulties, "for no man is better acquainted than he is with the *sunna* [usages] of times past."[47]

His pupil, Maᶜmar, is authority for the statement that in the library of the caliphs were piles of books (*dafātir*) containing the writings or notes of al-Zuhrī, for he is quoted as saying, "We were of the opinion that we had heard much from al-Zuhrī till al-Walīd was killed; for then volumes from his treasure chambers [khazāʾin] were loaded upon beasts of burden. He [Maᶜmar] means: filled with the learning of al-Zuhrī."[48] Al-Zuhrī was the author of *Kitāb al-Maghāzī*,[49] ("Book of the Wars"), which is frequently quoted. According to his own

[44] Al-Dhahabī, *op. cit.*, p. 67. See anecdotes on him in Horovitz, *op. cit.*, continued in *ibid.*, January, 1928, pp. 46 ff., indicating his changing attitude.

[45] Al-Dhahabī, *op. cit.*, p. 69.

[46] *Ibid.*, p. 72; al-Bukharī and others give variants of the story; see Horovitz, *op. cit.*, p. 41, and, for an estimate of his character and literary activities, pp. 46–50.

[47] Ibn Khallikān (De S.), II, 582; Huart, *op. cit.*, p. 62.

[48] Ibn Saᶜd, II*b*, 136; see also al-Dhahabī, *op. cit.*, p. 71 and note. Maᶜmar ibn Rāshid here quoted was also the author of a *Book of Wars* (Horovitz, *op. cit.*, p. 168); he died 154 A.H. (Horovitz, *op. cit.*, pp. 48 f.; Sprenger, "Von Kremer's Edition of Wāḳidī," *op. cit.*, p. 211).

[49] Ḥājjī Khalīfa, §§ 10513 and 12464.

statement as recorded by al-Ṭabarī,[50] he wrote also a list of the caliphs with their ages, which Margoliouth calls one of the very earliest attempts at written history.[51] Al-Zuhrī is also quoted as saying that he started to write a work on the North Arabian clans which he never completed.[52] The same man who had commissioned him to write it also asked him to compose a biography (*sīra*) of the Prophet.[53] Al-Zuhrī's books, perhaps because of royal patronage, seemed to have been more adequately published and preserved than those of some of his contemporaries, for a scholar of the time of Al-Manṣūr (ruled 754–75 A.D.) said, quoting some traditions: "Al-Zuhrī informed me." Asked where he had met al-Zuhrī, he answered: "I have not met al-Zuhrī, but I found a book of his at Jerusalem."[54] His influence on Moslem studies was considerable: among his pupils were al-ᶜĀmirī and Mālik ibn Anas, two outstanding canon lawyers. Sprenger was of the opinion that al-Zuhrī and one of his teachers, Shuraḥbīl ibn Saᶜd, were influential in giving the biography of the Prophet a stereotyped pattern from which subsequent writers never departed.[55]

Another historian, most of whose life was spent under the Umaiyads, was Abū Mikhnaf (d. 154/744). He was the author of more than thirty historical monographs, considerable parts of which are preserved by al-Ṭabarī. Although most of the independent writings which have come down under his name are probably forgeries, it may be that the one on the death of Ḥusain, the son of ᶜAlī, manuscripts of which exist in several libraries, is genuine.[56] One sees in the treatises of Abū Mikhnaf a continuation of the episodal type of historical writing begun by ᶜUrwa. When Hishām asked al-ᵓAᶜmash to write on the virtues of ᶜUthmān and the sins of ᶜAlī, he probably expected this sort of little treatise. In a collection of traditions on ᶜUmar II there

[50] Al-Ṭabarī, II, 428; *The Years of the Caliphs* is twice quoted by Ṭabarī, *ibid.* and p. 1269.

[51] D. S. Margoliouth, *Early Development of Mohammedanism* (New York, 1914), p. 4.

[52] *Kitāb al-Aghānī* (Bulaḳ, 1284–85 A.H.), XIX, 59, referred to by al-Dhahabī, *op. cit.*, p. 68.

[53] *Al-Aghānī, loc. cit.*

[54] Sprenger, *Origin and Progress of Writing*, p. 328, as from al-Khatīb al-Baghdādī.

[55] *Ibid.*, pp. 202–10; Muir, *op. cit.*, I, xxxviii.

[56] Brockelmann, *op. cit.*, I, 65; *Encyc. Islam*, art. "Abu Mikhnaf"; De Slane's n. 17, p. 448, to Ibn Khallikān IV, 446; Sprenger, *Report of Researches into Muhammadan Libraries of Lucknow* (Calcutta, 1896), p. 3; *Encyc. Brit.* (9th ed.), art. "Ṭabari," p. 2; *Fihrist*, I, 93.

are preserved two letters, one from that caliph asking Sālim ibn ᶜAbd Allāh ibn ᶜUmar to write a biography (*sīra*) of his grandfather ᶜUmar I and the author's reply, promising to accede to the request.[57] From these indications, as well as from the writings of al-Zuhrī, it is apparent that the scope of historical writings was beginning to broaden to include subject matter other than that dealing directly with the career of the Prophet.

Several other early historians are quoted frequently by later authors. Sprenger considered Abū Isḥāḳ (d. 127 or 128 A.H., at an advanced age) and Abū Mijlaz (d. shortly after 100 A.H.) of great importance, for they represent a different line of tradition than that followed by Ibn Isḥāḳ and Ibn Hishām. They are quoted by al-Bukharī and Ibn Saᶜd; nearly the whole of Ibn Hibbān's biography of Mohammed was taken from Abū Isḥāḳ.[58] Abū Maᶜshar (d. 170/786–7), author of a work on *maghāzī*, spent part of his life under the Abbasids, but lived at Medina until 160, hence his work probably represents the studies of that school. He is quoted by al-Wāḳidī, Ibn Saᶜd, and al-Ṭabarī, who depended on him for chronological data.[59]

Al-Suyūṭī preferred the *maghāzī* by Mūsā ibn ᶜUḳba (d. 141/758) to any other, which indicates that this early history was still extant in Egypt in the fifteenth century.[60] Nineteen excerpts from it exist in a college notebook of a student who lived at Damascus in the fourteenth century, which is preserved at Berlin.[61] Mūsā was a student of al-Zuhrī, on whose opinions he depended greatly, and, as seen above, he utilized the writings of Ibn ᶜAbbās, the Prophet's cousin.[62]

Along with strictly religious history, based on the traditions collected by recognized authorities, the Umaiyad period witnessed an interest in other sorts of historical literature, much of which was hardly more than folklore.

The report that Ziyād, the foster-brother of Muᶜāwīya, composed a

[57] Ibn ᶜAbd al-Ḥakam, *Sīrat ᶜUmar ibn ᶜAbd al-ᶜAzīz . . . .* (Cairo, 1346/1927), p. 125.

[58] Sprenger, "Von Kremer's Edition of Wāḳidī," *op. cit.*, pp. 219 f.

[59] *Encyc. Islam*, Horovitz art. "Abū Maᶜshar."

[60] Sprenger, "Von Kremer, etc.," *op. cit.*, p. 219; Mālik ibn Anas also had a very high estimate of Mūsā's work (see Horovitz, *Islamic Culture*, April, 1928, p. 165).

[61] E. Sachau, "Das Berliner Fragment des Mūsā ibn ᶜUḳba," in *Sitzungsberichte der Königlich Preussischen Akademie der Wissenschaften*, 1904, p. 445.

[62] See *AJSL*, LII (1935–36), 249.

book on the pretensions of Arab families, which he intended as a weapon for his descendants in case their origin was ever attacked, is somewhat dubious, although the book is mentioned in the *Fihrist*[63] as the first book of calumny.[64] If genuine, it is indicative of the general interest in genealogical studies, which had practical utility as well as serving to satisfy the inordinate family and tribal pride of the Arabs. It is noteworthy that the literary historian al-Ṣūlī (d. 946 A.D.) says that Ziyād was the first person to copy books, apparently meaning professionally. Genealogical lists served as an army roll, for state pensions and the shares in plunder were apportioned according to the participation of families in the conquests of Islam. Criticism of traditions, consisting largely of the study of the lives, characters, and connections of those who transmitted them, gave further impetus to genealogical studies. Reporters were arranged in classes (*tabaḳāt*). Then as now the preparation of genealogies furnished opportunities for forgeries. A poor but celebrated authority on the companions and life of Mohammed, Shuraḥbīl ibn Saᶜd (d. 123 A.H.), turned his reputation to account. Sprenger said of him, "If a man made him a handsome present, he assured him his father or grandfather or some member of his family was close to the Prophet, and woe to the ancestors of those who did not pay."[65] It is unfortunate that extreme poverty and possibly failing mental powers in old age drove him to such dubious practices, which have tarnished his reputation, for the work of his younger days, especially on *maghāzī*, was regarded as dependable. Mūsā ibn ᶜUḳba refers to the lists Shuraḥbīl wrote of the names of the emigrants to Medina and of those who had participated in the battles of Badr and Uhud.[66]

The need of preserving genealogies led to the establishment of a rolls office. At first, public records for Syria were kept in Greek by Christian scribes, and in Persian for the eastern provinces. Al-Balādhurī says ᶜAbd al-Mālik ibn Marwān first ordered the state registers

[63] *Fihrist*, p. 89, ll. 10 ff.

[64] Huart, *op. cit.*, p. 60; Brocklemann, *op. cit.*, I, 64; I am indebted to Miss Nabia Abbott, of the Oriental Institute, for drawing my attention to al-Ṣūlī's remark on Ziyād as a copyist; see al-Ṣūlī, *Adab al-Kuttāb* (Cairo, 1341), p. 122.

[65] *Op. cit.*, pp. 203 f.; see also p. 201, and Horovitz, *Islamic Culture*, 1927, pp. 552 f.; Ibn Saᶜd, V, 228, 321; al-Dhahabī, ed. Fischer, in *ZDMG*, XLIV, 437; Ibn Hajar, IV, 321.

[66] Ibn Hajar, X, 361; see also IV, 321, for commendation of his knowledge of *maghāzī*; cf. Horovitz, *op. cit.*, p. 552.

to be written in Arabic in the year 81/700,[67] but Barhebraeus says the change from Greek to Arabic was made under Walīd ibn ᶜAbd al-Mālik.[68] Al-Ḥajjāj, the governor of Iraq, transferred the register from Persian to Arabic about A.D. 700.[69] State archives, of course, are not strictly libraries, but their existence indicates a recognition of the value of preserving written records of public affairs.

We have noticed the rise of *maghāzī* literature, histories of the early wars of conquest, and biography (*sīra*) from the pens of serious scholars. At the same time a more popular and legendary variety also flourished, the hearers of which demanded no authorities. A great deal of it was highly fanciful and was originated and perpetuated by popular story-tellers (*ḳuṣṣāṣ*), who recited such tales for the edification and amusement of those who gathered in public houses, on street corners, and at mosques, particularly on festal occasions. Stories of the birth and infancy of Mohammed were especially popular. Much as such tales were enjoyed by the common people, they and their relators were frowned upon by religious authorities, and the *ḳuṣṣāṣ* were not infrequently forbidden to hold forth in mosques. Official disapprobation, however, had little or no effect on the propagation of this pious form of entertainment, and some of the stories were even committed to writing. It is related that the caliph ᶜAbd al-Mālik, seeing his son reading such a book, commanded it to be burned and ordered him to study the Koran instead.[70] In addition to strictly Moslem literature, the Umaiyads relished stories of Arab antiquity and the history of other peoples. Al-Masᶜūdī has a charming account of how Muᶜāwiya was in the habit of giving audience to his people, great and small, daily after the evening prayer and meal; then "he devoted a third of the night to the history of the Arabs and their famous battles, the histories of foreign peoples, their kings and their governments, the biographies of monarchs, including their wars and stratagems and methods of rule and other matters connected with

[67] *Origins of the Islamic State*, trans. P. Hitti (New York, 1916), p. 301.

[68] *The Chronography of Gregory Abûl-Faraj* (*Barhebraeus*), trans. from Syriac by Budge (Oxford, 1932), p. 106.

[69] Al-Balādhurī, *op. cit.*, pp. 465 f.; *Fihrist*, p. 242, gives accounts of the transfer of both registers to Arabic. Al-Suyūṭī, *Ḥusn al-Muḥāḍarah* (Cairo, 1299) II, 9 seems to say that Arabic was first used for the Egyptian *diwān*'s sometime between 86 and 90 A.H.

[70] Nicholson, *op. cit.*, p. 247.

ancient history." After sleeping the second third of the night, the caliph had pages, in whose charge they were intrusted (evidently the royal librarians and readers), bring in books (*dafātir*, a Persian word for "notebooks" or "books"), in which were biographies of kings and accounts of their battles and tactics, which they read to him.[71] These may have been the *Book of the Kings and Past Events* referred to in the *Fihrist*.[72] There it is said that Muᶜāwiya summoned from Ṣanaᶜāᵓ, in the Yemen, ᶜUbaid ibn Sharya to recount to him narratives of past events and the kings of the Arabs and foreigners, after which he commanded them to be recorded. The *Fihrist* also mentions a book of proverbs by the same writer. One of his historical works was much read as late as the fourth (tenth) century, when it was known to al-Masᶜūdī and al-Hamdānī.[73] Krenkow, however, believes that ᶜUbaid is a fictitious person and that both the *Book of Kings* and the *Book of Proverbs* are to be identified with the *Relation of ᶜUbaid Ibn Sharya*, which was actually the work of Ibn Isḥāḳ and revised by Ibn Hishām, as was his biography of the Prophet.[74]

Another Yemenite, who supplied several of the Umaiyad caliphs with a considerable amount of historical, legendary, and biblical lore, and of whose reality there is no question, was Wahb ibn Munabbih (d. 110/728). He is the source from which Moslems have derived much of their knowledge of the ancient world, including that of the South Arabian civilizations. Wildly fanciful stories have been told of his erudition. For instance, he had read ten thousand chapters of the *Wisdom of Luḳmān;* seventy, seventy-two, seventy-three, or even ninety-two of the scriptures of Jews and Christians. Much of the material he recounted was highly legendary, and in later times stories of dubious origin were attributed to him, so that some have considered him merely an audacious liar.[75] The fault, however, lies rather with the nature of the material he transmitted and the use made of his

[71] Al-Masᶜūdī, *Le praires d'or*, ed. Barbier de Meynard [Paris, 1869]), V, 77 f.; see also Nicholson, *op. cit.*, pp. 194 f. The distinction between the activities of the first and last thirds of the night may be that in the first the caliph listened to recitals of history, whereas later he was read to from books. We have other allusions to caliphs' librarians reading to them. This does not necessarily imply that these rulers were illiterate.

[72] P. 89.

[73] Goldziher, *op. cit.*, I, 182 f.

[74] Krenkow, "The Two Oldest Books on Arabic Folklore" (cont.), *Islamic Culture*, April, 1928, pp. 234–36.

[75] See De Slane's estimate of him in *Ibn Khallikān*, III, 673 nn.

name in after-years than with Wahb himself, for he appears to have been a man of piety and integrity.[76] At any rate, he is a source upon which subsequent historians drew heavily. Krenkow has recently edited his *Book of the Crowns concerning the Chronicles of the Kings of Himyār*,[77] revised by Ibn Hishām, who misused and enlarged it in the same fashion as he did the *Sīra* by Ibn Isḥāḳ. Krenkow calls this work "the oldest book in profane Arabic literature which has been preserved" and "the only epic the Arabs have produced," carrying the story of the Arabs from creation to the time of Islam.[78] Wahb was acquainted with the legend of Alexander the Great (*Dhuʾl-Ḳarnain*), although he makes him a Yemenite king, and there are other evidences for non-Semitic origins of some of his stories. It is obvious that he had read both Jewish and Christian literature, canonical and apocryphal, but much as he was indebted to his ancient sources, the distinctive quality of the book itself is due to "the exuberant imagination of the author, which has never been equaled again in Arabic literature."[79] The *Tījān*, as well as the above-mentioned *Relation of ʿUbaid ibn Sharya*, served two purposes: to celebrate the glorious past of South Arabia and to furnish information on the nations of the past who are alluded to in the Koran.[80] Several other books covering a wide range of subject matter are ascribed to Wahb. His writings were handed down by his pupils and members of his own family. A grandson, ʿAbd al-Munʿim ibn Idrīs (d. 229 A.H.), devoted himself to their preservation.[81] His *Kitāb al-Mubtada*, used by al-Thaʿlabī in the version of ʿAbd al-Munʿim, is attributed to the latter in the *Fihrist*.[82] It gave the origin of man according to biblical accounts, and stories of prophets and saints of the past, so that it forms a sort of introduc-

[76] Horovitz gives very sympathetic sketches of Wahb's character and literary activities in his article, "Wahb ibn Munabbih," in *Encyc. Islam.*, and in "The Earliest Biographies, etc.," in *Islamic Culture*, 1927, pp. 553–59.

[77] For a résumé of *Al-Tījān* see Krenkow, *op. cit.*, January, 1928, pp. 55–89, and cont. April, 1928, pp. 204–36. This work is referred to by Yāḳūt, *op. cit.*, VII, 232, as *The Book of the Crowned Kings of Himyār and Reports and Stories concerning Them and Their Sepulchres and Their Poems*; see Horovitz, "Earliest Biographies," *op. cit.*, p. 557.

[78] Krenkow, *op. cit.*, pp. 232 f.

[79] *Ibid.*, p. 233. For the frequent confusion of the Alexander legend with that of other heroes see *Encyc. Islam*, arts. "Dhūʾl-Ḳarnain," "Iskandar," "Iskandar Nāma." Some version of the Alexander legend was known to Mohammed and utilized in the Koran in *Sūra* xviii on Mūsā, vss. 59 ff.; also vss. 82 ff. on Dhūʾl-Ḳarnain.

[80] Krenkow, *op. cit.*, pp. 55 and 232 ff.

[81] *Encyc. Islam*, art. "Wahb ibn Munabbih," p. 1084.

[82] P. 94.

tion to the history of revelation which culminates in the Prophet of the Arabs. This is probably the same work which Ḥājji Khalīfa called the *Kitāb al-Israīlīyāt*, for Yāḳūt says that Wahb "took much from old books which are known as Israīlīyāt."[83] Two works containing wise sayings, the *Ḥikma* and the *Manᶜiza*, are mentioned and were known in Spain in the sixth century A.H.[84] A translation of the Psalms of David, a theological work, *Kitāb al-Ḳadar*,[85] and a historical work, the *Futūḥ*,[86] are attributed to him. Becker discovered among the papyri of the Schott-Reinhardt collection a Fasciculus from a biography of Mohammed by Wahb dealing with events before the flight of Medina. As has been mentioned, this twenty-seven-page papyrus book, written on fifty-three sides, is the oldest Arabic book manuscript in existence. It is dated *dhuᵓl-ḳaᶜda*, 229 A.H.[87] Horovitz observed that although the Heidelberg fragment adds little new information, it is important as establishing "the fact that early in the year 100 A.H. or earlier the biography of the Prophet was narrated exactly as in later works."[88] It appears, therefore, that the tradition that Wahb dealt with distinctly Moslem subjects, as well as ancient lore, is founded on fact.[89]

The popularity enjoyed by Wahb is but one indication that the Arabs had by this time become interested in antiquity. Al-Masᶜūdī says he saw in 303 A.H. at Iṣtakhr a valuable book on the sciences of the Persians and the history of their kings, which had belonged to the royal library. It was taken by the Arabs in conquest, and in 113 A.H. was translated for Hishām ibn ᶜAbd al-Mālik. Al-Masᶜūdī drew some of his information on Persian history from this book.[90]

CHICAGO, ILLINOIS

83 Yāḳūt, *op. cit.*

84 Ibn Saᶜd, VII*b*, 97; *Bibliotheca Arabico-Hispana*, ed. Codera and Ribera (1895), IX, 129 and 294.

85 Yāḳūt, *op. cit.*

86 Ḥājjī Khalīfa, § 8932; on the writings of Wahb see Horovitz, "Earliest Biographies," *op. cit.*, pp. 555–57.

87 Becker, *op. cit.*, I, 8 f.

88 Horovitz, *op. cit.*, p. 559. This helps to substantiate Sprenger's thesis that the pattern of the biographies was set very early, and in the light of it one must perhaps qualify the statement that the oldest biography extant is Ibn Isḥāḳ's in the recension of Ibn Hishām.

89 According to Ibn Saᶜd, VII*b*, 97, the studies of Wahb embraced "narratives of the Prophet, of the pious and the Banū Israīl."

90 *Kitāb al-Tanbīh*, ed. De Goeje (Leyden, 1894), p. 106.

[*To be continued*]

ARABIC BOOKS AND LIBRARIES IN THE UMAIYAD PERIOD—*Concluded*

RUTH STELLHORN MACKENSEN

Moslems of the Umaiyad period also turned to literature of the pre-Islamic days in the desert. As mentioned above, Wahb prepared collections of wise sayings and the *Fihrist* credited ᶜUbaid with having written a book of proverbs. The same book[91] mentions another work on the same subject (*Kitāb al-Amthāl*), by one ᶜIḳāla ibn Karīm al-Kilābī, written in the days of Yazīd son of Muᶜāwiya (caliph 60–64/679–83). The author of the *Fihrist*, writing at the end of the fourth century after the Hijra, adds, "It is about fifty pages and I have seen it." The oldest collection of proverbs which survives is that of al-Mufaḍḍal al-Dabbī (d. 170/876, published at Stamboul in 1300). These fragments of the homely wisdom of the Bedawis appealed both to the general interest in the past and to the special interest of philologists, who found in them valuable sources for their minute linguistic studies, as well as legendary and historical material.[92]

Even more enthusiastic was the gathering and study of ancient poetry. Although the formal collecting of it was the special province of the philologists, poetry also had a popular appeal. Accordingly, Hammād al-Rāwīya received a present of 100,000 dirhems from the caliph Walīd ibn Yazīd for his recital in one sitting of twenty-nine hundred odes composed before Mohammed.[93] This reciter is remembered chiefly for his collection, known as the *Muᶜallaḳāt.* His ability to judge poetry and poets, to detect plagiarisms and borrowings, was highly respected. Although a contemporary, al-Mufaḍḍal al-Dabbī, accused him of introducing his own verses into ancient poems, none possessed the critical ability to detect forgeries.[94] Unfortunately, many others succumbed to the same temptation, the

[91] *Fihrist*, p. 90.

[92] *Encyc. Islam*, art. "Mathāl"; Brockelmann, *op. cit.*, I, 67; Goldziher, *op. cit.*, II, 204.

[93] Ibn Khallikān (De S.), I, 470.

[94] *Aghānī*, V, 172, ll. 16 ff.; see art. on him in *Encyc. Islam*, and Nicholson, pp. 132–34.

recognition of which fact has thrown suspicion of late on the authenticity of all poetry purporting to come from the early days.[95]

The cultivation and study of pre-Islamic as well as contemporary verse during the Umaiyad period is so well known and has been treated so frequently by modern scholars that I shall restrict myself here chiefly to indications of the existence of poetry in writing. Sir Charles Lyall, whom few have equaled in appreciation and knowledge of ancient Arabic poetry, said:

> It seems probable that the greater part, at any rate of pre-Islamic verse which has survived to us, was already in writing by the middle of the 4th century: either in the shape of *dīwān*'s, or collections consisting entirely of pieces by the same author, or of tribal aggregates, containing all the occasional pieces composed by members of one tribe or family, perhaps with the addition of the traditions which link them together, and grouped about the occasions which called them forth.[96]

In the same article Lyall refers to *dīwān*'s as "a sort of library," that is, they represent efforts to collect, arrange, and preserve hitherto stray and scattered verses in a permanent form. Whether kept in the memory or in writing, these collections were the means whereby the old poetry passed on to later generations. Undoubtedly much was lost as the Arabs spread from the confines of their peninsula, but it is due to these early attempts at collecting that anything at all survives. Yunus the *kātib*, a singer of Persian origin whom Walīd ibn Yazīd brought to court from Medina, in 742 A.D. composed a *Book of Song* which served as a model for the more famous one (*Kitāb al-Aghānī*) of Abū˒l-Faraj al-Isfahānī (d. 967 A.D.)[97]

Al-Farazdak (b. 20, d. 110 or 114 A.H.), in a poem belonging to the famous exchange of satires (*naḳā˒iḍ*), between himself and Jarīr lists twenty-two poets, most of whom flourished before Mohammed, whom he claims as masters in his art, and speaks of their verses as in writing.[98] He mentions owning a complete edition of the odes of Labīd, the latter years of whose life were spent under Islam.[99]

[95] For instance, see Tāḥā Ḥusain, *Al-Shi˓r al-Jāhilī* (Cairo, 1926), and *Al-Adab al-Jāhilī* (Cairo, 1927); Margoliouth, "The Origins of Arabic Poetry," *JRAS*, 1925, pp. 417–49, from whom the Arabic scholar drew his theory.

[96] *Some Aspects of Ancient Arabic Poetry*, reprinted from the *Proceedings of the British Academy* (Oxford, 1918), VIII, 10.

[97] Huart, *op. cit.*, pp. 47 f.

[98] *The Naḳā˒id of Jarīr and al-Farazdak*, ed. A. A. Bevan (Leyden, 1905–7), I, Part II, 200 f., with reference to the writing of the poems in vs. 61.

[99] *Ibid.*, vs. 57.

Dhūᶜl-Rumma (78–117 A.H.), a Bedawi poet of the same period, although able to write, considered it unbecoming (*ᶜaib*) a nomad.[100] However, he dictated his composition to his *rāwīs*, who wrote them down, for he said, "A book does not forget or alter words or phrases which have taken the poet a long time to compose."[101]

The poetess Laila al-Akhyaliyyā and the poet al-Nābigha engaged in a poetic quarrel of the usual sort, in which each lampooned the tribe of his rival. The tribe of al-Nābigha took offense at some of Laila's verses and lodged a complaint with the ruler of Medina, by whom ᶜUmar I or ᶜUthmān is probably meant. The intrepid poetess, hearing of their plan, added further fuel to the fire by appending the following verses to her satire.

> News has reached me that a tribe at Shaurān is urging forward
> jaded riding camels.
> Night and morning is their embassy journeying with a sheet
> of writing to get me flogged,
> What a bad piece of work [on their part]!

Professor Krenkow points out that the people who were to lodge the complaint brought the offending piece of poetry to the arbitrator in writing.[102]

Al-Ṭabarī quotes a certain ᶜAbd Allāh ibn ᶜAlī as saying he had collected the *dīwān*'s of the Banū Marwān (the Marwānid branch of the Umaiyad house), and adds that no *dīwān* more complete or authoritative than that of Hishām is to be seen.[103] Several members of the royal house displayed poetic talents; outstanding among them were Yazīd (caliph 680–83 A.D.), son of Muᶜāwiya and his mother Maisūn, who at Damascus sang of her longing for the freedom of desert life.[104] The greatest of them all was al-Walīd II (caliph 743–44 A.D.), a poet probably of equal rank with the famous Abū Nuwās (d. *ca.* 810 A.D.).

A son of Jamᶜa, the daughter of the poet al-Kuthayyir (d. 723 A.D.), is cited as authority for the statement that among the books of his father, containing the verses of al-Kuthayyir, a certain poem was

[100] *Aghānī*, XVI, 121, l. 9.

[101] Krenkow, "The Use of Writing for the Preservation of Ancient Arabic Poetry," in *A Volume of Oriental Studies Presented to E. G. Browne* (Cambridge, 1922), p. 266.

[102] *Ibid.*, p. 263; the verses and episodes are given in *Aghānī*, IV, 134, ll. 7–11.

[103] Al-Ṭabarī, II, 1732, under the year 125.

[104] Nicholson, *op. cit.*, pp. 195 f.

found.[105] Probably many families prized little libraries of songs, and it is more than likely that the royal family owned a considerable quantity of poetry, both from the bygone days which they admired so greatly and the products of the numerous singers who flocked to their court and enjoyed their patronage. Most famous of these were Jarīr and al-Farazdak, whose poetic scolding match (as Nicholson aptly translates *muhājāt*) lasted for years and excited the enthusiasm of all classes of society. The verses which each flung at his rival were caught up by their respective partisans, who disputed endlessly about their merits. The court and even the army, according to a picturesque story in the *Aghānī*, entered the fray with zest.[106] A third poet, al-Akhṭal, who had come from Hira to Damascus, where he was a great favorite, sided with al-Farazdak and also engaged in *naḳā'iḍ* with Jarīr.[107]

Although the court of the caliphs drew most of the best-esteemed bards of the day, poetry also flourished in the Hijāz. A distorted picture of the times ensues if one presses too far the contrast between the free and easy life of the Umaiyads and their followers and the stern Puritanism of the faithful of Medina. With all their preoccupation with matters religious, the inhabitants of that sacred city had their lighter moments, or perhaps more accurately one should say that Medinese society was of two kinds: one seriously devout and the other frivolous and luxury-loving. As elsewhere it is likely that some individuals enjoyed moments of gaiety as well as others of religious zeal. Mālik ibn Anas seems to have once had ambitions as a poet, but because of his lack of personal beauty, turned to law. The oft married Sukaina (d. 117/735), a great granddaughter of the Prophet, was a leader of fashion; a hairdress she affected was copied by those who wished to dress *à la Sukaina*. She was easily one of the most outstanding women of her time. Her personal courage, chastity, fastidiousness, and dignity, as well as her pride in her own beauty, her

[105] Krenkow, *op. cit.*, p. 266, from *Aghānī*, VIII, 30.

[106] *Aghānī*, VII, 55, ll. 12 ff.; see Nicholson, pp. 239 f. Professor D. B. Macdonald draws my attention to the Scotch expression "flyting" as the equivalent of *muhājāt*.

[107] In one of the Akhṭāl's poems he refers to ancient manuscripts in the simile, "Just as if they were, through the length of time which has passed, decayed leaves of a book which are spread out" (*Dīwān*, p. 156, l. 4, quoted by Krenkow, "The Use of Writing, etc.," *op. cit.*, p. 264). On the poets of the Umaiyad period see Nicholson, pp. 235 ff., and Huart, pp. 46 ff.

daughter whom she decked with jewels, and her ancestry are elaborated by numerous writers. Anecdotes are related to illustrate her wit and fondness for perpetrating jokes and hoaxes.[108] As the daughter of the gifted poetess Rahab bint ᶜImr al-Ḳais ibn ᶜAdī, she was devoted to poetry, and her good taste and judgment brought the best poets of the day to her door. Ibn Khallikān preserves a story of how she pointed out the artificiality of the sentiments expressed in the verses of ᶜUrwa ibn Uzaina, a poet and traditionalist of the tribe of Laith (d. 118/736). Meeting him one day, she asked him if he were the author of the verses

> When I feel in my heart the flames of love, I try to cool its ardor by draughts of water. Could I ever succeed in cooling with water the exterior of my heart, how should I extinguish the fire which rages in its interior?

He admitted they were his, and she asked him again if he had composed the following:

> When I revealed to her the secret of my love, she replied, "You used to desire [secrecy and] concealment when with me; be veiled then [as to your passion]: see you not how many are around us?" To this I answered, "The love I bear you and [the pains] I feel have already cast a veil over my sight."

The poet acknowledged these also as his, on which the lady said to the slave girls standing around her, "You are free, if such verses ever came from a heart wounded by love!"[109] So great was the esteem in which Sukaina was held, her burial was delayed several hours, the governor having sent word that it be postponed until his arrival.[110]

Her character and activities are typical of one aspect of the life of those who found or were forced to accept Medina as a pleasant place of retirement from the political turmoil of the Syrian capital. It must be admitted that for many, including even members of the Umaiyad house, this retirement to Medina was far from voluntary. A considerable group who for various reasons were unwelcome at the caliph's court in Damascus sought to make their practical exile as pleasant as possible, at the same time being conscious that Medina was no longer the center of the Moslem world. The more active and politically

108 See *Aghānī*, XVII, 94, 97, 101; Ibn Khallikān (De S.), I, 581 ff.

109 Ibn Khallikān, *ibid.*

110 *Encyc. Islam*, art. "Sukaina bint al-Ḥusain."

ambitious considered a life of gaiety and ease in the "provinces" a sorry substitute for participation in the affairs of state. Men of the caliber of ᶜAbd al-ᶜAzīz and ᶜAbd al-Mālik frankly chafed at their confinement and sought means to end it. At any rate, they had the good fortune to possess the means of passing their time agreeably, for the booty which fell to their lot from the wars of conquest enriched many families who lived in a luxury unknown in pre-Islamic days, except to those Arabs who had come in contact with Persia and Byzantium. They owned beautiful palaces, gardens, and rich meadows in and near the city. Part of the population consisted of the devout, who were drawn to make Medina their home because of its sacred memories. Happy in the comparative quiet and seclusion of the sacred city, they devoted themselves to the study of tradition, upon which they built an elaborate legal and ritual system. Honored by this group, but not necessarily always an integral part of it, were numerous descendants of Mohammed. The career of Sukaina is evidence that at least some members of the family of the Prophet participated in the social life of Medina, the luxury of which became notorious.[111] This was the golden age of Medina, sung by poets who passed back and forth between the Hijāz and Syria.[112] ᶜUrwa, whose encounter with Sukaina has just been related, in the company of several other poets once paid a visit to the court of Hishām ibn ᶜAbd al-Mālik. ᶜUrwa, a placid soul, whose poems on contentment circulated widely, was recognized by the caliph, who quoted some of his verses, and said, "I do not see that you act in conformity to your words, for you have now come from Hijāz to Syria in search of favors."

"Commander of the Faithful!" replied the poet, "You have given me a good lesson and reminded me of that which the lapse of time has caused me to forget."

He left at once and, mounting his camel, set off for Medina. That night Hishām noticed his absence and realized the probable consequences. "That man is a member of the tribe of Ḳuraish and his words are wisdom; he came to see me, but I repulsed him and refused to grant him what he required; he is also a poet and I shall be exposed to his satires."

[111] *Aghānī*, XXI, 197, l. 19; al-Ṭabarī, II, 1910.

[112] *Encyc. Islam*, art. "Madīna."

He sent off at once a messenger after ᶜUrwa with a present of two thousand dinars, who overtook the poet at his house. ᶜUrwa received him and the gift and said, "Give my salutation to the Commander of the Faithful, and ask him what he now thinks of my verses: I toiled for favors and was called a liar; I then returned home and they came to me."[113]

Although poetry enjoyed a tremendous popularity in Umaiyad days, it was also put to practical use by the philologists, who found in the ancient lines the material for their studies. The invention of Arabic grammar is traditionally assigned to Abūᵓl-Aswad al-Duᵓalī (d. *ca.* 69/688–89), of Baṣra, who is said to have received his original idea from the caliph ᶜAlī. It is more likely that other reports which trace the suggestion to Ziyād ibn Abīhī are more dependable though less devout. Various stories are told to account for the need of this science; the element of truth in them seems to be that Persian converts, of whom there were many in Baṣra, so mutilated their newly adopted language that it was necessary to introduce a formal study of Arabic grammar. The tradition further credits Abūᵓl-Aswad with having composed a grammatical treatise, and this is confirmed by that careful scholar al-Nadīm, who says in the *Fihrist,* describing a most unusual library he was once privileged to examine:

> I discovered also in these papers a proof that grammar was invented by Abūᵓl-Aswad; it was a document of four sheets on Chinese paper, I believe, and bearing this title, "Discourse on the Governing and the Governed Parts of Speech, by Abūᵓl-Aswad, in the Handwriting of Yaḥya ibn Yaᶜmar" (one of the grammarian's disciples); underneath were inscribed in old characters (*bi khaṭṭ ᶜatīk*) these words, "This is the handwriting of such a one, the grammarian." Then followed a note by al-Naḍar ibn Shumail.[114]

The school of grammarians thus started at Baṣra continued to flourish and was, from the end of the eighth century on, in constant rivalry with the school of Kūfa. Scholars of both places, however finespun their theories and distinctions, ultimately referred to

[113] Ibn Khallikān (De S.), I, 582 f.

[114] P. 41. This same library prized autographs of several early grammarians and philologists, among them one by Abū ᶜAmr ibn al-ᶜAlā; see *Encyc. Islam*, art. "Abūᵓl-Aswad"; art. on "Abūᵓl-Aswad" by Ibn Khallikān (De S.), I, 662 ff., and notes. Note here how the traditions of ᶜAlī's and Ziyād's connections with the beginnings of the science are combined.

pre-Islamic usage as preserved in poetry for their proofs and sanctions. From the beginning at Baṣra,[115] philologists busied themselves with collecting and writing down the verses still to be heard on the lips of the Bedawis of the desert, who spoke the purest Arabic. The collection of poetry owned by one of the founders of the schools of Baṣra, Abūʾl-ᶜAmr ibn al-ᶜAlāʾ al-Māzinī, has been referred to before.[116] He was unusually conscientious in his methods, although he confessed forging at least one verse.[117] Ibn Khallikān has several delightful anecdotes about him, one to the effect that each day he spent a coin for a new water-pitcher and another for a fresh nosegay. At evening he gave the latter to a maid, who tore the flowers to bits to perfume the water used by the household.[118] His candor and sense of humor concerning his studies are well illustrated. One said to him, "Tell me of the work you composed on the subject which you call *Arabism;* does it contain all the language of the desert Arabs?" Abūʾl-ᶜAmr answered that it did not, and his questioner then asked, "How do you manage when the Arabs furnish you with examples contrary to your own rules?" To this Abūʾl-ᶜAmr replied, "I follow the majority of the cases and call the rest dialects."[119]

It appears from this conversation that he wrote some sort of treatise, based on his collection of sayings and poems.[120] The commentary of al-Sukkarī on the *dīwān* of Zuhair ibn Abī Sulma says that in addition to books Abūʾl-ᶜAmr also collected ancient coins which had been found.[121]

The activities of Arabic philologists were but one aspect of the study and elucidation of the Koran which paralleled the study and collecting of traditions. The father of Koranic exegesis was ᶜAbd

115 Lyall was of the opinion that the search for poetry was more active at Kūfa, which was near Ḥīra, where Arabic writing and literature were cultivated in pre-Islamic times. Kūfa was also the headquarters of ᶜAlīʾ. See Lyall's editicn of the *Mufaḍḍalīyāt* (Oxford, 1918), II, xii f.

116 See above.

117 *Encyc. Islam*, art. "Abūʾl-ᶜAmr ibn al-ᶜAlāʾ."

118 Ibn Khallikān (De S.), II, 401.

119 *Ibid.*, p. 402.

120 See also *Fihrist*, pp. 28 and 41 l. 2.

121 Manuscript of the German Oriental Society, information from a personal communication from Professor Krenkow. On his library see also J. Zaidan, *History of Islamic Civilization* (Cairo, 1922), III, 47, as from Ḥājjī Khalīfa. On the schools of Baṣra and Kūfa see Nicholson, *op. cit.*, pp. 342 ff.

Allāh ibn ᶜAbbās, Mohammed's cousin. The date of his death is given variously as 68/687–8 or 69 or 70. Once governor of Baṣra under ᶜAlī, he proved unscrupulous, and, following the assassination of the latter, he found it advisable and agreeable to attach himself to Muᶜāwiya. Thereafter he devoted himself to literary pursuits. Politically an opportunist, he was hardly more dependable as a scholar. He and a much-quoted traditionalist, Abū Huraira (d. 57, 8 or 9 A.H.) fabricated so many tales to suit their several purposes that even their contemporaries could not have failed to recognize them as little better than audacious, though pious, liars. In spite of the fact that the Koran is said to contain all knowledge needful to mankind, Ibn ᶜAbbās, like many others, drew on Jewish and Christian traditions and scriptures, although gathered secondhand. A South Arabian Jew, Kaᶜb ibn Mātiᶜ, furnished him with much of his information. According to Barhebraeus, the gospels had been translated into Arabic for the Amīr ᶜAmr ibn Saᶜd, by John I, patriarch of Antioch, known as John of Sedras, who came to the archepiscopal throne in A.D. 631 and died in 648.[122] Ibn ᶜAbbās is one of the few Meccans reputed to have been able to write before the days of Islam. His library of notes as we have seen, was drawn upon by several scholars.[123] Whether or not the commentary attributed to him in al-Kalbī's redaction and presumably quoted by al-Thaᶜlabī (d. 427/1036), of which several manuscripts exist,[124] actually goes back to him, it is likely that he made some sort of compilation. Fr. Buhl, in an article on him in the *Encyclopedia of Islam*, says, "He did not however confine himself to relating occasional traditions and to answering questions put to him; he welded his tales into a great system which took into account the creation, the history of mankind, and the pre-Islamic times."[125] A commentary is also ascribed to Saᶜīd ibn Jubair (d. 95/714), who was noted for his piety and learning.[126] The writings of the earliest Koranic

[122] *Chronicon Ecclesiasticum*, ed. Abbeloos and Lamy (Paris, 1872–77), I, 275. Is the Amīr referred to ᶜAmr ibn Saᶜīd al-Ashdaḳ, a nephew of Marwān who was put to death 70/689–90 because of his ambitions for the caliphate? See the *Encyc. Islam* art. on him; also *Encyc. Brit.* (9th ed.), art. "Syriac Literature," by Wright, p. 839.

[123] See above; Sprenger, *Das Leben*, I, xciv.

[124] Printed in Bombay, 1302 A.H.

[125] See also Nicholson, pp. 144 f.; Brockelmann, 1, 90, Sprenger, *Das Leben, etc.*, pp. cvi–cxv. On the undependability of Ibn ᶜAbbās and Abū Huraira see also III, lxxxii ff., and Caetani, *Annali dell'Islām* (Milan, 1905), I, 47–51.

[126] *Fihrist*, p. 34, ll. 6–7.

exegetes have not come down intact, but are incorporated in the enormous commentary of al-Ṭabarī (d. 922 A.D.).

At Damascus especially Moslems came into contact with Christian learning, and the beginnings of Moslem theology and philosophy are doubtless due, at least in part, to this influence. The simple faith of early Islam became self-conscious when brought up against another religion possessed of an elaborate system of doctrine and ritual, as well as a scripture collected in a real book, giving a biography of its founder. Christians were employed regularly by Muᶜāwiya and succeeding caliphs of his house, and not a few rose to positions of influence at court. Sergius, the father of John of Damascus, the last great theologian of the Greek church, for a long time served them as treasurer. Later his son became *wazīr*—a position he held until he withdrew from active affairs to a life of contemplation. John's writings and those of his pupil, Theodorus Abucara, contained treatises on Islam in the form of debates between Christians and Moslems. A common introduction, "When the Saracen says to you such and such, then you will reply . . . . ," would indicate that discussion between exponents of the two religions was common at Damascus.[127] Professor Arnold said, "The very form and arrangement of the oldest rule of faith in the Arabic language suggest a comparison with similar treatises of St. John of Damascus and other Christian fathers."[128]

Two of the earliest sects of Islam arose in Syria, the Ḳadarites and the Murjites. The latter are so called because they postpone or defer judgment against sinful Moslems until the day of final reckoning, and in fact this sect denied the orthodox doctrine of eternal punishment and emphasized the goodness of Allah and his love for mankind. This position agrees with the teaching of the Eastern church as formulated by John of Damascus. The Ḳadarites on their part dissented from the predestinarianism which characterized Mohammed's teaching in the latter part of his life and which was accepted by most of his followers, and preached instead the doctrine of free will. Once more the influence of Eastern Christianity is evident. Eventually the Ḳadarite position merged with that of the Muᶜtazilites.[129] How much

[127] Macdonald, *op. cit.*, pp. 131 f.

[128] *The Preaching of Islam* (New York, 1913), p. 74; see also von Kremer, *Kulturgeschichtliche Streifzüge auf dem Gebiete des Islams* (Leipzig, 1873), p. 8.

[129] Macdonald, *op. cit.*, pp. 131 ff., and arts. Ḳadar and Ḳadarīya in *Encyc. Islam;* Arnold, *op. cit.;* Nallino, "Sul nome di Qadariti," in *Rivista degli studi orient.*, VII, 461 ff.;

actual writing was done by these early theologians is questionable. Whatever was done probably took the form of short treatises, of which the religious exhortation written by al-Ḥasan of Baṣra (d. 110/728–9)[130] to the caliph ᶜUmar II may be regarded as typical. The versatile Wahb ibn Munabbih is said to have written on *Ḳadar*. Krenkow suggests that part of this work may be preserved in the *Tījān*, of which the earlier portions in their present form are full of discussions on *Ḳadar*.[131]

Of course it must not be forgotten that several Arab tribes had accepted Christianity before the time of Mohammed, as in the case of the Lakhmids and Ghassanids, and part of the influence of Christian thought may perhaps be traced to them. Most of the Christian Arabs eventually accepted Islam, but even those who remained loyal to their old faith lived in contact with Moslems, as did the poet Akhtal, of Hira, who flourished at the court of Damascus. Moslem mysticism also developed from contacts with Christian hermits and monks who were scattered throughout Arabia, Syria, and Iraq.[132] Some of the Christian Arabs had come in contact with Greek thought, as is to be seen in the case of George, who was ordained bishop of the Monophysite Arabs in Iraq in A.D. 686. He lived at ᶜĀḳōlā—that is, Kūfa—and died in 724. He wrote extensively on theology and philosophy, his main work being a version of the *Organon* of Aristotle, with commentary.[133]

The precise degree and nature of Christian influence on Moslem thought at Damascus of course cannot be ascertained. Professor Macdonald has said, "We are not to think of the Moslem divines as studying the writings of the Greek fathers, but as picking up ideas from them in practical intercourse and controversy."[134]

Wensinck, *The Muslim Creed* (Cambridge, 1932), pp. 51 f. A modern Moslem reviewing this last work disagrees with this position and suggests rather that John of Damascus was influenced by Islam (review in *Islamic Culture*, April, 1933, p. 337).

130 For the text of this treatise see von Kremer, *Geschichte der herrschenden Ideen des Islams* (Leipzig, 1868), p. 22.

131 Krenkow, "The Two Oldest Books . . . . ," *op. cit.*, p. 232.

132 See my art., "Background of the History of Moslem Libraries," in *AJSL*, LII, No. 2 (January, 1936), p. 106.

133 Sarton, *Introduction to the History of Science* (Baltimore, 1927–31), I, 493; Wright, art. "Syriac Literature," *Encyc. Brit.* (9th), p. 841.

134 *Op. cit.*, p. 132.

A most vexed and probably never to be settled question is that of the transmission of Greek philosophy and science, much of which was in the hands of the Christians of Syria and Egypt, to the Arabs during the Umaiyad period. This centers about the problem of the dependability of several statements to the effect that the prince Khālid ibn Yazīd (665–704 or 8 A.D.), a grandson of Muᶜāwīya, caused translations to be made of Greek books on alchemy, medicine, and astronomy (or astrology). According to the *Fihrist* (written 987, author d. 995 A.D.), the first translations made under Islam from one language to another were the work of a group of Greek philosophers of Egypt who translated from Greek and Coptic for Khālid, "the philosopher of the family of Marwān who was a lover of the sciences."[135] On page 244 of the same work a certain Stephen the Elder, who has not been identified with any certainty, is said to have translated for the prince. Khālid was the first to investigate the books of the ancients on alchemy. He was an eloquent orator, a poet, a man of enthusiasm and judgment. He caused books on medicine, astrology, and alchemy to be translated, and was himself the author of several books and treatises and verses on alchemical matters. Al-Nadīm, the author of the *Fihrist*, says he saw three works of Khālid's, one book in long and short recensions, in all, about five hundred pages of his compositions. Having been deprived of the hope of the caliphate, his art became his solace, in which some say he was successful; "Allah knows best whether it is true!" Nevertheless his undertakings were not due to selfish motives but for the benefit of his brethren and companions.[136] Among the writings of al-Madāʾinī (d. 225 A.H.) there was one commenting on an ode by Khālid.[137]

Earlier writers knew something of Khālid's studies. Ibn Kutaiba (d. probably 276/889 or a few years earlier) refers to him as the most learned among the Kuraish in the various sciences, and as a poet.[138]

[135] *Fihrist*, p. 242.

[136] *Ibid.*, p. 354; on p. 353 he is listed among the philosophers. Contrary to this representation of him as living in retirement, numerous references in Arabic histories indicate that he continued to have some interests in public affairs. According to one account, it was he who advised ᶜAbd al-Mālik to forbid the use of Greek coins and to mint money bearing the name of Allah. As a result, this caliph began to coin dinars and dirhems in 76 A.H. See Ibn al-Athīr under the year 76 (Tornberg ed.; Leyden, 1851–76), p. 337.

[137] *Fihrist*, p. 104, ll. 5–6.

[138] *Ibn Coteiba*, "Handbuch der Geschichte, etc.," ed. Wüstenfeld (Göttingen, 1850), p. 179.

Abū'l-Faraj al-Isfahānī (d. 967 A.D.) speaks of his devotion to alchemy and quotes some verses presumably by him.[139] Al-Mas'ūdī (d. 956 A.D.) gives three verses consisting of a recipe for making gold.[140] According to a late writer, Ḥājjī Khalīfa (d. 1656 A.D.), these are from an alchemical poem of some 2,315 verses, called *The Paradise of Wisdom on the Science of Alchemy*.[141]

After the publication of the *Fihrist*, writers continued to mention the scientific or pseudo-scientific and poetic gifts of the young prince; some barely refer to him, others give fairly long biographical sketches. Yāḳūt (d. 1229 A.D.)[142] says he recited traditions on the authority of his father, al-Zuhrī and others, but adds no new information on his medical, alchemical, or poetical writings. The same may be said of the notices of Ibn al-Ṭiḳṭaḳā,[143] writing in A.D. 1300, and Ibn Taghribirdī (probably d. 874/1469). The latter mentions a report that he composed *Ḥadīth al-Sufyānī*.[144] Ibn Khallikān (d. 1282 A.D.) praises his scientific skill and knowledge, which are exemplified by the quality of his writings. This author also tells us that Khālid studied alchemy with a Greek monk named Marianos.[145] Ḥājjī Khalīfa (seventeenth century) refers to Khālid frequently, noticing the translations made for him and his writings, and links his name with that of Geber.[146] Ibn al-Ḳiftī (d. 1248 A.D.) does not list him among the philosophers and scientists, but quotes one Ibn al-Sinbādī, a scientist, as seeing in the royal library of the Fatimids of Cairo in 435/1044 a bronze globe made by Ptolemy, which bore an inscription to the effect that it had been in the possession of Khālid ibn Yazīd ibn Mu'āwīya.[147]

No Arabic writer except Ibn Khaldūn (d. 1406 A.D.) has anything except words of praise for Khālid. Ibn Khaldūn, however, questions these favorable reports of his abilities, doubting whether a prince of

139 *Aghānī*, XVI, 88 f.; XVIII, 89.

140 Al-Mas'ūdī, *Les prairies d'or*, VIII, 176.

141 IV, 413, § 9016.

142 *Op. cit.*, IV, 165–69.

143 *Al-Fakhrī*, ed. Ahlwardt (Gotha, 1860), p. 164.

144 *Annales*, ed. Juynboll and Matthes (Leyden, 1851), I, 245 f. and 554. The supplanting of the Sufyānid branch of the Umaiyad house by the Marwānids on the accession of Marwān ibn al-Ḥakam appears to have given rise to an Imāmite party expressing its hopes in a sort of *Mahdi*, al-Sufyānī. The *Aghānī* (XVI, 88) says that Khālid was the first to start this. See *Encyc. Islam*, art. "Al-Mahdi," by Macdonald, p. 114.

145 Ibn Khallikān (De S.), I, 481 ff.

146 Ḥājjī Khalīfa, III, 94–95, 97, 592, § 7114; IV, 413, § 9016; V, 87, 280; VI, 53, § 12698.

147 *Ta'rīkh al-Hukamā'*, ed. Lippert (Leipzig, 1903), p. 440.

the Umaiyad house could have comprehended the theoretical and practical aspects of subjects, which presuppose much knowledge and study.[148]

Most Western scholars, until very recently, have accepted the more favorable reports, seemingly ignoring Ibn Khaldūn's criticism.[149] In part they may have been influenced by a Latin treatise on alchemy, *Liber de compositione alchemiae,* translated from Arabic by Robert of Chester in A.D. 1144. It purports to be the work of Khālid (*Calid, King of the Egyptians*), edited by Morienus Romanus, a hermit of Jerusalem. However, the work actually belongs to a much later period than that of Khālid.[150] His name is also connected with the *Book of Crates,* which is said to have been translated for or under him, but this Arabic rendering of a Greek work can be no earlier than the end of the eighth century, and probably belongs to the ninth.[151]

Julius Ruska, in his detailed study of all the reports of Khālid's scientific activities and the extant works purporting to come from his hand, has rejected the whole as a legend. He points to the fact that later writers—for instance, Ibn Khallikān and Ḥājjī Khalīfa—knew many more details about him than did the earlier al-Masᶜūdī and al-Nadīm, although even in the *Fihrist* one finds the legend-building tendency at work. Ruska concludes that although it is possible that Khālid employed Egyptian scholars, there is no positive evidence of his scientific activity, and his connection with the Greek monk Morianus is entirely unwarranted.[152] Ruska's study has served to clear away the mass of legend which has long surrounded the memory of the young Umaiyad prince. Obviously there was a tendency to attach his name to anything which hinted of learning in the Umaiyad

148 *Prolegomena,* Arabic text (Bulaḳ, 1274/1857), p. 261, ll. 11 ff.; Quatremere's text in *Notices et extraits,* XVIII, 193 = De Slane's French translation, XXI, 209.

149 M. Bertholet, *La chimie au Moyen Âge* (Paris, 1893), III, 2 ff.; Le Clerc, *Histoire de la médecine arabe* (Paris, 1876), I, 61 ff.

150 See Sarton, *op. cit.,* II, 176; J. Ruska, *Arabische Alchemisten,* I: *Chālid Ibn Yazīd Ibn Muᶜāwiya* (Heidelberg, 1924), pp. 31 ff.

151 Bertholet (*op. cit.*) gives the text and translation of the *Book of Crates;* see Sarton, I, 495; Ruska, *op. cit.,* pp. 12 ff.

152 See Ruska's entire study, especially conclusions; also Sarton, I, 495; L. Thorndike, *Magic and Experimental Science* (New York, 1923), pp. 214 ff. E. J. Holmyard (*Makers of Chemistry* [Oxford, 1931], pp. 43 ff.), points out that the story of Khālid is valuable as showing what Mohammedan chemists believed about the origin of alchemy in Islam.

period. As illustrative, one may quote from Krenkow's article on Arabic libraries in the *Encyclopedia of Islam:*

> The earliest record of anything like a public library is connected with the name of Khālid ibn Yazīd ibn Muᶜāwiya, who devoted his life to the study of Greek sciences, particularly alchemy and medicine. We are told that he caused such books to be translated, and when an epidemic occurred at the beginning of the reign of ᶜUmar ibn ᶜAbd al-ᶜAzīz, he commanded the books to be fetched out of the library [*Khizāna*] to be made available for the people.[153]

Khālid, according to most authorities, died 85/704 and certainly not later than 90/708–9, whereas ᶜUmar II was caliph 99/717 to 101/720.

It appears, however, that Ruska, like Ibn Khaldūn, is reluctant to attribute learning to an Umaiyad. The Arabic historian obviously admired the early Abbasids and their efforts in behalf of scholarship and regarded their predecessors as little better than ignorant Bedawis; Khālid was a prince of the Umaiyad house, therefore he could not possibly have had any intellectual interests. Granted that much which has been attributed to Khālid is absolutely unfounded, the question remains, How did the legend arise? We know that the Abbasids did all in their power to blot out the memory of the Umaiyads, and when that failed, to falsify their memory. Accordingly, writers of that period, and subsequently, seldom attribute any virtue to the members of the previous dynasty. Hence, unless there was some element of truth to the stories of Khālid's activity, some genuine tradition of scholarly interest, including the beginning of translations from Greek works, too well known and persistent to be ignored, it is difficult to see why the reputation of the prince did not suffer with the rest of his family. The fact that the author of the *Fihrist,* on the whole a sober and careful investigator of the history of Arabic literature and scholarship, gives Khālid a place among the learned men of Islam, is greatly in favor of believing that there was something to the tradition. Al-Nadīm's details, doubtless as Ruska suggests, belong to popular legend. Whether they were genuine or not, we must accept his word for the existence at his time of writings purporting to come from Khālid.

It is of course possible that the fact that he never attained the

153 Art. "Kitāb-khāna," p. 1045, Arabic source not given.

coveted caliphate prejudiced the Abbasids in his favor, so that he became in their eyes one like themselves, a philosopher-prince and a patron of learning. However, for their purposes it would have been far better to have represented all the Umaiyads as entirely unlearned and indifferent to scholarly matters. Ibn Khaldūn, a late historian, agreed with the attitude of the Abbasid writers, and saw no reason to exempt Khālid from his general condemnation of the Umaiyads.

Khālid probably was not much of a scientist, for his interest in alchemy is the most persistent part of the tradition, but it is certainly not impossible that an Umaiyad prince, deprived of political aspirations, may have turned to the Greek studies current among the non-Moslem residents of Damascus and Egypt. We have seen that intercourse between Moslems and Christians was very free in the days of the Umaiyads. Others of the dynasty were devoted to poetry and to secular history. Khālid, having once been accepted as exceptional among the Umaiyads, his reputation grew by leaps and bounds.

Arabic historians preserve a few other hints that this period was not entirely devoid of a knowledge of foreign literature and learning. We have noticed this in the case of historical, biblical, and legendary lore. Barhebraeus says of Walīd ibn ᶜAbd al-Mālik (caliph 705–15 A.D.); "This Khalīfah was well versed in outside [i.e., alien or profane] learning."[154] The *Fihrist* mentions a medical work, the *Pandects* (*Kitāb al-Kunnāsh*), written in Syriac by a certain Aaron (*Ahrun*) the priest, consisting of thirty discourses, which was translated by a physician Māsīrjīs, who added two more chapters.[155] The latter is listed as a translator from Syriac to Arabic and the author of two books. Al-Nadīm gives no indication of dates except that Aaron lived at the beginning of the Moslem era. Barhebraeus adds that Aaron, a contemporary of the Prophet, was an Alexandrian, whose *Kunnāsha fīʾl-Ṭibb* ("Principles of Medicine") is "found with us in Syriac."[156] In this place Barhebraeus calls the man who added to the work Sirjīs, but later[157] refers to him as Māsirjiwaih, a physician of Baṣra, a Syrian as to language and a Jew by religion, who translated Aaron's work in the days of Marwān I (64/683—65/685) and adds an anecdote on him

[154] *Chronography, etc.*, p. 106.

[155] *Fihrist*, p. 297.

[156] *Chronicles* (Beirut ed.), p. 157; Pococke ed. (text), p. 159; (trans.), p. 99.

[157] Beirut ed., p. 192; Pococke (text), p. 198; (trans.), p. 127.

from a contemporary. This historian took his information from Ibn Juljul al-Andalusī, whom Ibn al-Ḳifṭī and Ibn Abī Uṣaibiʿa quote more fully.[158] They have substantially the same information on Aaron[159] as does the *Fihrist.* Both have fairly long sketches on the translator, which differ but slightly. Ibn al-Ḳiftī calls him Māsirjiwaih, with the alternative Māsīrjīs, and says he was a Jew of Baṣra, living in the time of ʿUmar II,[160] learned in medicine, who translated for this caliph Aaron's medical work, the *Pandects,* "the most excellent of ancient books of the time." Then he follows with a quotation from Ibn Juljul which says that Māsīrjīs made the translation in the days of Marwān, which was found by ʿUmar in the royal library (*khazāʾin al-kutub*). The caliph ordered the book brought out and placed it in his place of prayer (*muṣallā*) after which he consulted Allah as to the desirability of bringing it out to the Moslems (to publish it, one manuscript, instead of *Moslems,* has "concerning its being brought out in Arabic"). After forty days had elapsed, apparently the verdict was favorable, for he caused it to be brought out to the people and published. Ibn Juljul says that Abū Bakr Mohammed ibn ʿAmr related this story to him in the Ḳarmūni Mosque in the year 359.[161]

This story of ʿUmar bringing out a medical book from the royal collections to the people, which amounts to publishing the work, bears some resemblances to that quoted above about Khālid bringing out books from the library (*khizāna*) to make them available to the people. Both events are placed in the reign of ʿUmar II. Are they two versions of the same affair, and is there some hint of supposed magical efficacy in a book on medicine?

Professor H. G. Farmer, of Glasgow, says that the manuscript of the *ʿArḍ Miftaḥ al-Nujūm,* of Hermes, in the Ambrosian Library is dated 743 (A.D.); of it I have been unable to locate any more information.[162] If the date is genuine (is it the equivalent in the Arabic era to 743?),

[158] Ibn al-Ḳifṭī, *op. cit.,* pp. 324 ff.; Ibn Abī ʾUṣaibiʿa, *ʿUyūn al-Anbā fī Tabaḳāt al-Aṭibbā,* compiled A.D. 1245 (Cairo, 1882), I, 163 f.

[159] Ibn al-Ḳifṭī, p. 80; Ibn AbīʾUṣaibiʿa, I, 109, l. 15.

[160] Ibn Abī ʾUṣaibiʿa simply places him in the Umaiyad period, I, 163, l. 26, and lists a work by his son ʿIsā (*ibid.,* 1, 204).

[161] Ibn Abī ʾUṣaibiʿa has Tarmudhī mosque. Ibn al-Ḳifṭī adds two anecdotes on Māsīrjīs found also in Ibn Abī ʾUṣaibiʿa, I, 163, ll. 31 f., and 164, ll. 11 f.

[162] H. G. Farmer, *Historical Facts for Arabian Musical Influence* (London, 1930), p. 273; this title is mentioned in the *Fihrist,* p. 267, and Ibn Al-Ḳifṭī, p. 403.

it means that this manuscript of an astrological work is a century older than the Heidelberg papyrus mentioned above (229/844) and is valuable evidence for the beginnings of translations from Greek. These various indications of the first use of foreign literatures seem to suggest that the Arabs first interested themselves in what must have appeared to them as the practical sciences: medicine, astrology, and alchemy, and only later (and perhaps thereby) were attracted to the more abstract sciences and philosophy. Barhebraeus quotes the Ḳādī Ṣāᶜd ibn Aḥmad al-Andalusī (d 462–1070) to the effect that during the Umaiyad period the only science (other than their own language and law) which attracted the attention of the Arabs was medicine. Although cultivated only by certain individuals, it was generally approved because of its universal utility.[163] Muᶜāwiya's study of history was also motivated by considerations of practicality, for he was especially devoted to accounts of the military tactics and state craft of rulers of the past.

As one reviews the various types of literature which were cultivated in the Umaiyad period, it becomes apparent that it was not, as is so often supposed, one characterized by the dearth of literary activity, except for poetry. The cultivation of poetry, both ancient and contemporary, was most characteristic of the age, but several types of prose writings also had their beginnings. Much was done under royal patronage, but Medina was also a center for the poets of the Hijāz and students of religious matters. In Iraq, Baṣra and later Kūfa were the homes of scholars and poets, and from Ṣanaᶜāᵓ in the Yemen came men versed in ancient lore. The question of the beginnings of Arabic literature in Egypt also requires investigation, but, as Becker points out, they are quite obscure. It is most unlikely that all remnants of interest in Greek studies should have vanished when Egypt became a Moslem province. If there is anything to the Khālid tradition, it points to Egypt as the source of his study and one of the sources for the knowledge of Greek works in general. The Hermes text points in the same direction. ᶜAbd Allāh, son of the conqueror of Egypt, Laith ibn Saᶜd and Ibn Lahīᶜa, are names connected intimately with the propagation of Moslem traditions, especially of an eschatological tinge. A papyrus page (*ṣaḥīfa*) of ᶜAbd Allāh ibn ᶜAmr, dealing with

[163] Probably from his "History of the Learned etc.," Pococke ed. (text) p. 246; (trans.), p. 160.

the final judgment, has survived, passing under the name of Ibn Lahīᶜa.[164] Egypt therefore appears to have shared with the rest of the Umaiyad empire a growing interest in both religious and foreign studies and literature. However, these were not isolated centers, for, as in later times, singers, story-tellers, and scholars passed to and fro. Caliphs called them to the courts of Damascus or wrote them requesting information. Much was still passed on by word of mouth, but there was a real beginning in the preservation of literature by means of writing. One finds at once serious attempts to preserve the old, and real creative activity. Whether the early books were merely collections of students' notes and little treatises in the form of letters or more formal books, of which there were at least a few, the collecting of them, the recognition that such materials were worth keeping, can legitimately be considered the beginning of Moslem libraries. One may therefore speak of the libraries, even though few, of the caliphs and private individuals. The preservation of source materials is as truly a function of a library as is the treasuring of formally published books. If anything, at this stage of Arabic literary history the source material, consisting of the notes of scholars, taken from the lips of a few surviving companions, and the jotting-down of poetry from those who still remembered the ancient songs, are of greater importance than the actual books written at the time. Subsequent generations used and re-used the old material. But of books in our sense there were probably more than the fragmentary records and the exceedingly few survivals would suggest. A great age of intellectual and literary activity such as the early Abbasid period does not burst full blown without some earlier preparation. The Umaiyad caliphs are said to have owned a volume of poetry composed in honor of the Lakhmid kings of the Christian Arabs of Hira, which had been put into writing for al-Nuᶜmān III (d. 605 or 7 A.D.), the last ruler of this pre-Moslem dynasty. It was written on boards and buried in his palace, where it was found by Mukhtār ibn Abī ᶜUbaid in 65 A.H. when he was hunting for concealed treasure.[165] This book and the Persian history, alluded

[164] See *Encyc. Islam*, art. of L. H. Becker, "Egypt," pp. 19–20; Becker, *Papyri Schott-Reinhardt*, I, 9.

[165] Al-Suyūṭī *Muzhir fī ᶜulūm al-lugha* (Cairo, 1282), I, 121; II, 237; al-Jumaḥī *Ṭabaḳāt*, ed. Hell, p. 10, ll. 13 ff.; Ibn Jinni *Khaṣāʾiṣ* (Cairo, 1914), I, 393. Margoliouth doubts the historicity of this report, and suggests that if it really goes back to Ḥammād al-Rāwiya, to whom it is accredited, it was intended to account for his immense knowledge of pre-Islamic verse (see "The Origins of Arabic Poetry," *JRAS*, 1925, p. 428).

to by Masᶜūdī, suggest that books may have been, not infrequently, found in and preserved from the loot of the early wars of conquest.

In the *Kitāb al-Jumahir fī Maᶜrifat al-Jawahir* ("Book of Precious Stones"), by al-Bīrūnī, the manuscript of which Krenkow is preparing for publication, this versatile scholar, writing in the first half of the fifth century (early eleventh), mentions a book on jewels, written in the time of ᶜAbd al-Mālik (685–705 A.D.) which had fallen into his hands. This book actually gave prices of precious stones which al-Bīrūnī cites on occasions.[166] The writing of such a book in the Umaiyad period is most significant evidence for the state of literature at the time, for it is not the sort of thing likely to be produced when the writing of books was in its infancy and uncommon. It bespeaks a fairly advanced state of literary activity and furnishes one more bit of proof that religious studies and poetry were not the sole preoccupations of the writing and reading world.

One must be ever on guard lest he accept uncritically the estimate of the Umaiyads foisted upon the world by their successors, the brilliant but often unscrupulous Abbasids. Without any desire to whiten the reputation of the caliphs at Damascus, who undoubtedly deserve many of the harsh accusations hurled at them both by their contemporaries and by succeeding generations, it is well to recognize that they were not utterly unworthy.

Muᶜāwīya, the founder of the dynasty, was as astute a political and military leader as any in Moslem annals, and he was not devoid of an appreciation for literature. Susceptible to the charms of poetry, he knew how to utilize poets to further his own designs. By his patronage he won the support of the poets whom Lammens refers to as the journalists of the period. "To win them over was to have a good press and at the same time gained their tribes to the cause of order, for the tribes usually agreed with the ideas spread by their bards."[167] Part of his purpose was to swing public opinion in favor of his intention to name his son Yazīd as his successor, thereby making the caliphate hereditary. Yazīd was himself a poet and the friend of poets, and his father did not hesitate to exploit this bond of loyalty. In utilizing the

[166] Private communication from Professor Krenkow. He utilizes al-Bīrūnī's book in his article, "The Oldest Western Account of Chinese Porcelain," in *Islamic Culture*, July, 1933, pp. 464 ff.

[167] *Encyc. Islam*, art. "Muᶜāwīya," pp. 619–20.

poets as agents of propaganda, Muʿāwīya anticipated the common practice of later caliphs and lesser princelings and imitated the example of the Prophet. Mohammed, although avowedly the enemy of many singers of his day and objecting violently to any implication that he was himself merely another poet, found in Ḥassān ibn Thābit an invaluable ally. Ḥassān frequented the courts of the Ghassānid and Lakhmid kings and the fair at ʿUkāẓ in the days before Mohammed came to the front. After the Prophet's repeated successes marked him as the coming leader of the Arabs, Ḥassān threw in his lot with the new cause. He readily answered the lampoons of unbelieving poets and brought about the conversion of the tribe of Tamīm, after defeating its champions in a poetic contest. He continued to support the cause of the first three caliphs and is the founder of Moslem religious verse.[168] Margoliouth says that a copy of the poems of Ḥassān was kept at Medina and was regularly renewed whenever the writing showed signs of fading.[169]

Although these considerations have led us far afield from the precise history of Moslem libraries, it is hoped they have made clear how these libraries, which rapidly became a characteristic institution in the intellectual and cultural life of Islam, grew from two roots. They are based in part on the example of the libraries of the world into which Islam spread, and are at the same time the natural outgrowth of the method by which their own literature was collected. The Koran resulted from the desire to preserve the revelations received by Mohammed from on high, and the great *dīwān*'s from the gathering of poetic fragments of pre-Islamic days, and traditions, history, and law from the collecting of records of the words and deeds of the Prophet.[170]

Chicago, Illinois

[168] *Ibid.*, art. "Ḥassān ibn Thābit"; Hirschfeld's Introduction to his edition of the *Dīwān of Ḥassān ibn Thābit* ("Gibb Series" [Leyden, 1910]).

[169] *Early Development*, p. 89; no Arabic authority cited. For estimates of the intellectual life and the state of education in the Umaiyad period see H. Lammens, *La Syrie* (Beirut, 1921), chap. vi; *Encyc. Islam*, arts. "Masdjid" sect. "Mosque as an Educational Center," p. 351), "Umaiyads," and "Muʿāwīya"; Muir, *Annals of the Early Caliphate* (London, 1883), p. 46.

[170] Since this article was accepted for publication the literature on the subject has increased considerably. The article will be brought up to date in a short note at a future time.

[*Concluded*]

SUPPLEMENTARY NOTES TO "ARABIC BOOKS AND LIBRARIES IN THE UMAIYAD PERIOD"

The following notes are additions to my previous article, "Arabic Books and Libraries in the Umaiyad Period" (*AJSL*, July, 1936, pp. 245 ff.; July, 1937, pp. 239 ff.; October, 1937, pp. 41 ff.), which, it is hoped, will be useful to those interested in Umaiyad contributions to Islamic civilization. The numbers correspond to those of the footnotes to which they are supplementary.

NOTE 29. R. Strothmann, "Das Problem der literarischen Persönlichkeit Zaid ibn ᶜAlī," *Der Islam*, XIII (1923), 1 ff. The text of the legal compendium was published by Griffini, *Corpus iuris di Zaid ibn ᶜAlī* (Milan, 1919).

NOTE 73. Al-Masᶜūdī (d. A.D. 956) states (*Murūj al-Dhahab*, IV, 89) that the *Book of Kings* by ᶜUbaid ibn Sharya circulated widely in his day; it was used by Ḥamdānī (d. A.D. 945) in his *Iklīl* and later in the historical commentary to *The Ḥimyarite Ode*, probably also written by the author of the ode, Nashwān ibn Saᶜīd al-Ḥimyarī (d. A.D. 1177) (see Nicholson, *Literary History of the Arabs*, p. 13). The present form of the *Relation* of ᶜUbaid, which consists of answers to questions asked by Muᶜāwiya, agrees with the statement of the *Fihrist*, p. 89, to the effect that this caliph summoned him to court to ask him for historical information, after which he caused it to be recorded. Taken with the above-mentioned use of this work, there seems to be considerable evidence for its authenticity and the historicity of its author. It is published as a supplement to the *Tījān* of Wahb ibn Munabbih in the recension of Ibn Hishām (Hyderabad, A.H. 1347) (see Brockelmann, *Geschichte der arabischen Literatur*, Suppl. I [1937], pp. 100 f.).

NOTE 107. See also Brockelmann, *op. cit.*, Suppl. I, pp. 76 ff.

NOTE 126. The *Fihrist*, p. 34, also refers to a *Tafsīr* by Al-Ḥasan of Baṣra (d. 110/728–29). His glosses were collected in commentary form by ᶜAmr ibn ᶜUbaid (d. 145/762) (see G. Bergsträsser, "Die Koranlesung des Ḥasan von Baṣra," *Islamica*, II [1926], 11–57). The chief source for Ḥasan's comments is the *Itḥāf* of Al-Bannāᵓ (d. A.H. 1117), published at Cairo, A.H. 1317 (see also Brockelmann, *op. cit.*, Suppl. I, pp. 102 f.).

NOTE 130. Other tractates by Al-Ḥasan have come to light recently, *Risāla Lālelī*, MS 1703, published in *Le Monde oriental*, VII, 97; for a Turkish translation of it see Brockelmann, *op. cit.*, Suppl. I, p. 103. His work on *Ḳadar* (Köprülü, MS 1589, and an abridgment Aya Sofya MS 3998) is published and discussed by H. Ritter, "Studien zur Geschichte der islamischen Frömmigkeit I, Ḥasan al-Baṣrī," *Der Islam*, XXI (1933), 1–83. Its significance is dealt with by J. Obermann, "Political Theology in Early Islam," *JAOS*, LV (1935), 138–62. These tractates agree with other indications for the nature of early Arabic prose literature, the writings of ᶜUrwa and ᶜUbaid ibn Sharya, in being in the form of brief treatises written in response to inquiries, usually from caliphs. The letter of ᶜAbd al-Malik ordering him to vindicate himself from charges made by certain unnamed persons that he was teaching subversive doctrine is prefixed to the *Ḳadar Risāla.* The abridgment, apparently sent to the caliph by Al-Ḥajjāj, governor of Iraq, is accompanied by a note of warm commendation of Al-Ḥasan (see Obermann, *op. cit.*, pp. 140–43). Like all Al-Ḥasan's writings, it is a devout and emotional homily rather than a systematic presentation of his subject.

It is apparent that Al-Ḥasan's teachings on free will were of political significance. Obermann points out that the *terminus ad quem* for the writing of this work is 86/705, the year in which ᶜAbd al-Malik died, and the hitherto friendly relations between the governor and Ḥasan were severed (*ibid.*, p. 141). We have other indications that about the turn of the century the *Ḳadar* controversy had become an acute issue with political as well as religious implications. In 699 Maᶜbad al-Juhanī was martyred because of his teachings on free will, by order of ᶜAbd al-Malik or Al-Ḥajjāj. His pupil Ghaylān al-Dimashḳī met the same fate in 730 at the hands of Hishām, a son of ᶜAbd al-Malik. (For a letter of reproof addressed to ᶜUmar II by Al-Dimashḳī and his controversy with Hishām see M. Horten, *Die philosophischen Systeme .... im Islam* [Bonn, 1912], pp. 122 ff.) The late professor A. V. W. Jackson (*Zoroastrian Studies* [New York; 1928], pp. 238–40) drew attention to the report that Maᶜbad learned the doctrine of *Ḳadar* from a Persian AbūYūnas Snsūyh or Sinbūya (Maḳrīzī, *Khiṭaṭ* [Cairo, A.H. 1326], IV, 181, ll. 25–27; Al-Shahrastānī, *Book of the Religious and Philosophical Sects,* Arabic text, ed. Cureton [Leipzig, 1923], I, 17, trans. Th. Haarbrücker [Halle, 1850], I, 25; see also Browne, *Literary History of Persia,* I, 282 f.; A. von Kremer, *Streifzüge,* p. 9, n. 1), and raises the question whether Muslim teachings on free will may not have been influenced by Zoroastrianism, to which the doctrine at some time became essential, as well as by Christian and Neo-Platonic thought.

Ḥasan was of Persian extraction and lived in Baṣra, a city open to Persian influence. It is noteworthy that Iraq and Persia were frequently the scenes of politico-religious disaffections, the dangers of which to Umaiyad prestige were fully recognized by the caliphs. During the reign of ᶜAbd al-Malik the vigorous and ruthless measures of Al-Ḥajjāj and his lieutenants were needed to eliminate the rival caliph ᶜAbd Allah ibn al-Zubair, who exercised considerable influence in Iraq, to suppress the ᶜAlid party of Al-Mukhṭār ibn Abī ᶜUbaid at Kufa and the militant Azraḳites, whose zeal endangered the peace of the Persian provinces. This last was hardly settled when the governor of Sijistān, ᶜAbd al-Raḥmān, revolted and was subdued only after two years of vigorous campaigning (see *Encyclopedia of Islam,* arts. "ᶜAbd al-Malik" and "Al-Ḥadjdjādj"; P. K. Hitti, *History of the Arabs* [London, 1937], pp. 206 ff.).

It is not surprising that ᶜAbd al-Malik, who was most concerned to bring about the unification of the empire, viewed with apprehension the charges lodged by some of his supporters that the saintly Ḥasan of Baṣra was guilty of religious views which were inimical to the solidarity of the state. Obermann sees correctly that the doctrine of individual self-responsibility was not merely an academic question but might easily undermine the authority of the state and especially Umaiyad domination (*op. cit.*, p. 145). He does not, however, suggest that Ḥasan's views might have been of Persian origin, and therefore congenial to, or possibly the expression of, Persian opposition to Arab arrogance. Rather, Obermann denies that the *Ḳadar* ideology is of foreign origin and stresses the point that Ḥasan's teachings show no Jewish, Christian, or Greek influence, except in so far as such elements can be detected in the Koran, for Ḥasan bases his arguments on the authority of revealed scripture (*ibid.*, pp. 147 [n. 29] and 157–58 [n. 72]).

It is significant, nevertheless, as Obermann points out, that Ḥasan accuses his opponents of using their doctrine of predeterminism as an excuse for their "sinful appetites and treacherous iniquities," a statement which agrees with other evidence that this was a favorite justification of government officials for corrupt practices (Ibn Ḳutaiba, *Kitāb al-Maᶜārif*, ed. Wüstenfeld, p. 225). Furthermore, one of the men who brought these offenses to the attention of Ḥasan was his friend, and possibly pupil, the abovementioned martyr, Maᶜbād al-Juhanī (Obermann, *op. cit.*, pp. 150 and 153; on the relations of the two men see Ibn Ḳutaiba, *op. cit.*).

An amusing touch is lent to the controversy by Ḥasan's charge that his critics are actually ignorant of proper Arabic usage and by his temerity in enlightening them by quotations from poetry and popular expressions (*ibid.*, p. 152). Does not this also give us a glimpse into the deep-set antagonism between the "pure Arabs" and their Persian converts?

Another work on *Ḳadar* was composed by a contemporary of Al-Ḥasan, also of Persian extraction, Wahb ibn Munabbih (they both died 110/728–29), who, however, is quoted as saying that, after consulting some seventy prophetic writings, he regretted ever having written this book (Yaḳūt, *Irshad*, VII, 232). He is included in the list of Ḳadarites headed by Maᶜbād (Ibn Ḳutaiba, *op. cit.*, p. 301). The text of his *Kitāb al-Ḳadar* is lost, unless, as Krenkow suggests, it is incorporated in the early pages of the *Tījān*, where there is considerable discussion of the subject (F. Krenkow, "Two Oldest Books, etc.," *Islamic Culture*, II [1928], 232). One cannot but wonder whether his retraction was not due to political pressure. He was imprisoned during the last years of his life and flogged to death by order of the governor of the Yemen, Yusuf al-Thakafī, who, like his famous son Al-Hajjāj, was a vigorous inquisitor of political and religious malcontents (Horovitz, art. "Wahb ibn-Munabbih," *Encyclopedia of Islam*, and *Islamic Culture*, I [1927], 553 ff.). Wahb's family, though settled in the Yemen since the time of Khusraw Anushirwan, apparently maintained connections with Persia, for he says that he had occasion from time to time to go to Herat to look after family affairs (Krenkow, *op. cit.*). The *Tījān* shows familiarity with Iran and some acquaintance with the more eastern provinces; in fact, his folklore, which Krenkow notes is scarcely Semitic, may be Central Asian. It should also be noted that Wahb flourished at the time of the Muslim conquests of Transoxania.

Is it not more than likely that Umaiyad persecutions of the *Ḳadarite* heresy were due to a recognition of its Persian connections combined with its possible justification of too independent thought and activity? Both were a menace to the state. The *Ḳadarite* movement eventually gave birth to the Muʿtazilite, so warmly espoused by the Abbasids Al-Maʾmūn and Wāthiḳ, both of whom had Persian leanings, and Persian Shiʿite doctrine to the present contains many Muʿtazilite elements. A saying attributed to Mohammed, but which, as Professor Macdonald points out, must be later than the rise of the *Ḳadarīya*, says: "The *Ḳadarites* are the Mājūs [Zoroastrians] of the people" (*Encyclopedia of Islam*, art. "Ḳadarīya").

Coming from a Persian background, it does not appear improbable that Wahb and Ḥasan had consciously or unconsciously stressed those aspects of Mohammed's teachings which were most congenial to the Zoroastrian thought of their time. Their mystical personal piety doubtless played a part, too, and it is surely not a coincidence that Persia has ever been a congenial home for Ṣūfī doctrine and practice. At any rate, Ḥasan's tractate and the *Ḳadar* passages in the *Tījān* should be studied from the viewpoint of possible Zoroastrian influence. Certainly, one must take into account *all* the systems of thought which were current in the atmosphere in which Muslim theology developed.

It has usually been assumed that contacts with the teachings of John of Damascus are responsible in large measure for the *Ḳadarite* heresy. This Byzantine theologian, who died sometime before 754, was born at the end of the seventh century, just at the time when Maʿbād suffered martyrdom, Ḥasan was being questioned as to his teachings on *Ḳadar*, and Wahb retracted his writings on the same subject. Hence the movement is earlier than the active years of John. It has been noted that a modern Muslim critic of Wensinck's *Muslim Creed*, which presents the view of the influence of Greek theology on Muslim, suggests rather that John was influenced by Islam (see *AJSL*, LIV [1937], 51, n. 129).

Is it too daring to suggest that Zoroastrian teachings on free will, directly or more probably indirectly, brought about the *Ḳadarite* heresy, which in turn colored in some degree the thinking of John and was finally mediated to Christian scholasticism through the twelfth-century Latin translation of his *De orthodoxa fide*, which is known to have influenced Peter the Lombard and Thomas Aquinas? The subject merits investigation by someone familiar with Zoroastrian, Muslim, and Christian thought. The problem of the possible influence of Persian teachings on Mohammed is more remote but also pertinent.

NOTE 138. J. Ruska draws attention to the evidence furnished by Al-Rāzī's *Kitāb al-Shawāhid* (not yet published) that *ca.* A.D. 900 the legends of Khālid's alchemical studies were already established. Ruska is still very emphatic in his opinion that the Khālid tradition is baseless and holds that there can have been no scientific activity before the time of the early Abbasids. Further, he asserts that the translations of medical and astronomical texts must have preceded the alchemical ("Alchemy in Islam," *Islamic Culture*, XI [1937], 32 and 36). It is my belief that we now have evidence of beginnings, during the Umaiyad period, in both of these sciences, as well as in alchemy.

Manuscripts are still extant of Avicenna's Persian translation of an ode on the preservation of health by Tayādhūḳ (d. *ca.* A.H. 90), court physician to Al-Ḥajjāj. He is also credited with a large work on the preparations of medicines (Ibn abī Uṣaibiʿa, I, 121; Ibn al-Ḳifṭī, p. 105; *Fihrist*, p. 303; *Catalogue of the Arabic and Persian Manuscripts in the Oriental Public Library at Bankipore* [Calcutta, 1910], IV, 165, No. 108, iii).

H. E. Stapelton and M. Meyerhof have recently brought to light information which suggests far greater scientific activity in the Umaiyad period than was supposed at the time my former article was written. Stapelton, in a letter to the editor of *Isis*, gives a preliminary report of his investigation of the alchemical manuscripts in the libraries of India. His findings are most significant for the genuineness of the Khālid tradition and the relations of the studies of Jābir and Jaʿfar al-Ṣādiḳ to those of the Umaiyad prince. Khālid was born A.D. 672, and, from a fifteen-line extract of a poem, apparently addressed by him to his cousin Yazīd II, at or after the time of the latter's accession, it is certain that he survived at least until A.D. 720 and lived in Damascus. In it he claims to have succeeded in the practice of alchemy. A manuscript in the Aṣāfīyah library in Hyderabad makes it clear that he acquired some of his knowledge from the monk Mariyānos, from whom Jābir's learning was derived through two intermediaries. Stapelton is now convinced that the alchemical treatises in the Rampur Library, with which he and Azo dealt years ago, are probably authentic and not forgeries as has long been supposed (see "Further Notes on the Arabic Alchemical Manuscripts in the Libraries of India," *Isis*, XXVI [1936], 127–31, and "Note on the Arabic Manuscripts in the Aṣāfīyah Library, Hyderabad," *Archeion*, XIV, 57–61, where he lists manuscripts of two or three treatises by Khālid). Stapelton suggests that the contents of these Indian manuscripts will clear up details on the transference of alchemical knowledge current in pre-Islamic times in Alexandria and northern Mesopotamia to the Arabs through Khālid and Jābir. The statement (*AJSL*, LIV [1937], 55) on the date of Khālid's death must be corrected in the light of these findings, which also make more probable the tradition of his literary and scientific activities at Damascus under ʿUmar II (*ibid.*, quoted from *Encyclopedia of Islam*, art. "Kitāb-khāna," p. 1045). Information on the Arabic source of this Khālid tradition would be appreciated.

Meyerhof offers very suggestive evidence for one path by which the learning of Alexandria, especially on the medical side, reached the Moslem world.

It becomes increasingly clear that the Umaiyad rulers played a considerable role in the beginnings of Arabic scientific interests and the translation of Greek words. Al-Mascūdī (d. A.D. 956, *Tanbīh*, p. 122) states that the ancient center of philosophical teaching was transferred, in the days of cUmar II, from Alexandria to Antioch and from there to Harrān in the time of Mutawakkil. A quotation from the autobiography of Al-Fārābī (d. A.D. 950) preserved by Ibn abī Uṣaibica (II, 135) agrees with this. According to both statements, the school at Antioch finally dwindled down to one teacher and two pupils before it was moved to Harrān. Ibn abī Uṣaibica (I, 116 f.) also gives a brief sketch of a Christian physician, Ibn Abjar, who as the confidant of cUmar II accepted Islam at the caliph's hand. He was the head of the Alexandrian school which cUmar moved to Antioch and which later went to Harrān. Finally, Meyerhof found confirmation for these statements in the unique Cairo manuscript of the *Useful Book in Medicine*, by cAlī ibn Riḍwān (d. after A.D. 1067), who repeatedly insists that the last Byzantine emperors persecuted the philosophers of Egypt and neglected the sciences, whereas several of the caliphs, particularly cUmar II, Hārūn al-Rashīd, and Al-Ma᾿mūn, were great patrons of every kind of scientific activity. Ignoring the anti-Christian touch, it is noteworthy that Ibn Riḍwān brackets the name of the Umaiyad caliph with those of the two foremost patrons of Greek science among the Abbasids.

None of these Arabic sources explains why the school was removed from its ancient center to Syria, but Meyerhof suggests that it is "possible that the rapid decay of Alexandria cut off from Mediterranean commerce after the Arab occupation prevented the purchase of indispensable Greek manuscripts while Antioch had during the intervals between the long Byzantine-Arabic wars, intercourse and commerce with the Byzantine Empire" ("Transmission of Science to the Arabs," *Islamic Culture*, January, 1937, pp. 19–21). He does not believe that such a school was of an official character, for both orthodox Christians and Moslems distrusted Hellenic science. It would be interesting to know something of the activity of the scholars at Antioch during Umaiyad times, but, to judge from the later interests of both pagan and Nestorian Christian scholars at Harrān, it seems likely that the study of Greek texts continued. Whether there was also a beginning of translations into Syriac and Arabic is not stated.

Al-Fārābī's report carries the scientific tradition from Harrān on to Baghdad. This scientist, who Al-Mascūdī says was the heir of the scientific learning of this school, makes a point of the continuity of the scholarly tradition at Alexandria from Greek through Roman and Christian times to the days of Islam and states that the basis of instruction consisted of copies of Aristotle's works made from still earlier manuscripts dating from the very days of the philosopher himself. Hence, when he speaks of the last three members of the school leaving Antioch taking *the books* with them, it appears that he wishes to stress the reliability of the texts transmitted by the school as well as the continuity of learning. Therefore, although Al-Fārābī does not say so explicitly, the inference seems to be that a quantity of books was carried to Antioch from Alexandria at the time the school was moved by ᶜUmar II.

Are we not justified in seeing the schools at Antioch and Harrān as the connecting links between the Museon of Alexandria and the House of Wisdom (*Bait al-Ḥikma* or *Dār al-ᶜIlm*) of Baghdad? (See my previous article in *AJSL,* Vol. LII [October, 1935, and January, 1936], where the relations between the Moslem scientific academies and the school of Alexandria are discussed.)

None of these four reports collected by Meyerhof appears to use the term "House of Wisdom," but we have one hint that it was known in Umaiyad times. Wahb ibn Munabbih, who, as we have seen, wrote under Umaiyad patronage, in the *Tījān* says that, when King Solomon was on his way to visit Bilḳīs the first time, her governor at Najrān—one of the wisest men of the day—assembled the people in the *Dār al-ᶜIlm* to try the reputed wisdom of the Hebrew king. Where did Wahb get the idea of an "Abode of Learning" as a place of assembly for the discussions of wise men? (Ibn Hishām, *Kitāb al-Tījān* [Hyderabad, 1347/1928], p. 154; *Islamic Culture,* April, 1928, p. 83.)

NOTE 145. Ruska (*Islamic Culture,* January, 1937, pp. 35 f.), notes that the Rāzī manuscript is evidence that Stephanos appears as Khālid's instructor in the older version of the legend, but that both the Stephanos and the Marianos forms were known in the tenth century.

NOTE 157. Meyerhof says Māsīrjīs was a Persian Jew, probably a pupil of the great school at Jundīshāpūr. If correct, this raises the question of the possible influence and activities of this center of Sassanian-Hellenistic learning during the Umaiyad period. A unique manuscript (Aya Sofya 4838) of the abridgment of his *Fī Abdāl al-Adwiya* ("On Substitutes for Remedies") is still extant (Meyerhof, *op. cit.,* p. 22).

NOTE 162. Professor H. G. Farmer writes me that the Ambrosian manuscript (C. 86. 1) of the *ᶜArḍ Miftāḥ* of Hermes states that it was translated into Arabic *Dhuᵓl-Kaᶜda,* A.H. 125/September 743.

NOTE 165. A unique manuscript of a work by the geographer Ibn al-Faḳīh, photographed by E. E. Herzfeld in the library of the Meshhed shrine (fol. 94*b*) quotes a very reliable early historian, Hishām ibn al-Kalbī (819 A.D.), as saying that he copied the entire introduction of a book which had been confiscated from the luggage of the Sassanian princess Behāfrīd and translated for the governor Al-Ḥajjāj. The introduction also states that the work was composed for Kavāt (about A.D. 500), and, judging from the citations in the Meshhed manuscript, it contained a collection of all sorts of strange information on the various districts of Iran, including a characterization of the climate and inhabitants of each. Professor Herzfeld draws attention to a Pahlavi pamphlet dealing with the towns of Iran entitled *Shahrihā ē Ērān,* and the fact that the source for the chapter "On the Nature of the Mountains" in the *Bundahishn* is given as the *Ayātkārihā ē Shahrihā.* Various historical remarks suggest that it was written during the reign of Kavāt. Herzfeld is convinced that the corresponding chapters on rivers, lakes, and seas must have been derived from the same source, however much they may have been altered. He concludes that both the pamphlet on the towns and the quotations in the *Bundahishn* are fragments of the original "Baedeker" which the princess carried on her travels. It is to be hoped that the Ibn al-Faḳīh manuscript will soon be published (E. E. Herzfeld, *Archeological History of Iran* [London, 1935], pp. 105 f.; the text of the Pahlavi work has been published with an English translation by J. Markwart, *A Catalogue of the Provincial Capitals of Eranshahr*, ed. G. Messina [Rome, 1931]).

In "A New Pahlavi Inscription," *AJSL*, LIII (January, 1937), 126–44, Professor M. Sprengling presented a preliminary publication of a Pahlavi inscription found by the Oriental Institute Expedition on the Kaaba of Zoroaster in 1936. This portion of a *notitia dignitatum* of the Sassanid empire he dated to the early years of Narseh, but now, according to a private conversation, he is convinced it is from the reign of Shahpuhr I and is an earlier example of the same type of literature as the *Shahrihā ē Ērān*. The usefulness of such a catalogue to Al-Ḥajjāj as governor of the Eastern Provinces is obvious.

Princess Behāfrīd's book adds another bit of evidence for the preservation of books taken as loot in the early days of Muslim conquest and belies the implication, in the famous words imputed to Umar I, that the Arabs destroyed all books that fell into their hands.

Far more significant, the translation of it for Al-Ḥajjāj suggests that Arabic geographical literature grew out of the administrative needs of the Umaiyad government. It has been seen above, note 130, that even the *Ḳadar* controversy was not merely the academic discussion of theologians, detached from practical affairs, but had far-reaching political implications and cannot be properly understood unless it is related to the social process. See my article (*AJSL*, LIV [October, 1937], 58) for a brief discussion of the practical considerations which first stimulated an interest in various intellectual pursuits which in turn resulted in the development of several departments of Arabic prose literature.

According to T. W. Arnold (*Painting in Islam* [Oxford, 1928], p. 63), the geographer Abū Isḥak al-Iṣṭakhrī (middle of the tenth century) describes a manuscript on the history of the Persian kings which he saw in a castle in northern Persia, containing pictures of the Sassanian kings, which seems to have resembled the manuscript seen by Al-Masᶜūdī about the same time at Iṣṭakhr and which he said was taken as loot in A.H. 113 and translated into Arabic for Hishām ibn ᶜAbd al-Malik. Al-Masᶜūdī describes the miniatures in some detail (*Tanbīh*, pp. 106 ff.; see *AJSL*, LIII [July, 1937], 250). One wonders whether the pictures were of more than passing interest to the Umaiyad caliphs and whether Persian painting exercised any influence in the Moslem world before the time of the Abbasids. The murals at Ḳuṣair ᶜAmra and the mosaics in the mosque at Damascus indicate that the Umaiyad princes were not a little charmed by representational art (Alois Musil, *Ḳuṣajr ʿAmra* [Wien, 1907], Band II, plates; Eustache de Lorey et M. van Berchem, *Les Mosaïques de la mosquée des Omayyades à Damas* [Paris, 1930]).

NOTE 170. It becomes increasingly apparent that a re-estimate of the Umaiyad period is imperative for a proper understanding of the cultural history of Islam. Such a study must utilize the rapidly accumulating archeological evidence for the architecture of the period, any scraps of information dealing with the intellectual and social life of the time, and, above all, necessitates a critical re-examination of the historical records. The publication undertaken by the School of Oriental Studies of the Hebrew University of Balādhurī's *Ansāb al-ashrāf wa akhbārahum*, hitherto inaccessible to most scholars, will furnish new material and a valuable check on the more biased accounts (Vol. V, ed. S. D. F. Goitein [Jerusalem, 1936]; see the review by G. Sarton, *Isis*, XXVI [1936–37], 457 f.). The work of Balādhurī (d. A.D. 892), although produced under Abbasid patronage, exhibits a surprising degree of objectivity in the treatment of the deposed dynasty. This is probably due in part to the debt of Balādhurī, for his history of the caliphs, to Al-Madāʾinī (d. A.D. 840), much of whose information according to Yaḳūt (VI, 94, l. 8) was drawn from ʿAwāna (d. A.D. 764–65), who wrote in the interests of the Umaiyads (Goitein, *op. cit.*, Preface, pp. 15 f.).

These notes and the article to which they are supplementary are intended to draw attention to rather than to solve some of the problems of the intellectual history of the Umaiyad period which need thorough investigation. It is probable that we shall soon be in a position to realize that the dark age between the downfall of the Sassanids and the establishment of the Persianized Abbasids at Baghdad had been exaggerated. In the first place, the Arab conquest should not be viewed as the eruption of hordes of uncultivated savages, for the Arabs of the "Days of Ignorance" were possessed of a culture of their own, however much its values differed from those of the settled man, and Arabia was in far closer touch with the movements of civilization than has often been supposed. Second, the more truly Arab Umaiyads played a considerable role in the making of Islamic civilization—that strange distillation of ancient Greek and oriental cultures to which the Arabs contributed much more than simply a book and a language. A knowledge of the nature of that civilization is an essential part in the task of understanding our own complex heritage, for the debt of the Western world to the medieval Near East is only recently coming to be appreciated. (For a general survey of Umaiyad history see P. K. Hitti, *History of the Arabs* [London, 1937], chaps. xvii–xxii; on the intellectual and artistic interests see chap. xxi and Brockelmann, *op. cit.*, Suppl. I, pp. 76–106.)

RUTH S. MACKENSEN

CHICAGO

19

THE LIBRARY OF AL-ḤAKAM II AL-MUSTANṢIR AND THE CULTURE OF ISLAMIC SPAIN

David Wasserstein

The library amassed in Cordoba by the second Umayyad caliph there, al-Ḥakam II al-Mustanṣir (*reg.* 350/961-366/976), has attracted the admiration and the hyperbole of writers from that ruler's own time up to the present. From Ibn Ḥazm, in the fifth/eleventh century, who claimed (just plausibly) to have known the eunuch in charge of the collection, to Ribera, in this century, they unite in claiming that the library contained some four hundred thousand books (Ar. *mujallad*, though that word is as potentially vague as the English 'book'), and that the catalogue alone filled forty four volumes, of twenty pages each, listing nothing but titles[1]. (It is perhaps just worth noting, parenthetically, that these figures work out at two hundred and twenty seven items on each side of every single page of the catalogue, a fact which seems to have caused no difficulty for anyone from Ibn Ḥazm to Ribera.)

Such figures are, of course, quite meaningless, and relate to reality only insofar as they serve as indications that the library was, by the standards of the writers concerned, very large. For comparison we may note that a major library, housed in the Dār al-Ḥikma in Cairo and similarly enjoying a form of state support, apparently contained only six and a half thousand works when it was catalogued in 435/1045[2]; another, in Baghdād, dating from only a few years after the death of al-Ḥakam (that is, from 381/991 or 383/993), contained 'more than 10,000 books'[3]. Other large collections in Spain itself also existed, both in the time of the Umayyads and in the later cultural florescence of the fifth/eleventh century. We hear of such libraries intermittently in the large biographical dictionaries, and in one case, that of the vizier of Zuhayr, the Slav ruler of Almeria in the first third of the fifth/eleventh century (*ob.* 429/1038), the number of items is said to have been 400,000, just as in the case of the library of al-Ḥakam. The coincidence is striking. We know nothing of the fate of this collection - or for that matter of its contents[4].

Not much remains of the library of al-Ḥakam. A single manuscript, a copy of a work on religious law, has survived to our own days, and was found and identified by Lévi-Provençal in the library of the mosque of the Qarawiyyīn, in Fes, in 1934[5]. Apart from manuscripts themselves, we can point to texts of which copies are known to have been in the library. A history of Egypt and the Maghrib written in Spain under al-Ḥakam was dependent on a similar work lent to the author by al-Ḥakam[6]. A third manuscript, a 120-part copy of the works of al-Shāfiʿī, with a good *isnād* going back directly to the author, apparently 'ended up in the possession' of al-Mustanṣir[7]. I think that I have been able to demonstrate the existence of a translation into Arabic of a summary of the Talmud in al-Ḥakam's library, and part of that translation, though not, alas, in the original library copy, may survive[8]. We know also of other works: there will presumably have been two copies of the book on *materia medica* of Dioscorides, the Greek copy that was sent to Spain with an embassy from Constantinople, and the revised Arabic translation of it made at the Cordoban court[9]. There will, in the same way, presumably have been two copies, one in Latin and one in Arabic, of the *Seven Books Against the Pagans* of Orosius (the Arabic translation survives in the library of Columbia University, and has apparently been published recently in Beirut)[10]. We can be fairly sure of the presence of third/ninth and fourth/tenth century Spanish Arabic translations of parts of the New Testament, and also of at least the Psalms from the Old Testament[11]. And the account of his travels in Christian Europe by Ibrāhīm b. Yaʿqūb al-Ṭurṭūshī is likely to have been there too[12]. The *Kitāb al-Aghānī*, of which we know that al-Ḥakam paid 1000 dinars of gold for the first copy, was definitely there; and a legal commentary by Abū Bakr al-Abharī al-Mālikī, for which he is said to have paid a similar sum[13]. Another category of such works is made up of those texts which were composed for al-Ḥakam or under his patronage: we can trace perhaps a dozen of these, and they include a curious mixture of subjects: works of linguistic interest, history and legal study jostle others on *ḥadīth* and obstetrics[14].

All this is not to mention references to works which al-Ḥakam is said to have made notes in (of which more in a moment), nor works that can be assumed to have been in the library - the Qur'ān, and works connected with it, legal texts and so on; nor is it to mention works that are known to have been brought to Spain, to al-Ḥakam's court, by scholars attracted there by that caliph's munificence and patronage; these include not only actual manuscripts but also works whose texts were brought in the memories of such scholars as al-Qālī, and dictated there to local scholars. A list of such works is given by Ibn Khayr in his *Fahrasa*[15]. Although it is confined largely to belletristic works, it extends considerably the range as well as the number of works which we can identify with some degree of certainty as having been in the library. And a number of other specific texts could doubtless be traced by a systematic trawl through the sources for the period.

If we confine ourselves to an examination of works of which copies can be shown to have been in al-Ḥakam's possession, thus excluding works (like the Qur'ān) which we must assume to have been there but whose presence we cannot demonstrate, then we can name, at the moment, probably not much more than around fifty works in the library of al-Ḥakam. This is not much for a great library, although it does not compare too unfavourably with what we can do for some other great libraries and collections of the past. The ancient library of Alexandria (which a recent report suggests UNESCO is planning to rebuild) contained somewhere between 100,000 and 700,000 volumes; although not a single one of these survives, we can name quite a respectable number (though these of course represent a tiny proportion of the whole)[16]. Of the contents of the libraries of medieval England, according to Ker and his continuators, we can trace surviving books amounting to some six and a half thousand (although it should be remembered both that this refers to actually surviving books and that these come from about five hundred different libraries, and from a period of several centuries, right up to the invention of printing)[17]. If comparisons have any meaning in such a context, two or three score works of which copies are known to have been in al-Ḥakam's library, of which one single manuscript survives, while respectable, is not a lot.

Al-Ḥakam's library was not the first great collection in the Islamic world. We have the libraries in Cairo and Baghdād, mentioned above, which were roughly contemporary with al-Ḥakam's; and we have, more importantly, the famous *Bayt al-Ḥikma* established in Baghdād by the ʿAbbāsid caliph al-Ma'mūn in the third/ninth century: although the primary purpose of that institution was not to serve as a repository for books, it did nonetheless fulfil at least some of the important functions of a great library, and is in significant respects, most importantly that of its function as a focus for a great deal of cultural activities, to be compared with the library of al-Ḥakam[18].

Why then is this Spanish library so important? It was probably not much larger than most of the other great royal libraries of the Islamic middle ages; although it contained some notable first editions, the real weight and significance of these will have faded with time; and, as will be seen, the fate of the library was, except in one important feature, not all that different from those of other great collections of the period. The answer of this question seems to lie not so much in the collection's size as in a combination of other features, in the functions which it existed and aimed to fulfil and in the place which it occupied in the overall policies of al-Ḥakam himself as ruler, policies both related to the library and completely unrelated to it or to its aims as a cultural phenomenon.

In histories of Islamic Spain the reign of al-Ḥakam is usually presented as a one-paragraph interlude between the fifty-year reign of his father ʿAbd al-Raḥmān III al-Nāṣir (300/912-350/961) and the long first reign of his son Hishām II al-Mu'ayyad (366/976-399/1009). The first of these brought unity to Islamic Spain, re-created the caliphal institution in Cordoba, and laid the foundation for a strong, wealthy and internationally influential Islamic state in the Iberian peninsula. The latter, under the tutelage of his mayor of the palace, the great *ḥājib* al-Manṣūr Muḥammad Ibn Abī ʿĀmir, presided over a long period of at least surface success for the Cordoban state. The reign of al-Mustanṣir, by contrast, is generally dismissed by historians as scarcely worthy the attention of scholars: 'Abd al-Raḥmān's son and successor ... was a great scholar and bibliophile, and little interested or concerned to make changes in the structures constructed by his father ... This was in part a consequence of the ruler's lesser interest in personal involvement in such affairs ...'[19]. Al-Ḥakam's main interest is seen to have been books, and he is thus not really a serious actor on the political scene.

Part of the reason for such an impression is, of course, the fact that historians of Islam have tended to prefer the political over most other types of historiography; and part, too, is the result of the fact that al-Ḥakam reigned for only sixteen fairly untroubled and prosperous years, while between them his father and his son reigned for three politically tumultuous quarters of a century. Then, again, father and son were present, so to speak, at the birth pangs and the death throes of the Umayyad caliphal institution in Cordoba. Al-Ḥakam was in a sense the Isaac of his dynasty, poised pointlessly and uncomfortably between its Abraham and its Jacob, and, like Isaac, he has tended to attract such little attention as he has received mainly by virtue of being apparently not terribly interesting.

In one sense, there might be little trouble with such a view of al-Ḥakam, but as one looks more closely at his activities as a ruler alongside his activities as a patron of culture a problem arises. Put simply, the routine picture of al-Ḥakam as a genial old bibliophile wandering between the shelves, pottering about and making notes in manuscripts, just does not march happily with the other equally routine picture of him as efficient administrator, political calculator and manipulator, and marshaller of armies from the Pyrenees deep into North Africa. In the ways in which they have been drawn in the past, these pictures do not match; as pictures of a single man, equally, they must do so. The solution to this problem, it seems to me, stares at us out of the evidence: it is not just that al-Ḥakam the efficient ruler was also a bibliophile, nor that he acted as a patron. He was both, but he was also a prince, and as a prince he was a patron with a purpose. The cultural policies of middle Umayyad tenth-century al-Andalus were clear and unambiguous and as much the product of intelligent calculation and political ambition as of princely taste.

Al-Ḥakam's taste for education was formed early. He enjoyed, like many others of his house in Spain before him, and like his son later, the tuition of a number of the best scholars and teachers available. We can identify roughly a dozen of these in the sources[20]; and probably half that number among the teachers whom he employed for his son[21]. Although he came to the throne late, at the age of forty six or forty seven, he had begun to collect books very much earlier, and to patronise both the copying and the outright composition of books. We can trace his studies back to his early teens, and follow him in the latter role, that of patron, almost as soon as he enters his twenties[22]. When the famous littérateur al-Qālī came to Spain in 330/942, he did so in response to an invitation issued by a twenty five year old.

From what little we know of the contents of his library and of the activities of some of those whom he employed, we can see a little of al-Ḥakam's tastes: of the works from his library whose identities we can be sure of, one is a work, or a collection of works, by al-Shāfi'ī, and another is a summary, in Arabic, of the Talmud - both of these strange works for a Muslim prince in a state dominated exclusively by Mālikī doctrines to be interested in[23]. We possess more than a dozen explicit references to specific notes made by him in his manuscripts (and one possibly in a manuscript belonging to someone else), generally notes connected with the backgrounds or the biographical details of various scholars, *qāḍī*s and others[24]. He appears to have had a special interest in the history of Islamic Spain (not perhaps very surprisingly), and in topics related to religion, more particularly religious law, but this interest was not in any sense exclusive or intolerant: quite apart from the interest in Judaism and in Shāfi'ī law for which we have evidence mentioned above, we also have material showing a broad interest in poetry and in other more purely belletristic types of literary writing, exemplified by his patronage, at a very great geographical remove, of the *Kitāb al-Aghānī*.

All this was from one point of view personal activity, but it went hand in hand with other more public activities characteristic of a truly great library. It is clear from what we know of it that al-Ḥakam's was far from being merely the private (and fabulous) collection of a learned prince. The library served as the focus of a whole nexus of cultural activities which helped to lay the foundations for the massive explosion of literary productivity in Islamic Spain associated with the century and a quarter following al-Ḥakam's death in 366/976. It is in connection with this that the caliph's involvement with the library and its related work and institutions should be considered. Books from his library were lent out[25]. Outsiders appear to have enjoyed some degree of access to books held there (the value of this should not be exaggerated: one person who derived some heretical views from a book in al-Ḥakam's library was executed for them on the caliph's order[26]). The library's needs called for the employment of numerous copyists of manuscripts, of other people to check the accuracy of copies made there, of librarians, of translators of different types[27]. The interests of the ruler himself encouraged the acquisition of books on a very wide range of subjects, and despite the official intolerance it is clear that in philosophical and theological areas there were large numbers of works which did not accord with the ruling orthodoxy[28]. As a part of the ruler's (and hence we may say the state's) institutions, the library must have served as a link in the educational network for the Spanish and the non-Spanish alike in Cordoba. The biographical dictionaries show us al-Ḥakam welcoming foreign scholars and teachers to Cordoba, and, as a centre through which new works, whether local or foreign in origin, could be made available, the library helped to channel the energies and interests of local scholarship along the same lines as in the main centres of Arabo-Islamic culture to the east.

What was all this for? What aims did it serve? Can we in fact plausibly claim that the personal scholarly interests of this prince represent more than an uneconomic (if creditable) drain on the privy purse of tenth-century Islamic Spain? I think that we can point to a pattern in all this that serves to make the activity of the prince as patron consistent with his activity as a ruler.

The main need felt by al-Ḥakam as a ruler was to maintain the strength and the cohesion of the Umayyad state centred on Cordoba. In doing this he was perpetuating the stategic policy aims formulated by his father, 'Abd al-Raḥmān III al-Nāṣir. These called for a difficult balancing act: in the desire to establish a strong and independent Islamic Spain under Umayyad rule, it was necessary both to imitate the models, both cultural and political, provided by Baghdād, as the real centre of the Islamic world, and at the same time to stress the fact that Spain was both separate from Baghdād and also somehow different[29]. Accepting Baghdād wholly implied admitting the illegitimacy of the Umayyad regime in Spain; rejecting Baghdād, on the other hand, in the name of Umayyad legitimacy in Spain and in the rest of the Islamic world, meant consigning Spain to eternal backwater provinciality. Neither suited a resurgent Spain facing a weakened Baghdād. The solution was to proffer a Spain that was the same, only more so. That is why, when the Būyid vizier Ibn ʿAbbād, on reading Ibn ʿAbd Rabbihi's work *al-ʿIqd al-Farīd*, said, 'This is our own merchandise being served back to us', he was missing the essential point of this famous Andalusian anthology of oriental literature: that work, through its structure and through its highly programmatic introduction, laid stress on the directness and the legitimacy of the Spanish Umayyads' inheritance of authority in Islam as a whole from their oriental predecessors[30]. In this sense, by making oriental materials the lasting touchstone for quality in later Andalusian literary production, the author, in the name of his Spanish Umayyad masters, was also laying claim to the literary excellences of the oriental part of the Islamic world. As heirs to it, and as the successors also of such writers as Ibn ʿAbd Rabbihi, the littérateurs of Umayyad Spain, with al-Ḥakam himself at their head, sought both to distance themselves from Baghdād, the capital of their rivals, and to compete with it as the centre of their own world[31].

This picture of a great library acting as the hub for a wide range of cultural activities with a deliberate policy in view fits very neatly with the other picture provided by the normative politico-military style of Islamic Spanish history, that of al-Ḥakam as the leader of a resurgent Umayyad state in the peninsula, powerful and influential outside its own frontiers within its end of the Mediterranean basin[32]. Is this picture correct? More precisely, perhaps, while political and military advantage might be produced quite rapidly, cultural preeminence seems to take longer - it calls for more than just paying professors more in one place than they can command in another: how was it possible for such developments to occur under al-Ḥakam? Why should Spain have been able so relatively quickly to emerge as a major centre of Islamic culture?

The answer to this appears to lie in a combination of features, first, and most important, the conversion of non-Muslims to Islam. The model for the rate of conversion proposed some years ago by Bulliet is not without its difficulties and problems, not least in its application to Spain[33]; but for all the difficulties it does seems to offer a persuasive account, if not a total explanation, of what happened in this area as far as Spain is concerned. If Bulliet is right, the massive wave of conversion to Islam in Spain will have been largely complete by the reign of al-Ḥakam. Along with conversion, going in advance of it and keeping largely in parallel with its momentum, the process of arabicisation, linguistic acculturation, of the majority of the population, both Muslim and non-Muslim, appears to have been largely complete by this time as well[34]. The numbers of people involved or expecting to be involved in the majoritarian culture of Spain were vastly greater than ever before (The first in the great series of Spanish biographical dictionaries, that of Ibn al-Faraḍī, covers precisely the fourth/tenth century, and for good reason); at the same time, and here we approach the second feature of this hypothesis, it was necessary for the regime to claim convincingly that it represented some form of Islamic legitimacy to its subjects[35]. As the regime of a provincial backwater it could do so only by accepting permanent insignificance and the danger of disappearance. Brilliance offered a happier solution.

In facing this problem, al-Ḥakam was in the fortunate position that the ʿAbbāsid caliphate, as offering the only other major form of Sunnī Muslim orthodoxy, was not only too far away to matter but also too weak to be of any real significance as a challenge to Cordoba. Bulliet has identified the historical moment of which this period is a paradigm[36]: when Islam has not only become the religion of the overwhelming majority, or something like the overwhelming majority, of the population of a territory but also reached a stage where its elimination has begun to appear a manifest impossibility, he sees this as the stage when the significance of Islamic unity, the unity of the *umma* provided by the figure of the caliph and the institution of the caliphate, begins rapidly to lose weight. In cultural terms, this argument can be applied here with considerable force: by the middle of the fourth/tenth century, Islam had become so solidly implanted in Spain as to appear irremovable; the *real* significance of Baghdād, as the seat of the symbols of unity in the Islamic world, begins to decline; but the Umayyads still need their own local legitimation, and they still need to offer their subjects something of the symbols of unity, and they are able to provide this only by appearing to be more Catholic than the ʿAbbāsids. The result is the awkward balancing act between distancing and imitation.

A hypothesis of this sort squeezes the old bibliophile into the same skin as the adroit politician. It would be good to have some supporting evidence for it, in the form of some programmatic declaration by the caliph or by his officials or paid writers, to demonstrate its analytical value. Such material naturally does not exist. But it is possible, nonetheless, to suggest that there is one control that apparently confirms its general validity.

The fourth/tenth century is precisely the period, I have argued elsewhere, where we have to look for the seeds of the tremendous vitality of the Jewish Golden Age in Spain, both Muslim and, later, Christian[37]. It is in this period that there took place the separation of Cordoba, in Jewish terms, from Babel, Babylon, the great centre of oriental Jewish life up till that time.

Babylon, Mesopotamia, centred in Baghdād, was the seat of a declining Jewish exilarchate, generally parallel to the caliphate for the Jews of the Islamic world. In many of its features, the Jewish separation in Spain from the east mirrors, or appears to parallel, what was happening in the Muslim world at the same time. And so far as we are able to judge of this, it seems to have done so with at least the tacit blessing of the state: the scale and quality of the revolution in Spanish Jewish life in the fourth/tenth century are inconceivable without the structural support of a patron; the great leader and patron of the Jewish community in fourth/tenth century Islamic Spain, Hasdai ibn Shaprut, was an official of the government, close to the caliph, and indeed himself a participant in at least one of the major cultural enterprises of the arabophone society in which he lived, the revised Arabic translation of Dioscorides. It seems to be the case that the Jewish revolution of fourth/tenth century Spain is a sub-set of the overall Iberian separatist revolution of that period.

The deliberate distancing of the Muslim and of the Jewish worlds of Spain from the east, their appropriation of the cultural heritages both of Judaism and of Islam for Spain, appear to have been integral elements in the creation of a new view of that country on the part of Muslim and Jew there. All that was inconceivable before that time and without the preconditions offered by both the special situation of the Umayyad regime in that country and the processes of arabicisation and islamisation there up to the middle of the fourth/tenth century.

Al-Ḥakam's library did not survive him very long. After his death, in 366/976, power in the state was taken over by the *ḥājib* al-Manṣūr, and al-Ḥakam's son and successor, Hishām II al-Mu'ayyad, was reduced to a cipher. In order to encourage the support of the *'ulamā'*, al-Manṣūr purged the library of its works on philosophy and of much of its theological contents, on grounds of heresy[38]. A few decades later, in the upheavals that marked the downfall of the Manṣūrid dictatorship and the beginning of the end for the Umayyad dynasty, the rest of the library was dispersed, taking, we are told, six months to be removed from its building[39]. In a sense, the burning of some of the books by al-Manṣūr and the dispersal of the rest a generation afterwards underline the value and the significance of the library as a centre for the spreading of ideas and for the infiltration of new books and new ways of thinking in Spain, recognising as they do the potential for danger that the library represented. But the library, and its founder, I think, should be viewed in a broader perspective.

The library, seen as I have suggested it should be, is an argument for a thoroughgoing re-assessment of al-Ḥakam and of his reign. He is usually seen as a bibliophiliac querk in an otherwise (at least up till his own time) fairly sound dynasty. This view comes, I think, largely from the fact that we tend to see his bibliophilia as a personal interest and activity, whatever its effects. Unlike the societies of the ancient world, or for that matter the modern world, where proper state institutions, corporations and the like, could stand behind such work as the activities of a great library, in the medieval Islamic world this was not possible. Even mosques, and mosque schools, did not have the means, as they did not by and large bear the responsibility, for this. For these activities to be undertaken, it was necessary to have a ruler who could act as patron. For such a ruler to provide the patronage, it was necessary that he be a ruler of the type of al-Ḥakam - that is to say, not just a civilised and cultured eccentric with a love of books (That sort of eccentricity does not act on such a scale by itself), but a ruler with an eye to his state's interests.

The library of al-Ḥakam was in effect a great state institution, and should be viewed as that. In its quality as a state institution, its activity and the support given to it by the state, through the ruler, should be interpreted not, or not just, in the old-fashioned clichés of purely cultural history, but also in terms of the relationship which they reveal between culture and politics. Cultural policies are on occasion general and vague; and on occasion they have very specific and detailed aims. In this case, I should suggest, we are faced with a commingling of the general and the specific in a major area of cultural politics.

Notes

* University College, Dublin, Ireland

1 Ibn Ḥazm, quoted in al-Maqqarī, *Analectes sur l'Histoire et la Littérature des Arabes d'Espagne*, ed. R.P.A. Dozy, G. Dugat, L. Krehl and W. Wright, Leiden, 1855-61 (repr. Amsterdam, 1967), I, 249-50, 256 (dependent on Ibn Khaldūn and Ibn al-Abbār); J. Ribera, *La Enseñanza entre los Musulmanes Españoles. Bibliofilos y Bibliotecas en la España musulmana*, Córdoba (Publicaciones de la Real Academia de Córdoba),1925[3], 107 (where the figures of 50 folios per volume should be corrected to twenty). See also S.M. Imamuddin, *Hispano-Arab Libraries*, Karachi (Pakistan Historical Society, memoir no.4), 1961, 3-6. On libraries in the Islamic world more generally, see Y. Eche, *Les Bibliothèques arabes publiques et semi-publiques en Mésopotamie, en Syrie, et en Egypte au moyen âge*, Damascus, 1967.

2 *Encyclopaedia of Islam* (= *EI*)[2], II, 126-27, art. *Dār al-Ḥikma* (by D. Sourdel).

3 *EI*[2], II, 127, art. *Dār al-'Ilm* (by D. Sourdel).

4 Al-Maqqarī, *Analectes*, II, 359, where 400,000 is given as the number of *dafātir* in his collection, which are then distinguished from the 'defective' ones in it, which are said to be 'innumerable'.

5 E. Lévi-Provençal, 'Un manuscrit de la bibliothèque du calife al-Ḥakam II', *Hespéris*, 18, 1934, 198-200. The manuscript is a copy of the *Mukhtaṣar* of Abū Muṣ'ab b. Abī Bakr al-Zuhrī, made by Ḥusayn b. Yūsuf for al-Ḥakam in Sha'bān 359/June-July 970.

[6] Ibn al-Faraḍī, *Ta'rīkh 'Ulamā' al-Andalus*, ed. F. Codera, 2 vols., Madrid (Bibliotheca Arabico-Hispana, 7-8), 1890, I, p. 6.

[7] *Ibid.*, II, pps. 69-70, no. 1634.

[8] D. Wasserstein, 'An Arabic Version of *Abot* 1:3 from Umayyad Spain', *Arabica*, 34, 1987, 370-74.

[9] Cf. E. Lévi-Provençal, *Histoire de l'Espagne Musulmane*, Paris-Leiden, III, 1967, 230, 508; C.E. Dubler, *La 'Materia Medica' de Dioscorides: Transmisión medieval y renacentista*, I, Barcelona, 1953.

[10] See 'U. 'Abd al-Raḥmān Kuḥayla, 'Kitāb al-Tawārīkh li-Bawlūs Ūrūsiyyūs wa-Tarjamatuhu al-Andalusiyya', *Majallat al-Ma'had al-Miṣrī lil-dirāsāt al-Islāmiyya fī Madrid*, 23, 1985-86, 119-37; H. Daiber, 'Orosius' *Historiae Adversus Paganos* in arabischer Überlieferung', in: J.W. van Henten [& others] (edd.), *Tradition and reinterpretation in Jewish and early Christian literature: Essays in honour of J.C.H. Lebram*, Leiden, 1986, 202-249; Orosius, *Ta'rīkh al-'Ālam*, ed. 'Abd al-Raḥmān Badawī, Beirut, 1982 (I owe these references to the kindness of Professor P.Sj. van Koningsveld); G. Levi della Vida, 'La traduzione araba delle storie di Orosio', *Al-Andalus*, 19, 1954, 257-93.

[11] H. Goussen, 'Die christlich-arabische Literatur der Mozaraber', *Beiträge zur christlich-arabischer Literaturgeschichte*, IV. Heft, Leipzig, 1909, 1-31; E. Tisserant (and D. de Bruyne), 'Une feuille arabo-latine de l'épître aux Galates', *Revue Biblique*, 7, 1910, 321-43; H.S. Gehman, 'The Arabic Bible in Spain', *Speculum*, 1, 1926, 219-21; D.M. Dunlop, 'Ḥafṣ b. Albār - the last of the Goths?' *Journal of the Royal Asiatic Society*, 1954, 137-51; id., 'Sobre Ḥafṣ Ibn Albār al-Qūṭī al-Qurṭubī', *Al-Andalus*, 20, 1955, 211-13; A.S. Tritton, 'The Old Testament in Muslim Spain', *Bulletin of the School of Oriental and African Studies*, 21, 1958, 392-95, is concerned mainly with a later period. See also P.Sj. van Koningsveld, *The Latin-Arabic Glossary of the Leiden University Library. A contribution to the study of Mozarabic manuscripts and literature*, Leiden (Asfār I), 1977, esp. cap. 3, pps. 44-60.

[12] On this traveller see now *EI²*, III, 991, art. *Ibrāhīm b. Ya'kūb al-Isrā'īlī al-Ṭurṭūshī* (by A. Miquel), with bibliography; B. Lewis, *The Muslim Discovery of Europe*, London, 1982, 315, n. 10.

[13] Cf. al-Maqqarī, *Analectes*, I, 250.

[14] See, for examples, Ibn al-Faraḍī, I, p. 404, no. 1398 (Muḥammad b. al-Ḥārith al-Khushanī: 'he composed for the Commander of the Faithful al-Mustanṣir billāh [may God have mercy upon him] many books; I have heard that he compiled a hundred *dīwāns* for him, and he composed for him a book on the [great] men of al-Andalus, which we have quoted from here wherever it is so stated'); p. 69, no. 236 (Isḥāq b. Salama al-Qaynī, author of a history of Islamic Spain ordered by al-Ḥakam); for further references on him see F. Pons Boigues, *Los Historiadores y Geógrafos Arábigo-Españoles, 800-1450 A.D.*, Madrid, 1898, repr. Amsterdam, 1972, p.100, no. 66, no. 2); pps.113-14, no. 396 (Khālid b. Sa'd, author of a work on the great men of al-Andalus); al-Ḍabbī, *K. Bughyat al-Multamis*, ed. F. Codera and J. Ribera, Madrid (Bibliotheca Arabico-Hispana, 3), 1885, pps. 500-01, no. 1506 (Ya'īsh b. Sa'id b. Muḥammad al-Warrāq, author of a work on *ḥadīth*); *EI²*, I, 628 ('Arīb b. Sa'd, author of *K. Khalq al-Janīn wa-Tadbīr al-Ḥabālā wal-Mawlūd*, a work on obstetrics); al-Zubaydī, *Ṭabaqāt al-Naḥwiyyīn wal-Lughawiyyīn*, ed. M. Abū al-Faḍl Ibrāhīm, Cairo (Dhakhā'ir al-'Arab, 50), 1984², 18 (a work on biographies of grammarians, with its dedication to al-Mustanṣir); Ibn Khayr, *Fahrasa*, 2 vols., ed. J. Ribera, Saragossa (Bibliotheca Arabico-Hispana, 9-10), 1894-95, p. 125 (Qāsim b. Aṣbagh, author of a work on *fiqh*); Ibn al-Faraḍī, I, p. 7, and I, p. 216, no. 777 (Muḥammad b. Aḥmad Ibn Mufarraj, author of a biographical work, cf. also Pons, *Historiadores*, pps. 82-83, no. 43).

[15] Ibn Khayr, *Fahrasa*, pps. 395-97 ('a list of the names of the books of poetry and the names of the poets which Abū 'Alī Ismā'īl b. al-Qāsim al-Baghdādī [= al-Qālī] brought [*scil.* to Spain], excluding those works, other than these, which he brought but which he taught in Qayrawān [on the way to Spain]'); 398-400 ('and the *akhbār* which Abū 'Alī al-Baghdādi brought'; from the list it can be seen that the word *akhbār* here refers simply to prose works in general).

[16] Cf. *Oxford Classical Dictionary*, Oxford, 1970², art. *Libraries*; P.M. Fraser, *Ptolemaic Alexandria*, Oxford, 1972, I, 328-29; II, 485-86.

[17] N.R. Ker, *Medieval Libraries of Great Britain: a list of surviving books*, London (Royal Historical Society Guides and Handbooks, no. 3), 1964², x-xi, xxvii.

[18] See now M.G. Balty-Guesdon, *Le* Bayt al-Ḥikma *de Baghdad*, mémoire de D.E.A., Université de Paris III - Sorbonne Nouvelle, année universitaire 1985-1986 (dactylographié). I am grateful to Mme Balty-Guesdon for permitting me to consult this work.

[19] Cf. my *The Rise and Fall of the Party-Kings: Politics and Society in Islamic Spain, 1002-1086*, Princeton, 1985, 38.

[20] For al-Ḥakam's teachers see Ibn al-Faraḍī, I, p. 128, no. 442; pps. 142-43, no. 492; pps. 251-52, no. 896; p. 287, no. 1041; pps. 297-98, no. 1068; pps. 348-49, no. 1230; pps. 353-54, no. 1247; p. 354, no. 1249; II, p. 41, no. 1543; al-Zubaydī, *Ṭabaqāt*, p. 284, no. 234; p. 298, no. 266; p. 303, no. 276 (the last three described as employed to teach al-Nāṣir's *walad*, which need not by any means refer to al-Mustanṣir but the reading *wuld* would permit such an interpretation); al-Maqqarī, *Analectes*, II, 256.

[21] Cf. Pons, *Historiadores*, p. 83, no. 44; Ibn Khayr, *Fahrasa*, p. 79; Ibn al-Faraḍī, I, p. 47, nos. 163, 164; pps. 47-48, no. 165; p. 89, no. 308; p. 111, no. 390; pps. 113-14, no. 396; p. 128, no. 442; pps. 142-43, no. 492; p. 383, no. 1355; II, pps. 56-57, no. 1595.

[22] Ibn al-Faraḍī, II, p. 41, no. 1543, is a biography of a man who taught both al-Nāṣir and al-Mustanṣir, dying in 317/929, when al-Mustanṣir was only 14 (cf. also al-Zubaydī, *Ṭabaqāt*, p. 284, no. 234). For two others of his teachers who died when he was still very young, cf. also al-Zubaydī, *op. cit.*, p. 298, no. 266; Ibn al-Faraḍī, I, pps. 251-52, no. 896.

[23] For the work of al-Shāfi'ī, cf. Ibn al-Faraḍī, II, pps. 69-70, no. 1634; for the Talmud, cf. *supra*, at n. 8.

[24] Cf. Ibn al-Faraḍī, I, p. 89, no. 308; p. 111, no. 390; p. 128, no. 442; p. 188, no. 681; pps. 212-13, no. 769; p. 266, no. 952; p. 288, no. 1045; pps. 293-94, no. 1060; pps. 314-15, no. 1122; p. 335, no. 1195; II, pps. 9-10, no. 1430; p. 21, no. 1459; p. 61, no. 1605.

[25] Cf. Ibn al-Faraḍī, I, p. 6; II, pps. 9-10, no. 1430.

[26] Cf. n. 8, *supra*.

[27] E.g., Ibn al-Faraḍī, I, p. 47, no. 163; p. 364, no. 1290; p. 368, no. 1307.

28 Cf., for the reaction to this, the account of al-Manṣūr's purging of the library's contents after al-Mustanṣir's death given by a writer of the mid-eleventh century: Ṣā'id of Toledo, *Kitāb Ṭabaqāt al-Umam*, ed. L. Cheikho, Beirut, 1912, pps. 66-67 (= trans. R. Blachère, Ṣâ'id al-Andalusî, *Kitâb Ṭabaḳāt al-Umam (Livre des Catégories des Nations)*, Paris [Publications de l'Institut des Hautes Etudes Marocaines, t. xxviii], 1935, pps. 125-126); cf. also M. Isabel Fierro Bello, *La Heterodoxia en al-Andalus durante el Periodo Omeya*, Madrid (Cuadernos de Islamología, I), 1987, 161-62.

29 Cf. *The Rise and Fall of the Party-Kings* (*supra*, n. 19), pps. 23-38.

30 *Ibid.*, 25-26; *EI*², III, 676-77 (art. *Ibn 'Abd Rabbih*, by C. Brockelmann).

31 Cf. al-Mustanṣir's boast about his country reported by Ibn al-Faraḍī, I, pps. 113-14, no. 396: 'If the orientals boast of Yaḥyā b. Mu'īn to us then we can boast of Khālid b. Sa'd to them'; and cf. also the publicity and generosity attending the welcomes given to oriental scholars arriving in Spain: e.g., Ibn al-Abbār, 'Apéndice a la edición Codera de la «Tecmila» de Aben al-Abbār', ed. M. Alarcón and C.A. González Palencia, *Miscelánea de Estudios y Textos Árabes*, Madrid, 1915, 147-690, at pps. 336-37, no. 1290; Ibn al-Faraḍī, I, p. 230, no. 822; pps. 261-62, no. 932.

32 On this see generally Lévi-Provençal, *op. cit.* (supra, n. 9), II, 1950², 165-96.

33 R.W. Bulliet, *Conversion to Islam in the Medieval Period, an Essay in Quantitative History*, Cambridge, Mass., 1979, esp. cap. 10, pps. 114-27.

34 Cf. my 'The Linguistic situation in al-Andalus', to appear in the proceedings of the first international colloquium on the *kharjas*, Exeter, 1987.

35 Cf. *The Rise and Fall of the Party-Kings*, 27-29, 33-36.

36 Bulliet, *op. cit.*, cap. 11, pps. 128-38, 'The consequences of conversion'.

37 'The Jewish Community of Tenth-Century Spain', to appear in the proceedings of the Second Solon Symposium, Oxford, 1988.

38 Cf. *supra*, n. 28.

39 Cf. Lévi-Provençal, *op. cit.*, II, 318, and *ibid.*, n. 1; cf. also al-Maqqarī, *Analectes*, I, 256.

INDEX

Note: Transliteration and spelling follow those of individual chapters.

Index created by Meg Davies (Fellow of the Society of indexers)